SAGE
Premium
Video

- SAGE Premium Video **EXCLUSIVELY CURATED FOR THIS TEXT**
- **BRIDGES BOOK CONTENT** with application & critical thinking
- Includes short, auto-graded quizzes that **DIRECTLY FEED TO YOUR LMS GRADEBOOK**
- Premium content is **ADA COMPLIANT WITH TRANSCRIPTS**
- Comprehensive media guide to help you **QUICKLY SELECT MEANINGFUL VIDEO** tied to your course objectives

The Hallmark Features

A COMPLETE LEARNING PACKAGE

Small Business Management equips students with the tools they need to navigate the important financial, legal, marketing, managerial, and operational decisions to sustain a competitive advantage in small business.

- **EXPERIENTIAL LEARNING ACTIVITIES** bring the application of "what" and "how" alive to students

- **WHAT WOULD YOU DO?** presents students with a dilemma to solve using concepts and tools from the chapter

- **CREATING COMPETITIVE ADVANTAGE** provides streetwise best practices for succeeding in a competitive business environment

- **HOW TO... VIDEOS** focus on basic concepts to further clarify and enhance understanding of common, basic business needs

- **SMALL BUSINESS IN ACTION VIDEOS** showcase stories and interviews from a wide variety of small business owners

SAGE Publishing:
Our Story

Founded in 1965 by 24-year-old entrepreneur Sara Miller McCune, SAGE continues its legacy of making research accessible and fostering **CREATIVITY** and **INNOVATION**. We believe in creating fresh, cutting-edge content to help you prepare your students to thrive in the modern business world and be **TOMORROW'S LEADING ENTREPRENEURS**.

- By partnering with **TOP BUSINESS AUTHORS** with just the right balance of research, teaching, and industry experience, we bring you the most current and applied content.

- As a **STUDENT-FRIENDLY PUBLISHER**, we keep our prices affordable and provide multiple formats of our textbooks so your students can choose the option that works best for them.

- Being permanently **INDEPENDENT** means we are fiercely committed to publishing the highest-quality resources for you and your students.

SMALL BUSINESS
MANAGEMENT

SEVENTH EDITION

Sara Miller McCune founded SAGE Publishing in 1965 to support the dissemination of usable knowledge and educate a global community. SAGE publishes more than 1000 journals and over 800 new books each year, spanning a wide range of subject areas. Our growing selection of library products includes archives, data, case studies and video. SAGE remains majority owned by our founder and after her lifetime will become owned by a charitable trust that secures the company's continued independence.

Los Angeles | London | New Delhi | Singapore | Washington DC | Melbourne

SMALL BUSINESS
MANAGEMENT

Creating a Sustainable Competitive Advantage

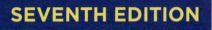

SEVENTH EDITION

Timothy S. Hatten

Colorado Mesa University

Los Angeles | London | New Delhi
Singapore | Washington DC | Melbourne

⑤SAGE

FOR INFORMATION:

SAGE Publications, Inc.
2455 Teller Road
Thousand Oaks, California 91320
E-mail: order@sagepub.com

SAGE Publications Ltd.
1 Oliver's Yard
55 City Road
London EC1Y 1SP
United Kingdom

SAGE Publications India Pvt. Ltd.
B 1/I 1 Mohan Cooperative Industrial Area
Mathura Road, New Delhi 110 044
India

SAGE Publications Asia-Pacific Pte. Ltd.
18 Cross Street #10-10/11/12
China Central Square
Singapore 048423

Acquisitions Editor: Maggie Stanley
Senior Content Development Editor: Darcy Scelsi
Editorial Assistant: Alissa Nance
Production Editor: Jane Martinez
Copy Editor: Taryn Bigelow
Typesetter: C&M Digitals (P) Ltd.
Proofreader: Laura Webb
Indexer: Amy Murphy
Cover Designer: Karine Hovsepian
Marketing Manager: Sarah Panella

BRIEF CONTENTS

©iStock.com/Rawpixel

DETAILED CONTENTS

©iStockphoto.com/imtmphoto

PART II: PLANNING IN SMALL BUSINESS

©iStockphoto.com/jetcityimage

PART III: EARLY DECISIONS

©iStockphoto.com/nilimage

©iStockphoto.com/NicoElNino

PART IV: FINANCIAL AND LEGAL MANAGEMENT

Chapter 8: Accounting Records and Financial Statements   190

©iStockphoto.com/PeopleImages

©iStockphoto.com/benedek

PART V: MARKETING THE PRODUCT OR SERVICE

©iStockphoto.com/g-stockstudio

©iStockphoto.com/Steve Debenport

©iStockphoto.com/BernardaSv

PREFACE

Are you thinking about starting your own business some day? For many students, preparation for small business ownership begins with a course in Small Business Management. My goal as an instructor (and the purpose of this text) is to help students fulfill their dreams of becoming entrepreneurs and achieving the independence that comes with small business success.

The theme of this book revolves around creating and maintaining a *sustainable competitive advantage* in a small business. Running a small business is difficult in today's rapidly evolving environment. At no other time has it been so important for businesses to hold a competitive advantage. Every chapter in this book can be used to create your competitive advantage—whether it be your idea, your product, your location, or your marketing plan. Running a small business is like being in a race with no finish line. You must continually strive to satisfy the changing wants and needs of your customers. This book can help you run your best race.

The writing style is personal and conversational. I have tried to avoid excessive use of jargon by explaining topics in simple, understandable language. The book is written in the first person, present tense, because I, the author, am speaking directly to you, the student. I believe that a good example can help make even the most complex concept more understandable and interesting to read. To strengthen the flow of the material and reinforce important points, examples have been carefully selected from the business press and small business owners I have known.

New to this Edition

In preparing this seventh edition, I incorporated suggestions from instructors and students who used the previous edition. In addition, an advisory board of educators from around the country was consulted to help me determine the best ways to meet the needs of students in this course. Here are some of the changes that have been made in this edition:

You know all the material that is normally called "end-of-chapter" pedagogy? I didn't leave it at the end of the chapter—questions for review, discussion, and critical thinking have been moved to the section where the content is covered. I call the approach of blocking Learning Objectives, content, examples, review, and assessment material together "Concept Modules." I hope you like them.

Two Experiential Learning Activities have been added to each chapter to emphasize the application of what you have just learned to running a small business.

The latest information on topics critical to small business has been added. These topics include

- Balance of Life for Small Business Owners
- Creativity, Innovation, and Integrity in Small Business
- Feasibility Studies
- Lifestyle Entrepreneurs

- The Gig Economy

- Crowdfunding

- Valuation of Small Business

- Online Customer Acquisition Costs

- Small Business Harvest

- Risk Management in Small Business

- And, of course, facets of online business, web development, social media, and mobile presence have been added in many chapters/concept modules throughout the book.

New feature boxes highlight important issues in small business management. The four types of boxed features used are *Creating Competitive Advantage*, *Issues in Small Business*, *Tech in Action*, and *What Would You Do?* In this edition, the number of boxes was reduced to avoid reader confusion, and the length of boxes was shortened to hold readers' attention. (Believe it or not, a rumor exists that some students actually skip reading these highlight boxes. Of course, you would never do this and risk missing some of the juiciest stories.) Here is what to expect in each type of highlight box:

- **Creating Competitive Advantage:** These real-world stories come from streetwise business practitioners who know how it's done and are willing to share the secrets of their success. Building a competitive advantage is the primary theme of this book.

- **Issues in Small Business:** New to this edition, these boxes bring attention to the latest developments and topics facing small businesses.

- **Tech in Action:** Another brand new box contains cutting-edge information on how entrepreneurs use social media and other technology to build their businesses.

- **What Would You Do?** As part of the effort to build Concept Modules, these boxes provide students with a scenario similar to the content they are reading at that moment and are asked to describe, well, what they would do. Clever, eh?

In addition to the highlight boxes, new and revised examples, issues facing small business, and pedagogical tools that bring self-employment to life have been included all through the body of the book.

- Some notable examples of small business owners (some of which have businesses that are no longer small, but they started that way):
  - Andrew Paradise—Skillz
  - Alex and Andrew—4Ocean
  - Roni and Ken DiLullo—Doggles
  - Jon Kourn/Brian Acton—WhatsApp
  - Jorge Oden—Wow, you HAVE to read about the device this auto mechanic created to reduce childbirth deaths in developing countries.
  - Don Sadoway—This chemistry professor developed a radical new battery (and business) that can store power from alternative energy sources like solar and wind.
  - Leigh-Kathryn Bonner—Bee Downtown
  - Daniel Katz—No Cow

- Topics you will find that tell the stories of small businesses include
  - Creating a small business start-up on campus
  - Building a business model
  - Analyzing what to do if you create a tattoo removal cream
  - Crowdfunding cases from Indiegogo and Kickstarter
  - Illuminating the path to innovation
  - Using big data for small businesses
  - Pricing with anchors, bumps, and charms
  - Pricing by Spotify to attract college students
  - Making the most of financial dashboards in the cloud
  - Building podcasts for your small business
  - Making LinkedIn your go-to place for hiring
- The pedagogical features of this book are designed to complement, supplement, and reinforce material from the body of the text. The following features enhance critical thinking and show practical small business applications:
  - Chapter opening vignettes, *Creating Competitive Advantage*, and extensive use of examples throughout the book show you what *real* small businesses are doing.
  - Each chapter is broken into Concept Modules, each with its own Learning Objective that directly correlates to the topic being covered. These objectives are then revisited and summarized at the end of the chapter.
  - A running glossary in the margins highlights important terms as they appear in the text.
  - Questions for review and discussion allow you to assess your retention and comprehension at the end of Concept Modules. More questions designed to spark critical thinking prompt you to apply what you have learned to realistic situations.
  - Experiential Learning Activities is a new feature of this edition. These offer you the opportunity to "roll up your sleeves" and discover what it's really like in the trenches.
  - Chapter Closing Cases present real-life business scenarios, allowing you to think critically about the management challenges presented and to further apply chapter concepts.

Every effort has been made to prevent "new edition bloat." Attention has been paid to items to delete as well as what to add to stay current and streamlined. Special attention has been paid to sharpen the focus of the book to make it about "small business," not crossing into the related but separate topic of "entrepreneurship."

New to this Edition: Chapter by Chapter

Chapter 1: Small Business: An Overview

- New chapter opening case highlighting Skillz Inc.
- Added discussion of microbusinesses
- Added coverage of the Small Business Act

- Provided new examples throughout

- Expanded discussion of innovation

- Added feature *Issues in Small Business*: Lighting the Fuse of Innovation

- Added Experiential Learning Activities: Competitive Advantage and Advantages/ Disadvantages; Creative Destruction

Chapter 2: Small Business Management and Entrepreneurship

- New chapter opening case on Bacon Boxes and Ephemeral (think tattoos)

- New *Issues in Small Business*: The Balance of Life in Small Business

- *Creating Competitive Advantage*: Are You Ready? (formerly *Entre-Perspectives*)

- New *Tech in Action*: Big Data for Small Business

- New Concept Module 2.4: Creativity and Innovation in Small Business has been added; this includes incorporation of content from the old Concept Module 12.1: Product: The Heart of the Marketing Mix

- Added Experiential Learning Activities: Stages of Preparing for Small Business Ownership; Forms of Ownership

- New Chapter Closing Case: The Organic Nonprofit: Feet First

Chapter 3: Social Entrepreneurs, Ethics, and Strategic Planning

- New chapter opening case highlighting up-and-coming social entrepreneurs

- Broadens discussion of social entrepreneurship and the role it plays in business and the triple bottom line

- *Entre-Perspectives* on Competitive Intelligence changed to *Creating Competitive Advantage* and expanded upon

- Added Experiential Learning Activities: Small Business Ethics; Creating Competitive Advantage

- New Chapter Closing Case: Bill Daniels: A Man Whose Word Was His Bond

Chapter 4: The Business Plan

- New chapter opening case featuring Brad Powell of RedBoard

- The new Concept Module 4.1 focuses on the business plan and expands the discussion of its importance and role in planning a new business.

- The new Concept Module 4.2 provides an updated discussion of contemporary business models with an added discussion of conducting feasibility analysis.

- Revised feature *Issues in Small Business*: Feasible, Viable, Good Idea?

- Revised feature *Issues in Small Business*: How Does Your Plan Rate?

- New Concept Module 4.5 focuses on creation of a pitch

- New feature *Tech in Action*: PowerPoint Alternatives

- Added Experiential Learning Activities: The Business Plan Sequence; The Business Plan

- New Chapter Closing Case: TrailerWalla: Evaluating an Opportunity

Chapter 5: Franchising

- New chapter opening case featuring the College Hunks Hauling Junk
- Updated franchising statistics
- Added timeline of franchising
- New feature *What Would You Do?* College Hunks Hauling Junk
- New feature *Issues in Small Business*: What Do You Need to Know?
- New feature *Tech in Action*: Techno-Franchise
- New feature *Creating Competitive Advantage*: Millennial Franchisees
- Added Experiential Learning Activities: Business Format or Product Distribution Franchise; Franchise Requirements Evaluation

Chapter 6: Taking Over an Existing Business

- New chapter opener on buying a business
- New feature *Tech in Action*: Buy an Online Business . . . Online
- Expanded discussion of methods used to value a business
- New feature *Issues in Small Business*: Small Business Flip
- New feature *Creating Competitive Advantage*: *Shark Tank* Acquisition Launch
- Added Experiential Learning Activities: Advantages/Disadvantages of Buying a Business; Tangible and Intangible Assets
- New Chapter Closing Case: A Question of Value

Chapter 7: Starting a New Business

- New chapter opening case on Christopher Mitchell and Thomas Dickerson of Geopipe and Derek Johnson of Tatango
- New feature *Issues in Small Business*: Start-Up Challenges
- New feature *Tech in Action*: There's an App for That
- Added discussion of e-commerce and use of apps
- New feature *Creating Competitive Advantage*: Entrepreneurs Solve Big Problems
- Added Experiential Learning Activities: New Types of Businesses/Fast-Growth Companies; Start-Up Costs
- New Chapter Closing Case: Trend Pie: Turning a Social Media Network into a Business

Chapter 8: Accounting Records and Financial Statements

- Expanded discussions on accounting and accounting needs/issues
- *'Trep Connection* converted to *Tech in Action* feature
- Updated information on accounting software packages—Peachtree to Sage 50
- *Reality Check* converted into *Issues in Small Business*
- *Entre-Perspectives* converted to *Creating a Competitive Advantage*

- Added Experiential Learning Activities: Financial Statement Account Identification; Ratio Analysis Decision-Making
- New Chapter Closing Case: Superior Engineering in Texas: Stay or Go?

Chapter 9: Small Business Finance

- New chapter opening case on crowdfunding
- New feature box *Issues in Small Business*: Mobile Money
- New feature box *Tech in Action*: Crowdfunding
- Added Experiential Learning Activities: Finance Terminology; Finding Capital for the Start-Up

Chapter 10: The Legal Environment

- New chapter opening case on counterfeiting
- New feature *Issues in Small Business*: Small Business Legal Worries
- New feature *Creating Competitive Advantage*: Choosing an Attorney
- Converted *Reality Check* into *Tech in Action*: IP App Protection?
- New Concept Module 10.5: Forms of Business Organization; moved here from Chapter 2
- Added Experiential Learning Activities: Contracts; Form of Business Ownership

Chapter 11: Small Business Marketing: Strategy and Research

- New chapter opening case about Alex Schulze and Andrew Cooper of 4Ocean
- New feature *Creating Competitive Advantage*: Online Video Marketing
- New feature *Issues in Small Business*: Target Markets of One
- New feature *Tech in Action*: PPC or SEO?
- Added Experiential Learning Activities: Small Business Marketing: Strategy and Research Decision Making; Small Business Marketing: Strategy and Research Target Market
- New Chapter Closing Case: Active Analog Fun Business

Chapter 12: Small Business Marketing: Location

- Chapter 12 from the sixth edition has been eliminated—some content moved into Chapter 16.
- Formerly Chapter 13 with a title change from "Place" to "Location"
- New feature *Creating Competitive Advantage*: Location, Location, Location
- New feature *Issues in Small Business*: New Way We Work
- New feature *Tech in Action*: If You're Not Online, You Don't Exist
- Added Experiential Learning Activities: Small Business Marketing: Location Channels of Distribution; Small Business Marketing: Location

Chapter 13: Small Business Marketing: Price and Promotion

- Formerly Chapter 14
- New chapter opening case about online market influencers
- New feature *Issues in Small Business*: The Danger with Discounts
- New feature *Creating Competitive Advantage*: Anchors, Bumps, and Charms
- New feature *Tech in Action*: Online Big Dogs
- Added Experiential Learning Activities: Small Business Marketing: Pricing and Promotion Breakeven Analysis; Small Business Marketing: Promotion

Chapter 14: Professional Small Business Management

- Formerly Chapter 16
- New chapter opening case on Bee Downtown and No Cow
- New feature *Tech in Action*: Podcasts: Listen, Learn, and Tell
- New feature *Issues in Small Business*: Leadership in a Small Business
- New feature *Creating Competitive Advantage*: Advantageous Culture
- Added Experiential Learning Activities: Management: Four Functions; Management Leadership

Chapter 15: Human Resource Management

- Formerly Chapter 17
- New chapter opening case on "digital nomads"
- New feature *Creating Competitive Advantage*: Keeping Your Most Valuable Asset
- New feature *Tech in Action*: Finding Employees via LinkedIn
- Eliminated discussion of temporary employees and professional employer organizations
- New feature *Issues in Small Business*: Handling Harassment
- Added Experiential Learning Activities: Human Resource Management: Interviewing; Human Resource Management: Dismissing Employees
- New Chapter Closing Case, Building a Team at Tagit

Chapter 16: Operations Management

- Heavily revised chapter incorporating the newest trends and technologies in operations management. Some content from former Chapter 12 has been integrated into this chapter.
- New feature *Tech in Action*: Small Businesses Impact the IoT
- New feature *Issues in Small Business*: Women in Manufacturing
- New feature *Creating Competitive Advantage*: Lean Manufacturing
- Concept Module on purchasing placed in this chapter
- Concept Module on inventory management placed here, moved from old Chapter 12
- Added Experiential Learning Activities: Operations Management; Operations Management: Productivity

Digital Resources

SAGE edge™

SAGE offers an exceptionally robust set of offerings for both student and instructor resources, all accessible from each title's companion website. The Student Study Site is completely open access, making it as easy as possible for your students to use. The Instructor Teaching Site is verified and password-protected, offering you both peace of mind and a wealth of support for your courses.

SAGE edge for Students

Use the Student Study Site to get the most out of your course! Our Student Study Site at **edge.sagepub.com/hatten7e** is completely open access and offers a wide range of additional features

- Mobile-friendly **eFlashcards** reinforce understanding of key terms and concepts that have been outlined in the chapters.
- Mobile-friendly **web quizzes** allow for independent assessment of progress made in learning course material.
- **Business Plan Guide and sample business plans** to help in writing your business plan and sample business plans for your reference and review.
- **Video and multimedia links** that appeal to students with different learning styles.

SAGE edge for Instructors

Calling all instructors! It's easy to log on to SAGE's password-protected Instructor Teaching Site at **edge.sagepub.com/hatten7e** for complete and protected access to all text-specific Instructor Resources for *Small Business Management: Creating a Sustainable Competitive Advantage*, Seventh Edition. Simply provide your institutional information for verification and within 72 hours you'll be able to use your login information for any SAGE title!

Password-protected **Instructor Resources** include the following:

- An **electronic test bank** contains multiple choice, true/false, short answer, and essay questions for each chapter and provides you with a diverse range of pre-written options as well as the opportunity for editing any question and/or inserting your own personalized questions to effectively assess students' progress and understanding.
- Editable, chapter-specific **Microsoft® PowerPoint® slides** offer you complete flexibility in easily creating a multimedia presentation for your course. Highlight essential content and features.
- **Sample course syllabi** for semester and quarter courses provide suggested models for use when creating the syllabi for your courses.
- **Business Plan Guide and sample business plans** to help in writing your business plan and sample business plans for your reference and review.
- **Instructor's manual** containing lecture notes that summarize key concepts on a chapter-by-chapter basis to help you with preparation for lectures and class discussions, teaching tips to provide some additional ideas for integrating classroom content, suggested answers to Concept Check questions, notes for use of the experiential learning activities, and case notes.

- **Video and multimedia links** that appeal to students with different learning styles.
- A set of **graphics from the text**, including tables and figures, in PowerPoint, .pdf, and .jpg formats for class presentations.

SAGE Coursepacks

SAGE coursepacks for Instructors make it easy to import our quality content into your school's LMS. Intuitive and simple to use, it allows you to

Say NO to . . .

- required access codes
- learning a new system

Say YES to . . .

- using only the content you want and need
- high-quality assessment and multimedia exercises

For use in: Blackboard, Canvas, Brightspace by Desire2Learn (D2L), and Moodle

Don't use an LMS platform? No problem, you can still access many of the online resources for your text via SAGE edge.

SAGE coursepacks include

- Our content delivered directly into your LMS

- **Intuitive, simple format** that makes it easy to integrate the material into your course with minimal effort

- Pedagogically robust **assessment tools** that foster review, practice, and critical thinking, and offer a more complete way to measure student engagement, including

  - Diagnostic chapter **pre tests and post tests** that identify opportunities for improvement, track student progress, and ensure mastery of key learning objectives

  - **Test banks** built on Bloom's Taxonomy that provide a diverse range of test items with ExamView test generation. Questions are also correlated to the current AACSB Standards.

  - **Activity and quiz options** that allow you to choose only the assignments and tests you want

  - **Instructions** on how to use and integrate the comprehensive assessments and resources provided

- **Instructor's manual** containing lecture notes that summarize key concepts on a chapter-by-chapter basis to help you with preparation for lectures and class discussions, teaching tips to provide some additional ideas for integrating classroom content, suggested answers to Concept Check questions, notes for use of the experiential learning activities, and case notes.

- **Assignable SAGE Premium Video** (available via the interactive eBook version, linked through SAGE coursepacks) that is tied to learning objectives, curated, and produced exclusively for this text to bring concepts to life and appeal to different learning styles, featuring

- ○ **Corresponding multimedia assessment options** that automatically feed to your gradebook.

- ○ *How To* animated videos highlight key concepts in running a small business and provide explanations of how to implement the concepts.

- ○ *Small Business in Action* videos present interviews with small business owners, providing insight and tips on the everyday practice of running a small business.

- Comprehensive, downloadable, easy-to-use *Media Guide in the Coursepack* **for every video resource**, listing the chapter to which the video content is tied, matching learning objective(s), a helpful description of the video content, and assessment questions

- **Multimedia content** includes links to video, audio, web, and data that are tied to learning objectives and enhance exploration of key topics to make learning easier

- Editable, chapter-specific **PowerPoint® slides** that offer flexibility when creating multimedia lectures so you don't have to start from scratch but you can customize to your exact needs

- **Sample course syllabi** with suggested models for structuring your course that give you options to customize your course in a way that is perfect for you

- **Integrated links to the interactive eBook** that make it easy for your students to maximize their study time with this "anywhere, anytime" mobile-friendly version of the text. It also offers access to more digital tools and resources, including SAGE Premium Video

- Selected tables and figures from the textbook

ACKNOWLEDGMENTS

SAGE would like to thank the following reviewers:

Martin Bressler, Southeastern Oklahoma State University

Mike Cairns, College of Marin

Macgorine Cassell, Fairmont State University

Violet Christopher, Antelope Valley College

Robin R. Davis, Claflin University

Gustavo Demoner, West Los Angeles College

Stephanie Kloos Donoghue, Pace University

JoAnn Flett, Eastern University

Janice S. Gates, Western Illinois University

Tomeka Harbin, Delta State University

Marcos Hashimoto, University of Indianapolis

Melissa Houston, Thomas University

Lisa Kahle-Piasecki, Tiffin University

Brent H. Kinghorn, Texas A&M University–Kingsville

George Kleeb, Great Basin College

Gail Knell, Cape Cod Community College

Leanna Lawter, Sacred Heart University

Frank Liselli, Farmingdale State College

John Pappas, Lake Forest College

Linda J. Ridley, City University of New York, Hostos Community College

Matthew Rivaldi, San Diego Community College

Larry Woods, University of Mount Olive

Lee J. Zane, Rider University

Special thanks are also due to Morgan Bridge of Colorado Mesa University for developing the How To videos as well as the video quizzing that accompanies this text.

ABOUT THE AUTHOR

 **Timothy S. Hatten** is a professor at Colorado Mesa University in Grand Junction, Colorado, where he has served as the chair of business administration and director of the MBA program. He received his Ph.D. from the University of Missouri–Columbia, his M.S. from Central Missouri State University, and his B.A. from Western State College in Gunnison, Colorado. He is a two-time Fulbright Scholar. He taught small business management and entrepreneurship at Reykjavik University in Iceland and Copenhagen Business Academy in Denmark and business planning at the Russian-American Business Center in Magadan, Russia.

Dr. Hatten has been passionate about small and family businesses his whole life. He grew up with the family-owned International Harvester farm equipment dealership in Bethany, Missouri, which his father started. Later, he owned and managed a Chevrolet/Buick/Cadillac dealership with his father, Drexel, and brother, Gary.

Since entering academia, Dr. Hatten has actively brought students and small businesses together through the Small Business Institute program. He works closely with the award-winning Business Incubator Center in Grand Junction, Colorado. He approached writing this textbook as if it were a small business. His intent was to make a product (in this case, a book) that would benefit his customers (students and faculty).

Dr. Hatten is fortunate to live on the Western Slope of Colorado where he has the opportunity to share his love of the mountains with his family.

Please send questions, comments, and suggestions to thatten@coloradomesa.edu.

THE
CHALLENGE

PART I

SMALL BUSINESS

An Overview

When you visualize "small business" do you think of old-fashioned diners or touristy little T-shirt shops? While those may be small businesses they certainly don't represent the entire genre—especially if *you* are not interested in diners or T-shirts.

How about working in, or owning a business that requires employees to do something that would get them fired in about every other business? Playing video games on their phones. Andrew Paradise created the company Skillz with the requirement that every person in the business (including him) has to play video games a minimum of 35 times per week. Every employee that plays at least 50 times enters a raffle to choose the lunch menu for catered office lunch on Fridays. Overachievers like Don Kim regularly play over 500 times each week—which has earned him the nickname "Beast."

Why would a small business want its people to play video games? Because Skillz provides the online venue for organizing game tournaments, arranging competitions, managing entry fees and payouts to winners, and catching ringers, hackers, and cheats. Most participants just play for fun, but 10 percent pay entry fees ranging from $.60 to $20 per game. Of the entry fees, 86 percent goes to the prize pool, 7 percent goes to game developers, and 7 percent goes to Skillz.

How big a deal can seven percent be to the company that started in 2012? In 2013, that 7 percent meant $108,144 in revenue. In three short years 12 million registered users in 180 countries took that 7 percent to $54 million in annual revenue!

Amazingly, more time is spent playing video games than physical sports, and eSports could soon become bigger than the NFL, NBA, MLB, and NHL combined. Skillz is well positioned by providing the platform for over 3,000 eSport game development companies. Nielsen estimates there are 191 million eSports enthusiasts, of which 61 percent are Millennials.

Andrew Paradise wants to own a unique spot in online gaming—not first-person shooters that take computer horsepower to operate. Rather, Paradise focuses exclusively on mobile devices better suited for games like Bubble Shooter, Doodle Jump, Color Switch, bowling, even dominoes and solitaire.

Paradise's small business Skillz illustrates points that you will see throughout the pages and chapters to come—all you need is to find a niche in a market, have the skills to create a competitive advantage, and small business does not have to be boring.

Sources: David Whitford, "The Skillz to Conquer," *Inc.*, September 2017, 20–25; Eric Schurenberg, "500 Dreams Come True. Are You Listening, Washington?" *Inc.*, September 2017, 14; Miriam Aguirre, "Esports' Future is Female," September 5, 2017, https://venturebeat.com/2017/09/05/esports-future-is-female.

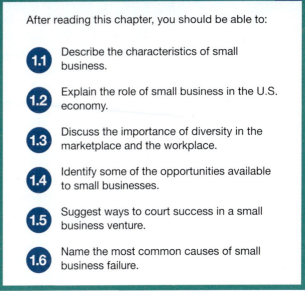

LEARNING OUTCOMES

After reading this chapter, you should be able to:

1.1 Describe the characteristics of small business.

1.2 Explain the role of small business in the U.S. economy.

1.3 Discuss the importance of diversity in the marketplace and the workplace.

1.4 Identify some of the opportunities available to small businesses.

1.5 Suggest ways to court success in a small business venture.

1.6 Name the most common causes of small business failure.

Concept Module 1.1: What Is Small Business?

- **LO 1.1: Describe the characteristics of small business.**

As the driver of the free enterprise system, small business generates a great deal of energy, innovation, and profit for millions of Americans. While the names of huge Fortune 500 corporations may be household words pumped into our lives via a multitude of media, small businesses have always been a central part of American life. In his 1835 book *Democracy in America*, Alexis de Tocqueville commented, "What astonishes me in the United States is not so much the marvelous grandeur of some undertakings as the innumerable multitude of small ones." If

> Master the content at
> **edge.sagepub.com/ Hatten7e**
> **$SAGE edge™**

de Tocqueville were alive today, aside from being more than 200 years old, he would probably still be amazed at the contributions made by small businesses.

The U.S. Small Business Administration (SBA) Office of Advocacy estimates there were 28.8 million businesses in the United States in 2006. Census data show that only 20 percent (5.8 million) of those 28.8 million businesses have employees, and 80 percent (23 million) do not.[1] The IRS estimate may be overstated because one business can own other businesses, but all of the businesses are nevertheless counted separately. What a great time to be in (and be studying) small business! Check out the following facts. Did you realize that small businesses

- Represent more than 99.7 percent of *all* employers?

- Employ 48 percent of all private sector employees?

- Pay 41.2 percent of total U.S. private payroll?

- Created 63.3 percent of net new jobs over the past 20 years?

- Represented 98 percent of all identified exporters and produced 33 percent of the known export value in FY2017?[2]

- Produce 16 times more patents per employee than large firms?

- Create more than 50 percent of private gross domestic product (GDP)?

- Hire 42 percent of high-tech workers (such as scientists, engineers, and computer programmers)?

- Are about 50 percent home based and 2.9 percent franchises?[3]

Small businesses include everything from the stay-at-home parent who provides day care for other children, to the factory worker who makes after-hours deliveries, to the owner of a chain of fast-food restaurants. The 28.8 million businesses identified by the SBA included more than 9 million Americans who operate "sideline" businesses, part-time enterprises that supplement the owner's income.[4] Another 12 million people make owning and operating a small business their primary occupation. Seven million of these business owners employ only themselves—as carpenters, independent sales representatives, freelance writers, and other types of single-person businesses. The U.S. Census Bureau tracks firms by number of employees. The firms included in the census figures are those that have a tangible location and claim income on a tax return. Figure 1.1 shows that 57 percent of employer firms (established firms with employees) have fewer than 5 employees. Slightly more than 128,000 businesses have 100 employees or more. Most people are surprised to learn that of the millions of businesses in the United States, only approximately 23,000 businesses have 500 or more workers on their payroll.

Size Definitions

The definition of **small business** depends on the criteria used for determining what is "small" and what qualifies as a "business." The most common criterion used to distinguish between large and small businesses is the number of employees (Figure 1.1). Other criteria include sales revenue, the total value of assets, and the value of owners' equity. The SBA, a federally funded agency that provides loans and assistance to small businesses, has established definitions of business size that vary by industry. These definitions are based on annual sales revenues or number of employees, and they vary by industry codes assigned by the North American Industrial Classification System (NAICS).

small business
A business is generally considered small if it is independently owned, operated, and financed; has fewer than 100 employees; and has relatively little impact on its industry.

Almost All Established Firms Are Small Businesses, 2017

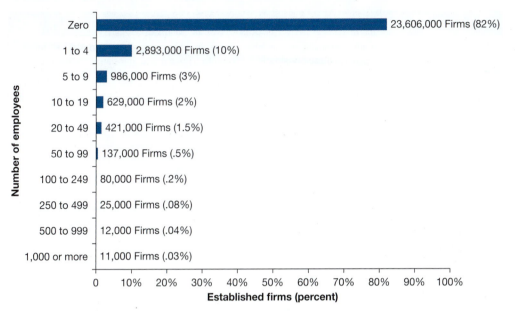

Source: U.S. Department of Labor, Bureau of Labor Statistics, "Business Employment Dynamics, Table G. Distribution of private sector firms by size class: 1993/Q1 through 2017/Q1," accessed December 2017, www.bls.gov/web/cewbd/table_g.txt

The SBA's Size Policy Board makes recommendations of business size eligibility based on economic studies. In establishing and reviewing business size standards, it considers the following factors:

- Industry structure analysis
- Degree of competition
- Average firm size
- Start-up cost
- Entry barriers, distribution of sales, and employment by firm size
- Effects of different size standard levels on the objectives of SBA programs
- Comments from the public on notices of proposed rule making[5]

Small business size standards vary by the industry within which the business operates: construction, manufacturing, mining, transportation, wholesale trade, retail trade, and service. In general, manufacturers with fewer than 500 employees are classified as small, as are wholesalers with fewer than 100 employees, and retailers or services with less than $6 million in annual revenue. Table 1.1 details more specific size standards.

Why is it important to classify businesses as big or small? Aside from facilitating academic discussion of the contributions made by these businesses, the classifications are important in that they determine whether a business may qualify for SBA assistance and for government set-aside programs, which require a percentage of each government agency's purchases to be made from small businesses.

Types of Industries

Some industries lend themselves to small business operation more than others do. In construction, for instance, the SBA classifies over 80 percent of companies in the industry as small. Manufacturing and mining industries have long been associated with mass employment,

Small Business Size Standards

Range of Size Standards by Industry
Construction: General building and heavy construction contractors have a size standard of $33.5 million in average annual receipts. Special trade construction contractors have a size standard of $14 million.
Manufacturing: For approximately 75 percent of the manufacturing industries, the size standard is 500 employees. A small number have a 1,500-employee size standard, and the balance have a size standard of either 750 or 1,000 employees.
Mining: All mining industries, except mining services, have a size standard of 500 employees.
Retail Trade: Most retail trade industries have a size standard of $7 million in average annual receipts. A few, such as grocery stores, department stores, motor vehicle dealers, and electrical appliance dealers, have higher size standards. None exceed $29 million in annual receipts.
Services: For the service industries, the most common size standard is $7 million in average annual receipts. Computer programming, data processing, and systems design have a size standard of $25 million. Engineering and architectural services have different size standards, as do a few other service industries. The highest annual receipts size standard in any service industry is $35.5 million. Research and development and environmental remediation services are the only service industries with size standards stated in number of employees.
Wholesale Trade: For all wholesale trade industries, a size standard of 100 employees is applicable for loans and other financial programs. When acting as a dealer on federal contracts set aside for small business or issued under the 8(a) program, the size standard is 500 employees, and the firm must deliver the product of a small domestic manufacturer.
Other Industries: Other industry divisions include agriculture; transportation, communications, electric, gas, and sanitary services; finance; insurance; and real estate. Because of wide variations in the structures of the industries in these divisions, there is no common pattern of size standards. For specific size standards, refer to the size regulations in 13 CFR § 121.201 or the table of small business size standards.

as well as mass production, yet SBA data show that over 40 percent of manufacturers and mining companies are classified as small. More than 65 percent of all real estate businesses are small. Just under two-thirds (62.3 percent) of arts, entertainment, and recreational service businesses are small.[6] The industry that employs the largest number of people in small business, however, is services. Seventy-one percent of all service businesses are small.

For purposes of discussion in this book, we will consider a business to be small if it meets the following criteria:

- *It is independently owned, operated, and financed.* One or very few people run the business.

- *It has fewer than 100 employees.* Although SBA standards allow 500 or more employees for some types of businesses to qualify as "small," the most common limit is 100.

- *It has relatively little impact on its industry.* New Belgium Brewing Company, maker of Fat Tire beer, brews about one million barrels generating annual revenue of $180 million. Although this is an impressive figure, the firm is still classified as a small business because it has little influence on Anheuser-Busch or Heineken, which had 2016 sales of $45.52 billion and $22.5 billion, respectively.[7]

Microbusinesses

While the SBA uses the broad size definition cited above, the Association for Enterprise Opportunity (AEO—a trade group dedicated to microbusinesses) and the U.S. Census

Bureau define microbusiness as one with fewer than five employees, including the owner.[8] For example, a law firm with two attorneys and a paralegal; the owner of a corner grocery store with a stock assistant and a clerk; an after-school tutor; a computer technician; or an independent truck driver. Historically, such businesses have been regarded as too small to count; today, microbusinesses are becoming too important to ignore.

How much impact could businesses with so few employees generate? For starters, they employ more people than are in the government sector—federal, state, and local levels combined. They employ more than twice as many people as those in manufacturing (Figure 1.2).

With a group of over 26 million, one would expect a lot of variation in owner type. Five types of microbusiness owners provide insight into groups that are similar. See Figure 1.3.

Technology creates all kinds of possibilities for microbusiness. We will discuss location-neutral businesses and co-working spaces later (in Chapter 12). These two factors combined with the desire by many to have more flexibility in hours worked and online platforms to facilitate transactions make microbusinesses a viable alternative.

©iStock.com/Maica

▼ FIGURE 1.2

Microbusiness Employment Compared to Industry Sectors

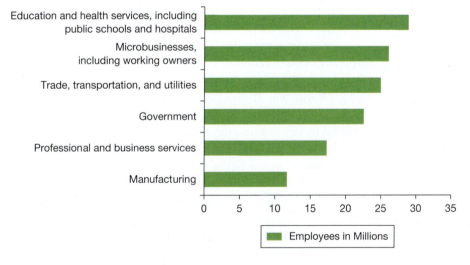

Employees in Millions

Concept Check Questions

1. How would you define *small business*?

2. Name a company that seems large but might be classified as small because it has relatively little impact on its industry.

3. What are the criteria commonly used to define small business?

Five Types of Microbusiness Owner

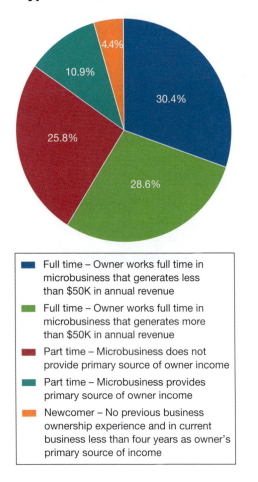

- ■ Full time – Owner works full time in microbusiness that generates less than $50K in annual revenue
- ■ Full time – Owner works full time in microbusiness that generates more than $50K in annual revenue
- ■ Part time – Microbusiness does not provide primary source of owner income
- ■ Part time – Microbusiness provides primary source of owner income
- ■ Newcomer – No previous business ownership experience and in current business less than four years as owner's primary source of income

Economy of scale
The lowering of costs through production of larger quantities.

marketing concept
The philosophy of a business in which the wants and needs of customers are determined before goods and services are produced.

service sector
Businesses in an economic sector that provide services, rather than tangible goods.

Concept Module 1.2: Small Businesses in the U.S. Economy

- **LO 1.2: Explain the role of small business in the U.S. economy.**

Until the early 1800s, all businesses were small in the way just described. Most goods were produced one at a time by workers in their cottages or in small artisan studios. Much of the U.S. economy was based on agriculture. With the Industrial Revolution, however, mass production became possible. Innovations such as Samuel Slater's textile machinery, Eli Whitney's cotton gin, and Samuel Colt's use of interchangeable parts in producing firearms changed the way business was conducted. Factories brought people, raw materials, and machinery together to produce large quantities of goods.

Although the early manufacturers were small, by the late 1800s businesses were able to grow rapidly in industries that relied on economies of scale for their profitability. **Economy of scale** is the lowering of costs through production of larger quantities. The more units you make, the less each costs. During this time, for example, Andrew Carnegie founded U.S. Steel, Henry Ford introduced the assembly line for manufacturing automobiles, and Cornelius Vanderbilt speculated in steamships and railroads. Although these individuals began as entrepreneurs, their companies eventually came to dominate their respective industries. The costs of competing with them became prohibitively high as the masses of capital they accumulated formed a barrier to entry for newcomers to the industry. The subsequent industrialization of America decreased the impact of new entrepreneurs over the first half of the 20th century.[9] Small businesses still existed during this period, of course, but the economic momentum that large businesses had gathered kept small businesses in minor roles.

The decades following World War II also favored big business over small business. Industrial giants like General Motors and IBM, and retailers like Sears, Roebuck and Company flourished during this period by tapping into the expanding consumer economy. President Franklin Roosevelt's New Deal programs aimed at economic development focused on government programs in conjunction with large businesses. Little attention was given to stimulate small business.[10]

In the late 1950s and early 1960s, another economic change began. Businesses began paying more attention to consumer wants and needs, rather than focusing solely on production. This paradigm shift was called the **marketing concept**—finding out what people want and then producing that good or service, rather than making products and then trying to convince people to buy them. With this shift came an increased importance ascribed to the service economy. The emphasis on customer service by businesses adopting the marketing concept started to provide more opportunities for small business. Today, the **service sector** of our economy makes up about 81 percent of total U.S. jobs, producing services for customers rather than tangible products.[11] The growth of this sector is important to small businesses because they can compete effectively in it.

In 1953, President Dwight Eisenhower signed the Small Business Act into law creating the Small Business Administration to "encourage" and "develop" small business growth, and to aid minorities and other disadvantaged people in securing loans and learning management

techniques. The act reads, "The essence of the American economic system of private enterprise is free competition. Only through full and free competition can free markets, free entry into business, and opportunities for the expression and growth of personal initiative and judgement be assured."[12]

By the early 1970s, corporate profits began to decline, while these large firms' costs increased. Entrepreneurs such as Steve Jobs of Apple and Bill Gates of Microsoft started small businesses and created entirely new industries that had never before existed. Managers began to realize that bigger is not necessarily better and that economy of scale does not guarantee lower costs. Other start-ups, such as Walmart and The Limited, both of which were founded in the 1960s, dealt serious blows to retail giants like Sears in the 1970s. Because their organizational structures were flatter, the newer companies could respond more quickly to customers' changing desires, and they were more flexible in changing their products and services.

▲ Service businesses dominate the U.S. economy and are primarily small.

The global economic crisis that began in 2007 had a tremendous impact on small business. Disruption of small business financing was significant due to the close connection between the business and the owner—with home second mortgages and lines of credit—putting the small business owner's home in play in case of loan default. Tactics for small business owners to deal with the credit squeeze revolved primarily around protecting cash flow to decrease dependence on external funding.

> "Managers began to realize that bigger is not necessarily better and that economy of scale does not guarantee lower costs."

What many countries, regions, and local governments have come to realize is the importance of small businesses to economic development. Increasingly, economic development experts are abandoning traditional approaches to economic development that rely on recruiting large employers with tax breaks, financial incentives, and other inducements. What works now is building businesses from the ground up and supporting growth of existing businesses. This approach accomplishes two goals:

1. Develop and support entrepreneurs and small business.

2. Expand and improve infrastructure and develop a skilled and educated workforce.

The economic development goal of enticing large firms to move are seldom reached—or at a long-term cost higher than the value of the jobs gained.[13] Chiquita Brands International (think bananas) accepted $22 million worth of state and local tax incentives to move its corporate headquarters to Charlotte, North Carolina, in exchange for bringing more than 400 jobs. It agreed to stay for 10 years. But after only 3 years, Chiquita decided to move to Cincinnati, Ohio, after a high-profile Twitter recruitment campaign. Feeling jilted, Charlotte economic development officials are now rethinking the incentives they will offer in the future. Commissioner Jim Puckett says "It's like my dad always told me, if the girl dates you for your money, etc., remember there is always someone with more of whatever she is looking for."[14]

Increased Business Start-Ups

Indeed, the rate of small business growth has more than doubled in the last 47 years. In 1970, 264,000 new employer businesses were started.[15] In 1980, that figure had grown to 532,000; it reached 585,000 in 1990, 574,000 in 2000, falling to 385,358 in 2010, and rebounding to 403,902 in 2014.[16] Although a lot of attention tends to be paid to the failure rate of small businesses, many people continue going into business for themselves. New businesses compared with closures are consistently close in number. While annual business closures were greater than start-ups for the years 2009–2011, the trend has reversed with 2014 seeing 403,902 start-ups versus 391,553 closures.[17]

Increasing Interest at Colleges and Universities

The growing economic importance of small business has not escaped notice on college and university campuses. In 1985, only 250 entrepreneurship courses were offered in the United States. By 2008, that number had grown to over 5,000.[18]

A recent study found that 61 percent of recent college graduates want to start their own business. Forty-five percent think it is very likely they will do so, and 20 percent have already started a business of their own before graduating. Even the 30 percent of graduates who concede it is highly unlikely they will be self-employed say they would like to do so. There is a gap between desire and reality indicated by half of those who want to start a business but believe that it's really feasible. Two-thirds admit they don't completely understand critical functions of starting a business, such as how to incorporate their business or write a business plan.[19]

> "In 1985, only 250 entrepreneurship courses were offered in the United States. By 2008, that number had grown to over 5,000."

What can explain this phenomenal growth of interest in small business at educational institutions? For one thing, it parallels the explosion in small business formation. For another thing, since mistakes made in running a small business are expensive in terms of both time and money, many prospective business owners attend school in order to make those mistakes on paper and not in reality.

Some students don't wait for graduation to take advantage of hot college trends—such as Miranda Wang with her company BioCellection. While an undergrad at Wharton, Wang knew that plastic works well for many applications, but that most plastic is never recycled because of difficulties in processing and remolding it. BioCellection's mission is "to focus on treating this plastic innovatively before it becomes pollution." Its first product is an artist's paint made from plastic bags.[20]

Concept Check Questions

1. This module discusses growth of interest in entrepreneurship on campuses, which causes some to wonder if entrepreneurship can be taught or are you born one. What do you think? Why?

2. Why is the service sector dominated by small businesses?

3. How would you show that small business is becoming a more important part of the economy?

Concept Module 1.3: Workforce Diversity and Small Business Ownership

- **LO 1.3: Discuss the importance of diversity in the marketplace and the workplace.**

Data from the Census Bureau Survey of Business Owners (SBO) and the Bureau of Labor Statistics show that women owned 9.1 million nonfarm U.S. businesses in 2016—an increase of 38 percent since 2002 (Figure 1.4). The trend toward self-employment is reflected in all nonwhite categories by large percentage gains, up to 22 percent in 2016.[21]

Trends of an aging population, increasing birthrate of minority groups, more attention to the needs and abilities of people with disabilities, and more women entering the workforce are changing the way our nation and our businesses operate. The intent of most civil rights law is to ensure all groups are represented and that discrimination is not tolerated. Wheels of change

U.S. Women Business Owners by the Numbers

Sources: "The 2017 State of Women-Owned Businesses Report," National Association of Women Business Owners, www.nawbo.org/resources/women-in-business-owner-statistics; icons from Alena Artemova, Alice Noir, and Wilson Joseph.

tend to move slowly, and inequities persist across wide ranges of groups of people, but progress is being made, especially among the self-employed.

The number of women-owned firms and their annual revenues:[22]

- Women-owned firms make up 39 percent of all privately owned businesses.
- They generate 14 percent of employment and 12 percent of total revenues.
- Twenty percent of firms with revenue of over $1 million are women owned.

The number of minority-owned firms and their annual revenues:[23]

- Asian-owned firms totaled 1,917,902 and generated $699.5 billion annual revenue.
- Black-owned firms totaled 2,584,403 and generated $150.2 billion annual revenue.
- Hispanic-owned businesses totaled 1,573,464 and generated $222 billion annual revenue.
- American Indian/Alaska Native–owned firms totaled 272,919 and generated $38.8 billion annual revenue.
- The rate of minority business ownership in 2016 was 22 percent, compared with 14.6 percent in 2012.

> "These data show that when faced with the choice of working for someone else or working for themselves, people from widely varied backgrounds choose the latter."

These data show that when faced with the choice of working for someone else or working for themselves, people from widely varied backgrounds choose the latter.

Resources exist to specifically assist women- and minority-owned businesses. The SBA 8(a) federal certification program promotes access for entrepreneurs who are socially or economically disadvantaged to federal contracts. SBA 8(a) certification provides women and minority business owners preference in bidding on federal and some state contracts. Professional organizations such as the Techstars Foundation, Code2040, 500 Startups, Black Founders, National Association of Women Business Owners (nawbo.org) and Women's Business Enterprise National Council (wbenc.org) provide networking, educational, and corporate contract information.[24]

The Value of Diversity to Business

Considering the number of problems most small business owners face, perhaps more of them will make the same discovery that Ernest Drew did in the following story: Diversity in the workplace can provide creative problem-solving ideas.

Ernest Drew, CEO of chemical producer Hoechst Celanese, learned the value of diversity during a company conference. A group of 125 top company officials, primarily white men, were separated into groups with 50 women and minority employees. Some of the groups comprised a variety of races and genders; others were composed of white men only. The groups were asked to analyze a problem concerning corporate culture and suggest ways to change it. According to Drew, the more diverse teams produced the broadest solutions. "They had ideas I hadn't even thought of," he recalled. "For the first time, we realized that diversity is a strength as it relates to problem solving."[25] Drew's conclusion that a varied workforce is needed at every level of an organization can be applied to businesses of any size.

Concept Check Questions

1. Is workforce diversity as important to small businesses as it is to big businesses? Why or why not?

2. From strictly a small business perspective (not social or emotional perspectives), why is diversity important?

3. How might an increase in women-owned small businesses drive change toward more equal pay for equal work in the workforce?

Concept Module 1.4: Secrets of Small Business Success

- **LO 1.4: Identify some of the opportunities available to small businesses.**
- **LO 1.5: Suggest ways to court success in a small business venture.**

When large and small businesses compete directly against one another, it might seem that large businesses would always have a better chance of winning. In reality, small businesses have certain inherent factors that work in their favor. You will improve your chances of achieving success in running a small business if you identify your competitive advantage, remain flexible and innovative, cultivate a close relationship with your customers, and strive for quality.

> "It may come as a surprise, but big businesses need small businesses—a symbiotic relationship (the type where both parties benefit) exists between them."

It may come as a surprise, but big businesses need small businesses—a symbiotic relationship (the type where both parties benefit) exists between them. For instance, John Deere relies on hundreds of vendors, many of which are small, to produce component parts for its farm equipment. Deere's extensive network of 3,400 independent dealers, comprising small businesses, provides sales and service for its equipment. These relationships enable Deere, the world's largest manufacturer of farm equipment, to focus on what it does best, while at the same time creating economic opportunity for hundreds of individual entrepreneurs.

Small businesses perform more efficiently than larger ones in several areas. For example, although large manufacturers tend to enjoy a higher profit margin due to their economies of scale, small businesses are often better at distribution. Most wholesale and retail businesses are small, which serves to link large manufacturers more efficiently with the millions of consumers spread all over the world.

competitive advantage
The facet of a business that is better than the competition's. A competitive advantage can be built from many different factors.

Competitive Advantage

To be successful in business, you have to offer your customers more value than your competitors do. That value gives the business its **competitive advantage**. For example, suppose you are a printer whose competitors offer only black-and-white printing. An investment in color printing equipment would give your business a competitive advantage, at least until your competitors purchased similar equipment. The stronger and more sustainable your competitive advantage, the better your chances are of winning and keeping customers. You must have a product or service that your business provides better than the competition, or the pressures of the marketplace may make your business obsolete (see Chapter 3).

Flexibility. To take advantage of economies of scale, large businesses usually seek to devote resources to produce large quantities of products over long periods of time. This commitment of resources limits their ability to react to new and quickly changing markets as small businesses do. Imagine the difference between making a sharp turn in a loaded 18-wheel tractor trailer and a small pickup truck. Now apply the analogy to large and small businesses turning in new directions. The big truck has a lot more capacity, but the pickup has more maneuverability in reaching customers.

> "Creativity is allowing yourself to make mistakes. Art is knowing which ones to keep." —Scott Adams

Innovation. Real innovation has come most often from independent inventors and small businesses. The reason? The research and development departments of most large businesses tend to concentrate on the improvement of the products their companies already make. This practice makes sense for companies trying to profit from their large investments in plant and equipment. At the same time, it tends to discourage the development of totally new ideas and products. For example, does Apple have an economic incentive to invent a product that makes iPhones obsolete? No, they have incentive to release lines of incremental new models with enough variations to get us to upgrade.

Small businesses have contributed many inventions that we use daily. The long list would include zippers, air conditioners, helicopters, computers, instant cameras, audiotape recorders, double-knit fabric, fiber-optic examining equipment, heart valves, optical scanners, soft contact lenses, airplanes, and automobiles, most of which were later produced by large manufacturers. In fact, many say the greatest value of entrepreneurial companies is the way they force larger competitors to respond to innovation. Small businesses innovate by introducing new technology and markets, creating new markets, developing new products, and nurturing new ideas—actions that larger businesses have to compete with, thereby requiring the larger businesses to change.

Economist Joseph Schumpeter called the replacement of existing products, processes, ideas, and businesses with new and better ones **creative destruction**. It is not an easy process. Yet, although change can be threatening, it is vitally necessary in a capitalist system.[26] Small businesses are the driving force of change that leads to creative destruction, especially in the development of new technology.[27]

> "Small businesses are the driving force of change that leads to creative destruction, especially in the development of new technology."

In 2001, General Electric was the most valuable company in the world. In 2017, it didn't make the top 50, and 5 of the top 10, Alphabet, Amazon, Facebook, Tencent, and Alibaba were start-ups or didn't exist in 2000.[28]

Small businesses play a major role in creating the innovation that Schumpeter discussed. Four types of innovation that small businesses are most likely to produce include

- *Product innovation:* Developing a new or improved product.

- *Service innovation:* Offering a new or altered service for sale.

- *Process innovation:* Inventing a new way to organize physical inputs to produce a product or service.

- *Management innovation:* Creating a new way to organize a business's resources.

creative destruction
The replacement of existing products, processes, ideas, and businesses with new and better ones.

The most common types of innovation relate to services and products. Thirty-eight percent of all innovations are service related, and 32 percent are product related. Interestingly, the

SBA found the majority of innovations originate from the smallest businesses, those with 1 to 19 employees. More than three-fourths of service innovations are generated by very small businesses, which also generate 65 percent of both product and process innovations. Small firms account for 14 percent of green technology patents and more than 32 percent of patents in both smart grids and solar energy. Recent research reported to the SBA's Office of Advocacy showed that small patenting firms produce 16 times more patents per employee as large patenting firms.[29]

The process of creative destruction is not limited to high-technology businesses or to the largest companies. A small business owner who does not keep up with market innovations risks being left behind. Creative destruction occurs in mundane as well as exotic industries, such as chains of beauty salons replacing barber shops.

The structure of small businesses set them up to be incubators for innovation—fewer decision makers, fewer employees, and lean business models are competitive advantages. When conditions change, small businesses can pivot and adapt. Still, innovation is not easy—even for small business owners. To make innovation a priority, small business owners need to

- *Take risks:* Staying in the pack is easier and safer in almost every situation, business or otherwise. Taking carefully calculated risks can lead to competitive advantage.

- *Take advantage of customer connections:* Proximity to customers gives small business owners access to good ideas that come from the people actually using their products/services.

- *Keep decision-making agile:* Few things kill innovation faster than multiple layers of decision makers or bureaucracy—neither of which is associated with small business.

- *Experiment and adapt:* Innovation comes from the habit of simply trying new things without expecting every new idea to be a success.

- *Hire for innovation:* The thinking of creative, forward-thinking people is contagious.[30]

Close Relationship to Customers. Small business owners get to know their customers and neighborhood on a personal level. This closeness allows them to provide individualized service and gives them firsthand knowledge of customer wants and needs. By contrast, large businesses get to "know" their customers only through limited samples of marketing research (which may be misleading). Knowing customers personally can allow small businesses to build a competitive advantage based on specialty products, personalized service, and quality, which enables them to compete with the bigger businesses' lower prices gained through mass production. For this reason, you should always remember that the rapport you build with your customers is of vital importance—it is what makes them come back again and again.

Getting Started on the Right Foot

Before starting your own business, you will want to make sure that you have the right tools to succeed. Look for a market large enough to generate a profit, sufficient capital, skilled employees, and accurate information.

Market Size and Definition. Who will buy your product or service? Marketing techniques help you find out what consumers want and in what quantity. Armed with this information, you can make an informed decision about the profitability of offering a particular good or service. Once you conclude that a market is large enough to support your business, you will want to learn what your customers have in common and how their likes and dislikes will affect your market, so as to serve them better and remain competitive.

Gathering Sufficient Capital. All too often, entrepreneurs try to start a business without obtaining sufficient start-up capital. The lifeblood of any young business is cash; starting on a

LIGHTING THE FUSE OF INNOVATION

While small businesses develop and commercialize much innovation, another source of initial innovations is primary research—which small businesses may still develop without their own research and development. Some sources of innovations include

- **Global Innovation Initiative**—This program provides grants to university consortia focusing on science, technology, engineering, and mathematics, or STEM-related issues of global significance that foster cutting-edge multinational research and strengthen institutional international partnerships.

- **America Makes**—America Makes supports and facilitates research collaboration among leaders from business, academia, nonprofit organizations, and government. Its research efforts are aimed at enabling technology transition from universities and government (i.e., basic research) through to commercialization.

- **National Network for Manufacturing Innovation**—NNMI is a network of research institutes that focuses on developing and commercializing manufacturing technologies through public–private partnerships between U.S. industry, universities, and federal

government agencies. The network currently consists of nine institutes:

1. National Additive Manufacturing Innovation Institute
2. Digital Manufacturing and Design Innovation Institute
3. Lightweight Materials Manufacturing Innovation Institute
4. Next Generation Power Electronics Institute
5. Institute for Advanced Composites Manufacturing Innovation
6. American Institute for Manufacturing Integrated Photonics
7. Flexible Hybrid Electronics Manufacturing Innovation Institute
8. Advanced Functional Fabrics of America
9. Smart Manufacturing Innovation Institute

Sources: Institute for International Education, Global Innovation Initiative, accessed August 28, 2018, https://www.iie.org/en/Programs/Global-Innovation-Initiative/About; America Makes, accessed August 28, 2018, https://www.americamakes.us; National Network for Manufacturing Innovation, accessed August 28, 2018, https://www.energy.gov/eere/amo/national-network-manufacturing-innovation.

financial shoestring hurts your chances of success. Profit is the ultimate goal, but inadequate cash flow cuts off the blood supply (see Chapter 8).

You may need to be creative in finding start-up capital. A second mortgage, loans from friends or relatives, a line of credit from a bank or credit union, or a combination of sources may be sufficient. Thorough planning will give you the best estimate of how much money you will need. Once you have made your best estimate, double it—or at least get access to more capital. You'll probably need it.

Finding and Keeping Effective Employees. Maintaining a capable workforce is a never-ending task for small businesses. Frequently, small business owners get caught up in the urgency to "fill positions with warm bodies" without spending enough time on the selection process. You should hire, train, and motivate your employees before opening for business (see Chapter 15).

Once established, you must understand that your most valuable assets walk out the door at closing time. In other words, your employees are your most valuable assets. It is their skill, knowledge, and information that make your business successful. These intangible assets are called **intellectual capital**.

Getting Accurate Information. Managers at any organization will tell you how difficult it is to make a decision before acquiring all the relevant information. This difficulty is compounded for the aspiring small business owner, who does not yet possess the expertise or experience needed to oversee every functional area of the business, from accounting to sales. Consult a variety of sources of information, from self-help books in your local library to

intellectual capital
The valuable skills and knowledge that employees of a business possess.

experts in your nearest Small Business Development Center. A more accurate picture can be drawn if you consider several vantage points.

Concept Check Questions

1. Why are small businesses more likely than large businesses to be innovative?

2. Explain the term *creative destruction*.

3. Is *creative destruction* just another economic theory for the foundation of capitalism? Build a case supporting your answer.

4. How can being close to your customers give you a competitive advantage?

5. How would the computer industry be different today if there were no businesses with fewer than 500 employees? Would personal computers exist?

6. This chapter discusses the evolution of small business in the U.S. economy. On the heels of the rapid growth in the popularity of internet businesses in the late 1990s, the ensuing bust in 2000, and the current trend away from online and toward mobile connectivity, what will be the next stage in small business's evolution? Is the internet just another business tool, or will it re-create the way business is done?

Concept Module 1.5: Understanding the Risks of Small Business Ownership

- **LO 1.6: Name the most common causes of small business failure.**

The decision to start your own business should be made with a full understanding of the risks involved. If you go in with both eyes open, you will be able to anticipate problems, reduce the possibility of loss, and increase your chances of success. The prospect of failure should serve as a warning to you. Many new businesses do not get past their second or third years. Running a small business involves much more than simply getting an idea, hanging out a sign, and opening for business the next day. You need a vision, resources, and a plan to take advantage of the opportunity that exists.

> "Running a small business involves much more than simply getting an idea, hanging out a sign, and opening for business the next day."

What Is Business Failure?

Even though business owners launch their ventures with the best of intentions and work long, hard hours, some businesses inevitably fail. Dun & Bradstreet, a financial research firm, defines a business failure as a business that closes as a result of either (1) actions such as bankruptcy, foreclosure, or voluntary withdrawal from the business *with a financial loss to a creditor;* or (2) a court action such as receivership (taken over involuntarily) or reorganization (receiving protection from creditors).[31]

> "Only those who dare to fail miserably can achieve greatly." —Robert Kennedy

How long do start-up businesses typically last? Of the businesses started in 2015, 79.9 percent survived 2016. About 50 percent see their fifth birthday. About one-third of establishments survive 10 years or longer.[32]

Causes of Business Failure

The rates of business failure vary greatly by industry and are affected by factors such as type of ownership, size of the business, and expertise of the owner. The causes of business failure are many and complex; however, the most common causes are inadequate management and financing (see Figure 1.5).

Although financial problems are listed as the most common cause of business failure, consider management's role in controlling them. Could business failure due to industry weakness

be linked to poor management? Yes, if the owner tried to enter an industry or market with no room for another competitor or responded only slowly to industry changes. High operating expenses and insufficient profit margins also reflect ineffective management. Finally, business failure due to insufficient capital suggests inexperienced management.

Inadequate Management. Business management is the efficient and effective use of resources. For small business owners, management skills are especially desirable—and often especially difficult to obtain. Lack of experience is one of their most pressing problems. Small business owners must be generalists; they do not have the luxury of specialized management. On the one hand, they may not be able to afford to hire the full-time experts who could help avert costly mistakes. On the other hand, their limited resources will not permit them to make many mistakes and stay in business. As a small business manager, you will probably have to make decisions in areas in which you have little expertise.

Small business managers are generally correct in pointing to internal factors as the reason for the failure of their businesses.[33] Figure 1.6 shows data on reasons small business founders gave for failures.[34] Internal problems are those more directly under the control of the manager, such as adequate capital, cash flow, facilities/equipment inventory control, human resources, leadership, organizational structure, and accounting systems.

The manager of a small business must be a leader, a planner, and a worker. You may be a "top gun" in sales, but that skill could work against you. You might be tempted to concentrate on sales while ignoring other equally important areas of the business, such as record keeping, inventory, and customer service.

No Website and No Social Media Presence. In the U.S. alone, about 88.5 percent of the population are online regularly and census numbers show that percentage continues to grow. A fact of business life in the 21st century is that if your customers (individual consumers or other businesses) cannot find you online or on social media the chances of them connecting with you are about zero.

▼ FIGURE 1.5
Causes of Business Failure

Source: Based on information from "Why Do Small Businesses Fail?" National Federation of Independent Business, March 20, 2017, www.nfib.com/content/resources/start-a-business/why-do-small-businesses-fail.

Causes of Small Business Failure Vary Widely

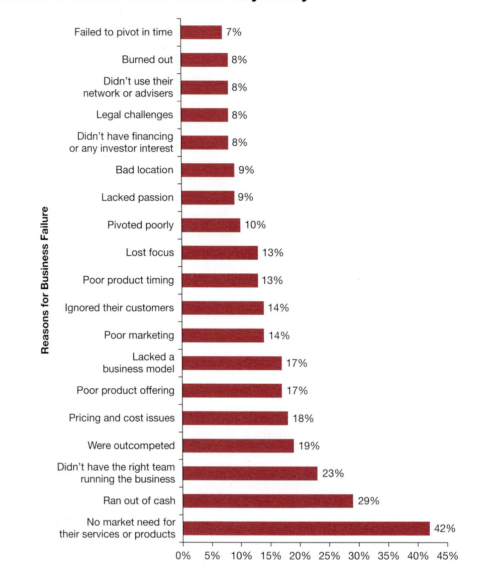

Source: Georgia McIntyre "What Percentage of Small Business Fail? (And Other Similar Stats You Need to Know)," Fundera Ledger, August 29, 2017, www.fundera.com/blog/what-percentage-of-small-businesses-fail

Inadequate Financing. Business failure due to inadequate financing can be caused by improper managerial control as well as shortage of capital. On the one hand, if you don't have adequate funds to begin with, you will not be able to afford the facilities or personnel you need to start up the business correctly. On the other hand, if you do possess adequate capital but do not manage your resources wisely, you may be unable to maintain adequate inventory or keep the balance needed to run the business.

There are a lot of ways to fail in business (Figure 1.6). You can extend too much credit. You can fail to plan for the future or not have strategic direction. You can overinvest in fixed assets or hire the wrong people. Identifying mistakes that can be made is merely one component of the problem. Figuring out how to avoid them is the hard part.[35]

Business Termination versus Failure

business termination
When a business ceases operation for any reason.

business failure
When a business closes with a financial loss to a creditor.

There is a difference between a **business termination** and a **business failure**. A *termination* occurs when a business no longer exists for any reason. A *failure* occurs when a business closes with a financial loss to a creditor. Reasons for a termination abound. The owner may have an opportunity to sell her business to someone else for a healthy profit, or be ready to move on to a new business or to retire, or she may have simply lost interest in the business. The market for the business's product may have changed or become saturated. Perhaps the owner has decided it would be more appealing to work for someone else. In other cases, businesses may change form. A partnership may be restructured as a corporation, or a business may move to a new location. Businesses that undergo such changes are considered terminated even though they continue in another form.

Mistakes Leading to Business Failure

No one likes to think about failing, yet many small business owners invite failure by ignoring basic rules for success. One of the most common mistakes is to neglect to plan for the future because planning seems too hard or time-consuming. Planning what you want to do with your business, where you want it to go, and how you're going to get there are prerequisites for a sound business. Of course, that doesn't mean you can't change your plans as circumstances dictate. Your plan should provide a road map for your business, showing you both the express-ways and the scenic routes—and the detours.

Another common mistake is failing to understand the commitment and hard work that are required for turning a business into a success. Having to work long hours and do things you don't enjoy because no one else is available to do them are part and parcel of owning a small business. Yet, when you have the freedom of being your own boss, the hard work and long hours often don't seem so demanding!

Still another mistake that small business owners make, particularly with rapidly growing businesses, is not hiring additional employees soon enough or not using existing employees effectively. There comes a point in the growth of a business when it is no longer possible for the manager to do it all, but she resists delegation in the belief that it means she is giving up control. It is important to recognize that delegating tasks to others isn't giving up control—it's giving up the execution of details.

The last type of mistake discussed here involves finances. Inaccurate estimates of cash flow and capital requirements can swamp a business quickly. Figuring the correct amount of money needed for starting a business is a tough balancing act: Asking for too little may hinder growth and actually jeopardize survival, whereas asking for too much might cause lenders or investors to hesitate. An important rule to remember in terms of arranging financing or calculating cash-flow projections is to figure the unexpected into your financial plans. In this way, you can have more of a cushion to fall back on if things don't go exactly according to plan. After all, without the right amount of capital, it's impossible to succeed.[36]

> "Inaccurate estimates of cash flow and capital requirements can swamp a business quickly."

Business failure, then, is a serious reality. How can a small business owner avoid it? Difficult changes may be needed, and change requires leaders to overcome all sorts of human dynamics, like inertia, tradition, and head-in-the-sand hoping that things will get better. Strategic moments require courage, or at least a lack of sentimentality, which is rare. It is in these moments that the best leaders find a mirror and ask themselves the defining question the late, great Peter Drucker posed nearly 40 years ago: "If you weren't already in your business, would you enter it today?" If the answer is no, Drucker said, you need to face a second tough question: "What are you going to do about it?" Every leader should heed this good advice and, if need be, follow it through to its conclusion, whether that will be to fix, sell, or close the business.[37]

Failure Rate Controversy

Almost everyone has heard the story about the supposedly high rate of failure for small businesses. "Did you know that 90 percent of all new businesses fail within one year?" the story usually begins, as if to confirm one's worst fears about business ownership. For educators

U.S. Business Start-Ups, Closures, and Bankruptcies

	Start-Ups	Closures	Bankruptcies
2014	403,902	391,553	26,983
2010	385,358	416,642	89,402
2005	644,122	565,745	39,201
2000	574,300	542,831	35,472
1995	594,369	497,246	50,516
1990	584,892	531,892	63,912

and business people, this piece of modern folklore is known as "the myth that would not die." Actually, only about 20 percent of all new businesses are forced to close their doors with a loss to creditors.[38] The rest either close voluntarily or are still in business. Over the past several decades, the number of new businesses that have opened has approached or exceeded the number that have closed. Table 1.2 shows a net increase in business formations (more businesses were started than stopped operations).

Sometimes researchers include business terminations in their failure-rate calculations, resulting in an artificially high number of failures. Economic consultant David Birch describes the misinterpretation of economic data as "like being at the end of a whisper chain. It's a myth everyone agrees to."[39] Fortunately for small business owners, this high number of failures is indeed a myth, not a fact.

Analysis of business closure data as part of the recent U.S. Census Bureau's Characteristics of Business Owners (CBO) reveals some interesting findings—including the finding that about one-third of closed businesses were successful at the time of their closure. The study represented a universe of about 17 million businesses with a sample of 78,147 businesses. It was one of the first major studies to include "closing while successful" as a possible outcome. That option could well challenge the failure myth, or the view that business closure is always negative. Entrepreneurs certainly devise exit strategies to close or sell a business before losses accumulate or to move on to other opportunities.[40]

Starting a business does involve risk, but the assumption of risk is part of life. In 2016, the divorce rate was 3.4 per 1,000 population.[41] The six-year graduation rate of bachelor's degree students in the United States is 59 percent (that is, 59 percent of first-time, full-time undergraduate students who started in 2009 or later had completed a bachelor's degree).[42] Would you decide not to get married because the divorce rate is too high? Were you afraid to go to college because of the dropout rate? The point to remember is that if you have a clear vision, know your product and your market, and devote the time and effort needed, your small business, like many others, can succeed.

Concept Check Questions

1. The text compares the failure rate for small businesses with the divorce rate in marriage and the student failure rate in college. Are these fair comparisons?

2. Describe four causes of small business failure. How does the quality of management relate to each of these causes?

3. Describe the techniques that a business with which you are familiar has used to prevent its failure.

4. Predict the future of small business. In what industries will it be most involved? What trends do you foresee? Will the failure rate go up or down? Will the importance of small business increase or decrease by the year 2020?

CHAPTER REVIEW

SUMMARY ▶▶

LO 1.1 Describe the characteristics of small business.

Small businesses include a wide variety of business types that are independently owned, operated, and financed. Although specific size definitions exist for each type of business, manufacturers with fewer than 500 employees, wholesalers with fewer than 100 employees, and retailers or services with annual revenues less than $3.5 million are typically considered small. By itself, each individual small business has relatively little impact in its industry.

LO 1.2 Explain the role of small business in the U.S. economy.

Small businesses provided the economic foundation on which the U.S. economy was built. Today these businesses are creating new jobs even as large businesses continue eliminating jobs. Small businesses are more flexible than large ones in the products and services they offer. Most real product innovations come from small businesses.

LO 1.3 Discuss the importance of diversity in the marketplace and the workplace.

As the population becomes more diverse, the owners and employees of small businesses are likewise becoming more diverse. Businesses owned by women and minorities are growing at a faster rate than the overall rate of business growth. Diversity is important in small business because a wide range of viewpoints and personal backgrounds can, at the least, improve problem solving.

LO 1.4 Identify some of the opportunities available to small businesses.

Small and large businesses need each other to survive—they have a symbiotic relationship. This relationship provides opportunities to small businesses in that they can supply needed parts to large manufacturers and can distribute manufactured goods. Moreover, small businesses often pick up functions that large businesses outsource. Other opportunities exist for small businesses where they enjoy the advantage of being able to profitably serve smaller niches than can their larger counterparts. For all these reasons, small businesses are rapidly becoming important players in international trade.

LO 1.5 Suggest ways to court success in a small business venture.

To prevent your small business from becoming another casualty noted in business failure statistics, you must begin with a clearly defined competitive advantage. You must offer a product or service that people want and are willing to buy. You must do something substantially better than your competition does it. You must remain flexible and innovative, stay close to your customers, and strive for quality.

LO 1.6 Name the most common causes of small business failure.

Ineffective and inefficient management, which shows up in many ways, is the number one cause of business failure. Inadequate financing, industry weakness, inexperience, and neglect are other major causes.

KEY TERMS ▶▶

business failure **18**

business termination **18**

competitive advantage **12**

creative destruction **13**

economy of scale **8**

intellectual capital **15**

marketing concept **8**

service sector **8**

small business **4**

EXPERIENTIAL LEARNING ACTIVITIES ▶▶

1.1: Competitive Advantage and Advantages/Disadvantages

LO 1.4: Identify some of the opportunities available to small businesses.

LO 1.5: Suggest ways to court success in a small business venture.

Instructions:

Students should form into groups of 3–5. Read the following scenario in your group, then, as a group, answer the questions that follow. Be prepared to write your answers on the white board and report your answers to the rest of the class.

Your best friend from high school has just texted you with his great new idea. He is going to begin a yard care business starting this October and he wants to hire you part-time to work for him. Your best friend knows little about running a business and also little about yard work, except what he has learned from doing yard work for his parents. Since you are currently taking a small business class, you know there are some questions your friend needs to consider.

1. What could be a competitive advantage your friend could bring to his business, taking into consideration there are already many successful yard care businesses in the area?

2. In order of importance, rank three reasons why your friend may be excited to have his own small business.

3. In order of importance, rank three challenges your friend will need to overcome in order for his small business to succeed.

After all groups have shared, what were the most frequently cited reasons for someone wanting to begin their own small business. What were the most frequently cited challenges that a small business owner must overcome?

1.2: Creative Destruction

LO 1.4: Identify some of the opportunities available to small businesses.

Take out a piece of paper and write down two plausible, yet creative, innovation ideas for each of the following categories in no more than 10 minutes.

- Product innovation
- Service innovation
- Process innovation
- Management innovation

After 10 minutes, form into groups of 3–5. In each group choose the best innovation from each category. Once the groups have chosen their best idea in each category, each group will write their innovations on the board and briefly explain the ideas.

After all groups have reported out their innovations, the class as a whole will choose the three best ideas for each category.

CHAPTER CLOSING CASE ▶▶

Small Business Lessons from the Movies

Movies are magical. They take us to new places, they spark our imagination, and they entertain us. Lessons from movies are open to interpretation that may differ from what the filmmaker ever intended. Steven Spielberg and George Lucas may have never intended to teach people how to run businesses, but let's step back, open our minds, and consider what we have seen that may solve problems in business. With some thought, we can come up with stories of communication, branding, ethics, customer service, and leadership applicable to starting and running a small business.

Here are some examples to get you started. Popcorn please . . .

It's a Wonderful Life (1946) OK, so we equate this one with Christmas, but consider the lesson of leading by example that director Frank Capra shows. It comes down to a confrontation between two businesspeople—Mr. Potter (Lionel Barrymore) wants to turn Bedford Falls into Pottersville, while George Bailey (James Stewart) puts his customers, employees, and family interest first by taking personal responsibility.

The Godfather, Parts I and II (1972, 1974) Not the most savory of mission statements, but these movies are about family business. There are lessons about loyalty and consequences. Many quotes are still used often in the business world—"go to the mattresses," "I'm gonna make him an offer he can't refuse," and "My father taught me many things . . . keep your friends close, but your enemies closer."

Steve Jobs (2015) Several movies have been made about the Apple founder, but this one doesn't flinch in covering successes and failures. The story of Steve Jobs is both profoundly inspiring and a bit scary when one sees what happens when a founder is the very soul of the company created.

Jerry Maguire (1996) After being jettisoned from a large firm, the title character (Tom Cruise) becomes a reluctant entrepreneur that brilliantly captures the manic-depressive roller-coaster ride of starting a business. With one employee and one client, Maguire literally has all his eggs in one basket to show that fewer clients and more personal attention are a good business strategy.

Wall Street (1987) This study of values compares and contrasts the differences between a father and a son. The small business lesson can be that "there are no shortcuts" in life or business. Just because you can visualize where you want to be does not mean that you can get there without paying dues.

A League of Their Own (1992) Just the tagline for the movie sets it up with a small business lesson: "To achieve the incredible you

have to attempt the impossible." Memorable quotes include "There's no crying in baseball," and "Of course this is hard." No matter how it appears—*every* business is hard. Don't complain.

The Pursuit of Happyness (2006) This biographical drama is based on entrepreneur Chris Gardner's one-year struggle with homelessness in the 1980s. Raising his son on the streets, we see his fierce commitment to his dream and duty to his son. Best quote? "Don't ever let somebody tell you . . . you can't do something. Not even me. . . . You got a dream . . . you gotta protect it. People can't do somethin' themselves, they wanna tell you 'you can't do it.' If you want somethin', go get it. Period."

Tucker: The Man and His Dream (1988) I, your author, admit personal bias on this one—I believe this is the *best business* movie *ever!* The best part is that the whole story is true. It's about an inventor who sets out to revolutionize the auto industry during World War II. It's got it all—business started in a barn, naysayers, faithful followers, time-crunched prototypes, creative technology advances, giant corporate adversaries, and failure. If you are in a class on small business/ entrepreneurship—watch this one.

You get the idea by now and yes, some of these were made before most students were born, but they are available as rentals. Some other contenders to consider include

Apollo 13 (1995)

Dead Poets Society (1989)

Elizabeth (1998)

Glengarry Glen Ross (1992)

Norma Rae (1979)

Office Space (1999)

One Flew over the Cuckoo's Nest (1975)

Twelve Angry Men (1957)

Twelve O'Clock High (1949)

Questions

1. What are your personal screen inspirations? What lessons do these or other movies provide in running a small business?

2. In addition to the movies cited in this closing case, think of other titles for business lessons such as *Risky Business*, *Pirates of Silicon Valley*, and *Monsters, Inc.* What lessons do they provide?

3. What movies portray leaders who think creatively, who keep their heads, who manage communication, and, as for failure, well, that's just not an option (a line from *Apollo 13*)?

4. Bearing in mind that the intent of movies is artistic, rather than educational, what movie lessons do you think illustrate the opposite of what a manager should do or say?

Sources: Lori Grant, "The 10 Best Business Movies," May 21, 2009, www.smartlemming.com/2009/05/the-10-best-business-movies; Mike Hofman, "Everything I Know about Leadership, I Learned from the Movies," *Inc.*, March 2000, 58–70; Leigh Buchanan, "Cinema for the Enterprising," *Inc.*, February 2007, 75–77. For more on this topic, see a recent book by Kevin Coupe and Michael Sansolo titled *The Big Picture: Essential Business Lessons from the Movies* (2010) from Brigantine Media.

## CHAPTER 2

SMALL BUSINESS MANAGEMENT AND ENTREPRENEURSHIP

E ntrepreneurs solve problems. That's really what they do—they identify problems and create a business to solve them. So, when's a good time to start solving problems? How about now?

You've heard stories of many famous entrepreneurs who dropped out of college to start their wildly successful business, insert Mark Zuckerberg or Steve Jobs story here. But you don't have to drop out to start a business.

Meet Kimberly and Logan

Kimberly Hruda and Logan Rae met while attending Florida Atlantic University. Rae made a bouquet—but not of flowers. Hers was made of bacon! The pair knew they were on to a good business idea so they launched Bacon Boxes in 2015. They grew their product line of savory treats distributed via an online direct to consumer business model. Bacon Boxes augments its direct e-commerce by offering pairing events and subscription boxes. Hruda and Rae soon moved into an industrial kitchen in Boca Raton. The pair has created gifts that are unique while also being environmentally sound.

Meet Seung

Seung Shin recognized a different kind of problem once his very traditional family saw his new tattoo for the first time. The $3,000 laser surgery process to remove his ink made him wonder if he could develop a

After reading this chapter, you should be able to:

2.1 Articulate the differences between the small business manager and the entrepreneur.

2.2 Discuss the steps in preparing for small business ownership.

2.3 Enumerate the advantages and disadvantages of self-employment.

2.4 Explain the role of innovation to small business.

permanent-yet-removable ink. Shin assembled a team of fellow New York University (NYU) students. Some 4 a.m. meetings and some all-nighter product development sessions led their company Ephemeral to win $75,000 in NYU's Stern School of Business 200K Entrepreneurial Challenge. Their goal of using existing tattoo equipment but delivering high-quality ink and an optional proprietary removal solution was achieved.

Sources: Yeho Lucy Hwang, "Meet This Year's Coolest College Startups Winner," *Inc.*, April 4, 2017, www.inc.com/yeho-lucy-hwang/meet-the-2017-coolest-college-startup; Helena Ball, "This Startup Wants You to Never Regret Getting a Tattoo," *Inc.*, April 7, 2016, www.inc.com/helena-ball/meet-incs-coolest-college-startup.html; "Ephemeral: Developer of Tattoo Ink with a Safe Removal Solution," *Inc.*, www.inc.com/profile/ephemeral.

Concept Module 2.1: The Entrepreneur–Manager Relationship

- **LO 2.1: Articulate the differences between the small business manager and the entrepreneur.**

What is the difference between a small business manager and an entrepreneur? Aren't all small business owners also entrepreneurs? Don't all entrepreneurs start as small business owners? The terms are often used interchangeably, and although some overlap exists between them, there are enough differences to warrant studying them separately.

In fact, entrepreneurship and small business management are both *processes*, not isolated incidents. **Entrepreneurship** is the process of identifying opportunities for which marketable needs exist and assuming the risk of creating an organization to satisfy them. An entrepreneur needs the vision to spot opportunities and the ability to capitalize on them. **Small business management**, by contrast, is the ongoing process of owning and operating an established business. A small business manager must be able to deal with all the challenges of moving the business forward—hiring and retaining good employees, reacting to changing customer wants and needs, making sales, and keeping cash flow positive, for example.

The processes of entrepreneurship and small business management both present challenges and rewards as the business progresses through different stages.

entrepreneurship
The process of identifying opportunities for which marketable needs exist and assuming the risk of creating an organization to satisfy them.

small business management
The ongoing process of owning and operating an established business.

Master the content at **edge.sagepub.com/Hatten7e**

⑤SAGE edge™

©iStockphoto.com/Slphotography

What Is an Entrepreneur?

An entrepreneur is a person who takes advantage of a business opportunity by assuming the financial, material, and psychological risks of starting or running a company. The risks that go with creating an organization can be financial, material, and psychological. The term *entrepreneur*, a French word that dates from the 17th century, translates literally as "between-taker" or "go-between."[1] It originally referred to men who organized and managed exploration expeditions and military maneuvers. The term has evolved over the years to have a multitude of definitions, but most include the following behaviors:

- *Creation.* A new business is started.

- *Innovation.* The business involves a new product, process, market, material, or organization.

- *Risk assumption.* The owner of the business bears the risk of potential loss or failure of the business.

- *General management.* The owner of the business guides the business and allocates the business's resources.

- *Performance intention.* High levels of growth and/or profit are expected.[2]

All new businesses require a certain amount of entrepreneurial skill. The degree of entrepreneurship involved depends on the amount of each of these behaviors that is needed. Current academic research in the field of entrepreneurship emphasizes opportunity recognition, social capital, and trust. For an interesting article reviewing the scholarly development of entrepreneurship topics, see "Is There Conceptual Convergence in Entrepreneurship Research?"[3]

> "An entrepreneur is a person who takes advantage of a business opportunity by assuming the financial, material, and psychological risks of starting or running a company."

Entrepreneurship and the Small Business Manager

Entrepreneurship involves the start-up process. Small business management focuses on running a business over a long period of time and may or may not involve the start-up process. Although you cannot study one without considering the other, they are different. In managing a small business, most of the "entrepreneuring" was done a long time ago. Of course, a good manager is always looking for new ways to please customers, but the original innovation and the triggering event that launched the business make way for more stability in the maturity stage of the business.

> "The manager of a small business needs perseverance, patience, and critical-thinking skills to deal with the day-to-day challenges that arise in running a business over a long period of time."

The manager of a small business needs perseverance, patience, and critical-thinking skills to deal with the day-to-day challenges that arise in running a business over a long period of time.

Concept Check Questions

1. What do entrepreneurs do that distinguishes them from other persons involved in business?

2. Imagine that the principal from the high school you attended called to invite you to make a presentation to a newly founded entrepreneurship club at the school. What would you tell this group of high school students about owning their own business as a career option?

Concept Module 2.2: A Model of the Start-Up Process

- **LO 2.2: Discuss the steps in preparing for small business ownership.**

The processes of entrepreneurship and small business management can be thought of as making up a spectrum that includes six distinct stages (Figure 2.1).[4] The stages of the entrepreneurship process are innovation, a triggering event, and implementation. The stages of the small business management process are growth, maturity, and harvest.

The **entrepreneurship process** begins with an *innovative idea* for a new product, process, or service, which is refined as you think it through. You may tell your idea to family members or close friends to get their feedback as you develop and cultivate it. You may visit a consultant at a local small business development center for more outside suggestions for your innovative business idea. Perhaps you even wake up late at night thinking of a new facet of your idea. That is your brain working through the creative process subconsciously. The time span for the innovation stage may be months or even years before the potential entrepreneur moves on to the next stage. Usually a specific event or occurrence sparks the entrepreneur to proceed from thinking to doing—a **triggering event**.

When a triggering event occurs in the entrepreneur's life, he or she begins bringing the organization to life. This event could be the loss of a job, the successful gathering of resources to support the organization, or some other factor that sets the wheels in motion.

Implementation is the stage of the entrepreneurial process in which the organization is formed. It can also be called the *entrepreneurial event*.[5] Risk increases at this stage of the entrepreneurial process because a business is now formed. The innovation goes from being just an idea in your head to committing resources to bring it to reality. The commitment needed to bring an idea to life is a key element in entrepreneurial behavior. Implementation involves one of the following: (1) introducing new products, (2) introducing new methods of production, (3) opening new markets, (4) opening new supply sources, or (5) industrial reorganization.[6]

Entrepreneurship is, in essence, the creation of a new organization.[7] By defining entrepreneurship in terms of the organization rather than the person involved, we can say that entrepreneurship ends when the creation stage of the organization ends. This is the point where the **small business management process** begins. The rest of this book will concentrate on the process of managing a small business from growth through harvest.

The small business manager guides and nurtures the business through the desired level of **growth.** The growth stage does not mean that every small business manager is attempting to get his or her business to Fortune 500 size. A common goal for growth of small businesses is to reach a critical mass, a point at which an adequate living is provided for the owner and family, with enough growth remaining to keep the business going.

The **maturity** stage of the organization is reached when the business is considered well established. The survival of the business seems fairly well assured, although the small business manager will still face many other problems and challenges. Many pure entrepreneurs do not stay with the business until this stage. They have usually moved on to other new opportunities before this point is reached. Small business managers, by contrast, are more committed to the long haul.

entrepreneurship process
The stage of a business's life that involves innovation, a triggering event, and implementation of the business.

triggering event
A specific event or occurrence that sparks the entrepreneur to proceed from thinking to doing.

implementation
The part of the entrepreneurial process that occurs when the organization is formed.

small business management process
The stage of a business's life that involves growth, maturity, and harvest.

growth
Achievement of a critical mass in the business, a point at which an adequate living is provided for the owner and family, with enough development remaining to keep the business going.

maturity
The stage of the organization when the business is considered well established.

▼ FIGURE 2.1

The Start-Up Process

The stages of entrepreneurship and small business management are unique and follow this sequence with few exceptions.

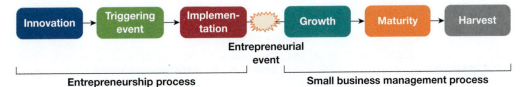

This stage could be as short as a few months (in the case of a fad product) or as long as decades. Maturity in organizations can be similar to maturity in people and in nature. It is characterized by more stability than that of the growth and implementation stages. Of course, organizations should not become too complacent or stop looking for new ways to evolve and grow, just as people should continue learning and growing throughout their lives.

In the **harvest** stage, the owner removes him- or herself from the business. Harvesting a business can be thought of as picking the fruit after years of labor. In his book *The 7 Habits of Highly Effective People*, Steven Covey says one of the keys to being effective in life is "beginning with the end in mind."[8] This advice applies to effectively harvesting a business also. Therefore, it is a time that should be planned for carefully.

The harvest can take many forms. For example, the business might be sold to another individual who will step into the position of manager. Ownership of the business could be transferred to its employees via an employee stock ownership plan (ESOP). It could be sold to the public through an initial public offering (IPO). The business could merge with another existing business to form an entirely new business. Finally, the harvest could be prompted by failure, in which case the doors are closed, the creditors paid, and the assets liquidated. Although made in a different context, George Bernard Shaw's statement, "Any darned fool can start a love affair, but it takes a real genius to end one successfully," can also apply to harvesting a business.

Not every business reaches all of these stages. Maturity cannot occur unless the idea is implemented. A business cannot be harvested unless it has grown.

Figure 2.2 adds **environmental factors** to our model to show what is going on outside the business at each stage of development. Management guru Peter Drucker points out that innovation occurs as a response to opportunities within several environments.[9] For example, other entrepreneurs might serve as role models when we are in the innovation and triggering-event stages. Businesses in the implementation and growth stages must respond to competitive forces, consumer desires, capabilities of suppliers, legal regulations, and other forces. The environmental factors that affect the way in which a business must operate change from one stage to the next.

The personal characteristics of the entrepreneur or the small business manager that are most significant in running a business will vary from one stage to the next. As you will see in the next section, personal characteristics or traits are not useful in predicting who will be a successful

harvest

The stage when the owner removes him- or herself from the business. Harvesting a business can be thought of as picking the fruit after years of labor.

environmental factors

Forces that occur outside of the business that affect the business and its owner.

▼ FIGURE 2.2

Environmental Factors Affecting the Start-Up Process

At each stage in the start-up-process, the small business owner must confront a new set of concerns. Here the arrows show what those concerns are and how they overlap.

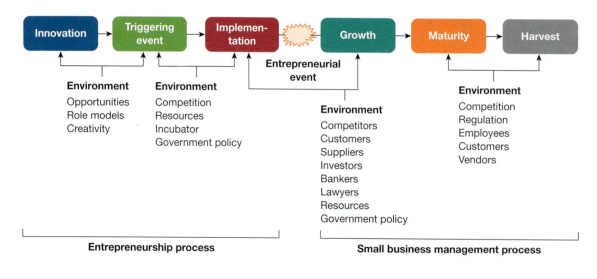

entrepreneur or small business manager, but they do affect the motivations, actions, and effectiveness of those running a small business (Figure 2.3). For example, in the innovation and triggering-event stages, a strong need to achieve, a high tolerance for ambiguity, and a willingness to accept risk are important for entrepreneurs. In the growth and maturity stages, the personal characteristics needed to be a successful small business manager are different from those needed to be a successful entrepreneur. In these stages the small business manager needs to be persevering, committed to the long run of the business, a motivator of others, and a leader.

The business also changes as it matures. In the growth stage, attention is placed on team building, setting strategies, and creating the structure and culture of the business. In the maturity stage, more attention can be directed to specific functions of the business. The people within the business gravitate toward, specialize in, and concentrate on what they do best, whether it's marketing, finance, or managing human resources.

▼ FIGURE 2.3

A Model of the Entrepreneurship/Small Business Management Process

In each stage of the start-up process, different personal characteristics will be more important to the owner as the business takes on new attributes. This models shows how entrepreneurial skills are required early in the process, then give way to management skills once the business is established.

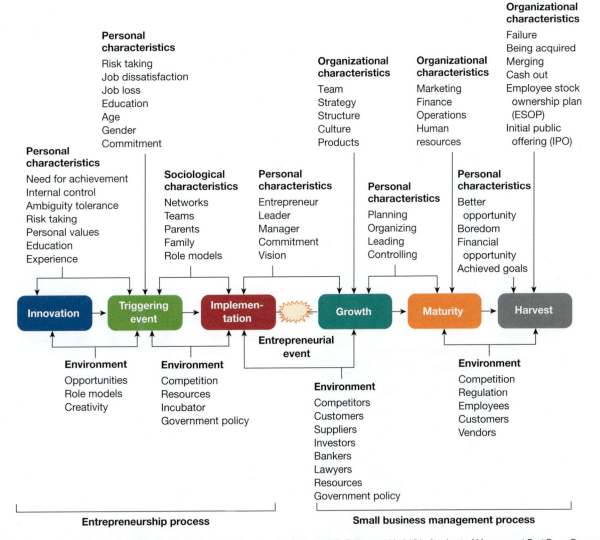

Source: Based on, with additions to, Carol Moore, "Understanding Entrepreneurial Behavior: A Definition and Model," in *Academy of Management Best Paper Proceedings,* edited by J. A. Pearce II and R. B. Robinson, Jr., 46th Annual Meeting of the Academy of Management, Chicago, 1989, 66-70. See also William Bygrave, "The Entrepreneurial Paradigm (I): A Philosophical Look at Its Research Methodologies," *Entrepreneurship: Theory and Practice,* Fall 1989, 7-25.

The purpose of the entrepreneurship and small business management model is to illustrate the stages of both processes and factors that are significant in each. The purpose of this book is to assist you as you proceed from the innovation stage through the management of your successful business to a satisfying harvest.

Concept Check Questions

1. Describe the significance of triggering events in entrepreneurship. Give examples.

2. How is small business management different from entrepreneurship?

3. Why would an entrepreneur be concerned about harvesting a business that has not yet been started?

Concept Module 2.3: Your Decision for Self-Employment

- **LO 2.3: Enumerate the advantages and disadvantages of self-employment.**

Readers of this text are probably considering the prospect of starting their own business now or at some time in the future. To help you decide whether owning a small business is right for you, we will consider some of the positive and negative aspects of self-employment. Then we will look at the reasons why other people have chosen this career path, what they have in common, and what resources they had available. Finally, we will address the issue of how you can prepare yourself for owning a small business.

Pros and Cons of Self-Employment

Owning your own business can be an excellent way to satisfy personal as well as professional objectives. Before starting your own business, however, you should be aware of the drawbacks involved as well as the payoffs. We will discuss the advantages first, such as the opportunity for independence, an outlet for creativity, a chance to build something important, and rewards in the form of money and recognition (see Figure 2.4).

▼ FIGURE 2.4

Small Business Owners Are Driven by a Variety of Motives

- Control Your Destiny
- Achieve Work/Life Balance
- Choose Who You Work With
- Take on Risk While Reaping Rewards
- Challenge Yourself
- Follow Your Passion
- Achieve Things Faster
- Connect With Clients
- Give Back to Community
- Pride in Building Something You Own

Source: Darren Dahl *"Top 10 Reasons to Run Your Own Business"* January 21, 2011, www.inc.com.

Opportunity for Independence. To many people, having their own business means having more control over their lives. They feel that they cannot reach their full potential working for someone else. Business ownership seems to offer a way to realize their talents, ambitions, or vision. This search for independence has led many people to leave jobs with large corporations and strike out on their own.

Opportunity for a Better Lifestyle. The desire to use one's skills fully is the most common motivation for self-employment. The idea is to provide a good or service that other people need while enjoying what you do. The lifestyle provided by owning your own business can make going to work fun. Working becomes a creative outlet that gives you the opportunity to use a combination of your previously untapped talents.

Also attractive to most entrepreneurs is the challenge presented by running their own business. Such people are often bored working for someone else. As a business owner, the only limitations you face arise from a challenge to your own perseverance and creativity, not from barriers placed before you by other people or the constraints of an organization.

About half of small business owners are motivated by familial concerns (refer again to Figure 2.4). They may feel not only that self-employment is the best way to provide for their children now, but also that their business is a legacy for their children. Children, in turn, may enter the family business out of self-interest or to help ease their parents' burden.

Opportunity for Profit. Less than 20 percent of small business owners express a desire to earn lots of money. Most people do not start businesses to get rich, but rather to earn an honest living. Nonetheless, the direct correlation between effort and compensation is a powerful motivation to work hard. The fact that you can keep all the money you earn is a strong incentive for many entrepreneurs.

Risks of Self-Employment. Small business ownership offers ample opportunities to satisfy your material and psychological needs, but it also poses certain risks of which you should be aware. Personal liability, uncertain income, long working hours, and frequently limited compensation while the business grows are some of the disadvantages of self-employment. Moreover, not having anyone looking over your shoulder may leave you with fewer places to turn for advice when the going gets tough. And even though you are your own boss, you are still answerable to many masters: You must respond to customer demands and complaints, keep your employees happy, obey government regulations, and grapple with competitive pressures.

The uncertainty of your income is one of the most challenging aspects of starting a business. There is no guaranteed paycheck at the end of the pay period, as exists when you are working for someone else. Your young business will require you to pump any revenue generated back into it. As the owner, you will be the last person to be paid, and you will probably have to live on your savings for a while. Going through the first year of business without collecting a salary is common for entrepreneurs.

THE BALANCE OF LIFE IN SMALL BUSINESS

Have you thought about, dreamed of, planned for work–life balance that you would create for your future small business? You're not alone—that mythical balance is a hot button for aspiring entrepreneurs. The problem is that it's more "myth" than "balance."

Fortunately, the topic of work–life balance is one of semantics and personal definitions. People who define work–life balance as having the "perfect" business that transitions into the "perfect" life are setting themselves up for disappointment due to unrealistic definitions and expectations.

Owners of small businesses get pulled in many directions because they are responsible for every facet of the business. Author Annie McKee states, "We tell ourselves that if we just 'meet this deadline,' get through the busy period or reach that next goal, *then* we will take care of ourselves. *Then*, we will have balance." All areas of life are about choices and true 50–50 balance seldom occurs because there are always new goals (both personal and professional), new deadlines, new passions.

What will likely work better for you is to work on optimizing work–life *integration*, rather than *balance*. Finding how you can best blend your desires to engage with your business, your family, your friends, your health, and your community is more realistic than truly making such areas "balance." We have a lot of moving pieces that are not the same size or importance but are all necessary for life to work. How can we do that?"

Connect. Small business owners are seldom "lone wolves." We operate best by having personal connections at our business, with our families, in our communities, so connect and be sure to listen to the people we are connected to. They will provide feedback to us when one area of our life is taking over (even before we realize it ourselves).

Create multitiered support systems. When you are living an integrated lifestyle, you need to be open to receive help from each area.

Get healthy. Exercise and sleep are critical to staying healthy, and the health of a small business owner is closely tied to the health of his/her business.

Practice tactical imbalance. As stated earlier, balance doesn't have to mean exactly equal. It's OK to go out of balance in certain areas while still remaining committed to everything. Just be aware of the imbalance and recover when you can.

Combine your commitments with prioritization. Starting and running a small business takes a lot of time. Period. Few people have ever had the conscious thought that their family is not their highest priority, but there are always sacrifices to achieve commitments in every area.

Sources: Amy Nassisi, "Stop Chasing Work-Life Balance and Strive for Work-Life Integration Instead," *Inc.*, December 7, 2017, www.inc.com; Nick Thomas, "Entrepreneurship is an Imbalancing Act of Business and Family," *Entrepreneur*, July 25, 2017, www.entrepreneur.com/article/296844; Rohit Prakash, "5 Ways to Keep You and Your Business Healthy," *Entrepreneur*, October 24, 2017, www.entrepreneur.com/article/299108; Heather Huhman, "'Work-Life Balance' is Backfiring on Employers," *Entrepreneur*, www.entrepreneur.com/article/302042.

The reliable, if dull, nine-to-five work schedule is another luxury that small business owners must do without. To get your business off the ground during the critical start-up phase, you may find yourself being the company president during the day and its janitor at night. Owning and running a business requires a tremendous commitment of time and effort. You must be willing to make sure everything that must be done actually gets done. In a study conducted by the Families and Work Institute, among the 3,500 small business respondents, 43 percent worked more than 50 hours per week, while 38 percent worked between 35 and 50 hours per week. (The same study also showed those same small business owners earned an average of $112,800 per year—so there *is* a payoff!)[10]

When you own a business, it becomes an extension of your personality. Unfortunately, it can also take over your life, especially at the beginning. Families, friends, and other commitments must sometimes take a backseat to the business. This problem is complicated by the fact that people often start businesses in their child-rearing years. Married couples going into business together face a volatile mix of business and marital pressures that do not always lead to happy endings.

Traits of Successful Entrepreneurs

©iStockphoto.com/vernonwiley

Since the early 1960s, researchers have tried to identify the personal characteristics that will predict those people who will be successful entrepreneurs. The conclusion of more than 30 years of research is that successful entrepreneurs cannot be predicted. They come in every shape, size, and color, and from all backgrounds. Still, in this section we will briefly examine some characteristics seen among individuals who tend to rise to the top of any profession. The point to remember when you are considering starting a business is that no particular combination of characteristics guarantees success. People possessing all the positive traits discussed here have experienced business failure. However, certain qualities seem to be prerequisites of success.

First, you need to have a *passion* for what you are doing. Caring very deeply about what you are trying to accomplish through your business is imperative. If you go into business with a take-it-or-leave-it, it-will-go-or-it-won't attitude, you are probably wasting your time and money. *Determination* is also critical. You must realize that you have choices and are not a victim of fate. You need to believe that you can succeed if you work long enough and hard enough. *Trustworthiness* is important to entrepreneurs because of their many interpersonal, institutional, or organizational relationships (often untested) under conditions of uncertainty.[11] Finally, you need a deep *knowledge* of the area in which you are working. Your customers should see you as a reliable source in solving their wants and needs. Virtually every successful entrepreneur possesses these four characteristics of passion, determination, trustworthiness, and knowledge.[12] In other words, perseverance, the technical skills to run a business, belief in yourself, and the ability to inspire others to trust you are all important for success.

A pioneer in entrepreneurial research, David McClelland identified entrepreneurs as people with a higher **need to achieve** than nonentrepreneurs.[13] People with a high need to achieve are attracted to jobs that challenge their skills and problem-solving abilities, yet offer a good chance of success. They equally avoid goals that seem almost impossible to achieve and those that pose no challenge. They prefer tasks in which the outcome depends on their individual effort.

Locus of control is a term used to explain how people view their ability to determine their own fate. Entrepreneurs tend to have a stronger internal locus of control than people in the general population.[14] People with a high internal locus of control believe that the outcome of an event is determined by their own actions. Luck, chance, fate, or the control of other people (external factors) are less important than one's own efforts.[15] When faced with a problem or a difficult situation, internals look within themselves for solutions. Internal locus of control is the force that compels many people to start their own businesses in an effort to gain independence, autonomy, and freedom.

Successful entrepreneurs and small business owners are innovative and creative. *Innovation* results from the ability to conceive of and create new and unique products, processes, or services. Entrepreneurs see opportunities in the marketplace and visualize creative new ways to take advantage of them.

How do entrepreneurs tend to view *risk taking*? A myth about entrepreneurs is that they are wild-eyed, risk-seeking, financial daredevils. While acceptance of financial risk is necessary to start a business, the prototypical entrepreneur tends to accept moderate risk only after careful examination of what she is about to get into.

Consider the case of Scott Schmidt, the entrepreneurial athlete who started what has become known as "extreme skiing." Basically, he jumps from 60-foot cliffs on skis for a living.

> "Virtually every successful entrepreneur possesses these four characteristics of passion, determination, trustworthiness, and knowledge."

need to achieve
The personal quality, inked to entrepreneurship, of being motivated to excel and choose situations in which success is likely.

locus of control
A person's belief concerning the degree to which internal or external forces control his or her future.

CREATING COMPETITIVE ADVANTAGE

ARE YOU READY?

Becoming an entrepreneur is not for everyone. In business, there are no guarantees. There is simply no way to eliminate all of the risks. It takes a special person with a strong commitment and specific skills to be successful as an entrepreneur.

Are you ready to start your own business? Use the following assessment questions to better understand how prepared you are. It is not a scientific assessment tool. Rather, it is a tool that will prompt you with questions and assist you in evaluating your skills, characteristics, and experience as they relate to your readiness for starting a business.

General

1. Do you think you are ready to start a business?
2. Do you have support for your business from family and friends?
3. Have you ever worked in a business similar to what you are starting?
4. Would people who know you say you are entrepreneurial?
5. Have you ever taken a small business course or seminar?

Personal Characteristics

6. Are you a leader?
7. Do you like to make your own decisions?
8. Do others turn to you for help in making decisions?
9. Do you enjoy competition?
10. Do you have willpower and self-discipline?
11. Do you plan ahead?
12. Do you like people?
13. Do you get along well with others?
14. Would people who know you say you are outgoing?

Personal Conditions

15. Are you aware that running your own business may require working more than 12 hours a day, 6 days a week, and maybe Sundays and holidays?
16. Do you have the physical stamina to handle a "self-employed" workload and schedule?
17. Do you have the emotional strength to deal effectively with pressure?
18. Are you prepared, if needed, to temporarily lower your standard of living until your business is firmly established?
19. Are you prepared to lose a portion of your savings?

Skills and Experience

20. Do you know what basic skills you will need in order to have a successful business?
21. Do you possess those skills?
22. Do you feel comfortable using a computer?
23. Have you ever worked in a managerial or supervisory capacity?
24. Do you think you can be comfortable hiring, disciplining, and delegating tasks to employees?
25. If you discover you do not have the basic skills needed for your business, will you be willing to delay your plans until you have acquired the necessary skills?

Source: Learning Center (website), U.S. Small Business Administration, n.d., www.sba.gov/services/training/onlinecourses/index.html.

Ski equipment companies sponsor him for endorsements and video production. If you saw him from the ski lift, you would say, "That guy is a maniac for taking that risk." The same is often said of other entrepreneurs by people looking in from outside the situation. Actually, Schmidt very carefully charts his takeoff and landing points, and he does not see himself as reckless. An analogy can be drawn between Schmidt's adventurous style of skiing and the risks of starting a new business.

Entrepreneurs carefully plan their next moves in their business plans. Once they are in the air, entrepreneurs must trust their remarkable talent to help them react to what comes their way as they fall. Entrepreneurs don't risk life and limb because they look for ways to minimize their risks by careful observation and planning, just as Schmidt precisely plans his moves. They commonly do not see unknown situations as risky, because they know their strengths and talents, are confident of success, and have analyzed the playing field. In similar fashion, Scott Schmidt doesn't consider himself reckless. He considers himself very good at what he does.[16] That is a typical entrepreneurial attitude.

Other traits that are useful in owning your own business are a high level of energy, confidence, an orientation toward the future, optimism, a desire for feedback, a high tolerance for ambiguity, flexibility/adaptability, and commitment. If one characteristic of successful entrepreneurs stands out above all others across all types of businesses, however, it would have to be their *incredible tenacity*.

> "If one characteristic of successful entrepreneurs stands out above all others across all types of businesses, however, it would have to be their incredible tenacity."

Preparing Yourself for Business Ownership

How do you prepare for an undertaking like owning your own business? Do you need experience? Do you need education? The answer to the latter two questions is always "yes." But what kind? And how much? These questions are tougher to answer because their answers depend on the type of business you plan to enter. The experience you would need to open a franchised bookstore differs from that needed for an upscale restaurant.

Entrepreneurs and small business owners typically have higher education levels than the general public. About 39.2 percent of new business owners have a bachelor's degree compared to 29.2 percent for the general population.[17] Exceptions do exist, however—people have dropped out of school and gone on to start successful businesses—so it is difficult to generalize. Even so, in a majority of cases we can conclude that more education increases the chances of success. Entrepreneurs and small business owners are almost without exception on perpetual journeys of self-education. Systems scientist Peter Senge said, "people with a high level of personal mastery are acutely aware of their ignorance, their incompetence, their growth, and they are deeply self-confident."[18]

Entrepreneurship and small business management are the fastest-growing classes in business schools across the country.[19] In 1971, Karl Vesper of the University of Washington found that 16 U.S. schools offered a course in entrepreneurship. In his 1993 update of that study, that number had grown to 370. Now the number of colleges and universities offering entrepreneurship classes around the globe is in the thousands. Some of the nation's top business schools, such as Babson, Brigham Young University, University of Michigan, Northeastern University, and Baylor University (ranked as the top five Best Undergrad Programs for Entrepreneurs by *Entrepreneur* magazine in 2017), as well as many other four-year colleges and community colleges, are offering degrees in entrepreneurship and small business management.[20] Until very recently, the leaders of most business schools argued that entrepreneurship could not be taught. Now, however, the increased academic attention is constructing a body of knowledge on the processes of starting and running small businesses, which proves that entrepreneurial processes can be and are being learned.

The Small Business Administration (SBA) and other nonacademic agencies offer start-your-own-business seminars to prospective entrepreneurs. Executive education programs offered through college extension departments provide curricula specifically designed for entrepreneurs and small business owners. These one-day to one-year programs provide valuable skills without a degree.

Obtaining practical experience in your type of business is an important part of your education. You can learn valuable skills from various jobs that will prepare you for owning your own business. For example, working in a restaurant, in retail sales, or in a customer service department can hone your customer relations skills, which are crucial in running your own business but difficult to learn in a classroom.

The analytical and relational skills that you learn in formal educational settings are important, but remember that your future development depends on lifelong learning. (*Commencement*, after all, means "beginning"—the beginning of your business career!) Finally, don't overlook hobbies and other interests in preparing for self-employment. Participating in team sports and student organizations, for instance, can cultivate your team spirit and facility in working with

BIG DATA FOR SMALL BUSINESS

Small business owners need data they can rely on to make decisions about running their business. Until fairly recently, small business had difficulty accessing what is known as big data—data from large databases. Now, not only can they access it, they can use big data to create a sustainable competitive advantage. Five reasons why data can give your small business a competitive advantage are

- **Data is a source for insights.** Business decisions that are not based on data analysis are called *opinions*. Data analysis and data visualization make decision-making possible in the quest for hidden opportunities.

- **You can leverage offline data.** While databases are full of search queries, clicks, and purchases all providing insights into what buyers do online, there is a wealth of data available from surveillance of in-store shoppers. Such as, what types of packaging, colors, displays, and locations influence consumer preferences and behaviors?

- **Data helps you manage your online reputation.** If consumers are only making a few posts to your company's social media, you can handle making direct comment responses. But, if there are thousands of comments and reviews, what do you do? NLP (natural language processing) techniques break down larger dynamics so you can create a Facebook application to retrieve and analyze public posts.

- **Data is fuel for AI research.** The search to perfect artificial intelligence is the current business Holy Grail being sought for business analytics. Your small business can access public and commercial databases, crowdsourcing data, and information from other data-driven businesses to automate your analysis of posts, comments, and searches.

- **Data is an instrument of personalization.** Since a fundamental advantage of small businesses is the closeness to their customers, data can now bring that advantage to the online world. Insights from data can allow you to deliver content that your customers find relevant based on their searches and products they have viewed. Personalization is a powerful tool in retaining customers.

By definition, big data is, well . . . huge. Small business owners need tools to gather, access, analyze, and display it. Some of the best tools include

- **Improvado.io.** This company was created to solve a major small business pain point—making sense of monitoring and reporting on digital ad campaigns. By connecting to the improvado.io platform, a small business owner can view social, search, and display marketing data via their widget-based dashboard.

- **Mixpanel.** This powerful tool allows you to follow the digital footprint of every user of your products across mobile and web devices. It lets you see what potential customers are doing on your site. You can see patterns of web usage over time or instantaneously about how users are engaging with what you build.

- **Jaspersoft.** As if there were not enough big data to analyze (currently 2.7 zettabytes, or one sextillion bytes), the volume of business data doubles every 1.2 years! How does a small business owner keep up? Jaspersoft provides a huge range of online analytical tools, available to manage piles of information.

- **Apache Hadoop.** Hadoop provides an open-source software framework with tools to store and access massive amounts of data.

Sources: Artur Kiulian, "In the Next Wave of Innovation, Big Data Is Your Competitive Advantage," *Entrepreneur*, October 10, 2017, www.entrepreneur.com/article/300119; Deep Patel, "10 Tools Helping Companies Manage Big Marketing Data," *Entrepreneur*, August 2, 2017, www.entrepreneur.com/article/298046; http://improvado.io/company/about; https://mixpanel.com/; https://www.jaspersoft.com/; http://hadoop.apache.org/.

others. Your marketing skills can be improved through knowledge of languages or fine art. Sometimes an avocation can turn into a vocation. For example, more than one weekend gardener has become a successful greenhouse owner.

Of course, no amount of experience or education can completely prepare you for owning your own business. Because every person, situation, and business is different, you are certainly going to encounter situations for which you could not have possibly prepared. Get as much experience and education as you can, but at some point you must "take off and hang on." You have to find a way to make your business go.

Concept Check Questions

1. If a friend told you that entrepreneurs are high-risk takers, how would you set the story straight?

2. Explain why people who own a small business may not enjoy pure independence.

3. If personal characteristics or personality traits do not predict who will be a successful entrepreneur, why are they significant to the study of entrepreneurship or small business management? Which characteristics do you think are most important?

4. Think of an activity that you love to do; it could be a personal interest or a hobby. How could you turn your passion for this activity into a business? What questions would you have to answer for yourself before you took this step? What triggering events in your personal life would it take for you to start this business?

Concept Module 2.4: Creativity and Innovation in Small Business

- **LO 2.4: Explain the role of innovation to small business.**

Innovation—those new, more efficient and effective products, processes, services, technologies, or models—is the catalyst for business growth. Small businesses make major contributions of innovation in the U.S. economy, largely due to the economic incentive that comes with successful commercialization.

Small innovative firms are 16 times more productive, in terms of patents per employee, than large innovative firms. Small businesses generate a full third of all patents in both smart grids and solar energy, and 15 percent of patents in batteries and fuel cells. They also account for 14 percent of all green technology patents.[21] The bottom line—small businesses are a big deal when it comes to innovation.

In a 2015 report titled *Small Innovative Company Growth—Barriers, Best Practices and Big Ideas*, Mark Harrison identified a six-stage model innovative company development process (Figure 2.5):

- **Discovery/Identified Market Need:** A small business owner generates an idea for an innovation based upon research, building on previous development, opportunity recognition of a market need, or customer feedback.

- **Technology Demonstration:** The small business owner shows due diligence in analyzing the idea to make sure it is viable. This can take the form of experiments, building prototypes, or market assessment.

- **Product Development:** The small business owner extends the testing from the previous stage (assuming positive results) in refining product design, pilot testing, and identifying production options and possible distribution channels.

- **Commercialization/Market Entry:** Once the small business owner has a viable product, it is time to begin the generation of revenue with heavy emphasis on marketing and selling. Refinements to the manufacturing processes are normal.

- **Early Stage Growth:** Successful product launch leads to small business growth and investment in materials, human resources, and infrastructure.

- **Economic Development Impact Growth:** In this stage, the small business generates significant revenue, increases hiring, likely makes capital investments in land and buildings, and pays higher taxes that support and enhance local economies.[22]

The Six Stages of the Innovation Process

The same report identified barriers and challenges specific to small businesses that are attempting to commercialize innovative products or technology:

- The amount of student debt held by graduating students prevents them from pursuing entrepreneurial opportunities.

- The amount of funding and support of research and development in the United States needs to increase to ensure continued innovation.

- Entrepreneurs often lack information regarding market needs and product research and development efforts.

- There is a shortage of engineering and production job talent.

- Access to capital still remains a large barrier for small business growth.

- Small innovative companies have difficulty in commercializing products.

- Technology diffusion and adoption is harder for small businesses.

- The high costs of acquiring equipment and implementing a new technology [are] a barrier to entry for small businesses.

- Small companies need access to more business opportunities.

- Innovations often result in legal and/or regulatory challenges or uncertainty.

- Small companies continue to face challenges to exporting their products and services.[23]

Product Innovation

Innovation can be seen in every facet of business, but for this small business discussion we are primarily limiting the scope to products. Remember that **product** means tangible goods, intangible services, or a combination of these (Figure 2.6). Hiring someone to mow your lawn is an example of the service end of the goods-and-services spectrum. In this case, you don't receive a tangible good. An example of a tangible good would be the purchase of a chair that is finished and assembled, but not delivered. Thus, in this case, you don't receive any services. Many businesses offer a combination of goods and services. Restaurants, for instance, provide both goods (food and drink) and services (preparation and delivery).

▼ FIGURE 2.6

Spectrum of Goods and Services

Most small businesses sell a combination of goods and services.

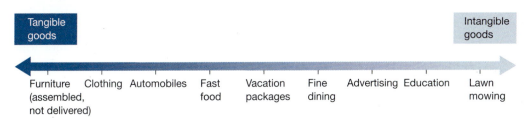

Product Satisfaction

When thinking about product innovation, it is useful to think about different levels of product satisfaction. Products are the "bundle of satisfaction" that consumers receive in exchange for their money. The most basic level of product satisfaction is its *core benefit*, or the fundamental reason why people buy products (Figure 2.7). For an automobile, the core benefit is transportation from point A to point B. With a hotel room, the core benefit is a night's sleep. To put this another way, people don't buy drills—they really buy holes.

The next level of product satisfaction is the *generic product*. For an automobile, the generic product is the steel, plastic, and glass. For the hotel, the building, the front desk, and the rooms represent the generic product.

The third level of product satisfaction is the *expected product*, which includes the set of attributes and conditions that consumers assume will be present. U.S. consumers expect comfortable seats, responsive handling, and easy starting from their cars. A hotel guest expects clean sheets, soap, towels, relative quiet, and indoor plumbing.

The *augmented product*, the fourth level of product satisfaction, is all the additional services and benefits that can distinguish your business. For example, night vision built into windshields, satellite-linked navigational systems in autos, and express checkout and health club facilities in hotels are product augmentations. Augmentations represent the sizzle that you sell along with the steak. The problem with product augmentations is that they soon become expected. When you have raised your costs and prices by adding augmentations, you open the door for competitors to come in and offer more of a generic product at a lower price. That's how the Motel 6 franchises became so successful—by offering a plain room for a low price when competitors were adding amenities that raised their cost structure and prices.

▼ FIGURE 2.7

Levels of Benefits Consumers Receive from Products

The benefits that consumers receive from products are represented by different product levels.

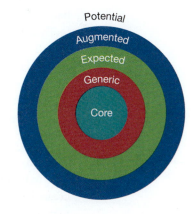

product
A tangible good, an intangible service, or a combination of these.

The fifth and final level is the *potential product*. It includes product evolutions to come. Not long ago, taking video with a cell phone or still camera was not possible. It soon became a product augmentation and, very quickly, expected.

Thus the products that you develop and sell in your small business are more than just a combination of tangible features. Always keep in mind which core benefits customers receive from your product, how the actual product satisfies those core needs, and how you can augment your products to make them more appealing.

Developing New Products

Trends like increased global competition and quickly changing customer needs have shortened product life cycles and increased the need for new products.[24] As a company's current products enter the stages of late maturity and decline, they need to be replaced with new ones in demand. What is new? Good question. Marketing consultant Booz Allen Hamilton groups new products into six categories:

1. *New-to-the-world products.* These are products that have not been seen before, which result in entirely new markets. Ken Fischer developed and patented a marine paint the U.S. Navy uses to keep its ships free of barnacles. The paint is made from a mixture of epoxy and cayenne pepper. Fischer came up with the idea for the paint after blistering his mouth on a Tabasco-covered deviled egg. He decided that animals would react the same way. He was right.[25]

2. *New product lines.* These are products that exist but are new to your type of business. For example, the addition of a coffee bar to your bookstore would be taking on a new product line.

3. *Extensions to existing product lines.* These are products that are extensions of what you already sell. For example, a small business that adds a new line of innovative tablet cases to its existing cell phone cases would represent a product-line extension.

4. *Improvements in, revisions of, or new uses for existing products.* These are products that have had their value increased. Take the example of WD-40 spray lubricant. Although it was originally developed to prevent rust by displacing water, so many new uses have been found for it that the WD-40 Company holds an annual "Invent Your Own Use" contest. Besides quieting squeaky hinges and freeing zippers, the product also removes gum stuck in hair or carpet, and sticky labels from glass, plastic, and metal. The Denver Fire Department even used WD-40 to free a nude burglary suspect who got stuck while attempting to enter a restaurant through an exhaust vent.

5. *Repositioning of existing products.* Entrepreneurial jargon typically calls this procedure "pivoting" but the process is the same. Many products and businesses are created with one purpose in mind but end up finding success in another arena—including Post-it Notes (originally created to mark pages in the inventor's church choir songbook) and Viagra (originally formulated to treat angina—chest pain associated with poor circulation to the heart).

6. *Lower-cost versions of existing products.* These are products that provide value and performance similar to those of existing products but at a lower cost. For example, food stands that sell hamburgers and hot dogs offer products similar to the big-name fast-food franchises but at a lower price, thereby enticing customers with their cost advantage.

Of course, increased risk is associated with the launch of new products. How many new products can you remember seeing on the shelves at the grocery store in the last year? Ten? Fifty? One hundred? Now think of how many of those you chose to adopt. However many you

remember, it was surely far less than the 10,000 new food products and 5,000 nonfood items introduced in grocery stores each year.[26] Many of those new products did not survive. Nevertheless, despite the risk, innovation is the key to success. Innovation is part of being proactive in the marketplace.

Inventor's Paradox

Consider the following scenario. You have developed a new product that fits into one of the six categories cited above. What are your options? The best alternative is to start and run your own business based on the new product—that option is the foundation of this whole book. But what other options exist?

Unfortunately, many product innovators believe they simply need to generate an idea for a new product, service, or process, and Uber-Corporation X will pay them massive amounts of money for this idea. Sorry to disappoint you, but ideas are worth very little in the business world. In fact, most companies strongly discourage inventors from approaching them with ideas. Why? Because they have been approached by hundreds of people who want to cash in on undeveloped ideas. Of course, some people have convinced members of a large corporation that they are serious inventors who have marketable ideas, but lightning has struck in the same place twice, too. Just don't count on it happening.

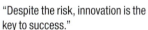

"Despite the risk, innovation is the key to success."

If you do gain an audience with a corporate representative to whom you can make a proposal and a presentation, you have a better chance of walking out with a **licensing agreement** than a check. Under a licensing agreement, the owner of intellectual property grants another person (or another company) permission to produce that product. In exchange, the inventor receives royalties, which constitute a percentage (generally 5 percent to 6 percent) of sales. The inventor relinquishes control over what the licensee does with the product. Your chances of getting a licensing agreement are greatly improved if you are already producing the product and have established a track record of sales. Your chances of getting a licensing agreement dwindle if you are seeking a license because you don't have enough money to develop the product yourself.

Another alternative for an inventor may be **private-label manufacturing**. For example, Sears does not own a factory in which it builds its Craftsman tools. Instead, the company engages other companies to make the tools to its specifications and puts the Craftsman brand on them. This is where you, the tool inventor, could enter the picture.

If you have designed a new tool that Sears does not currently have in its product line, you might be able to secure an agreement to produce that tool under the company's brand name. You will get only about one-half of the retail price, but at least you have a sales base from which to begin your operations. A serious downside to this strategy is that you have just one major customer, so your company's fortunes will hang on that firm's willingness to maintain the agreement.

Recall the Chapter 1 discussion of the symbiotic relationship between large and small businesses. Here is another possible connection where each party needs the other: Similar to private-label manufacturing, you could become an *OEM (original-equipment manufacturer)*, a company that makes component parts or accessories for larger items.[27] For example, your firm might produce circuit boards for computer manufacturers or custom knobs for cabinetmakers.

Importance of Product Competitive Advantage

Few would argue that the length of time many products have before they become obsolete has decreased rapidly over the past few years. Factors such as new technologies, increasing numbers of substitute products, quickly changing consumer tastes and preferences, and shifting

licensing agreement
An agreement in which the owner of intellectual property grants another person (or another company) permission to produce that product.

private-label manufacturing
Producing products under another company's name.

consumption patterns all play large roles in this rapid phase-out of existing products. Small businesses are more vulnerable to product obsolescence because they typically depend on fewer key products and have fewer resources with which to develop new ones. In addition, the niche markets that small businesses serve can dry up or be lured away by a larger, low-cost competitor. The optimal scenario for these businesses features a steady stream of new products being developed to replace existing ones as they pass through the product life cycle.

> "A sustainable competitive advantage is based on something that firm does better than others—a core competency."

Unfortunately, no one actually runs a business that operates within the optimal scenario. Instead, the best you can do is learn from other successful small businesses. A recent study illustrated some fundamental practices of small businesses that succeed in creating and retaining a competitive advantage. Notably, they maintain their focus on specialized products serving niche markets and rely on their existing core competitive advantage to enter new markets. A *sustainable competitive advantage* is based on something that firm does better than others—a *core competency*. To be classified as a core competency, a factor should satisfy three criteria:

1. Be applicable across a range of products.

2. Be difficult for competitors to duplicate.

3. Provide a fundamental and valuable benefit to customers.

Assuming their core competencies are intact, successful companies share some common characteristics that can be termed *best practices*. They

- *Leverage existing capabilities*—meaning they understand what they do well, and they use those skills to enter new markets.

- *Set team expectations*—getting your entire team together regularly (for example twice a month) to discuss each department's accomplishments and challenges.

- *Enter growth markets*—and thereby avoid cutthroat price competition and zero-sum games.

- *Manage without ego*—small businesses run on margins that are too thin for owners to believe that his/her ideas and processes are the best and only ways. Get feedback from your team.

- *Target niche markets*—by definition, niche markets are less crowded with competitors than mass markets, and customers in niche markets are willing to pay premiums for specialized products.

- *Diversify*—so as to spread risk, or, as the cliché goes, they don't put all their eggs in one basket.

- *Add new capabilities*—by building a set of skills, such as technology, marketing, or distribution.

- *Have clear and documented processes*—documentation leaves little room for miscommunications.

- *Keep the 3 P's in mind*—Marcus Lemonis builds solid operations with them in his show *The Profit*. So should you—process, people, and product.

- *Have low overhead*—because they have a lean management structure, and they avoid major new investments in buildings and equipment by adding extra shifts and overtime.[28]

Concept Check Questions

1. What factors might affect how long a product remains in each stage of the product life cycle? What can a small business owner do to extend each stage?

2. Many small businesses are built around one product. What risks does this approach impose? How can small business owners minimize those risks? How can a small business develop new products?

CHAPTER REVIEW

SUMMARY ▶▶

LO 2.1 Articulate the differences between the small business manager and the entrepreneur.

An entrepreneur is a person who takes advantage of an opportunity and assumes the risk involved in creating a business for the purpose of making a profit. A small business manager is involved in the day-to-day operation of an established business. Each faces significant challenges, but they are at different stages of development in the entrepreneurship/small business management model.

LO 2.2 Discuss the steps in preparing for small business ownership.

The entrepreneurship process involves an *innovative* idea for a new product, process, or service. A *triggering event* is something that happens to the entrepreneur that causes him to begin bringing the idea to reality. *Implementation* is the stage at which the entrepreneur forms a business based on her idea. The first stage of the small business management process is *growth,* which usually means the business is becoming large enough to generate enough profit to support itself and its

owner. The *maturity* stage is reached when the business is stable and well established. The *harvest* stage occurs when the small business manager leaves the business because of its sale, merger, or failure.

LO 2.3 Enumerate the advantages and disadvantages of self-employment.

The advantages of self-employment include the opportunity for independence, the chance for a better lifestyle, and the potential for significant profit. The disadvantages include the personal liability you would face should the business fail, the uncertainty of an income, and the long working hours.

LO 2.4 Explain the role of innovation to small business.

Product innovation is the catalyst for all business growth and small businesses make major contributions of innovation in the U.S. economy because they have more economic incentive to create truly innovative products than do large businesses. Innovation includes those new, more efficient and effective products, processes, services, technologies, or models.

KEY TERMS ▶▶

entrepreneurship **25**

entrepreneurship process **27**

environmental factors **28**

growth **27**

harvest **28**

implementation **27**

licensing agreement **41**

locus of control **33**

maturity **27**

need to achieve **33**

private-label manufacturing **41**

product **39**

small business management **25**

small business management process **27**

triggering event **27**

EXPERIENTIAL LEARNING ACTIVITY ▶▶

2.1: Stages of Preparing for Small Business Ownership

LO 2.2: Discuss the steps in preparing for small business ownership.

Using the information found in Chapter 2, which step in preparing for small business ownership is represented by each of the following scenarios?

1. Sally has a great idea for improving the efficiency of moving her product from Point A to Point B.

2. Kathy's business has now reached a critical mass, providing a living for herself and her family.

3. Robert's company has been in the community for over 20 years and is well established with several of his children now working in the family business.

4. Greg was just laid off from his company and now has time to pursue his business idea he has been thinking about for years.

5. John has spent the last two years developing, testing, and determining a production process for his amazing new carpentry tool. He is now ready to begin the production process, open the doors of his store, and sell his product.

6. After years of successfully owning her flower shop, Jenna has sold her business to a newly graduated college student. Jenna plans to pursue her painting passion.

7. Jamie has had a great idea for a new phone app for the last two years. She has shared her idea with her family and friends and everyone agrees it will be an awesome app.

8. Katie's restaurant has operated successfully for the last 15 years and is a community favorite. Her weekend crowd has many regular customers who enjoy Katie's well-known fish and chips.

9. After several years of hard work and dedication, Joe's automotive service has reached the point where Joe can quit his part-time job and devote all of his time to his automotive business. Joe now has a sufficient group of regular customers and can support himself and his family solely from the automotive business.

10. Kurt's boss has just offered him a promotion to regional manager, which should be a wonderful offer. However, if Kurt takes the promotion, he will no longer have time to implement his coaching clinics, which he has been planning for the last several months.

2.2: Innovation

LO 2.4: Explain the role of innovation to small business.

Invention is the creation of a new product or service. Innovation is making a current product or service better to fulfill a consumer need or want.

1. For the products listed to the right, list whether each product is an invention or an innovation.

2. After you have categorized each product, break into groups and brainstorm ideas for three products to develop further innovations. Explain the six stages of innovation used to make your product a success.

_____ A telephone in 1875

_____ A pizza place that now sells chocolate chip dessert pizzas

_____ The cell phone in 1973

_____ A machine linked to a computer that expertly cuts material into any design chosen

_____ An electronic textbook

_____ A metal key to your hotel room

_____ A curling iron

_____ Frisbee golf

_____ Christmas lights for outside your house

_____ Fitbit to track your steps taken

The Organic Nonprofit: Feet First

Aiden Roberts and Mason Fielder have been best friends since kindergarten. Raised in an upper-middle-class community, the boys enjoyed a rather idyllic boyhood. Every afternoon after school and most weekends were filled with some sort of sporting activity, usually soccer or baseball. Their families enthusiastically supported their efforts and enjoyed cheering them on from the stands. In their freshman year of high school, both Aiden and Mason were selected to play on the junior varsity soccer team.

Later that same year, they worked together with a local Rotary Club where Mason's father was a member, on a service learning project to help raise money to build clean water drinking wells in rural African villages. They enjoyed their work on the project and became interested in visiting Africa. The opportunity came in their junior year when they were offered the chance to participate in a 2-week-long Rotary International–sponsored exchange program with one of the villages. In a letter home to his parents, Aiden described how incredibly friendly the people were and how it felt really good to help them. "The kids loved the school supplies we delivered. You should have seen their faces. When we had some free time we played soccer with them. They don't have nets or really any sports equipment here, but we made it work," he wrote. The trip not only raised their awareness about the needs of the villagers in rural Africa; both boys were also struck by "how good we have it," as Mason put it.

Discussing it on the long trip back to the United States, they both agreed that they wanted to do more to help the kids they had come to know. "We can really do something to help those kids. We know so many people who would be willing to give them something," Aiden said. Before the plane landed, they had come up with an idea to collect used sports equipment and donations of new shoes and to send them back to the villages they had visited. "I think this is something people can really get behind, plus it connects all the things we love to do," Aiden commented.

"It won't look bad on a college application either," Mason kidded.

True to their word, the boys launched their program within days of getting home. They called it Feet Forward. They started with friends and family, collecting donations of used sports equipment and asking for money to buy some new pairs of shoes. They hosted a couple of small fund-raisers to raise the cash needed to purchase some new items and to cover the cost of shipments. Through Rotary, they connected with a missionary group that agreed to receive and disperse the equipment. Overall, getting the first shipment delivered took quite a bit more effort than either of the boys originally thought, but when they received some photos of the kids playing with the new balls and wearing the new shoes, they were both deeply satisfied. "We need to keep going with this," Mason said.

By the end of their senior year, the boys had coordinated two more shipments of donations. Although they did not have the time or money to return to Africa in person, they had received heartwarming letters back from people working on the ground, letting them know their goods were being dispersed to kids in need. The boys used their knowledge of social media to promote the work of the organization through Facebook pages, and one of their friends produced a YouTube video to share their story.

The local paper ran a story about their work, and they were presented with a leadership award by a local news station.

As their reach broadened and they found themselves getting larger donations from people they didn't know personally, Aiden's mom, Jeanne, suggested they set up a nonprofit so people could get a tax deduction for their donations to Feet Forward. Jeanne was a bookkeeper for a local insurance company and was growing concerned about the boys keeping accurate records of their donations. Using a template from the internet, Jeanne helped them get the paperwork together. They wrote a mission statement: The mission of Feet Forward is to take a team approach to provide, through charitable contributions, used and new sports equipment and supplies to children with limited resources.

Aiden was listed as president and CEO, and Mason was named chairman of the board. "Who knew I would be a CEO at 18?" Aiden ribbed Mason. They listed Jeanne as the treasurer, and they also named Mason's girlfriend, Brianna, and Aiden's brother, Jack, as members of the board of directors.

In the fall, Aiden and Mason went their separate ways with Aiden attending a small Jesuit school in the Northwest and Mason enrolling in an engineering program at a large southern university. They left the work of Feet Forward in the hands of Jack and some of his friends for the time being; however, they vowed to figure out a way to continue their work.

Aiden, a business major, was particularly interested in learning more about how he could combine his passion for Feet Forward with his interest in business ownership and corporate social responsibility. He was excited to be admitted to an incubator program for social entrepreneurs, and he enrolled in a course called Leadership and Social Enterprise. On the first day of the class, he was quick to share the story of Feet Forward with the group. A student named Sydney raised her hand to ask a question. "How do you know you are helping these people?" she asked. This kind of project seems like a handout not a hand-up."

Aiden was taken aback by the question. "Well, we were there, we saw that they needed these things, and so we sent them, simple as that. People really want to help, and we get good reports back from people on the ground," he answered.

"Yes, I'm sure you do, but how do you know they don't need other things more? You say it is simple, but I think you underestimate the complexity of the underlying issues. I've lived in Africa and seen how those kinds of donations just pile up because what people really need is a way to make a living so they can buy stuff for themselves. Do you have anyone from the villages on your board or advising you?" Sydney challenged Aiden.

"Well, logistically, that is sort of hard," Aiden began.

Sydney interrupted him. "In a way, what you are doing is really insulting," she proclaimed. "Projects like this don't help communities to develop; they just make people like you and your friends feel less guilty for having so much when others have so little."

Aiden couldn't help but feel defensive, but before he could respond, their professor intervened and suggested they use Aiden's group as a case study throughout the semester.

Discussion Questions

1. In your opinion, what are some things that motivate people to form nonprofits? Are some motivations better or nobler than others? Are good intentions enough?

2. How would you have approached launching Feet Forward? What kinds of information would you have gathered before engaging in such an endeavor? How would you plan it?

3. Do you think it was necessary for Aiden and Mason to form a nonprofit, or were there other organizational structures or strategies they could have considered?

4. Are there any things about the way the nonprofit was formed in the case that concern you? What, if anything, would you have done differently?

Source: Pat Libby and Laura Deitrick, "The Organic Nonprofit: Feet First," July 12, 2017, Sage Knowledge: Cases, http://dx.doi.org/10.4135/9781506371658.

PART II

PLANNING IN SMALL BUSINESS

CHAPTER 3

SOCIAL ENTREPRENEURS, ETHICS, AND STRATEGIC PLANNING

Entrepreneurs come in all shapes, sizes, ages, and backgrounds and have very different motivations. A unique set called "social entrepreneurs" are those who recognize opportunities and problems and then create organizations to find solutions with social, cultural, or environmental answers. Let's look at some examples from Forbes's "30 Under 30: Social Entrepreneurs" 2017 list:

- Ricky Ashenfelter, 29, cofounder of Spoiler Alert. Ashenfelter created a mission of ensuring that no surplus food goes to waste. He created a tech solution as a real-time marketplace for businesses, farms, and nonprofits to make food donations and sales.

- Corinne Clinch, 23, and Uriel Eisen, 24, cofounders of Rorus Inc. Clinch and Eisen (and many others) recognize the problem of hundreds of millions of people who lack safe drinking water. Rorus makes portable and household water filters that "work for people, rather than making them work for their water." Their filters are unique in being both cost effective and easy to use.

- Kathleen O'Keefe, 26, Kristof Grina, 26, Jeff Prost-Greene, 26, cofounders of Up Top Acres. Building on the trend of local sourcing, Up Top Acres takes a creative approach by operating four Washington, D.C., rooftop farms producing 60,000 pounds of food per year. This food is sold within the neighborhoods and nearby restaurants.

- Tina Hovsepian, 29, Cardborigami. After studying architecture, Hovsepian's mission is "to provide instant space to protect people from the elements through innovation and design." As the name implies, Cardborigami combines origami-inspired treated cardboard that is lightweight, sustainable, and insulated.

This group illustrates well the topics covered in this chapter: social entrepreneurship, ethics, and strategic planning.

Sources: Caroline Howard and Natalie Sportelli, "Meet the 2017 Class of 30 under 30," *Forbes*, January 3, 2017, https://www.forbes.com/30-under-30-2017/social-entrepreneurs/#1ab2648b1332; www.spoileralert.com; www.rorusinc.com/about/; http://uptopacres.com/; www.cardborigami.org.

Concept Module 3.1: Relationship Between Social Responsibility, Ethics, and Strategic Planning

- **LO 3.1: Explain the relationship between social responsibility, ethics, and strategic planning.**

What do concepts like social responsibility and ethics have to do with strategic planning in business? They are rarely covered together in textbooks, but the connection between them is especially strong in small businesses because of the inseparability of the owner and the business. The direction in which the business is heading is the same direction in which the owner is going. What is important to the business is what is important to the owner. In many cases, a small business is an extension of the owner's life and personality.

> "In many cases, a small business is an extension of the owner's life and personality."

Master the content at
edge.sagepub.com/Hatten7e
$SAGE edge™

Strategic planning is the guiding process used to identify the direction for your business. It spells out a long-term game plan for operating your business. **Social responsibility** means different things to different people. In this chapter, we will define it as the managerial obligation to take action to protect and improve society as a whole, while achieving the goals of the business. *Social responsibilities* are the obligations of a business to maximize the positive effects it has on society and minimize the negative effects. **Ethics** are the rules of moral values that guide decision making—your understanding of the difference between right and wrong.

Let's look at the relationship between social responsibility, ethics, and strategic planning in the following way: When you assess your company's external environment for opportunities and threats, you identify what you might do. When you look at your internal strengths and weaknesses, you see what you can do and cannot do. Your personal values are ingrained in the business; they are what you want to do. Your ethical standards will determine what is right for you to do. Finally, in responding to everyone who could be affected by your business, social responsibility guides what you should do.

The connection between social responsibility, ethics, and strategic planning is especially strong in small business. In fact, at a very fundamental level, they are more difficult to separate than to connect.

Concept Check Question

1. Using your own words, write a brief summary of the connection between social responsibility, ethics, and strategic planning in a small business setting.

Concept Module 3.2: Social Entrepreneurship

- **LO 3.2: Describe the impact of social entrepreneurship on small business.**

There was time not long ago when a person who wanted to make a difference in the world had to join a nonprofit. People who wanted to make money launched businesses. But now the directions are not so cut-and-dried as many nonprofits are being run like high-growth start-ups and traditional businesses are being built around social missions. The idea of "social entrepreneurship" has resonated loudly for the past decade. Many are adopting this concept at the intersection of business and society because many governmental and philanthropic efforts fall well below expectations. Social sector institutions are typically viewed as inefficient, ineffective, and unresponsive while business institutions are seen as narrowly focused and greedy.

The term **social entrepreneurship** has entered the language of business, building upon the definition of entrepreneurship we discussed in the previous chapter. Paul C. Light, of New York University, states, "A social entrepreneur is an individual, group, network, organization, or alliance of organizations that seeks sustainable, large-scale change through pattern-breaking ideas in what or how governments, nonprofits, and businesses do to address significant social problems."[1] What may be more memorable in understanding the difference between traditional entrepreneurs and social entrepreneurs is the word *why*. Traditional entrepreneurs build businesses to create a bottom-line financial profit. Social entrepreneurs measure a triple bottom line in tracking their success: people, planet, and profit.

Bill Drayton of social entrepreneur network Ashoka explains, "Social entrepreneurs are not content to just give a fish or teach how to fish—they will not rest until they have revolutionized the fishing industry."[2] For example, small business BioCarbon Engineering has a bold plan to reverse the course of deforestation from lumber, mining, agriculture, and urban expansion that removes 26 billion trees per year. Current reforestation efforts only replant 15 billion trees per year. BioCarbon is filling that deficit by using 3D mapping apps and drones mounted with a

social responsibility
The obligation of a business to have a positive effect on society on four levels—economic, legal, ethical, and philanthropic.

ethics
The rules of moral values that guide decision making, your understanding of the difference between right and wrong.

social entrepreneurship
The process of creation and innovation of a new business with the passion of a social, cultural, or environmental mission.

paintball-type shooting device loaded with pre-germinated seeds that literally make future trees rain from the sky.[3]

While the term social entrepreneur may be new, the concept is not. Social entrepreneurs have always existed, but companies like TOMS and Zipcar are evolving them into entirely new beings. Social entrepreneurship is obviously resonating with younger generations. A recent survey showed that:

- 73 percent of young professionals surveyed said they wanted a job that allows them to make a direct positive impact on their local community.

- 70 percent of young professionals surveyed indicated they're seeking to start their own business within five to ten years.[4]

A nonprofit called B Lab is creating a new legal structure to serve social entrepreneurs. Certified B corporations (as in benefit corporations) set rigorous standards of social and environmental performance, accountability, and transparency. B Lab states that B corporation certification is to sustainable business what LEED (Leadership in Energy and Environmental Design) certification is to green building or Fair Trade certification is to coffee. Delaware was the first state to pass benefit corporation legislation in July 2013, with 17 other states currently processing laws. B Lab founder Jay Coen Gilbert describes the "Evolution of Capitalism" in a Ted talk (search for it at www.ted.com).

Social Responsibility

The manager of a socially responsible business should attempt to make a profit, obey the law, act ethically, and be a good corporate citizen. Your level of commitment to these responsibilities and the strategic planning process you conduct form the heart of your business—the foundation and philosophy on which the business rests. Knowing what is important to you, your business, and everyone affected by its actions (social responsibility) is significant in deciding where you want to go and how to get there (strategic planning). The business you start or operate takes on a *culture*, or a set of shared beliefs, of its own. When you create a business, *your* values have a strong influence on the culture of the business you create. The values and culture of your business are demonstrated by your socially responsible (or irresponsible) actions.

There are four levels of social responsibility: economic, legal, ethical, and philanthropic.[5] Although the primary responsibility of a business is economic, our legal system also enforces what we, as a collective group or society, consider proper behavior for a business. In addition, the firm itself decides what is ethical behavior, or what is right beyond the bare minimum of strictly obeying a law. Finally, a business is expected to act like a good citizen and help improve the quality of life for everyone—a philanthropic obligation. Although all four of these obligations have always existed, ethical and philanthropic issues have received considerable attention recently.

Economic Responsibility

As a businessperson in a free enterprise system, you have not only the fundamental right but also the responsibility to make a profit. You are in business because you are providing a good or a service that is needed. If you do not make a profit, how can you stay in business? If you don't stay in business, how can you provide that good or service to people who need it?

Historically, the primary role for business has been economic. When entrepreneurs assume the risk of going into business, profit is their incentive. If you don't attend to the economics of your business, you can't take care of anything else. Therefore, the economic responsibilities of your business include a commitment to being as profitable as possible; to making sure employees, creditors, and suppliers are paid; to maintaining a strong competitive position; and to maintaining efficient operation of your business.

Economist Milton Friedman emphasizes the economic side of social responsibility. Friedman contends that business owners should not be expected to know what social problems should receive priority or how many resources should be dedicated to solving them. He states, "There is one and only one social responsibility of business: to use its resources and energy in activities designed to increase its profits so long as it stays within the rules of the game . . . [and] engages in open and free competition, without deception and fraud."[6] His point of view is that business revenues that are diverted to outside causes raise prices to consumers, decrease employee pay, and may support issues with which some of the business's stakeholders do not agree. Friedman quotes another believer in free enterprise, Adam Smith, who in 1776 said, "I have never known much good done by those who profess to trade for the public good."[7] Basically, Friedman's argument is that businesses should produce goods and services and let concerned individuals and government agencies solve social problems.

Legal Obligations

Above making a profit, each of us is expected to comply with the federal, state, and local laws that lay out the ground rules for operation. Laws can be seen as society's codes of right and wrong; in other words, laws exist to ensure individuals and businesses do what is considered right by society as a whole.

Some laws and regulations have unexpected consequences that place a heavier burden on small businesses than on large ones. How heavy? The first Small Business Regulations Survey conducted by the National Small Business Association found that the average small business spends at least $12,000 on regulation compliance per year. What does the average U.S. start-up spend on regulations in its first year? $83,019! Yikes. Other findings include 44 percent spend at least 40 hours per year dealing with federal regulations and 29 percent spend at least that much on state and local regulations. Forty percent have declined making a new small business investment because of some regulatory impact.[8]

Ethical Responsibility

Although economic and legal responsibilities are considered separate levels of obligation, they actually coexist because together they represent the minimum threshold of socially acceptable business behavior. *Ethics* are the rules of moral values that guide decision making by groups and individuals. They represent a person's fundamental orientation toward life—what he or she sees as right and wrong. Ethical responsibilities of a business encompass how the organization's decisions and actions show concern for what its stakeholders (employees, customers, stockholders, and the community) consider fair and just.

The literature of business ethics identifies four dominant ethical perspectives:

- *Idealism* includes religious and other beliefs and principles.

- *Utilitarianism* deals with the consequences of one's own actions.

- *Deontology* is a rule-based, or duty-based, principle.

- *Virtue ethics* is concerned with the character of an individual.[9]

As individuals, we resolve ethical issues by being guided by one of these perspectives. Research has shown that no single ethical perspective dominates among small business owners. Rather, they consider ethical considerations in general to be very important in the way they conduct their businesses, no matter which principle actually influences their individual behavior at a given time.

Changes in ethical standards and values usually precede changes in laws. We regularly see society's expectations changing, which leads to the passage of new laws. Changing values cause

GOOD BET

Some small businesses, by the very nature of what they produce or market, find it difficult to clarify how they plan to fulfill the four levels of social responsibility (economic, legal, ethical, and philanthropic). Through strategic planning, even companies in somewhat controversial and questionable industries can define how they will be socially responsible. Consider Grand Casinos of Minneapolis. As more and more states have legalized gambling in selected locations, Lyle Berman, CEO of Grand Casinos, has been there to develop and manage the casinos. His company has proved so successful that it ranked first on Fortune's list of America's 100 fastest-growing companies. Yet Grand Casinos' business—gambling—tends to arouse considerable controversy. Obviously, Berman could use strategic planning to help identify areas in which his company could fulfill its social responsibilities.

Question

1. You are in charge of strategic planning for Grand Casinos. The company wants to open and manage a casino in rural Iowa. Community residents have asked you and your strategic planning team to attend a town meeting to discuss the casino. You will need to prepare a description of how your company is fulfilling its social responsibility. Other members of the class will act as community residents. As a resident, prepare your questions and concerns for confronting the Grand Casinos team.

constant interaction between the legal and ethical levels of social responsibility. Even businesses that set high ethical standards and try to operate well above legal standards, however, may have difficulty keeping up with perpetually rising expectations.

Philanthropic Goodwill

Philanthropy is seen as the highest level of social responsibility. It includes businesses participating in programs that improve the quality of life, raise the standard of living, and promote goodwill in their communities. The difference between ethical responsibility and **philanthropic goodwill** is that the latter is seen not so much as an obligation but rather as a voluntary contribution to society to make it a better place. Businesses that do not participate in these activities are not seen as unethical, but those that do tend to be seen in a more positive light.

Philanthropic activity is not limited to the wealthy or to large corporations writing seven-figure donation checks. Average citizens and small businesses can be and are philanthropic. A small business can sponsor a local Special Olympics meet, contribute to a Habitat for Humanity project, lead a community United Way campaign, or sponsor a Little League baseball team. Albert Vasquez allows a church group to convert his Tucson, Arizona, El Saguarito Mexican food restaurant into a center of worship on Sunday mornings. When the father of an employee of Ultimate Software was killed by a drunk driver, the entire company got involved with Mothers Against Drunk Drivers. As lead sponsor for MADD events, the company has helped raise $1.25 million.[10]

Concept Check Questions

1. Social entrepreneurship includes a triple bottom line: people, planet, profit to measure success. Describe an example of a small business that practices the triple bottom line (besides the examples from the chapter).

2. Economist Milton Friedman states that businesses should concentrate on making profit and leave solving social problems to those who specialize in them. Do you agree or disagree? Explain.

3. How can a small business show that it is socially responsible? Think of evidence of social responsibility (like sponsoring a Little League team) that a small business can demonstrate.

philanthropic goodwill
The level of social responsibility in which a business does good without the expectation of anything in return.

Business ethics are seldom clearly labeled.

Concept Module 3.3: Ethics and Business Strategy

- **LO 3.3:** Discuss the importance of ethics for your small business.

Business ethics means more than simply passing moral judgment on what should and should not be done in a particular situation. It is part of the conscious decisions you make about the direction you want your business to take. It is a link between morality, responsibility, and decision making within the organization.[11]

The Ethics & Compliance Initiative (ECI) conducts its Global Business Ethics Survey annually and has become a leading source of research on ethics. Results from their 2018 survey found that when employees are encouraged to make decisions based on their company's stated values and standards, favorable ethics outcomes increased by 11 times. Employees who believed that their supervisors would hold them accountable for wrongdoing were twelve times more likely to create favorable ethics outcomes. Finally, when employees believed they were encouraged to speak up about misconduct, favorable ethics outcomes increased by fourteen times. This data clearly shows the value of what ECI calls a High Quality Ethics & Compliance Program (HQP). Learn more at www.ethics.org.[12]

When asked, "What does 'business ethics' mean to you?" the most cited answer was staying above the requirements of the law (see Figure 3.1).

While headline stories of ethical lapses gain much attention, the topic of ethics has been with us for centuries beginning with "Treat others as you want to be treated," or the Golden Rule. Henry Ford got it. He said "If there is any one secret of success, it lies in the ability to get the other person's point of view and see things from that person's angle as well as from your own."[13]

Codes of Ethics

code of ethics
The tool with which the owner of a business communicates ethical expectations to everyone associated with the business.

A **code of ethics** is a formal statement of what your business expects in the way of ethical behavior. It can serve as a guide for employee conduct to help employees determine what behaviors are acceptable. Because the purpose of a code of ethics is to let everyone know what is expected and what is considered right, it should be included in any employee handbook (see Chapter 15 on human resource management).

▼ **FIGURE 3.1**

Something Worth Thinking About

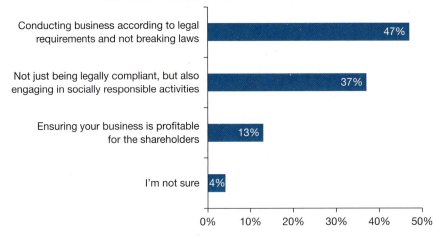

What Does "Business Ethics" Mean to You?

Response	Percent
Conducting business according to legal requirements and not breaking laws	47%
Not just being legally compliant, but also engaging in socially responsible activities	37%
Ensuring your business is profitable for the shareholders	13%
I'm not sure	4%

Source: Based on Lama Ataya, "How to Be an Ethical Leader," *Entrepreneur*, March 21, 2016, www.entrepreneur.com/article/272746.

Your code of ethics should reflect *your* ethical ideals, be concise so that it can be easily remembered, be written clearly, and apply equally to all employees, regardless of level of authority.[14] Your expectations and the consequences of breaking the code should be communicated to all employees. Small businesses, especially in fast-paced high-tech industries, often ignore formal codes of conduct because of their push for rapid growth. This mistake can cause expensive legal problems later.

An explicit code of ethics and the expectation that employees must adhere to it can reap many benefits for your small business, including the following:

- Obtaining high standards of performance at all levels of your workforce

- Reducing anxiety and confusion over what is considered acceptable employee conduct

- Allowing employees to operate as freely as possible within a defined range of behavior

- Avoiding double standards that undermine employee morale and productivity

- Developing a public presence and image that are consistent with your organization's ideals[15]

If you want to maintain and encourage ethical behavior in your business, it must be part of your company's goals. By establishing ethical policies, rules, and standards in your code of ethics, you can treat them like any other company goal, such as increasing profit or market share. Establishing ethical goals allows you to take corrective action by punishing employees who do not comply with company standards and by rewarding those who do. If your code of ethics is supported and strictly enforced by you and your management team, it will become part of your company's culture and will improve ethical behavior. Conversely, if your managers and employees see your code of ethics as a window-dressing, it will accomplish nothing. Don't just take a "three P's" approach—print it, post it, and pray they read it. Instead, talk about your code when it is implemented, review it annually, and use employee suggestions to improve it.[16]

Another recommendation is to include a *frequently asked questions (FAQs)* section in the code of ethics section of your employee handbook. Have these FAQs relate specifically to your industry, because many of your new employees will have the same questions.[17]

Ethics Under Pressure

Businesses face ethical dilemmas every day. How can they maintain high ethical standards when the effects of doing so will hit their bottom line?

> You run a construction company and receive a bid from a subcontractor. You know a mistake was made; the bid is accidentally 20 percent too low. If you accept the bid, it could put the subcontractor out of business. But accepting it will improve your chance of winning a contract for a big housing project. What do you do?[18]

Robert George, CEO of Medallion Construction Company of Merrimack, New Hampshire, was the manager who faced this dilemma. Medallion was bidding to become the general contractor for a $2.5 million public housing contract. An electrical contractor from the area submitted a bid that was $30,000, or 20 percent, lower than the quotes from four other subcontractors. Subcontractor bids come in only a few hours before the general contractors must deliver their bids so that subcontractors cannot be played off against one another. George was tempted to take the bid that he knew was a mistake because it would have almost guaranteed that Medallion would win the contract. Then he reconsidered for several reasons. Accepting the bid could have caused problems if the subcontractor went belly-up once the project was underway. Then

Medallion would have been forced to find a replacement, which might have caused time delays and cost overruns.

Aside from the pragmatic problems, the ethical ramifications troubled George. He asked himself, "Is it fair to allow someone to screw up when they don't know it and you do?" He decided the money wasn't worth the damage to his reputation of ruining a fellow small businessperson. George called the subcontractor and said, "Look, I'm not going to tell you what your competitors bid, but your number is very low—in my opinion, too low." The subcontractor withdrew his bid. Medallion still won the contract.

A year later, the same subcontractor submitted another low bid on a different project. This time the low bid was intentional. The subcontractor offered a 2 percent discount because he remembered how honestly George had treated him earlier. Sometimes high ethics can have material rewards. Having a reputation for high ethical standards can give you an "ethical edge," a competitive advantage for your business. Being known for doing what is right can help you attract talented people, win loyal customers, forge relationships with suppliers, and earn the public's trust.

You spend months trying to negotiate a deal to sell your equipment in Japan. You deliver your product as agreed, but the Japanese distributor tells you it is not what the customer expected. The distributor wants you to re-engineer the equipment even though it clearly meets the written specifications. What do you do?

David Lincoln is president of Lincoln Laser Company, a manufacturer located in Phoenix, Arizona. Lincoln thought he had a done deal with a distributor from Japan that had spent months scrutinizing Lincoln's $300,000 machine that scans printed circuit-board wiring for very small cracks or breaks. The distributor finally ordered eight machines. Unfortunately, the Japanese client wasn't happy after delivery. Lincoln said, "They thought it should inspect *every type* of printed circuit board, even though we explained repeatedly that it was suitable only for a certain class of boards." To change the machine so that it could inspect every type of circuit board would require Lincoln to have the software rewritten, pull engineers from another project, and borrow funds to pay for the additional work.

Lincoln's first instinct was to say, "This is what you agreed to; we supplied what we said we would. You bought it, so now pay up." He could have said "no" and been acting ethically according to common business practices in the United States. Instead, he decided to go beyond his basic obligation and do what he felt was the right thing under the circumstances. As Lincoln reflected on the differences between American and Japanese customers, he realized he had expected Japanese customers to act like American clients without taking into account the differences in adaptation levels between the two groups. In other words, he hadn't taken the time to become sensitive to cultural differences. Fortunately, Lincoln was able to secure financing to accommodate his customers—keeping the ethical principles, credibility, and Japanese market for his company intact.

Here are some more ethical situations to consider:

- You own a high-tech business in a very competitive industry. You find out that a competitor has developed a scientific discovery that will give it a significant competitive advantage. Your profits will be severely cut, but not eliminated, for at least a year. If you had some hope of hiring one of your competitor's employees who knows the details of its secret, would you hire him or her?

- A high-ranking government official from a country where payments regularly lubricate decision-making processes asks you for a $200,000 consulting fee. For this fee, he promises to help you obtain a $100 million contract that will produce at least $5 million of profit for your company. What do you do?

CREATING COMPETITIVE ADVANTAGE

COMPETITIVE INTELLIGENCE

Everyone needs to keep an eye on competitors. Fortune 500 companies have entire departments for competitive intelligence (CI), and CI consultants serve those departments. Small businesses are seen as too busy minding their own business to mind anyone else's. Actually, they need to keep closer track than large businesses because the impact of competitive moves are felt quicker and deeper.

SimilarWeb (www.similarweb.com) is a market intelligence solution designed to provide its business customers with insights to understand, track, and increase market share and provide insight into

- Benchmarking competitor performance
- Revealing competitors' online strategies
- Discovering opportunities you aren't leveraging today
- Identifying emerging trends (cross-channel)
- Understanding consumer intent

With this information from SimilarWeb and other competitive intelligence sources, small business owners need to

Determine who matters. Competitive intelligence does not have to take a lot of time or money, spies, or subterfuge. Focus on four or five competitors (more is overwhelming for small businesses).

Focus on what matters. When watching a competitor, what are you looking for? In CI jargon, you are tracking the Four Corners: (1) its goals or drivers (revenue or profit generators), (2) its management's assumptions about the market you compete within, (3) the strategies and tactics it uses to achieve its goals, and (4) its capabilities in accomplishing those goals.

Formalize the process. Create a simple repository for anyone on your staff to file information found and to be available to anyone who could benefit from it.

Gather intelligence. First stop: Google. But not just the search engine, set up email alerts about search terms (like competitor business name, owner name, or other unique key words) on news.google.com. When your carefully selected terms appear anywhere online, you are notified. Also check your competitors' websites for valuable information they may provide to you.

Source: Tom Popomaronis, "Market Intelligence: The Newest Way to Give Yourself a Competitive Advantage (That Ensures Survivability)," *Inc.*, October 30, 2017, www.inc.com; "How To: Keep Tabs on the Competition," *Inc. Guidebook*, April 2010, 53–56.

- You recently hired a manager who is having a problem with sexual harassment from another manager. She informs you, as the business owner, what is happening and tells you she is considering legal action. Unfortunately, you have been so busy dealing with incredible growth that you haven't had a chance to write formal policies. What do you do?

- An advertising agency has created and released a marketing and advertising campaign for your consumer product. The campaign has proven to be offensive to some minority groups (who do not buy your product), and those parties have expressed their objections. Sales for your product have increased by 45 percent since the campaign started. What do you do?[19]

Concept Check Questions

1. Define the purpose of a code of ethics, and write a brief code that would be suitable for a small business.

2. Explain how cultural differences between countries can have either a positive or a negative effect on an entrepreneur who is pursuing a contract either outside the United States or with persons of different ethnic backgrounds in the United States.

3. Although a certain practice may be widely accepted in the business community and be perfectly legal, does that necessarily mean it is always moral? Qualify your answer with examples.

4. Imagine your small business emits hazardous waste. Your industry signed an agreement with regulators to run all emissions through an expensive device to clean them. If you do not comply you will face sanctions. Also imagine the same scenario, but with no sanctions if you do not complete the costly cleanup. In which scenario do you think most business owners would be likely to avoid the cleanup?

Concept Module 3.4: Strategic Planning

- **LO 3.4a: Describe each step in the strategic planning process.**
- **LO 3.4b: Explain the importance of competitive advantage.**

Recall from Chapter 1 that poor management is the major cause of business failure. Since the first function of good management is good planning, a good **strategic plan** is a priority for the small business owner. Strategic planning is a long-range management tool that helps small businesses be proactive in the way they respond to environmental changes. The process of strategic planning provides an overview of your business and all the factors that may affect it in the next three to five years. It will help you formulate goals for your business so as to take advantage of opportunities and avoid threats. From your goals, you can determine the most appropriate steps you need to take to accomplish them—an *action plan*.

At the beginning of this chapter, the question was posed about the connection between social responsibility, ethics, and strategic planning. If the intent of the strategic planning process is to produce a working document for your business to follow, the relationship can be seen in this way: When you assess your company's external environment for opportunities and threats, you identify what you *might do*. When you look at the internal strengths and weaknesses, you see what you *can do* and *cannot do*. Your personal values are ingrained into the business; they are what you *want to do*. Your ethical standards will determine what is *right for you to do*. Finally, in responding to everyone who could be affected by your business, social responsibility guides what you *should do*. When viewed in this manner, social responsibility, ethics, and strategic planning are not only connected but also impossible to separate.

Writing a strategic plan generally involves a six-step process, as shown in Figure 3.2: (1) formulating your mission statement, (2) completing an environmental analysis, (3) performing a competitive analysis, (4) analyzing your strategic alternatives, (5) setting your goals and strategies, and (6) setting up a control system.

Yogi Berra once said, "You've got to be very careful if you don't know where you're going, because you might not get there."[20] Strategic planning is how entrepreneurs determine how to "get there."

Mission Statement

A **mission statement** provides direction for the company by answering a simple question: What business are we really in? The mission statement should be specific enough to tell the

strategic plan
A long-term planning tool used for viewing a business and the environments in which it operates in broadest terms.

mission statement
A description of the reason why an organization exists.

▼ FIGURE 3.2
Strategic Planning Process

A strategic plan can be drafted with six sequential steps.

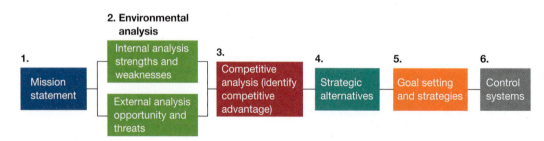

reader something about what the business is and how it operates, but it should *not* be a long, elaborate document detailing all of your business philosophies.

Does a small business need a mission statement in an age of Lean Launchpads? As with many business questions—the answer is "it depends." If it is a meaningless few sentences collecting dust somewhere, then the answer is "no." You don't need yet another exercise in corporate futility. If it can provide you a guiding light to help you through your darkest hours, then the answer is "yes."

By accurately describing the purpose, scope, and direction of your business, your mission statement communicates what you want your business to do and to be. It is the foundation on which all other goals and strategies are based. Without a concrete statement of organizational mission, the values and beliefs of a small business must be interpreted from the actions and decisions of individual managers.[21] The result may not be what you, as the owner, desire. Another value of a mission statement derives from the commitment you make by printing and publicizing your strategy and philosophy. You have more incentive to stick to your ideas and expect others to follow them if they are written down and shared than if you keep them to yourself.

For your mission statement to be a clearly articulated template of purpose, start with three keys:[22]

- **Simplify:** Management consultant and author Tom Peters writes that a company's mission statement should be 25 words or less in length.[23] This brevity will allow everyone in the organization to understand and articulate it.

- **Self-Igniting:** Your mission is about *you* and *your business*. Forget shifting the Earth's axis—write what inspires you.

- **Value Alignment:** Your meaning goes beyond money. If your small business is creative, then focus your mission on creativity. Your mission is tied to your competitive advantage.

Kickstarter's mission statement is "to help bring creative projects to life." Cofounder Yancey Strickler points out that it does not contain the word "crowdfunding" even though they were pioneers in that field.[24] It says what the business is and, by implication, what it is not. Kickstarter's focus has always been on its outputs. Every new tool and service that Kickstarter rolls out will support creative people in making their visions a reality.

Environmental Analysis

Large and small businesses alike must operate in constantly changing environments. The ability to adapt to change is a major determinant of success or failure for any business in a free enterprise system. Essentially, *environmental analysis* is the process in which a manager examines what is going on within any sector that could affect the business, either within the business or outside of it.

Environmental analysis is also called **SWOT analysis** because you examine strengths, weaknesses, opportunities, and threats. An analysis of the *internal* environment identifies strengths and weaknesses that exist within your own business. An analysis of the *external* environment identifies opportunities and threats—factors outside your control—that may affect your business.

Because of their speed, flexibility, and sensitivity to customer preferences, small businesses are in a position to quickly take advantage of changes in the environment. Environmental analysis is important to small businesses because they have fewer resources to risk. No business can afford many mistakes, but the larger the operation, the more breadth it generally has to absorb the cost of errors. A small business may be significantly affected by detrimental environmental changes that a larger business could more easily weather.

SWOT analysis
The step of strategic planning in which the managers identify the internal strengths and weaknesses of a business and the opportunities and threats that exist outside the business.

External Analysis. *Opportunities* are positive alternatives you may choose to help attain your company's mission. Although you should always be scanning for opportunities, you cannot pursue every one. Your strategic plan will help you identify those that are right for your business.

Threats are obstacles to achieving your mission or goals. They are generally events or factors over which you have no control: a change in interest rates, new government regulations, or a competitor's new product. Although you cannot control these threats, you can prepare for them or take positive action to cope with them. Threats and opportunities can be found by scanning developments in the following environments:

- *Economic.* Much of the economic data readily available on the international and national levels is very valuable to small businesses operating in smaller, more isolated markets. As a small business owner, you need to be aware of economic conditions that affect your target markets, such as unemployment rates, interest rates, total sales, and tax rates within your community.

- *Legal/regulatory.* Some factors can affect small businesses in more than one environment. For example, as many states legalize marijuana for medical and recreational uses, it is still (at this writing) illegal under U.S. federal regulations. There are small business opportunities, including many uses for industrial hemp, but many legal/regulatory complications remain.

- *Sociocultural.* What members of society value and desire as they pass from one life stage to another has an effect on what they purchase. For example, the increased popularity of tattoos among teens and twenty-somethings means opportunity for skin artists who are able to provide this service in a small business. Will the next opportunity for an entrepreneur be an innovative new process for removing those tattoos?

- *Technological.* Technology is the application of scientific knowledge for practical purposes. Few environmental forces have caused as much excitement in the business community as technological advances. For example, mobile apps are affording retailers an opportunity to connect with consumers in ways that go beyond the boundaries of brick and mortar businesses.

- *Competitive.* Actions of your competitors are considered forces within your competitive environment. You face a difficult task in not only tracking what your competitors are currently doing, but also predicting their reactions to your moves. If you drop the price of your product to gain more market share, will competing business managers react by holding their prices constant or by cutting their prices below yours? This situation could escalate into an expensive price war.

Are opportunities and threats easy to identify? No, and they never have been. Writer Mark Twain once said, "I was seldom able to see an opportunity until it had ceased to be one."

> "
> "Are opportunities and threats easy to identify? No, and they never have been. Writer Mark Twain once said, 'I was seldom able to see an opportunity until it had ceased to be one.'"
> "

Internal Analysis. An *internal analysis* assesses the strengths and weaknesses of your company. It identifies what it is that your company does well and what it could do better. Internal analysis is important for two reasons. First, since your personal opinion of your own business is sure to be biased (we tend to look at ourselves through the proverbial rose-colored glasses), you need an objective analysis of the capacity and potential of your business. Second, an internal analysis can help you match the strengths of your business with the opportunities that exist. The idea is to put together a realistic profile of your business to determine whether you can take advantage of opportunities and react to the threats identified in the environmental analysis. This isn't as easy as it sounds, because you have to view your environments not as if they are snapshots, but rather as several videos playing simultaneously. The key is to match opportunities that are still unfolding with resources that are still being acquired.

Although most of us have no problem identifying our strengths, some of us may need help realizing our weaknesses. The following diagnostic tests can help you evaluate your business realistically:

- Determine the principles that matter most to you and look for evidence of them in your business—do they show on your website, your business cards?

- Analyze the colors and images you choose to reflect who you are and the words you write on your "About Us" page, the podcasts you record, and videos you post.

- Visit your newest, lowest-level employee. Can he or she tell you why the business exists? Name major competitors? Say what you do well? List major customers? If not, your vision isn't coming across.

- Can that same employee describe what he or she is doing to contribute to your competitive advantage?

- Observe your business during work hours. Invent a reason to be where you can watch and hear what goes on. What impression do you get of the business?

- Select a few recent online reviews you have received. Reply to reviewers to open dialog with them about how they were treated by your business, and emphasize that you value their feedback.

- Ask a friend to visit your business as a mystery shopper. Would he or she come back again?[25]

Competitive Analysis

If you were forced to condense the description of your business down to the one factor that makes you successful and sets your business apart from all other similar businesses, you would recognize your competitive advantage, which is found by means of a *competitive analysis*. The heart of your company's strategy and reason for being in business is your competitive advantage. You must do *something* better than everyone else; otherwise, your business isn't needed. Furthermore, your competitive advantage must be sustainable over time to remain a benefit to you. If it can be easily copied by competitors, you have to find a new way to stay ahead.

Without analysis, competition will likely be viewed with bias. Competitors are rarely as slow, backward, and inferior in all areas as we would like to believe they are. Competition should be viewed as formidable and serious. In competitive analysis, you are trying to identify *competitive weaknesses*. In what areas is the competition truly weak and therefore vulnerable? Some bias may be removed if you are as specific as possible in writing your competitive analysis. For example, instead of saying that your competitors offer poor service, qualify your remarks with references to return policies, delivery, schedules, or fees.

For a practical application of competitive analysis that small business owners can use, try this: Rank your business and four competitors you have identified in the competitive areas of competition. Using Figure 3.3 as a guide, rank each business from 1 to 5, with 5 being the lowest and 1 the highest. Assign only one 1 per area, one 2, and so on. No ties are allowed, so you will end up with a ranked list of the five companies. This exercise will help you improve your competitive position and possibly point out new areas in which your business might enjoy a competitive advantage.

Competitive Areas of Comparison. These areas are for example only; add or delete areas that best apply to your business.

- *Image.* How do consumers perceive the reputation and the physical appearance of the business?

- *Location.* Is the business convenient to customers in terms of distance, parking, traffic, and visibility?

- *Layout.* Are customers well served with the physical layout of the business?
- *Atmosphere.* When customers enter the business, do they get a feeling that it is appropriate for your type of business?
- *Products.* Can customers find the products they expect from your type of business?
- *Services.* Do customers receive the quantity and quality of services they expect?
- *Pricing.* Do customers perceive the prices charged to be appropriate given the quality of the products sold? Do they receive the value they expect?
- *Advertising.* Does the advertising of the business reach its target market?
- *Sales methods.* Are customers comfortable with the methods the business uses to sell products?

Defining Your Competitive Advantage. Your strategic plan helps you define a competitive advantage by analyzing different environments, studying your competition, and choosing appropriate strategies. Advantages you have over your competitors could include price, product features and functions, time of delivery (if speed is important to customers), place of business (if being located near customers is needed), and public perception (the positive image your business projects). Remember, a competitive advantage must be sustainable. If competitors can easily copy it, then it is not a true competitive advantage.

Three core ideas are valuable in defining your competitive advantage. First, keep in mind any advantage is relative, not absolute. What matters in customers' minds is not the absolute performance of your product or service, but its performance compared with that of other products. For example, no toothpaste can make teeth turn pure white, but you could build an advantage if you developed toothpaste that gets teeth noticeably whiter than competing toothpastes do.

Second, you should strive for multiple types of competitive advantage. Doing more than one thing better than other businesses will increase the chances that you can maintain an advantage over a longer period of time.

Third, remember that areas of competition change over time. Customers' tastes and priorities change as products and the processes for making them evolve, as the availability of substitute products changes, and for a variety of other reasons that can affect your competitive advantage. For example, rather than focusing on sandwich ingredients, Jimmy John's changes their important metric with marketing messages revolving around "Freaky Fast." Although backing off a bit in the interest of public safety, they are still known for fast delivery in 15 minutes or less.[26]

▼ FIGURE 3.3

Competitive Analysis

Areas of Comparison	Your Business	Competitor A	Competitor B	Competitor C	Competitor D
1. Image	_____	_____	_____	_____	_____
2. Location	_____	_____	_____	_____	_____
3. Layout	_____	_____	_____	_____	_____
4. Atmosphere	_____	_____	_____	_____	_____
5. Products	_____	_____	_____	_____	_____
6. Services	_____	_____	_____	_____	_____
7. Pricing	_____	_____	_____	_____	_____
8. Advertising	_____	_____	_____	_____	_____
9. Sales Methods	_____	_____	_____	_____	_____
TOTALS	_____	_____	_____	_____	_____

TRACKING TO WIN

How can you analyze the competition? The process of gathering competitive intelligence doesn't have to be prohibitively expensive. A little effort and creativity combined with keeping your eyes open can yield a lot of information. Here are sources that can help small business owners gather information for compiling their competitive analyses:

- **Socedo (www.socedo.com).** Its mission is to bring social leads to every business in the world, so you can use it not only to generate leads on social media and engage those leads via Twitter and LinkedIn, you can also track what else is going on in your business sector.

- **Google Trends (www.google.com/alerts).** Gathering information does not get easier than this—you can set up Google alerts for any word (such as a competitor's company or product name) and Google will magically send competitive information to your inbox.

- **Twitter (www.twitter.com).** More low-hanging competitive information. Everyone wants more followers, so just about any information you desire is likely in the Twittersphere.

- **The Strategic and Competitive Intelligence Professionals (www.scip.org).** Described as a global community of business experts across industry, academia, and government who come together to build and share strategic intelligence, research decision-support tools, processes, and analytics capabilities. SCIP offers conferences, books, industry news, and certification, and tools for your business.

- **Trendwatching (www.trendwatching.com).** Tracking popular trends relating to your small business, such as demographics, pricing, and designs allows you to predict your (and your competitor's) next move.

Some nondigital tactics:

- Find trade association information—you will likely find its website and articles in trade publications.

- Listen to what your customers and salespeople say about competitors. These groups make the most frequent comparisons of you and the competition.

- Keep a file on key competitors. Information is useless unless you can access it easily. Include published information, notes of conversations, and competitors' sales, product, or service brochures. These readily available sources of information can help you determine how your competitors position themselves.

- Buy competitors' products and take them apart to determine their quality and other advantages. Consider incorporating the best elements of competing products into your own products. This process is called *reverse engineering* and is part of a process of establishing comparison standards called *benchmarking*.

Sources: Jeff Boss, "Stay Competitive with These 6 Sources of Up-to-Date Information," *Entrepreneur*, April 3, 2015, www.entrepreneur.com/article/244582; www.socedo.com/about; www.google.com/alerts; www.scip.org; www.trendwatching.com.

Five Basic Forces of Competition. Porter's five forces analysis has long been the standard beginning point for the examination of competition that exists within every industry. Analyzing these forces for your chosen industry can help you determine the attractiveness of the industry and the prospects for earning a return on your investment (Figure 3.4).

The degree of rivalry among existing competitors in Figure 3.4 refers to how passively or aggressively the businesses within an industry compete. If they consistently attack one another, the attractiveness of the industry is reduced because the potential to make a profit is decreased. For example, compare the airline industry, where strong rivalries produce low profits, with the packaged consumer goods industry, where companies try to attract different groups of customers.

The threat of new entrants in the figure is a function of how easily other businesses can enter your market, which keeps prices and profits down. If a certain type of food, such as Cajun bagels, becomes popular, very little prevents new bakeries from opening or converting to produce this popular item. Low barriers to entry reduce profitability for incumbents.

The bargaining power of suppliers affects the price you will have to pay to produce your goods. If the supplies in question are commodities carried by several companies, suppliers will have little power to raise the prices they charge. By contrast, if you have only one or two choices of vendors, or if you require very specialized goods, you may have to pay what the suppliers ask.

Five Forces of Competition

The interplay of competitive forces helps determine which products and companies succeed in the marketplace and which do not.

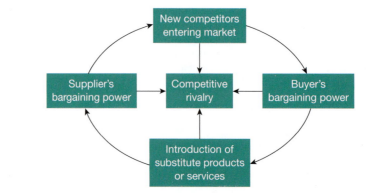

Adapted from Michael Porter, "Know Your Place," *Inc.,* September 9, 1991.

The bargaining power of buyers affects how much latitude you have in changing your prices. The more potential substitutes your buyers have, the more power they have to influence your prices or the extent of services you must provide to keep their business.

The threat of substitute products or services is determined by the options your customers have when buying your product or service. The greater the number of substitutes available, the more your profit margin can be squeezed. Overnight delivery services must consider the threat of fax machines and email, for example, even though they are entirely different ways to transmit messages.

Some have pointed out that the impact of digitalization requires that analog-era frameworks like Porter's five forces will need to be revisited. Traditional barriers to entry can be replaced with intangible barriers—such as relevant purpose, resounding mission, authenticity and trust—and these can have a power that no amount of industry prominence or cash can overcome.[27]

The following five fatal flaws are associated with misapplying strategic thinking to specific competitive situations:

- *Misreading industry attractiveness.* The highest-tech, most glamorous, fastest-growing field may not be the best for making a profit because of its attractiveness to competition.

- *Failing to identify a true competitive advantage.* Imitation can put you in the middle of the pack. Yet, being different from competitors is both risky and difficult.

- *Pursuing a competitive advantage that is not sustainable.* Porter recommends that if small businesses cannot sustain an advantage, the owner should view the business as a short-term investment rather than an ongoing enterprise. This business philosophy might be stated as "Get in, grow, and get out."

- *Compromising a strategy in an attempt to grow faster.* If you are fortunate enough to identify a significant competitive advantage, don't give it up in a quest to become more like your larger competitors. Remember what made you successful in the first place.

- *Not making your strategy explicit or not communicating it to your employees.* Writing your strategy down and discussing it with your key people sets up an atmosphere in which everyone in your organization feels compelled to move toward a common goal. Each of your employees makes decisions every day. If your overall strategy is to offer products at the lowest possible cost, decisions by everyone in your business need to reinforce that goal.[28]

Importance of Competitive Advantage. Having a competitive advantage is critical. Your small business must do *something* better than other organizations or it is not needed. To cope with a quickly changing competitive environment, small businesses need to be market driven.[29] Part of becoming market driven includes closely monitoring changing customer wants and needs, determining how those changes will affect customer satisfaction, and developing strategies to gain an edge. Small businesses cannot rely on the inertia of the marketplace for their survival.[30] When running a small business, you cannot solve problems simply by throwing money at them. Instead, you need to see your competitive environment with crystal clarity, then identify and secure a position you can defend.

In developing your competitive advantage, you will inevitably make decisions under conditions of uncertainty. This is the art, rather than the science, of marketing-related decision making. In his book *Marketing Mistakes,* Robert Hartley notes that we can seldom predict with any exactitude the reactions of consumers or the countermoves and retaliations of competitors.[31] Although it may be easy to play Monday-morning quarterback, viewing mistakes with 20/20 hindsight, we will do better to decide to learn from others' mistakes, especially when looking for a competitive advantage. Of course, no one ever deliberately set out to design a bad product or start a business that would fail. Nevertheless, what seems to be a good idea for achieving a competitive advantage often may not be, for one reason or another.

Benefits of Competitive Advantage. Gaining a sustainable competitive advantage can help you establish a self-sustaining position in the marketplace. Whether your edge comes from external factors (such as luck, the mistakes of a competitor, or new technologies and markets) or internal factors (such as lower cost efficiencies, innovation, exceptional skills, or superior resources), it can set up a cycle of success (Figure 3.5).[32]

Because of your competitive advantage, your customers will be more satisfied with your business than with your competitors' businesses. You will, in turn, gain market share. Increased market share translates into larger sales and profits, which then give you more resources for improving your products, facilities, and human resources—all of which allow you to improve your competitive advantage. As additional resources come into the business from outside the company, they can be used to build and fortify operational sources of advantage.[33] Businesses that don't gain competitive advantage, therefore, lose out in this cycle. Their customers receive less value and are less satisfied. Their market share, sales volume, and profit fall. Without profits, they have fewer resources to reinvest in the business, so positioning is difficult to maintain. The gap between follower and leader grows wider.

▼ FIGURE 3.5

Competitive Advantage Cycle

However it is created, a competitive advantage will increase your profit margins, providing more resources for your small business to use to strengthen itself.

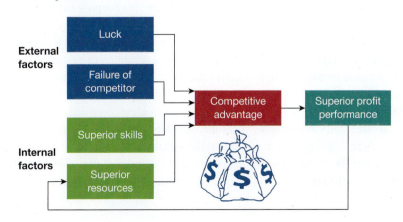

How to Create Competitive Advantage. Three generic strategies exist through which a business can gain a competitive advantage: lower cost, differentiation, and focus strategies.[34] Using *focus strategies* means aiming at a narrow segment of a market. By definition, all small businesses target niches or narrow market segments, so let's concentrate on the first two strategies.

You must find a way to lower your costs if you intend to compete primarily on price. If you try to compete on price without obtaining a cost advantage, your business is headed for trouble. Such an advantage can come from reduced labor costs, less expensive raw materials or supplies, more efficient distribution, or any number of other factors.

A competitive advantage based on *differentiation* means that your product or service is different from those offered by your competitors. Its value comes from the fact that you can show customers why your difference is better, not just cheaper. In this way, differentiation can effectively remove direct competition.

An advantage does not have to involve features of the product. It can come from anything your business does—including quality of products or services, customer service, and distribution. Research shows that creating a competitive advantage has four key components: the competitor identification process, the sources of the advantage, the positions of the advantage, and the performance outcomes achieved.[35]

To create a sustainable competitive advantage, your strategy must incorporate a combination of methods to continuously differentiate your product and to improve it in areas that make a meaningful difference to your customers.[36] But how can you keep up with the ever-changing tastes and preferences of your customers? There are so many questions about your customers you must try to answer. The products and services that people like and dislike at any particular time are shaped by hundreds of influences, many of which can't be identified. Nevertheless, you need to gather as many facts as possible about your markets in an objective and orderly manner. *Market research* offers a way to answer at least some questions about your customers' changing wants and needs, to help you create and hold on to your competitive advantage.

Strategic Alternatives

The process of defining *strategic alternatives* begins by identifying problems based on information gained in earlier steps. Next is the drafting of a list of alternatives. Thus, in this two-step process, you identify what is wrong and then determine what you can do about it.

Problem identification is the most difficult part of strategic planning. It takes thorough SWOT and competitive analyses and a lot of analytical thinking to pinpoint problems like a current strategy that no longer suits your environment or a mismatch between your strengths and an opportunity that you have discerned. Bracing up one of your weaknesses and preparing for an upcoming threat are tasks that demand your attention. If completion of your SWOT and competitive analyses identifies no major problems or new strategies needed, don't fix anything. Always look to be proactive, but don't ignore the possibility that keeping to the status quo might be the best choice.

Few problems can be solved with a single solution or with the first idea that comes to mind. Therefore, you should try to generate as many potential solutions as possible. Don't evaluate ideas as you generate them, as criticism stifles creativity. Only after you've exhausted the possibilities should you evaluate whether each alternative would solve your particular problem or work in your company. Once your list of alternative strategies is compiled, you need to consider their potential effects on your company's resources, environment, and people.

Although there is a strong temptation to list strategic alternatives informally in one's mind, research has shown that putting ideas down on paper leads to a wider range of alternatives and stimulates the creativity and insightful thinking that are the bases for good strategic change.[37]

Goal Setting and Strategies

Your mission statement sets the broadest direction for your business. SWOT and competitive analyses help you refine or change that direction, but the goals that you set must stem from your mission statement. Obviously, goals are needed before you can build a set of strategies. As the cliché goes, "If you don't put up a target, you won't hit anything." Goals need to be

- *Written in terms of outcomes rather than actions.* A good goal states where you want to be, not how you want to get there. For example, a goal should focus on increasing sales rather than on your intention to send one of your brochures to every address in town.

- *Measurable.* In order to tell whether you have accomplished a goal, you must be able to measure the outcome.

- *Challenging, yet attainable.* Goals that are too easy to accomplish are not motivating. Goals that are not likely to be accomplished are self-defeating and decrease motivation.

- *Communicated to everyone in the company.* A team effort is difficult to produce if some of your players don't know the goals.

- *Written with a time frame for achievement.* Performance and motivation increase when people have goals accompanied by a time frame as compared with open-ended goals.

Writing usable goals isn't easy at first. If you state that your goal is to be "successful," is that a good goal? It sounds positive; it sounds nice. But is it measurable? No. How can you tell whether you have achieved a goal such as this? You can't, because there is no defined outcome. There is also no time frame. Do you intend to be successful this year? By the time you are 90? Goals need the characteristics listed previously to be useful.

Although you will have only one mission statement, you will have several business-level goals that apply to your entire organization. Each functional area of your business (for example, marketing, finance, human resources, and production) will have its own set of specific goals that relate directly to achieving your business-level goals (Figure 3.6). Even if you are the only person performing marketing, finance, human resource management, and production duties, these areas of your small business must still be addressed individually, while your strategies are arranged in a hierarchy like this:

- Your *mission statement* describes who you are, what your business is, and why it exists.

- A *business-level goal* describes what you want your overall business to accomplish to achieve your company mission.

- A *function-level goal* describes the performance desired of specific departments (or functional areas, such as marketing, production, and so on) to achieve your business-level goals.

- A *strategy* is a plan of action that details how you will attain your function-level goals.

In the final stage of goal setting, specific strategies are developed to accomplish your goals. Function-level goals and strategies must coordinate with one another and with business-level goals for the business to run smoothly. For example, a marketing strategy of taking your brick-and-mortar small business online will bring in orders from all over the globe. Looking at the bigger picture, you must plan for the impact such a strategy will have, for example, on your production department's ability to increase capacity, your human resource department's acquiring and training the right new employees, and so on. Each functional area must see itself as an integral part of the entire business and act accordingly.

Levels of Goals

The goals you set for each functional area of your small business should help you achieve the overall goals of your business, which in turn issue from your mission statement.

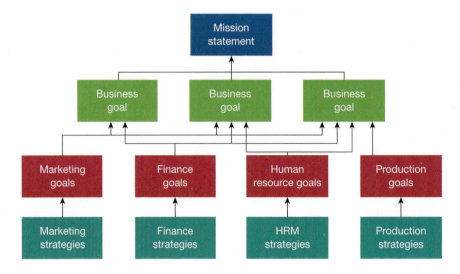

Control Systems

Planning for the future is an inexact science. Very rarely do the actual outcomes of your plans exactly match what you anticipated. When things don't turn out as you planned, you must ask, "Why was there a deviation?" Having a control process, in which you compare what actually happened with what you had originally planned, built into the strategic planning process will help answer this question.

Your strategic plan, including all of its separate parts, sets a standard of comparison for your business's actual performance. The purpose of control systems is to provide you with information to start the planning process all over again. After checking your controls, you either readjust the standards of your plan or create new goals for your plan, and off you go for another planning period. This is why goals must be (1) written in terms of outcomes rather than actions; (2) measurable; (3) challenging, yet attainable; (4) communicated; and (5) written with a time frame for achievement. You need to collect accurate data about what you have done so you can compare this information with your planned standards. Control systems don't need to be expensive and elaborate. They should be simple enough to become a natural part of your management process.

> "Your strategic plan, including all of its separate parts, sets a standard of comparison for your business's actual performance."

Strategic Planning in Action

Strategic plans are different from *business plans* (see Chapter 4). Business plans and strategic plans support each other and overlap to some degree, but they seek to accomplish different purposes. Business plans are written primarily to test the feasibility of a business idea, acquire financing, and coordinate the start-up phase. Strategic plans are needed both before the business is started and continuously while it is in operation to match the direction of the business with changes that occur within its environments.

Strategic planning addresses strategic growth—where you are going. Business planning addresses operational growth—how you will get there. Strategic planning looks outward from the business at the long-term prospects for your products, your markets, your competition, and so on. Business planning, or organizational growth, focuses on the internal concerns of your business, such as capital, personnel, and marketing. Eventually, the two plans will converge, as your long-term strategic goals will be strongly influenced by operational decisions made when the business was started. Strategic planning requires you to broaden your thinking and forces you to look at general issues over the next three to five years—countering the realities of the competitive world with concrete plans instead of wishful thinking. Most sections of a strategic plan will not be extremely detailed but will provide outlines for direction. A business plan, by comparison, needs to be as detailed as possible.

Planning is difficult; consequently, many small business owners would like to ignore it. The reason the planning process is difficult is because it forces you to identify realities that exist in a competitive world rather than relying on emotions, guesses, and assumptions.

What is the best kind of strategic or business plan to write? The one that you will *use*! A balance must be struck between floundering around with no direction or being stuck in an unrealistic, rigid planning process that strangles flexibility and is based on hard data that are not really hard. You need to remember that the *planning process* is actually more important and valuable than the plan that is created because of the *strategic thinking* required to write it.

When you begin writing the first draft of your plan, don't worry about the fine points of its structure—simply get your ideas down on paper. Once you have some elements of your plan written, you should revise it to reorder your ideas into a logical and clear format. An informal plan written in a format that you are comfortable with and will use is 100 percent better than a formal plan that fits someone else's definition of "correct" form but sits on a shelf.

Get advice and suggestions from as many sources as practical when you are formulating your plans. Ask colleagues, bankers, accountants, other executives, and lawyers for their input. If your business is already in operation, including employees in decisions is a great way to show them that their opinions count. They can all provide valuable insight to enhance your plans.

Concept Check Questions

1. Write a mission statement for a small business that not only functions as a strategic planning guide but also incorporates the company's philosophy of social responsibility and ethical standards.

2. Why is environmental analysis more crucial to the small business owner than to larger corporations?

3. You are an entrepreneur and wish to perform a self-evaluation of your business environment. How would you go about this task? Be specific about what you hope to discover through the evaluation of your employees, product, management, and so on.

4. What is the value of competitive analysis to the small business owner? What sorts of things should you know about your competition, and what analytical methods can you use to find out this information?

5. Goal setting is a major part of the entrepreneur's business plan. Outline specific methods for setting goals that are realistic, fit into the overall mission of the company, and can be related to the strategic planning process that is in place at the organization

6. What does strategic planning mean to the small business owner? How does the size of the organization affect the strategic planning process, and how much input should be sought from outside sources while outlining the strategic plan?

CHAPTER REVIEW

SUMMARY ▶▶

LO 3.1   Explain the relationship between social responsibility, ethics, and strategic planning.

The social responsibility and ethics of your business are the commitments you make to doing what is right. Strategic planning is the process of deciding where you want your business to go and how it will get there. All three concepts work together to form the foundation on which your entire business rests.

LO 3.2   Describe the impact of social entrepreneurship on small business.

You have an economic responsibility to make your business profitable. Without profit, your business cannot contribute anything to society. Your legal obligation to obey the law describes the minimal behavior expected for your firm to be part of society. Your ethical responsibility covers your obligation to do what is right. Philanthropic goodwill is contributing to others without expecting anything in return.

LO 3.3   Discuss the importance of ethics for your small business.

Business ethics encompasses more than deciding what should and should not be done in a particular situation. It supplies the fundamental basis for the course you want your business to take. A code of ethics offers a way for you to communicate your ethical expectations to everyone involved in your business. The code should represent your ethical ideals, be concise enough to be remembered, be written clearly, and apply to everyone in the organization.

LO 3.4a   Describe each step in the strategic planning process.

LO 3.4b   Explain the importance of competitive advantage.

The strategic planning process includes defining your mission statement, conducting an environmental analysis (internal and external, or SWOT, analysis), analyzing the competition and defining your competitive advantage, identifying strategic alternatives, setting goals, and establishing systems to measure effectiveness. A competitive advantage is the facet of your business that gives your company an edge over the competition. The strategic plan helps you to identify and establish competitive advantage by analyzing the environment and the competitive landscape.

KEY TERMS ▶▶

code of ethics **54**	philanthropic goodwill **53**	strategic plan **58**
ethics **50**	social entrepreneurship **50**	SWOT analysis **59**
mission statement **58**	social responsibility **50**	

STUDENT STUDY SITE ▶▶

edge.sagepub.com/hatten7e

⑤SAGE edge™ Sharpen your skills with SAGE edge!

SAGE edge for Students provides a personalized approach to help you accomplish your coursework goals in an easy-to-use learning environment. You'll find mobile-friendly eFlashcards and quizzes as well as multimedia resources to support and expand on the concepts presented in this chapter.

EXPERIENTIAL LEARNING ACTIVITIES ▶▶

3.1: Small Business Ethics

LO 3.3: Discuss the importance of ethics for your small business.

Answer the following questions:

1. Stacy's sister is getting married in less than a month. Since Stacy does not live close to her sister, they use Facebook to discuss wedding plans. Stacy regularly spends a couple of hours a day messaging back and forth with her sister on small wedding details while

she is at work since she does not have good internet service at home. Which of the following is most accurate?

A. Stacy is not practicing unethical behavior at work.

B. Stacy should not use company resources, including Stacy's time on personal plans while at work.

C. Stacy should only message her sister on Stacy's breaks or at lunch.

2. Bob has a company credit card since he frequently takes clients out to lunch. He has been working with a group of clients for several years now and knows some of them well. One client, that he considers a friend, asks to bring his brother along to their upcoming business lunch since his brother is in town. Bob knows the client is expecting Bob and the company to pay for lunch. What does Bob do in this situation?

A. Bob says sure since he does not want to lose the client and this is the first time he has done this.

B. Bob tells the client he can pay for the client's lunch but not the lunch of the brother.

C. Bob says sure and then when the bill comes, Bob uses the company credit card to pay for Bob's lunch and pays for the brother's lunch out of his own pocket.

3. You and Sally have been working on a major project together that could very well lead to a promotion. Sally came up with a great idea yesterday that really made a huge difference in the success of the project. Sally is out sick today and your boss comes in and congratulates you on having such a great idea for the project. What do you do?

A. Accept the congratulations and elaborate on the idea adding some of your input.

B. Say thanks but the idea really belongs to Sally.

C. Say nothing now but in the formal presentation acknowledge that the idea was Sally's.

4. You bus tables at a local restaurant that makes all food fresh every day. So at the end of every night, any leftover food, which is perfectly good, is thrown away. It is against company policy to take any food home. However, those of you working the night shift divide the food each night and take it home so the perfectly good food does not go to waste.

A. This is perfectly acceptable since the food that you do not take will be thrown away.

B. This is perfectly acceptable since everyone is doing it.

C. This is not acceptable since it goes against company policy.

5. You see your coworker, who has been with the company for ten years, put a ream of paper and several pens and highlighters in her bag on Friday afternoon as she is preparing to leave. As you think about it, you realize you saw her doing the same thing last Friday. You ask your coworker sitting beside you about what you saw and she just laughs and makes the statement that everyone occasionally takes office supplies.

A. You say nothing since it is none of your business and the coworker has been at the company much longer than you.

B. You speak to the coworker who took the office supplies about what you saw.

C. You speak to your supervisor about what you saw.

After you have answered the five questions individually, form into groups and discuss the answers. In your group, you will discuss (1) your personal answer and (2) what impact each answer will have on the company.

3.2: Creating Competitive Advantage

LO 3.4b: Explain the importance of competitive advantage.

Break into groups of 4–5 students. There must be one smart phone or laptop in each group.

Each group must find the mission statements for seven companies. These companies should produce products used by the students on a frequent basis. Write down the mission statements as the group finds them on the internet. A good place to look for the mission statement is the company home page. Also, for each company, discuss and write down what the group thinks the competitive advantage is for that company.

Once both the mission statements and the competitive advantages are written down, using the information in the text, analyze each mission statement and give it a grade of 1–10, with 10 being the highest ranking. Support the ranking from the information found in the text and be prepared to discuss and defend the group ranking.

Once the mission statements are ranked, discuss why the highest-ranking one was chosen by the group. For each company, discuss *how* the competitive advantage chosen will remain sustainable and *why* that particular competitive advantage will remain sustainable. Support the answer from the information found in the text and be prepared to discuss and defend the reasons chosen.

Bill Daniels: A Man Whose Word Was His Bond

Bill Daniels was an extraordinarily successful businessman whose professional career centered on integrity, honesty, respect, and a fair outcome for all involved. His ethical standards were practiced daily throughout his life from his first business in Casper, Wyoming, to his cable business success in Denver, Colorado, to the Bill Daniels Foundation he created, one of the largest foundations in the Rocky Mountain region. Bill Daniels was known as a man whose word was his bond.

Part I

Bill Daniels was born in Greely, Colorado, in 1920 and grew up during the Depression. After attending the New Mexico Military Institute and serving as a combat pilot during two world wars, Daniels began his first business in the early 1950s. He opened a small insurance agency in Casper, Wyoming, the Bill Daniels Company Insurance. When one of Daniels's clients filed a final claim for $11,000 due to a loss the client had sustained, Daniels discovered the insurance company he had represented and written the policy on had declared bankruptcy. The policy that Daniels had written was worth nothing. Daniels felt personally liable since he had sold the insurance policy to the client and the client had purchased the policy based upon Daniels's representation and word. Bill Daniels felt terrible. Eleven thousand dollars was a huge loss. Daniels knew he had done nothing wrong professionally; yet the client had made the purchase based upon Daniels's advice and it was the client who now had no insurance coverage.

1. What are the legal requirements since Daniels sold the policy? From a business perspective, what is Daniels's obligation to the client? What is the ethical course of action for Daniels to take in this situation? What would you do if you were Daniels?

Part II

Bill Daniels was an avid sports fan who loved to win. He was involved with the American Basketball Association (ABA), serving as president, and in 1970 he purchased the Los Angeles Stars. The Los Angeles Stars, however, were losing money due to low attendance at the Los Angeles Sports Arena. In order to boost support, the new owner, Bill Daniels, moved the defending ABA Western Division playoff champions to Salt Lake City, Utah, where a very supportive new fan base received the team enthusiastically. Over the next five years, the now Utah Stars played to a new ABA fan attendance record. Salt Lake City was proud and supportive of its new and winning professional basketball team. However, even though the Utah Stars were doing well on the court, the finances of the Utah Stars were not doing nearly as well. During the sixteenth game of the 1975 season, with no money to pay the players, the Utah Stars were finished and the franchise was canceled. This decision affected not only the players but also the fans, creditors, and season vendors. The fans were out their season tickets, the creditors were out the dollars they had loaned to the Stars, and the vendors were out their season contracts. With the ending of the Utah Stars, professional basketball was no longer present in Salt Lake City, impacting the community both socially and economically. The revered team was gone. The courts dismissed Daniels's financial obligation as the team's owner. However, Daniels felt he was letting the players, fans, and everyone connected with the Utah Stars down, including the Salt Lake City community. He felt terrible as his winning team failed financially.

2. What are the legal requirements since Daniels owns the Utah Stars? From a business perspective, what is Daniels's obligation to the players, fans, creditors, and vendors? What is the ethical course of action for Daniels to take in this situation? What would you do if you were Bill Daniels?

Part III

Question for discussion in debriefing both sections of the case:

3. Doing the right thing can often be more difficult and expensive than taking short-cuts. Describe how building integrity and a reputation for ethical behavior can be worth the time and money in creating a competitive advantage for a business?

CHAPTER 4

THE BUSINESS PLAN

Brad Powell developed software specifically for credit unions for over 20 years so he knew the industry well—especially the unique problems it faced. One of the biggest sources of office stress and business disruption was an audit of the credit union.

Powell states, "When credit unions respond to a regulatory examination, it can be a nightmare to get the right people involved, get the right answers and respond in a timely manner. If they overlook the slightest detail, it can make things worse rather than better." So he created a software package and founded RedBoard to ease that stress and disruption.

Like any start-up, Powell had to determine the business model that would be best for his new business and for his customers. He had options such as a freemium model, a pay-as-you-go model, a subscription-based model, or a software-as-a-service model. The way to choose one should be determined by which model delivers the most value to the customer.

- Freemium model. This combination of "free" and "premium" has become the dominant business model among internet start-up and mobile app developers. Users get basic features at no cost and get more functions for a subscription fee.

- Pay-as-you-go model. With this model, the user pays on the basis of what is actually consumed.

- Subscription model. The point of this model is to sign long-term contracts with customers so they will be consuming the product well into the future.

- Software-as-a-service (SaaS) model. This model, unique to the software industry, is one

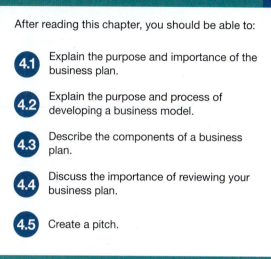

LEARNING OUTCOMES

After reading this chapter, you should be able to:

4.1 Explain the purpose and importance of the business plan.

4.2 Explain the purpose and process of developing a business model.

4.3 Describe the components of a business plan.

4.4 Discuss the importance of reviewing your business plan.

4.5 Create a pitch.

of the three main categories of cloud computing in which the customer does not purchase the software, but rather pays for a license to use it.

In Brad Powell's case, he determined the best business model for everyone was an annual subscription. He created real value for his customers with pricing set so RedBoard paid for itself 20 times over annually. That return on investment (ROI) makes for easy purchase decisions.

We will look at other business models available for small businesses in this chapter.

Sources: Ian Altman, "Here's How to Choose Which Business Model Is Right for You," *Inc.*, August 24, 2017, www.inc.com; Vineet Kumar, "Making 'Freemium' Work," *Harvard Business Review*, May 2014, hbr.org/2014/05/making-freemium-work; Alan Gleeson, "Examples of Well-Known Business Models," accessed July 15, 2018, Bplans Blog, articles.bplans.co.uk/starting-a-business/examples-of-well-known-business-models.

Concept Module 4.1: Every Business Needs a Plan

- **LO 4.1: Explain the purpose and importance of the business plan.**

Successful small business owners know where they want to go and find a way to get there. To see their dreams of owning a profitable business become a reality, they know they must plan each step along the way. Starting a business is like going on vacation—you don't reach your destination by accident. Whether you want to hike through Denali National Park in Alaska or sell frozen yogurt to tourists in Miami, you need a map and adequate provisions.

A **business plan** is a written document that demonstrates persuasively that enough products or services can be sold at a profit for your firm to become a viable business. Planning is an essential ingredient for any successful business. Although we all create mental plans, those thoughts need to be committed to writing before starting a business.[1] A written plan can help us find omissions and flaws in our ideas by allowing other people to critically review and analyze them.

> **business plan**
> A document describing a business that is used to test the feasibility of a business idea, to raise capital, and to serve as a road map for future operations.

Master the content at
edge.sagepub.com/Hatten7e

A business plan tells the reader what your business objectives are; *when, where, why,* and *how* your business will accomplish its objectives; and *who* will be involved in running the business. When planning, you must define the goals of your business, determine the actions that need to be taken to accomplish those goals, gather and commit the necessary resources, and aim for well-defined targets. A business plan can mean the difference between running a business proactively and reactively. When NASA launched Apollo 7, the first manned spacecraft to land on the moon, it didn't aim at the moon. Instead, NASA pointed the rocket to the point in space where the moon would be, factoring in the time needed to get there. Similarly, a business plan should aim at the point where you want your business to be in the future.

The Purpose

The three primary reasons for writing business plans are (1) to help you determine the feasibility of your business idea, (2) to attract capital for starting up the business, and (3) to provide direction for your business after it is in operation.

Proving Feasibility. Writing a business plan is one of the best ways to prevent costly oversights. Committing your ideas to paper forces you to look critically at your means, goals, and expectations. Many people thinking of starting a small business get caught up in the excitement and emotions of the process. It is truly an exciting time! Unfortunately, business decisions based purely on emotion are often not the best long-term choices.

Wanting to have a business does not automatically mean that a market exists to support your desire. You may love boats and want to build a business around them, but if you live 100 miles from the nearest body of water and are unwilling to move, it is unlikely that you can create a viable boat business. Norm Brodsky is a successful entrepreneur who writes a column in *Inc.* magazine titled "Street Smarts." Brodsky states, "The initial goal of every business is to survive long enough to see whether or not the business is viable—no matter what type of business, or how much capital you have. You never know for sure if a business is viable until you do it in the real world."[2] Writing your plan can help remove strong personal emotions from the decision-making process. You need to be passionate about the business you are in, but emotion must be balanced and tempered with logic and rationality.

Attracting Capital. Almost all start-ups must secure capital from bankers or investors. One of the first questions a banker or investor will ask when approached about participating in a business is "Where is your plan?" You need to appreciate the bankers' position. They have to be accountable to depositors for the money entrusted to their care. Bankers in general are financially conservative, so before they risk their capital, they will want assurances that you are knowledgeable and realistic in your projections. Therefore, a complete business plan is needed before you can raise any significant capital. Your business plan will show you know what you are doing and have thought through the problems and opportunities. Potential investors will also have questions about your plan. They will want to know when your business will break even, when it will be profitable, and if your numbers are real.[3]

> "Free or inexpensive business-planning assistance is available to entrepreneurs from such sources as Small Business Development Centers."

Providing Direction. Business plans should provide a road map for future operation. "Can't see the forest for the trees" and "It's difficult to remember that your initial objective was to drain the swamp when you're up to your hips in alligators" are clichés that well apply to starting a small business in that so much of your time can be consumed by handling immediate problems ("management by spot fire" or paying attention to the latest dilemma to flare up) that you have trouble concentrating on the overall needs of the business. By having a road map to guide you over the long term, you are more likely to stay on course. Free or inexpensive business-planning assistance is available to entrepreneurs from such sources as Small Business Development Centers.

Don't misunderstand—providing direction does not mean that directions (and plans) don't change. Craig Knouf understands that point very well. He calculates he has revised his original business plan more than 120 times since he first wrote it in 1997 for Associated Business Systems, an office equipment supplier in Portland, Oregon. Knouf meets with his seven vice presidents to take a look at the 30-page document every month to review current goals and every quarter for three-month goals, and he holds a two-day meeting annually to discuss long-term objectives. Knouf says, "If you only looked at the plan every quarter, by the time you realize the mistake, you're five months off. You're done. You're not going to get back on track."[4]

The Practice: Guidelines for Writing a Business Plan

No rigid formula for writing business plans exists that would fit every new business. Plans are unique to each business situation. Even so, some general guidelines should be followed.

Consider Your Audience. You need to show the benefit of your business to your reader. Investors want their money to go into market-driven businesses, which satisfy the wants and needs of customers, rather than technology-driven ones, which focus more on the product or service being offered than on what people want.[5]

Keep It Brief. Your business plan should be long enough to cover all the major issues facing the business, yet not look like a copy of *War and Peace*. Your final plan should be complete, yet concise. Including financial projections and appendixes, it should be less than 40 pages long. Your first draft will probably be longer, but you can sharpen your ideas by editing the final document to 40 or fewer pages.

Point of View. Try to write your business plan in the third person (do not use *I* or *we*). This approach helps maintain objectivity by removing your personal emotions from the writing process.

Create a Professional Image. The overall appearance of your business plan should be professional and attractive, but not extravagant. Having your document laser printed on white paper, with a colored-stock cover, dividers, and spiral binding, is perfectly acceptable. Think of the message your business plan will send to bankers and investors. For example, having it bound in leather with gold leaf–trimmed pages is not a good sign. Does the plan's appearance suggest that you really need the money or will spend it wisely? Conversely, what might potential investors think of a business plan scratched out on a Big Chief tablet with a crayon? Would it look as if you were really serious about your business?

As you write the first draft of your plan, have several people who are not involved in your business read your work to get their initial reactions. Do they quickly grasp the essence of your proposal? Are they excited about your idea? Do they exclaim, "Wow!"? Getting feedback while you are still writing the plan can help you refine your work and get the reader to say, "Wow!"

Where to Get Help. Who should write the business plan for your proposed venture? You should! The person who is best qualified and who receives the most benefit from the planning process is the person who is going to implement the plan. It is *your* business, after all, and it needs to be *your* plan. With that stated, can you get aid in writing the plan? Of course you can, and you should seek such help if you need it. Here are some sources:

- The Small Business Administration home page at www.sba.gov
- Your local Small Business Development Center
- A local SCORE (Service Corps of Retired Executives) chapter
- Your local chamber of commerce

- A nearby college or university

- One of the many paperback guides written on business plans available at any bookstore

Computer software is available to perform many functions of our daily lives. We can balance our checkbook or design our dream house using software, for example. Although software packages can make our lives easier, you need to be careful not to use one to generate a "cookie-cutter" business plan. Filling in a few blanks on a master document does not produce a workable business plan any more than a paint-by-numbers kit produces valuable art. Because your business will be different from others, you need to emphasize your competitive advantage and show your objectives.

This is not to imply that you should not use word-processing, spreadsheet, or graphics packages to produce your plan. You should, because they can be extremely helpful. Instead, this caveat applies to "canned" business plans. If you wish to investigate business-planning software, check out JIAN's BizPlan Builder Interactive and Palo Alto Software's Business Plan Pro, but remember writing a business plan is as much an art as it is a science.[6]

Concept Check Questions

1. Why wouldn't a 100-page business plan be four times better than a 25-page business plan?

2. Should you write a business plan even if you do not need outside financing? Why or why not?

3. Who should write the business plan?

4. If successful companies like Pizza Hut have been started without a business plan, why does the author claim they are so important?

5. Why do entrepreneurs have trouble remaining objective when writing their business plans?

6. Why do some prospective business owners refuse to plan?

7. When you reach the point in your career when you are ready to start your own business (or your next one), will you write a business plan before beginning? Why or why not? If you would choose to start a business without a business plan, what would be an alternative for testing feasibility?

Concept Module 4.2: Business Models and Feasibility Analysis

- LO 4.2: Explain the purpose and process of developing a business model.

The world of business plans has changed in recent years. Historically, entrepreneurs would write a business plan, make pitches with it to investors, gather resources, and start building product, hoping the business would reach profitability before a major problem caused the business to fail.

The problem with traditional business planning is the assumption that it is possible to identify and solve all problems a business will face *before* the business is started—a shaky assumption at best. Boxer Mike Tyson was asked about his opponents' prefight strategies and quipped, "Everybody has a plan until they get punched in the mouth." Business planning translation: It is hard to anticipate how one will respond to adversity.

The new approach to building a business from scratch is termed "lean start-up" and is geared toward getting a new product into the hands of consumers as quickly as possible.[7] The fundamental driver of lean start-ups is to Build–Measure–Learn. Turn your idea into something tangible quickly to get feedback on what works and what does not work. Once those measurements are seen, the entrepreneur can then "pivot" or move the product design in the appropriate direction. Learning about what customers want along the way during the design process accelerates the feedback loop.

The term *business model* covers a wide range of formal and informal descriptions of all the core aspects that are important to a business. A good business model answers questions like "Who is the customer?" "What does the customer value?" but most important, it answers the question "How do we make money in this business?"[8]

As addressed in the chapter opener, there are many variations in creating a business model for generating revenue, including

- **Product is free, generate revenue from advertisers.** Think Facebook. The problem is generating enough users to make advertising worthwhile.

- **Freemium model.** Think LinkedIn. Offer basic function for free and make more services available for more money. The challenge is to differentiate and convert users.

- **Base price on cost plus margin.** This is a traditional model—build a product then charge two to five times what it cost to make.

- **Subscription model.** Customers pay little up front with monthly or annual payments so revenue is ongoing.

- **Break even on base, make money on disposables.** Think razor blades or ink jet printer cartridges.

- **Nonrevenue model.** Think Twitter, in which outside investors cover business costs and business valuation goes up with the number of users.[9]

From the very beginning an entrepreneur's idea for a new business is based on a hypothesis—a good guess. A quicker way of testing these hypotheses (before writing a comprehensive business plan), created by Alexander Osterwalder and Yves Pigneur, is called the business model canvas. This diagram walks the entrepreneur through questions that answer how the business creates value for itself and its customers. At their website, www.businessmodelgeneration.com/canvas, you can watch a two-minute video and download the one-page canvas to test your ideas.

The building blocks for the business model canvas are

- Value Proposition
  - *What problem are we helping the customer solve?*
  - *Which customer need are we satisfying?*
  - *What value are we delivering to the customer?*
- Customer Segments
  - *For whom does this product create value?*
  - *Who are our most important customers?*
- Channels
  - *What communications, distribution, and sales channels do customers prefer?*
  - *What channels are used now?*
  - *Which channels are most cost and time efficient?*

- Customer Relations
  - *How do we get and keep new customers?*
  - *How do our customer relations fit with the rest of our model?*
- Key Resources
  - *What assets do we need in order to offer our value proposition?*
- Key Activities
  - *What do we have to DO in order to offer our value proposition?*
- Key Partnerships
  - *Who are our key partners and suppliers?*
  - *What activities do we need to outsource to partners?*
  - *What resources do we need from partners?*
- Cost Structure
  - *What do key activities and resources cost?*
  - *What other costs are needed to build our model?*
- Revenue Streams
  - *What are customers willing to pay for our value propositions?*
  - *What do they currently pay to solve the same problem?*
  - *How many revenue streams run into our model?*[10]

Feasibility Analysis

Another planning tool that fits somewhere between building business models and writing full-blown business plans is a **feasibility study**. If your business idea checks out upon building all the blocks of a business model, a feasibility study continues to flesh out all the possibilities with each step representing a go/no-go decision.

Business models and feasibility studies answer the question "Will this business idea work?" As each step in the study leads to a "yes" answer to this question, then your response is to "go" to the next step. A step that generates a "no" answer to that question is likely a "no-go" to the feasibility of the business idea. If the business model and feasibility studies are all "go," then the business plan will answer the question, "*How* will this business idea work?"

Business opportunities and ideas differ, and so will the testing of their feasibility, but the following guidelines provide a good foundation for the aspects to probe.[11]

Description of the Business Idea

- Identification and exploration of business scenarios. Does my plan clearly identify and explain my business idea?

- Identify alternative business models for the business. How will it be organized? How will it generate profits? These may come from the idea assessment or market assessment that you may have already completed.

- Eliminate models that don't make sense.

- Flesh out the model(s) that appears to have potential for further exploration.

- Define the business.

- Describe the type and quality of product(s) or service(s) to be marketed.

feasibility study
A tool for assessing parts of the business plan and determining if the idea will work.

- Outline the general business model (i.e., how the business will make money).

- Define the operations including size, location, kind of inputs, and so on.

- Specify the time horizon from the time the project is initiated until it is up and running at capacity.

Market Feasibility. This can be based on a market assessment that you may have already completed.

- Describe the industry your business will be a part of.

- Describe the size and scope of the industry, market, and/or market segment(s).

- Estimate the future direction of the industry, market, and/or market segment(s).

- Describe the nature of the industry, market, and/or market segment(s). Is it stable or going through rapid change and restructuring?

- Identify the life cycle of the industry, market, and/or market segment(s). Is it emerging, growing, mature, declining?

- How competitive is the industry?

- Describe the industry concentration. Are there just a few large producers or many small producers?

- Describe the major competitors? Will you compete directly against them?

- Analyze the barriers to entry of new competitors into the market or industry. Can new businesses enter easily?

- Analyze the concentration and competitiveness of input suppliers and product/service buyers.

- Describe the price competitiveness of your product/service.

Market Potential

- Identify whether the product is to be sold into a commodity market or a differentiated product/service market.

- Identify the demand and usage trends of the market.

- Examine the potential for emerging, niche, or segmented market opportunities.

- Explore the opportunities to create a unique brand.

- Assess your potential market share.

- Describe access to market outlets.

- Identify the potential buyers of the product/service and the associated marketing costs.

- Investigate the product/service distribution system and the costs involved.

- Determine sales projections.

- Estimate sales revenue.

- Carefully identify and assess the accuracy of the underlying assumptions in the sales projection.

- Project sales under various assumptions (i.e., different selling prices, services provided, etc.).

Technical Feasibility

- What are your facility needs?
- Estimate the size and type of production facilities needed.
- Investigate the need for related buildings, equipment, rolling stock, and so forth.
- Evaluate the suitability of production technology.
- Investigate and compare technology providers.
- Determine reliability and competitiveness of technology (proven or unproven, state of the art, etc.).
- Identify limitations or constraints of the technology.
- Investigate access to raw materials, transportation, labor, and production inputs (electricity, natural gas, water, etc.).
- Investigate potential emissions problems.
- Analyze other environmental impacts.
- Identify regulatory requirements.
- Explore economic development incentives.

Raw Materials

- Estimate the amount of raw materials needed.
- Investigate the current and future availability and access to raw materials.
- Assess the quality and cost of raw materials.
- Evaluate other inputs.
- Investigate the availability of labor including wage rates, skill level, and so on.
- Assess the potential to access and attract qualified management personnel.

Financial/Economic Feasibility

- Estimate the total capital requirements.
- Estimate capital requirements for facilities, equipment, and inventories.
- Estimate working capital needs.
- Estimate start-up capital needs until revenues are realized at full capacity.
- Estimate contingency capital needs due to construction delays, technology malfunction, market access delays, and so forth.
- Estimate other capital needs.

Estimate Equity and Credit Needs

- Estimate equity needs.
- Identify alternative equity sources and capital availability—family, producers, local investors, angle investors, venture capitalists, and so on.

- Estimate credit needs.

- Identify and assess alternative credit sources—banks, government (i.e., direct loans or loan guarantees), grants, and local and state economic development incentives.

- Budget expected costs and returns of various alternatives.

- Estimate the expected revenue, costs, profit margin, and expected net profit.

- Estimate the sales or usage needed to break even.

- Estimate the returns under various production, price, and sales levels. This may involve identifying "best case," "typical," and "worst case" scenarios.

- Assess the reliability of the underlying assumptions of the analysis (prices, production, efficiencies, market access, market penetration, etc.).

- Benchmark against industry averages and/or competitors (cost, margin, profits, ROI, etc.).

- Identify limitations or constraints of the economic analysis.

- Calculate expected cash flows during the start-up period and when the business reaches capacity.

- Prepare pro forma income statement, balance sheet, and other statements of when the business is fully operating.

Organizational/Managerial Feasibility

- Identify the proposed legal structure of the business.

- Outline the staffing and governance structure of the business.

- Identify the availability of skilled and experienced business managers.

Business Founders

- What key individuals will lead the project?

- Character matters—are the people involved of outstanding character?

- Do the founders have the "fire in the belly" required to take the project to completion?

- Do the founders have the skills and ability to build a successful business?

- Have the founders organized other successful businesses?

Next Step. After the feasibility study has been completed, you are faced with decisions about which course of action to pursue. Potential courses of action include

- Choosing the most viable business model, developing a business plan, and proceeding with creating and operating a business.

- Identifying which factors are questionable, calling for further study.

- Deciding that a viable business opportunity does not exist and moving to end the process.

- Following another course of action.

Concept Check Question

1. Assume you are visiting with your grandmother. She tells you she was watching *Shark Tank* on TV and heard them talking about business models working or not working. She asks you what a business model might be. How do you answer her?

Concept Module 4.3: Business Plan Contents

- **LO 4.3: Describe the components of a business plan.**

A business plan should be tailored to fit your particular business. Write the plan yourself, even if you seek assistance from lawyers, accountants, or consultants. In 40 or fewer pages, the plan should present your strengths clearly and in a logical order.

Although a plan's contents will vary from business to business, its structure is fairly standardized. Your plan should contain as many of the following sections as appropriate for your type of venture.[12] Not every business will require every one of these sections. For example, if your business is a start-up, it won't have a history section, but you can describe your management experience.

Cover Page

The cover page should include the name of the business, its address and phone number, and the date the plan was issued. If this information is overlooked, you have a problem if a potential investor tries to reach you to ask additional questions (or send a check).

> "A first-rate executive summary provides you with a two-sentence 'elevator pitch,' so named in case you should ever find yourself contained in an elevator with a venture capitalist and need to explain your business concept quickly."

Table of Contents

You want the business plan to be as easy to read as possible. An orderly table of contents will allow the reader to turn directly to the sections desired.

Executive Summary

The **executive summary** gives a one- to two-page overview of your entire plan. It is the most important section of the plan because readers do not want to wade through 35 to 40 pages to get the essential facts. If you do not capture the reader's attention here, he or she is not likely to read the rest of the plan.

The executive summary should include the following components:

- *Company information*—what product or service you provide, your competitive advantage, when the company will be formed, your company objectives, and the background of you and your management team.

- *Market opportunity*—the expected size and growth rate of your market, your expected market share, and any relevant industry trends.

- *Financial data*—financial forecasts for the first three years of operations, equity investment desired, and long-term loans that will be needed.

The information in the preceding list is a lot to condense into two pages, but all of it is important, and if you truly understand what you are writing about, you will find that you can explain it simply and succinctly. A first-rate executive summary provides you with a ninety-second "elevator pitch," so named in case you should ever find yourself contained in an elevator with a venture capitalist and need to explain your business concept quickly.[13]

Although the executive summary is the first section of the plan, it should be written last. You are condensing what you have already written into the summary, not expanding the summary to fill the plan. Here's a hint for writing the executive summary: As you compose all the other

executive summary
A condensed abstract of a business plan used to spark the reader's interest in the business and to highlight crucial information.

sections of the plan, highlight a few key sentences that are important enough to include in your executive summary. To see examples of executive summaries, refer to the complete plan included in Appendix A and the sample plans on this book's companion website.

Company Information

In this section, you should describe the background of your company, your choice of legal business form, and the reasons for the company's establishment. How did your company get to the point where it is today? Give the company's history by describing in some detail what your business does and how it satisfies customers' needs. How did you choose and develop your products or services to be sold? Don't be afraid to describe any setbacks or missteps you have taken along the way to forming your business. They represent reality, and leaving them out could make your plan and projections look "too good to be true" to lenders or investors.

Environmental and Industry Analysis

In the section on environmental and industry analysis, you have an opportunity to show how your business fits into larger contexts. An *environmental analysis* shows identified trends and changes that are happening at the national and international levels that may influence the future of your small business. Introduce environmental categories such as economic, competitive, legal, political, cultural, and technological arenas that affect and are affected by your business. Discuss the future outlook and trends within these categories. For example, a cultural trend of "Buy American" might create a competitive advantage for your small manufacturing business. Changes in the legal or political arena can provide opportunities as well. Suppose the Environmental Protection Agency (EPA) banned lead fishing sinkers because of possible contamination of water supplies. What if you had just created a line of fishing sinkers produced from some material other than lead?

While you generally cannot control such external environments, you can describe the opportunities that changes in them present in your business plan. As an entrepreneur, you have to understand the world in which you operate and how you can best assess the opportunities that arise there.

After completing the environmental analysis, you should do an *industry* analysis describing the industry within which your business operates. Here you will focus on specific industry trends. Describe industry demand—pertinent data will likely be readily available from industry trade publications or other published sources. How do you determine what other businesses or products should be included as part of your industry? One helpful way to draw the line between what and whom to include in your industry is to consider possible substitutes for your product. If you own a business that sells ice cream, do your customers view frozen yogurt or custard as a potential substitute for your frozen treats? If so, you should consider businesses that sell these products to be part of your industry. What competitive reactions and industrywide trends can you identify? Who are the major players in your industry? Have any businesses recently entered or exited the field? Why did they leave? Is the industry growing or declining? Who are the new competitors in the industry?

Lenders want to see that you have a clear understanding of how your industry operates. Specifically, which of Porter's five forces (threat of new entrants, bargaining power of customers, threat of substitutes, bargaining power of suppliers, and rivalry among existing competitors; see Chapter 3) are rated as high or low for the industry you intend to enter?[14]

The environmental and industry analyses are tricky sections of your business plan to write. As stated earlier, your plan must be concise, but in this section especially you must cover huge, comprehensive issues and factors that could fill volumes. Feel like you are being pulled in several different directions at once? Good—now you are starting to realize the complexity of what you are getting into. Think of the environmental and industry analysis section in the following way: As a small business owner, you have to be knowledgeable about all current and potential factors that could affect your business. Of course, the business plan is not the place to describe every possible development in detail. Instead, treat this section as if you are showing only the tip of the iceberg that represents your accumulated knowledge, and make it clear you are prepared to answer questions relating to less critical factors that you chose not to include in your business plan.

Products or Services

In this section, you can go into detail describing your product or service. How is your product or service different from those currently on the market? Are there any other uses for it that could increase current sales? Include drawings or photos if appropriate. Describe any patents or trademarks that you hold, as these give you a proprietary position that can be defended. Describe your competitive advantage. What sets your product or service apart as better than the competition's?

What is your product's potential for growth? How do you intend to manage your product or service through the product life cycle? Can you expand the product line or develop related products? In this section of your business plan, you can discuss potential product lines as well as current ones.

Marketing Research and Evaluation

You need to present evidence that a market exists for your business. A section on marketing research and evaluation, presenting the facts you have gathered on the size and nature of your markets, will tell investors if a large enough market exists and if you can be competitive in that market. State the market size in dollars and units. Give your sales forecast by estimating from your marketing research how many units and dollars' worth of your product you expect to sell in a given time period. That sales forecast becomes the basis for projecting many of your financial statements. Indicate your primary and secondary sources of data, and the methods you used to estimate total market size and your market share.

Target Markets and Market Segmentation. You must identify your target markets and then concentrate your marketing efforts on these key areas. These markets must share some identifiable need that you can satisfy. What do the people who buy your product have in common with one another? To segment your markets, you could use a demographic characteristic (for example, 18- to 25-year-old females), a psychographic variable (similar lifestyles, usage rate of product, or degree of loyalty), a geographic variable (anyone who lives within a five-mile radius of your business), or another variable. Describe actual customers who have expressed a desire to buy your product. What trends do you expect will affect your markets?

> "A danger of segmentation and target marketing is that it encourages the belief that those segments and markets will stay the same—they won't."

Market Trends. Markets and consumer tastes change, so you will need to explain how you will assess your customers' needs over time. A danger of segmentation and target marketing is that it encourages the belief that those segments and markets will stay the same—they won't. Specify how you will continue to evaluate consumer needs so you can identify market trends and, based on that information, improve your market lines and aid new product development.

Competition. Among three or four primary competitors, identify the price leader, the quality leader, and the service leader. Realistically discuss the strengths and weaknesses of each. Compare your products or services with those of competitors on the basis of price, product performance, and other attributes.

This section offers a good opportunity to include the SWOT analysis you completed in the strategic planning chapter (Chapter 3). Identify the strengths and weaknesses of your business and the opportunities and threats that exist outside your business.

Market Share. Because you have identified the size of your market and your competitors, you can estimate the *market share* you intend to gain—that is, the percentage of total industry sales. Market share can effectively be shown and explained using a pie chart.

Your job in writing the marketing-research section of your business plan is to convince the reader that a large enough market exists for your product for you to achieve your projected sales forecasts.

Marketing Plan. Your *marketing plan* shows how you intend to achieve your sales forecast. You should start by explaining your overall marketing strategy, identifying your potential markets, and explaining what you have decided is the best way to reach them. Include your *marketing objectives* (what you want to achieve) and the strategies you will use to accomplish these objectives.

Pricing as Part of Marketing Plan. Your pricing policy is one of the most important decisions you will have to make. The price must be "right" to penetrate the market, to maintain your market position, and especially to make profits. Compare your pricing policies with those of the competitors you identified earlier. Explain how your gross margin will allow you to make a profit after covering all expenses. Many people go into business with the intent of charging lower prices than the competition. If this is your goal, explain how you can follow this strategy and still make a profit—through greater efficiency in manufacturing or distribution of the product, lower labor costs, lower overhead, or whatever else allows you to undercut the competition's price.

You should discuss the relationship between your price, your market share, and your profits. For example, by charging a higher price than the competition, you may reduce your sales volume but realize a higher gross margin and increase your business's bottom line.

Promotion as Part of Marketing Plan. How will you attract the attention of and communicate with your potential customers? For industrial products, you might use trade shows and advertise in trade magazines, via direct mail, or through promotional brochures. For consumer products, you should describe your plans for advertising and promotional campaigns. You should also give the advertising schedule and costs involved. Examples of advertising or brochures may be included in the appendix of the business plan.

Place as Part of Marketing Plan. Describe how you intend to sell and distribute your products. Will you use your own sales force or independent sales representatives or distributors? If you will hire your own sales force, describe how it will be structured, the sales expected per salesperson per year, and the pay structure. Your own sales force will concentrate more on your products because it will sell them exclusively. If you will use sales representatives, describe how those individuals will be selected, the territories they will cover, and the rates they will charge. Independent sales representatives may also handle products and lines other than yours, but they are much less expensive for you because they are not your employees. Your place strategy should describe the level of coverage (local, regional, or national) you will use initially and as your business grows. It should include the channels of distribution you will use to get and to sell products.

Service Policies as Part of Marketing Plan. If you sell a product that may require service, such as cameras, copy machines, or bicycles, describe your service and warranty policies. These policies can be important in the customer's decision-making process. How will you handle customer service problems? Describe the terms and types of warranties offered. Explain whether you will provide service via your own service department, subcontract out the service work, or return products to the factory. Also state whether service is intended to be a profit center or a break-even operation.

Manufacturing and Operations Plan

The manufacturing and operations plan will stress elements related to your business's production. It will outline your needs in terms of facilities, location, space requirements, capital equipment, labor force, inventory control, and purchasing. Stress the areas most relevant to your type of business. For instance, if you are starting a manufacturing business, outline the production processes and your control systems for inventory, purchasing, and production. The business plan for a service business should focus on your location, overhead, and labor force productivity.

Geographic Location. Describe your planned geographic location and its advantages and disadvantages in terms of wage rates, unionization, labor pool, proximity to customers and suppliers, types of transportation available, tax rates, utility costs, and zoning. Again, you should stress the features most relevant to your business. Proximity to customers is especially important to a service business, whereas access to transportation will be of greater concern to a manufacturing business.

Facilities. What kinds of facilities does your business need? Discuss your requirements for floor space (including offices, sales room, manufacturing plant space, and storage areas), parking, loading areas, and special equipment. Will you rent, lease, or purchase these facilities? How long will they remain adequate: One year? Three years? Is expansion possible?

Make-or-Buy Policy. In a manufacturing business, you must decide what you will produce and what you will purchase as components to be assembled into the finished product. This is called the *make-or-buy decision*. Many factors go into this decision. In your business plan, you should justify the advantages of your policy. Describe potential subcontractors and suppliers.

> "Training can be a hidden cost that can turn a profit into a loss."

Control Systems. What is your approach to controlling quality, inventory, and production? How will you measure your progress toward the goals you have set for your business?

Labor Force. At the location you have selected, is there a sufficient quantity of adequately skilled people in the local labor force to meet your needs? What kinds of training will you need to provide? Can you afford to offer this training and still remain competitive? Training can be a hidden cost that can turn a profit into a loss.

Management Team

A good management team is the key to transforming your vision into a successful business. Show how your team is balanced in terms of technical skills (possessing the knowledge specific to your type of business), business skills (the ability to successfully run a business), and experience. As when building any other kind of team, the skills and talents of your management team need to complement one another. Include a job description for each management position, and specify the key people who will fill these slots. Can you show how their skills complement one another? Have these individuals worked together before? An *organization chart* can be included in the appendix of your plan to graphically show how these positions fit together. Resumes for each key manager should be included in the appendix.

State how your key managers will be compensated. Your chances of obtaining financing are very slim unless the managers are willing to accept substantially less than their market value for salary while the business is getting started. Managers must be committed to putting as many proceeds as possible back into the business.

Discuss the training your key people have had and may still need. Be as specific as possible on the cost, type, and availability of this management or technical training.

Like your managers, you may need professional assistance at times. Identify other people with whom you will work, including a lawyer, a certified public accountant, an insurance agent, and a banker. Identify contacts you have supporting you in these areas.

Anyone who is considering putting money into your business will scrutinize this section thoroughly. Therefore, your plan must answer the following questions about the management team members, which were first posed by Harvard professor William Sahlman:

- Where are the founders from?
- Where have they been educated?
- Where have they worked, and for whom?
- What have they accomplished—professionally and personally—in the past?
- What is their reputation within the *business* community?
- What experience do they have that is directly relevant to the opportunity they are pursuing?
- What skills, abilities, and knowledge do they have?
- How realistic are they about the venture's chances for success and the tribulations it will face?
- Who else needs to be on the team?
- Are they prepared to recruit high-quality people?
- How will they respond to adversity?
- Do they have the mettle to make the inevitable hard choices?
- How committed are they to this venture? At what price?
- What are their motivations?[15]

Timeline

Create a timeline outlining the interrelationships and timing of the major events planned for your venture. In addition to helping you calculate your business needs and minimize risk, the timeline is an indicator to investors that you have thoroughly researched potential problems and are aware of deadlines. Keep in mind that people tend to underestimate the time needed to complete projects. Your schedule should be realistic and attainable.

Critical Risks and Assumptions

All business plans contain implicit assumptions, such as how your business will operate, what economic conditions will be, and how you will react in different situations. Identification and discussion of any potential major trends, problems, or risks that you think you may encounter will show the reader that you are in touch with reality. These risks and assumptions could relate to your industry, markets, company, or personnel.

This section gives you a place to establish alternate plans in case the unexpected happens. If potential investors discover unstated negative factors after the fact, they may quickly question the credibility of both you and the business. Too many businesses are started with only a plan A and no thought about what will happen if X, Y, or Z occurs.[16] Possible contingencies that you should anticipate include the following scenarios:

- *Unreliable sales forecasts.* What will you do if your market does not develop as quickly as you predicted or, conversely, if your market develops too quickly? Each of these situations creates its own problems. Sales that are too low may cause serious financial problems. Sales that are too high may cause bottlenecks in production, difficulties in purchasing enough products from vendors or suppliers, trouble hiring and scheduling employees, or dissatisfied customers who must wait longer than they expected for your product or service.

- *Competitors' ability to underprice or to make your product obsolete.*
- *Unfavorable industrywide trends.* Not long ago, businesses that produced asbestos made up a thriving industry supplying products for automotive and building construction firms. Then reports linking asbestos with cancer drastically affected the demand for that product and virtually eliminated the industry.
- *Appropriately trained workers not as available as predicted.*
- *Erratic supply of products or raw materials.*
- *Any one of the 10,000 other things you didn't expect.*

Benefits to the Community

Your new business will affect the lives of many other people besides yourself. Describe the potential benefits to the community that the formation of your business could provide.

- *Economic development*—number of jobs created (total and skilled), purchase of supplies from local businesses, and the multiplier effect (which shows the number of hands that new dollars brought into the community pass through before exiting).
- *Community development*—providing needed goods or services, improving physical assets or the appearance of the community, and contributing to a community's standard of living.
- *Human development*—providing new technical skills or other training, creating opportunities for career advancement, developing management or leadership skills, offering attractive wages, and providing other types of individual growth.

Exit Strategy

Every business will benefit by devoting some attention to a succession plan. Before you begin your business is a good time to consider how you intend to get yourself (and your money) out of it. Do you intend to sell it in 20 years? Will your children take it over? How will you prepare them for ownership? Do you intend to grow the business to the point of an initial public offering? How will investors get their money back?

Financial Plan

Your financial plan is where you demonstrate that all the information from previous sections of your business plan, such as marketing, operations, sales, and strategies, can come together to form a viable, profitable business. Potential investors will closely scrutinize the financial section of your business plan to ensure it is feasible before they become involved. Projections should be your best estimates of future operations. Your financial plan should include the following statements (existing businesses will need historical statements and pro forma projections, whereas start-ups will have only projections):

- Sources and uses of capital (initial and projected)
- Cash flow projections for three years
- Balance sheets for three years

- Profit-and-loss statements for three years

- Break-even analysis

We will discuss how to prepare these documents in later chapters. (See Chapter 8 for cash flow projections, balance sheets, and profit-and-loss statements, and Chapter 9 for sources and uses of capital.) With the financial statements, you need to show conclusions and important points, such as how much equity and how much debt are included, the highest amount of cash needed, and how long the payback period for loans is expected to be.

Sources and Uses of Funds. The simple **sources and uses of funds** form shows where your money is coming from and how you are spending it (Figure 4.1).

Cash Flow Statement. The most important financial statement for a small business is the **cash flow statement**, because if you run out of cash, you're out of business. In a cash flow statement, working from your opening cash balance, you add all the money that comes into your business for a given time period (week, month, quarter), and then you subtract all the money you spend for the same time period. The result is your closing cash balance, which becomes your opening balance for the next time period (Figure 4.2).

You should project a cash flow statement by month for the first year of operation and by quarter for the second and third years. *Cash flow* shows you what the highest amount of working capital will be. It can be especially critical if your sales are seasonal in nature or cyclical.

sources and uses of funds
A financial document used by start-up businesses that shows where capital comes from and what it will be used for.

cash flow statement
A financial document that shows the amount of money a business has on hand at the beginning of a time period, receipts coming into the business, and money going out of the business during the same period.

▼ FIGURE 4.1

Sources and Uses of Funds Worksheet

A sources and uses of funds worksheet shows where money comes from and what it is used for.

Sources of Funds:	
Debt:	
Term loans	$ _____
Refinancing of old debt	_____
Lines of credit	
Line 1	_____
Line 2	_____
Mortgage	_____
Equity:	
Investments	_____
Total Sources:	$ _____
Uses of Funds:	
Property	$ _____
Inventory	_____
Equipment (itemize)	_____
	_____
	_____
Working capital	_____
Cash reserve	_____
Total Uses:	$ _____

▼ FIGURE 4.2

Sample Components of a Cash Flow Statement

A cash flow statement shows how money enters and exits your business.

Opening cash balance	
Add:	Cash receipts
	Collection of accounts receivable
	New loans or investment
	Other sources of cash
	Total receipts
Less:	Utilities Salaries
	Office supplies
	Accounts payable
	Leased equipment
	Sales expenses
	Loan payments
	General expenses
	Total disbursements
Cash increase (or decrease)	
Closing cash balance	

Balance Sheet. The **balance sheet** shows all the assets *owned* by your business and the liabilities, or what is *owed* against those assets (Figure 4.3). The difference between the two is what the company has *earned*, or the net worth of the business, which is also called *capital*. From the balance sheet, bankers and investors will calculate some key ratios, such as debt-to-equity and current ratio (see Chapter 8), to help determine the financial health of your business. You need to prepare balance sheets ending at each of the first three years of operation.

Profit-and-Loss Statement. Don't expect the pro forma for your business plan to be a finely honed, 100 percent accurate projection of the future. With a **profit-and-loss statement**, your objective is to come up with as close an approximation as possible of what your sales revenues and expenses will be. In making your projections, it is helpful to break sales down by product

▼ FIGURE 4.3

Balance Sheet

A balance sheet shows what you own and whom you owe.

	For year ended [month] [day], [year]		
	Year 1	**Year 2**	**Year 3**
Current Assets			
Cash	$ _____	$ _____	$ _____
Accounts Receivable	_____	_____	_____
Inventory	_____	_____	_____
Supplies	_____	_____	_____
Prepaid Expenses	_____	_____	_____
Fixed Assets			
Real Estate	_____	_____	_____
Equipment	_____	_____	_____
Fixtures and Leasehold Improvements	_____	_____	_____
Vehicles	_____	_____	_____
Other Assets			
License	_____	_____	_____
Goodwill	_____	_____	_____
TOTAL ASSETS	$ _____	$ _____	$ _____
Current Liabilities			
Accounts Payable	_____	_____	_____
Notes Payable (due within 1 year)	_____	_____	_____
Accrued Expenses	_____	_____	_____
Taxes Owed	_____	_____	_____
Long-Term Liabilities			
Notes Payable (due after 1 year)	_____	_____	_____
Bank Loans	_____	_____	_____
TOTAL LIABILITIES	$ _____	$ _____	$ _____
NET WORTH (assets minus liabilities)	$ _____	$ _____	$ _____

line (or types of services) and then determine a best-case scenario, a worst-case scenario, and a most-likely scenario somewhere between the two extremes for each category. This practice helps create realistic projections. Remember that lenders and investors (especially venture capitalists) are professionals at picking apart business plans.[17]

Start preparing this statement in the left-hand column to show what your sales and expenses would be under the worst conditions (Figure 4.4). Assume that you have difficulty getting products, that the weather is terrible, that your salespeople are out spending all their time playing golf instead of selling, and that the state highway department closes the road that runs in front of your only location for repairs. Imagine anything bad that can happen will happen. Now, in the right-hand column, make projections assuming everything goes exactly your way. What would your sales and expenses be if customers with cash in their hands are waiting in line outside your door every morning at opening time, if suppliers rearrange their schedules so that you never run out of stock, and if competitors all close their doors for a month of vacation just as you are beginning operations? This is a lot more fun, of course, but not any more likely to happen than the first scenario—although either could happen. Your most realistic estimate will fall between these two extremes in the center column.

▼ FIGURE 4.4
Profit-and-Loss Statement
Projecting the best and the worst that could happen helps you calculate what your profits or losses are likely to be.

Sales:	Low	Most Likely	High
Product/service line 1	$ _____	$ _____	$ _____
Product/service line 2	_____	_____	_____
Product/service line 3	_____	_____	_____
Product/service line 4	_____	_____	_____
TOTAL SALES REVENUE			
Cost of Goods Sold:			
Product/service line 1	_____	_____	_____
Product/service line 2	_____	_____	_____
Product/service line 3	_____	_____	_____
Product/service line 4	_____	_____	_____
TOTAL COST OF GOODS SOLD	$ _____	$ _____	$ _____
GROSS PROFIT	$ _____	$ _____	$ _____
Expenses:			
Variable:			
Payroll	$ _____	$ _____	$ _____
Sales commission	_____	_____	_____
Freight and delivery	_____	_____	_____
Travel and entertainment	_____	_____	_____
Semivariable:			
Advertising/promotion	_____	_____	_____
FICA/payroll tax	_____	_____	_____

(Continued)

(Continued)

	Low	Most Likely	High
Supplies	$ _____	$ _____	$ _____
Telephone	_____	_____	_____
Fixed:			
Rent	_____	_____	_____
Utilities	_____	_____	_____
Property taxes	_____	_____	_____
Dues and subscriptions	_____	_____	_____
TOTAL EXPENSES			
Profit before depreciation	_____	_____	_____
Depreciation	_____	_____	_____
NET PROFIT	$ _____	$ _____	$ _____

Note: Expense items for your business will vary from these three categories. For illustration purposes only.

Question and test your projections. Is there enough demand for you to reach your sales goal? Do you have enough space, equipment, and employees to reach your sales goal? Break your sales down into the number of units, then the number of units bought per customer, and then the number of units sold per day. When viewed this way, you may find that every person in town would have to buy eight bagels per day, 365 days per year, for you to achieve your sales projections for your proposed bagel shop. (Yes, real business plans get written with such projections.) Obviously, you would need to revise your goal, expand your menu, do more to control your expenses, or convince people to eat more bagels than is humanly possible for your business to succeed in meeting such a projection.

Break-Even Analysis. How many units (or dollars' worth) of your products or services will have to be sold to cover your costs? A *break-even analysis* will give you a sales projection of how many units (or dollars' worth) need to be sold to reach your break-even point—that is, the point at which you are neither making nor losing money (Figure 4.5; see also Chapter 13).

▼ FIGURE 4.5

Break-Even Analysis

At what point will you make money?

1.	Total sales	$ _____
2.	Fixed costs	$ _____
3.	Gross margin	$ _____
4.	Gross margin as percentage of sales (line 3/line 1)	_____ %
5.	Breakeven sales (line 2/line 4)	$ _____
6.	Profit goal	$ _____
7.	Sales required to achieve profit goal [(line 2 + line 6)/line 4]	$ _____

FEASIBLE, VIABLE, GOOD IDEA?

A full-blown business plan is not always needed. A feasibility study is an abbreviated planning process to determine whether to proceed with the next step in creating a new venture or launching a new product. The goal is to identify any "make or break" issues that would argue against an action or suggest whether a favorable outcome can be achieved.

STEP 1: SWOT Analysis

As covered in Chapter 3, begin by considering all strengths, weaknesses, opportunities, and threats for the purpose of positioning strengths with external opportunities and internal weaknesses away from threats.

STEP 2: Financial Feasibility

Can you gather data that shows the business or product generates more money than it will cost (in a reasonable time period)? If not, why investigate further?

STEP 3: Marketing Feasibility

Can your business opportunity generate a high enough sales volume to justify all other necessary costs—and can the target market be reached so they will buy?

STEP 4: Resource Feasibility

Even if your idea passes the previous tests, you still won't succeed if you cannot muster all resources (personnel, raw materials, money, etc.).

STEP 5: Technology Feasibility

Is the platform of the proposed business based on technological superiority capable of providing a solid customer experience?

STEP 6: Other Aspects

Finally, consider specific factors such as appropriate location for business, adequate suppliers and vendors, and costs versus benefits.

A feasibility study will indicate if it is possible to turn an idea into a business, but what you are REALLY looking for is if it will be *viable*. Viability means that something is not only possible but also profitable.

Sources: Sawaram Suthar, "Is the Future of Customer Service Omnichannel or Multichannel?" *Entrepreneur,* May 22, 2018, www.entrepreneur.com/article/313806; "Feasibility Study," *Inc.,* April 27, 2010, www.inc.com/encyclopedia; Brad Sugars, "How to Research Your Market," *Entrepreneur,* March 2, 2007, www.entrepreneur.com/article/175276; and Tamara Monosoff, "Get Your Product to Market in 6 Steps," *Entrepreneur,* May 7, 2009, www.entrepreneur.com/article/201526.

To reinforce your financial projections, you may want to compare them to industry averages for your chosen industry. Robert Morris Associates, now known as Risk Management Association, publishes an annual index, RMA's *Annual Statement Studies,* showing industry averages of key manufacturing, wholesale, and retail business groups. Compare your projected financial ratios with industry averages to give the reader an established benchmark (see Chapter 8).

Appendix

Supplemental information and documents not crucial to the business plan, but of potential interest to the reader, are gathered in the appendix. Resumes of owners and principal managers, advertising samples, brochures, and any related information can be included. Different types of information, such as resumes, advertising samples, an organization chart, and a floor plan, should each be placed in a separate appendix and labeled with successive letters of the alphabet (Appendix A, Appendix B, and so on). Be sure to identify each appendix in your table of contents (for example, "Appendix A: Advertising Samples").

Concept Check Questions

1. Why is the executive summary the most important section of the business plan?

2. What are some of the key elements to be included in the Marketing section?

3. Why is the Critical Risks and Assumptions section important to lenders/investors?

Concept Module 4.4: Review Process

- **LO 4.4: Discuss the importance of reviewing your business plan.**

Writing a business plan is a project that involves a long series of interrelated steps. Beginning with your idea for a business, you want to determine its feasibility through the creation of your business plan. The technique illustrated in Figure 4.6 will allow you to identify the steps you need to take in writing your plan. Steps connected by lines show that lower-numbered steps need to be completed before moving on to higher-numbered ones. Steps that are shown as being parallel take place simultaneously. For example, steps 6 through 10 can be completed at the same time, and all must be accomplished before you can estimate how much capital you need in step 11.

Like any project involving a number of complex steps and calculations, your business plan should be carefully reviewed and revised before you present it to potential investors. After you have written your plan, rate it yourself the way lenders and investors will evaluate it (see Issues in Small Business, "How Does Your Plan Rate?").

Business Plan Mistakes

Often we can learn from the mistakes of others. Writing business plans is no exception. Bankers and investors who assess hundreds of business plans each year look for reasons to reject the proposals. This practice helps them to weed out potentially unworthy investments and to identify the likely winners—the most organized, focused, and realistic proposals. Your business plan says a lot about your level of financial and professional knowledge. How can you keep investors focused on your ideas while keeping your plan out of the "reject" pile? It helps to avoid the most common errors.

- *Submitting a "rough copy."* Your plan should be a cleanly typed copy without coffee stains and scratched-out words. If you haven't worked your idea out completely enough to present a plan you're proud of, why should the investor take you seriously?

- *Depending on outdated financial information or industry comparisons.* It is important to be as current as possible to convince the investor you are a realistic planner.

- *Trying to impress financiers with technojargon.* If you can't express yourself in common language in your business plan, how will you be able to market it?

- *Lacking marketing strategies.* Getting your product or business known by potential buyers is key. "We'll just depend on word-of-mouth advertising" won't cut it.

- *Making unsubstantiated assumptions.* Explain how and why you have reached your conclusions at any point in the plan. Don't assume the competition will roll over without a fight or that phenomenal growth will begin the moment you get the money.

- *Being overly optimistic.* Too much "blue sky and rainbows" will lead the investor to wonder if your plan is realistic. Describe potential pitfalls and your strategies to cope with them.

- *Misunderstanding financial information.* Even if you get help from an accountant in preparing your financial documents, be sure you understand and can interpret what they say.

- *Ignoring the macro-environment.* How will competitors react to your business? What other economic factors are likely to change? Considering the business climate and environment will help demonstrate the breadth of your understanding.

- *Avoiding or disguising potential negative aspects.* If you fail to mention possible problems, or misrepresent them, you will give the impression that you are either naive or devious, and lenders find neither trait especially charming.

- *Having no personal equity in the company.* If you aren't willing to risk your own money in the venture, why should the investor? A vested interest in the business will help to convince potential lenders that you will work as hard as possible to make the business succeed. Or, if you have invested only $1,000, is it reasonable to seek $20 million in capital?[18]

Business Plan

Writing a business plan is a long process of progressive steps that generally follow the sequence shown here.

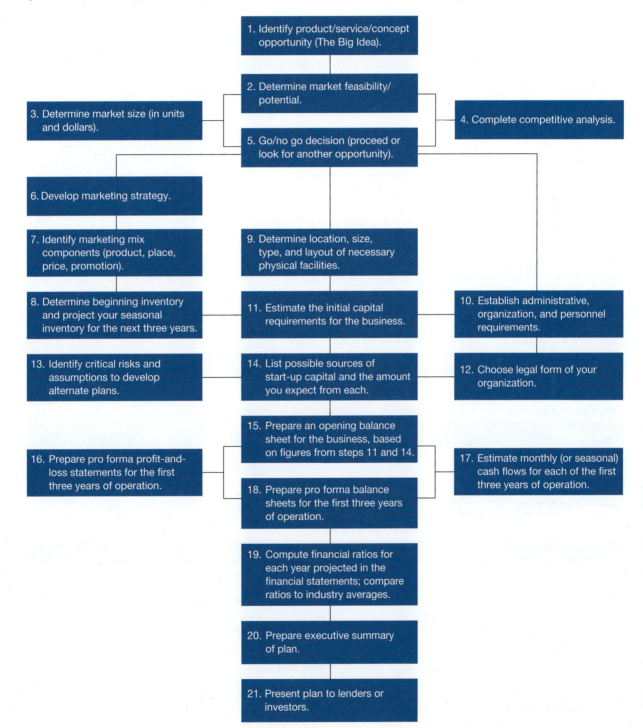

1. Identify product/service/concept opportunity (The Big Idea).
2. Determine market feasibility/potential.
3. Determine market size (in units and dollars).
4. Complete competitive analysis.
5. Go/no go decision (proceed or look for another opportunity).
6. Develop marketing strategy.
7. Identify marketing mix components (product, place, price, promotion).
8. Determine beginning inventory and project your seasonal inventory for the next three years.
9. Determine location, size, type, and layout of necessary physical facilities.
10. Establish administrative, organization, and personnel requirements.
11. Estimate the initial capital requirements for the business.
12. Choose legal form of your organization.
13. Identify critical risks and assumptions to develop alternate plans.
14. List possible sources of start-up capital and the amount you expect from each.
15. Prepare an opening balance sheet for the business, based on figures from steps 11 and 14.
16. Prepare pro forma profit-and-loss statements for the first three years of operation.
17. Estimate monthly (or seasonal) cash flows for each of the first three years of operation.
18. Prepare pro forma balance sheets for the first three years of operation.
19. Compute financial ratios for each year projected in the financial statements; compare ratios to industry averages.
20. Prepare executive summary of plan.
21. Present plan to lenders or investors.

HOW DOES YOUR PLAN RATE?

On the following checklist, take the perspective of a potential lender or investor who is rating your business plan. Give each section a grade ranging from A to F, with A being the best grade. Would you want to invest your money in a business that doesn't earn an A in as many categories as possible? Use your rating to identify areas that can be improved.

Section	
Business Description	Characteristics of an A-Level Plan
Company	Simply explained and feasible
Industry	Growing in market niches that are presently unsatisfied
Products	Proprietary position; quality exceeds customer's expectations
Services	Described clearly; service level exceeds customer expectations
Previous success	Business has past record of success
Competitive advantage	Identified and sustainable
Risks turned into opportunities	Risks identified; how to minimize risks is shown
Orientation of business	Market oriented, not product oriented
Marketing	
Target market(s)	Clearly identified
Size of target market(s)	Large enough to support viable business
User benefits identified	Benefit to customers clearly shown
Management Team	
Experience of team	Successful previous experience in similar business
Key managers identified	Managers with complementary skills on team
Financial Plan	
Projections	Realistic and supported
Rate of return	Exceptionally high; loans can be paid back in less than one year
Participation by owner	Owner has significant personal investment
Participation by others	Other investors already involved
Plan Packaging	
Appearance	Professional, laser-printed, bound, no spelling or grammatical errors
Executive summary	Concise description of business that prompts reader to say, "Wow!"
Body of plan	Sections of plan appropriate and complete
Appendixes	Appropriate supporting documentation
Plan standardized or custom	Plan custom-written for specific business, not "canned"

WHAT WOULD YOU DO?

IT'S YOUR SHOW

Your telephone rings early one morning. It is your small business/entrepreneurship professor, who tells you he just received notification that he has won the first Nobel Prize in Entrepreneurship. His plane leaves soon for Stockholm, where he will pick up the award, so he won't be in class today. Because you are one of the star students in this class, the professor asks you to conduct today's class, covering Chapter 4, "The Business Plan." Write an outline of how you would teach this class and what you would cover to effectively teach this material. Would you lecture? How would you keep discussion going? Would you show business plan samples? Where would you find them? Would you show web pages? Which ones? You can do anything (except cancel class!) that your professor would do, but *what would you do*?

Concept Check Questions

1. Talk to the owner of a small business. Did he or she write a business plan? A strategic plan? If he or she received any assistance, where did it come from?

2. You are an investor in small businesses, and you have three business plans on your desk. Which of the following potential business owners do you think would be the best bet for an investment (if you could pick only one)?

   a. A recent college grad, full of energy and ideas, but short on experience

   b. A middle-management corporate refugee desiring a business of her own after experiencing frustration with bureaucratic red tape

   c. A serial entrepreneur who has previously started seven businesses, three of which were huge successes and four of which failed, losing the entire investment.

Concept Module 4.5: The Pitch

- **LO 4.5: Create a pitch.**

Your business model is created. It proves feasible. You've produced a beautiful business plan. Now the offers to fund your business come rolling in, right? Nope. Your next step to self-employment is to pitch your idea in order to receive whatever it is you need—probably outside funding and customers.

Your pitch needs to be polished and super-prepared because you never know when you will be making it next. The person sitting next to you on a flight may be a big deal investor. The person with whom you struck up a casual conversation with at the coffee shop may be exactly the type of person you have been trying to sell to.

Kevin O'Leary of the television show *Shark Tank* is no stranger to pitches. When asked the difference between good ones and bad ones, he identifies three attributes. First, "Be able to explain the opportunity in 90 seconds or less. Sixty seconds or less is better."[19] You have to identify what it is that you do, why it works, and why it's a huge opportunity. He likes to cite the example of Wicked Good Cupcakes—a nonpatented, nonproprietary commodity product. "But these two women came up and said, 'We bake cupcakes. We put them in mason jars, seal them, and FedEx them to you as a gift.'" He wrote the check.

Second, you have to sell why *you* are the person to make this plan work. Ideas are cheap—execution is difficult. So, even when an investor hears a good idea, her immediate question is about the entrepreneur's execution skills. Sell what makes you the right person to invest in.

Third, O'Leary says, "Know your numbers—this one is the killer. You've got to know your numbers cold. What's the size of the market, how fast is it growing, what's the break-even analysis, what's your margin?"[20]

There is no set template, format, or order that pitches come in, but Jeff Haden of *Inc.* magazine identifies some stages and steps you need to consider.[21]

Stage 1: Understand what makes a compelling pitch—the 30,000-foot view.

- Know to whom you are pitching (and tailor your pitch accordingly). An effective pitch is not memorized and delivered verbatim. While the essence of your small business will not change, the specific aspects potential customers are looking for will not be the same hooks that will catch partners, lenders, or investors.

- Understand the person's needs and motivations. Everyone responds to solutions to problems they face. In your pitch, your challenge is to show how you are the solution. So, if you have developed and are pitching the next killer app, resist the temptation to talk about features, or worse, about issues you ran into developing the coding. Pitch how this app solves the other person's problems and they will become motivated.

- Get past the superficial needs of your market. Doing a deeper dive into understanding their problems gives you more authenticity in talking about how to solve them.

Stage 2: Gather the tools and resources that will make your pitch stand out—the tools to make it happen.

- Create a beautiful and powerful presentation. The heart of your pitch is your pitch deck, a "pack" of slides to bring your presentation to life. While PowerPoint is the best-known presentation software, it may not be the best for what you need. Take a look at the Tech in Action box in this chapter for alternatives.

- Have the latest version of a model of your product. The more physical senses you can involve, the better you can communicate and excite your audience. If it can be touched, smelled, tasted, heard, seen—make it happen. If you are in the design phase include a page schematic or screen blueprint called a website wireframe. If you are making a tangible product, go to a local Makerspace, Incubator, or Co-working space with a 3-D printer to make a model.

- Get testimonials from users or investors. The currency exchanged via social media is the clout that a person who uses your product brings. Talking with as many people experienced with your product as you can gives you sound bites for your pitch.

- Get video. You've heard that "a picture is worth a thousand words"? So, what's a video worth? Well, we don't have a cliché answer yet, but it's a lot. A tight, entertaining, informative video embedded into your pitch is a powerful tool.

Stage 3: Build your winning pitch deck—Now tell your story (literally). Stories play better than dry presentations. Your slides cover all the information previously addressed, but highlights include the following:

- After a catchy intro, get right to telling the story of what problem you and your business are addressing, and how your product/service/technology is the solution to said problem. Address the key components of your market—how big, who they are, percentage of market share you plan to capture.

- Why you? This is not the section to be shy or humble. Objectively address competitors. Do you have anything proprietary that can be protected? How will you market?

- Describe yourself and tell your story.

POWERPOINT ALTERNATIVES

Since PowerPoint was the first and most widely used presentation software, many assume it is the best, but actually it is limited in options to customize or design. Fortunately, there are alternative packages for you to make a big impact for your pitch deck.

- **Prezi.** If you want visual impact and customization then Prezi is for you. Prezi has a "zooming user interface" that puts entire slides in motion and is heavy with images, graphics, and motion to draw attention. That flexibility comes at a cost in time to move the learning curve, but it can be cool.

- **Slidebean.** Check out this outstanding, well-rounded presentation package. You can create, share, and display your pitch deck via email or provide links for tracking and analytics.

- **Wideo.** Simpler and more intuitive than PowerPoint, Wideo takes a different approach by creating presentation video that can be uploaded to your website or YouTube.

- **PowToon.** While maybe not the best for every audience, PowToon creates animated videos and presentations. It is colorful and engaging and creates video without coding.

Sources: Andy Saks, "10 PowerPoint Alternatives That Make Your Presentation Memorable," Spark Presentations, April 26, 2016, www.sparkpresentations.com/powerpoint-alternatives; Sarah Bennett, "6 of the Best PowerPoint Alternatives for Exciting Presentations," July 19, 2016, https://slidebean.com/blog/design/powerpoint-alternatives; www.powtoon.com/home.

- Describe what you have accomplished so far.

- Make your ask, and make it clear. What do you need—a strategic partner? An investment?

- The hardest part—go back and ruthlessly edit. You've got a lot to cover in 10 to 20 slides, so cut.

Stage 4: Tweak your pitch for different targets—The deck described so far has been targeted toward a typical investor presentation. It can easily be adjusted for other groups.

- Customer pitch. Emphasize the problem/solution, but back off on market data. The competitive advantage will be more important than your business model.

- Elevator pitch. This is the pitch that everyone has heard of—imagine you enter an elevator with Warren Buffet and you have 60 seconds to explain your deal before the elevator doors open and your dream investor walks away. You obviously cannot rely on slides—get to the point. Even though time is tight, you don't want to sound like you're regurgitating a script. Stick to results and benefits. Have an ask and provide a way to contact you for follow-up.

Stage 5: Prepare to deliver your pitch.

- Anticipate questions. If you can come up with questions then you can develop answers before they are asked. To accomplish this you have to forget everything you know about this whole deal. Look at everything with "fresh eyes."

- Prepare for objections. Objections are not a bad thing—they mean that your audience is interested but needs more information.

- Rehearse. Confidence comes from familiarity so make your roommates listen to you make your pitch, and coworkers, and your parents, and your recreation league basketball team— you get the idea—anyone who will listen is good practice. Record yourself on video (and watch it).

1. Identify three attributes your pitch should address in 90 seconds or less.

2. Describe what makes a pitch compelling.

3. Should your pitch be memorized word-for-word? Why or why not?

CHAPTER REVIEW

SUMMARY ▶▶

LO 4.1   Explain the purpose and importance of the business plan.

Business plans are important to raise capital, provide a road map for future operations, and prevent omissions.

LO 4.2   Explain the purpose and process of developing a business model.

Business models answer questions like "Who is the customer?" "What does the customer value?" and "How do we make money?" Business models and feasibility analyses are valuable exercises to show *that* the business can make money before the business plan shows *how*.

LO 4.3   Describe the components of a business plan.

The major sections of a business plan include the cover page, table of contents, executive summary, company information, environmental and industry analysis, products or services,

marketing research and evaluation, manufacturing and operations plan, management team, timeline, critical risks and assumptions, benefits to the community, exit strategy, financial plan, and appendix.

LO 4.4   Discuss the importance of reviewing your business plan.

Like any project involving a number of complex steps and calculations, your business plan should be carefully reviewed and revised before you present it to potential investors. After you have written your plan, evaluate it as you think lenders and investors will.

LO 4.5   Create a pitch.

Your pitch is the presentation you make to investors, customers, or others in order to communicate the value of your business plan. One of the key components is your pitch deck.

KEY TERMS ▶▶

balance sheet **92**	executive summary **84**	sources and uses of funds **91**
business plan **75**	feasibility study **80**	
cash flow statement **91**	profit-and-loss statement **92**	

STUDENT STUDY SITE ▶▶

edge.sagepub.com/hatten7e

$SAGE edge™ Sharpen your skills with SAGE edge!

SAGE edge for Students provides a personalized approach to help you accomplish your coursework goals in an easy-to-use learning environment. You'll find mobile-friendly eFlashcards and quizzes as well as multimedia resources to support and expand on the concepts presented in this chapter.

EXPERIENTIAL LEARNING ACTIVITIES ▶▶

4.1: The Business Plan Sequence

LO 4.3: Describe the components of a business plan.

Break into groups of 4–5 students. Each group must place the following list of business plan items in the correct sequence for writing a business plan. Figure 4.6 will be helpful and is the basis for the activity. In one to two sentences, explain the rationale for the order chosen for each step.

After the group has arranged their list of items, the group will then join another group and discuss the order chosen. Each group may make two changes in their order, based upon feedback received from the other group. Be prepared to justify/explain the rationale used in choosing the order.

Be prepared to share with the entire class, once the final order has been selected.

_____ Finalize the executive summary.

_____ Choose one of the following or a variation: sole proprietorship, partnership or corporation.

_____ Decide the initial dollar amount needed to begin the business.

_____ Determine the size and location of facilities needed for the successful operation of the business.

_____ Plan the amount of cash needed for the first three years of operations.

_____ Analyze the amount and where funding could possibly be obtained.

_____ Decide if the idea is actually one to pursue.

_____ Decide how many dollars the idea will generate.

_____ Determine how the start-up business compares to industry ratios.

_____ Present final plan to potential investors.

_____ Prepare alternative plans to address potential threats and risks.

_____ Prepare estimates of the balance sheet for the next three years.

4.2: The Business Plan

LO 4.5: Create a pitch.

Break into groups of 2–3 students. Each group must choose an appropriate current product that the group or someone in the group uses on a regular basis. The group has just inherited this product and now must obtain funding to grow product sales. Develop an elevator pitch (90 seconds) to give to potential investors.

For example, the group just inherited a name brand shoe. The group's goal is to grow the market for this shoe and obtain the needed outside funding to accomplish this goal.

The group must come up with elevator pitch for the product focusing on the following areas as outlined in the text:

1. Clear product goal
2. Benefits of the product
3. Specific expected results
4. Requested dollar amount

After the group has developed the elevator pitch, someone in the group needs to be prepared to share the pitch with the entire class.

One group in the class will act as the potential investors, asking questions and making the decision on whether or not funding was obtained.

CHAPTER CLOSING CASE ▶▶

TrailerWalla: Evaluating an Opportunity

In the summer of 2015, several innovative business ideas were given a platform in a business plan competition organized by a prominent business school in India, the Indian Institute of Management Kashipur. As was the norm, once the presentations were finished, students gathered around the judges and venture capitalists over tea, trying to build informal contacts and seek more in-depth feedback on their ideas.

Amidst this buzz, Ramesh Reddy stood in a corner pondering why his idea had not even reached the semifinal stage in the competition. Was he chasing an opportunity that did not exist? Or did he fail to appropriately communicate his idea's value? He was convinced that the former was not the case. It was time to return to the drawing board and look at the proposed business model. He was determined to convince investors of the viability of his idea.

TrailerWalla: The Origins

Ramesh had always been a cinema aficionado. A catchy trailer, notes from a soundtrack song from an upcoming movie, or an eye-catching cinema poster were enough to get Ramesh enthused about knowing more about a movie. Like many others in his community, Ramesh eagerly anticipated new movies—both Bollywood and regional films—and his employer even allowed him and his coworkers to miss work on the opening day of a major film. He was one of thousands of movie fans in India, many of whom loved the cinema so much that they would watch regional movies—those in regional dialects such as Tamil that appealed mostly to speakers of that language—even if they did not speak the language of the film. Although Ramesh spoke Hindi, he liked all non-Hindi movies, but primarily Tamil-, Telugu-, Kannada-, and Malayalam-language movies.

On his way to work one day in January 2013, Ramesh happened to see a movie poster (see Figure 1) that intrigued him greatly. Unfortunately, he was unable to read the movie name because it was written in a language unknown to him. For many days, Ramesh tried to find the movie on Google and YouTube but was unsuccessful.

To search for the movie, Ramesh had to have a film name, but he only had an image in his head! He tried to describe the poster to his friends but was unable to elicit an adequate response. The movie poster refused to leave his mind and he was determined to find out the name. After days of random guesses and what felt like endless searching, Ramesh finally found a name to put to the poster: "Vishwaroopam." The Tamil movie featured Bollywood superstar Kamal Haasan and appealed to multiple audiences, including those who spoke Hindi.

This experience planted an idea in Ramesh's mind. In a country like India, where thousands of regional movies in different languages were released every year, it was almost impossible to keep track of every movie that was set to hit the big screen. To a large extent, movie trailers worked to pique potential audience interest. These commercialized previews could make or break the potential audience's impression of an upcoming movie. Despite the power of movie trailers, there was no single platform where users could easily search for their desired trailers. Ramesh had searched for such a website, but it did not exist. This was the gap that Ramesh aspired to fill. He wanted to build and promote a website dedicated to showcasing the movie trailers in India in their various languages. There was a huge opportunity to capture, with regional movies being released in over 22 official languages in India.

Ramesh's business idea, therefore, was born out of his passion to promote good cinema and connect it with potential audiences. When coining the name for his website, Ramesh wanted it to be intrinsically associated with the popularity of Bollywood. He hit upon the name "TrailerWalla"—the word *walla* was a commonly used suffix in Hindi, meaning *the provider*. TrailerWalla was going to be a one-stop shop for Indian audiences searching for regional movie trailers in different languages.

Designing and Testing the Website

Ramesh began designing TrailerWalla.com shortly after his mystery movie experience. With the help of his friends, who were software engineers, Ramesh designed the interface of the website. The site offered updated listings of the movies to be released each week and provided links to the trailers on YouTube. Ramesh was able to use trailers in this way without copyright or royalty payments because TrailerWalla did not house the movie trailers on its site; it simply directed visitors to YouTube to see the trailers of their choice. Although the trailers were linked in their original languages, basic details about the movies were offered in English and many of the films offered English subtitles. On TrailerWalla users could search for movie trailers by release date, language, actor, topic, and genre, while the home page featured all the trailers for the most recent release date.

In order to test the technical infrastructure, the website went live from June to November 2013. During that time, Ramesh manually pasted YouTube links to all the new movie trailers onto the website. To gather feedback and suggestions, Ramesh showed the website to his friends and several potential users during those first six months. Other Indian websites emerged that ran movie trailers, including desimartini.com and bollywoodmdb.com. However, these sites featured very limited trailers from Bollywood and virtually ignored the soaring regional movie industry.

Building on the Business Idea

Ramesh reviewed his plan in his mind. He had full faith that his website would be successful because he had evaluated the Indian movie industry and believed that his idea served a target market and met the requirements of the industry and potential website users. He had conducted primarily secondary research via website searches and consultation with business experts, but he had also conducted some primary market research in consultation with peers and professors and other film fans using his initial site and Facebook page. The site was positioned to support the film industry (e.g., did not violate copyright laws, offered links to marketing pieces that the film industry wanted publicized, potentially increasing audiences and revenues) and to support film audiences (e.g., compiled trailers in a way that helped audiences navigate hundreds of movie releases, supported regional movie audiences by publicizing regional movies).

Next Steps: Resources and Revenues

Yet some questions remained unanswered surrounding TrailerWalla's offerings, resources, and potential revenues. How would Ramesh reach out to a larger audience without adequate financial funding? Would it be a good idea to seek funding at this point, or would it be better to demonstrate the commercial success of TrailerWalla to some extent before seeking funding? How would the website generate revenue after its launch? How would TrailerWalla fund expanded offerings? Would TrailerWalla solicit advertisements or would movie theaters or production companies pay to place their trailers on the site? Would Ramesh sell the site's analytics to film companies to inform their investments and new movie making or marketing? Would the site allow users to watch a movie trailer and then link to the movie theaters showing the movie and allow users to buy tickets? Would the site link to local businesses in the area of cinemas and allow visitors to plan experiences around their movie going?

How would TrailerWalla establish a sustained competitive advantage? Would TrailerWalla focus on a single regional market or target all Indian audiences? Would dubbing or translation services be added to the site to appeal to certain audiences? Would the site rely on linked material or incorporate original and source content? Would the service be exclusive to website users or would it also be offered as a mobile application with links to other businesses and services?

First Steps

Ramesh was confident that his design and vision for the site would attract production houses and distributors to showcase their trailers on the site in the future. Furthermore, with an increasing number of regional movies being dubbed in Hindi and shown by mainstream movie channels, the trend and the demand for Hindi films was on the rise, thereby offering significant growth potential for TrailerWalla. How could this business idea born out of a personal need be successfully commercialized? TrailerWalla needed to find the right first steps for launching its business.

Discussion Questions

1. Is the opportunity presented in this case worth undertaking? When and why should a personal interest be treated as an opportunity?

2. What are some of the initial challenges Ramesh might face in launching his idea into a business? How can Ramesh overcome those challenges?

3. Conduct an environmental and internal resource analysis for TrailerWalla. Use the analyses to suggest if the case opportunity is worth pursuing.

4. What key information would Ramesh need to make a TrailerWalla business plan fundable?

Source: Safal Batra, "TrailerWalla: Evaluating an Opportunity," Sage Knowledge: Cases, January 5, 2017, http://dx.doi.org/10.4135/9781526411099.

PART III

EARLY DECISIONS

## CHAPTER 5

FRANCHISING

©iStockphoto.com/jetcityimage

One hot summer day in 2003, two college buddies, Nick Friedman attending Pomona College and Omar Soliman at University of Miami, borrowed a beat-up cargo van and started hauling stuff to help people move, take items to donate or recycle, or even dispose of property for some extra money.

The next summer, the pair became cofounders of College Hunks Hauling Junk. But starting a business is one thing, growing a sustainable entity is another. Growth costs money and takes time. Friedman recalls, "It would have probably cost us about $100,000 to open up in each of the different markets that we now operate in. But franchising actually gives us a cash injection each time somebody buys a franchise from us." Thus, the solution became clear: Franchising.

By developing their business while still in college, they took advantage of resources they had at their fingertips. Friedman advises, "Instead of paying a consultant to evaluate your model to determine if it is franchisable, you can meet with a knowledgeable professor. For marketing materials, computer programming, or PR, look to students taking applicable classes who will work for a fraction of the cost that companies would charge."

One of the first challenges was their mindset—they didn't expect hauling junk to turn into a real business, so they didn't even think of licenses and permits. But how many times must you get pulled over by authorities and threatened with arrest or slapped with fines before you get your documentation in place? Not too many, as it turns out.

After only two years, 20 franchisees were generating $10 million and employing 100 students. The 2017 Inc. 5000 list shows revenue had grown to $46.9 million.

The toughest sale in franchising is finding the first person to see the vision and write a check. The initial franchisee to pay the $35,000 franchise fee? Another student who wanted a business, but didn't want to start from scratch.

Sources: College Hunks Hauling Junk and Moving (website), accessed January 1, 2018, www.collegehunkshaulingjunk.com/about; "Inc. 5000 2017: The Full List," *Inc.*, September 15, 2017, https://www.inc.com/inc5000/list/2017; Joel Holland, "Why Stop at Just One?" *Entrepreneur*, August 30, 2009, www.entrepreneur.com/article/203098; "Nick Friedman: How I Started College Hunks Hauling Junk," *Entrepreneur*, November 16, 2010, www.entrepreneur.com/article/217546.

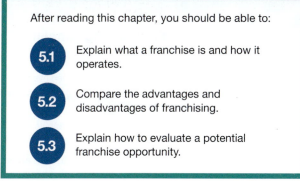

LEARNING OUTCOMES

After reading this chapter, you should be able to:

5.1 Explain what a franchise is and how it operates.

5.2 Compare the advantages and disadvantages of franchising.

5.3 Explain how to evaluate a potential franchise opportunity.

Concept Module 5.1: About Franchising

- **LO 5.1: Explain what a franchise is and how it operates.**

Over the past 50 years or so, franchising has become a very attractive means of starting and operating a small business. Some of the most familiar franchises are McDonald's, H&R Block, AAMCO Transmissions, GNC (General Nutrition Centers), and Dairy Queen. A **franchise** is an agreement that binds a **franchisor** (a parent company of the product, service, or method) with a **franchisee** (a small business that pays fees and royalties for exclusive rights to local distribution of the product or service). Through the franchise agreement, the franchisee gains the benefit of the parent company's expertise, experience, management systems, marketing, and financial help. Franchisors benefit because they can expand their operations by building a base of franchisees rather than by using their own capital and resources.

Background

Franchises have experienced considerable growth since the 1950s. However, contrary to popular belief, the concept did not originate with McDonald's. In fact, franchises have existed since the early 1800s, and variations from much earlier (Figure 5.1).

In the 1830s, Cyrus McCormick was making reapers, and Isaac Singer began manufacturing sewing machines. As America's economic system began to shift from being based on agriculture

franchise
A contractual license to operate an individually owned business as part of a larger chain.

franchisor
The parent company that develops a product or business process and sells the rights to franchisees.

franchisee
The small businessperson who purchases the franchise so as to sell the product or service of the franchisor.

▼ FIGURE 5.1

Franchising Timeline

900–1400	Medieval Europe and Feudal Times—European crowns would franchise government land to nobles and churches in exchange for armies, taxes, and toll roads.
1400–1600	Renaissance Era—European explorations into the New World were financed via franchise agreements, including the 1609 Dutch East India Company agreement with Henry Hudson.
1700s	Colonial America—Benjamin Franklin formed a "co-partnership" with Thomas Whitmarsh in a printing press business. Franklin entered into dozens of such franchise agreements for printing companies across the colonies.
1850s–1900s	Industrial Revolution—Isaac Merritt Singer provided manufacturing equipment to local independently owned textile businesses in 1851 and received a share of their profits. Coca-Cola franchised the first bottling plant in 1901.
1940s–1950s	Post-WWII Boom—While many types of franchised business began in this era, it was restaurants that took off. Dairy Queen grew from 10 to 2,600 locations between 1941 and 1950. In 1952, Richard and Maurice McDonald franchised their second location.
2017	Franchising Today—More than 800,000 U.S. businesses are franchised, reaching almost every industry.

Sources: Michael Guta, "The History of Franchising," Small Business Trends, January 25, 2018, https://smallbusinesstrends.com; Michael Seid, "The Evolution of Franchising," Franchise Update, May 20, 2006, www.franchising.com; Michael Seid, "Everything You Need to Know About Franchises," The Balance, August 16, 2017, www.thebalance.com.

> "Franchised businesses directly produced almost 9 million jobs—roughly the same number of people employed by all manufacturers of durable goods."

and small business to being based on industry and big business, business methods needed to change as well. Early manufacturers also had to provide distribution of their products. To do so, they faced the choice of setting up a company-owned system or developing contracts with independent firms to represent them. The choice was not an easy one. Direct ownership guaranteed complete control and ensured quality levels of service. On the other hand, direct ownership was expensive and difficult to manage. McCormick and Singer were two of the first to use agents in building sales networks quickly, at little cost to themselves.[1] This use of exclusive agents laid the groundwork for today's franchising. The exclusive contractual agreement between franchisor and franchisee has evolved past agency, but it has become a viable business alternative.

Franchising Today

Today franchising is found in almost every industry (Figure 5.2). More than 801,000 U.S. businesses are franchised. A study titled *Economic Impact of Franchised Businesses: 2016* for the International Franchise Association reported on economic activity that happened (1) within franchised businesses and (2) because of franchised businesses. The study found that franchised businesses

- generated annual sales of $868 billion.

- made up nearly 15.3 percent of the U.S. private sector economy.

- accounted for 40 percent of all retail sales.

- directly produced almost 9 million jobs—roughly the same number of people employed by all manufacturers of durable goods.

- supported more than 25 million jobs and $1.2 trillion private nonfarm GDP.[2]

Not All Franchises Sell French Fries

The number of franchise establishments by business lines shows a wide diversity of products and services.

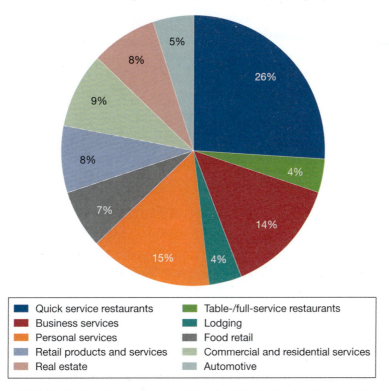

■ Quick service restaurants	■ Table-/full-service restaurants
■ Business services	■ Lodging
■ Personal services	■ Food retail
■ Retail products and services	■ Commercial and residential services
■ Real estate	■ Automotive

Source: Based on IHS Markit, *Franchise Business Economic Outlook for 2017*, study for the International Franchise Association Educational Foundation, January 2017.

Franchising Systems

There are two types of franchises: product-distribution franchises and business-format franchises. Producers, wholesalers, and retailers use these two forms to distribute goods and services to consumers and other businesses.

Product-Distribution Franchising. **Product-distribution franchising** allows the franchisee (or dealer) to buy products from the franchisor (or supplier) or to license the use of its trade name. This approach typically connects a single manufacturer with many dealers. The idea is to make products available to consumers in a specific geographic region through exclusive dealers. Soft-drink bottlers and gasoline stations, for example, use this type of franchising. Auto manufacturers also use this system to make their cars, service, and parts available. Your local Chevrolet dealer, for instance, has full use of the Chevrolet trade name, brand names (like Corvette), and logos (like the bow tie symbol) to promote the dealership in your area. Product franchisors regulate their franchisees' locations to avoid excessive competition between them. As a consequence, Chevrolet would not allow a new dealership that sells its products to set up across the street from your established local dealer.

Business-Format Franchising. **Business-format franchising** is more of a *turnkey* approach to franchising. In other words, the franchisee purchases not only the franchisor's product to sell but also the entire way of doing business, including operation procedures, marketing packages, the physical building and equipment, and full business services. Business-format franchising is commonly used in quick-service restaurants (56.3 percent), lodging (18.2 percent), retail food (14.2 percent), and table/full-service restaurants (13.1 percent).

product-distribution franchising
A type of franchising in which the franchisee agrees to purchase the products of the franchisor or to use the franchisor's name.

business-format franchising
A type of franchising in which the franchisee adopts the franchisor's entire method of operation.

Concept Check Questions

1. What is the difference between a franchise, a franchisee, and a franchisor?

2. How would you explain the difference between franchises and other forms of business ownership?

3. Why would you prefer to buy a franchise than to start a new business or buy an existing business?

4. Why is franchising important in today's economy?

5. What is the difference between product-distribution franchises and business-format franchises? Give an example of each that has not been cited in the text.

6. After having read about entrepreneurship in Chapter 2, would you consider someone who buys a franchise to be an entrepreneur? Does franchising stifle entrepreneurship?

Concept Module 5.2: Why Open a Franchise?

- **LO 5.2: Compare the advantages and disadvantages of franchising.**

If you are considering the purchase of a franchise, you should compare its advantages and disadvantages to those of starting a new business or buying an existing nonfranchised business (see Chapters 6 and 7). You should also determine whether the unique characteristics of franchising fit your personal needs and desires. Some small business owners would rather assume the risk and expense of starting an independent business than have to follow someone else's policies and procedures. Others prefer the advantages a franchise's proven system can provide. Sometimes it makes sense not to reinvent the wheel (see Table 5.1).

▼ TABLE 5.1

Advantages and Disadvantages of Franchising

Franchisee's Perspective	Franchisor's Perspective
Advantages	**Advantages**
1. Proven product or service	1. Expansion with limited capital
2. Marketing expertise	2. Multiple sources of capital
3. Financial assistance	3. Controlled expansion
4. Technical and managerial assistance	4. Motivated franchisees
5. Opportunity to learn the business	5. Bulk-purchasing discounts
6. Quality control standards	
7. Efficiency	
8. Opportunity for growth	
Disadvantages	**Disadvantages**
1. Fees and profit sharing	1. Loss of control
2. Restrictions of freedom	2. Sharing profit with franchisees
3. Overdependence or unsatisfied expectations	3. Potential for disputes with franchisees
4. Risk of fraud or misunderstanding	
5. Termination of the agreement	
6. Performance of other franchisees	

Advantages to Franchisee

For the franchisee, there are eight major advantages of franchising: proven product or service, marketing expertise, financial assistance, technical and managerial assistance, opportunity to learn the business, quality control standards, efficiency, and opportunity for growth.[3]

Proven Product. The most valuable advantage to a franchisee is that you are selling a proven product or service. Customers are aware of the product; they know the name, and they know what to expect. For example, travelers may not know anything about the Ramada Inn in Colorado Springs, but they know Ramada's reputation and are more likely to stay there than at some independent, unknown motel.

Marketing Expertise. Franchisors spend millions of dollars on national or regional advertising to help build an image that independent businesses could not afford. Franchisors also develop print, broadcast, and point-of-purchase advertising. Local franchisees do share in these advertising costs, usually based on their gross revenues, but it is still a great advantage to have access to the marketing expertise of the franchisor at relatively low cost.

> "The most valuable advantage to a franchisee is that you are selling a proven product or service."

Financial Assistance. Some franchisors provide financial assistance to new franchisees. This assistance typically comes in the form of trade credit on inventory or overhead reduction by the franchisor's choosing, purchasing, and owning buildings and real estate.

Professional Guidance. A franchisee can receive managerial and technical assistance not available to an independent business. You can benefit from the accumulated years of experience and knowledge of the franchisor. Most franchisors provide training, both as preparation for running the business and as instruction after the business gets off the ground. This training can allow a person without prior experience to be successful in owning a franchise. A good franchisor is available to provide day-to-day assistance and professional guidance should a crisis arise. In addition, franchisees can receive a great deal of technical help regarding store layout and design, location, purchasing, and equipment.

Opportunity to Learn. Although it is not usually advisable to go into a business in an unfamiliar field, franchising can provide an opportunity to become successful doing exactly that. Thus, franchising can be helpful for a mid-career change of direction. In fact, some franchisors prefer their franchisees not to have experience in that particular field. They prefer to train their business owners from scratch so there are no bad habits to break.

Recognized Standards. Franchisors impose quality standards for franchisees to follow, a feature that might not seem advantageous at first glance—if independence is your motive for self-employment, why would you want to meet standards set by someone else? The benefit, though, is the practice ensures consistency to customers. Consumers can walk into a McDonald's anywhere in the world and know what to expect. A franchisor's quality control regulations help franchisees to maintain high standards of cleanliness, service, and productivity. As a franchisee, you will benefit from standardized quality control, because

COLLEGE HUNKS HAULING JUNK

Y ou're convinced purchasing a franchise is your method of choice for becoming a small business owner. Before you jump in, though, you'd better do your homework. For this exercise, we'll first present some basic information about possible franchise operations; then it's your turn.

You were introduced to College Hunks Hauling Junk in the chapter opener. You know this franchisor began business in 2003 and started franchising in 2005. Its business is providing all kinds of local moving, cleaning, and recycling. It ranked at number 260 on the 2017 Entrepreneur 500 list. There are 79 franchisee locations throughout the United States, 3 of which are owned by the company and 3 franchisees outside the United States.

You think you are a H.U.N.K.S. (which stands for honest, uniformed, nice, knowledgeable, and service—that's you, right?), but are not sure you are ready to proceed. What are the financial requirements and ongoing fees (like initial investment, franchise fee, royalty fee)?

Questions

1. Find the information you would need to make a decision about whether you want to be a franchisee or not.

2. What would be included in a business plan draft outline?

3. Divide the class into teams to discuss the merits and potential drawbacks of this franchise.

---

if another franchisee in your organization provides inferior service, it will affect attitudes toward *your* business.

Efficiency. Because of increased efficiency, a franchise can sometimes be started and operated with less capital than it takes to start an independent business. Franchisors have already been through the learning curve and worked most of the bugs out of the process. Inventory needs, such as what to stock and what will sell quickly, are known before you open the doors, so you won't waste money on equipment, inventory, or supplies you don't need. Many franchisors often provide financial resources for start-up and working capital for inventory if a franchisee is low on cash.

Potential for Business Growth. If you are successful with a franchise, you will often have the opportunity to multiply that success by expanding to other franchises in other locations. Most franchisors have provisions to open other territories.

These eight advantages share a common theme—the opportunity to benefit from someone else's experience. In other words, as a franchisee, you have the chance to learn from someone else's mistakes.

> " "As a franchisee, you have the chance to learn from someone else's mistakes." "

Disadvantages to Franchisee

Of course, franchising has its drawbacks, too. You must give up some control, some decision-making power, and some freedom. Other disadvantages to the franchisee include fees, problems caused by overdependence on the franchisor or by not receiving what was expected from the franchisor, the possibility of fraud or misunderstanding, termination of the agreement, and the potentially negative effects of poor performance by other franchisees.

Cost of Franchise. The services, assistance, and assurance in buying a franchise comes at a price. Every franchisor will charge a fee and/or a specified percentage of sales revenue (see Table 5.2). The disadvantage to the franchisees is that they are usually required to raise most of the capital before they begin operations. The total investment can range from $500 for a windshield repair franchise to $45 million for a Hilton Inn.

Getting In: Top New Franchises of 2017

Franchise	Franchise Fee	Initial Investment	Royalty + Advertising Fee (percentages)
Mosquito Joe	$30K	$66K–127.5K	10% + 2%
Blaze Pizza	$30K	$398K–990K	5% + 2%
uBreakiFix	$40K	$60K–220K	8%
Office Evolution	$35K	$217K–749K	7.5% + 3%
Amada Senior Care	$42K–48K	$85K–178K	5% + 1%
MY SALON Suite	$50K	$371K–959K	5.5% + 1%
Realty ONE Group	$25K	$53K–220K	2%
Apex Fun Run	$49.5K	$80.5K–113K	8%
iLoveKickboxing	$50K–100K	$157K–398K	6% + 1%
Nekter Juice Bar	$35K	$201K–452K	6% + 2%

Source: "Franchise 500," *Entrepreneur*, September 2017, 134–199, www.entrepreneur.com/franchise500.

These fees and percentages may begin to seem excessive after you have been in business for a while and see how they affect your bottom line. It is not uncommon for franchisees to be grateful for the assistance a franchisor provides in starting the business, only to become frustrated by the royalties that have to be paid a few years later.

Restrictions on Freedom or Creativity. The restrictions placed on their freedom may be a problem for some franchisees. Most people open their own businesses because they have a desire for independence, but franchises have policies and procedures that must be followed to maintain the franchise agreement. Also, the size of your market will be limited by territorial restrictions. Although you may feel some products, promotions, or policies are not appropriate for your area, you will have little recourse after the franchise agreement has been signed.

Overdependence or Unsatisfied Expectations. Even though a franchisee is bound by contractual agreement, overdependence on the franchisor can still pose a problem. Franchisors do not always know what is best for every set of local conditions. The franchisee must be willing and able to apply his or her own managerial decisions in running the business in the way best suited to the local market and avoid being overly dependent on the franchisor's guidance. The flip side of overdependence is dealing with a franchisor that does not provide all the assistance the franchisee expected.

Risk of Fraud or Misunderstanding. Less-than-scrupulous franchisors have been known to mislead potential franchisees by making promises that are not fulfilled. To avoid being taken in by a fraudulent franchise, consult an attorney and talk with as many current franchisees as possible. Do not think that because the agreement looks standard it is unnecessary for you to understand every section. Look especially at the fine print.

Problems of Termination or Transfer.

Difficulty in terminating the franchise agreement or having it terminated against your will can be a disadvantage to the franchisee. Before entering into the franchise, you should understand the section of the agreement that describes how you can get out of the deal. For instance, what if you want to transfer your rights to a family member, or sell the franchise to someone else, or otherwise terminate your agreement? What provisions does the contract make for you to renew the agreement? Most franchise agreements cover a specific period of time—typically 5 to 20 years. Some may be renewed in perpetuity if both parties agree. Otherwise, both sides must consider franchise renewal when the term of the agreement expires. Check the agreement to see whether the franchisee has a *right of first refusal*, which means the franchisee must decline to continue the agreement before the franchisor can offer the franchise to someone else. Check whether the franchisor must provide *just cause* for termination or must give a definite reason why the agreement is not being continued. Remember that a franchise is a contract. Any questions regarding it should be directed to your legal counsel.

> "Remember that a franchise is a contract. Any questions regarding it should be directed to your legal counsel."

Poor Performance of Other Franchisees.

Poor performance on the part of other franchisees can lead to problems for you. If the franchisor tolerates substandard performance, a few franchisees can seriously affect the sales of many others. Customers view franchises as an entire unit, because the implicit message from franchises is that "we are all alike"—for good or ill. If customers are treated unsatisfactorily in one location, they are likely to believe the same treatment will occur elsewhere.

Advantages to Franchisor

Now let's look at franchising from the franchisor's perspective. First, we will consider the positive aspects: smaller capital investment required than if outlets were formed independently, multiple sources of capital coming into the business, expansion of the business happening much faster than if the franchisor were in business alone, synergy created by a group of motivated franchisees, and volume discounts for bulk purchasing.

▲ After years of franchise dominance, the Subway system ran into problems due to a series of scandals.

©iStockphoto.com/Bank1T

Expansion with Smaller Capital Investment.

From the perspective of the franchisor, the biggest advantage of offering franchises is the expansion of its distribution sources with limited equity investments. The franchise fees from franchisees provide capital to the franchisor. The franchisor therefore does not have to borrow from lenders or attract outside investors. For a business with limited capital, franchising, in which franchisees share the financial burden, may be the only viable way to expand.

Multiple Sources of Revenue.

Franchisors often build several sources of revenue into their franchise agreements. These sources might include the franchise fee, which is paid when the agreement is signed; a percentage of the franchise's monthly gross operating revenues; and revenue from selling the necessary products and supplies to the franchisees. For example, a fast-food restaurant franchisee could have a franchise fee of up to $200,000; pay 3 to 8 percent of monthly gross sales as a royalty fee; and be required to purchase all food items (from hamburger to condiments), office supplies, and restaurant supplies (napkins, coffee filters, and paper cups) from the franchisor.

Controlled Expansion. When compared with the expansion of a corporate chain, expanding via franchising can be accomplished with a simpler management structure. Very rapid growth of a corporation can be more of a problem than an opportunity, however, if the growth outpaces central management's capacity to control and monitor it. When this happens, problems with inconsistency, communications, and especially cash flow generally appear. Although franchisors still face these problems to some degree, the franchise network reduces them.

Motivated Franchisees. Because franchisees own their own business, they are almost always more highly motivated to make it succeed than an employee working for someone else. Franchisees have a direct personal interest in the entire operation, so they are inspired to perform and thus create positive synergy within the franchise.

> "Franchisees have a direct personal interest in the entire operation, so they are inspired to perform and thus create positive synergy within the franchise."

Bulk Purchasing. Centralized purchasing of products and supplies allows franchisors to take advantage of volume discounts, because they are buying for all the franchise locations. This economy of scale can increase profit margins and hold down costs for franchisees.

Disadvantages to Franchisor

Problems exist in every method of business operation, and franchising is no exception. Loss of control over the business is the biggest disadvantage faced by franchisors. Other potential problems relate to profit sharing and disputes with franchisees.

Loss of Control. Franchisees who do not maintain their businesses reflect poorly not only on other franchisees, but also on the franchisor. Although the franchisor does control the organization to the limit specified by the franchise agreement, franchisees are still independent businesspeople. After the franchise agreement has been signed, the franchisor must get permission from franchisees before any products or services are changed, added, or eliminated. Permission is often negotiated individually. This system makes it difficult for the franchisor to adapt products to meet changing customer needs, especially if a wide variety of consumer tastes are being served over a large geographic area.

One way franchisors have dealt with this problem is by establishing some company-owned units. Because these sites are not independently owned businesses, the franchisor can test-market new products, services, and procedures in them. In this way, the franchisor can track and respond to changing customer needs, as well as use these units as examples when negotiating with franchisees.

Profit Sharing. If franchisees are able to recover their initial investment within two or three years, they could enjoy a 30 to 50 percent return on investment. This return can provide motivation for the franchisees, but it represents profit the franchisor is not making with a company-owned unit.

Franchisee Disputes. Friction between franchisees and franchisors may arise over such issues as payment of fees, expansion, and hours of operation. These potential conflicts point to the importance of good communication between both sides and the need to have a clearly written franchise agreement.

Concept Check Questions

1. What are the biggest advantage and the biggest disadvantage of franchising from the perspective of a franchisee? How about as a franchisor? Justify your answer.

2. What do you expect to get in return for paying a franchise fee?

Concept Module 5.3: Selecting a Franchise

- **LO 5.3: Explain how to evaluate a potential franchise opportunity.**

Choosing the right franchise is a serious decision. Investing in a franchise represents a major commitment of time and money. Before taking the plunge into franchising, determine what you need in a business and evaluate what several different franchises can offer you and your customers.

> "Before taking the plunge into franchising, determine what you need in a business and evaluate what several different franchises can offer you and your customers."

Evaluate Your Needs

The choice of which franchise to buy is not an easy one. You need to find a franchise opportunity that matches your interests, skills, and needs. Ask yourself the following questions to determine whether franchising is the appropriate route to small business ownership for you:

- How much equity capital will you need to purchase the franchise and operate it until your income equals your expenses? Where are you going to get it?

- Are you prepared to give up some independence of action to secure the advantages offered by the franchise?

- Do you really believe you have the innate ability, training, and experience to work smoothly and profitably with the franchisor, your employees, and your customers?

- Are you ready to make a long-term commitment to working with this franchisor, offering its product or service to your public?[4]

Do Your Research

Inc., Fortune Small Business, the *Wall Street Journal,* and *Entrepreneur* are general business periodicals that contain advertising and articles related to franchising. Trade journals and magazines that specialize in franchising include *Franchise, Franchising Opportunities World,* and *Quarterly Franchising World.*

Trade associations can be valuable sources of information when you are investigating franchise opportunities. The major trade association of franchising is the International Franchise Association (IFA), which can be found at www.franchise.org. The IFA is a leading source of information for franchisors and franchisees alike, offering publications that contain industrywide data as well as company-specific information. Also check *The Franchise Handbook,* which gives you an idea of the requirements, expectations, and assistance available for each franchise at www.franchisehandbook .com. Figure 5.3 shows examples of the types of franchise descriptions you can find in this handbook.

Other Information Sources. The American Franchisee Association (AFA), based in Chicago (www.franchisee.org), and the American Association of Franchisees and Dealers (AAFD), headquartered in San Diego (www.aafd.org), are trade associations that provide information and services, represent the interests of members, and were formed to help negotiate better terms and conditions from franchisors. The AAFD has developed a franchisee bill of rights as a code of ethical business conduct for franchised businesses.

On Yahoo!, under the business and economy category of Small Business Information, you will find a link to another source of franchise information, called FranNet. FranNet (www.frannet.com) can provide you with the information needed to help you select the right franchise. You can find additional information on franchises by using any of the popular search engines and doing a key word search for "franchise." Better yet, go to a full-text online database like ABI-INFORM, Business Source Premier, or Lexis-Nexis to search for general and company-specific information on franchises.

You might also want to check out the Better Business Bureau's website (www.bbb.org/bbb). There you'll find a publications directory, membership list, and contact information for Better Business Bureaus nationwide. You can also access the bureau's newsletter, check the scam alerts, and even file a complaint online.

▼ FIGURE 5.3

Franchise Information

Examples of information available about Entrepreneur's Franchise 500 companies.

McDonald's – Ranked #1 on 2018 Franchise 500

2915 Jorie Blvd.,
Oak Brook, IL 60523
www.mcdonalds.com

Company Bio: Ray Kroc, a milkshake mixer salesman, ventured to California in 1954 to visit McDonald's hamburger stand, where he heard they were running eight mixers at once. Kroc was impressed by how rapidly customers were served and, seeing an opportunity to sell many more milkshake machines, encouraged brothers Dick and Mac McDonald to open a chain of their restaurants. Kroc became their business partner and opened the first McDonald's in Des Plaines, Illinois in 1955. McDonald's and the Golden Arches have since become an internationally-recognized symbol of quick-service hamburgers, fries, chicken, breakfast items, salads, and milkshakes.

# of U.S. Franchised Units: 13,109

# of Franchised Units Outside U.S.: 18,827

# of Company Owned: 5,075

In Business Since: 1955

Franchising Since: 1955

Franchise Fee: $45,000

Initial Investment: $1,008,000–$2,214,080

Liquid Cash Requirement: $500,000

Ongoing Royalty Fee: 4%

Ad Royalty Fee: 4%+

Financing Options: McDonald's has relationships with third-party sources which offer financing to cover the following: equipment.

Training: On-the-job training 6–24 months; Classroom training 75 hours; Additional training at local McDonald's restaurant.

Support: Newsletter; Meetings/Conventions; Grand Opening; Online Support; Security/Safety Procedures; Field Operations; Site Selection; Proprietary Software; Franchisee Intranet Platform; Co-op Advertising; Ad Templates; National Media; Regional Advertising; Social Media; Loyalty Program App.

(Continued)

(Continued)

Dunkin' Donuts – Ranked #3 in 2018 Franchise 500

130 Royall St.,
Canton, MA 02021
www.dunkindonuts.com

Company Bio: In 1946, Bill Rosenberg founded Industrial Luncheon Services, a company that delivered meals and snacks to workers in the Boston area. The success of Industrial Luncheon Services convinced Rosenberg to start the Open Kettle, a doughnut shop in Quincy, Massachusetts. Two years later, the Open Kettle changed its name to Dunkin' Donuts.

Today, Dunkin' Donuts stores can be found in over 32 countries and they serve 70 varieties of doughnuts, along with hot and cold coffee drinks, bagels, breakfast sandwiches, and other baked goods. Dunkin' Donuts parent company, Dunkin' Brands Inc., also franchises Baskin-Robbins, and the two concepts are sometimes co-branded.

# of U.S. Franchised Units: 8,948

# of Franchised Units Outside U.S.: 3,402

Company-Owned Units: 0

In Business Since: 1950

Franchising Since: 1955

Franchise Fee: $40,000–$90,000

Initial Investment: $228,620–$1,691,200

Net Worth Requirement: $250,000

Liquid Cash Requirement: $125,000

Ongoing Royalty Fee: 5.9%

Ad Royalty Fee: 2-6%

Financing Options: Veteran incentive of 20% off franchise fee for first five traditional restaurants

Training: On-the-job training 219–324 hours; Classroom training 68–73 hours

Support: Purchasing Co-ops; Newsletter; Meetings/Conventions; Grand Opening; Online Support Security/Safety Procedures; Field Operations; Proprietary Software; Franchisee Intranet Platform; Co-op Advertising; Ad Templates; National Media; Regional Advertising; Social Media; SEO; Website Development; Email Marketing; Loyalty Program App.

Still another source of franchise information is the Institute of Management and Administration's website (http://ioma.com/ioma), which provides links to hundreds of other business sites, including many industry-specific resources.

Questions to Ask. When you have a general idea of the franchise you are interested in, contact the company and ask for a copy of its *disclosure statement* (discussed shortly). Before you sign the required contracts with a chosen franchisor, talk to current and former franchisees. They can provide priceless information that you could not learn anywhere else.

Once you have found a franchise you would consider buying (or possibly a few from which to choose), evaluate the opportunities represented by asking yourself the following questions:

- Did your lawyer approve the franchise contract you are considering after he or she studied it paragraph by paragraph?

WHAT DO YOU NEED TO KNOW?

A good place to get information about a particular franchise is from the people who are currently running one. Ask the following questions to get the real scoop:

- What does the business cost to operate on a monthly basis?

- How long did it take to break even?

- How profitable is the franchise?

- How much does the company charge for advertising fees? (Be careful if this number is more than 1 to 3 percent of gross sales.)

- Does the money go toward ads in the local market or mainly toward building the parent company's national image? (You should expect about 50 percent to benefit the local franchisee.)

- How many units have failed?

- How rapid is unit turnover?

- How many stores does the parent company own? (About 25 percent is acceptable. Too many could weaken franchisee bargaining power; too few could indicate a weak system.)

- Would you buy the franchise again? (The bottom line.)

Remember when you are talking with these current franchise owners that many of them are struggling to internally validate the decision they have made regarding this business. They will often tell you things are going great, sales are up, and they would definitely do it all over again. They may be trying to convince themselves. To get a realistic picture of what you are facing, push them to tell you exactly how much profit they have made in each year of operation. Might you have to go two years without making a profit? Could you do that?

Sources: Fran Finders, "Questions to Ask a Current Franchisee," www.franfinders.com/franchise-information; Gordon Tredgold, "7 Questions You Should Ask If You Want to Start a Franchise," *Inc.*, June 8, 2017, www.inc.com.

- Does the franchise call on you to take any steps that are, according to your lawyer, unwise or illegal in your state, county, or city?

- Does the franchise give you an *exclusive territory* (discussed later in this chapter) for the length of the franchise, or can the franchisor sell a second or third franchise in your territory?

- Is the franchisor connected in any way with any other franchise company handling similar merchandise or services? If so, what is your protection against this second franchisor organization?

- Under what circumstances can you terminate the franchise contract and at what cost to you, if you decide for any reason at all that you wish to cancel it?

- If you sell your franchise, will you be compensated for your goodwill, or will the goodwill you have built into the business be lost by you?

Evaluate what the franchisor will offer you and your customers by asking the following questions about the franchisor:

- How many years has the firm offering you a franchise been in operation?

- Does it have a reputation for honesty and fair dealing among the local firms holding its franchise?

- Has the franchisor shown you any certified figures indicating exact net profits of one or more going firms that you personally checked with the franchisee(s)?

- Will the firm assist you with
  - A management training program?
  - Capital?
  - An employee training program?
  - Credit?
  - A public relations program?
  - Merchandise ideas?
- Will the firm help you find a good location for your new business?
- Is the franchising firm adequately financed so that it can carry out its stated plan of financial assistance and expansion?
- Is the franchisor a one-person company or a corporation with experienced management trained in-depth (so there will always be an experienced person at its head)?
- Exactly what can the franchisor do for you that you cannot do for yourself?
- Has the franchisor investigated you carefully enough to assure itself that you can successfully operate one of its franchises at a profit to both of you?
- Does your state have a law regulating the sale of franchises, and has the franchisor complied with that law?

Analyze the Market

What do you know about your market—the people buying your product or service? In answering the following questions, you can determine whether a franchise is the best way to match what the franchisor has to offer with your skills and your customers' needs:

1. Have you made any study to determine whether the product or service you propose to sell under franchise has a market in your territory at the prices you will have to charge?

2. Will the population in your proposed territory increase, remain static, or decrease over the next five years?

3. Will the product or service you are considering be in greater demand, in about the same demand, or in less demand five years from now?

4. What competition already exists in your territory for the product or service you contemplate selling?
   a. Nonfranchise firms?
   b. Franchise firms?

> "Will the product or service you are considering be in greater demand, in about the same demand, or in less demand five years from now?"

disclosure statements
Information that franchisors are required to provide to potential franchisees.

Disclosure Statements

Franchisors are required by the Federal Trade Commission (FTC) to provide **disclosure statements** to prospective or actual franchisees. Comparing disclosure statements from each franchise you are considering will help you identify risks, fees, benefits, and restrictions involved. Figure 5.4 provides a sample table of contents for a disclosure statement. The entire document can be several hundred pages long. As a prospective franchisee, you should read the document carefully and consult a lawyer to review the franchise agreement. Disclosure statements identify and provide information on the following 23 items:

1. *The franchisor.* Information identifying the franchisor and its affiliates and describing their business experience. This section provides a description of the company and its history.

2. *Business experience of the franchisor.* Information identifying and describing the business experience of each of the franchisor's officers, directors, and management personnel responsible for franchise services, training, and other aspects of the franchises in the franchise program.

3. *Litigation.* A description of the lawsuits in which the franchisor and its officers, directors, and management personnel have been involved.

4. *Bankruptcy.* Information about any previous bankruptcies in which the franchisor and its officers, director, and management personnel have been involved in the past 15 years.

5. *Initial fee.* Information about the initial franchise fee and other initial payments that are required to obtain the franchise. The franchisor must also tell how your fee will be used and whether you must pay in one lump sum or can pay in installments. If every franchisee does not pay the same amount, the franchisor must describe the formula for calculating the initial fee.

6. *Other fees.* A description of the continuing payments that franchisees are required to make after the franchise opens, and the conditions for receiving refunds.

7. *Estimate of total initial investment.* The franchisor must provide a high-range and a low-range estimate of your start-up costs. Included expenses would cover real estate, equipment and other fixed assets, inventory, deposits, and working capital.

8. *Restriction of sources of products and services.* Information about any restrictions on the quality of goods and services used in the franchise and where they may be purchased, including restrictions requiring purchases from the franchisor or its affiliates.

9. *Franchisee's obligations.* This item provides a reference table that indicates where in the franchise agreement franchisees can find the obligations they have agreed to.

10. *Financing.* This item describes the terms and conditions of any financing arrangements offered by the franchisor.

11. *Franchisor's assistance, advertising, computer systems, and training.* This section describes the services the franchisor will provide to the franchisee.

12. *Exclusive territory.* A description of any territorial protection or restrictions on the customers with whom the franchisee may deal. Franchisees of Subway sandwich shops and other franchises have alleged that the franchisor has placed franchises too close together and overlapped territories. This practice cuts into the sales volume and market size of individual stores.

13. *Trademarks.* This section provides information about the franchisor's trademarks, service, and trade names.

14. *Patents, copyrights. and proprietary information.* This section gives information about how the patents and copyrights can be used by the franchisee.

15. *Obligation to participate in the actual operation of the franchise business.* This section stipulates that the franchisee must participate in the actual operation of the business.

16. *Restrictions on what the franchisee may sell.* This section deals with any restrictions on the goods and services the franchisee may offer.

17. *Renewal, termination, transfer, and dispute resolution.* This section tells you when and whether your franchise can be renewed or terminated and what your rights and restrictions are when you have disagreements with your franchisor.

18. *Public figure arrangements.* A disclosure of any involvement by celebrities or public figures in promoting the franchise. If celebrities are involved, you need to be told if they are involved in actual management and how they are being compensated.

19. *Financial performance representations.* Here the franchisor is allowed, but not required, to provide information on unit financial performance.

20. *Information about franchisees.* You will receive information about the present number of franchises; the number of new franchises projected; and the number that have been terminated, chose not to renew, or were repurchased. Franchisors must give you the names, addresses, and phone numbers of all franchisees located in your state; contact several of them.

21. *Franchisor financial statements.* The audited financial statements of the franchisors are included to show you the financial condition of the company.

22. *Contracts.* This item provides all the agreements the franchisee will be required to sign.

23. *Receipts.* Prospective franchisees are required to sign a receipt that they received the Franchise Disclosure Document.[5]

The FTC has revised the *Franchise Disclosure Document (FDD)* several times in the past 25 years. The changes were intended to replace much of the "legalese" wording of disclosure statements with plain English and to provide more standardized information for comparing franchises. The FDD still has a way to go before it qualifies as "easy reading," but stay with it. This is a very important document to understand.[6] Don't assume that the disclosure statement tells you everything you need to know about the franchise. It is a good start, but it does not constitute full due diligence.

When you receive a disclosure statement, you will be asked to sign and date a statement indicating that you received it. The franchisor may not accept any money from you for 10 working days from the time you sign the disclosure. This cooling-off period allows you the time to study, evaluate, and prepare your financing.[7]

> "Don't assume that the disclosure statement tells you everything you need to know about the franchise."

The Franchise Agreement

The **franchise agreement** is a document that spells out the rights and obligations of both parties in a franchise. This contract defines the precise, detailed conditions of the legal relationship between the franchisee and the franchisor. Its length, terms, and complexity will vary from one franchise and industry to another, so as to maintain the delicate balance of power between franchisees and franchisors.[8] It may or may not be possible for you to negotiate the contents of the contract, depending on how long the franchisor has been established and what the current market conditions are.

You should remember that the franchisor wrote the contract and that most of the conditions contained in it are weighted in the franchisor's favor. Read this document carefully yourself, but never sign a franchise agreement without getting your lawyer's opinion. Make sure your attorney and accountant have experience with franchising. Some of the most important topics you should understand in franchise agreements are fees to be paid, ways in which the agreement can be terminated or renewed, and your rights to *exclusive territory* (discussed later in this chapter).

Franchise, Royalty, and Advertising Fees. The **franchise fee** is the amount of money you have to pay to become a franchisee. Some agreements require you to have a percentage of the total franchise fee from a nonborrowed source, meaning, obviously, that you can't

franchise agreement
The legal contract that binds both parties involved in the franchise.

franchise fee
The one-time payment made to become a franchisee.

Franchise Disclosure Document

Table of Contents

Section

1. Franchisor and Any Predecessors

2. Identity and Business Experience of Persons Affiliated with the Franchisor

3. Litigation

4. Bankruptcy

5. Developer's/Franchisee's Initial Franchise Fee or Other Initial Payment

6. Other Fees

7. Franchisee's Initial Investment

8. Obligation of Franchisee to Purchase or Lease from Designated Sources

9. Obligations of Franchisee to Purchase or Lease in Accordance with Specifications or from Approved Suppliers

10. Financing Arrangements

11. Obligations of the Franchisor: Other Supervision, Assistance, or Services

12. Exclusive Area or Territory

13. Trademarks, Trade Names, and Service Marks

14. Patent and Copyrights

15. Obligation of Franchisee to Participate in the Actual Operations of the Franchise

16. Restrictions on Goods and Services Offered by Developer/Franchise

17. Renewal, Termination, Repurchase, Modification, and Assignment of the Franchise Agreement and Related Information

18. Arrangements with Public Figures

19. Statement of per-Franchise Average Gross Sales and Ranges of Gross Sales for the Year Ended Month, Day, Year

20. Other Franchises of the Franchisor

21. Financial Statements

22. Contracts

23. Receipts

EXHIBIT A   Franchise Agreement

EXHIBIT B   Area Development Agreement

EXHIBIT C   Preliminary Agreement

EXHIBIT D   Royalty Incentive Rider

EXHIBIT E   Disclosure Acknowledgment Statement

EXHIBIT F   List of Franchisees as of Month, Day, Year

EXHIBIT G   List of Franchisees Who Have Ceased Doing Business in the One-Year Period Immediately Preceding Month, Day, Year

EXHIBIT H   Financial Statements of Franchisor

borrow that amount. Agreements may or may not allow you to form a corporation to avoid personal liability.

Royalty fees are usually a percentage of gross sales you pay to the franchisor. Remember that royalties are calculated from gross sales, not from profits. If your business generates $350,000 of sales and the royalty fee is 8 percent, you have to pay $28,000 to the franchisor whether you make a profit or not. And you still have all your other operating expenses to cover.

When comparing two franchises, look at the combination of franchise fees and royalties. For example, suppose franchise X charges $25,000 for the franchise fee and a 10 percent royalty (not including advertising fees), and franchise Y charges a $37,500 franchise fee with a 5 percent royalty (no advertising fees, either). Assume gross sales for each franchise would be $250,000 per year. The total fee you would pay for either would be $50,000 for the first year. But for each year after the first, you would pay $25,000 ($250,000 × 10%) with franchise X and only half that with franchise Y ($250,000 × 5%).

If the franchise agreement requires you to pay advertising fees, you want to be sure that a portion of your fee goes to local advertising in your area. If you operate a franchise on the outer geographic fringe of the franchise's operations, the franchisor could spend all of your advertising dollars where there is a greater concentration of other franchises, but none of *your* customers.

When it comes to total fees in franchising, you generally get what you pay for. If a deal looks too good to be true (unlimited potential earnings with no risk), it probably is.[9]

Termination of the Franchise Agreement.
The agreement should state how you, as the franchisee, could lose your franchise rights. Also described should be the franchisee's obligations if you choose to terminate the agreement. Make sure the franchisor must show "good cause" to terminate the agreement—that is, there must be a good reason to discontinue the deal. Some states require a good-cause clause.

Terms and Renewal of Agreement.
The franchise contract includes a section that specifies how long the agreement will remain in effect and what renewal process will apply. Most franchise contracts run from 5 to 15 years. Will you have to pay a renewal fee or, possibly worse, negotiate a whole new franchise agreement? Because fees and royalties are generally higher for well-established franchises, your royalties and fees would probably increase if you have to sign a new agreement 10 years from now.

Exclusive Territory.
You need to know the geographic size of the territory and the exclusive rights the franchisee would have. Franchisors may identify how many franchises a territory can support without oversaturation and then issue that many, regardless of the businesses' specific locations. Rights of first refusal, advertising restrictions, and performance quotas for the territory are addressed in this section.[10]

This issue of *exclusive territory* is the subject of much controversy in the franchising world. Patrick Leddy, Jr., had run a Baskin-Robbins franchise for 13 years when he learned the franchisor was planning to open a new store less than two miles away from his site. He protested, but Baskin-Robbins opened the new store anyway. Leddy's sales plunged. When he tried to sell his store, he could not find a buyer because of his declining sales. Many franchisees cited examples like Leddy's case when they called for a federal law to prevent what they called widespread unfair treatment by franchisors.[11]

In reviewing the franchise opportunity, a potential franchisee should gather and verify the accuracy of the information included in the franchise agreement and all other information provided by the franchisor. This process is called **due diligence**. It means doing your homework and investigating the franchise on your own, rather than accepting everything the franchisor

royalty fees
The ongoing payments that franchisees pay to franchisors—usually a percentage of gross sales.

due diligence
The process of thoroughly investigating the accuracy of information before signing a franchise (or any other) agreement.

TECHNO-FRANCHISE

©Shutterstock.com/TY Lim

In the near-future world of franchise restaurants, robots and drones are likely to remain more of a novelty than something mainstream. But, that does not mean technology is not going to be a major factor.

CaliBurger, based in Pasadena, California, already uses robots to flip hamburgers. Zume, a pizza parlor in Northern California uses robots to make pies. And, even creepier is H.A.R.L.A.N.D., a robotic Colonel Sanders that KFC has installed in a few drive-thru locations to interact with customers in a Kentucky drawl.

Counterintuitive? Yes, but understandable. Digital convenience in the front of operations increases the volume of orders, average order amount, and customized orders—requiring more workers in the kitchen. Table service and delivery takes human interaction. OK, how

about drone or driverless vehicles—maybe, but not on a large scale for some time.

Many prognosticators have predicted that such technology will replace low-wage employees in fast-food restaurants. Is a fast-food restaurant completely devoid of human workers imminent? Would that be what customers really want?

Panera Bread provides some data addressing those questions. They have had mobile and kiosk ordering in all of its 2,000 Panera 2.0 stores since 2014. Do you still see workers in those green aprons when you visit Panera? Yep, a bunch of them—bringing food to tables, cleaning, packaging food for "to go" orders, and running registers. Turns out Panera 2.0 stores actually employ more humans after automating operations than locations without automation. Labor costs increased from 29.7 percent of sales to 32.5 percent.

Bottom line impact of technology on franchises? While they are seldom on the cutting edge of technology, franchises understand the most important thing they offer is value and a pleasant customer experience. That requires cleanliness, comfort, and a nice environment. The Bureau of Labor Statistics predicts 11 percent growth of jobs in food preparation and service from 2014 to 2024. So, fast-food jobs do not appear to be in danger of being replaced by robots in the near future. As for the 22nd century? That's your guess.

Sources: Nancy Kruse, "Will Automation Replace Restaurant Workers?" *Nation's Restaurant News,* September 11, 2017, 12; Elizabeth G. Dunn, "Gearing Up: When Will Robots Finally Take Over the Fast-Food Business?" *Entrepreneur,* May 30, 2017, www.entrepreneur.com/article/294575; Heather Lally, "The Future Will be Personalized," *Restaurant Business,* September 2017, 47–49.

says at face value. This is a big commitment, so you should investigate matters thoroughly. Some information you can find yourself; some you will need professional assistance to gather and interpret.

Get Professional Advice

Consult a lawyer and a certified public accountant (CPA) before you sign any franchise agreement. Ask your CPA to read the financial data in the company's disclosure statements to determine whether the franchisor would be able to meet its obligation to you if you buy a franchise. Then ask a lawyer who is familiar with franchise law to inform you of all your rights and obligations contained in the franchise agreement—it *is* negotiable, but you have to push. Query your lawyer about any state or local laws that would affect your franchise. The cost of consulting professionals is small compared to the amount of time and money you will invest in a franchise. Do not assume that the disclosure statement tells you everything you need to know about the franchise. That is not the intent of the document.

> "The cost of consulting professionals is small compared to the amount of time and money you will invest in a franchise."

MILLENNIAL FRANCHISEES

Franchisors are working to clear up some misconceptions about the Millennial generation—because they like what they see. One misconception is that Millennials are only young people—the upper age is currently 34. The Millennial generation is one of the most diverse, so they are difficult to generalize. And generalizations create misconceptions on topics like credit card debt, student debt, and avoidance of hard work—none of which apply across the entire group. Millennials have a lot to offer to franchising. Notable findings from a Small Business Development Center study include

- 59 percent of Millennials indicate that with the right idea and resources they would start a business within the next year.

- 61 percent of Millennials believe the best job security comes from owning your own business.

- 51 percent of Millennials would absolutely want help with a business development plan.

- 45 percent of Millennials say access to capital is the biggest barrier to starting a business.

- More than 13 million Millennials cite not knowing where to go for help to start or run a business as the top reason that keeps them from starting their own business.

- All of the above point toward a solid match between Millennials and franchising. Franchising provides Millennials (and everyone else) with more guidance and assistance when compared with starting a similar business from scratch. The International Franchise Association (IFA) is taking steps to attract this generation to invest in franchising by highlighting return-on-investment potential, transparent business practices, and technologies that streamline business.

First and foremost in the mutual attraction between Millennials and franchises is technology. As digital natives, Millennials are masters of technology and franchised businesses can greatly benefit by capitalizing on these skill sets. Creating new avenues for Millennials to engage and communicate with franchisors is imperative, as the IFA recognized when it customized a website for its NextGen initiative (http://nextgenfranchising.org/).

Franchisors need to understand what Millennials actually want. Research from PricewaterhouseCoopers shows that when going into business, Millennials desire

- Feedback: Millennials want to know how their performance rates and what to do better. Franchisors need to change previous approaches to franchisee feedback for Millennials.

- Training: Millennials don't want to be left adrift. They want training and mentorship to set their direction and speed their progress. This is an area franchises do better than any other form of business.

- Freedom: Millennials have a need to implement new ideas and try new things without restrictions of rules and regulations. This is another area for change from standard franchise procedures.

Sources: AJ Agrawal, "Are Millennials the Future of Franchises?" *Inc.*, May 16, 2016, www.inc.com; Danny Rivera, "The Impact of Millennials on the Franchise Industry," *Franchising World*, April 2016, 32; Miriam L. Brewer, "Millennials in the Workplace: NextGen Students in Franchising," *Franchising World*, July 2017, 16; Evan Hackel, "Keys to Recruiting and Keeping Millennial Franchisees," *Franchising World*, November 2017, 15.

Concept Check Questions

1. Is the disclosure statement the *only* source of information you need to check out a potential franchise? Why or why not?

2. After reading about the topics included in a franchise agreement, who do you think controls most of the power in a franchise: the franchisee or the franchisor? Explain.

3. What are potential sources of conflict between franchisees and franchisors?

4. You are worried someone else will buy a specific franchise in your area before you do. Would it be appropriate to sign the franchise agreement before talking to your lawyer or accountant if you intend to meet with them later? Explain.

5. If you are the franchisee of a bookstore and are offered twice the business's book value to sell it to a third party, should you or the franchisor collect the additional money? Take a position and justify it.

6. Explain how a franchise could be considered a partnership. What makes a franchise agreement simpler than a partnership that you would start with another individual?

7. What is a royalty fee?

CHAPTER REVIEW

SUMMARY ▶▶

LO 5.1   Explain what a franchise is and how it operates.

Franchising is a legal agreement that allows a franchisee to use a product, service, or method of the franchisor in exchange for fees and royalties. A franchisee is an independent businessperson who agrees to operate under the policies and procedures set up by the franchisor.

LO 5.2   Compare the advantages and disadvantages of franchising.

There are eight major advantages of franchising from the franchisee's perspective: proven product or service, marketing expertise, financial assistance, technical and managerial assistance, opportunity to learn, quality control standards, efficiency,

and opportunity for growth. The primary disadvantages to the franchisee include fees, restrictions on his or her freedom to operate the business, overdependence on the franchisor, unsatisfied expectations of the franchisor, termination of the agreement, and poor performance of other franchisees.

LO 5.3   Explain how to evaluate a potential franchise opportunity.

To evaluate a franchise opportunity, you should send for a copy of the company's disclosure statement (the company is required to send it to you), research the company through business periodicals, talk to current and former franchisees, and check out the franchisor's reputation with the International Franchise Association.

KEY TERMS ▶▶

business-format franchising   **111**

disclosure statements   **122**

due diligence   **126**

franchise   **109**

franchise agreement   **124**

franchisee   **109**

franchise fee   **124**

franchisor   **109**

product-distribution franchising   **111**

royalty fees   **126**

STUDENT STUDY SITE ▶▶

edge.sagepub.com/hatten7e

$SAGE edge™ Sharpen your skills with SAGE edge!

SAGE edge for Students provides a personalized approach to help you accomplish your coursework goals in an easy-to-use learning environment. You'll find mobile-friendly eFlashcards and quizzes as well as multimedia resources to support and expand on the concepts presented in this chapter.

EXPERIENTIAL LEARNING ACTIVITIES ▶▶

5.1: Business Format or Product Distribution Franchise

LO 5.2: Compare the advantages and disadvantages of franchising.

Break into groups of 4–5 students.

For each franchise business listed below, decide if the franchise is a business format franchise or a product distribution franchise. In one to two sentences, explain the rationale for the type of franchise chosen.

_____ McDonald's

_____ The UPS Store

_____ Great Clips

_____ RE/MAX LLC

_____ Jimmy John's Gourmet Sandwiches

_____ Pizza Hut LLC

_____ Planet Fitness

_____ Hampton by Hilton

_____ Merry Maids

_____ The Flying Locksmiths

After the group has chosen the type of franchising for each business and justified the choice in a couple of sentences, determine one franchise advantage and one franchise disadvantage for each of the listed businesses.

Be prepared to share with the entire class.

5.2: Franchise Requirements Evaluation

LO 5.3: Explain how to evaluate a potential franchise opportunity.

Break into groups of 4–5 students. Each group must have at least one student with a smart phone. Have the students answer the questions below for each franchise listed.

Once the group has answered the questions on each franchise, as a group they must select which franchise they would choose to open. The group must justify their decision in choosing that franchise.

Be prepared to share with the entire class.

Franchises

- Edible Arrangements
- KFC US LLC
- Jiffy Lube Int'l. Inc.
- College Nannies + Sitters + Tutors
- Spring-Green Lawn Care

Answer the following questions for each franchise listed above.

1. What is the initial investment, net worth requirement, and liquid cash requirement?

2. What type of job training and/or classroom training is available?

3. What is the initial franchise fee and ongoing royalty fee?

4. Where are the primary locations of the franchises—the United States or abroad?

5. What is one interesting fact about the franchise?

CHAPTER CLOSING CASE ▶▶

Extreme Garage Makeover

Marc Shuman tries to solve a problem common to most every homeowner—getting to their cars without tripping over tools and toys or hurdling barbecue grills and bikes. "Garages can be a lot more than just a place to dump junk," says Shuman.

Shuman's solution to the war on clutter is a "garage organizational system" consisting of patented slotted wall panels and an array of modular attachable cabinets, shelves, bike racks, and workbenches—all styled in the same light-gray steel and plastic and bearing the yellow GarageTek logo.

Marc describes himself as a "neat freak" and devised an early version of the slotted wall panel while running his family's store-fixture manufacturing company on Long Island. He and a partner adapted the panels and tested them out on his mother-in-law's two-car garage, which was packed with 30 years' worth of junk. "The transformation was just staggering," he says.

Selling the panels at home-improvement stores such as Home Depot and Lowe's was tempting, but eventually Shuman decided to build a garage-makeover business. He could envision

GarageTek experts going to customers' homes, designing and installing organization systems—complete with cabinets, shelves, bike racks, and workbenches. Custom work justifies a premium price so margins would be higher. No one sold such garage systems, but it would not be difficult to copy the idea so Shuman needed to be the first in the market and get big fast. Franchising seemed like the best way to do both.

Shuman placed an ad in the *Wall Street Journal* soliciting franchisees. The phone started ringing. His attorney advised him to choose carefully, but Shuman's first-mover advantage could be lost quickly so he approved anyone that met minimal standards. Franchisees invested between $200,000 and $250,000 up front, including a $50,000 licensing fee, and promised to pay 6 percent of gross sales as an annual royalty, plus another 4 percent for advertising. He expected that to be enough to purchase supplies, buy newspaper ads, and turn a profit within 18 months. Franchisees received three days of basic training and a manual written by Shuman. "If they had the money and a strong sales and marketing background, we felt they were qualified," Shuman says.

All went smoothly—at first. In the first half of 2001, GarageTek franchises opened in Connecticut, New Jersey, and New York. By 2003, 57 franchises had sprung up in 33 states, and annual revenue at the corporate office was on track to top $12 million. In the summer of 2003, Shuman detected 15 franchisees who were struggling. One franchisee in California begged Shuman to send executives out west to train his staff. Another complained that Garage-Tek's suggested marketing method—ads in local newspapers—was ineffective, costing as much as $500 per lead. Desperate for help, Shuman enlisted iFranchise Group, a consulting firm in Homewood, Illinois, to help him develop a strategy. Top managers began benchmarking successful franchisees for tactics that worked best. Franchisees wondered where their royalty and franchise fees were going.

GarageTek's target market is owners of houses worth an average of $350,000 or more, or roughly the top 20 percent of the nation's 50 million houses with garages. The company's average sale (including design, components, and installation) is $4,500.

About three-quarters of GarageTek's franchisees were doing well. But, of course that means that 25 percent were losing money or barely breaking even. Complaints from disgruntled franchisees were pouring in. Shuman and crew were struggling to create operational systems that would help the unprofitable franchises get back on track, but they were losing ground. The picture painted by financial statements made Shuman start to think about closing the failing locations and get it over with.

Shuman and his managers knew they needed more data before making major decisions, so they compiled a spreadsheet with information on every GarageTek franchise, including the size and demographics of each territory, overhead costs, pricing models, management assessments, and the amount of capital being invested by owners. Two trends became apparent: The failing franchises were either underfunded or being run by non-owner managers hired by hands-off investors.

Shuman knew that he bore some of the blame for approving marginal franchisees in the first place and that GarageTek training and support had not been first rate. At the same time, the struggling franchisees were at fault too. Shuman, who had a reputation for being a tough boss, was torn. He, his management team, and the consultant from iFranchise all wanted to close the doors of struggling locations.

But legally, pulling franchise agreements could get messy. GarageTek's contract clearly stated the franchisor could shut down franchises that failed to meet specific sales goals. But Shuman's attorney warned that that could cause more problems. "I envisioned a bloodbath," Shuman says.

Questions

1. What problems would GarageTek face if it closed failing franchises? Lawsuits, damage to its reputation, harm to its public image?

2. Is shuttering the failed franchises the right move for Shuman? What are his other options?

Sources: Stephanie Clifford, "Case Study: Hooked On Expansion," *Inc.*, March 2006, 44–50; Patricia Mertz Esswein, "Extreme Makeover: Garage," *Kiplinger's Personal Finance*, July 2005; Patrick J. Sauer, "Garage Makeover," *Inc.*, July 2007, 7; and Joseph Rosenbloom, "Space Man," *Inc.*, May 2002.

## CHAPTER 6

TAKING OVER AN EXISTING BUSINESS

O K, so you're taking this class or reading this book because you want to create the next "Uber for [insert your favorite service here]," but there may be other ways for you to get there. The timing may be much better for you to buy an existing business or take over one that is family-owned.

Think of the demographics in the United States. How many of the huge Baby Boomer generation are close to retirement age? The California Association of Business Brokers predicts that with Boomers holding more than 12 million privately owned businesses, 70 percent of them will likely change hands in the next few years—that's a LOT of opportunity for young entrepreneurs. The Bureau of Labor Statistics says that by 2022, 25.6 percent of the workforce will be Baby Boomers and 46 percent will be Millennials.

Statistics show the average person will change jobs 10 to 12 times during his or her career. It is a trend that continues to accelerate. This statistic means that transitions need to be meaningful and fulfilling. The reasons for all of these transitions can vary greatly, but for this chapter we will focus on young business owners purchasing an existing business from an older generation . . . or younger family members taking over a family business from an elder generation.

LEARNING OUTCOMES

After reading this chapter, you should be able to:

6.1 Compare the advantages and disadvantages of buying an existing business.

6.2 Propose ways of locating a suitable business for sale.

6.3 Explain how to measure the condition of a business and determine why it might be offered for sale.

6.4 Differentiate between tangible and intangible assets, and assess the value of each.

6.5 Calculate the price to pay for a business.

6.6 Discuss factors that are important when finalizing the purchase of a business.

6.7 Describe what makes a family business different from other types of businesses.

Sources: Krista Stein, "Forget Startups—Just Buy a Small Business from a Retiring Entrepreneur," *Fast Company*, November 16, 2016, www.fastcompany.com; Todd Berger, "7 Ways to Bridge the Boomer–Millennial Gap," *Entrepreneur*, December 14, 2014, www.entrepreneur.com/article/240725; Michelle Wu, "The How-To: Making Successful Transitions to the Next Chapter in Your Life," *Entrepreneur*, January 3, 2018, www.entrepreneur.com/article/306838.

Concept Module 6.1: Business-Buyout Alternative

- **LO 6.1: Compare the advantages and disadvantages of buying an existing business.**

Suppose you are a prospective small business owner. You possess the necessary personal qualities, managerial ability, and capital to run a business, but you haven't decided on the approach you should take to get into business. If you aren't inheriting a family business, then you have three choices for getting started:

- You may buy out an existing establishment.

- You may acquire a franchise business.

- You may start a new firm yourself.

This chapter discusses the many factors to be considered in buying an existing business and taking over a family business.

Master the content at
**edge.sagepub.com/
Hatten7e**

$SAGE edge™

Advantages of Buying a Business

The opportunity to buy a firm already in operation is appealing for a number of reasons. Like franchising, it offers a way to avoid some beginners' hazards.[1] The existing firm is already functioning—maybe it is even a proven success. Many of the serious problems typically encountered by start-ups should have been either avoided or corrected by now. The ongoing business is analogous to a ship after its "shakedown cruise," a new automobile after the usual small adjustments have been made, or a computer program that has been "debugged." But remember one thing: Just as there are no perfect ships, cars, or software programs for sale out there, neither are there any perfect businesses on the market. You are searching for an opportunity, so *some* flaws in a business can make it more attractive. You just have to be able to correct them while keeping all the parts that work going strong.

> "Just as there are no perfect ships, cars, or software programs for sale out there, neither are there any perfect businesses on the market."

Buying an existing business is a popular way for would-be owners to acquire a small business. At any given time, there are tens of thousands of small businesses available for sale in dozens of industries and many, many sectors. But not every type of small business for sale is right for every buyer. How do you know if a business for sale is right for you?

- **Personal Interests.** Start-ups can begin from expanding a hobby or personal passion. Not so with buying a business. Your acquired business will immerse you into specific work for an extended period of time—be sure you're going to enjoy it.

- **Skills, Talents, and Experience.** Passion is great, but it's not enough. Be honest with yourself in what you can actually do.

- **Capital Requirements.** Some industries (like manufacturing) just take more cash than others. Do your resources realistically match the money needed?

- **Market Research.** Buying a business is one of those many decisions that must be made on data—not emotions.

- **Business Network.** Your personal business network will be a valuable source of customers and strategic partnerships so buying a business outside your network means starting from scratch—delaying achievement of your goals.[2]

One of the messages in this chapter is to make your decision about purchasing a business based on analytics as much as possible. Don't let emotions cloud your business decisions. There are several advantages to buying an existing business as compared with the other methods of getting into business. Because customers are used to doing business with the company at its present address, they are likely to continue doing so once you take over. If the business has been making money, you will break even sooner than if you start your own business from the ground up. Your planning for an ongoing business can be based on actual historical figures, rather than relying on projections, as with a start-up. Your inventory, equipment, and suppliers are already in place, managed by employees who already know how to operate the business. Financing may be available from the owner. If the timing of the deal occurs when you are ready to buy a business and the owner needs to sell for a legitimate reason, you may get a bargain (see Table 6.1).

> "Don't let emotions cloud your business decisions."

Disadvantages of Buying a Business

Could this business that you're considering buying be what is called in the used-car business a "lemon"? Most people don't sell their cars until they feel the vehicle needs considerable mechanical attention. Is the same true of selling businesses?

Advantages and Disadvantages of Buying a Business

Advantages
1. Customer base is established.
2. Location is already familiar to customers.
3. Planning can be based on known historical data.
4. Supplier relationships are already in place.
5. Inventory and equipment are already in place.
6. Employees are experienced.
7. Possibility of owner financing exists.
8. Quick entry is available.
9. Control systems are already in place (e.g., accounting, inventory, and personnel controls).
10. Business image is already set in minds of customers.

Disadvantages
1. Business image may be difficult to change.
2. Employees may be ones you would not choose.
3. Business may not have operated the way you like and could be difficult to change.
4. Inventory or equipment may be obsolete.
5. Financing costs could drain your cash flow and threaten the business's survival.
6. Business's location may be undesirable, or a good location may be about to become not so good.
7. Potential liability exists for past business contracts.
8. Misrepresentation is possible (yes, the person selling the business may be lying).

There are disadvantages to buying an existing business as a way to become your own boss (see Table 6.1 again). The image of the business already exists and may prove difficult to change should you desire to improve it. The employees who come with the business may not be the ones whom you would choose to hire. The previous owners may have established precedents that can be difficult to change. The way the business operates may be outmoded. The inventory or equipment may be outdated. The purchase price may create a burden on future cash flow and profitability. You may pay too much for the business due to misrepresentation or inaccurate appraisal. The business's facilities or location may not be the best. You may be held liable for contracts left over from previous owners.

Concept Check Questions

1. What are some arguments for buying an established business rather than starting one yourself?

2. Should one ever consider purchasing a presently unsuccessful business (that is, a business with relatively low or no profits)? Explain.

▲ Online business sites contain thousands of businesses for sale.

Concept Module 6.2: How Do You Find a Business for Sale?

- **LO 6.2:** Propose ways of locating a suitable business for sale.

If you have decided you're interested in purchasing an existing business and have narrowed your choices down to a few types of businesses, how do you locate one to buy? Perhaps you are currently employed by a small business. Is there a chance it may be available for purchase sometime soon? Because you know the inner workings of the business, it might be a good place to start. Newspaper advertising is a traditional place for someone who is actively trying to sell a business to start marketing it. Don't stop your quest with the newspaper, however, because many good opportunities are never advertised. Word of mouth through friends and family may turn up businesses that don't appear to be available through formal channels.

People who counsel small businesses on a regular basis, such as bankers, lawyers, accountants, and Small Business Administration representatives, can be good sources for finding firms for sale. Real estate brokers often have listings for business opportunities, which include real estate and buildings. Trade associations generally have publications that list member businesses for sale.[3]

Don't overlook a direct approach to finding a business. If you have been a regular customer of an establishment and have an attraction to it, why not politely ask the owner if he or she has ever thought of selling it? The timing may be perfect if the owner is considering a move to another part of the country or is exploring another new business. Perhaps this is an unlikely way to find a business, but what do you have to lose by asking?

Nearly every city has one or more **business brokers**. Most inspect and appraise a business establishment offered for sale before listing and advertising it. Some also assist a buyer in financing the purchase, but not all of them will provide you with the same level of service. A few will work very hard for you in trying to find a business that matches your talents and needs. Most will tell you what is available at the moment, but not much more than that. Some will do you more harm than good. Remember, business brokers normally receive their commission from the seller, so their loyalty is to the seller, not to you.

Unfortunately for prospective buyers, the market is rife with "business opportunity" scams. As with any scam, the individuals most likely to be targeted are those venturing into unknown territory and trusting the wrong people. The practice of selling unprofitable (and unfixable) businesses to unwary buyers has been around as long as business itself. The ruse is most common in the retail field, where a single business unit can wreck a dozen or more owners through successive sales and resales to a steady stream of newcomers, each confident he or she can succeed where others have failed.

Naturally, the brokers who promote these sales make more in commissions the more frequently the business changes hands. Check for recommendations from bankers, accountants, and other businesspeople who have used the broker in the past. You need to be on guard to keep from being included among that group immortalized by the late P. T. Barnum, who allegedly said, "There's a sucker born every minute."

Brokers must take classes and pass examinations to become *certified business intermediaries* (CBIs). To find a reliable business broker, check the International Business Brokers Association at www.ibba.org.

Curtis Kroeker, general manager of bizbuysell.com and bizquest.com (two of the largest and most heavily trafficked business-for-sale sites online) recommends five important tools and resources every business buyer should consider:

business brokers
A business intermediary that brings sellers of their businesses together with potential buyers.

- **Business Brokers**—invaluable source of information (even on opportunities that are not publicized) and navigator of obstacles that always arise.

BUY AN ONLINE BUSINESS . . . ONLINE

Going into business leaves everyone with a lot of questions, especially for online businesses. Do you have the resources for building your brand? Can you monetize your idea (can it generate more money than it costs)? Can you develop a solid business model?

Buying an existing online business rather than starting one may be your answer to questions like these. Of course, having early questions answered means you still have to successfully manage the business—but it does allow you to go right to business development and growth. If buying an online business is right for you, what are your options?

- **Exchange**—*exchange.shopify.com* is a cool marketplace to buy and sell online businesses. You can search by category like "fashion and apparel," "sports and recreation," or "electronics and gadgets." You can also search by selling price such as "$0 to $250" or "$500 to $2,500." With such an online marketplace you get accurate data on revenue or online traffic to analyze.

- **Direct purchase**—If you have a specific online business in mind to buy you can contact the owner to check interest in selling it. Find the owner either via the business About Us tab or do a "who.is" search of domain names or IP addresses. Before initiating contact you can begin due diligence with sites like *www.semrush.com*, for analytics reports about online strategies in display, advertising, organic and paid searches, and backlinks. You can also check backlinks (quality, quantity, and relevance of backlinks indicate how much traffic a site receives) via Open Site Explorer (*moz.com/researchtools*).

- **Online business broke**—Are you bored with the idea of shopping for a business in the old-fashioned ways, such as through classified ads and business brokers? Then go online—specifically, go to *www.bizbuysell. com*, a very comprehensive site for buying or selling a business that offers a database of thousands of established businesses for sale. You begin by choosing where you want your business to be. All 50 states, plus Africa, Asia, Australia/New Zealand, Canada, the Caribbean, Central America, Europe, and South America, are represented. Next, you choose the type of business that interests you. You can choose all business categories or pick from retail, service, manufacturing, wholesale, construction, transportation, finance, and several other miscellaneous categories.

Sources: Jonathan Long, "Three Ways to Buy an Established Online Business," *Entrepreneur*, July 17, 2017, www.entrepreneur.com/article/297209; Thomas Smale, "4 Ways to Find an Online Business for Sale," *Entrepreneur*, September 2, 2015, www.entrepreneur.com/article/250185.

- **Online Tools**—for example, www.bizbuysell.com offers valuation reports based on tens of thousands of currently offered and sold businesses (comparables or "comps"). Similar in format, but different business listings for sale are found on www.businessbroker.net. Not vetted like the previous sites, but good for localized listings is www.craigslist.com.

- **Appraisal Experts**—rules of thumb and online valuation guides are great starting points, but savvy buyers hire appraisal experts with experience in the industry and geographic area.

- **Legal Counsel**—can you purchase a business without hiring an attorney? Yes. Should you? Oh no. There are too many legal details that can nuke a deal and put you in jeopardy after the sale. You need an attorney to draft purchase agreements, contracts, and many other documents.

- **Accountants and Other Financial Advisers**—buyers need more financial eyes on the deal to help determine how much you can afford to spend and help you secure capital. Plus, they will assist in analyzing the financial statements of the target business.[4]

Concept Check Question

1. Discuss the advantages of working through a business broker. What precautions should one take when dealing with a business broker?

Concept Module 6.3: What Do You Look for in a Business?

- **LO 6.3:** Explain how to measure the condition of a business and determine why it might be offered for sale.

To successfully analyze the value of any business, you should have enough experience to recognize specific details that are most relevant to the type of business. You need enough knowledge to take the information provided by sales, personnel, or financial records and (1) evaluate the past performance of the business and (2) predict its probable future development. You need objectivity to avoid excess enthusiasm that might blind you to the facts.

At a minimum, you should ask the following questions to gather information about the business you are considering buying:

- **History:** How long has the business existed? Who founded it? How many owners has it had? Why have others sold out?

- **Inventory:** What is the current status of all products and materials? What is present now? What existed at the end of the previous fiscal year? Have the inventory appraised, keeping in mind you do not have to accept the value set by the seller. The salability and value are major points of negotiation.

- **Tax returns for the past five years:** Investigate how comingled the seller's personal and business dealings had been—were business funds used to purchase personal items or trips? You and your accountant need to analyze returns to get an accurate financial net worth for the business.

- **Financial statements for the past five years:** Compare these with the seller's tax returns to determine the true earning power of the business. What is the profit record? Is profit increasing or decreasing? What are the true reasons for the increase or the decrease?

- **Sales records:** Yes, sales revenues are on the financial statements, but you need to evaluate sales by month for the past 48 months. Analyze by product line and by other factors such as cash sales versus credit. This will give you a picture of the seasonality of the business and trend lines. Do further analysis on the top 10 (or whatever break number makes sense) customers. It's fine if the seller does not want to identify them by name—a code is fine since you are more interested in trends.

- **Contracts and legal documents:** This would include all leases, purchase agreements with suppliers, sales contracts with customers, union contracts, and employment contracts. If the business involves intellectual property, such as patents, have those documents analyzed by a specialist. Real estate leases are especially sensitive since location can be a huge competitive advantage for your small business. What are the terms and length of the lease? Is it transferable? Does the landlord have the right of first refusal (i.e., does the landlord have to approve you?)? Can the lease be renewed?

- **List of liabilities:** You are looking for liens by creditors against any assets. There may be claims such as employee benefits or out-of-court settlements still being paid off that do not show up on financial statements that a savvy accountant can find.

- **List of accounts receivable:** While A/R are on the balance sheet, you need to see an aging schedule breaking them down by 30, 60, and 90+ days. The longer accounts are outstanding, the less value they have.

- **List of accounts payable:** You need to see a schedule just like accounts receivable because of the impact on cash flow.

- **Sales taxes:** When buying the assets of a business, you can avoid responsibility for the seller's debts and liabilities—except *sales taxes*. If the seller has been underreporting (or not paying) sales taxes, the state can (and will) come after you for the entire amount owed. You can sue the seller and get a settlement, but if that person has skipped the country, you are stuck. Do not pay a cent for a business until you have a *clearance certificate* from the state tax authority (ask your lawyer).

- **Furniture, fixtures, and equipment:** FF&E is a standard comparison for what you are physically buying. As with inventory, the valuation, condition, age, and whether equipment is purchased or leased have an impact on value.

- **Marketing:** How has the seller communicated with customers? Get copies of all advertising and sales literature. This will give you insight into the image of the business and how customers perceive it.

- **Suppliers:** Are there dependable sources of supply for all the inventory, supplies, or materials the company needs? Evaluate current price lists and discount schedules.

- **Organizational chart of current employees:** Since employees are a valuable asset, you need to understand how they work together. You need to be especially careful to see if key people are willing to remain. Are any salaries inflated, or does the seller have a relative on the payroll who does not work for the business?

- **Industry and market region trends:** What about present and future competition? Are new competitors or substitute materials or methods visible on the horizon? What is the condition of the area around the business? Are traffic routes or parking regulations likely to change?

- **Key ties:** Does the present owner have family, religious, social, or political connections that have been important to the success of the business?

- **Seller's plans:** Why does the present owner want to sell? Where will the owner go? What is he or she going to do? What do people (customers, suppliers, local citizens) think of the present owner and of the business?

- **Buy or build:** How does this business, in its present condition, compare with one you could start and develop yourself in a reasonable amount of time?[5]

Due Diligence

For the buyout entrepreneur, preparation is the key to a successful business purchase. You need to analyze your own skills, find good advisers, write a business plan, and, most important, do due diligence. Due diligence means investigating financial, organization, and asset information (including physical and intellectual property) relating to the business for sale. Think of due diligence as doing your homework. Many prospective buyers mistakenly view due diligence as a financial review, but in fact it goes far beyond the numbers. This step comprises a complete investigation and review of a business that begins the moment you become interested in a business.

Due diligence begins by addressing the overall financial health of the company. What trends have occurred with revenues, expenses, and profit margins? Have they grown, stagnated, or declined? Will the products become obsolete in the foreseeable future? If a small business does not have audited financial statements signed by an accountant (and many don't), then insist on seeing the owner's tax returns (because it's more difficult to lie about those documents). Beyond inspecting the owner's financial documents, you should visit the local county courthouse to check for any existing or pending litigation or liens filed against the business or its owners. The Better Business Bureau can tell you about past or current complaints.

> "You need to analyze your own skills, find good advisers, write a business plan, and, most important, do due diligence"

▲ Due diligence represents the 'homework' a buyer does before purchasing a business.

Although the financial scandals of the past few years have centered on large corporations, they have created a heightened level of skepticism about mergers and acquisitions of all sizes of businesses—and increased the emphasis placed on due diligence.[6] The Sarbanes-Oxley Act increases the extent to which executives are held responsible for the accuracy of their company's financial statements. Because business buyers may be liable for any financial-reporting discrepancies found after the business purchase, they have a strong incentive to be thoroughly knowledgeable about the firm's accounting practices.[7]

Since buying a business is risky no matter how much due diligence is performed, a new type of insurance has recently been developed to shift some risk to a third party. This insurance, consisting of *representations and warranties policies*, covers financial losses suffered if a seller makes false claims in the representations and warranties section of a sale contract.[8]

General Considerations

If you aspire to try entrepreneurship by buying an existing business, don't rush into a deal. Talk with the firm's banker and verify account balances with its major customers and creditors. Be sure you get any verbal understandings in writing from the seller.

> "Be sure you get any verbal understandings in writing from the seller."

Put the earnest money in escrow with a reputable third party. Before an agreement to purchase is signed, have all papers checked by your accountant and attorney.

If the business you are buying involves inventory, you need to be familiar with the *bulk-sales provisions* of the Uniform Commercial Code. Although the law varies from state to state, it generally requires a seller to provide a list of all business creditors and amounts due to each buyer. You, as the buyer, must then notify each creditor that the business is changing hands. This step protects you from claims against the merchandise previously purchased.

Why Is the Business Being Sold?

When the owner of a business decides to sell it, the reasons he gives to prospective buyers may be somewhat different from those known to the business community, and both of these explanations may be somewhat different from the actual facts. There are at least as many factors that could contribute to the sale of a business as there are reasons for business liquidations. Be careful. Business owners who are aware of future problems (such as a lost contract for a strong line of merchandise or a new law that will affect the business unfavorably) may not tell you everything they know. For a prospective buyer, a discussion with the firm's customers and suppliers is recommended. Check with city planners about proposed changes in streets or routing of transportation lines that might have a serious effect on the business in the near future.

Although anyone can be misled or defrauded, a savvy business buyer with good business sense will rely on his or her ability to analyze the market, judge the competitive situation, and estimate the profits that could be made from the business, rather than relying on the present owner's reasons for selling. These "reasons" are often too difficult to verify.

One point to consider as you search for a business is the list of alternatives in which you could invest your money, such as the stock market, money market funds, or even a savings account. By viewing the purchase of a business as an investment, you can compare alternatives on the same terms.

Financial Condition

A study of the financial statements of the business will reveal how consistently the business has rewarded its previous owner's efforts. As a prospective purchaser, you must decide if the income reported thus far would be satisfactory to you and your family. If it is not, could it be increased? You will want to compare the firm's operating ratios with industry averages to identify where costs could be reduced or more money is needed.

The seller's books alone should not be taken as proof of stated sales or profits. You should also inspect bank deposits for at least five years or for as long as the present owner has operated the business.

> "A study of the financial statements of the business will reveal how consistently the business has rewarded its previous owner's efforts."

When analyzing the financial statements of the business, don't rely strictly on the most recent year of operation. Profits can be artificially pumped up and expenses cut temporarily for almost every business. Check whether the business employs the same number of people as in previous years; most businesses can operate shorthanded for a while to cut labor expenses. Maintenance on equipment, vehicles, or the building can be cut to increase short-term profit figures. Profits that appear on the books may also be overstated by insufficient write-offs of bad debts, inventory shortages and obsolescence, and underdepreciation of the firm's fixed assets.

Ask to see the owner's tax returns. This request shouldn't create a problem if everything is legitimate. Compare bills and receipts with sales tax receipts. Reconcile past purchases with the sales and markup claimed. Make certain that all back taxes have been paid. Make sure that interest payments and other current obligations are not in arrears.

Realize the financial information you need in order to analyze the overall condition of the business is sensitive information to the seller, especially if the two of you don't know each other. You can decrease the seller's suspicions about your using this information to aid a competing business or for some other improper use by writing a *letter of confidentiality*.

Independent Audit. Before any serious discussion of purchasing a business takes place, an *independent audit* should be conducted. This exercise will identify the condition of the financial statements. You will want to know whether the business's accounting practices are legitimate and whether its valuation of inventory, equipment, and real estate is realistic.

Even audited statements need some subjective interpretation, however. For example, owners may underreport their income for tax reasons. A family member may be on the payroll and paid a salary although unneeded by the business. Business owners who use a company car or a credit card for nonbusiness purposes also misrepresent their business expenses.

Profit Trend. The financial records of the business can tell you whether sales volume is increasing or decreasing. If it is going up, which departments or product lines account for the increased volume? Did the increased volume lead to increased profitability? In other words, what is the *profit trend*! Many businesses have failed by concentrating on selling a high volume of goods at such low margins that making net profits proved impossible.

If the sales volume is decreasing, is it due to the business's failure to keep up with competition or its inability to adjust to changing times? Or is the decline simply due to a lack of effective marketing?

Interpret net profit of the business you are considering in terms of the amount of capital investment you will have to make in the business as well as sales volume. In other words, a $5,000 annual net profit from a business that requires a $10,000 investment and sales of $20,000 is much more attractive than a business that generates the same profit but requires a $100,000 investment and sales of $200,000.[9]

Expense Ratios. Industry averages comparing expenses to sales exist for every size and type of business. Industrywide *expense ratios* are calculated by most trade associations, many commercial banks, accounting firms, university bureaus of business research, and firms like Dun & Bradstreet and Robert Morris Associates, now Risk Management Association (RMA).

For example, RMA publishes industry averages for 392 specific types of businesses in the manufacturing, wholesale, retail, and service sectors in its *Annual Statement Studies: Financial Ratio Benchmarks*. Comparisons are made in terms of percentages of assets, liabilities, and income data. RMA also provides industry averages of 16 common financial ratios, such as current ratio, quick ratio, sales/working capital, and sales/receivables. (These and other financial ratios are explained further in Chapter 8.)

Imagine you are interested in buying a health club. The location is good, the advertising has caught your attention for several months, and the club boasts state-of-the-art equipment. You are very excited about the possibilities and are now looking over the financial statements. You divide the total current assets by the total current liabilities to calculate the club's *current ratio*, which shows the ability of a business to meet its current obligations. Let's suppose you get a current ratio of 0.5 for this business.

Now you want to get an idea of management performance, which is shown by the *operating ratio*, so you divide the profit before taxes by total assets and multiply by 100 (to convert to a percentage). This computation gives you 4.8 percent. You ask yourself, "Are a current ratio of 0.5 and an operating ratio of 4.8 percent good or bad for a health club?" They could be either. You need something to compare them with to tell you whether they are in line. You go to the library at a nearby university to compare your figures with RMA industry averages. You look in the RMA reports under "Service—Physical Fitness Facilities," where you find the median current ratio listed at 0.9 and the median percentage profit before taxes divided by total assets at 7.5 percent. Your figures are well below the industry averages, so you decide to dig deeper to find out why such large deviations exist between the business you are interested in buying and the average for other similar-sized businesses in the health club industry.

Expense ratios are standards or guides for comparison. Their effective use depends on your ability to identify existing problems and to change conditions that have caused any ratios to be appreciably lower than the standard.

Other Measures of Financial Health. Profit ratios are excellent indicators of a business's worth, but you should also examine other aspects of its financial health. A complete financial health examination consists of the calculation and interpretation of a variety of other financial ratios in addition to those relating to profit. Of particular interest to you and your accountant will be the following factors:

1. The working capital and the cash flow of the business (is there enough of both to adequately keep the business going?)

2. The relationship between the firm's fixed assets and the owner's tangible net worth

3. The firm's debt load, or leverage

Another key factor in business valuation is what other companies in your industry have sold for. Each year, *Inc.* magazine, in partnership with Business Valuation Resources of Portland, Oregon, publishes an issue that contains a comprehensive business valuation guide with graphics and tables that illustrate which types of companies are selling for a premium or below their annual revenue. For example, companies in the life sciences, energy, financial services, and technology sectors boast high sale prices and robust sale multiples.[10]

SMALL BUSINESS FLIP

Which is easier—building an entire car or changing a flat tire? OK, so not a tough quiz question, but what does it have to do with small business? Think about starting a business from scratch versus fixing one with some problems.

You've seen TV shows about flipping houses (buying fixer-uppers, fixing them, then selling them for profit) and maybe flipping used cars. Much more overlooked, but the same concept is flipping existing businesses. If you can find a business with problems that you have the skills to solve—it could have flip potential. Not everyone has the skills to make a successful flip, but those who do apparently like it. According to a report on bizbuysell.com, 58 percent of all business sellers have owned and sold multiple businesses previously.

Buying a business to flip is different from buying one for long-term ownership. Some characteristics you should consider as you evaluate candidate businesses are

- **Industry:** Some types of businesses are always hotter than others—health care, fitness, data storage and security, and travel are currently still active.
- **Value:** Every business owner tries to buy low, sell high, but that is the mantra of business flipping.

- **Cash Flow:** As opposed to long-term business building in which asset value is significant, for a flip you are looking for a company with slow current cash flow that you could crank up quickly.
- **Low Barriers:** There is a time value of money in business flipping. If the business requires specialized skills or long cash-to-cash cycles, then the barriers may be too high for you to acquire or fix in order to flip within a year or two. So, unless you have the specific credentials this rules out things like an architecture firm or law firm.
- **Growth Potential:** This is a biggie for flipping. Can your changes turn this business around in a short time? Is it a business that can net you $10,000 a month or only $3,000? If it is running at 25 percent of capacity, how quickly can you get it to 80 percent?
- **Make Sure It's a Great Deal (for You):** You make money on the buy, not the sell. If you fall in love—fall for the deal, not the business.

Sources: Bob House, "Flipping a Small Business," *Inc.*, July 15, 2016, www.inc.com; Mike Kalis, "Starting a Business Is Hard So Try Flipping One Instead," *Entrepreneur*, October 1, 2015, www.entrepreneur.com/article/251245; Brad Sugars, "A Fix-and-Flip Business-Buying Checklist," *Entrepreneur*, December 6, 2012, www.entrepreneur.com/article/225149.

Concept Check Questions

1. When buying an established business, what questions should you ask about it? From whom might you seek information about the business?

2. What factors warrant special attention in appraising a firm's (a) inventory, (b) equipment, and (c) accounts receivable?

3. What should a prospective buyer know about the seller's inventory sources and other resource contacts? How is this information obtained?

4. You are analyzing the financial records of a business you have been thinking about buying. You discover that although the firm has excellent current and quick-asset ratios by industry standards (meaning its current assets are higher than its current liabilities), its cash is low, and it hasn't paid its bills on time. What might have caused this problem? Would it influence your decision to buy the business?

Concept Module 6.4: What Are You Buying?

- **LO 6.4: Differentiate between tangible and intangible assets, and assess the value of each.**

When buying an existing business, you need to realize the value of that business comes from what the business owns (its assets and what it earns), its cash flow, and the factors that make the business unique, such as the risk involved (Figure 6.1).

What Should You Pay?

The price you offer for a business should begin with adding the value of tangible and intangible assets to the profit potential of the business.

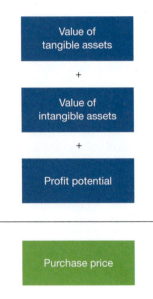

Tangible Assets

The **tangible assets** of a business, such as inventory, equipment, and buildings (Figure 6.2), are generally easier to place a fair market value on than intangible assets, such as trade names, customer lists, and goodwill. If the firm is selling its accounts receivable, you should determine how many of these accounts are collectible and discount them accordingly. Receivables that are 120 days or older are not worth as much as those less than 30 days old, because the odds are greater that you will not collect them. This process is called *aging accounts receivable*. Of the other tangible assets of a business that are up for sale, inventories and equipment should be examined the most closely, because they are most likely to be outdated and therefore worth less than what the seller is asking.

Inventory. Inventory needs to be timely, fresh, and well balanced. One indication the business has been well managed is an inventory of goods people want; that are provided in the proper sizes, designs, and colors; and are priced to fit local buying power and purchasing habits.

Your biggest concern about inventory should be that you aren't buying *dead stock* (merchandise that has no, or very little, value) that the seller has listed as being worth its original value. The

tangible assets
Assets owned by a business that can be seen and examined.

▼ FIGURE 6.2

Types of Tangible Assets

loss in value of dead stock should be incurred by the original buyer, and you must ensure the loss is not passed on to you as part of the sale.

Equipment. It is important that a business be equipped with current, usable machines and equipment. *Book value* (discussed under "What Are the Tangible Assets Worth?" later in this chapter) of electronic office equipment, especially computers, becomes outdated quickly. A cash register designed for the bookkeeping requirements of a generation ago, for example, will not record the information now required for tax reporting or scan UPC codes for efficient inventory control.

Often the usefulness of the firm's equipment was outlived long ago and its value depreciated. The owner may have delayed so long in replacing equipment it has no trade-in value, and without this discount the owner finds the price of new equipment to be exorbitant. This reason alone could lead to his or her decision to sell the business. Anything the owner makes on the fixtures and equipment is new, clear profit, an extra bonus on his or her period of operation.

Intangible Assets

Businesses are also made up of **intangible assets** that may have real value to the purchaser. Among these are goodwill; accounts receivable; favorable leases and other advantageous contracts; and patents, copyrights, and trademarks.

Goodwill. Goodwill is an intangible asset that enables a business to earn a higher return than a comparable business with the same tangible assets might generate. Few businesses that are for sale have much goodwill value.

We all know businesses in existence for years that have not established enough goodwill for the average customer to see the business as being "special." If strong competition existed, such companies would have been driven out of business long ago. From a consumer-preference standpoint, they are at the bottom of the scale. This public attitude cannot be changed quickly. A good name can be ruined in far less time than it takes to improve a bad one.

A successful business has goodwill as an asset. Taking over a popular business brings with it public acceptance that has been built up over a period of many years, which is naturally valuable to the new owner. (Goodwill is discussed further later on in this chapter.)

> "A good name can be ruined in far less time than it takes to improve a bad one."

Accounts Receivable. Not all accounts receivable are created equal. Those that have been owed the longest are worth less because they are the least likely to be collected. In other words, the longer someone takes to pay his or her account, the more likely it is this person will never pay the debt. Therefore, in valuing a business for sale, you need to reduce the cash value of long overdue accounts so as to reflect the odds that they will not be paid.

Determining how much to reduce the value of old accounts should be based on the debtor company's past payment trends. In the hypothetical example of a company we'll call Fabio's Floral Wholesalers, accounts receivable 30 days and younger have a 100 percent likelihood of being paid. Accounts 31 to 60 days old have historically had a 70 percent probability of being paid, those 61 to 90 days old have had a 50 percent probability of being paid, and those older than 90 days have had a 25 percent probability of being paid (Table 6.2). These percentages were determined by looking at the company's accounts receivable history—a fair and logical request to make of the business owner.

You can see there's a significant difference in the aged value and the book value of the accounts receivable: $52,500! When you're buying an existing business, play it smart and be sure to value accounts receivable accurately.

Leases and Other Contracts. A lease on a favorable location is a valuable business asset. If the selling firm possesses a lease on its building, or if it has any unfulfilled sales contracts, you should

intangible assets
Assets that have value to a business but are not visible.

goodwill
The intangible asset that allows businesses to earn a higher return than a comparable business with the same tangible assets might generate.

Accounts Receivable History

Accounts Receivable	Probability Percentage	Book Value	Aged Value
30 days and younger	100%	$75,000	$75,000
31 to 60 days	70%	$50,000	$35,000
61 to 90 days	50%	$30,000	$15,000
Over 90 days	25%	$30,000	$7,500
Total Value		$185,000	$132,500

determine whether the lease and other contracts are transferable to you or whether they must be renegotiated.

Patents, Copyrights, and Trademarks. *Intellectual property*—which includes patents, copyrights, and trademarks—can also be a valuable intangible asset. *Patent rights* give protection to your machine, your process, or a combination of the two against unauthorized use or infringement for only a limited period of time, after which they are open to use by others. Thus it is important for the prospective buyer of an existing business to determine precisely when the firm's patent rights expire and to value these rights based on the time remaining.

Copyrights offer the best protection for books, periodicals, materials prepared for oral presentation, advertising copy, pictorial illustrations, commercial prints or labels, and similar intellectual property. Unlike patent rights, copyrights are renewable.

Registered *trademarks* protect you against unauthorized use or infringement of a symbol, such as the Mercedes-Benz star or McDonald's arches, used in marketing goods. The function of trademarks is to identify specific products and to create and maintain a demand for those products. Because trademark protection lasts as long as the trademark is in continuous use, you should consider its value when purchasing a business that owns a trademark.

Personnel

When purchasing a business, you should regard the people working there as being equally important as profits and production. Retention of certain key people will keep a successful business going. New employees rarely come in as properly trained and steady workers. To help you estimate expenses related to finding, hiring, and training new employees, you will want to know if there are enough qualified people presently employed. Will any of these people depart with the previous owner? Are any key individuals unwilling or unable to continue working for you? The loss of a key person or two in a small business can have a serious impact on future earnings.

The Seller's Personal Plans

As a prospective purchaser of an existing business, you should not feel that all sellers of businesses have questionable ethical and moral principles. Nevertheless, you should remember that *Caveat emptor*—"Let the buyer beware"—has been a reliable maxim for years. There are laws against fraud and misrepresentation, but intent to defraud is usually very difficult to prove in court.

You can reduce your risk by writing protective clauses into contracts of sale, such as a **noncompete clause**, in which the seller promises not to enter into the same kind of business as a competitor within a specified geographic area for a reasonable number of years. If the seller resists agreeing to such a clause, it may be a signal he or she intends to enter into a similar business in the future.

noncompete clause
A provision often included in a contract to purchase a business that restricts the seller from entering the same type of business within a specified area for a certain amount of time.

For a noncompete clause to be legally enforced, it must be reasonable. For example, setting a 25-mile noncompete zone when selling a New York City business would take in a market of about 20 million people—probably an unreasonable restraint that might prevent the seller from earning a living in the future.

An example of a noncompete clause would read as follows:

> Seller shall not establish, engage in, or become interested in, directly or indirectly, as an employee, owner, partner, agent, shareholder, or otherwise, within a radius of 10 miles from the city of _____, any business, trade, or occupation similar to the business covered by this sales agreement for a period of three years. At the closing the seller agrees to sign an agreement on this subject in the form set forth in Exhibit _____.[11]

Concept Check Questions

1. Does every business for sale have an intangible asset of goodwill? Explain.

2. Which type of asset would be more difficult to value—tangible or intangible? Why?

Concept Module 6.5: How Much Should You Pay?

- LO 6.5: Calculate the price to pay for a business.

Even if you don't plan to buy an existing business, the methods of evaluating one are useful to know so you can appraise the success of a firm. But if you are planning to buy a business, certain additional factors come into play. When you make a substantial financial investment in a business, you should expect to receive personal satisfaction as well as an adequate living. A business bought at the wrong price, at the wrong time, or in the wrong place can cost you and your family more than the dollars invested and lost. After you have thoroughly investigated the business, weighed the information collected, and decided the business will satisfy your expectations, a price must be agreed on.

Small Business Valuation

Small business valuation is a tricky subject—a "subjective science."[12] The science part is what you learn in earning finance degrees or business valuation credentials. The subjective part considers every buyer's and seller's circumstances as being different and that multiple people can see the same financial documents and interpret them differently. If you are selling, you don't want to set the asking price so high that you turn off interest. Nor do you want to leave money on the table.

The intersection of formal scientific parts and subjective applied parts of valuation gets a little confusing. For example, the term *fair market value* is widely accepted by certified public accountants, certified valuation analysts, and the IRS. The definition of fair market value is

> the price, expressed in terms of cash equivalents, at which property would change hands between a hypothetical willing and able buyer and a hypothetical willing and able seller, acting at arms length in an open and unrestricted market, when neither is under compulsion to buy or sell and when both have reasonable knowledge of the relevant facts.[13]

Sounds reasonable. But, this stiff definition does not fit *you*. You are not hypothetical, you have real, specific goals you want to accomplish. You do have compulsions—in the real marketplace you have to move quickly and decisively because of competitors. I'll bet you even have specific knowledge not known by everyone that will give you a competitive advantage.

Determining the purchase price for a business involves analyzing several important factors: (1) valuation of the firm's tangible net assets; (2) valuation of the firm's intangible assets, especially any goodwill that has been built up; (3) expected future earnings; (4) market demand for the particular type of business; and (5) general condition of the business (including location, industry, company size, completeness and accuracy of its records, employee esprit de corps, and physical condition of facilities).[14]

There are key numbers to value your company. In this example we'll say the company you are trying to sell has $4 million in annual revenue and $400,000 net income. For simplicity we'll say EBITDA (earnings before interest, taxes, depreciation, and amortization) is also $400,000. Historically, you have increased revenue about 10 percent each year, and EBITDA runs about 10 percent of your revenue. Buyers are especially interested in

1. **Multiple of revenue.** Buyers consider what the future stream of cash flows from your company will be worth. A buyer who thinks your business is worth five times EBITDA will value it at $2 million. The common term for this value would be "5x."

2. **Growth in revenue.** Even though your business has grown at 10 percent, buyers will likely make more conservative projections. In this example, if we assume a 5 percent compounded growth rate your $4 million annual revenue will grow to $5.2 million over the next five years.

3. **Amount of leverage.** Because your business generates nice positive cash flow and would be able to service new debt, a buyer can exercise more leverage rather than use more of his or her own cash. In this case, we can assume an investor can finance half of the purchase price using $1 million in cash for a $2 million business.

Other factors affecting financial buyers include tax implications for both buyer and seller, and cost of interest paid on debt.[15]

Approaches to Small Business Valuation

One of the reasons business valuation is such a complicated issue is that there are many acceptable valuation methods. Rather than using a "one-size-fits-all" valuation approach, buyers and sellers have to pick one (or more) to fit the circumstances of the sale.

Asset-based business valuation is a straightforward method in which the value of the business is determined by the total value of the company's tangible and intangible assets minus its debts. For example, a landscaping business has assets like mowers, trimmers, tractors, trailers, trucks, and so on, and these have a value that could be totaled. This valuation method typically generates the lowest value for a business because it ignores other factors that can influence the price—like revenue. So it's commonly used for liquidating closed businesses, but not so much for thriving ones.

Price multiples business valuation is the quickest way to get a ballpark price for a small business market value. Multiples can be made on revenue or free cash flow. Free cash flow is calculated by subtracting the seller's income and benefits from EBITDA. Once you have selected the appropriate number you apply the appropriate multiplier. The trick is finding the correct multiple based on industry or business type. Analysis from bizbuysell.com shows the average U.S. sales price for sold businesses is 0.6 times revenue and 2.4 times cash flow.[16] The biggest upside of using multiples is the ability for the potential buyer to translate the purchase into earnings that can be converted into an informed return on investment (ROI). For small businesses, you have to use some sanity check as revenue multiples can get a little wild. A fast-growing small business can relatively easily go from $300k to $600k in revenue, but that makes a huge difference in the multiple.[17]

asset-based business valuation
A method of determining the value of a business based on the worth of its assets.

price multiples business valuation
A method of determining the value of a business based on applying specific appropriate multiples to revenue or free cash flow.

Discounted cash flow is often considered the preferred tool with which to value businesses. What sets this approach apart from the other approaches is that it is based on future operating results rather than on historical operating results. As a result, companies can be valued based on their future cash flows, which may be somewhat different than the historical results, especially if the buyer expects to operate some aspects of the business differently. Discounted cash-flow analysis consists of projecting future cash flows (generally for five years) before debts are subtracted and after taxes are paid. A *discount rate* (expressed as a percentage that represents the risk associated with the investment) is then derived and applied to the future cash flows and *terminal value* (a current value for a company's long-term future cash flows). This detailed analysis depends on accurate financial projections and specific discount-rate assumptions. For the purpose of this explanation, don't get as hung up on specific calculations as understanding the concept: (1) how much profit the business is expected to make in the future, and (2) how reliable those estimates are.[18]

Multiple method business valuation is based on a formula that applies a weighting factor to the owner-benefit figure of the previous year(s) in order to arrive at a possible purchase price. The *owner benefit* is a combination of several factors:

Pretax Profit + Owner's Salary + Additional Owner Perks + Interest + Depreciation.

Most small businesses will sell for a one- to three-times multiple of this figure. Granted, this is a wide range, so how do you determine which multiple to apply? Use a multiple of 1 for those businesses where the seller is "the business"—such as consulting businesses, professional practices, and one-person businesses. Multiples of 3 are more appropriate for businesses that have been in existence for several years, have demonstrated sustainable growth, boast a solid base of clients, own assets that will not have to be replaced in the immediate future, and are involved in growth industries, among other things.

Comparables approach is a technique to look at the value of comparable companies that have recently sold. By identifying and evaluating recent examples of businesses that have sold in your industry and geographic location, you can develop a good sense of a likely sales price for your business in question.

Tina Aldatz, who sold her Foot Petals shoe-accessory company for $14 million says "Entrepreneurs have a tendency to place value in the potential. But this doesn't work for bankers and bean counters who only want cold, hard facts and figures—and you have to be OK with that. Otherwise, it's very difficult to become comfortable with any number."[19]

Even the best valuation tools for placing a value on a business for sale can only deliver two numbers—an asking price and an offering price. What's in between? Negotiation . . . finding the amount that will make both parties get to "I accept." Some tips for negotiation include the following:[20]

- Stay rationally focused on the issue being negotiated. Don't try to sidestep issues to avoid telling the truth. Norm Brodsky advises, "The more forthright you are with the other party, the more likely you are to arrive at a satisfactory outcome."[21]

- Exhaustive preparation is more important than aggressive argument. The more knowledge you have of a situation, the better you will be able to negotiate. The more you are able to demonstrate you know what you are talking about and are reasonable, the more you will be able to set discussion parameters.

- Think through your alternatives. The more options you feel you have, the better a negotiating position you'll be in.

- Spend less time talking and more time listening and asking good questions. Sometimes silence is your best response.

discounted cash flow
Valuation method based on future cash flows the business is projected to make.

multiple method business valuation
A formula that applies a weighting factor based on the benefit the selling business owner has generated.

comparables approach
A valuation technique to look at the value of comparable companies that have recently sold.

- Embrace your fear. Bob Woolf, sports and entertainment attorney, stated that "95 percent of the folks you'll ever negotiate with feel just as nervous and, yes, as *scared* as you do."[22]

- Let the other side make the first offer. If you're underestimating yourself, you might make a needlessly weak opening move.

- Have confidence. You probably underestimate your experience. We all negotiate every day—the skills you develop back-and-forth with spouses, colleagues, children, professors, and fellow airplane passengers all improve your business negotiation skills.

The magic number you and the seller both agree upon may not exist for every deal. Be prepared to walk away from *every* deal, or you're not really negotiating.

What Are the Tangible Assets Worth?

The worth of tangible assets is what the balance-sheet method of valuation seeks to establish. Their value is determined based on one of three factors:

- *Book value.* What the asset originally cost or what it is worth from an accounting viewpoint; the amount shown on the books as representing the asset's value as a part of the firm's worth.

- *Replacement value.* What it would cost to buy the same materials, merchandise, or machinery today; relative availability and desirability of new items must be considered.

- *Liquidation value.* How much the seller could get for this business, or any part of it, if it were placed on the open market.

There are significant differences in these three approaches to determining value. Book value may not hold up in the marketplace. Buildings and equipment may not be correctly depreciated, whereas land may have appreciated. Replacement value may not be a reliable figure because of opportunities to buy used equipment. It is significant as a measure of value only in comparison to what it would cost to start your own business. Liquidation value is the most realistic approach in determining the value of tangible assets to the buyer of a business. It may represent the lowest figure that the seller would be willing to accept.

You have to determine the value of the following physical assets before serious bargaining can begin:

- Cost of the inventory adjusted for slow-moving or dead stock
- Cost of the equipment less depreciation
- Supplies
- Accounts receivable less bad debts
- Market value of the building

Don't make an offer for a business based on the seller's asking price. You may feel as if you got a real bargain if you talk the seller down to half of what he or she is asking—but half might still be twice as much as the business is worth.[23]

What Are the Intangible Assets Worth?

An established business may be worth more than the sum of its physical assets, and its owner may be unwilling to sell for liquidation value alone. The value of a business's intangible assets is difficult to determine. Intangible assets are the product of a firm's past earnings, and they are the basis on which its earnings are projected.

Goodwill is the term used to describe the difference between the purchase price of a company and the net value of the tangible assets. Goodwill is the most difficult asset to value at a price the seller will think is fair. It includes intangible but very real assets with real value to the prospective purchaser. Goodwill can be regarded as (1) compensation to the owner for his or her losses on beginner's mistakes you might have made if you had started from scratch and (2) payment for the privilege of carrying on an established and profitable business.[24] When justified, goodwill should be small enough to be made up from profits within a reasonably short period.

What is goodwill worth? To determine a company's goodwill, you can start by using the income-statement method of valuation. To do so, you should capitalize your projected future earnings at an assumed rate of interest that would be in excess of the "normal" return (earnings adjusted to remove any unusual occurrences like a lawsuit settlement or a one-time gain from the sale of real estate) in that type and size of business. The *capitalization rate* is a figure assigned to show the risk and expected growth rate associated with future earnings.

For example, suppose the liquidation value of the firm's tangible net assets is $224,000 and the normal before-tax rate of return on the owner's investment in this business is 15 percent, or $33,600 per year. We will assume the actual profit during the past few years has averaged $83,600, exclusive of the present owner's salary (which may have been overstated or understated).

From the profit, we will deduct a reasonable salary for the owner or manager—what he or she might earn by managing this type of business for someone else. If we assume a going-rate annual salary of $40,000, then the excess profit to be capitalized (that is, the amount of profit based on goodwill) is $10,000 ($83,600 minus $40,000 salary minus a normal profit of $33,600).

The rate of capitalization is negotiated by the buyer and the seller of the business. It should be appropriate to the risk taken. The more certain you are of the estimated profits, the more you will pay for goodwill. The less certain you are (the higher you perceive your risk to be), the less you will pay.

If you assume a 25 percent rate of return on estimated earnings coming from goodwill, then the value of the intangible assets is $10,000/0.25, or $40,000. Usually this relationship is expressed as a ratio or multiplier of 4, "four times (excess) earnings." You would expect to recover the amount invested in goodwill in no more than four years. When you put these two figures together, you come up with an offering price of $264,000 for the business—net tangible assets of $224,000 at liquidation value plus goodwill valued at $40,000.

If the average annual net earnings of the business before subtracting the owner's salary is $73,600 or less, then there is no goodwill value. Even though the business may have existed for a long time, the earnings would be less than you could earn through outside investment. In that case, your price would be determined by capitalizing the average annual profit (net earnings minus all expenses and owner's salary) by the normal or expected rate of return on investment in this business. For example,

$$\text{Profit} = \$73,600 - \$40,000 = \$33,600$$

$$\text{Offering Price} = \$33,600/0.15 = \$224,000.$$

Valuing goodwill is a highly subjective process. The value of intangible assets comes down to what you think they are worth and what you are willing to pay. You will need to negotiate with the seller to reach a consensus.

> "Goodwill is the term used to describe the difference between the purchase price of a company and the net value of the tangible assets."

Concept Check Questions

1. Which is more important in appraising a business: profitability or return on investment? Discuss.

2. Discuss the ways in which the tangible assets of a business may be valued. What is the most realistic approach to determining a business's true value? Why?

3. What is goodwill, and how may its value be determined?

4. How can a buyer determine the rate of return to use in evaluating the worth of a business?

Concept Module 6.6: Buying the Business

- **LO 6.6: Discuss factors that are important when finalizing the purchase of a business.**

To complete the purchase of your business, you need to negotiate the terms of the deal and prepare for the closing.

Terms of Sale

After a price for the business has been agreed upon, the terms of sale need to be negotiated. Few buyers are able to raise the funds required to pay cash for a business. A lump-sum payment may be in neither the buyer's nor the seller's best interests for tax reasons, unless the seller intends to reinvest in another business. Paying in installments is often the most practical solution.

By building installment payments into your cash-flow projection, you should be assured that the business can be paid for out of earnings. Installments assure the seller that his investment in the business will be returned on a tax-deferred basis, as opposed to paying all taxes at one time with a lump-sum payment. With an installment sale, the seller has some motivation to help with the buyer's success.

A seller may need to take steps to make the business more affordable. One way to do so is by *thinning the assets*. That is, the seller can adjust the assets to be more manageable for the new owner in one or more of the following ways:

- Separate real estate ownership from business ownership. The new owner leases rather than purchases the building. The buyer has less to borrow, and the seller receives a steady rental income.

- Lease equipment and/or fixtures in the same manner as real estate.

- Sell off excess inventory.

- Factor accounts receivable or carry the old accounts.

> "If you are buying the stock of a business rather than just the assets, you need protection from unknown tax liabilities."

If you are buying the stock of a business rather than just the assets, you need protection from unknown tax liabilities. The best way to accomplish this is to place part of the purchase price (anywhere from 5 percent to 30 percent) in an escrow account. This *holdback money* is earmarked to pay for any corporate liabilities, including taxes owed, that arise after the deal has closed.

Closing the Deal

When you and the seller have reached an agreement on the sale of the business, several conditions must be met to ensure a smooth, legal transaction. Closing can be handled by using either a settlement attorney or an escrow settlement.

CREATING COMPETITIVE ADVANTAGE

SHARK TANK ACQUISITION LAUNCH

Do you watch ABC's *Shark Tank*? Of course you do; if not, start now!

On the show, the sharks hear entrepreneurial pitches and decide which ones to invest in. It is about taking risks and growing businesses. As the adage goes "If you don't take risks, you will always work for someone who does."

Shark Kevin O'Leary often (and callously) tells struggling entrepreneurs they have to take risks. When he was asked about his biggest risk. He answered, "You only need one to work. I've invested in a wide, diverse range of companies and people. I've got over 44 of them now, and every once in a while one hits big." The big risk . . . and big hit for O'Leary was Plated. Back in 2015, Josh Hix and Nick Taranto went on *Shark Tank* asking for $500,000 for 5 percent equity and on-air struck a deal with Mark Cuban. That deal fell apart, but on *Beyond the Tank* O'Leary was impressed with their development and invested. In 2017, Plated was acquired by grocery chain Albertson's for $300 million . . . and a 1,346 percent ROI for O'Leary.

Plated was founded by Hix and Taranto to take advantage of a meal-kit delivery service craze. They box fresh ingredients and step-by-step instructions so anyone can create "amazing" meals at home.

Hix states that "Acquisition was never the goal—I believe that if you start a company with any goal other than solving a real problem and impacting the world, you're stacking the odds against you (and they're already long odds!!)." The pair spent about four years exploring relationships to find the right partner. Meeting with the Albertson's team, it became apparent they had a match. That partnership was the outcome of a wild ride and a long, deliberate process, years in the making—with a stop on TV.

Sources: David Brown, "Shark Tank'ers, Plated, Bite Off Acquisition," *Inc.*, September 29, 2017, www.inc.com; Jonathan Small, "The Biggest Risk 4 Judges on 'Shark Tank' Ever Took," *Entrepreneur*, September 29, 2017, www.entrepreneur.com/slideshow/301063; Catherine Clifford, "Founder of Food Start-up Plated, Which Just Sold for $300 Million: 'Dealing with Rejection Is a Necessity'" CNBC Make It, September 26, 2017, www.cnbc.com/2017/09/25/plated-founder-on-how-to-deal-with-rejection.html.

A *settlement attorney* acts as a neutral party by drawing up the necessary documents and representing both the buyer and the seller. Both parties meet with the settlement attorney at the agreed-upon closing date to sign the papers after all the conditions of the sale have been met, such as financing being secured by the buyer and a search completed to determine whether any liens against the business's assets exist.

In an *escrow settlement,* the buyer deposits the money, and the seller provides the bill of sale and other documents to an escrow agent. You can find an escrow agent at most financial institutions, such as banks and trusts that have escrow departments, or through an escrow company. The escrow agent holds the funds and documents until proof is shown that all conditions of the sale have been satisfied. When these conditions are met, the escrow agent releases the funds and documents to the rightful owners.

Concept Check Question

1. What is meant by "thinning the assets"? Cite examples.

Concept Module 6.7: Taking Over a Family Business

- **LO 6.7: Describe what makes a family business different from other types of businesses.**

A fourth route into small business (besides starting from scratch, buying an existing business, or franchising) is taking over a family business. This alternative offers special opportunities and risks.

What Is Different about Family Businesses?

Family businesses are those in which two or more members of the same family control, are directly involved in, and own a majority of the business. From Berkshire Hathaway and

Wal-Mart to small stores everywhere, family businesses account for about 70 percent of all businesses in the United States and are responsible for nearly 50 percent of the U.S. gross domestic product (GDP).[25] They are obviously an important part of our economy, but what makes them different from nonfamily businesses? Two critical factors are (1) the complex interrelationships of family members interacting with one another and interacting with the business, and (2) the intricate succession planning needed.

Harper Lee reminds us in *To Kill a Mockingbird*, "You can choose your friends, but you can't choose your family." Let's look at four reasons why it may be a good idea to start a family-owned business—and four reasons why it may not:[26]

Advantages:

- Loyalty to each other is highly likely, which creates a significant support system. Employees outside the family may be good workers, but they are looking out for themselves first. Family members are in for the long haul.

- Family members provide greater flexibility to each other in business settings than do nonrelated workers. For example, taking off an extra day to celebrate an anniversary or leaving early for a dance recital are not under the same scrutiny.

- The fact that your business is family owned is a great marketing point. Customers often prefer to frequent a family business more than faceless nonlocal corporations.

- Especially during the early years, operating expenses can be lower. Outside employees aren't as excited about working for free or minimal compensation to get the business off the ground.

Disadvantages:

- Harper Lee has already reminded us that we can't choose family, and there may well be people who are not the best fit. Family members may be lazy, dishonest, unreliable, or just plain unskilled. Firing a family member is not easy and includes a whole new level of awkward at holiday celebrations.

- Within every family lie rivalries and divisions. Patterns of behavior and dispute settlement tactics from youth are not appropriate for solving business problems.

- Among the less obvious of family disadvantages are limited viewpoints and perspectives. Everyone having common business philosophies and getting along would seem to be a good thing—but is it always? Blind spots can be dangerous.

- Family businesses generally lack clear business structure. Families take an "all hands on deck" mentality and believe everyone is of equal importance. This approach can diffuse solid decision-making processes.

We discussed the failure rate of small businesses in Chapter 1, where it was pointed out that most businesses do not survive to see their 20th birthday. Family-owned businesses are much hardier, but still not invincible. For each generation, the odds of a business surviving decline. Thus one way to measure business success, beyond revenues generated, profits earned, or societal impact, would be longevity. Ever wonder what the oldest family business in the United States might be? Perhaps not, but it's an interesting question. Making the list of the top 100 are some household names like number 68, Levi Strauss (founded 1853), and number 88, Anheuser-Busch (founded 1860).

But the hands-down endurance award goes to a business that has lasted through 74 *generations* and was started in 1623! Zildjian Cymbal Company of Norwell, Massachusetts, was founded in Constantinople by Avedis I, who discovered a metal alloy that created superior-sounding, more durable cymbals. The sultan named him "Zildjian," Armenian for "cymbalsmith."

▲ Zildjian Cymbal Company has existed in the same family since 1623.

The Zildjian family arrived in the United States in 1910, moving here to escape persecution of Christian Armenians in their native land. The company was brought here in 1929. It was good timing, as Avedis Zildjian III was able to supply his cymbals to the jazz drummers of the day. Those instruments have remained synonymous with hot drummers throughout the Jazz Age, the big band era, and today's rock and roll. Avedis's son Armand applied new technology to the company's traditional approach by creating a modern factory.

As you might have guessed, not all has gone smoothly over the past 385-plus years. When company leader Avedis died in 1979, his sons Robert and Armand locked horns in a nasty courtroom battle for control over the company (cymbaling rivalry?). Robert left Zildjian and set up a competing cymbal company, Sabian, in Canada. He was legally barred from referencing the family history or name in his business or even using the letter "Z" in his company name.

Today Armand's daughters Craigie (the company's CEO) and Debbie (vice president of human resources) are the first female chiefs in Zildjian's long history.

Complex Interrelationships

When you run a family business, you have three overlapping perspectives on its operation (see Figure 6.3).[27] For example, suppose a family member needs a job. From the family perspective, you would see the business as an opportunity to help one of your own. From the ownership perspective, you might be concerned about the effect of a new hire on profits. From a management perspective, you would be concerned about how this hire would affect nonfamily employees.

▼   FIGURE 6.3

Overlapping Perspectives of a Family Business Owner

The family business owner views the business and what goes on within it from three different overlapping perspectives.

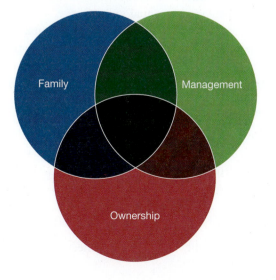

Everyone involved in a family business will have a different perspective, depending on each person's position within the business. The successful leader of this business must maintain all three perspectives simultaneously.

Planning Succession

Many entrepreneurs dream of the time when they will be able to "pass the torch" of their successful business on to their children. Unfortunately, many factors, such as jealousy, lack of interest, or ineptitude, can cause the flame to go out. Less than one third of family businesses survive through the second generation, about 12 percent make it through the third generation and 3 percent operate into the fourth generation or beyond.[28] The major cause of family business failure is lack of a business succession plan; only 44 percent have a written plan. There appear to be four reasons for family inability to create such a document:

1. It is difficult for senior family members to address their own mortality.

2. Many senior family members are worried that the way younger family members run the business will not maintain its success. Only 20 percent are confident of the next generation's commitment to the business.[29]

3. Transfer of control is put off until too late because of seniors' concern for their personal long-term financial security.

4. Seniors (like most small business owners) are too personally tied to the business and lacking in outside interests to be attracted to retirement.[30]

If the potential successor wants to take over the family business, she must gain acceptance and trust within the organization (see Figure 6.4). When a family member enters the business, he is not usually immediately accepted by nonfamily employees. This skepticism increases when that person moves up to a leadership position within the business. The successor must earn credibility by showing that she is capable of running the business. Only after being accepted and earning credibility will the new manager have legitimate power and become successful as the new leader.[31]

Family businesses need to establish good governance practices that separate the family from the business in order to manage internal talent or attract talented outsiders. Governance, even for small family businesses, can mean developing a level of professionalism.

How do you decide the right leaders for a family firm? All talent, and especially family members, must be assessed on competencies, potential, and values.

Competencies most frequently identified include strategic orientation, market insight, results orientation, customer impact, collaboration and influence, organizational development, team leadership, and change leadership. Leaders of family businesses need to understand the ownership dynamics, including that the company is important to multiple generations.[32]

General Family Business Issues

Because family businesses have situations and problems unique to them, they need a set of policies that are not needed in other types of businesses. Such a set of policies can help prevent problems such as animosity from nonfamily employees, which can decrease their motivation and productivity.[33]

- To be hired, family members must meet the same criteria as nonfamily employees.

- In performance reviews, family members must meet the same standards as nonfamily employees.

Business Succession Planning

- Maintain alignment throughout organization
- Be open and communicate plans and goals to all members of organization
- Maintain objectivity
- Ask for feedback from others in the organization
- Involve the board in the planning
- Develop a clear strategy and operations plan
- Begin to foster a healthy climate to the change in ownership

- Communicate vision of portfolio to next generation
- Communicate plan for succession of family members to rest of company

- Skill development of successor
- Talent management of successor
- Mutual development of portfolio plan

- Implement vision of portfolio
- Communicate vision to all family members
- Exert confidence in abilities and communicate aspirations

- Separate family from business
- Assess competencies and values of successors
- Open and clear communication
- Establish clear order to decision-making

Source: Based on Reddal, "Succession Planning Framework." Retrieved from https://www.entrepreneur.com/article/254614

FAMILY FEUD

A family in the Pacific Northwest owns a retail-clothing store. Two brothers work in the business, and their mother is president of the company. Sibling rivalry was a problem while the boys were growing up, and now that they are in the family business together, it is reappearing. In addition to her role as president, the mother often finds herself playing the role of referee and "chief emotional officer" when the young men fight. The continued rivalry between the brothers and the mother's need to intervene between them has interfered with a normally functional business. The family realizes its business system is entangled with its family system, but they are not sure what to do about it.

Questions

1. What should the mother do to help her family (and her business) operate more normally?

2. Would bringing in a nonfamily manager with direct-line control over each brother help or cause more problems? How can they ever decide who will eventually take over control of the business?

- Family members should be supervised by nonfamily employees when possible.

- If family members are younger than age 30, they are only eligible for "temporary" employment (less than one year).

- No family member can stay in an entry-level position permanently.

- All positions will be compensated at fair market value.

- For family members to seek permanent employment, they must have at least five years' experience outside the company. Family members must prove their worth to another employer to be useful here.[34]

- It's important to set clear boundaries within the workplace, such as referring to people by name rather than relationship ("Mary" rather than "Mom") and not discussing family drama at the office.[35]

Want more information about family businesses? Check out www.fambiz.com (more than 300 articles on family business issues and additional links) and www.familybusinessmagazine.com/index.html (*Family Business* magazine online).

Concept Check Question

1. A mother believes that all of her family's children should have equal ownership of the family business regardless of their participation in the business. The father sees the situation completely differently; he believes the children who are actively involved should receive more ownership. How can this dispute be resolved?

CHAPTER REVIEW

SUMMARY ▶▶

LO 6.1 Compare the advantages and disadvantages of buying an existing business.

The advantages of buying an existing business include the fact that it is an already functioning operation, customers are used to doing business with it, and you will break even sooner than if you started from the ground up. The disadvantages include the difficulty of changing the business's image or the way it does business, outdated inventory and equipment, too high a purchase price, poor location, and liabilities for previous contracts.

LO 6.2 Propose ways of locating a suitable business for sale.

Newspaper advertising is one source for finding a business for sale, and word of mouth through friends and family may be another. Bankers, lawyers, accountants, real estate brokers, business brokers, and Small Business Administration representatives can be other good sources.

LO 6.3 Explain how to measure the condition of a business and determine why it might be offered for sale.

Profitability, profit trends, comparison of operating ratios to industry standards, and total asset worth are all measures of the financial health of a business. There are as many reasons for selling a business as there are businesses to sell. As a prospective buyer, you must cut through what is being said to determine the reality of a situation. You must develop an ability to analyze a market and estimate potential profits and worth.

LO 6.4 Differentiate between tangible and intangible assets, and assess the value of each.

Tangible assets are those that can be seen and examined. Real estate, inventory, and equipment are important tangible assets. Intangible assets, though unseen, are no less valuable. Goodwill; leases and contracts; and patents, copyrights, and trademarks are examples.

LO 6.5 Calculate the price to pay for a business.

The offering price to pay for a business is calculated by adding the adjusted value of tangible assets to the value of intangible assets (including goodwill, if appropriate).

LO 6.6 Discuss factors that are important when finalizing the purchase of a business.

Once the price of a business is agreed upon, the terms of sale need to be negotiated—including setting up installment provisions and thinning of the assets. Before the closing date, the buyer puts an agreed-upon amount of money into an escrow account.

LO 6.7 Describe what makes a family business different from other types of businesses.

The two primary differences between family businesses and other businesses are the complex interrelationships among family members and their interaction in the business, and the intricate succession planning needed.

KEY TERMS ▶▶

STUDENT STUDY SITE ▶▶

edge.sagepub.com/hatten7e

$SAGE edge™ Sharpen your skills with SAGE edge!

SAGE edge for Students provides a personalized approach to help you accomplish your coursework goals in an easy-to-use learning environment. You'll find mobile-friendly eFlashcards and quizzes as well as multimedia resources to support and expand on the concepts presented in this chapter.

EXPERIENTIAL LEARNING ACTIVITIES ▶▶

6.1: Advantages/Disadvantages of Buying a Business

LO 6.1: Compare the advantages and disadvantages of buying an existing business.

Read the following scenario and create a table that lists the advantages and disadvantages of buying this established business. When you have completed your assessment, break into groups of 3–5 and discuss your assessment. Make sure to focus on advantages/disadvantages, not just what you would prefer to do in the case.

Karli has just finished her culinary degree and is looking forward to starting her own bakery. Elaborately decorated and wonderfully decadent cakes as well as unique wedding cakes are her specialty. A family friend (Nicole) owns a small bakery, which Nicole has run successfully for over 20 years. The bakery has focused on breads and rolls with seasonal desserts also offered. The bakery has a loyal customer base, which is needed since the bakery is two blocks off the main avenue that goes through town. The kitchen was updated five years ago so all equipment is new and energy efficient. Five loyal employees have worked for the bakery for years, one an established bookkeeper who has developed a wonderful inventory system. Nicole is very excited with the prospect of Karli buying her business.

However, Karli has also found an empty building on Main Street where she could start her business from scratch. She could then design and develop the business entirely the way she wants, which she finds very appealing. The building is empty, so Karli would need to purchase equipment, counters, tables, and so forth. Karli does not know which way to go in starting her own bakery.

After reading through the scenario, answer the following questions.

1. What are the advantages/disadvantages of buying the established business?

2. What would you do if you were Karli?

6.2: Tangible and Intangible Assets

LO 6.4: Differentiate between tangible and intangible assets, and assess the value of each.

LO 6.5: Calculate the price to pay for a business.

Complete the below activity. Be prepared to share with other students and/or the entire class.

For each item listed below, decide if the item is an intangible asset or a tangible asset. Then provide one method to assess the value of the item. Be prepared to justify your valuation method choice.

Item	Intangible/Tangible	Valuation Method
Inventory		
Customer list		
Equipment		
Favorable leases		
Goodwill		
Accounts receivable		
Buildings		
Patents		
Key personnel		

CHAPTER CLOSING CASE ▶▶

A Question of Value

Chris Angelis looked at his watch—he would have enough time. At this point in his career he knew about Washington, D.C., traffic and how to leave enough time so that he was never late. He hoped the guy he was meeting—Charlie Peters—was equally conscientious. Chris was founder and chief executive officer (CEO)

of two companies that dealt in respiratory health, and Charlie was an entrepreneur who had developed a homeopathic product that might be the basis for a lucrative business partnership. Chris was on his way to meet Charlie to structure a deal.

History

Chris Angelis had originally practiced and taught in the field of respiratory care and extracorporeal circulation before joining a major pharmaceutical company in New England in

1985. From 1985 to 1990, Chris held six positions of growing responsibility while he oversaw the successful launch of three new products in the United States, and the development of the global strategy that salvaged the company's failing flagship product.

After a series of professional successes, Chris chose to strike out on his own. He founded his first company, Strategic Implications International (SII), which provided strategic consultancy and marketing support to health care organizations. SII quickly became phenomenally successful through organic growth, mergers, and acquisitions before it was acquired in 1998 by a company that is now a division of Cardinal Health Inc.

In 1992, Chris met physicians Mike Kale and Bill Sager—they had served as consultants to SII while it was producing educational programming for pharmaceutical giant Glaxo Inc. (now GSK). Mike and Bill believed, based on their experience, that they could improve the way doctors are educated about new medicines and treatment, and that this education could be supported by the pharmaceutical industry because it would be beneficial for pharmaceutical products. Such education had to appeal to doctors—it could not merely be marketing—it had to illustrate the way these solutions helped patients, be inclusive of all available products, and be fairly balanced. The idea was to create innovative and relevant educational content using novel yet appropriate formats delivered by and to a network of doctors. Mike and Bill Sager were specialists in allergy and asthma, and they started to implement their vision in that niche.

Mike and Bill had sought Chris out based on his reputation and expertise, and because they "needed a business guy" to run the operation. In late 2003 Chris agreed to join them and to form SMA. Chris would serve as the new company's CEO. SMA was

incorporated in 2004, and used the original concept of education created for physicians by physicians to grow and expand. The organization now encompasses multiple therapeutic specialties and an ever-expanding network of physician advisers spanning the globe. Chris Angelis continues to serve as the CEO of SMA and oversees this continued growth while Mike Kale and Bill Sager maintain their strong link to clinical practice and serve as independent consultants to SMA.

In 2006, Chris formed PharmaSciences in partnership with a Hong Kong–based concern that owned the patent to a promising compound with many possible applications in the pharmaceutical industry worldwide. Chris would serve as CEO. PharmaSciences' main product was a chemical compound that was designed to provide more effective delivery of medicines to mucous membrane surfaces (e.g., nose and mouth). Their product, MuAd™, is a patented muco-adhesive pharmaceutical composition, developed on the basis of a synthetic polymer. Muco-adhesive solutions, in general, establish reversible contact with the mucosal surface, which enhances the effect of drugs dissolved in them. Unlike other bioadhesive drug delivery systems (gels, powders, microparticles, and liposomes) muco-adhesive solutions possess the property of fluidity, which enables them to cover maximal mucosal area when placed on its surface.

MuAd™ offers a means to achieve an optimal adhesiveness to fluidity ratio for whatever drug or substance is being delivered using MuAd™. This is done in production using the patented processing methods of PharmaSciences.

The Companies

SMA

SMA was in the business of knowledge and education. In the highly regulated and highly complex world of pharmaceutical marketing, SMA had a team of in-house experts and key opinion leaders across a variety of medical domains. These were people who understood what clinicians want and need because they were clinicians themselves. It also meant that they knew about the pressures and values of clinicians, and could therefore "speak to them in their own language." This enhanced the message credibility, and as such the impact of any educational programs SMA created.

Products have different marketing needs from prelaunch planning to mature product life-cycle management, and so SMA

positioned itself to possess knowledge appropriate to each stage and for each stakeholder. For example, for newer products SMA had in-house experts and clinical advisers to help with the design of the actual clinical development programs. As a product became viable, more interaction had to happen with regulatory bodies. This was a particularly nuanced issue, and so SMA's clinical advisers also had to be knowledgeable about regulatory strategy. They provided guidance for New Drug Application and Investigational New Drug submissions, and could deliver expert testimony as necessary for the U.S. Food and Drug Administration (FDA) and other regulatory authorities. This was another reason that it was critical that members of the SMA advisory team be made up of highly respected, practicing clinicians.

PharmaSciences

Whereas SMA had marketing expertise, PharmaSciences had a patented product that was proven effective as a medicine delivery vehicle using clinical trials. Their product, MuAd™, had been clinically tested with different respiratory medicines, and studies reinforced the product's effectiveness. It was found to qualify for a Class I designation, which means that it is well tolerated and virtually devoid of any mucosal irritation. The legitimacy of the product was bolstered by the rigorous research behind it. Another important finding was that MuAd™ increased the potency of certain drugs. This finding was important for

drugs where the efficacy could change over time and continual use. By pairing these medicines with MuAd™, patients were effectively able to have longer congestion-free periods using the compound because smaller and less frequent doses would yield a similar clinical effect.

In sum, *in vitro* and *in vivo* studies have shown that MuAd™ was a useful and usable product. But there were two additional advantages of the MuAd™ compound. The company's patented technology includes the methodology and devices required to assess and adjust the optimal muco-adhesive properties. This would allow fine-tuning of drug delivery. In addition, the significant advantage to licensees is that MuAd™ has been developed for existing pharmaceutical compounds. Securing

Nose-Clear

Charlie Peters had inherited a nasal-clearing formula from his grandmother. It was basically a mixture of hot peppers that was minimally irritating but very effective for sinus congestion and headache. It was one of two homeopathic products with similar ingredients targeting the same market.

Nose-Clear had launched in 2005, and had been praised for its effectiveness. By 2007 it had cumulative U.S. sales of $1.3 million, largely due to direct-to-consumer magazine and commercial radio advertising campaigns. But by 2008 sales had

drug approvals based on existing data of older drugs is easier than those of new compounds. In addition, licensees are afforded new patents to drugs with expired or expiring patents, helping them with their life-cycle management strategies.

fallen below $100,000. Advertising and promotion had ceased, and retail presence was minimal. Most sales came from online purchases. Clearly this was a company in need of help.

Nose-Clear was effectively a mom-and-pop shop running on a shoestring budget that contracted all manufacturing and related expertise to third parties. It had tried unsuccessfully to attract partners and/or capital to fund the operation, but so far had been unable to do so.

Deal or No Deal?

The way Chris saw it, investment in Nose-Clear had a lot of potential because of the size of its market. Seventy-two million people use headache and sinus/allergy medications, with an estimated $13 billion market in the United States and $20 billion market worldwide. Right now, Nose-Clear was one of hundreds of branded and generic over-the-counter products for relief of sinus congestion and headache. But the treatment was homeopathic, a medical system based on the belief that the body can cure itself. In some demographics, homeopathies are appealing for minor medicinal treatment. This trait also made it cheaper and easier to manufacture, and free of regulatory entanglements. However, this strength was also a liability.

The first problem had to do with the nature and strength of the claims one could make about Nose-Clear's effectiveness. People are naturally (and legitimately) suspicious of inflated effectiveness claims in homeopathic products because there is no third-party scrutiny or review. The second is that because Nose-Clear was homeopathic, it was not patentable. Nothing that you can make from natural ingredients is patentable. But MuAd™ *was* patented. By combining Nose-Clear with MuAd™ you would have a new, patentable product. The way the law works, if you add something to your patented compound, the entire formulation is now patentable.

So what kind of deal should be structured? There were many options.

The simplest deal would be just to buy Charlie out. Give him $X for the formula and be done with it. It would require some market analysis to figure out what a reasonable valuation of this product could be. At the same time, Chris already had two companies; did he want to run a third? There would need to be a good reason to do that. There was also the question of whether Charlie was

just in it for the money. This was his grandmother's recipe, and so maybe he was attached to the idea of making it into a product himself. Or maybe he wanted to be CEO. In talking to Charlie, he definitely seemed to have ambitions and aspirations.

If Charlie really wanted to be in control, then they could set up his company as a wholly owned subsidiary company. Here again, the parent company (whether SMA or PharmaSciences) would be in a position to extract all the value from this product. Again, there was risk. Both of Chris's companies had reputations to uphold, and Charlie was a bit of an unknown in terms of his management competence. But Chris would really hold all the cards if one of his companies owned Nose-Clear; and maybe Charlie could be groomed. Or maybe Charlie was not looking to be groomed, and would not be okay with being "CEO junior."

Charlie could be given more autonomy if instead of a wholly owned subsidiary, they formed a joint venture. This would almost certainly be more attractive to Charlie as it would make him more of an equal partner. Of course, there was a huge cost to that, for what was Charlie really bringing to the table? Chris had the contacts, the know-how, and the capital resources to make this venture work. With a joint venture, he would almost surely get less of the profits for lack of control of the process. But maybe that risk could be mitigated.

Of course, they could just establish a buyer–supplier relationship. Chris provides access to marketing, branding, clinical tests, and production services, and Charlie pays for it. This could be straightforward, but the upfront work was daunting. How was Charlie going to pay for anything given his meager earnings from this product? They could charge royalties on the back end, but then how would Charlie get his operation up and running?

Analytical Questions

1. Based on the case, what are the identified risks and rewards for Chris in terms of working with Nose-Clear?

2. What are the risks and rewards for Charlie in terms of working with Chris?

3. Below is a list of possible negotiable issues that can be used to structure a deal. Use these to create potential offerings for Charlie under each of the business structures (buyout, wholly owned subsidiary, joint venture, and buyer–supplier).

a. Be sure to articulate an ideal but realistic deal (your goal) and a minimally acceptable deal (your resistance point).
b. Are there any other issues that you could add to expand the pie?
c. Having looked at the different business structures, which one would you advocate and why?
d. Could you develop a hybrid structure for this partnership?

Negotiable issues (although each could potentially break down into sub-issues as well):

- Ownership percentage of any jointly owned organization

- Royalties for sale of product

- Profit sharing on sale of product

- Licensing fee for services (marketing, clinical, and production)

- Pay for service

- Marketing support in terms of advertisement

- Branding support in terms of product

- Clinical tests on efficacy of product

- Production management of product

- Exclusivity in terms of markets and products, as well as subsequent deals

- Managerial control of the various business functions

- Introduction to key opinion leaders.

Discussion

Given your choice of business deal, what information should you be looking for as the deal is executed in order to minimize your risk and maximize your return? Put differently, how will you identify whether your original business deal is optimal once you begin to work with Charlie?

Source: Matthew A. Cronin, "A Question of Value," Sage Knowledge: Cases, January 2, 2018, http://dx.doi.org/10.4135/9781526445568.

## CHAPTER 7

STARTING A NEW BUSINESS

©iStockphoto.com/Cecilie_Arcurs

C hristopher Mitchell and Thomas Dickerson began as online friends, then became real-life friends, and then started a volunteer group together teaching students at Brown University how to program. Finally, they were each exploring projects trying to put the real world into video games. The pair mentally incubated the problem until cofounding Geopipe to automatically create immersive, expansive, virtual, highly detailed 3D models of the real world. Partially inspired by the world-building game Minecraft, the pair created Geopipe to solve problems for game designers, real-world architects, and real estate professionals.

College is a great time to create a start-up business. While still in college you have time and resources to research and test potential business concepts. It's the best time to start a new business, because no matter what happens, you will still be able to eat and sleep with a roof over your head. Derek Johnson founded Tatango to sell group text messaging while still in college. Here are some quotes from Johnson about starting a business while still in college:

- Identify a problem. "Ask people what keeps them up at night."

- Zero in and start small. "Pick a problem people will pay to fix with a product or service. Find something you can do with minimal capital and human resources and don't worry about getting big right away."

- Be the best. "If you struggle to come up with a simple, clear answer to the question of what you do best, you need to narrow your focus more."

LEARNING OUTCOMES

After reading this chapter, you should be able to:

7.1 Discuss the advantages and disadvantages of starting a business from scratch.

7.2 Describe types of new businesses and discuss the characteristics commonly shared by fast-growth companies.

7.3 Evaluate potential start-ups and suggest sources of business ideas.

7.4 Explain the most important points to consider when starting a new business.

- Do the research. "Fast-track product testing by surveying and selling to students and using college resources and faculty."

- Just do it. "The biggest hurdle is going forward with an idea. A lot of people stop at the idea point and think too hard about the product and say, 'I don't know.'"

- Be ready to sacrifice. "You are going to miss out on some of your social life, which isn't fun. But when you graduate, you will be doing something you love. I have worked my ass off to be where I am today and I realize it's going to take a lot more work to get where I want to go."

Sources: Tim Crino, "Meet the Coolest College Startups of 2018," *Inc.*, March 7, 2018, www.inc.com; Diana Ransom, "America's Coolest College Startups 2014," *Inc.*, accessed April 6, 2014, www.inc.com; Joel Holland, "What's Your Problem?" *Entrepreneur*, May 2010, https://www.entrepreneur.com/article/206150.

Concept Module 7.1: About Start-Ups

- **LO 7.1: Discuss the advantages and disadvantages of starting a business from scratch.**

Starting a business from the ground up is more difficult than buying an existing business or a franchise because nothing is in place. There are also more risks involved. To many people, however, the process of taking an idea through all the steps, time, money, and energy needed to become a viable business is the essence of being a business owner. The period in which you create a brand-new business is an *exciting* time.

Master the content at
**edge.sagepub.com/
Hatten7e**

$SAGE edge™

As we have seen in previous chapters, small business owners cross a wide spectrum of groups so there is no such thing as a "typical" owner or small business. But some interesting insights about small business owners include

- The median age for a U.S. small business owner is 50.3 years.[1]
- 36 percent are female.[2]
- Over a third have a four-year college degree (39 percent), but 28 percent have no more than a high school diploma; 33 percent have some college.[3]
- 77.5 percent of small business proprietors own their own home.[4]
- 49 percent of Millennials intend to start their own business in the next three years.[5]
- The median annual revenue for all U.S. small businesses is $390,000.[6]

Would you prefer to be totally independent? Can you set up an accounting system that is readable to you and acceptable to your bank and the Internal Revenue Service? Can you come up with a promotional campaign that will get you noticed? Are you willing to devote the time and resources needed to succeed? Can you find sources of products, components, or distribution? Can you find employees with the skills your business will need? If so, you may be ready to start your own business.

Advantages of Starting from Scratch

When you begin a business from scratch, you have the freedom to mold your new creation into whatever you feel is appropriate. Other advantages of starting from scratch include the ability to create your own distinctive competitive advantage. Many business owners thrive on the challenge of beginning a new enterprise. You can feel pride when creating something that didn't exist before and in realizing your own goals. The fact that the business is all new can be an advantage in itself—there is no carryover baggage of someone else's mistakes, location, employees, or products. You establish your own image.

> "The fact that the business is all new can be an advantage in itself—there is no carryover baggage of someone else's mistakes, location, employees, or products."

Disadvantages of Starting from Scratch

The risk of failure is higher with a start-up than with the purchase of an existing business or franchise. You may have trouble identifying market needs in your area that you are able to satisfy. You must make people aware that your business exists—it can be tough to get noticed. Also, you must deal with thousands of details you didn't foresee, from how to choose the right vendors, to where to put the coffeepot, to where to find motivated employees.

Concept Check Question

1. Compare and contrast the advantages and disadvantages of starting a business from the ground up. Be sure to include different types of businesses in your analysis.

Concept Module 7.2: Types of New Businesses

- **LO 7.2: Describe types of new businesses and discuss the characteristics commonly shared by fast-growth companies.**

No matter what type of business you are starting, your most important resource is your time. Nothing happens until you make it happen. You have to create and build on the enthusiasm

START-UP CHALLENGES

Starting a business from scratch brings its own unique set of challenges and problems. Understanding (or at least identifying) those challenges can help one prepare for them. Some common pitfalls include

- **Being the visionary:** As a start-up founder, you're expected to have the initial ideas, more ideas when competitors challenge, and more ideas of how to respond when your team hits a wall. The need for creative ideas under a time crunch creates pressure— the less experience you have, the more the pressure.

- **Ambiguity:** Start-ups come with a lot of questions— How long before you are profitable? When can you get a paycheck? What if customers don't like your product as much as you do? Self-employment means you will have less job security, so long-term plans are hard to make.

- **Loneliness:** Not often discussed as a facet of entrepreneurship, so many small business owners are not prepared for loneliness. Teammates can provide

some insight, but not complete support. Employees are in a different category, so they ultimately remain at arm's length. Family members want to help but are limited. Entrepreneurship is a lonely profession.

- **Managing work and home:** Start-up owners often have problems balancing the demands of the business and needs of a family. The stress of each bleeds over to the other making the small business owner feel pressure around the clock.

- **Decision-making:** Speaking of stress, this is probably one of the most stressful items on this list. Decision fatigue is a real thing and comes from the hundreds of decisions (big and little) that must be made each day.

Sources: Larry Alton, "The 8 Biggest Challenges for New Entrepreneurs," *Entrepreneur*, January 7, 2016, www.entrepreneur.com/article/254721; Matt Hunckler, "12 Challenges Startup Culture Must Overcome in Order to Thrive in 2017," *Forbes*, March 22, 2017, www.forbes.com; Kristie Lorette, "Start-Up Business Problems," Small Business Chron, March 10, 2018, http://smallbusiness .chron.com.

that will attract others to your idea and your business. In the beginning, the only thing you have is your vision, and only you will be responsible for its success.

As the service industry plays an ever-greater role in the U.S. economy, start-up businesses are becoming increasingly popular. The reason? Service businesses tend to be more **labor intensive**, or dependent on the services of people, as opposed to manufacturing businesses, which are more **capital intensive**, or dependent on equipment and capital.

Start by finding out all you can about your industry and trade area from books, newsletters, trade publications, magazines, organizations, and people already in business. After all your questions are answered and your investigation is complete, if you are ready for the challenge, you will find several possible routes for starting your business.

Let's look at a few of those routes that people take, aside from seeking to achieve the typical goal of a low-growth, stable start-up that will provide the small business owner with a comfortable, modest living.

Online Businesses

Nothing has changed the small business landscape quite like the internet. It is the ultimate in making one-to-one connections—which is where small businesses have always thrived. You can begin an **online business** with relatively low overhead and potentially reach markets all over the world. But keep in mind that the internet, though a powerful tool, doesn't make all other business metrics obsolete. You still have to make a profit, keep employees happy and motivated, provide customer service, and offer a product that inspires customers to turn over their hard-earned money to obtain it. Contrary to popular opinion at one time, electronic business is not all about "click here to buy." Business models online have evolved into "click here to get more information," "click here to start the just-in-time inventory flow," or "click here to

labor intensive
A business that is more dependent on the services of people than on money and equipment.

capital intensive
A business that depends greatly upon equipment and capital for its operations.

online business
A business that shares information, maintains customer relationships, and conducts transactions by means of telecommunications networks.

let a new employee go through the orientation process." In other words, online has evolved into part of a multichannel marketing strategy that benefits from traditional business models and lessons that don't have to be thrown out with the emergence of new media.

Square and BigCommerce conducted a comprehensive research project titled *Onmi-Channel Retail in 2017*, looking at online shopping behavior in the United States. Some key findings included[7]

- Fifty-one percent prefer to shop online over in-store (broken down by generation: 67 percent of Millennials; 56 percent of Gen Xers; 41 percent of Baby Boomers; 28 percent of seniors).

- Millennials and Gen Xers shop online 6 hours per week on average compared with 4 hours average for older generations.

- Men spent 28 percent more time online than women.

- Thirty percent of Americans shop online at least weekly.

- Eighty percent of Americans shop online at least monthly.

- Forty-six percent of small businesses do not have their own website.

- Thirty-four percent of total businesses sell via their own website.

Describing online business in a few paragraphs is a difficult task, because one simple model does not exist. Your e-biz may be something as simple as taking a current avocation (like tying flies for fishing or making custom pillows) and selling your concoctions on eBay or Etsy, business to consumer. You may not ever personally touch a product, but provide value by connecting other businesses, business to business. In these few paragraphs we won't get into the technical details of mips, megs, and browsers. You, as a webpreneur, will need an understanding of the leading edge of technology. Unfortunately (or fortunately), that edge moves so quickly that we can't do it justice here. What we can cover here are basic characteristics that a successful web business must possess.

- ***It's not just retail.*** E-commerce still accounts for only a modest 9.1 percent ($119 billion) of total retail sales ($1,304B) as of Q4 2017.[8]

- ***Target a niche community.*** Don't be everything to everyone. Knowing and serving the needs of one specific group of people means you can narrow your product/service. For example, the Sneaky Chef makes a line of healthy food specifically for children and targets parents who are concerned about food options for their kids.[9]

- ***Be mobile.*** Being online is not enough. For the 2017 holiday shopping season, U.S. shoppers spent $35.9 billion via smartphones and tablets. More than half of online traffic to websites came from mobile. Small retailers had higher sales conversion using mobile.[10]

- ***Logistics are huge.*** When people buy online, something usually has to get shipped. As online business has grown, so have companies that specialize in key functions like order fulfillment, logistics, and warehousing; so, you can outsource.

- ***The Holy Grail of passive income.*** Active income is directly connected with the performance of some activity. Activities that require you to directly exchange your time for money *once*. Passive income means exchanging your time once and getting paid over and over. Passive income is not easy—requiring upfront investment of time and often months or years before income is produced.[11] Online ways to generate passive income? Start a blog,

THERE'S AN APP FOR THAT

©iStockphoto.com/jpopba

E-commerce is getting bigger every year. During the 2017 holiday season, online shopping increased 18.1 percent over the 2016 holiday season (with total sales up 4.9 percent). Keep in mind that consumer e-commerce spending is still less than 2 percent of U.S. GDP (gross domestic product) in 2018. But data show that the future of e-commerce is in mobile apps.

App Annie (www.appannie.com) is an app research and reporting service that bills itself as the only data platform supporting the entire app life cycle. It reports that consumers spend 3 hours a day in apps, use 40 different apps each month, and spend $86 billion in app store purchases annually. In 2017, consumers spent 44 percent more time on the top digital-first shopping apps (like Amazon, Wish, Etsy, and Zulily) than they did the previous year.

Why? Because e-commerce apps make internet shopping easier (if they are done well). Since mobile shopping is not new, small businesses have to stand out to monetize. How?

1. **Satiate consumers' desire for instant gratification with snackable moments.** Consumers use mobile in quick bursts, not prolonged sessions—so grab attention instantly. For example, Tophatter is designed to deliver a 90-second shopping experience to take advantage of "stolen moments" like checkout lines or television commercials.

2. **Shrink your checkout time from minutes to seconds.** Time is crucial for mobile shopping, which is why Amazon created the one-click checkout. If a purchase is taking too long, consumers will abandon the shopping cart. Fifty-eight percent of us have abandoned mobile checkouts that take too long.

3. **Drive discovery with push notifications.** Data from Localytics show that 52 percent of smartphone users have chosen to enable push notifications on their phones. These are an effective way to promote products, remind shoppers of items left in carts, or bring back absent users. Just remember to not trip over the fine line that separates engaging and annoying customers.

A mobile caveat—users and customers are not the same. A user is anyone using your app for any purpose: searching for data, mere entertainment, serendipity, an experiment, a hobby, or just killing time. When people actually pay for your app, they cross the line to becoming a customer. Active daily users of an average app drop by 77 percent within the first three days after installation. After a month, the number grows to 90 percent. The 10 percent who remain are your actual customers.

Sources: Ashvin Kumar, "3 Ways Ecommerce Companies Can Capitalize on Apps," *Entrepreneur,* March 16, 2018, www.entrepreneur.com/article/310376; Pratik Kanada, "Mobile App Myths: Do You Still Believe Them?" June 22, 2017, www.entrepreneur.com/article/296230; Statistica, "B2C E-Commerce as Percentage of GDP in the United States from 2009–2018," accessed September 2018, www.statista.com/statistics/324582/b2c-e-commerce-as-percentage-of-gdp-usa/; www.appannie.com.

write an e-book, create an online course, be an affiliate marketer, create a smartphone app, own rental property, generate YouTube video tutorials.[12]

- *Use the internet to save money.* E-business is as much about reducing costs as it is about generating revenue. Creating value-chain efficiencies and meeting increasing customer expectations is what e-biz is about.

- *Build your competitive advantage.* E-business can be boiled down to four ideas: accelerating the *speed* of business, reducing *costs*, enhancing *customer* service, and improving the business *process*.

Home-Based Businesses

According to the Small Business Administration (SBA), home-based businesses made up 52 percent of all U.S. small businesses in 2017.[13] The number of people running businesses from home now tops 15 million. Homepreneurs range from Alex Andon manufacturing jellyfish tanks in his house (he even raises jellyfish in one of his bathtubs) to Sheri Reingold teaching 90 students piano in her home (probably not all at once). Two points stand out as advantages for this type of business: schedule flexibility and low overhead.

The common perception of home businesses is that they are mere hobbies or sideline businesses of little economic consequence. But data show there are 38 million home-based businesses in the U.S. The vast majority—70 percent—report they work full-time in their home business. Forty-four percent were started with less than $5,000. About 20 percent generate revenues between $100,000 and $500,000. Finally, as many homepreneurs as already exist, many more people want to join their ranks—70 percent of Americans would prefer to be self-employed.[14]

Kwame Tutuh used to teach second grade. Now he teaches child safety and runs an Ident-A-Kid business out of his Fulton County, Georgia, home. His business produces identification cards so parents can quickly provide the child's photograph, fingerprints, and description to authorities if a child is abducted or lost. Tutuh's franchise agreement gives him exclusive territory to contract with schools and day care centers for access to photograph and gather data on children. At his home office, he uses a laptop, proprietary software, a digital fingerprint scanner, and other minimal equipment to produce as many as 200 cards at a time. Tutuh states, "I'm in the perfect sector. The economy can be at its worst but we're still going to do whatever it takes to protect our children."[15]

Running a business out of your home can provide flexibility in your personal life, but it takes serious organization and self-discipline. Let's look at some of this approach's advantages and disadvantages.

Advantages of a Home-Based Business.
Advantages of a **home-based business** include the following:

- Control over work hours
- Convenience
- Ability to care for domestic responsibilities (such as children, parents, or the household)
- Low overhead expenses
- Lack of workplace distractions (coworkers popping in, chatting around the coffee machine)
- Decreased commute time
- Tax advantages

Disadvantages of a Home-Based Business.
Disadvantages of a home-based business include the following:

- Difficulty setting aside long blocks of time
- Informal, cramped, insufficient workspace at home
- Demands on family members to cooperate
- Lack of respect (people may think you are unemployed or doing this as a hobby)
- Domestic interruptions (houses can get noisy and crowded)
- Lack of workplace camaraderie (houses can get quiet and lonely)
- Zoning issues[16]

home-based business
A popular type of business that operates from the owner's home, rather than from a separate location.

What kind of businesses can you run from your home? Some possibilities include specialty travel tour planner, computer consultant, personal shopper, clothing alteration service, concierge service, website consultant, event planner, cart or kiosk business, translation service, feng shui consultant, pet sitting, and technology writer.[17]

Starting a Business as a Side Gig

New terms and new approaches to work are becoming more common in the business vernacular—terms like "side hustle" and "gig economy." Side hustles are not for everyone because they take time, energy, and other resources. They can also get one into trouble if the side gig detracts from a primary job with a current employer. Make sure you completely understand your current company policies and any agreements you signed, such as an employment contract, nondisclosure agreement, or noncompete clause.

Still, side gigs represent great opportunities to test before making a permanent commitment. There are even many platforms that connect professionals with gigs like Gigster, Upwork, and WriterAccess.[18] Many people start businesses while keeping their regular jobs. A recent study by Inuit estimates that the gig economy is on track to grow to 43 percent of the U.S. workforce by 2020.[19] Another study by McKinsey Global Institute showed that up to 162 million people in the United States and Europe are involved in some form of independent work.[20]

Author Dorie Clark says, "Consider entrepreneurship as an insurance policy for your career. Maybe you've wanted to start a food blog in your off-hours, or to offer personal or professional coaching to friends on the side. Whatever form it takes, creating such 'side streams' of income enables you to take more control of your career, your finances, and your life."[21]

A lot of different industries and skill sets are good fits for gigs, including[22]

- App-based gigs: drivers (like Uber), personal concierge, personal shopper, handyman

- Seasonal manual labor

- Professional services: writing, marketing, accounting

- Technology-based gigs: social media consultant, app developer, sell services on Fiverr

- Talent: musician, dancer, actor, personal trainer

- Create an online course: teach a skill via Udemy or Teachable

- Do domestic jobs: walk dogs, offer child care, clean houses, wash and detail cars

- Sell products on eBay, Etsy, or Craigslist

Jason Quey didn't quit his day job when he launched his footwear and clothing business at age 22. Working as a freelance marketer, he generated an impressive $211,000 revenue the first year. He was very careful not to use company time of his primary employer to work his side business, but he learned a lot about online marketing from his primary job that was useful in his side gig. Quey found that keeping his day job was a great way to develop skills, make valuable connections, and provide stability while he launched his side business.[23]

> "Working a full-time job while getting a business off the ground may require superhuman organizational skills and discipline, yet it can offer some notable advantages."

Working a full-time job while getting a business off the ground may require superhuman organizational skills and discipline, yet it can offer some notable advantages. A transitional period can allow you to test the waters without pursuing complete immersion in the marketplace. You can also prepare yourself psychologically, experientially, and financially, so that when—or if—you leave your primary job, you will have a running start.

Fast-Growth Start-Ups

Not every new business can be or desires to be a **hypergrowth** company like, for example, the top company on the 2013 Inc. 500 list, Fuhu, which had a three-year growth rate of 43,148 percent! It is informative to see what characteristics and statistics these fast-growth companies shared in *Inc.*'s database (see Figure 7.1).

hypergrowth
Businesses that are intentionally structured to grow at exceptional rates. Scalability is key to creating such growth.

1. ***They rely on team effort.*** In contrast to low-growth firms, most fast-growth companies are started by partnerships. In an increasingly complex and competitive environment, teams can deal with a much wider range of problems than can an individual operating alone. Fifty-six percent of the fast-growth CEOs started with partners or cofounders.

▼ FIGURE 7.1

Inc. 500 by the Numbers

Information about the CEOs and companies included in the Inc. 500 provides some interesting insights.

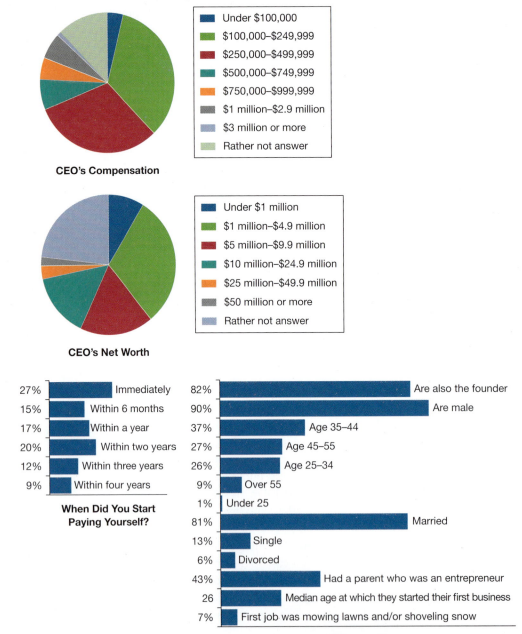

CEO's Compensation

- Under $100,000
- $100,000–$249,999
- $250,000–$499,999
- $500,000–$749,999
- $750,000–$999,999
- $1 million–$2.9 million
- $3 million or more
- Rather not answer

CEO's Net Worth

- Under $1 million
- $1 million–$4.9 million
- $5 million–$9.9 million
- $10 million–$24.9 million
- $25 million–$49.9 million
- $50 million or more
- Rather not answer

When Did You Start Paying Yourself?

27%	Immediately
15%	Within 6 months
17%	Within a year
20%	Within two years
12%	Within three years
9%	Within four years

CEOs at a Glance

82%	Are also the founder
90%	Are male
37%	Age 35–44
27%	Age 45–55
26%	Age 25–34
9%	Over 55
1%	Under 25
81%	Married
13%	Single
6%	Divorced
43%	Had a parent who was an entrepreneur
26	Median age at which they started their first business
7%	First job was mowing lawns and/or shoveling snow

2. **They're headed by people who know their line of work.** A majority of the CEOs of high-growth companies had at least 10 years of experience in the industry. In contrast, owners of low-growth companies typically have just a few years of prior experience.

3. **They're headed by people who have started other businesses.** Research shows that 63 percent of the founders of high-growth companies had previously started other companies, and 23 percent had started three or more businesses. This compares to only 20 percent of all business owners who had been self-employed previously. Some 61 percent started in the founder's home.

4. **They're making big bucks.** The 445 men and 57 women who run Inc. 500 companies take risks and are handsomely rewarded for their derring-do. Average first-year compensation was $92,000. Forty percent take home more than $500,000 annually, and more than 20 percent have generated a net worth in excess of $7.5 million.

5. **They're high-tech.** Of the fast-growth companies, 41 percent use new technology to achieve a competitive advantage. Another 40 percent say that new technology gives them somewhat of an edge.

6. **They're better financed—but not by much.** This factor is more difficult to measure because of the subjectivity in determining what "well financed" means. Sixty-one percent of Inc. 500 companies started with an investment of less than $10,000, and 20 percent began with between $10,000 and $49,999. Only 11 percent had initial start-up capital exceeding $100,000. Eighty-seven percent of Inc. 500 companies were self-funded.

7. **They have exit strategies.** The majority of CEOs (66 percent) plan to sell their business to outside investors. Going public is the exit strategy for 28 percent, while 23 percent plan to sell out to partners. Seventeen percent plan to pass the business on to children, and 16 percent intend to transfer ownership to employees via Employee Stock Ownership Plan (ESOP).[24]

Concept Check Questions

1. Define *hypergrowth* companies, and evaluate the reasons for their phenomenal rate of growth. What are the most valid explanations for the rate of success found in these companies?

2. Many entrepreneurs test the waters of a market by starting a sideline business. What are the advantages and disadvantages of selling items on internet auctions like eBay? Is a person who regularly has 20 or 25 items for sale at any given time an entrepreneur? What types of products would be most appropriately sold in this manner?

Concept Module 7.3: Evaluating Potential Start-Ups

- **LO 7.3: Evaluate potential start-ups and suggest sources of business ideas.**

The first thing you need to start your own business is an idea. Of course, not every idea is automatically a viable business opportunity. You must be able to turn your idea into a profitable business. How do you tell when an idea is also an opportunity? Where do people come up with viable business ideas that are opportunities?

Business Ideas

Although there is no shortage of ideas for new and improved products and services, there is a difference between ideas and opportunities. Are all ideas business opportunities? No. A business opportunity is attractive, durable, timely, and anchored in a product or service that creates or adds value for its buyer or end user. Many ideas for new products and businesses do not add value for customers or users. Maybe the time for the idea has yet to come, or maybe it has already passed.

Consider the idea for a new device for removing the crown caps that were common on bottles of soft drinks for many years. You could concoct an exotic and ingenious tool that would be technically feasible to produce, but is there an opportunity to build a business from it? Not since soft drink and beer companies switched to resealable bottles and screw-off tops to solve the same consumer problem that your invention does. Good idea—but no opportunity.

An idea that is too far ahead of the market can be just as bad as one that is too far behind. In 1987, Jerry Kaplan left his job as a software writer for Lotus Development to start Go Computers because he thought the world was ready for portable, pen-based computers. He had some big-time backing from IBM and AT&T, which together pitched in $75 million to help with the start-up. Kaplan had a vision of salespeople, lawyers, insurance adjusters, and millions of other people writing away on Go computers as if they were paper. Unfortunately, consumers at the time found that computers could not recognize their handwriting or convert it into print. The market was ready, but the technology was not. Now, two and a half decades later, many consumers regularly use iPads and tablet computers that are not that different from what Kaplan envisioned. Even with a great idea, a talented leader, and strong financial backing, Go Computers sold only 20,000 units and lasted only three years—it was ahead of its market. When Go closed, Kaplan said that he believed that "a new class of computing devices will come into being ... it's just a question of when."[25] He was right—just look around today at the success of handheld computers. But a start-up, even one with substantial resources, can't wait for technology or markets to catch up with an idea.

Harvard Business School professor Clayton M. Christiansen, in his book *The Innovator's Dilemma: When New Technologies Cause Great Firms to Fail*, discusses how some innovations *sustain* industries—offering better performance, more features, and everything that existing customers are seeking. Other innovations **disrupt** industries—bringing out useful products that people have never seen before.[26]

You've probably heard of the term **window of opportunity**. These windows constantly open and close (sometimes rapidly) as the market for a particular product ("product" meaning either goods or services) or business changes. Products go through stages of introduction, growth, maturity, and decline in the **product life cycle**. During the introduction stage, the window of opportunity is wide open because little or no competition exists. As products progress through this cycle, competition increases, consumer expectations expand, and profit margins decline so that the window of opportunity is not open quite as wide (see Figure 7.2).

> "An idea that is too far ahead of the market can be just as bad as one that is too far behind."

disrupt
In business context, disruption is making significant changes to the way business is done in a specific industry.

window of opportunity
A period of time in which an opportunity is available.

product life cycle
Stages that products in a marketplace pass through over time.

▼ FIGURE 7.2

The Window of Opportunity at Various Stages

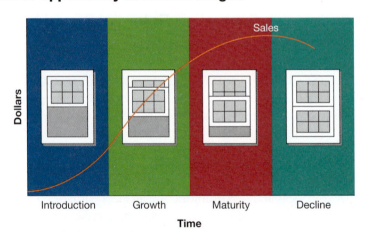

Optimally, you want to get through while the window is still opening—if the opportunity is the right one for you. To decide whether you should pursue an opportunity, ask yourself the following questions about your business idea:

- Does your idea solve a consumer want or need? This answer can give you insight into current and future demand.

- If there is a demand, are there enough people who will buy your product to support a business? How much competition for that demand exists?

- Can this idea be turned into a *profitable* business?

- Do you have the skills needed to take advantage of this opportunity?

- Why hasn't anyone else done it? If others have, what happened to them?

In the idea stage of your thinking (before you actually pursue an opportunity), you should discuss your idea with a wide variety of people to get feedback on it. Although praise may make you feel good at this stage, what you really need are people who can objectively look for possible flaws and point out the shortcomings of your idea.

Your final decision as to whether your idea represents an opportunity that you should pursue will come from a combination of research and intuition. Both are valuable management tools, but don't rely exclusively on either. Although research has kept some good ideas from becoming products or businesses, it has kept many more bad ones from turning into losing propositions. Do your homework; thoroughly investigate your possibilities. At the same time, don't get "analysis paralysis," which prevents you from acting because you think you need more testing or questioning—while the window of opportunity closes. Managerial decision making is as much an art as it is a science. Sometimes you will have to make decisions without the benefit of having every last shred of possible evidence. Get all the information that is practical, but also listen to your gut instincts.

Where Business Ideas Come From

Creativity is important to small business success. The Network Solutions Small Business Success Index provides data on where owners get their ideas. Not surprisingly, customers provided business ideas for over two-thirds. Other sources included newspapers and trade journals, competitors, and employees[27] (see Figure 7.3).

Top Five Sources of Start-Up Ideas

Prior Work Experience. Experience can be a wonderful teacher. Working for someone else in your area of interest can help you avoid many errors and begin to build competitive advantages. It gives you the chance to ask yourself, "What would I do differently, if I ran this business?"

One start-up may even lead to another. Seeing opportunities for new ventures after starting the first business is known as the **corridor principle**.[28] Entrepreneurs start second, third, and succeeding businesses as they move down new venture corridors that did not open to them until they got into business. As we saw with fast-growth start-ups, 63 percent of fast-growth CEOs had started other companies in the past, suggesting that one idea really does lead to another.

Research shows that big ideas occur to small business owners almost twice as often after the business is already running as before it begins.[29] This trend illustrates that experience pays off whether you are working for someone else or for yourself.

Hobbies and Avocations. Turning what you do for pleasure into a part-time or full-time business is a possibility you should consider. It helps ensure your business will be one that you enjoy and understand. If you enjoy fishing, could you potentially use your skills to become a guide? If you love pets, could you channel your affections into a dog-grooming or pet-sitting business?

Julian Bayley has turned an ice-carving hobby into a nice little business. When Elton John hosted his annual White Tie and Tiara charity gala at his mansion near Windsor Castle, ordinary dishes would not do. He called on Bayley's Canadian company, Ice Culture, to use its computer-aided machinery to mill caviar hors d'oeuvre trays for his 450 guests. Bayley has come a long way from his ice-carving hobby to designing and building a $45,000 computer-guided router modified for shaping crystal-clear ice. He also developed an ice lathe that can produce ice vases and oversized bottles—pretty cool.

corridor principle
The idea that opportunities become available to an entrepreneur only after the entrepreneur has started a business.

Chance Happening (Serendipity). **Serendipity** means finding something valuable that you were not looking for. Sometimes business opportunities come to you unexpectedly. The ability to recognize them takes an open mind, flexibility, a sense of adventure, and good business sense.

Brother and sister Ethan and Abby Margalith had to borrow a truck in the summer of 1973 to move a few things to a local swap meet. Both were just out of high school and out of work. While driving the truck to the swap meet, the pair realized that moving could be their summer job. Their first truck was a 1944 weapons carrier they got for free by rescuing it from a mudslide. Starving Students Movers, Inc. became the low-priced alternative to other movers that were characterized by full uniforms and high prices. The Margaliths used their sense of humor in their advertising—one ad stated that they offered "24-hour service for lease breakers." Even without knowing what they were doing, they had more business than they could handle. Ethan has stated that it wasn't until he got to law school that he realized he and his sister were really running a business. He finished law school but decided the moving business was fun, exciting, and profitable, so he stayed in the field with his sister. Starving Students has locations from California to Virginia. The company has proudly moved families, companies, government agencies like the U.S. Secret Service and the FBI, and even celebrities like Cher, Jerry Seinfeld, and Tom Hanks— and it all started with digging a truck out of the mud![30]

> "Sometimes business opportunities come to you unexpectedly. The ability to recognize them takes an open mind, flexibility, a sense of adventure, and good business sense."

Concept Check Questions

1. Explain the concept of *window of opportunity* as it relates to new start-ups, from idea conception through the final decision about whether to turn the idea into a reality.

2. Entrepreneurs get their ideas for business start-ups from various sources. Name these sources, and identify the ones most likely to lead to success.

3. What are some examples of consumer preferences and values? What are some examples of things the new business owner can do to ensure capturing some of the market for the good or service being produced?

4. What criteria do you see as most critical in differentiating an idea from an opportunity?

Concept Module 7.4: Getting Started

- **LO 7.4: Explain the most important points to consider when starting a new business.**

Most of the topics involved in starting your own business are covered in detail in other sections or entire chapters of this book. Let's look at what else is needed to get a business off the ground.

What Do You Do First?

You must first decide you want to work for yourself rather than for someone else. You need to generate a number of ideas for a new product or service, something people will buy, until you come up with the right opportunity that matches your skills and interests.

Whether you are starting a business because you have a product or service that is new to the world or because it is not available locally, you must get past some basic questions: Is there a need for this business? Is this business needed here? Is it needed now? These questions address the most critical concern in getting a business off the ground—the feasibility of your idea. Owning a business is a dream of many Americans, but there is usually a gap between that dream and bringing it to reality. Careful planning is needed to bridge that gap.

Serendipity
A fortunate discovery made by unplanned means.

CREATING COMPETITIVE ADVANTAGE

ENTREPRENEURS SOLVE BIG PROBLEMS

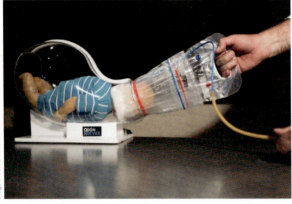

Diego Giudice/The New York Times/Redux

Jorge Odon was a 59-year-old auto mechanic trying to win a bet with a buddy that he could extract a cork from an empty bottle of wine without breaking it. He ended up developing a device that can save the lives of hundreds of babies being born (especially in developing countries) and their mothers.

Odon did what you probably do when faced with a problem—he went to YouTube. He found the bar trick clip showing that you tilt the bottle, stuff a plastic bag down the neck and blow into the opening. The bag balloons in the bottle wrapping tightly around the cork - give it a pull and POOF—the bag and cork pops out.

Satisfied with winning the bet, Odon went to bed. A middle-of-the-night idea snapped him awake. What if this trick could help delivering babies. He went to his garage (how many great entrepreneurship stories involve garages? A lot!) and put innovation and creativity to work. He patented a device cleverly called the Odon Device, and presented it to medical experts in his native Argentina. Eventually he was encouraged to enter his device in the World Health Organization (WHO) Saving Lives at Birth competition. He won $250k.

Entrepreneurs solve problems - this one is massive: every day approximately 800 women die from childbirth hemorrhage and babies asphyxiate. The vast majority of these preventable deaths occur in developing countries. Currently, the device is still in testing, but tests in Argentina have been hopeful and it should be on the market in a couple of years.

A car mechanic watches YouTube and stretches out of his comfort zone to save babies ... pretty cool. See Odon tell his story in a 2012 TED talk.

Sources: "The Mechanic, The Cork—and a Genius Idea," *Toronto Star*, September 28, 2013, A1; Leigh Buchanan, "The Innovation Story of the Year," *Inc.*, November 15, 2013, www.inc.com; "It's the Birth of an Idea," *Sun* (UK), December 30, 2013.

Importance of Planning to a Start-Up

Before you launch your business, you should write a comprehensive *business plan* (see Chapter 4). A business plan not only helps you determine the direction of your business and keeps you on track after it opens, but also will be required if you need to borrow money to start your business. It shows your banker you have seriously evaluated the business opportunity and considered how you will be able to pay back the loan.

In addition to writing your business plan, you need to decide and record other important steps in starting your business.

- **Market analysis.** For your small business to be successful, you must get to know your market by gathering and analyzing facts about your potential customers so as to determine the demand for your product. Market analysis takes time and effort, but it does not have to be statistically complex or expensive. Who will buy your product? What do your customers have in common with one another? Where do they live? How much will they spend?

- **Competitive analysis.** Your business needs a competitive advantage that separates it from your competitors. Before you can develop your own uniqueness, you need to know what other businesses do and how they are perceived. An exercise to help you remove some of the subjectivity of the competitive analysis process begins with identifying four of your direct competitors and setting up a grid on which you will rank your business as it compares to those competitors.

- **Start-up costs.** How much money will you need to start your business? Before you can seek funding, you must itemize your expected expenses (see Figure 7.4). Although some of these expenses will be ongoing, others will be incurred only when you start the business. There will be many expenses that you do not expect; therefore, add 10 percent to your subtotal to help offset them.

- **Capital equipment assets.** Assets such as computers, office equipment, fixtures, and furniture—capital equipment assets—have a life of more than one year. List the equipment you need along with the rest of your start-up costs. Beware of the temptation to buy the newest, most expensive, or fastest equipment available before you open your doors. You don't have any revenue yet, and more small businesses have failed due to lack of sales than due to lack of expensive "goodies." Is good used equipment available? Should you lease rather than buy? If sales do materialize, you can replace used equipment with new items by paying for them from actual profits.

- **Legal form of business.** As you will see in Chapter 10, when starting a business you need to consider the appropriate legal form of business: sole proprietorship, partnership, or corporation. Your decision will be based on tax considerations, personal liability, and cost and ease of organizing.

- **Location of business.** Consider how important the location of your business is to your customers (see Chapter 12). If customers come to your business, your location decision is

▼ FIGURE 7.4

How Much Money Will You Need?

Initial Capital Item	Estimated Cost
Capital equipment	_____
_____	_____
_____	_____
_____	_____
Beginning inventory	_____
Legal fees	_____
Accounting fees	_____
Licenses and permits	_____
Remodeling and decorating	_____
Deposits (utilities, telephone)	_____
Advertising (preopening)	_____
Insurance	_____
Start-up supplies	_____
Cash reserve (petty cash, credit accounts)	_____
Other expenditures:	_____
_____	_____
_____	_____
Subtotal start-up expenses:	$ _____
Add 10% safety factor:	_____
TOTAL START-UP EXPENSES	$ _____

critical. If your business comes to them, or if you don't meet with customers face-to-face, location is a less critical decision.

- *Marketing plan.* The marketing decisions you need to make before you open your business include who your customers are, how you will reach your potential customers, what you will sell them, where it will be available, and how much it will cost (see Chapter 13).

As you see, some important aspects of starting your business are not included in the business plan. Now let's look at what your business will focus on, how you will approach customer service, what licenses you will need to acquire, and what kinds of taxes you must withhold to begin business.

How Will You Compete?

Before you begin your small business, consider what you want to be known for. Because no business can be all things to all people, you need to determine what your customers value and then strive to exceed their expectations. For instance, if your customers value low prices, you must set up your business to cut costs wherever possible, so that you can keep your prices low. If your customers value convenience, you need to set up your business with a focus on providing speed and ease of use for them.

In providing value to your customers, we can identify three grounds on which companies compete: operational excellence, product leadership, and customer intimacy.[32] In choosing to focus on one of these disciplines, you are not abandoning the other two. Instead, you are defining your position in consumers' minds. Visualize your choice by picturing each discipline as a mountain on which you choose to compete by raising the expectation levels of customers in that area (see Figure 7.5). By becoming a leader in that discipline, you will be better able to defend against competing companies below you on that figurative mountain.

Companies that pursue **operational excellence** know their customers value low price, so they concentrate on the efficiency of their operations in an effort to hold down costs. They don't have the very best products or cutting-edge innovations. Instead, they strive to offer good products at the lowest price possible. Dell Computer is an example of a company that competes on operational excellence.

Companies that are **product leaders** constantly innovate to make the best products available even better. This kind of commitment to quality is not inexpensive, but product leaders know that price is not the most important factor to their customers. New Balance athletic shoes are known for their technical excellence, not for their inexpensive price or their customer service.

Companies that focus on developing **customer intimacy** are not looking for a onetime sale. Rather, they seek to build a long-term, close working relationship with their customers. Their customers want to be treated as if they are the company's only customer. The Lands' End operator you speak with on the telephone sees records of clothing sizes, styles, and colors from your

operational excellence
Creates a competitive advantage by holding down costs to provide customers with the lowest-priced products.

product leaders
A business that creates a competitive advantage based on providing the highest-quality products possible.

customer intimacy
Maintaining a long-term relationship with customers through superior service that results in a competitive advantage.

▼ FIGURE 7.5

On Which Mountain Will You Compete?

When setting up your small business, you must decide how you will satisfy your customers. Do you need to offer them the best product, the best price, or the best service?

Operational Excellence (low price)

Product Leadership (high quality)

Customer Intimacy (service)

previous orders as soon as you call. Customer-intimate companies offer specific rather than general solutions to their customers' problems.

Customer Service

Your business relationship with your customers does not end with the sale of your product or service. Increasing your level of customer service and adopting professional standards in this area are critical endeavors, especially in an industry where all competitors appear to be the same. Satisfying the customer is not a means to achieve a goal—it *is* the goal. Customer service can be your competitive advantage.

The importance of a start-up business providing an emphasis on the highest-quality customer service cannot be overstated. Very often the difference between one business and another is the people in it—and the way they treat customers. What is really different between car rental companies? They have basically the same cars. The prices, contracts, and advertisements are all nearly identical. The difference appears when someone answers the telephone. How long does it take to answer? Is the person's voice pleasant and professional, or hostile and bored? Does he have quick access to the information the customer called for, or does he offer to call back and never does? Does she take the time to understand the customer's needs and make truly helpful suggestions, or does she just try to push any car on the customer? Customer service can be a huge competitive advantage.[33]

> "Very often the difference between one business and another is the people in it—and the way they treat customers."

Licenses, Permits, and Regulations

If your business has no employees, you have fewer legal requirements to meet. First, let's look at the common requirements for all businesses. You need to file your business name with the secretary of state of the state in which you are forming your business. This step ensures that the name you have chosen for your business is not registered by another company. If it is, you will have to find another name for your business.

You must obtain the appropriate local licenses from the city hall and county clerk's office before you start your business. Find out if you can operate your business in the location you have picked by checking local zoning ordinances. You may also need a special permit for certain types of businesses. For example, if your business handles processed food, it must pass a local health department inspection.

Most states collect sales tax on tangible property sold. If your state does, you must apply for a state sales-tax identification number to use when paying the sales taxes you collect. Contact the department of revenue in your state for information regarding their requirements. Many types of businesspeople, such as accountants, electricians, motor vehicle dealers, cosmetologists, and securities dealers, require specific licenses. These licenses are obtained from the state agency that oversees the particular type of business.

Very few small businesses are likely to need any type of federal permit or license to operate. If you will produce alcohol, firearms, tobacco products, or meat products, or give investment advice, contact an attorney regarding regulations.

Taxes

When your business begins operation, you must make advance payments of your estimated federal (and possibly state) income taxes. Individual tax payments are due in four quarterly installments—on the fifteenth day of April, June, September, and January. It is important that you remember to set money aside from your revenues so it will be available when your quarterly taxes are due. The Internal Revenue Service is not known for its sense of humor if funds are not available.

If your business is a sole proprietorship, you report your self-employment income on IRS Form 1040 Schedule C or C-EZ, or Schedule F if your business is farming. A partnership reports partnership income on IRS Form 1065, and each partner reports her individual share of that income on Schedule SE and Schedule E. Corporations file tax returns on IRS Form 1120. Any payment in excess of $600 made for items like rent, interest, or services from independent contractors must be shown on Form 1096, and copies of Form 1099 must be sent to the people you paid.

When you begin employing other people, you become an agent of the U.S. government and must begin collecting income and Social Security taxes. You must get a federal employer identification number, which identifies your business for all tax purposes. Your local IRS office can supply you with a business tax kit that contains all of the necessary forms. You must withhold 7.51 percent of an employee's wages for Social Security tax, and you must pay a matching 7.51 percent employer's Social Security tax. You pay both halves of the tax on a quarterly basis when you submit your payroll tax return.

If a person provides services to your business but is not an employee, he is considered to be an **independent contractor**. Independent contractors are considered to be self-employed; therefore you do not have to withhold Social Security taxes, federal or state income taxes, or unemployment taxes from their earnings—an obvious advantage to you. Because of the advantages of classifying a person as an independent contractor rather than an employee, the IRS imposes stiff penalties on businesses that improperly treat employees as independent contractors.

You must deposit a percentage of each employee's earnings for federal and state unemployment tax purposes with a federal tax deposit coupon. The federal unemployment tax rate is 6.2 percent of the first $7,000 paid per employee, but a credit of up to 5.4 percent is allowed for state unemployment tax. In reality, only 0.8 percent goes toward the federal tax. The state rate you pay depends on the amount of claims filed by former employees. The more claims, the higher your unemployment tax will be, within certain limits.

Concept Check Questions

1. Give some examples of things the new entrepreneur should immediately investigate to ensure to the maximum extent possible that the business will "get off the ground."

2. Is a business plan really necessary for a very small start-up business? How much market analysis and competitive analysis should the new entrepreneur conduct prior to start-up?

3. What are some of the tangible resources the new entrepreneur might need in order to go into business? What are some options for obtaining capital for a business that is brand new and therefore has no financial history?

4. Discuss the legal ramifications of starting your own business. Where should the new entrepreneur seek information and advice regarding laws that govern the type of business that is being promoted?

5. After start-up, what is the *single* most important tool the small business owner has at his disposal to ensure the success of the business? Why is it so crucial?

independent contractor
A person who is not employed by a business and, unlike employees, is not eligible for a benefit package.

CHAPTER REVIEW

SUMMARY ▶▶

LO 7.1 Discuss the advantages and disadvantages of starting a business from scratch.

When starting a business from scratch, the small business owner is free to establish a distinct competitive advantage. There are no negative images or prior mistakes to overcome, as may occur when purchasing an existing business. The creation of a new business builds pride of ownership. However, the risk of failure is higher for a start-up because there are more uncertainties regarding the size and existence of a market for the business.

LO 7.2 **Describe types of new businesses and discuss the characteristics commonly shared by fast-growth companies.**

E-businesses have completely changed the small business landscape. Other types of new businesses include home-based businesses and part-time businesses. Some small businesses start with the intention of becoming hypergrowth companies. These companies are generally led by teams of people with prior experience in starting that type of business (usually high-tech manufacturing). They are well financed and constantly looking for opportunities to expand into new markets.

LO 7.3 **Evaluate potential start-ups and suggest sources of business ideas.**

When a new product idea is introduced to the market, the window of opportunity is open the widest (assuming it is a product that people want and will buy), because little competition exists. As a product progresses through the product life cycle, the window of opportunity closes, as more competition enters the market and demand declines.

Most people get ideas for new businesses from their prior employment. Turning a hobby or outside interest into a business is also a common tactic. Ideas may come from other people's suggestions or spring from information gained while taking a class. Sometimes business ideas even occur by chance.

LO 7.4 **Explain the most important points to consider when starting a new business.**

The entrepreneur needs to begin by questioning the feasibility of her idea. Then, to bridge the gap between dream and reality, careful planning is needed. Entrepreneurs need to carefully consider the costs of starting a new business, and they must analyze the market and competitive landscape to ensure that their competitive advantage really exists.

Providing customers with outstanding service during and after the sale of a product is of utmost importance in business start-ups. Customer service is the basis for establishing a long-term relationship with customers.

Start-ups also have legal requirements. Entrepreneurs must file the business name with the state of origin and obtain local business licenses and any industry-specific permits required. They must also apply for a tax identification number to collect and process sales taxes, if necessary.

KEY TERMS ▶▶

capital intensive **167**	hypergrowth **172**	product leaders **180**
corridor principle **176**	independent contractor **182**	product life cycle **174**
customer intimacy **180**	labor intensive **167**	serendipity **177**
disrupt **174**	online business **167**	window of opportunity **174**
home-based business **170**	operational excellence **180**	

STUDENT STUDY SITE ▶▶

edge.sagepub.com/hatten7e

⑤SAGE edge™ Sharpen your skills with SAGE edge!

SAGE edge for Students provides a personalized approach to help you accomplish your coursework goals in an easy-to-use learning environment. You'll find mobile-friendly eFlashcards and quizzes as well as multimedia resources to support and expand on the concepts presented in this chapter.

EXPERIENTIAL LEARNING ACTIVITIES ▶▶

7.1: New Types of Businesses/Fast-Growth Companies

LO 7.2: Describe types of new businesses and discuss the characteristics commonly shared by fast-growth companies.

Read the scenario below and answer the questions that follow. Be prepared to explain and discuss your answers and the reasoning behind your answers.

Shannon S. has been the CEO of a successful high-tech company for the last seven years. She is also the sole care provider of her elderly parents, who are requiring more and more attention as they age. She lives in a large metro area where her commute time can easily be an hour each morning and each evening. Her bachelor's and master's degrees are in engineering/computer science. In her spare time, she has developed a software program that allows a person to catalogue and value all their personal belongings using their smart phone and her software program. All that is required is for a person to walk around the rooms in their house and videotape their belongings. The smart phone then communicates with the software program, which checks the personal belongings against values in its database. The software program then lists and totals the values on all belongings, providing a professional-looking list of items and values, suitable for insurance companies, wills, estate lawyers, and so forth. Shannon is hoping both insurance companies as well as individuals will be interested in her product. Her ultimate goal is to sell her proprietary software to a major insurance company, once her product is established.

In preparing her sales pitch, Shannon is trying to decide which type of business would be most effective: e-business, home-based business, or a side business. She is also wondering if there is potential for this business to become a fast-growth start-up, which would assist her in obtaining needed financing.

Questions:

1. Shannon is trying to decide which type of business would be most effective: e-business, home-based business, or a side business. List advantages and disadvantages of the above choices.

2. Which type of business would you ultimately recommend and why?

3. Which characteristics of fast-growth start-ups does Shannon have currently?

7.2: Start-Up Costs

LO 7.4: Explain the most important points to consider when starting a new business.

Read the scenario below and determine the start-up expenses for Brian's business.

Brian is a recent college graduate with a degree in construction management. He is a nontraditional student with 10 years of construction experience, which complements his college degree. He has a beautiful little girl whom he adores and who loves to act out children's stories. His living room frequently becomes a castle, a working ranch, a science laboratory, or a gymnastic facility and more. As a result of this regular transformation, Brian has basically lost the use of his living room so he has developed a business idea to solve his problem. He will build custom playhouses sturdy enough to last a lifetime. His playhouses will have movable features that will quickly transform the playhouse into a child's scene of choice. He has approached an investor with his idea, and the investor was intrigued to the point of asking Brian to come back with start-up costs. Brian needs assistance in developing this initial list that will allow him to obtain the needed funding to begin his new business.

Brian knows he needs the following tools and supplies: construction hand tools, skill saw, handsaw, power drill, and sawhorses that will cost approximately $300. Wood, nails, paint, and other supplies for each playhouse will be approximately $800, depending upon the size of the playhouse. Brian wants to build two complete playhouses for his beginning inventory. He has a lawyer on retainer who will charge him $300 for legal fees and his accountant has agreed to set up his accounting on QuickBooks for $250. His insurance cost will be around $150 a month for the business insurance needed. He plans to use social media for advertising so will need around $100 a month to promote his business and he knows he needs $400 in his cash reserve to cover other incidentals as he begins; however, he has decided not to include this amount right now. He also needs to hire a designer to come up with interior decorating ideas. He knows a college student who has agreed to charge Brian $200 for a basic design and decoration. Brian will also need a new laptop and printer to devote to the business, which will cost around $1,000.

What amount should Brian bring to his potential investor as his start-up costs?

CHAPTER CLOSING CASE ▶▶

Trend Pie: Turning a Social Media Network into a Business

Victor Ricci grew up and went to high school in Rhode Island. He ran varsity track and held down several summer jobs. Like most other kids his age, he also had several social media accounts and enjoyed posting funny messages on various sites. In 2013, during his senior year, something amazing happened. He posted a life-hack video to his Vine account showing him using a water bottle to separate the egg yolk from the whites of an egg (https://www.youtube.com/watch?v=jLJU6qju61s). The video went viral and, with a few more successful videos, his became one of the trendiest accounts on the site, with more than 1.4 million followers. As a result, he also became part of an extensive network of young people that is able to influence what people watch on social media sites such as Twitter and YouTube.

Victor soon realized that his status and his contacts with other social media personalities could be leveraged to create a business. Digital ad spending was projected to grow to $100 billion by 2020. Much of this growth was coming from social media and, in particular, from Twitter. Studies showed, in fact, that 49 percent of Twitter users followed brands and companies, compared to just 16 percent of social network users overall. Twitter, therefore, was becoming a major target for companies seeking brand and product awareness. Finally, advertising experts reported that budgets for "influencer" marketing were expected to double over the next two years. This was a growing trend in marketing and Victor wanted to try to get a piece of the action.

With this idea in his head, Victor began to study both competitors and potential gaps in the market. He noted three major types of competitors. The first was Twitter itself, which offered companies the chance to post sponsored tweets. While this worked fairly well for larger companies with professional marketing and communications staff, it produced rather poor results for smaller firms that had less training in how to get the right messages out to their targeted audiences. A second type of competitor consisted of influencer marketing companies that specialized in using stars from the worlds of music, film, or sports to push products and brands. These were strong competitors but were only available to clients able to pay the high fees these celebrities charged for their services. Finally, the third type of competitor consisted of a mixed group of marketing companies that more or less specialized in influencer marketing (Social Chain, Collab, Tapjoy, Speaker). These companies all used different social media personalities with large followings to promote their clients' products. Here, he felt he had a chance to build a competitive advantage.

He saw that there was quite a bit of confusion in the market regarding both how customers were charged and how influencers were paid. Most service agencies followed a traditional model, invoicing customers at the end of the month for the number of messages produced and paying influencers according to the results obtained. There were several problems with this model, however. It was still unclear how to measure the results of influencer marketing campaigns and what clients should expect from their investments. The impact of a campaign could also vary substantially over the course of a month, with enthusiastic responses at the start and less interest at the end. This meant that clients often felt that they were paying more than necessary for what they were getting. At the other end, influencers were not being paid fairly for the messaging they were sending to their networks. In fact, if a campaign did not produce the desired results, the clients would still be charged for the work done while the influencers might not get paid at all. This situation had created a great deal of bad will among both marketers and influencers.

Developing the Right Business Model

Victor decided that he needed to do things differently if he wanted to compete in this new world of influencer marketing. By this time, he was enrolled at Seton Hall University. He decided to major in marketing and was taking courses in entrepreneurship. As he learned more about business and start-ups, he also began to work on a suitable business model for his start-up.

The model he came up with involved running daily campaigns rather than monthly ones. He thought that campaigns should be adapted continuously to follow the trends in any particular market. No campaign would be effective if you waited a month, or even a week, to analyze the results. He therefore decided to charge a flat fee for each daily campaign regardless of the results achieved. Clients would be asked to pay this fee up front, one day in advance of the campaign. Victor would then create the campaign and contact the needed influencers for the next day. The results of each campaign would be monitored in real time and, together with his clients, he could decide whether to continue, change, or stop a campaign day by day. In the same way, Victor decided that he would pay his influencers a daily flat fee for their services based on a percentage of what he was paid by the clients. But he also needed to manage his influencers well to make sure they implemented his campaigns correctly and in a timely manner. He therefore needed an efficient system that would allow him to have revenues and fees flowing in and out on a daily basis and to monitor the campaigns and their results in real time.

As he began to work on this system out of his dorm room at Seton Hall, he got his first paying client. It was an app called Drunk Mode. The manager of the company, Josh, offered him $2,000 to run a Twitter campaign to get the app trending in the app store. It turned out that Victor had to spend almost twice as much as what he was paid, the second half coming from his personal savings, to get the results the client was expecting. He also had to work much harder than he expected to find the right messaging. But his reputation depended on the campaign being a success. In the end, the app got more than the expected downloads and Josh was happy. He booked additional campaigns for the following days and weeks and also starting referring other clients to Victor. Just as important, this experience allowed Victor to experiment with different types of messaging and to test his administrative systems, which would allow him to keep control of both finances and campaign results.

The Early Challenges

Following this initial start, in 2015 Victor established a limited liability company (LLC). He named the venture Trend Pie. For the first months, he had a continuous flow of clients that provided him with a steady income. As his business grew, however, Victor confronted several challenges. The first was time management.

Victor found himself spending at least 25 hours per week on the phone or on his computer managing the business. His schoolwork began to suffer, along with his athletic performance and his personal relationships. After a particularly harsh argument with his girlfriend, he decided that it was time to get help.

In his mind, Victor was not ready to take on a partner in the business. He did not think the business was big enough and he felt that a future partner should be someone who had something significant to offer to grow the business. Right now, he just needed an employee interested in earning a part-time salary by helping him manage the flow of messages with the influencers.

Victor tweeted out his needs. After reviewing a few of the candidates who responded to his tweet, Victor decided on Carl. He was young, a high social media consumer, and was already handling some accounts on Twitter with hundreds of thousands of followers. More than that, Carl was eager to learn and willing to put in the time without asking for equity. Yet Victor also realized that Carl would have access to a great deal of proprietary information about the business and that he needed to protect his assets in case things did not work out with Carl. Victor therefore contacted a small business lawyer who helped him to draft both a salary package for Carl and an agreement that included nondisclosure, noncompete, and nonsolicitation clauses. Carl was paid on a month-to-month basis based on his workload and time spent. Victor now had his first employee.

The second challenge Victor faced came as quite a shock to the system. He had been using PayPal both to receive payments from his clients and to pay his influencers. But one day, late in the evening, just as he was about to send out payments to his influencers for the next day's campaigns, PayPal blocked his account. This problem risked damaging his reputation both with his clients (i.e., the word would quickly get out that he might not be capable of managing large campaigns and of guaranteeing results) and his network of influencers (i.e., they might begin to think that he didn't keep his word as promised).

Victor quickly called PayPal to find out why his account had been frozen. It turned out that the account had been flagged for suspicious activity since there were large quantities of money going in and out of the account every day without any registered invoices or receipts to account for the movements. Victor then realized that the informal mechanisms he used to deal with his clients and suppliers were no longer tenable. Up to then, he had been working on the basis of verbal agreements and personal trust. But the size of the company and the customer base now demanded more formalized mechanisms to regulate conditions and payments with his clients. Again, he contacted his lawyer who was quickly able to draw up a standard contract that he could present to each of his clients. He called his influencers to explain why their payments were delayed that day. By the next day, the contracts had been signed, the influencers were paid, and he was up and running again. But the experience had taught him a lesson about the importance of formal contracts in a business setting.

Scaling Up

With the business growing, Victor needed to hire a few more employees to help him in the business. He assigned Carl full responsibility for handling contracts with the influencers, while his new recruit, TJ, was given responsibility for handling client relationships. He later hired Barbara as a general office manager, although the office remained a virtual space; the team was still working out of their homes or dorm rooms. But at least he had employee contracts in place and hiring new people was relatively simple.

Now he was set up for a much bigger scale. But how could he achieve that? The business was growing well but was nowhere near what he could handle with the new team and processes. He therefore had to seek out new clients. He reached out to his first client, Josh, who by now had launched other businesses and had a solid network of connections in the tech world. He offered Josh a small amount of equity in Trend Pie in exchange for help in finding him new and larger clients. Over the following months, Josh helped to secure many new and important clients, and he also helped get Trend Pie press coverage in media outlets such as *Entrepreneur*, *Adweek*, and Tech.co. By early 2017, the business was managing between 35 and 40 campaigns every month for an average fee of $2,000, which was a highly competitive price on the market. He had reached his first major objective of $1,000,000 in revenues less than two years after launching the business and had developed a loyal base of influencers who were happy to work with him. His clients were also happy with the results they were achieving, which included higher than average impressions, user engagement rates, and monthly retention of users. While a majority of the clients' fees went to pay his influencers, the rest could be used to pay his expenses (salaries, office costs, travel, legal, insurance) and to reward him with a small profit; at this point, he was making about $2,500 profit after expenses each month. But he knew the business had much greater potential for growth. Victor figured that if he could run at least 100 campaigns per month, the business could make something closer to $30,000 per month in profits after expenses.

Decisions/Opportunities

In May 2017, Victor graduated and needed to decide what to do with his business.

He considered several alternatives, including

1. Grow the business and bring on new partners to help it grow.

2. Keep the company as a part-time activity while Victor and the others work at other jobs.

3. Sell the business.

Multiple companies had begun to show interest in buying the business from Victor. But because he was still unsure about what he wanted and had no idea how to measure the value of the company for an acquisition, he had put off meeting these potential buyers. His team was young and they were all eager to gain experience running other types of businesses or working in other companies. But they also realized that they had a good thing going. The time had come to make a decision.

Discussion Questions

1. In what ways does Trend Pie represent a typical entrepreneurial venture?

2. What do you think about the actions Victor has taken to protect his business ideas and to ensure the continued growth of his business?

3. What lessons can be learned from the case about starting an internet company?

4. What should Victor do with the business after graduation?

Source: Pamela Adams and Victor Ricci, "Trend Pie: Turning a Social Media Network into a Business," Sage Knowledge: Cases, January 2, 2018, http://dx.doi.org/10.4135/9781526447258.

PART IV

FINANCIAL AND LEGAL MANAGEMENT

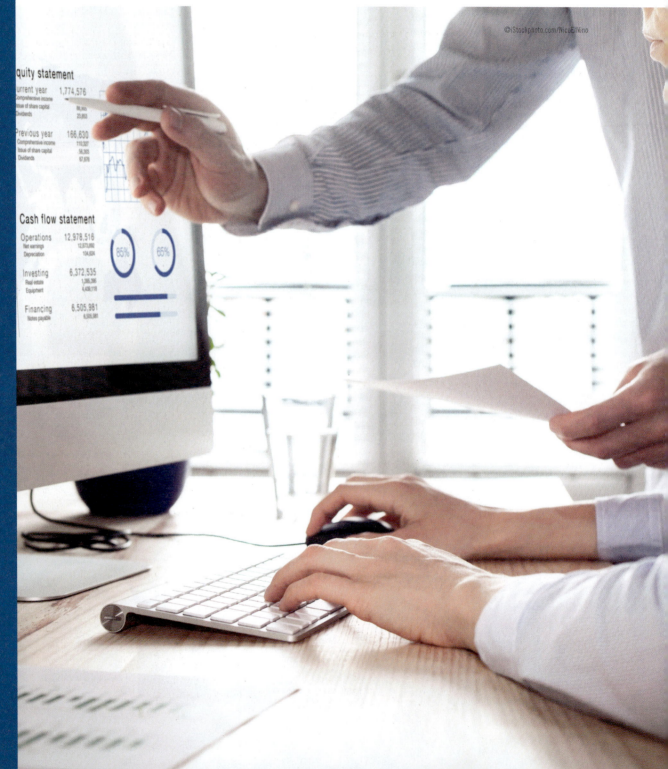

CHAPTER 8

ACCOUNTING RECORDS AND FINANCIAL STATEMENTS

So why should a small business owner, busy with developing a product or service, marketing, hiring employees, and the host of other tasks necessary for the success of the company worry about the accounting records and review the financial statements? After all, isn't that what the accountant is hired to do? The accounting records that become the necessary information for the financial statements can provide important and timely information that small business owners need in order to make appropriate decisions. The information can also be used to do quick checks and make sure the company is on track to make a profit. In fact, analyzing the financial statements can be a bit like playing detective.

For example, when Krispy Kreme Doughnuts was founded in 1937 by Vernon Rudolph in Winston-Salem, North Carolina, the doughnuts were produced to sell to local grocery stores. The doughnuts soon became so popular that Vernon cut a hole in the wall of the building where he was producing the doughnuts so he could sell directly to the customer—a doughnut drive-through. With the popularity of the doughnut, expansion soon occurred with the majority of the new stores started as franchises. Today, Krispy Kreme has pulled an impressive recovery after a financial roller-coaster ride. Sales peaked in 2005 with $1.07 billion across 344 U.S. stores dropping to $468 million rebounding to $758 million in 2017 from 1,172 locations.

So if a prospective small business owner was considering opening a Krispy Kreme franchise, what pieces of financial detective work might she want to consider? Headlines state that Krispy Kreme profit trends are up, but sales fluctuate and are generally down—with lots of speculation about reasons. How could answers to questions be found?

A company's financial statements can provide a prospective franchisee a wealth of information. Looking at recent annual reports for Krispy Kreme (KK), located at www.sec.gov, some interesting pieces of information come to light. For example, the company counts as revenue four areas: company store sales, domestic franchise revenue, international franchise revenue, and KK supply chain revenue. The annual reports also have a section containing details on the KK supply chain, stating that the "KK Supply Chain produces doughnut mixes and manufactures our

doughnut-making equipment, which all factory stores are required to purchase."

So now after a little financial detective digging and delving into financial statements, could it be that as long as Krispy Kreme was opening new franchises and selling the required equipment to those franchises, revenues were increasing, even if the sales of doughnuts were dropping? Since the KK supply chain was counted as revenue, the dollars that franchises were spending were helping to increase company revenues. However, a prospective franchisee would be more concerned about doughnut sales since that would be the profit producer for the small business owner. As Americans become more health conscious, doughnuts are certainly not on the menu and Krispy Kreme doughnut sales may well continue to fall. So, maybe with this new information provided by the financial statements, a prospective franchisee might want to more carefully consider this business opportunity.

Financial statements can provide a wealth of information for small business owners interested in franchising or small business owners as they compare their company to a much larger company. This process and these financial documents, as well as ratio analysis, will be further discussed in the chapter. Good luck playing financial detective.

Sources: Annual reports, Form 10-K, Krispy Kreme, found at www.sec.gov/edgar, http://www.krispykreme.com/history.html, http://investor.krispykreme.com/overview.cfm; Rose Leadem, "10 Crazy Things You Never Knew About Krispy Kreme," *Entrepreneur*, January 5, 2017, www.entrepreneur.com/slideshow/287321; Jon Marcus, "Krispy Kreme Fell Apart, Then Came Back Strong. Here's How," *Entrepreneur*, September 14, 2017, www.entrepreneur.com/article/298165.

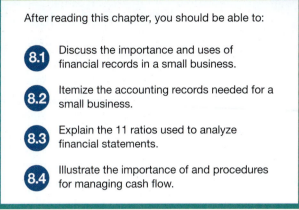

LEARNING OUTCOMES

After reading this chapter, you should be able to:

8.1 Discuss the importance and uses of financial records in a small business.

8.2 Itemize the accounting records needed for a small business.

8.3 Explain the 11 ratios used to analyze financial statements.

8.4 Illustrate the importance of and procedures for managing cash flow.

Master the content at
edge.sagepub.com/
Hatten7e

$SAGE edge™

Concept Module 8.1: Small Business Accounting

- **LO 8.1: Discuss the importance and uses of financial records in a small business.**

Are you intimidated by the thought of accounting systems, with row after row and column after column of numbers? If you are, you aren't alone. But you shouldn't be frightened by or dread the numbers of your business, because accounting isn't about making rows and columns of numbers. Rather, it is about organizing and communicating what's going on in your business. Think of numbers as the language of business.

> "The accounting process helps you to translate numbers—the language of business—into plain English."

Computers help us take piles of raw *data* and turn them into usable *information* with which to make managerial decisions. For example, consider a marketing research project you have conducted. You have received thousands of completed questionnaires, each with 20 responses. You would have a very difficult time interpreting these thousands of pages because they contain raw, unprocessed data. If you were to enter all of these data into a statistical program on a computer, however, you could organize them into means, trends, and a few meaningful numbers—in other words, into *information* that would enable you to make marketing decisions.

Accounting systems accomplish a similar purpose. Think of the many piles of checks, receipts, invoices, and other papers your business generates in a month as data. Everything you need to know about the financial health of your business is contained in those piles, but it is not in an easily usable form. Accounting systems transform piles of data into smaller bites of usable information by first recording every transaction that occurs in your business in *journals*, then transferring (or posting) the entries into *ledgers* (both of which are described in this chapter). The process is basically the same whether you use pencil and paper or an accounting program on a personal computer. From the ledger you make *financial statements* like a balance sheet, income statement, and statement of cash flow. These statements communicate how your business is faring much better than the stacks of papers with which you started.

In the last step in the accounting process, you take certain numbers from your financial statements to compute key *ratios* that can be compared to industry averages or historical figures from your own business to help you make financial decisions. The intent of this chapter is not to turn you into an accountant, but rather to help you understand the communication process—or accounting language—better (see Figure 8.1). The accounting process helps you to translate numbers—the language of business—into plain English.

So how is a new business owner supposed to get the accounting process started? How can you create an orderly system from nothing without having prior expertise in accounting? Many business owners start by purchasing a simple accounting software package (see the *Tech in Action* box on the "Small Business Dashboard" later in this chapter). Another stellar piece of advice is to pay an accounting firm that specializes in small businesses to set up your accounting system. You don't have to use the firm to handle all of your accounting needs like payroll preparation, tax form preparation, and creation of monthly financial statements, although you could. Money would be wisely spent getting a system that will work for your business from the very beginning—as opposed to throwing all receipts, invoices, and paperwork into a shoebox and panicking when the time comes to file quarterly taxes. Do yourself and your business a favor, and get started correctly by using the services of a professional.

As your small business grows, so do its accounting functions. Of course, you do not need a chief financial officer, or even a full-time bookkeeper, when first starting out. You will likely start out with a part-time, external-service professional who will set up your accounting system.[1] Choosing this accounting professional upon whose advice you will depend is a big decision. Some guidelines for helping you make this decision include

accounting
The system within a business for converting raw data from source documents (like invoices, sales receipts, bills, and checks) into information that will help a manager make business decisions.

Accounting Process

An accounting system works via a cycle to convert raw data into usable information for making decisions about how to run your small business.

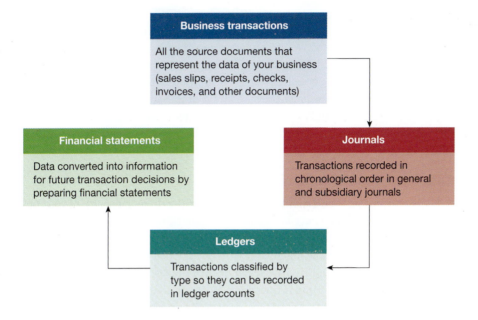

- *Ask what kinds of businesses the accountant works with.* For example, restaurants and food service businesses have rules that they must follow regarding wages and tips. Does the accountant know the ins and outs of your industry?[2]

- *How does the accounting firm bill for services?* Some bill hourly, some as a flat rate. Submitting your previous year's tax return will help the accountant develop a quote for what your estimated expenses would be.

- *What are the accountant's credentials?* A certified public accountant (CPA) has passed comprehensive certification requirements. While credentials are important, finding an accountant whose experience fits your business is more important.

- *How accessible will they be?* You don't want an accounting firm that closes after April 15.

- *How well does this accountant communicate with you?* Ed Lyon, cofounder of the American Institute for Certified Tax Coaches states, "We tend to think of accountants as numbers people, but a good accountant does more than just figure the numbers. A good accountant will communicate what the numbers mean to us."[3]

- *Does the accountant's conservative/aggressive approach fit with your philosophy?* Some accountants push for every deduction possible. Some are so sensitive to triggering an audit that deductions, such as home office allowance, will be passed. You and your accountant need to be at the same point on the comfort spectrum.

- *Can you look over my QuickBooks?* Many CPAs get irritated with a client's QuickBooks when preparing tax returns because a lot of people don't do a good job of tracking income and expenses. Fixing messes takes time, and time is a premium for accountants in tax season.

- *What if I get audited?* You want expertise if the IRS sends you an audit notice. You need to know in advance what your accountant's role will be. CPAs and tax attorneys will handle your case themselves. Bookkeepers and part-time accountants probably won't or can't.

How Important Are Financial Records?

Financial records are important to businesses for several reasons. Remember when we discussed common reasons for failure of small businesses in Chapter 1? Most of the mismanagement decisions that spell the doom of many small businesses are related to financial and accounting issues.

All too often, the last thing small business owners think of is careful accounting, but it should really be the first issue addressed. While you are plagued with a lot of worries—from making payroll to buying products to selling your services—you can put yourself at a competitive disadvantage by not being accounting oriented from the beginning. Many small business owners don't hire an accountant right away because they are afraid of the cost, but many accounting firms specialize in small businesses and are available at reasonable prices. It's like the advice you have probably heard your whole life: Getting things right the first time costs less than fixing mistakes the second or third time.

Accurate Information for Management

You need to have accurate financial information to know the financial health of your business. To make effective management decisions, you must know things like how much your accounts receivable are worth, how old each account is, how quickly your inventory is turning over, which items are not moving, how much your firm owes, when debts are due, and how much your business owes in taxes and FICA (Social Security taxes). Good records are needed to answer these and many other similar questions. Without good records, these questions are impossible to answer. Accurate financial records also allow you to identify problems and make needed changes before the problems become a threat to your business.

Banking and Tax Requirements

The information on your financial statements is needed to prepare your tax returns. If the Internal Revenue Service audits your business, you will be expected to produce the relevant accounting records and statements.

Bankers and investors use your financial statements to evaluate the condition of your business. If you need the services of either, you must not only produce statements, but also be ready to explain and defend their contents.

Concept Check Question

1. How can financial records allow you to identify problems in your business?

Concept Module 8.2: Small Business Accounting Basics

- **LO 8.2: Itemize the accounting records needed for a small business.**

The accounting system provides you with information for making decisions about your small business. To access this information, you need to understand which entry systems you can use and how accounting equations work. Your accounting system should be easy to use, accurate, timely, consistent, understandable, dependable, and complete.

Double- and Single-Entry Systems

Accounting systems revolve around three elements: assets, liabilities, and owner's equity. **Assets** are what your business owns. **Liabilities** are what your business owes. **Owner's equity** is what you (the owner) have invested in the business (it can also be called *capital* or *net worth*).

As the name implies, with a **double-entry accounting** system, all transactions are recorded in two ways—once as a *debit* to one account and again as a *credit* to another account. Every "plus" must be balanced by a "minus." So, for example, a transaction shows how assets are affected on one side and how liabilities and owner's equity are affected on the other.

A double-entry accounting system increases the accuracy of your system and provides a self-checking audit. If you make a mistake in recording a transaction, your accounts will not balance, indicating that you need to go back over the books to find the error. Debits must always equal credits. To increase an asset, you debit the account. To increase a liability or equity, you credit the account.

A **single-entry accounting** system does exist and may be used by small sole proprietorships. With a single-entry system, you record the flow of income and expenses in a running log, basically like a checkbook (Figure 8.2). It allows you to produce a monthly statement but not to make a balance sheet, an income statement, or other financial records. The single-entry system is simple but not self-checking, as is a double-entry system.

Popular computer programs like Quicken employ a single-entry accounting system. These programs provide attractive features like the ability to track expense categories, post amounts to those accounts, and print reports, but they are still pretty much electronic check registers. Many small, one-person businesses begin with them because of their simplicity and then graduate to more powerful, full-feature systems like the Sage 50 or Great Plains accounting programs. Other advantages include the ability to integrate your online bank account, create a tracking system of who has done what in record keeping, and also limit or provide access to information to specific employees or your accountant. There is no one-size-fits-all computer accounting program that is suitable for all small businesses. You may have to adjust your system as your business grows.

On the subject of beginning simply: *Always* use separate checkbooks for your business and your personal life. Avoid the temptation to combine the two by thinking that "the business money and personal money are all mine—I'll just keep them together." At some point you will need to separate them, which can be very difficult to do later. Also, write checks instead of paying for items with cash. They serve as an accurate form of record keeping. Finally, reconcile your bank accounts monthly, and make sure all errors are corrected.

Accounting Equations

As stated earlier, numbers are the language of business. Three equations are the foundation of that language:

$$\text{Assets} = \text{Liabilities} + \text{Owner's equity}$$

$$\text{Profit} = \text{Revenue} - \text{Expenses}$$

$$\text{Cash flow} = \text{Receipts} - \text{Disbursements}$$

The first equation, Assets = Liabilities + Owner's equity, is the basis of the *balance sheet*. Any entry you make on one side of the equation must also be entered on the other side to maintain a balance. For example, suppose you have a good month and decide to pay off a $2,000 note you took out at the bank six months ago. You would credit your cash account (an asset) by $2,000 and debit your notes payable account (a liability) by $2,000. Your balance sheet remains in equilibrium. Of course, any equation can be rearranged if you understand it. For example,

$$\text{Owner's equity} = \text{Assets} - \text{Liabilities}$$

You can also think of this equation as follows:

$$\text{What you have} = \text{What you own} - \text{What you owe}$$

double-entry accounting
An accounting system in which every business transaction is recorded in an asset account and a liability or owner's equity account so that the system will balance.

single-entry accounting
An accounting system in which the flow of income and expenses is recorded in a running log, basically like a checkbook.

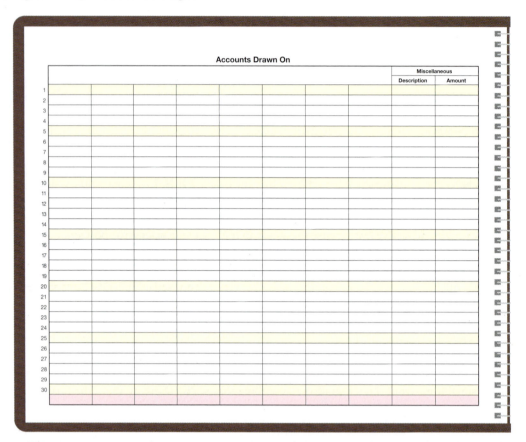

▼ FIGURE 8.2

Single-Entry Account Ledger

SMALL BUSINESS DASHBOARD IN THE CLOUD

Accounting systems of any type provide information for managers to make informed decisions. Think of driving a vehicle—your eyes are constantly moving from gauges to horizon to gauges to mirror. Right? Same thing in driving a business—eyes watching many things and directions at once, and accounting provides the dashboard.

Cloud-based accounting can save time in entering data and generating accounting statements, can improve the traceability of income and expenses (which could prove important for audits), and can increase the timeliness and frequency of your accounting statements. Cloud-based software, or software as a service (SaaS), provide access to technology on a subscription basis. The software provider hosts all necessary databases and servers, allowing a small business owner access to their data 24/7 via an internet connection.

Selecting appropriate hardware and accounting software can pose a major challenge. To facilitate your decision-making, let's examine some of the better-known accounting packages.

QuickBooks Cloud or Pro (www.quickbooks.com)

QuickBooks is popular accounting software created primarily for small and medium-sized businesses to automate all accounting functions. Small business owners (especially those with little training in accounting) find QuickBooks helpful in tracking customer, vendor, and employee financial data. Multiple users can access and collaborate in real time.

Sage 50 Complete Accounting (www.sage.com)

Sage 50 offers accounting software packages that range from simple to complex, comprehensive systems on a subscription basis. In addition to tracking accounting data, packages can be added to perform financial tasks such as job costing or equipment tracking needed for specific industries. With cloud hosting, users can use any internet-connected device and enjoy real-time collaboration of multiple users simultaneously. Templates are included to create over 100 reports and financial statements.

Keep in mind that your choice of an accounting software package depends on the size of your business and its accounting needs. Generally speaking, the more features and customization options provided in the package, the more expensive it will be and the more complex to install and use.

Other cloud small business accounting software options include FreshBooks, Xero, Zoho, and Kashoo.

Sources: Kathy Yakal, "The Best Small Business Accounting Software of 2018," *PC Magazine*, January 15, 2018, www.pcmag.com; Emmanuel Mathew, "How to Choose the Best Cloud Accounting Software for Small & Mid-Size Businesses," *Entrepreneur*, July 7, 2016, www.entrepreneur.com/article/278671; Jen Cohen Crompton, "3 Benefits of Cloud-Based Accounting Tools for Small-Business Owners," *Entrepreneur*, December 14, 2016, www.entrepreneur.com/article/273941.

The second equation, Profit = Revenue – Expenses, represents the activity described on the *income statement*. In other words, the money you get to keep equals the money your business brings in minus what you have to spend.

The third equation, Cash flow = Receipts – Disbursements, is the basis of the *cash flow statement*. The money you have on hand at any given time equals the money you bring in minus what you have to pay out.

We will discuss the balance sheet, the income statement, and the cash flow statement in more detail later in this chapter.

Cash and Accrual Methods of Accounting

One decision you need to make in your accounting system is whether to use cash or accrual accounting. The difference between the two relates to how each shows the timing of your receipts and your disbursements.

Most businesses use the **accrual-basis method** of accounting. With this method, you report your income and expenses at the time they are earned or incurred, rather than when they are collected or paid. Sales you make on credit are recorded as accounts receivable that have not yet been collected. The accrual method also allows you to record payment of expenses over a period of time, even if the actual payment is made in a single installment. For example, you may pay for insurance once or twice a year, but you can record the payments on a monthly basis.

accrual-basis method
A method of accounting in which income and expenses are recorded at the time they are incurred rather than when they are paid.

With the **cash-basis method** of accounting, you record transactions when cash is actually received and expenses are actually paid. The cash method is simpler to keep than the accrual method. Although it may be appropriate for very small businesses, for businesses with no inventory, or for businesses that deal strictly in cash, the cash method can distort financial results over time.

Taxpayers can generally adopt any permissible accounting method, as long as it clearly reflects income. You should not use the cash basis if your business extends credit, because credit sales would not be recorded as sales until you receive payment. Also, your accounts payable would not be recorded as an expense until the bill is paid.[4]

What Accounting Records Do You Need?

To turn data into management information, you need to follow certain guidelines, or standards, called **generally accepted accounting principles (GAAP)**. The group that monitors the appropriateness of these principles is the Financial Accounting Standards Board (FASB; see www.fasb.org). The GAAP guidelines are intended to create financial statement formats that are uniform across industries. Because business is complex, flexibility in GAAP methods is acceptable as long as consistency is maintained within the business. In November 2017 the American Institute of CPAs issued a Financial Reporting Framework for Small- and Medium-Sized Entities regarding non-GAAP financial statements that are worth discussing with your accountant.[5]

Journals and Ledgers. Your accounting actually begins when you record your raw data—from sources such as sales slips, purchase invoices, and check stubs—in journals. A **journal** is simply a place to write down the date of your transactions, the amounts, and the accounts to be debited and credited. You will have several journals, such as sales, purchases, cash receipts, and cash disbursements journals.

At some regular time interval (daily, weekly, or monthly), you will post the transactions recorded in all your journals in a general ledger. A **general ledger** is a summary book for recording all transactions and account balances. One of the advantages of using a computerized accounting system is that it can perform the monotonous task of posting electronically. To speed the posting process and to facilitate access to accounts, each account is assigned a two-digit number. The first digit indicates the class of the account (1 for assets, 2 for liabilities, 3 for capital, 4 for income, and 5 for expenses). The second digit is assigned to each account within the class. For example, your cash account could be assigned account number 11. The first 1 shows that the account is an asset, whereas the second 1 means that it is your first asset listed. Your inventory could be assigned the account number 13, meaning that it is the third asset listed.

At the end of your accounting period or fiscal year, you will close and total each individual account in your general ledger. At this point, or at any time you wish if you are using a computerized accounting package, you can prepare your financial statements to see where your business stands financially. The three most important statements for providing financial information about your business are the income statement, the balance sheet, and the statement of cash flow.

Income Statement. The **income statement**, also called the *profit-and-loss (P&L) statement*, summarizes the income and expenses your company has totaled over a period of time (see Figure 8.3). The income statement illustrates the accounting equation of Profit = Revenue – Expenses. This statement can generally be broken down into the following sections:

- Net sales
- Cost of goods sold
- Gross margin

Stereo City Income Statement for Year Ended December 31, 2014

Income		Percentage of Sales
Net Sales	$450,000	100.00
Cost of Goods Sold	270,000	60.00
GROSS PROFIT ON SALES	$180,000	40.00
Expenses		
Selling Expense		
Advertising	$12,000	2.67
Delivery and Freight	10,000	2.22
Sales Salaries	25,000	5.56
Miscellaneous Selling Expenses	1,000	0.22
Administrative Expense		
Licenses	$150	0.03
Insurance	2,400	0.53
Nonsales Salaries	38,000	8.44
Payroll Taxes	6,300	1.40
Rent/Mortgage	12,400	2.76
Utilities	6,000	1.33
Legal Fees	1,500	0.33
Depreciation	42,000	9.33
Miscellaneous Administrative Expenses	500	0.11
TOTAL EXPENSES	$157,250	34.94
INCOME FROM OPERATIONS	$22,750	5.06
Other Income		
Interest Income	$300	0.07
Other Expenses		
Interest Expense	$15,000	3.33
NET PROFIT (LOSS) BEFORE TAXES	$8,050	1.79
INCOME TAXES	$3,220	0.72
NET PROFIT (LOSS) AFTER TAXES	$4,830	1.07
NOTE:		
Cash Flow from Operations Equals Net Profit or Loss after Taxes plus Depreciation	$46,830	

- Expenses

- Operating income

- Net income (or loss)

Not only does the income statement show an itemization of your sales, cost of goods sold, and expenses, but it also allows you to calculate the percentage relationship of each item of expense to sales. Including these percentages on your financial statements produces a **common-size financial statement**. Common-size financial statements are valuable tools for checking the efficiency trends of your business by measuring and controlling individual expense items.

Consider the example of Stereo City, a retail company that sells home electronic equipment. Stereo City's net sales for the accounting period covered by Figure 8.3 were $450,000. The business had a 40 percent gross profit (or margin), which means that, out of net sales, Stereo City acquired $180,000 with which to cover its operating expenses. Total expenses were $157,250 (34.94 percent of sales). After adding interest income and deducting interest expenses and taxes, the company's net profit—the bottom line—was $46,830.

Balance Sheet. While the income statement shows the financial condition of your business over time, the balance sheet provides an instant "snapshot" of your business at any given moment (usually at the end of the month, quarter, or fiscal year; see Figure 8.4). A balance sheet has two main sections—one showing the assets of the business and one showing the liabilities and owner's equity of the business. As explained previously in the Accounting Equations section, these two sides must balance.

▼ FIGURE 8.4

Stereo City Balance Sheet December 31, 2014

Assets		Percentage of Total Assets
Current Assets:		
Cash	$3,500	1.08
Accounts Receivable	12,000	3.71
Inventory	125,000	38.64
Prepaid Expenses	5,000	1.55
Short-Term Investments	10,000	3.09
Total Current Assets	$155,500	48.07
Fixed Assets:		
Building	$150,000	46.37
Equipment	25,000	7.73
Leasehold Improvements	20,000	6.18
Other Fixed Assets	15,000	4.64
Gross Fixed Assets	$210,000	64.91
Less: Accumulated Depreciation	42,000	12.98
Net Fixed Assets	$168,000	51.93
Total Assets	$323,500	100.00

common-size financial statement
A financial statement that includes a percentage breakdown of each item.

Liabilities and Owners' Equity		Percentage of Liability and Equity
Current Liabilities:		
Accounts Payable	$75,000	23.18
Accruals	7,500	2.32
Current Portion of Long-Term Debt	17,500	5.41
Other Current Liabilities	5,000	1.55
Total Current Liabilities	$105,000	32.46
Long-Term Liabilities:		
Mortgage Loan	$93,000	28.75
Term Loan	39,500	12.21
Total Long-Term Liabilities	$132,500	40.96
Total Liabilities	$237,500	73.42
Owners' Equity:		
Paid-in Capital	$75,000	23.18
Retained Earnings	11,000	3.40
Total Owners' Equity	$86,000	26.58
Total Liabilities and Owners' Equity	$323,500	100.00

On Stereo City's sample balance sheet, you will see a column of percentages of total assets, liabilities, and owner's equity. As with the common-size income statement, these percentages on the common-size balance sheet can indicate accounts and areas that are out of line compared to industry averages, such as those published by Financial Research Associates, Risk Management Association (RMA), or trade associations.

Statement of Cash Flow. The **statement of cash flow** highlights the cash coming into and going out of your business. It is summarized by the accounting equation of Cash flow = Receipts – Disbursements (see Figure 8.5). The importance of tracking and forecasting your cash flow is difficult to overstate because it is often more critical to survival of the business than profits. Many businesses show considerable profit but have problems paying their bills—meaning that they have a cash flow problem.

It is common for new businesses to experience a situation in which more cash goes out than comes in, which is called *negative cash flow*. This condition is not too alarming if it happens when the business is very young or if it happens only occasionally. However, if you experience negative cash flow regularly, you may be *undercapitalized*, which is a serious problem.[6] Managing your cash flow will be covered in more detail later in this chapter.

What If You Are Starting a New Business?. If you are starting a new business, you don't have historical data to compile in financial statements. Even so, you must estimate how much money you will need, what your expenses will be at different sales levels, and how much money you can expect to make. Financial planning and budgeting are important parts of the business-planning

statement of cash flow
A financial statement that shows the cash inflows and outflows of a business.

▶ FIGURE 8.5

Stereo City Statement of Cash Flow for Year Ending December 31, 2019

	October	November	December	January	February	March	April	May	June	July	August	September	Total
Cash Receipts:													
Retail Receipts (a)	$46,875	$46,875	$46,875	$28,125	$28,125	$28,125	$37,500	$37,500	$37,500	$37,500	$37,500	$37,500	$450,000
Interest Income				100				100				100	300
Total Cash Receipts	$46,875	$46,875	$46,875	$28,225	$28,125	$28,125	$37,500	$37,400	$37,500	$37,500	$37,500	$37,400	$450,300
Cash Disbursements:													
Cost of Goods Sold (b)	$28,125	$28,125	$28,125	$16,875	$16,875	$16,875	$22,500	$22,500	$22,500	$22,500	$22,500	$22,500	$270,000
Sales Expenses	2,403	2,403	2,403	1,562	1,562	1,562	2,083	2,083	2,083	2,083	2,083	2,090	25,000
Advertising	1,000	1,000	1,000	1,000	1,000	1,000	1,000	1,000	1,000	1,000	1,000	1,000	12,000
Insurance	0	400	0	0	400	0	0	400	0	0	400	0	2,400
Legal and Accounting	0	0	375	0	0	375	0	0	375	0	0	375	1,500
Delivery Expenses	1,042	1,042	1,042	625	625	625	833	833	833	833	833	834	10,000
**Fixed Cash Disbursements	4,328	4,328	4,328	4,328	4,328	4,328	4,328	4,328	4,328	4,328	4,128	4,328	51,930
Mortgage (c)	1,033	1,033	1,033	1,033	1,033	1,033	1,033	1,033	1,033	1,033	1,033	1,037	12,400
Term Loan (d)	1,466	1,466	1,466	1,466	1,466	1,466	1,466	1,466	1,466	1,466	1,466	1,466	17,592
Total Cash Disbursements	$39,596	$40,197	$39,972	$26,889	$27,489	$27,264	$33,243	$33,843	$33,618	$33,243	$33,843	$33,630	$402,822
Net Cash Flow	$7,279	$6,679	$6,904	$1,337	$637	$862	$4,258	$3,758	$3,883	$4,258	$3,658	$3,971	$47,478
Cumulative Cash Flow **FCD	$7,279	$13,957	$20,861	$22,197	$22,834	$23,695	$27,953	$31,710	$35,593	$39,850	$43,508	$47,478	

Fixed Cash Disbursements:	October	November	December	January	February	March	April	May	June	July	August	September	Total
Utilities	$6,000												
Nonsales Salaries	38,000												
Payroll Taxes and Benefits	6,300												
Licenses	150												
Misc. Selling Expenses	1,000												
Miscellaneous	480												
Total FCD	$51,930												
Avg. FDC per month	$4,328												
Cash on Hand:													
–Opening Balance	$3,500	$10,779	$17,457	$24,361	$25,697	$26,334	$27,195	$31,453	$35,210	$39,093	$43,350	$47,008	
–Cash Receipts	46,875	46,875	46,875	28,225	28,125	28,125	37,500	37,400	37,500	37,500	37,500	37,400	
Cash Disbursements	(39,596)	(40,197)	(39,972)	(26,889)	(27,489)	(27,264)	(33,243)	(33,843)	(33,618)	(33,243)	(33,843)	(33,630)	
Total = New Cash (e) Balance	$10,779	$17,457	$24,361	$25,697	$26,334	$27,195	$31,453	$35,210	$39,093	$43,350	$47,008	$50,978	

(a) This assumes that all sales are collected in the month the sale is made.

(b) This is just the Cost of the goods row from the monthly income projection worksheet. Cost of Goods is calculated as 40 percent of the estimated total sales for the month.

(c) The mortgage payments (including both principal and interest) are for a $93,000 15-year loan at 10.6 percent. You can use the spreadsheet function @ PMT () to calculate this: Payment = @ PMT (loan amount, rate per month, number of months) = @ PMT (93,000, 106/12, 15*12)

(d) The loan is $39,500 for 2 V2 years at 8.5 percent. The amount shown includes both principal and interest and is calculated as follows: Payment = @ PMT (39,500, 85/12, 2.5*12)

(e) A typical strategy for established businesses with fairly predictable revenues and expenses is to open an account such as a "Money Market Deposit Account" with their bank. This account, which is interest earning, is used to store excess cash balances and cover cash shortages.

process. Making financial projections can reveal whether you should even start the business. Are the financial risks you are about to take worth the *realistic* return you can expect? Such projections are made in **pro forma financial statements**, which are either full or partial estimates, because you are making projections rather than recording actual transactions. (*Pro forma* is Latin meaning "for the sake of form.") Because these statements help you determine your future cash needs and financial condition, a new business should prepare them at least every quarter, if not every month.

In preparing pro forma statements, you need to state the assumptions you are making for your projections. How did you come up with the numbers? Did you grab them out of the air? Did the owner of a similar (but noncompeting) business share his actual numbers for you to use as a base? Are they based on industry averages, such as RMA's *Annual Statement Studies*? The closer the numbers are to what will really happen, the more useful the statements are for decision-making.

> "Making financial projections can reveal whether you should even start the business. Are the financial risks you are about to take worth the *realistic* return you can expect?"

Using Financial Statements to Run Your Small Business

Creating financial statements is one thing, but using them to make informed decisions to run your small business is another. Here's an analogy: When you are driving a vehicle, how do you know when something needs attention? By looking at the instruments on your dashboard. Think of financial statements as your instruments for running your business. Just as in driving, to make correct management decisions you need to know what to look at and when to check. Here's a Financial Status Checklist for checking the gauges:

Daily

1. Check your cash balance on hand.

2. Check your bank balance.

3. Calculate daily summaries of sales and cash receipts.

4. Note any problems in your credit collections.

5. Record any money paid out.

Weekly

1. *Cash flow.* Update a spreadsheet of regular receipts and disbursement entries. The discipline required by this endeavor will help you see what is going on in your business and help you to plan for any cash deficiencies.

2. *Accounts receivable.* Note especially slow-paying accounts.

3. *Accounts payable.* Note discounts offered.

4. *Payroll.* Calculate the accumulation of hours worked and total payroll owed.

5. *Taxes.* Note when tax items are due and which reports are required.

Monthly

pro forma financial statements
Financial statements that project what a firm's financial condition will be in the future.

1. If you use an outside accounting service, provide records of your receipts, disbursements, bank accounts, and journals.

2. Review your income statement.

3. Review your balance sheet.

4. Reconcile your business checking account.

5. Balance your petty cash account.

6. Review federal tax requirements and make deposits.

7. Review and age your accounts receivable.

Concept Check Questions

1. You need to write a business plan for a start-up business. How do you come up with the numbers for your pro forma financial statements? Do you just guess and make them up? (*Hint*: The process starts with a sales forecast.)

2. Explain the difference between cash and accrual accounting.

3. Assets = Liabilities + Owner's equity. How would you restate this equation if you wanted to know what your liabilities are? Your owner's equity?

4. What purpose do GAAP and FASB serve for a small business owner?

Concept Module 8.3: Analyzing Financial Statements

- **LO 8.3: Explain the 11 ratios used to analyze financial statements.**

Your ability to make sound financial decisions will depend on how well you can understand, interpret, and use the information contained in your company's financial statements. This section gives an overview of the most common form of financial analysis: ratio analysis.

Ratio Analysis

Suppose that two entrepreneurs are comparing how well their respective businesses performed last year. The first entrepreneur, Ms. Alpha, determines that her store made 50 percent more profits last year than the store owned by the second entrepreneur, Mr. Beta. Should Ms. Alpha feel proud? To answer this question, we need more information.

The profit figures tell us only part of the story. Although generating 50 percent more profits *seems* good, we need to see how profit relates to other aspects of each business. For example, what if Ms. Alpha's store is four times the size of Mr. Beta's store? Or what if Ms. Alpha's store made three times as many sales as Mr. Beta's store? Now does 50 percent more profit seem as good?

The reality is that fair comparisons can be made only when we demonstrate the relationships between differing financial accounts of the businesses. The relationships that show the relative size of some financial quantity to another financial quantity of a firm are called **financial ratios**. Four important categories of financial ratios are the liquidity, asset utilization, leverage, and profitability ratios.[7] It is important to use more than one ratio from each of the four categories of ratios and to use all categories when analyzing your company. Just like you check more than just the gas gauge on the car before a trip, each of the categories of ratios and the types of comparison provide differing insight into the financial workings of your business.

> "The profit figures tell us only part of the story."

Using Financial Ratios

Financial ratios by themselves tell us very little. For purposes of analysis, ratios are useful only when compared to other ratios. Three types of ratio comparisons can be employed: benchmarking analysis, which compares firms to industry leaders; industry average analysis, which

financial ratios
Calculations that compare important financial aspects of a business.

DO YOU HAVE A BUSINESS OR A HOBBY?

If your sideline business produces revenue but consistently loses money, be careful—the IRS could consider your writing, woodwork, artwork, or crafts to be a hobby. A lot of people are running sideline businesses in what has become known as the gig economy—so, what difference does it make if you have a business or a hobby? Your tax liability is the difference.

- If you have a hobby, you report all income from the sale of your paintings, woodworking, baking, web design, and so on, but your deductions are limited to the income generated. You have to itemize your deductions (not take standard deduction) as miscellaneous. You can only claim any amount in excess of 2 percent of your adjusted gross income.

- If you have a business, again all your income is reported, but legitimate business expenses may offset. Business expenses are fully deductible on Schedule C of your tax return. If your direct costs exceed your business income, you can use that loss to offset your other income on Form 1040.

How does the IRS determine whether you have a business or a hobby? The agency presumes that if you show a profit in three of the past five years, you have a business. If you fail the three-of-five-year test and can't demonstrate the following bulleted factors, you have a hobby. To classify your operation as a business, you have to prove a profit motive. In order to make this determination, consider the following factors:

- Does the time and effort put into the activity indicate an intention to make a profit?

- Does the taxpayer depend on income from the activity?

- If there are losses, are they due to circumstances beyond the taxpayer's control or did they occur in the start-up phase of the business?

- Has the taxpayer changed methods of operation to improve profitability?

- Does the taxpayer or his/her advisers have the knowledge needed to carry on the activity as a successful business?

- Has the taxpayer made a profit in similar activities in the past?

- Does the activity make a profit in some years?

- Can the taxpayer expect to make a profit in the future from the appreciation of assets used in the activity?

Not all hobbies are created equal when it comes to turning them into potential businesses. Collecting navel lint—probably not so much. Making unique jewelry that you can sell on Etsy—maybe. Be sure to start small in testing the time required and demands your business is going to make. When the realities of that time and those demands sink in and if you still enjoy your hobby, it may be a signal to start growing it into a business. Finally, you have to monetize. Get your first sale, whether it's a $10 jar of yummy salsa or a $2,000 wedding photo shoot. That first sale is the toughest and most important one you'll ever make.

Source: Jeffrey Hayzlett, "Is It a Hobby or a Business? 5 Things You Need to Know to Monetize Your Hobby," *Entrepreneur*, February 27, 2017, www.entrepreneur.com/article/289750; Larry Alton, "How to Turn Your Hobby Into a Profitable Business Venture," *Entrepreneur*, December 28, 2016, www.entrepreneur.com/article/286813; Rhett Power, "Questions to Ask Yourself Before Turning Your Hobby into a Business," *Inc.*, June 1, 2017, www.inc.com; Dorcas Chen-Tozun, "4 Steps to Turn Your Hobby into a Business," *Inc.*, October 6, 2017, www.inc.com.

---

compares firms' financial ratios to the industry averages; and trend analysis, which compares a single firm's present performance with its own past performance, preferably for more than two years.

Benchmarking is taking an industry leader or major competitor, computing their ratios, and then comparing the small business to that firm. Since ratios take away the size differential, even a new start-up can compare itself to the best in the industry and set financial targets based upon industry leaders.

Industry average analysis is often done by comparing an individual firm's ratios against the standard ratios for the firm's industry. Such industry ratios may be found in resources available in most college or large public libraries. Look for RMA's *Annual Statement Studies* or Dun & Bradstreet's *Industry Norms and Key Business Ratios*. Another good source is *Financial Studies of the Small Business* from Financial Research Associates.

industry average analysis
A comparison of a firm's financial ratios to the industry averages.

Table 8.1 shows an example of the financial ratio information located in RMA's *Annual Statement Studies*. At the top of the page in that publication are column headings showing the amount of sales for your type of company. Choose the column that matches the sales figure on your income statement. Looking down the column you will find three sets of numbers for each ratio listed. These three numbers provide a range so you can determine how close your company is to meeting the industry numbers. For example, the *current ratio* for the industry represented in the table shows 0.7, 1.5, and 3.9. If the current ratio for your company is 1.48, you are falling right in the middle of the numbers but are not anywhere close to the top or the best in the industry. Your company (Stereo City) could easily use more liquidity (more cash). When using the RMA tables, make sure you calculate your ratios using the same formulas as the RMA, which they provide.

Trend analysis involves comparing your own numbers to your numbers from last year and the year before. Trends can be seen using this analysis that can show a small business owner where changes need to occur in order to keep the company profitable. If there is potential trouble in any of the four main areas of analysis (liquidity, asset utilization, leverage, and profitability), managers will have time to correct these problems before the problems become overbearing. The key to potential solutions is found in the ratios themselves. For example, if the trend analysis shows that the firm's liquidity is diminishing, the managers will want to take action to enhance the firm's liquidity position.

▼ TABLE 8.1

Comparing Company and Industry Ratios

	Stereo City	Industry
Liquidity		
Current Ratio	1.48	3.9
		1.5
		.7
Quick Ratio	0.29	.6
Asset Utilization		
Average Collection Period	9.7	13.1
Total Asset Turnover	1.39	3.5
Leverage		
Debt Ratio	73.0	74.3
Times Interest Earned	1.5	1.1
Profitability		
Return on Assets[a]	1.49	2.5

Source: Based on RMA's *2014–2015 Annual Statement Studies*; NAICS 443142 Retail Electronics Stores, 925.

[a]Uses pretax profit.

Liquidity Ratios

Liquidity ratios are used to measure a firm's ability to meet its short-term obligations to creditors as they come due. *Liquidity* refers to how quickly an asset can be turned into the amount of cash it is actually currently worth—the more quickly it can become cash, the more liquid it is said to be. The financial data used to determine liquidity are the firm's current assets and current liabilities found on the balance sheet. There are two important liquidity ratios: the current ratio and the quick (or acid-test) ratio.

Current Ratio. The **current ratio** measures the number of times the firm can cover its current liabilities with its current assets. The current ratio assumes that both accounts receivable and inventory can be easily converted to cash. Current ratios of 1.0 or less are considered low and indicative of financial difficulties. Current ratios of more than 2.0 often suggest excessive liquidity that may be adverse to the firm's profitability.

$$\text{Current ratio} = \frac{\text{Current assets}}{\text{Current liabilities}}$$

Using Stereo City's balance sheet, we compute the company's current ratio as follows:

$$\frac{\$155,000}{\$105,000} = 1.48$$

Thus Stereo City can cover its current liabilities 1.48 times with its current assets. Another way of looking at this ratio is to recognize that the company has $1.48 of current assets for each

trend analysis
A comparison of a single firm's present performance with its own past performance, preferably for more than two years.

liquidity ratios
Financial ratios used to measure a firm's ability to meet its short-term obligations to creditors as they come due.

current ratio
A financial ratio that measures the number of times a firm can cover its current liabilities with its current assets.

$1.00 of current liabilities. When compared to the middle industry average number of 1.5 from the RMA table, Stereo City is only off by two cents compared to the industry and far above the low number of 70 cents. So Stereo City is doing reasonably well in the area of liquidity, with some room for improvement, when including inventory in the calculation. Short-term creditors should not be concerned that Stereo City will not be able to meet its current obligations.

Quick Ratio. The **quick (acid-test) ratio** measures the firm's ability to meet its current obligations with the most liquid of its current assets. The quick ratio is computed as follows:

$$\text{Quick ratio} = \frac{\text{Current assets} - \text{Inventory}}{\text{Current liabilities}}$$

Using the data from Stereo City's balance sheet, we compute the quick ratio as

$$\frac{\$155,000 - \$125,000}{\$105,000} = 0.29$$

Stereo City has only $0.29 in liquid assets for each $1.00 of current liabilities. The company obviously counts on making sales to pay its current obligations. When compared to the industry average of .60, Stereo City is much less liquid than other companies, and short-term creditors, like suppliers, may be concerned about the ability of Stereo City to pay its accounts payable on time making them less likely to extend credit to Stereo City.

Asset Utilization Ratios

Asset utilization ratios measure the speed with which various assets are converted into sales or cash. These ratios are often used to measure how efficiently a firm uses its assets. Four important asset utilization ratios exist: inventory turnover, average collection period, fixed asset turnover, and total asset turnover.

Inventory Turnover. **Inventory turnover** measures the liquidity of the firm's inventory—how quickly goods are sold and replenished. The higher the inventory turnover, the more times the firm is selling, or "turning over," its inventory. A high inventory ratio generally implies efficient inventory management. The optimal speed of inventory turnover depends upon the type of business. For example, you would want Krispy Kreme to have a high inventory turnover. A high-end jewelry story may not turn over their inventory more than once or at most, twice a year. Inventory turnover is computed as follows:

$$\text{Inventory turnover} = \frac{\text{Cost of goods sold}}{\text{Inventory}}$$

Using data from Stereo City's income statement and balance sheet, we compute the inventory turnover as

$$\frac{\$270,000}{\$125,000} = 2.16$$

Thus, Stereo City restocked its inventory 2.16 times last year. When compared to the industry average turnover number of 8.7, Stereo City is not selling their products close to the number of times of the competition. Increasing sales should become a primary focus for the company.

Average Collection Period. The **average collection period** is a measure of how long it takes a firm to convert a credit sale (internal store credit, not credit card sales) into a usable form (cash). All firms that extend credit must compute this ratio to determine the effectiveness of their credit-granting and collection policies. High average collection periods usually indicate many uncollectible receivables, whereas low average collection periods may indicate overly restrictive credit-granting policies. The average collection period is computed as follows:

$$\text{Average collection period} = \frac{\text{Accounts receivable}}{\text{Average sales per day}}$$

Using the data from Stereo City's balance sheet and income statement, we compute the average collection period as

$$\frac{\$12,000}{\$450,000 \, / \, 365} = 9.93$$

Stereo City collects its receivables in fewer than 10 days. The industry average is 13.1 days, so it is taking Stereo City less time to collect credit sales than other companies in the industry, which should have a positive impact on cash flow.

Fixed Asset Turnover. The **fixed asset turnover** ratio measures how efficiently the firm is using its assets to generate sales. This ratio is particularly important for businesses with a lot of equipment or buildings since it is measuring the effectiveness of these assets in generating sales. A low ratio can indicate that sales are off due perhaps to marketing efforts that are ineffective or that the equipment being used is older and requiring increasing downtime for maintenance. The fixed asset turnover ratio is calculated as follows:

$$\text{Fixed asset turnover} = \frac{\text{Sales}}{\text{Net fixed assets}}$$

Using the data from Stereo City's income statement and balance sheet, we compute the fixed asset turnover ratio as

$$\frac{\$450,000}{\$168,000} = 2.68$$

Stereo City turns over its net fixed assets 2.68 times per year, compared to the industry average of 33.5. This ratio shows that Stereo City is not using its fixed assets, property, plant, and equipment nearly as efficiently as the industry.

Total Asset Turnover. The **total asset turnover** ratio measures how efficiently the firm uses all of its assets to generate sales, so a high ratio generally reflects good overall management. A low ratio may indicate flaws in the firm's overall strategy, poor marketing efforts, or improper capital expenditures. Total asset turnover is calculated as follows:

$$\text{Total asset turnover} = \frac{\text{Sales}}{\text{Total assets}}$$

Using the data from Stereo City's income statement and balance sheet, we compute the total asset turnover as

$$\frac{\$450,000}{\$323,500} = 1.39$$

fixed asset turnover
An asset utilization ratio that measures how efficiently a firm is using its assets to generate sales.

total asset turnover
An asset utilization ratio that measures how efficiently the firm uses all of its assets to generate sales; a high ratio generally reflects good overall management.

Stereo City turns its assets over 1.39 times per year, compared to the industry average of 3.5, which indicates that Stereo City has some major issues with the efficient use of its assets. If any of the other asset utilization ratios are not on target, the total asset turnover ratio will be off also, so it is not surprising that this ratio confirms the activity problems Stereo City is currently experiencing.

Leverage Ratios

Leverage ratios measure the extent to which a firm uses debt as a source of financing and its ability to service that debt. The term *leverage* refers to the magnification of risk and potential return that come with using other people's money to generate profits. Think of the increased power that is gained when a fulcrum is moved under a simple lever. The farther the fulcrum is from the point where you are pushing on the lever, the more weight you can lift. The more debt a firm uses, the more financial leverage it has. Two important leverage ratios are the debt ratio and the times-interest-earned ratio.

Debt Ratio. The **debt ratio** measures the proportion of a firm's total assets that is acquired with borrowed funds. Total debt includes short-term debt, long-term debt, and long-term obligations such as leases. A high ratio indicates a more aggressive approach to financing and is evidence of a high-risk, high-expected-return strategy. A low ratio indicates a more conservative approach to financing. The debt ratio is calculated as follows:

$$\text{Debt ratio} = \frac{\text{Total debt}}{\text{Total assets}}$$

Using the data from Stereo City's balance sheet, we compute the debt ratio as

$$\frac{\$237,5000}{\$323,500} = 0.73$$

This ratio indicates that the company has financed 73 percent of its assets with borrowed funds. That is, $0.73 of every $1.00 of funding for Stereo City has come from debt. The industry average is .74 so Stereo City is using slightly less debt than the average in the industry.

Times-Interest-Earned Ratio. **Times interest earned** calculates the firm's ability to meet its interest requirements. It shows how far operating income can decline before the firm will likely experience difficulties in servicing its debt obligations. A high ratio indicates a low-risk situation but may also suggest an inefficient use of leverage. A low ratio indicates immediate action should be taken to ensure that no debt payments will go into default status. Times interest earned is computed as follows:

$$\text{Times interest earned} = \frac{\text{Operating income}}{\text{Interest expense}}$$

Using the data from Stereo City's income statement, we compute times interest earned as

$$\frac{\$22,750}{\$15,000} = 1.52$$

Thus the company has operating income 1.52 times its interest obligations compared to the industry average of 1.1 times. Stereo City can easily make its interest obligations compared to the industry, which will be viewed as a good sign by any potential lenders.

leverage ratios
Financial ratios that measure the extent to which a firm uses debt as a source of financing and its ability to service that debt.

debt ratio
A leverage ratio that measures the proportion of a firm's total assets that is acquired with borrowed funds.

times interest earned
A leverage ratio that calculates the firm's ability to meet its interest requirements.

READY TO EXPAND?

The popularity of soccer as a participation sport attracted Leo Hernandez and Gil Ferguson to open an indoor soccer arena with retail shops selling soccer-related merchandise. Last year's financial statements for their business OnGoal are shown here. Leo and Gil are hoping to expand their business by opening another facility. However, before they approach banks or potential investors, they need to look closely at what the accounting statements show them.

Questions

1. Calculate liquidity, asset utilization, leverage, and profitability ratios for OnGoal.

2. Pair off and compare your ratios. Discuss which of the ratios look weak and which look positive. Develop a one-page explanation of the company's ratios you can show to potential lenders.

OnGoal Balance Sheet
December 31, 20--

Assets		
Current Assets:		
Cash	$7,120	
Accounts Receivable	2,400	
Merchandise Inventory	18,200	
Prepaid Expenses	3,040	
Total Current Assets		$40,760
Fixed Assets:		
Fixtures	$16,800	
Less Accumulated Depreciation	3,600	
Building	78,000	
Less Accumulated Depreciation	7,800	
Equipment	12,000	
Less Accumulated Depreciation	4,000	
Total Fixed Assets		$91,400
Total Assets		$132,160
Liabilities/Equity		
Current Liabilities:		
Accounts Payable	$6,000	
Notes Payable	4,000	
Contracts Payable	8,000	
Total Current Liabilities		$18,000
Fixed Liabilities:		
Long-Term Note Payable	$75,000	
Owners' Equity:		
Shares Held by Hernandez and Ferguson	$39,160	
Total Liabilities/Equity		**$132,160**

(Continued)

OnGoal Income Statement

Year Ended December 31, 20--

Sales		$178,000
Cost of Goods Sold:		
Beginning Inventory, January 1	$18,000	
Purchases During Year	22,000	
Less Ending Inventory, December 31	18,200	
Cost of Goods Sold		$21,800
Gross Margin		$156,200
Operating Expenses:		
Payment on Building Note	$34,000	
Salaries	68,000	
Supplies	7,460	
Advertising/Promotion	3,000	
Insurance Expense	18,000	
Utilities Expense	10,000	
Miscellaneous Expenses	4,000	
Total Operating Expenses		$144,460
Net Profit from Operations		$11,740

Profitability Ratios

Profitability ratios are used to measure the ability of a company to turn sales into profits and to earn profits on assets committed. Additionally, profitability ratios allow some insight into the overall effectiveness of the management team. There are three important profitability ratios: net profit margin, return on assets, and return on equity.

Net Profit Margin. The **net profit margin** measures the percentage of each sales dollar that remains as profit after all expenses, including taxes, have been paid. This ratio is widely used as a gauge of management efficiency. Although net profit margins vary greatly by industry, a low ratio may indicate that expenses are too high relative to sales. Net profit margin can be obtained from a common-size income statement or computed with the following formula:

$$\text{Net profit} = \frac{\text{Net income}}{\text{Sales}}$$

Using the data from Stereo City's income statement, we compute the net profit margin as

$$\frac{\$4,830}{\$450,000} = 0.0107$$

This company actually generates .01 cent of after-tax profit for each $1.00 of sales.

profitability ratios
Financial ratios that are used to measure the ability of a company to turn sales into profits and to earn profits on assets and owner's equity committed.

net profit margin
A profitability ratio that measures the percentage of each sales dollar that remains as profit after all expenses, including taxes, have been paid.

Return on Assets. Also known as *return on investment*, **return on assets** indicates the firm's effectiveness in generating profits from its available assets. The higher this ratio is, the better. A high ratio shows effective management and good chances for future growth. The return on assets is found with the following formula:

$$\text{Return on assets} = \frac{\text{Net profit after taxes}}{\text{Total assets}}$$

Using the data from Stereo City's income statement and balance sheet, we compute the return on assets as

$$\frac{\$4,830}{\$323,500} = 0.0149$$

This company generates approximately 1.5 cents of after-tax profit for each $1.00 of assets the company has at its disposal. The industry average is 2.5, again indicating that Stereo City may not effectively be using its assets compared to the industry.

Return on Equity. The **return on equity** measures the return the firm earned on its owner's investment in the firm. In general, the higher this ratio, the better off financially the owner will be. However, return on equity is highly affected by the amount of financial leverage (borrowed money) used by the firm and may not provide an accurate measure of management effectiveness. The return on equity is calculated as follows:

$$\text{Return on equity} = \frac{\text{Net profit after taxes}}{\text{Owner's equity}}$$

Using the data from Stereo City's income statement and balance sheet, we compute the return on equity as

$$\frac{\$4,830}{\$86,000} = 0.0562$$

This company generates a little more than 5.5 cents of after-tax profit for each $1.00 of owner's equity. This ratio tells a business owner if he or she is receiving enough return from invested money. Compared to the industry average of 41.8, Stereo City is not making a comparable return for its investors. In the Stereo City example, 5.5 percent return is not much for the risk involved. That $86,000 could be placed in a relatively safe investment like a corporate bond, where it could earn a much higher return with less risk. This kind of information can tell a business owner whether a business is a good investment compared with other alternative uses for her money.

After reviewing all the ratios, from the data we can conclude that Stereo City potentially has three major problems.

First, Stereo City's quick ratio is only about half the industry average. This could mean the company has the possibility of liquidity issues if the inventory does not sell in a timely manner. Short-term creditors may be reluctant to extend credit for supplies being purchased, which would force Stereo City to a cash-only basis for purchases.

Second, Stereo City appears to have a problem with selling inventory. The company needs to focus on increasing sales and turning over their inventory. Increasing marketing efforts or training salespeople may both be options to fix this problem.

Third, Stereo City's total asset turnover, fixed asset turnover, and return on asset ratios are considerably below the industry averages. The likely cause is that the firm has insufficient

return on assets
A profitability ratio that indicates the firm's effectiveness in generating profits from its available assets; also known as return on investment.

return on equity
A profitability ratio that measures the return the firm earned on its owner's investment in the firm.

sales to support the size of the business. The company must work harder to increase sales or more efficiently use its current assets. If the small business owner does not make productive changes soon, Stereo City may face serious financial difficulties and even closure of the business.

Because ratio analysis has revealed that Stereo City needs to increase its liquidity, increasing current assets (especially cash and short-term investments) and decreasing current liabilities are possible solutions. Any action that boosts the firm's liquidity helps to avoid the risk of Stereo City's becoming insolvent because of diminishing liquidity.

Reviewing financial ratios annually can help you circumvent difficult situations before they have the opportunity to occur. Thus ratio analysis allows small business owners and managers to become proactive directors of the financial aspects of their ventures.

Concept Check Questions

1. Define the term *leverage* as it applies to accounting.

2. How can profitability ratios provide insight into the effectiveness of management? Liquidity ratios? Asset utilization ratios? Leverage ratios?

3. The sales projection for your retail business is $650,000. The industry average for the asset turnover ratio is 5. How much inventory (total assets) should you plan to stock?

Concept Module 8.4: Managing Cash Flow

- **LO 8.4: Illustrate the importance of and procedures for managing cash flow.**

Each business day, approximately a dozen U.S. small businesses declare bankruptcy. The majority of these business failures are caused by poor cash-flow management. Companies from the smallest start-ups to the largest conglomerates all share the same need for positive cash flow. A company that does not effectively manage its cash flow is poised for collapse.

Cash Flow Defined

"A company that does not effectively manage its cash flow is poised for collapse."

The accounting definition of **cash flow** is the sum of net income plus any non-cash expenses, such as depreciation and amortization. This treatment of cash flow is largely misunderstood by many small business owners. A more "bottom-line" approach is to define cash flow as the difference between the actual amount of cash a company brings in and the actual amount of cash a company disburses in a given time period.

The most important aspects of this refined definition are the inclusion of the terms *actual cash* and *time period*. The goal of good cash flow management is to have enough cash on hand when you need it. It doesn't matter if your company will have a positive cash balance three months from now if your payroll, taxes, insurance, and suppliers all need to be paid today.

Cash flow management requires as much attention as developing new customers, perfecting products and services, and engaging in all other day-to-day operating activities. The basic strategy is to maximize your use of cash. This means not only ensuring consistent cash inflows, but also developing a disciplined approach to cash outflows.

Could your cash flow management system be computerized? As noted earlier in the chapter, single-entry general ledger accounting software packages are certainly easy to use. However, these packages can provide an unrealistic view of your business's cash flow. In a single-entry system, all cash coming into the business is put on the left-hand side of the ledger, and cash flowing out of the business appears on the right-hand side. However, if your business has accounts receivable or accounts payable, a single-entry system can fool you into thinking you have enough cash on hand to meet expenses or to pursue business expansion.

cash flow
The sum of net income plus any noncash expenses, such as depreciation and amortization, or the difference between the actual amount of cash a company brings in and the actual amount of cash a company disburses in a given time period.

Cash Flow Fundamentals

The first step in cash-flow management is to understand the purpose and nature of cash flow. Why do you need cash flow? How is cash flow generated? How do firms become insolvent even though they are profitable? To answer these questions, we need to look at the motives for having cash, the cash-to-cash cycle, and the timing of cash inflows and outflows.

Motives for Having Cash. A firm needs cash for three reasons: (1) to make transactions, (2) to protect against unanticipated problems, and (3) to invest in opportunities as they arise. Of these, the primary motive is to make transactions—to pay the bills incurred by the business. If a business cannot meet its obligations, it is insolvent. Continued insolvency leads directly to bankruptcy.

Businesses, like individuals, occasionally run into unanticipated problems. Thefts, fires, floods, and other natural and human-made disasters affect businesses in the same way they affect individuals. Those businesses that have "saved for a rainy day" are able to withstand such setbacks. Those that have not planned ahead often suffer—and may even fail—as a result.

Finally, sometimes a business is presented with an opportunity to invest in a profitable venture. If the business has enough cash on hand to do so, it may reap significant rewards. If not, it has lost a chance to add to its cash flow in a way other than through normal operations.

Each of these three motives is important to understand, as they combine to create the proper mentality for the cash flow manager. If a firm does not proactively manage its cash flow, it will be exposed to many risks, any of which may spell disaster.

Cash-to-Cash Cycle. The **cash-to-cash cycle** of the firm, sometimes known as the *operating cycle*, tracks the way cash flows through the business. It identifies how long it takes from the time a firm makes a cash outlay for raw materials or inventory until the cash is collected from the sale of the finished good. Figure 8.6 shows a typical cash-to-cash cycle.

The firm begins with cash that is used to purchase raw materials or inventory. It will normally take some time to manufacture or otherwise hold finished goods until they sell. As sales are made, cash is replenished immediately by cash sales, but accounts receivable are created by credit sales. The firm must then collect the receivables to secure cash.

The cash flow process is continuous, with all activities occurring simultaneously. When the process is operating smoothly, cash flow is easy to monitor and control. However, for most firms, it is often erratic and subject to many complications, which makes cash flow management a challenge.

Timing of Cash Flows. The major complication of cash flow management is timing. While some cash inflows and outflows will transpire on a regular schedule (such as monthly interest

> **cash-to-cash cycle**
> The period of time from when money is spent on raw materials until it is collected from the sale of a finished good.

▼ FIGURE 8.6

Cash-to-Cash Cycle

A chart of the cash-to-cash cycle of your small business shows the amount of time that passes between spending money for raw materials or inventory and collecting money on the sale of finished goods.

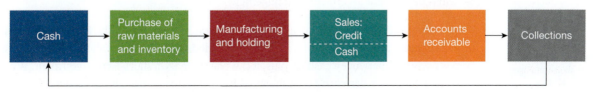

OPENING THE BOOKS

Open-book management (OBM) is going strong, in spite of recessions and skeptics. Small businesses are finding that if employees have access to and understand financial statements, better decisions—from the kind of mechanic tape used to negotiating sales—can be made by employees. Once thought off-limits to all but owners, OBM encourages small business owners to share critical financial information with employees regularly, which then allows better decision-making throughout the company. When employees know and understand the numbers, they can measure their contributions to the company's bottom line and assess how their performance can make a difference in those numbers.

One of the first proponents of OBM was Jack Stack, president and CEO of Springfield Remanufacturing Company. In *The Great Game of Business,* he states that you need to teach employees the rules of the game, give them the information (the financials) they need to play the game, and make sure they share in the risks and rewards.

Joel Gascoigne, CEO of Buffer, a social media management company saw his business growing rapidly so he boosted staffing accordingly—from 34 to 94 employees in a year. Unfortunately, the impact on productivity from more employees didn't materialize. Even though he was generating sales of $875,000 per month by the beginning of 2017, he would be broke in five months. He had to lay off employees, AND explain how he had

failed, how the company's finances suffered, and how he'd fix it—to his customers, employees and investors. Gascoigne had committed to running a totally transparent company and he couldn't back off.

Employees at Texas Air Composites in Cedar Hill, Texas, found numerous ways to cut expenses when buying shop supplies, like finding tape that was $2.50 a roll instead of $15 that did the same job. Once employees became aware of the costs through OBM, they were willing to take steps to curtail costs.

OBM is all about giving employees not only access to financial information but also control and incentive to change that financial information to positively impact the company, which then also benefits the employee.

Does OBM work? Entrepreneurs who are baring their company souls to the world often wonder, "Who is reading this stuff?" Even if audiences are small for a small business's financial statements, the point of OBM is much bigger. The fact that a company is willing to disclose so much information breeds a level of trust that is impossible to buy.

Sources: Clint Carter, "Should You Let Your Clients (or Your Staff) See Your Financials?" *Entrepreneur,* January 23, 2017, www.entrepreneur.com/article/286638; Dori Meinert, "An Open Book" *HR Magazine,* April 2014, 42–46; Carolee Colter and Melanie Reid, "Opening the Books," *Natural Foods Merchandiser,* May 2013, 22.

income or payroll costs), other cash flows occur on no schedule whatsoever. For example, when a firm needs to make periodic purchases of capital equipment, which are not part of the daily cash-to-cash process, it will cause a major disruption in the firm's cash flow.

Even though a firm might send out all of its billings to credit customers at one time, you can be sure these customers will not all pay at the same time. Uncollected receivables may count as revenue on an accrual-based income statement, but they are worthless from a cash flow standpoint until they turn into real money.

The small business owner needs to become well versed in the patterns of cash inflows and outflows of the firm. The nuances of timing become critical. A few tools are available that can assist in this process, which we will now discuss.

Cash Flow Management Tools

Once you have a good idea about the purpose and nature of cash flow, you are ready to take steps to manage it. Using cash budgets and aging schedules to control the inflow and outflow of cash is paramount for effective management.

cash budgets
A plan for short-term uses and sources of cash.

Cash Budgets. **Cash budgets** (also known as *cash forecasts*) allow the firm to plan its short-term cash needs, paying particular attention to periods of surplus and shortage. Whenever the firm is likely to experience a cash surplus, it can plan to make a short-term investment. When the firm is expected to experience a cash shortage, it can plan to arrange for a short-term loan.

A cash budget typically covers a one-year period that is divided into smaller intervals. The number of intervals is dictated by the nature of the business. The more uncertain the firm's cash flows are, the more intervals are required. Using monthly intervals is common, but some firms require daily cash budgets.

The cash budget requires the small business owner to determine all the known cash receipts and outflows that will occur during the year. Both the amount of cash involved and the cycle's length of time must be disclosed. This information is then put into a format like that shown in Table 8.2. The table lists some of the most common types of cash inflows and outflows experienced by a typical small business. Its categories should be modified to fit the particulars of each individual business. The most important point is to include all relevant sources of and demands for cash.

▼ TABLE 8.2

Cash Budget Format

	January	February	March	April	May
Beginning Cash					
Cash Receipts (Income):					
Cash Sales					
Receivable Collections Interest					
Owner Contributions					
Other Receipts					
Total Income					
Cash Outflows (Expenses):					
Cash Purchases					
Payment of Accounts Payable					
Wages and Salaries					
Payroll Taxes					
Advertising					
Office Supplies					
Rent/Mortgage					
Utilities					
Telephone					
Insurance					
Legal/Accounting					
Taxes and Licenses					
Interest Payments					
Loan Principal Payments					
Dues and Subscriptions					
Travel					
Miscellaneous Expenses					
Total Cash Outflows					
Ending Cash (Beginning Cash + Receipts – Expenses)					

Many businesses find that adding a *reconciliation* component to the bottom of the cash budget is helpful. This reconciliation summarizes the total cash inflows and outflows for the period. When this summary is combined with the beginning cash balance, you have the current cash status of the firm. Because there will be some minimum cash balance required to begin the next period, the ending cash figure is compared to this minimum figure. If there is a positive difference (ending cash minus minimum cash balance), the firm has cash to invest. If there is a negative difference, the firm must arrange for financing before beginning the new cycle.

By forecasting the inflows and outflows of cash, the small business owner will have a picture of when the firm will have cash surpluses and cash shortages. This knowledge allows the cash flow to be managed proactively rather than reactively.

Cash budgeting is, however, not always easy to do. As noted earlier, there are always disruptions to the process. Unforeseen cash outflows and inconsistent cash inflows plague many small businesses.

Aging Schedules. **Aging schedules** are listings of a firm's accounts receivable according to the length of time they are outstanding. A **macro-aging schedule** simply lists categories of outstanding accounts with the percentage of accounts that fall within each category (see Table 8.3). This schedule allows the small business owner to forecast the collection of receivables. Suppose the firm made credit sales of $10,000 three months ago, $12,000 two months ago, and $5,000 last month, and that it predicts it will make credit sales of $7,500 this month. Expected receivables collections for this month will be $(0.25 \times \$7,500) + (0.5 \times \$5,000) + (0.2 \times \$12,000) + (0.05 \times \$10,000) = \$7,275$. This is the amount the cash flow manager will place in the Receivables Collection slot of the cash budget for that month.

The **micro-aging schedule** offers another approach to showing receivables. This technique lists the status of each credit customer's account (usually in alphabetical order). It allows the small business owner to concentrate his collection efforts on the specific companies that are delinquent in their payments (see Table 8.4).

This aging schedule is invaluable for controlling receivables. Not only do you have the same information as shown in the macro-aging schedule, but you also have specific information on each credit customer that will enable you to make decisions about extending credit in the future.

Strategies for Cash Flow Management

Once the small business owner understands some of the basic tools of cash flow management, she should develop a strategy for the firm. Which accounts should be concentrated on? At what

▼ TABLE 8.3

Macro-Aging Schedule

Age of Receivables	Percentage
0–30 days	25
31–60 days	50
61–90 days	20
Over 90 days	5

aging schedules
A listing of a firm's accounts receivable according to the length of time they are outstanding.

macro-aging schedule
A list of accounts receivable by age category.

micro-aging schedule
A list of accounts receivable showing each customer, the amount that customer owes, and the amount that is past due.

▼ TABLE 8.4

Micro-Aging Schedule

Customer	Amount	Current	1–30	Past-Due Days 31–60	61–90	+90
Aardvark Supply	$1,500	$1,000	$200	$500	$2,250	
Beaver Trucking	2,250					
Canary Labs	1,000	500	500			
. . .						
Total	11,000	5,000	750	3,000	2,250	
Percentage	100	45	7	27	21	

intervals are cash budgets needed? What information is available or needs to be made available to track cash flow? Is the firm's bank providing services to assist in cash flow management? The answers to these questions, among others, help shape cash flow strategy.

Accounts Receivable. The first place to look for ways to improve cash flow is in accounts receivable. The key to an effective cash flow management system is the ability to collect receivables quickly. If customers abuse your credit policies by paying slowly, any future sales to them will have to be COD (cash on delivery) until they prove that you will receive your money in a reasonable amount of time.

Receivables have inherent procedural problems in most small businesses. Information often gets lost or delayed between salespeople, shipping departments, and the accounting clerks who create the billing statements. Most firms bill only once a month and may delay that step if workers are busy with other activities.

Managing your accounts receivable is an important step in controlling your cash flow. You need a healthy stream of cash for your small business to succeed. The following tips can help you accelerate the flow:

- *Establish sound credit practices.* Never give credit until you are comfortable with a customer's ability to pay. You can get a credit report from Dun & Bradstreet to indicate a purchasing company's general financial health.

- *Process orders quickly.* Ensure that each order is handled on or before the date specified by the customer. Unnecessary delays can add days or weeks to customer payments.

- *Prepare the invoice the same day as the order is received.* Especially on large amounts, don't wait until some "billing date" just because that's when you normally do it.

- *Send the invoice the same day it is prepared.* The sooner the bill is sent, the sooner it is likely to be paid. When possible, send the invoice with the order.

- *Offer discounts for prompt payment.* Give customers an incentive to pay sooner. Trade discounts typically amount to 1 to 2 percent if the bill is paid within 10 days.

- *Aggressively follow up on past-due accounts.* Call the customer as soon as a bill becomes past due, and ask when payment can be expected. Keep a record of customer responses and follow-up calls. For customers with genuine financial problems, try to get even a small amount each week.

- *Deposit payments promptly.* Accelerate receipt of checks by using a bank lockbox.

- *Negotiate better terms from suppliers and banks.* Improving cash flow also includes slowing the rate of money going out.

- *Keep a tight control on inventory.* Items sitting in inventory tie up money that could be used elsewhere. Be sure that deep discounts on volume purchases can financially justify the drain they will put on cash flow.

- *Review and reduce expenses.* Take a hard look at all expenses. What effect will an expense have on your bottom line?

- *Pay bills on time, but not before they are due.* Unless you receive enough trade discount incentive to pay early, don't rush to send payments.

- *Be smart in designing your invoice.* Make sure that the amount due, due date, discount for early payment, and penalty for late payment are clearly laid out.[8]

Inventory. Inventory is another area that can drain cash flow. According to James Howard, chairman of the board of Asset Growth Partners, Inc., a New York City financial consulting firm for small businesses, inventory costs are often overlooked or understated by small businesses. "A typical manufacturing company pays 25 to 30 percent of the value of the inventory for the cost of borrowed money, warehouse space, materials handling, staff, lift-truck expenses, and fixed costs."[9]

Cash flow determines how much inventory a firm can safely carry while still allowing sufficient cash for other operations. The inventory-turnover ratio lends insight into this situation. If, for example, a firm has an inventory ratio of 12, it has to keep only one month's worth of projected sales in stock before enough cash returns to pay for the next month's worth of inventory. By comparison, if the firm has a ratio of 4, it must keep three months' worth of projected sales on the shelves. This system ties up cash for as much as 90 days. In this case the firm should try to find suppliers that have terms extending to 90 days. Otherwise, it may have to borrow to meet current cash needs. The cash flow management goal is to commit just enough cash to inventory to meet demand.

Accounts Payable. Another cash flow management tool is trade terms. Under trade terms a small business owner works with his suppliers to establish when, how much, and under what conditions payments are made to suppliers. This allows small business owners to more effectively control cash outlays, since a major part of cash often goes to paying suppliers. Vendors, when approached up-front, are often more than willing to work out a payment schedule that benefits the small business owner if it also insures they get paid on a basis they can depend upon.

Banks. Ideally, your bank should be your partner in cash flow management. The small business owner should request the firm's bank to provide an *account analysis*. This analysis shows the banking services the business used during the month, the bank's charge for each service, the balances maintained in all accounts during the month, and the minimum balances required by the bank to pay for the services.

A review of the account analysis will indicate whether any excess account balances are on deposit. These should be immediately removed and invested. Also, your firm may be better off removing all account balances that are earning little or no interest and reinvesting them at higher rates, even if it means having to pay fees for bank services.

Finally, determine how quickly checks that your firm deposits in the bank become available as cash. Banks normally require delays of up to two business days. They should have an *availability schedule*, and the small business owner needs to request one from each bank in the area to determine whether his bank is competitive. Remember—the faster a deposited check becomes available as cash, the sooner your business has use of the money for other purposes.

Other Areas of Cash Flow Concern. Although inventory, receivables, and bank services are the most likely places in which to concentrate cash flow management strategies, several other areas also deserve attention:

- *Compensation.* Look for duplication of effort and lack of productivity within the firm's workforce. Cut personnel hours in those areas to save on wage and payroll tax costs.

- *Supplies.* Review all petty cash accounts. Show employees the cost of supplies by marking the cost of each item, such as tablets, on the boxes.

- *Deliveries.* Keep track of local delivery costs to the business. It may be cheaper to hire a part-time worker to pick up supplies than to pay other companies to deliver items.

- *Insurance.* Ask insurance carriers about ways to reduce premiums. One independent grocery store reduced premiums for its stock personnel by 15 percent simply by requiring them to wear supports while working.

- *Borrowing.* Take the cost of borrowing into account when determining operational expenses. Even short-term loans can have a large effect on profit and cash flow.

The process of cash flow management may seem confusing to you in the beginning, but you may find it relatively easy to monitor once everything is in place. Armed with a cash budget, aging schedules, and a set of feasible strategies, you can avoid cash flow problems and maximize your use of this precious resource.

Concept Check Questions

1. If you were setting up open-book management in your business, what would you teach employees to make it work?

2. Explain the difference between macro-aging and micro-aging accounts receivable schedules.

3. Cash flow has been described as the lifeblood of a business. How would you explain this description to someone who does not understand business finance?

4. Cash flow is more important than profit for a small business. Why? If your income statement shows a profit at the end of the month, how can anything be more important than that?

CHAPTER REVIEW

SUMMARY ▶▶

LO 8.1   Discuss the importance and uses of financial records in a small business.

You need financial records so you can make managerial decisions on topics concerning how much money is owed to your business, how much money you owe, and how to identify financial problems before they become serious dilemmas. Financial records are also needed to prepare your tax returns and to inform your banker and investors about your business's financial status. Without accurate financial records, you cannot exercise the kind of clear-sighted management control needed to survive in a competitive marketplace.

LO 8.2   Itemize the accounting records needed for a small business.

The accounting records of your small business need to follow the standards of generally accepted accounting principles (GAAP). From your source documents, such as sales slips, purchase invoices, and check stubs, you should record all the transactions in journals. Information from your journals should then be posted in (transferred into) a general ledger. Financial statements like your balance sheet, income statement, and statement of cash flow are produced from the transactions in your general ledger.

LO 8.3   Explain the 11 ratios used to analyze financial statements.

Ratio analysis enables you to compare the financial condition of your business to its performance in previous time periods or to the performance of similarly sized businesses' performance within your industry. Four important types of financial ratios discussed in this chapter are liquidity (current and quick, or acid-test, ratios), asset utilization (inventory turnover, average collection period, fixed asset turnover, and total asset turnover), leverage (debt and times interest earned), and profitability ratios (net profit margin, return on assets, and return on equity).

LO 8.4   Illustrate the importance of and procedures for managing cash flow.

Cash flow is the difference between the amount of cash actually brought into your business and the amount paid out in a given period of time. Cash flow represents the lifeblood of your business because if you do not have enough money to pay for your operating expenses, you are out of business.

KEY TERMS ▶▶

accounting **192**	assets **194**	average collection period **208**
accrual-basis method **197**	asset utilization ratios **208**	
aging schedules **218**		cash-basis method **198**

STUDENT STUDY SITE ▶▶

edge.sagepub.com/hatten7e

⑤SAGE edge™ Sharpen your skills with SAGE edge!

SAGE edge for Students provides a personalized approach to help you accomplish your coursework goals in an easy-to-use learning environment. You'll find mobile-friendly eFlashcards and quizzes as well as multimedia resources to support and expand on the concepts presented in this chapter.

EXPERIENTIAL LEARNING ACTIVITIES ▶▶

8.1: Financial Statement Account Identification

LO 8.2: Itemize the accounting records needed for a small business.

The balance sheet, income statement, and statement of cash flows are key financial statements.

For each item below, identify under which statement the item would be listed by checking the corresponding box. It is possible an item could fall under more than one financial statement. Once you have completed this, construct an income statement and a balance sheet from the items below.

Item to Classify	Balance Sheet	Income Statement	Statement of Cash Flows
Revenue			
Current Assets			
Owner's Equity			
Salary Expense			
Net Fixed Assets			
Cost of Goods Sold			
Taxes			
Total Liabilities and Owner's Equity			
Depreciation Expense			

Item to Classify	Balance Sheet	Income Statement	Statement of Cash Flows
Notes Payable			
Net Income			
Accumulated Depreciation			
Beginning Cash			
Accounts Payable			
Interest Expense			
Long-Term Debt			
Increase in Taxes Payable			
Accounts Receivable			
Inventory			
Earnings before Interest and Taxes			
Plant and Equipment			
Salaries Payable			
Earnings before Taxes			
Long-Term Assets			
Current Liabilities			
Total Assets			

8.2: Ratio Analysis Decision-Making

LO 8.3: Explain the 11 ratios used to analyze financial statements.

The following table provides account balances for a firm we'll call Jim's Company. Not all possible account balances are provided.

1. Fill in the blanks in the table to the right by calculating the ratios indicated based on the account balances you've been given.

Cash	$1,500
Accounts Receivable	2,500
Inventory	4,300
Total Debt	18,000
Current Assets	11,000
Cost of Goods Sold	3,500
Accounts Payable	6,500
Current Liabilities	14,750
Annual Sales	25,000 (Divide this number by 365 to get average sales per day)
Total Assets	24,000
Net Income	3,100
Owner's Equity	6,000

2. Compare the ratios you have calculated to the industry averages that are listed in the second column, and answer the following questions:

   a. If you were a banker, would you loan Jim money to repair his equipment, based only on the numbers? Why?

   b. If you were an investor, would you invest in Jim's Company, based only on the numbers? Why?

   c. If you were Jim, what two areas of your business would you be most concerned about immediately? And what are some ideas that could be implemented to address those concerns?

	Jim's Company	Industry Average
Current Ratio		1.6
Quick Ratio		.95
Inventory Turnover		1.4 (times/year)
Average Collection Period		35 days
Debt Ratio		.45
Profit Margin		.10
Return on Assets		.12
Return on Equity		.10

CHAPTER CLOSING CASE ▶▶

Superior Engineering in Texas: Stay or Go?

Thad Lepp, chief operating officer at Superior Engineering Services (SES), thumbed through the regional sales report for 2013. On the whole, it looked as though the worst was over. Sales were up in every region except for the Midwest, but the Texas figures were troubling. Despite the Lone Star State's potential, Superior had been unable to penetrate the market there in any meaningful way. Texas was contributing only 2 percent of company revenues. It had been almost 10 years since Superior opened offices in San Antonio and Fort Worth. How much longer should the company work to cultivate this market? Was there enough of an upside to warrant staying the course? Should Superior jettison this market to focus on areas closer to its base of operations in North Carolina? These were questions that would certainly come up when Superior's executive team held its regular quarterly meeting.

The Engineering Services Industry

The engineering services industry provides studies, design, construction management, and consulting for facilities in support of all sectors of the economy (e.g., residential, commercial, government, transportation, health care, education). The industry was active in all developed (and some undeveloped) portions of the United States.

The engineering services industry consists of many small companies that typically restrict their activities to regional markets, while larger firms have a global presence. The industry was fragmented with the four largest firms controlling less than 14 percent of the industry sales. Despite the low concentration, the 50 largest firms generated approximately 40 percent of industry sales. As the recession deepened and construction projects plunged, many small firms were forced to cease operations. The industry was further fragmented by over 90,000 self-employed professionals; however, they constituted only a very small proportion of industry sales.

The industry was highly dependent on the real estate and government sectors of the U.S. economy. Construction activity and sales declined during the recession beginning in 2007 and continued through 2013 largely due to cuts implemented in a government sequestration. Since 2011, the industry had shown signs of recovery as businesses began to invest in new facilities. However, the federal government scaled back spending on capital projects. Competition was high due to the large number of competitors within the industry. Clients typically made their purchase decisions for engineering services based on reputation for service and quality, experience on previous projects, and price. The demand for engineering services in the United States consisted of industrial and manufacturing projects, transportation, commercial, federal, government, residential, project management, and municipal utilities.

The Texas market had added 24,000 construction jobs as of August 2013, roughly 14 percent of the 168,000 added nationwide. Job growth in Dallas, Houston, and Austin was twice the national average. Furthermore, in 2013, three of the top 10 U.S. metro markets with the highest number of housing starts were in Texas.

Superior Engineering Services

Superior Engineering Services' (SES) headquarters was in Holly Springs, North Carolina, just outside Raleigh. The employee-owned company, founded in 1987, grew to include 45 locations with just over 1,100 employees by 2014. The offices were primarily along the Eastern Seaboard (Florida to Pennsylvania), but it also had offices in Indiana, Ohio, and Texas.

The company services spanned geotechnical, environmental, and facilities engineering and construction materials testing. For example, in widening one city's beltway, Superior provided geotechnical engineering and inspection for drilled shafts and retaining walls. For the reconstruction of a fire-damaged building, the company provided petrographic analysis of concrete columns and load testing of existing pile foundations. Services it provided to a metro rail project included construction materials testing and quality control of drilled shafts. The company's clients included architects and engineers, facility owners, and general contractors, as well as state, local, and federal government.

Thad knew that the "Texas question" was not as straightforward as the numbers might indicate. Superior's recent executive meeting illustrated the complexities of the situation. One of the standing agenda items was a report from each business unit on its financial and nonfinancial status. After Barney Williams, regional manager of the Texas operation, gave yet another report laced with more red than black ink, the room grew silent. Was someone going to comment, or would they be able to avoid unpleasantness? Not surprisingly, the Mid-Atlantic manager, Mike Mangione, asked "How much more money de we need to lose before we cut our losses?" He grabbed a copy of the Texas balance sheet and pointed to the negative shareholders equity. "After all these years, we're still running a $1 million deficit in retained earnings, and that doesn't even include the personal injury litigation we settled for $3 million," he continued. Seeing his chance, Phil Collins, the Florida regional manager, said, "Texas is too far from any of our other operations, making the span of control difficult. Furthermore, we can't seem to convince any of our most experienced managers to take on the challenge of turning it around."

It went downhill from there. The CEO, Mike Matthews, launched into his defense of the Texas operation with a lecture on the great potential offered by the state, an apology for some early tactical errors, and an affirmation of his commitment to stick it out in Texas. All the regional managers looked relieved when Mike's executive assistant announced that lunch had arrived. The call to lunch had broken the tension, but managers continued the discussion in small groups around the restrooms and in the buffet line. Thad made a mental note that this scene was like the 1993 movie *Groundhog Day* all over again, except that at Superior, the situation never improved—the Texas question came up again and again.

Before the afternoon session began, Thad scanned Superior's rather erratic sales growth (see Figure 1).

▼ FIGURE 1

Superior Engineering Sales Growth by Region, 2008–2013

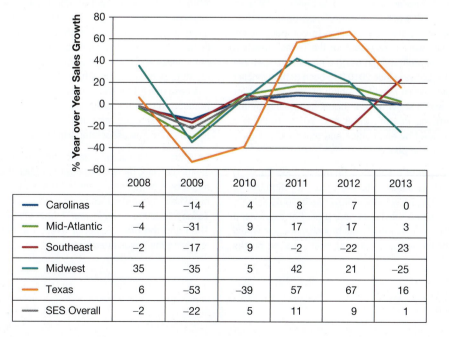

	2008	2009	2010	2011	2012	2013
Carolinas	−4	−14	4	8	7	0
Mid-Atlantic	−4	−31	9	17	17	3
Southeast	−2	−17	9	−2	−22	23
Midwest	35	−35	5	42	21	−25
Texas	6	−53	−39	57	67	16
SES Overall	−2	−22	5	11	9	1

Source: Adapted from information provided by the company.

FIGURE 2

Regional Offices' Percentage Contribution to Superior Sales, 2008

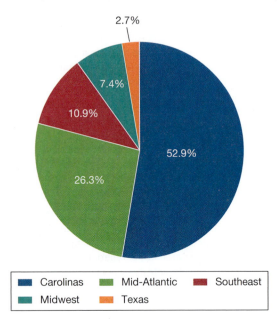

Source: Adapted from information provided by the company.

Note: Figure 2 shows the contributions by each office for 2008. Texas contributed only 2.7 percent, while the Carolina office contributed 52.9 percent.

FIGURE 3

Regional Offices' Percentage Contribution to Superior Sales, 2013

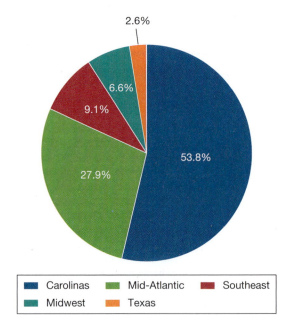

Source: Adapted from information provided by the company.

Note: Figure 3 shows the contributions by each office for 2013. Texas contributed 2.6 percent and the Carolina office 53.8 percent.

Growth percentages for Texas varied, with some higher and some lower than those at other offices over the same time period but on a much smaller dollar sales volume. Superior's total sales for 2013 were over $119 million, but the Texas operation had never contributed more than $3.1 million to company sales. Furthermore, profits were nonexistent for the Texas operation with the average net profit margin being a negative 16 percent from 2007 to 2013. Losses since 2010 had been getting smaller with the net profit margin reaching a high of −1.5 percent for 2013. Figures 2 and 3 show the contributions to sales by the various sales offices in both 2008 and 2013. The basic contributions provided by each office had remained relatively consistent over the time period.

Thad scanned Superior's selected financials (see Table 1) hoping to gain further insight into the Texas question. As he glanced at the figures, he wondered how much would actually be saved by eliminating the Texas operation. For example, it wasn't clear to Thad whether the Texas branch managers would be reassigned or terminated. His best guess, based on the CEO's comments in defense of the Texas operation, was that only one manager would be retained, at a cost of about $140,000. The equipment used in Texas was getting older, and the cost of transporting it to a new location would probably be more than it was worth. Thad thought it could be disposed of at its book value. Thad seemed to recall that this was the last year of the lease and that negotiations to extend it would occur next quarter. Since each branch operated essentially as a strategic business unit (SBU) Thad knew that Superior would not need to reabsorb any of the overhead costs or business development (BD) and marketing attributed to the Texas branch. Likewise, the other income associated with Texas would be eliminated.

As Thad made his way back into the conference room, he seemed to have more questions than when the day began. Texas might be a huge contributor to Superior's bottom line one day, but when? Were the losses incurred over the 10-year effort in Texas relevant to going forward? What other numbers might help Thad and the other Superior executives make a decision on resolving the Texas question?

Selected Financials Comparing Consolidated and Texas, 2013

	Superior Consolidated	Superior Texas Only
Sales (net of bad debt)	$119,893,314	$3,175,025
Cost of services	$70,004,181	$2,290,204
Gross margin	$49,889,133	$884,821
Expenses		
General overheads	$30,080,474	$1,089,424
Branch managers	$8,267,966	$240,390
Depreciation	$1,495,266	$35,972
Rent	$5,306,605	$210,619
BD & marketing	$1,293,453	$34,208
Total expenses	$46,443,764	$1,610,613
Net income (loss) from operations	$3,445,369	$(725,792)
Other income	$(1,672,465)	$(93,203)
Net income before taxes	$1,772,904	$(818,995)
Taxes	$655,977	$(303,028)
Net income (loss)	$1,116,927	$(515,967)

Source: Adapted from information provided by the company.

Note: Superior's sales totaled $119.8 million with just over $1 million net income. Texas generated just over $3 million in sales producing a loss of $515,967.

Discussion Questions

1. Reconcile the executive team's lamentations regarding Texas's poor performance with Figures 1–3 in the case.

2. Why has Texas struggled to be profitable? What does a vertical analysis of Superior's financials suggest about the Texas operation versus Superior as a whole?

3. What would the Texas branch's financials look like if it maintained Superior's overall gross margin?

4. What would the Texas financials look like if its pricing was similar to the company's as a whole?

5. What should Superior's executive team focus on to answer the Texas question? What additional information might they need?

SMALL BUSINESS FINANCE

A source of finance for small businesses that is growing like crazy is called crowdfunding. Crowdfunding is all about getting many individuals to give a small donation—like $10, $50, $100, maybe more. This is where social media meets business funding (more on this later in the chapter).

The campaign that made Kickstarter break away from other crowdfunding sites was the Pebble E-Paper Watch. The first affordable smartwatch on the market raised $10.2 million from 69,000 backers in just 37 days. It also was the first to demonstrate production problems in filling large orders on a short timeline—taking 10 months to get watches to backers after the campaign ended.

One of the most challenging aspects of a small business is acquiring the funding necessary to open your doors for the very first time and to keep your business running until you start to produce positive cash flow. Dollars needed by your new start-up range from rent, to equipment, to production of your product, to hiring employees, to paying for needed licenses and permits. Where does a budding entrepreneur look for the financing so desperately needed?

There are several sources of financing available for small business owners. The more exotic-sounding sources are called angels and venture capitalists. Both groups are willing to loan dollars for great new ideas; however, both have

requirements that must be met before the dollars are provided. Data from the National Venture Capital Association, indicates only about 6,600 companies receive angel/seed or early-stage venture capital out of 400,000 start-ups—about 2 percent. Other sources of funding include banks and the Small Business Administration. While finding money for your small business may sometimes feel an insurmountable hurdle, that is seldom the case. A viable business idea targeting a substantial market of buyers has a great chance of finding funding. Let's take a look at your options.

Sources: Mary Ellen Biery, "Focus on Your Business, Not on Venture Capital," *Forbes*, July 2, 2017, www.forbes.com; Michael Lev-Ram and Kurt Wagner, "Crowdfunding Tries to Grow Up," *Fortune*, May 2013, 40; Wil Schroter, "Top 10 Business Crowdfunding Campaigns of All Time, *Fortune*, April 16, 2014.

LEARNING OUTCOMES

After reading this chapter, you should be able to:

9.1 Determine the financing needs of your business.

9.2 Define basic financing terminology.

9.3 Explain where to look for sources of funding.

Concept Module 9.1: Funding for Small Business

• **LO 9.1: Determine the financing needs of your business.**

Although some entrepreneurs are well versed in determining their need for capital and knowing where to find it, the failure of many businesses can be traced to undercapitalization, not having the funds available to get started and carry you through until your business starts to produce a positive cash flow. A common approach is "not to worry about it" until the situation gets out of hand. However, every small business owner should understand how to define the amount of funding required to efficiently operate his business. Furthermore, the ability to be a proactive manager of the financial aspects of a business is of paramount importance when the economy takes a downturn. As you've seen in earlier chapters, when circumstances change quickly, you must be prepared to adapt to the new milieu. About 63 percent of small businesses that have employees carry some amount of debt from traditional lenders like banks.[1] According to the National Federation of Independent Business (NFIB), online, nonbank lenders (such as crowdfunding, crowdlending, and online platform lenders like Kabbage) have become viable alternatives in 2018. About 44 percent of small businesses who take advantage of these alternative finance routes need loans under $50,000 and 76 percent need less than $250,000.[2] This chapter covers issues of financing that every business owner should understand before starting a business so your company does not become a failed-business statistic.

Because service businesses often require the purchase of fewer fixed assets at start-up than do retailers or manufacturers, they can offer a good route to self-employment. Providing

Master the content at
**edge.sagepub.com/
Hatten7e**

§SAGE edge

outsourcing services for larger companies can be lucrative and can be anything from payroll to human resource management to information technology. The processes most often outsourced, according to an article in *Credit Management*, are "information technology, payroll, finance, personal assistants and receptionists."[3] For small business service firms this trend means new opportunities. How? It's a win-win situation for all parties involved. For the outsourcing firm, this approach offers a way to reduce operating costs, because providers of a single type of service have a lower cost structure resulting from economies of scale. For the small service business, it's a prime market to exploit.

Initial Capital Requirements

The fundamental financial building blocks for a small business owner are recognizing (1) what assets are required to open the business; (2) what will be required to put your business plan in action; (3) which expenses cannot be changed and must be paid, called fixed costs; and (4) knowing how these costs will be financed. This knowledge relates to the business's *initial capital requirements*. Recall from Chapter 8 the importance of the balance sheet. The balance sheet lists the investment decisions of the business owner in the asset column and the financing decisions in the liabilities and owner's equity columns. The financing necessary to acquire each asset required for the business must come from either owner-provided funds (equity) or borrowed funds (liabilities).

The process of determining initial capital requirements begins with identifying the short-term and long-term assets as well as the expenses, including fixed costs necessary to get the business started. Once you have this list, you must then determine how to pay these costs necessary to get your business up and running.[4]

> "Each business must have its assets in place—cash, inventory, patents, equipment, buildings, whatever it needs to operate—before it ever opens its doors."

Defining Required Assets

Each business must have its assets in place—cash, inventory, patents, equipment, buildings, whatever it needs to operate—before it ever opens its doors. Typical **short-term assets** include cash and inventory but may also include prepaid expenses (such as rent or insurance paid in advance) and a working capital (cash) reserve. Because many businesses are not profitable in the first year or so of operation, having a cash reserve with which to pay bills can help you avoid becoming insolvent.

The most common **long-term assets** are buildings and equipment, but these assets may also include land, leasehold improvements, patents, and a host of other items. Each of these assets must be in the business *before* the enterprise earns its first dollar of sales. This means you must carefully evaluate your situation to determine exactly what has to be in place for the business to operate effectively. A useful exercise to help accomplish this task is to prepare a list of the assets the business would have if money were no object. Next, review this "wish list" to determine the essential assets that are needed to operate the business on a "bare-bones" basis. Finally, estimate the cost of these assets under each scenario.

After carefully completing this exercise for all assets, you will end up with a list of assets with a minimum-dollar investment and another list of assets needed for the dream business. Often your actual business will wind up somewhere in the middle of those two lists as you make final decisions.

Expenses should be carefully evaluated, especially fixed costs. Fixed costs must be paid, even if the business has no revenue and can cause serious challenges for a small business owner. These costs are items like a five-year lease on the building you have just rented. That lease amount may have to be paid, depending upon the lease agreement, even if you shut your doors. Developing a plan to pay for these costs is important and a part of your initial capitalization requirements.

short-term assets
Assets that will be converted into cash within one year.

long-term assets
Assets that will not be converted into cash within one year.

With the final list of required assets and fixed costs and corresponding dollar costs in hand, you can then determine your financing requirements. Remember that each dollar of assets must be supported by a dollar of equity or liability funds. Expenses must also be paid. How much equity can you contribute personally to the enterprise? Note that this contribution does not necessarily have to be all in the form of cash.

The final step in the process is to subtract the total dollar value of the owner's equity from the total dollar value of the required assets. Generally, this step yields the dollar amount that must come from other sources. Sometimes there will be more owner's equity than needed to finance the required assets. More commonly, however, businesses will need additional capital to finance the required assets. This additional capital will come from one or more sources, which are most likely external to the business.

It may not take as much start-up money as you might think to launch a new business. The amount of capital needed to start small businesses with employees and nonemployee firms can be seen in Table 9.1.

▲ **TABLE 9.1**

Start-Up Dollars

	Small Business with Employees	Nonemployer Firms
Less than $5K	22.5%	39.5%
$10K–$24,999K	14.2%	7.1%
$50K–$99K	11.5%	2.8%
$250K–$999K	7.3%	1.8%

Source: U.S. Small Business Administration, Office of Advocacy, "FAQs about Small Business Finance," April 2016, www.sba.gov.

What Lenders Look For

When an entrepreneur decides to seek external financing, she must be able to prove creditworthiness to potential providers of funds. A traditional guideline used by many lenders is the *five C's of credit*, where each "C" represents a critical qualifying element:

1. *Capacity.* Capacity refers to the applicant's ability to repay the loan. It is usually estimated by examining the amount of cash and marketable securities available, and both historical and projected cash flows of the business. The amount of debt you already have will also be considered.

2. *Capital.* Capital is a function of the applicant's personal financial strength. The net worth of a business—the value of its assets minus the value of its liabilities—determines its capital. The bank wants to know what you own outside of the business that might be an alternate repayment source.[5]

3. *Collateral.* Assets owned by the applicant that can be pledged as security for the repayment of the loan constitute collateral. If the loan is not repaid, the lender can confiscate the pledged assets. The value of collateral is not based on the assets' market value, but rather is discounted to take into account the value that would be received if the assets had to be liquidated, which is frequently significantly less than market value (see Table 9.2).

4. *Character.* The applicant's character is considered important in that it indicates his apparent willingness to repay the loan. Character is judged primarily on the basis of the applicant's past repayment patterns, but lenders may consider other factors, such as marital status, home ownership, and military service when attributing character to an applicant.

The lender's prior experience with applicant repayment patterns affects its choice of factors in evaluating the character of a new applicant.

5. *Conditions.* The general economic climate at the time of the loan application may affect the applicant's ability to repay the loan. Lenders are usually more reluctant to extend credit in times of economic recession or business downturns.

Additional Considerations

Potential investors will want to know more about you and your business than just the five C's. For start-ups, simply having a good idea will not be enough to convince many investors to risk their capital in your business. You will need to show that you are a competent manager with a track record of prior business success. If possible, you should have an informal board of directors made up of people whom you may contact for assistance. Potential members of such a board might include bankers, attorneys, certified public accountants (CPAs), and successful business owners.

> "You will need to show that you are a competent manager with a track record of prior business success."

If yours is a growing or emerging business, you will need to stand ready to provide well-audited financial statements and show a solid record of earnings. It is difficult to attract investors without proven performance and a high likelihood of continued growth and success. The old adage, ''You have to have money to make money,'' is largely true in the area of financing. However, it might be amended to say, ''You have to show an ability to make money to attract money.''

A common myth suggests that the sheer strength of a business idea can win funding for a venture. In reality, a banker's first question is often ''How much money can you put in?'' Bankers are not venture capital partners; they will expect you to put in at least 25 percent of total project costs, and perhaps much more if the loan is viewed as a risky one.[6] Remember the ratios we calculated in the last chapter? Your debt/net worth ratio if you are a new business should be at least 2 to 1, with the business owner putting up at least 33 percent of the assets needed.

▼ **TABLE 9.2**

General Approximation of Different Forms of Collateral Valuations

Collateral Type	Bank	Small Business Administration
House	(Market value × 0.75) – mortgage balance	(Market value × 0.80) – mortgage balance
Car	Nothing	Nothing
Truck and heavy equipment	Depreciated value × 0.50	Same
Office equipment	Nothing	Nothing
Furniture and fixtures	Depreciated value × 0.50	Same
Inventory; perishables	Nothing	Nothing
Jewelry	Nothing	Nothing
Other	10%–50%	10%–50%
Receivables	Under 90 days × 0.75	Under 90 days × 0.50
Stocks and bonds	50%–90%	50%–90%
Mutual funds	Nothing	Nothing
IRA	Nothing	Nothing
CD	100%	100%

Source: U.S. Small Business Administration, "Borrowing Money," www.sba.gov.

Concept Check Questions

1. Define "initial capital requirements." How can you determine these?

2. What are the five C's of credit, and how do lenders use them?

Concept Module 9.2: Basic Financial Vocabulary

• **LO 9.2:** Define basic financing terminology.

Before an entrepreneur can begin looking for sources of funds, she needs to understand the terminology associated with the two basic types of funds, debt and equity.

Forms of Capital: Debt and Equity

Debt funds (also known as *liabilities*) are borrowed from a creditor and, of course, must be repaid. Using debt to finance a business creates **leverage**, which is money you can borrow against the money you already have (see Chapter 8). The goal in using leverage is to put in a little money and get back a lot more. Leverage can enable you to greatly increase the potential returns expected as you invest your equity in the business. Increased leverage also increases risk. Of course, debt funding can also consume the future cash flows generated by the business and potentially magnify losses. The interest payment on debt becomes a fixed cost that must be paid. Debt creates the risk of your becoming technically insolvent if you cannot make each debt payment on time. Continued nonrepayment of debt will ultimately lead to the bankruptcy of the business. Debt is burdensome, particularly when the economy is in a downturn, which is why some business owners shed it as quickly as possible.

Equity funds, by contrast, are supplied by investors in exchange for an ownership position in the business. They need not be repaid. Providers of equity funds forgo the opportunity to receive periodic repayments in hopes of later sharing in the profits of the business. As a result, equity financing does not create a constraint on the cash flows of the business. However, equity providers usually demand a voice in the management of the business, thereby reducing the business owner's autonomy to run the business as he would like.

It is easy to see that the decision to seek outside funds is both critical and complex. Therefore, a more detailed view of each kind of financing is presented in this chapter. Figure 9.1 contains

> **leverage**
> The ability to finance an investment through borrowed funds, increasing both the potential for return and the level of risk.

Where Capital Comes From

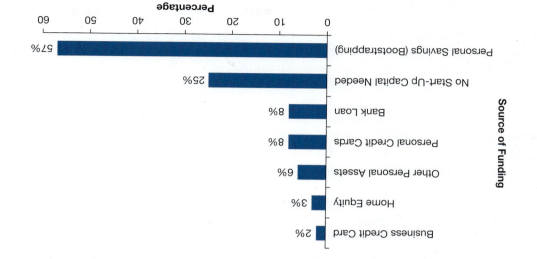

Source of Funding

Source	Percentage
Personal Savings (Bootstrapping)	57%
No Start-Up Capital Needed	25%
Bank Loan	8%
Personal Credit Cards	8%
Other Personal Assets	6%
Home Equity	3%
Business Credit Card	2%

Percentage

Source: U.S. Small Business Administration, Office of Advocacy, "FAQs about Small Business Finance," April 2016, www.sba.gov.

the Small Business Administration (SBA) Office of Advocacy data. In particular, the bar graph shows the sources of capital used by small businesses.

Debt Financing. Three important parameters associated with **debt financing** are the amount of principal to be borrowed, the loan's interest rate, and the loan's length of maturity. Together they determine the size and extent of your obligation to the creditor. Until the debt is repaid, the creditor has a legal claim on a portion of the business's cash flows. Creditors can demand payment and, in the most extreme case, force a business into bankruptcy because of overdue payments.

The **principal** of the loan is the original amount of money to be borrowed. Minimizing the size of the loan will reduce your leverage and your financial risk. The pro forma balance sheet estimates the amount of funds needed (see Chapter 8). The amount you need to borrow is the difference between the total of pro forma total assets and total owner's equity.

The **interest rate** of the loan determines the "price" of the borrowed funds. In most cases it will be based on the current prime rate of interest. In the past, the *prime rate* was defined as the rate of interest banks charge their "best" customers—those with the lowest risk. More recently, it has developed into a benchmark for determining many other rates of interest. Interest rates for small business loans are normally the prime rate plus some additional percentage points. For example, if the prime rate is 8.5 percent, a bank might offer small business loans at "prime plus four," or 12.5 percent. Additional factors, such as default risk and maturity (or length of loan), will also affect the cost of a loan.

---

debt financing
The use of borrowed funds to finance a business.

principal
An amount of money borrowed from a lender.

interest rate
The amount of money paid for the use of borrowed funds.

ISSUES IN SMALL BUSINESS

MOBILE MONEY

Mobile payments have become immensely popular for businesses of all size, but small businesses can especially benefit. Platforms like Venmo have simplified the process of transferring funds. Financial solutions allow people to pay businesses for goods and services, pay other individuals, and split bills while transferring money instantly.

So, the evolution of money has gone from barter, coin, paper, plastic, and now . . . smartphone! Small businesses have the incentive to make transactions with customers as easy, simple, and quick as possible. NFC (near field communication) allows customers to avoid fumbling for cash, checks, or wait for invoices. Projections from Business Insider expect mobile payments to hit $503 billion by 2020, and that by 2025, 75 percent of all transactions will be cashless. Reasons why small business should adopt mobile payment technology:

- **Convenience for customers.** If contactless payment is available, nearly three-quarters of U.S. consumers would use it for over 50 percent of their purchases. Thirty- to forty-four-year-olds in Australia and UK would use it for all purchases.
- **It's more secure.** Mobile wallets like Apple Pay, Android Pay, or Samsung Pay have customer credit card information stored, but each transaction is handled via a token with no card number attached. The token is security protected with a password or other technique.
- **Keep on the edge of new technology.** Research shows that consumers spend twice as much money and shop more often when using digital rather than traditional payments.
- **Bookkeeping is easier.** Cloud accounting packages used in conjunction with mobile payments eliminate paper receipts and invoices making their loss and forgetting a thing of the past.
- **Better customer experience.** Customers love decreasing time and effort in the checkout process. Since mobile payments are the finance tool of the future, small business should adopt sooner rather than later. Starbucks, known to be the pioneer of in-app mobile payments, states that over 25 percent of its U.S. transactions in 2016 were via smartphone.

Sources: Kimberly de Silva, "5 Reasons Why Your Business Should Use Mobile Payments," *Entrepreneur*, March 21, 2018, www.entrepreneur.com/article/310726; Jonathan Long, "6 Trends Impacting the Future of Payments," *Entrepreneur*, March 8, 2018, www.entrepreneur.com/article/310060.

Any interest payment becomes a fixed cost that must be paid. Remember the times interest earned ratio from Chapter 8? The times interest earned ratio calculates how many times you can make your current interest payment. If you miss an interest payment or two, you could be considered in default and the entire loan becomes due. Before you borrow, make sure you can make the interest payment on a timely basis.

The actual rate of interest the borrower will pay on a loan is called the *effective rate of interest*. It is often higher than the stated rate of interest for several reasons. A lender may require a *compensating balance*, meaning the borrower is required to keep a minimum dollar balance (often as much as 10 percent of the principal) on deposit with the lender. This requirement reduces the amount of funds accessible to the borrower and increases the actual rate of interest because over the life of the loan, the borrower pays the same amount of interest dollars but has fewer funds available.

The frequency with which interest is compounded can also increase the cost of a loan. *Compounding* refers to the intervals at which you pay interest. Lenders may compound interest annually, semiannually, quarterly, monthly, weekly, daily, or even continuously. For example, quarterly compounding involves four compounding periods within a year—one-fourth of the stated interest rate is paid each quarter on the cumulative outstanding balance. The more compounding periods, the higher the effective rate will be. Financial institutions are required to inform borrowers of the effective rate of interest on all loans.

Whether a loan has a fixed rate or a variable rate of interest affects its ultimate cost. A **fixed-rate loan** retains the same interest rate for the entire length of time for which the funds are borrowed. With a **variable-rate loan**, the interest rate may fluctuate over time. Typically, the variable rate is tied to a benchmark such as the prime rate or federal funds rate. Every year (normally on the anniversary of the original loan date), the variable interest rate is adjusted according to changes in the benchmark.

A fixed-rate loan typically has a higher interest rate than the initial rate on a variable-rate loan. Therefore, the cost of a fixed-rate loan is higher in the first year (or longer). But because the variable interest rate could increase each year, it might eventually exceed the rate on the fixed loan by several percentage points. Thus a variable-rate loan represents much more of a gamble than a fixed-rate loan when borrowing for a long period of time. Your goal is to find the lowest possible effective interest rate, given your current circumstances, by investigating different funding sources. For example, a particular bank may have excess funds available to lend and be willing to offer lower rates than its competitors. A start-up business may want to consider a variable-rate loan to help offset its lower cash flows in the first year of operation.

The **maturity** of a loan refers to the length of time for which a borrower obtains the use of the funds. A short-term loan must be repaid within one year, an intermediate-term loan must be repaid within one to ten years, and a long-term loan must be repaid within ten or more years. Typically, the purpose of the loan will determine the length of maturity chosen. For example, you would use a short-term loan to purchase inventory that you expect to sell within one year. Once you sell the inventory, you repay the loan. For the purchase of a building, which presumably will serve the business for decades, a long-term loan is preferable. The maturity of the loan should essentially match the borrower's use of the loan proceeds.

The maturity of the loan also affects its interest rate. Ordinarily, the longer the maturity, the higher the rate of interest. The reason for this is that a lender must be compensated for the opportunity cost of not being able to use those loaned funds in other ways. As a consequence, lenders will add a "premium" to the price the borrower pays for a longer-maturity loan.

Your goal regarding loan maturity is to obtain as much flexibility as possible. On the one hand, a loan with a shorter maturity will usually have a lower rate of interest but must be repaid quickly, thus affecting cash flow more dramatically. On the other hand, a loan with a longer maturity has a higher rate but gives you more time to repay the loan, resulting in smaller payments and reduced constraints on your current cash flow. Flexibility is created by

fixed-rate loan
A loan whose interest rate remains constant.

variable-rate loan
A loan whose interest rate changes over the life of the loan.

maturity
The length of time in which a loan must be repaid.

maximizing the maturity of a loan while retaining the option of repaying the loan sooner than the maturity date, if cash flows allow. Make sure the lender does not charge a penalty for early repayment.

Consider the principal, effective rate of interest, and maturity very carefully when attempting to obtain debt financing. By ascertaining the proper amount of principal needed, comparing the effective rates of interest at your disposal, and matching the maturity of the loan with the projected availability of cash flows with which to make repayments, you will be able to make the greatest possible use of debt financing.

Advantages of Debt Financing:

- Easier to plan: Budgeting is easier since principal and interest are known.
- Appropriate timing: Loans can be structured for short-, medium-, or long-term, depending upon what you are funding.
- Tax deductions: Interest paid is tax deductible.
- Flexibility: Since the bank or lending institution does not hold ownership, they have no say in how to run your business.

Disadvantages of Debt Financing:

- Deadlines: Money must be paid back by a fixed date.
- Cash flow: Too much debt will create cash flow issues which will make repayment difficult.
- Investor potential: Too much debt will make you less attractive to investors if you choose to add equity funding later.
- Collateral: Business assets will be held as collateral and you, as business owner, will have to personally guarantee the business loan.

Equity Financing. As stated earlier, **equity financing** does not have to be repaid. There are no payments to constrain the cash flow of the business. There is no interest to be paid on the funds. Providers of equity capital wind up owning a portion of the business and are generally interested in (1) getting dividends, (2) benefiting from the increased value of the business (and thus their investment in it), and (3) having a voice in the management of the business.

Dividends are payments based on the net profits of the business and made to the providers of equity capital. These payments are made on a quarterly, semiannual, or annual basis. Many small businesses keep net profits in the form of retained earnings to help finance future growth, and dividends are paid only when the business shows profits above the amount necessary to fund projected new development.

Increased value of the business is a natural result of a successful business enterprise. As a successful business grows and prospers, the owners prosper as well. Because the providers of equity capital own a "piece of the action," the value of their investment increases in direct proportion to the increase in the value of the business. The investors are frequently not as concerned about dividends as they are about the business's long-term success. If the business is successful, the equity providers will have the opportunity to sell all or part of their investment for a considerable profit.

A voice in management is an additional consideration for providers of equity capital. The rationale underlying this concept is that because the owners of a business have the most to lose if the business fails, they are entitled to have a say about how their money is used. Not all equity providers are interested in running a business, of course, but many can

equity financing
The sale of common stock or the use of retained earnings to provide long-term financing.

dividends
Payments based on the net profits of the business and made to the providers of equity capital.

contribute important expertise along with their capital. They can enhance your business's chances of success.

Advantages of Equity Financing:

- Less risky: You don't have to pay it back.
- Long-term view: Investors tend to look longer term and not expect their investment back immediately.
- Growth potential: Your profits can go back into the business, rather than paying debt.
- Cash flow: You'll keep more cash in fist for building your business

Disadvantages of Equity Financing:

- Total cost: Giving up a percentage of ownership may cost more than you would pay for a loan.
- Less control: Giving up ownership means you'll have to give up some control including asking investors for decision approval.
- Irreconcilable differences: If you and your investors do not agree there will come a point when one of you will have to be bought out of the business.
- Time and effort: Finding the right investor(s) is not easy and the relationship has to be maintained.[8]

Other Loan Terminology

Two additional sets of terms that you will often encounter while searching for financing relate to *loan security* and *loan restrictions*. These terms can be of great importance and should be thoroughly understood.

Loan Security. **Loan security** refers to the borrower's assurance to lenders that loans will be repaid. If the entrepreneur's signature on a loan is not considered sufficient security by a lender, the lender will require another signature to guarantee the loan. Other individuals whose signatures appear on the loan are known as *endorsers*. Endorsers are contingently liable for the notes they sign. Two types of endorsers are comakers and guarantors.

Comakers create a joint liability with the borrower. The lender can collect from either the maker (original borrower) or the comaker. *Guarantors* ensure the repayment of a note by signing a guarantee commitment. Both private and government lenders often require guarantees from officers of corporations to ensure continuity of effective management.

Loan Restrictions. Sometimes called *covenants*, loan restrictions spell out what the borrower cannot do (*negative covenants*) or what she must do (*positive covenants*). These restrictions are built into each loan agreement and are generally negotiable—as long as you are aware of them.

Typical negative covenants preclude the borrower from acquiring any additional debt without prior approval from the original lender. Common positive covenants require that the borrower maintain some minimum level of working capital until the loan is repaid, carry some type of insurance while the loan is in effect, or provide periodic financial statements to the lender.

By understanding that lenders will sometimes require the additional assurance of an endorser and will likely create covenants on loan agreements, you can be better prepared to negotiate during the search for financing. Doing your homework and being prepared can improve your chances of successfully obtaining funds.[9]

> "Doing your homework and being prepared can improve your chances of successfully obtaining funds."

loan security
Assurance to a lender that a loan will be repaid.

Concept Check Question

1. What are the differences between debt funds and equity funds?

Concept Module 9.3: How Can You Find Capital?

- LO 9.3: Explain where to look for sources of funding.

Once you determine how much capital is needed for the start-up or expansion, you are ready to begin looking for capital sources. To prepare for this search, you need to be aware of what these sources will want to know about you and your business before they are willing to entrust their funds to you. You also need to understand the characteristics of each capital source and the process for obtaining funds from it.

Loan Application Process

Typically, to determine creditworthiness, a lending institution will collect relevant information from financial statements supplied by the applicant and by external sources, such as local or regional credit associations, credit interchange bureaus, and the applicant's bank. This procedure is known as *credit scoring*. If the applicant meets or exceeds some minimal score (set by the lender) on key financial and credit characteristics, the institution will be willing to arrange a loan. Personal credit scores range from 350 to 850, while business credit scores range from 0 to 100.[10] Most lenders hesitate to make loans to start-up businesses, however, unless either a wealthy friend or a relative will co-sign the loan, or unless loan proceeds will be used to purchase assets that could be repossessed and easily resold in case of default.

Sources of Debt Financing

The wide array of credit options available confuses many entrepreneurs. A thorough understanding of the nature and characteristics of these debt sources will help ensure that you are successful in obtaining financing from the most favorable source for you.

Commercial Banks. Most people's first response to the question "Where would you borrow money?" is the obvious one: "A bank." Commercial banks are the backbone of the credit market, offering the widest assortment of loans to creditworthy small businesses. Bank loans generally fall into two major categories: short-term loans (for purchasing inventory, overcoming cash flow problems, and meeting monthly expenditures) and long-term loans (for purchasing land, machinery, and buildings, or renovating facilities).

Most short-term loans are **unsecured loans**, meaning that the bank does not require any collateral as long as the entrepreneur has a good credit standing. These loans are often *self-liquidating*, which means the loan will be repaid directly with the revenues generated from the original purpose of the loan. For example, if an entrepreneur uses a short-term loan to purchase inventory, the loan is repaid as the inventory is sold. Types of short-term loans include lines of credit, demand notes, and floor planning.

A **line of credit** is an agreement between a bank and a business that specifies the amount of unsecured short-term funds the bank will make available to a business. The agreement allows the business to borrow and repay funds up to the maximum amount specified in the agreement. The business pays interest only on the amount of funds actually borrowed but may be required to pay a setup or handling fee. For start-up businesses or businesses where revenue is erratic, lines of credit can make the difference between business success and failure, as the line of credit can augment cash flow. But be aware that bank financing is not easy to get for small businesses—four out of five small business applications are turned down.[11] Alternative funding sources like OnDeck.com, Kabbage.com, and Lendingclub.com write small business lines of credit also.

Make sure you apply for the line of credit before you need it, not when you are experiencing cash flow problems.

A **demand note** is a loan made to a small business for a specific period of time, to be repaid in a lump sum at maturity. With this type of loan, the bank reserves the right to demand repayment of the loan at any time. For example, a bank might loan a business $50,000 for one year at 12 percent interest. The business would repay the loan by making one payment of $56,000 ($50,000 principal plus 0.12 × $50,000 interest) at the end of one year. The only reason a bank is likely to demand repayment sooner is if the business appears to be struggling and is potentially unable to repay the loan in full at the end of the specified time period.

Types of long-term bank loans include installment loans, balloon notes, and unsecured term loans. **Installment loans** are made to businesses for the purchase of fixed assets such as equipment and real estate. These loans are to be repaid in periodic payments that include accrued interest and part of the outstanding principal balance. In the case of many fixed assets, the maturity of the loan will equal the usable life of the asset, and the principal amount loaned will range from 65 to 80 percent of the asset's market value. For the purchase of real estate, banks will often allow a repayment schedule of 15 to 30 years and typically lend between 75 and 85 percent of the property's value. In every case, the bank will maintain a security interest in, or lien on, the asset until the loan is fully repaid.

Balloon notes are loans made to businesses in which only small periodic payments are required over the life of the loan, with a large lump-sum payment due at maturity. A typical balloon note requires monthly payments to cover accrued interest, with the entire principal coming due at the end of the loan's term. This scheme allows you more flexibility with your cash flow over the life of the loan. If you are unable to make the final balloon payment, a bank may refinance the loan for a longer period of time, allowing you to continue making monthly payments.

Unsecured term loans are made to established businesses that have demonstrated a strong overall credit profile. Eligible businesses must show excellent creditworthiness and have an extremely high probability of repayment. These loans are usually made for very specific terms and may come with restrictions on the use of the loan proceeds. For example, a bank might agree to lend a business a sum of money for a three-year period at a given rate of interest. As the business owner, you must then ensure the funds are used to finance some asset or activity that will generate enough revenue to repay the loan within the three-year time horizon.

Commercial banks remain a primary source of debt financing for small businesses.[12] The type, maturity, and other terms of each loan, however, are uniquely a function of the financial strength or creditworthiness of the borrower.

Commercial Finance Companies.

Commercial finance companies extend short- and intermediate-term credit to firms that cannot easily obtain credit elsewhere. Because these companies are willing to take a bigger risk than commercial banks, their interest rates are often considerably higher. Commercial finance companies perform a valuable service to small businesses that have yet to establish their creditworthiness. Among the most common types of loans provided by commercial finance companies are floor planning, leasing, and factoring accounts receivable.

Floor planning is a special type of loan used particularly for financing high-priced inventory items, such as new automobiles, trucks, recreational vehicles, and boats. A business borrowing money for this purpose is allowed to display the inventory on its premises, but the inventory is actually owned by the bank. When the business sells one of the items, it will use the proceeds of the sale to repay the principal of the loan. The business is generally required to pay interest monthly on each item of inventory purchased with the loan proceeds. Therefore, the longer it takes the business to sell each item, the more the business pays in interest expenses. This is one instance in which the short-term loan is a **secured loan**. That is, the assets purchased with the loan proceeds serve as collateral.

demand note
A short-term loan that must be repaid (both principal and interest) in a lump sum at maturity.

installment loans
A loan made to a business for the purchase of fixed assets such as equipment and real estate.

balloon notes
A loan that requires the borrower to make small monthly payments (usually enough to cover the interest), with the balance of the loan due at maturity.

unsecured term loans
A loan made to an established business that has demonstrated a strong overall credit profile.

floor planning
A type of business loan generally made for "big-ticket" items. The business holds the item in inventory and pays interest, but it is actually owned by the lender until the item is sold.

secured loan
A loan that requires collateral as security for the lender.

CROWDFUNDING

Financing business start-ups was pretty much limited to loans and contributions from investors for many years—until a thoroughly modern, highly democratized approach called crowdfunding came along providing access to funding to musicians, artists, nonprofits, and businesses. There are about 600 of these sites worldwide, but the two biggies in the field are Kickstarter and Indiegogo (www.kickstarter.com and www.indiegogo.com).

Crowdfunding is about persuading LOTS of individuals to give you a small donation—$10, $50, $100, maybe more. Crowdfunding advocates believe it is a viable way for people to use the internet to fund virtually anything from documentary films to puppetry school tuition. But as more for-profit small businesses attempt to raise money for their start-up, regulators are moving in to make sure investors are protected and rewarded for taking financial risks. From the beginning Indiegogo and Kickstarter were a platform to seek donations in return for special rewards like free products or a say in product design.

The vast majority of backers (49 percent) pledge between $11 and $50, while another 21 percent pledge $51 to $100, so not huge money from any single person. About 30 percent of supporters are between the ages of 18 and 29, and 27 percent are between 30 and 49—factors you might consider when writing your product pitch.

Most pitches do not reach their goal, but many success stories exist. Ryan Grepper's Coolest Cooler saw 62,642 individual backers pledge $13,285,266! How did he do it? He made a great video showcasing all the cool features of his innovative product. Pledges ranged from $5 = a Thanks Forever, to $2,000 = Grepper flies to donor's home to bartend a party. Too many people set lofty goals only to fall short. And in crowdfunding close does not count. If you don't hit your set goal, you get nothing.

Indiegogo gets a 5 percent platform fee on any money raised through its site, plus processing fees per transaction for credit card processing. At Kickstarter, pledged money is collected only if entrepreneurs or artists meet their fundraising goals—with Kickstarter getting a 5 percent cut.

Some factors to ensure a successful crowdfunding campaign:

- Have some passionate friends and family get the campaign started.

- When you give perks in exchange for money pledged, make sure they are cool.

- Show that you have your personal funds invested.

- A great video that is concise and contains a compelling "ask" makes a huge difference.

Sources: Young Entrepreneur Council, "Here's What You Can Learn about Crowdfunding Backers," *Inc.*, March 16, 2018, www.inc.com; Lissa Harris, "Why Some Small Business Owners Are Turning to Crowdfunding to Save Their Company," *Entrepreneur*, December 15, 2017, www.entrepreneur.com/article/304407; Kendall Almerico, "5 Ways to Learn the Nuts and Bolts of Crowdfunding," *Entrepreneur*, September 19, 2017, www.entrepreneur.com/article/296366; "The Basics of Crowdfunding," *Entrepreneur*, accessed March 21, 2018, www.entrepreneur.com/article/228125.

Leasing is a contract arrangement whereby a finance company purchases the durable goods needed by a small business and rents them to the small business for a specific period of time. The rent payment includes some amount of interest. Due to current tax laws, this activity is very lucrative for finance companies and often allows entrepreneurs to have the use of state-of-the-art equipment at a fraction of the cost.

Another important type of loan available from commercial finance companies is accounts receivable **factoring**. Under this arrangement, a small business either sells its accounts receivable to a finance company outright or uses the receivables as collateral for a loan. The purchase price of the receivables (or the amount of the loan) is discounted from the face value of what the business is owed to allow for potential losses (in the form of unpaid accounts) and for the fact that the finance company will not receive full repayment of the loan until sometime in the future.

Typically, the finance company will either purchase the receivables for or will lend the small business somewhere between 55 and 80 percent of the face value of the business's accounts receivable, based on their likelihood of being paid in a timely manner. If a finance company purchases the receivables outright, it will collect payments on them as they come due. If the small business uses its receivables as collateral for a loan, in a process known as *pledging*, as the business collects these accounts due, the proceeds are forwarded to the finance company to repay the loan.

factoring
The practice of raising funds for a business through the sale of accounts receivable.

Factoring has historically been viewed as one of the least desirable approaches to financing, but competition from new small and mid-sized factors is changing that perception. Technology is also changing the funding mechanism that has existed for 4,000 years. BlueVine offers invoice factoring, which allows a business owner to tap into capital trapped in unpaid invoices. BlueVine runs a web-based platform powered by world-class risk and data science technology transforming factoring into a fast, convenient, and flexible form of online financing.[13]

Insurance Companies. For some entrepreneurs, life insurance companies have become a principal source of debt financing. The most common type of loan, **policy loans**, are made to entrepreneurs based on the amount of money paid in premiums on an insurance policy that has a cash surrender value. Although each insurance company varies its methods for making these loans, a typical arrangement is for the insurance company to lend up to 95 percent of a policy's cash surrender value.

The collateral for the loan is the cash the business owner has already paid into the policy. In essence, the insurance company is lending the business owner his own money. Because the default risk is virtually zero (defaulting on the loan merely reduces the cash surrender value of the policy), the rate of interest is often very favorable.

If an entrepreneur has been paying premiums into a whole-life, variable-life, or universal-life policy, it is likely the option to borrow funds against it will be available. Term insurance policies, however, have no borrowing capacity. One caution about this type of borrowing is that the amount of insurance coverage is usually reduced by the amount of the loan.

Federal Loan Programs. Government lending programs exist to stimulate economic activity. The underlying rationale for making these loans is that the borrowers will become profitable and create jobs, which in turn means more tax dollars in the coffers of government agencies providing the funds for the loans. The most active government lender is the Small Business Administration, a federal agency. **SBA loan** programs include the 7(a) loan guaranty program, the Microloan Program, the Small Business Investment Company program, and the 504 loan program. For full descriptions of all SBA loan programs, see www.sba.gov/smallbusinessplanner. Then go to "finance start-up" and the "SBA's role." The majority of these loan funds go to service, retail, and manufacturing businesses (see Figure 9.2).

Guaranteed loans are generally known as the 7(a) program. Under this program, private lenders—usually commercial banks—make loans to entrepreneurs that are guaranteed up to 85 percent of loans up to $150,000 and up to 75 percent of loans above $150,000 by the SBA. This means the lender's risk exposure is reduced by the amount of the SBA guarantee. The SBA's 7(a) maximum loan amount is $2 million with SBA maximum exposure of $1.5 million.

To be eligible for the 7(a) program, a business must be operated for profit and must fall within the size standards set by the SBA (see Chapter 1). Loans cannot be made to businesses engaged in speculation or real estate rental. Existing businesses must provide, among other things, financial statements for the past three years and financial projections for the next three years. Start-up businesses must provide three years of projected financial statements, a feasible business plan, and proof of adequate investment by the owners (generally about 20 to 30 percent equity).

Successful applicants pay interest rates up to 2.25 percent above the prime rate for loans with maturities of less than seven years and interest rates up to 2.75 percent above the prime rate for loans with maturities of seven years or longer. The borrower must repay the loan in monthly installments, which include both principal and interest. The first payment may be delayed up to six months, and the loans do carry prepayment fees under certain conditions.[14]

The 504 loan program provides small businesses with funding for fixed assets when conventional loans are not possible. These funds are distributed through a **certified development company**, which is a nonprofit organization sponsored either by private interests or by state or

policy loans
A loan made to a business by an insurance company, using the business's insurance policy as collateral.

SBA loan
A loan made to a small business through a commercial bank, of which a portion is guaranteed by the Small Business Administration.

certified development company
A nonprofit organization sponsored either by private interests or by state or local governments.

Who Gets the SBA Loans?

The SBA guarantees $10.5 Billion in 7(a) business loans. The average loan is $250,656 with a maturity of 11.5 Years; 21 percent of the loans went to businesses less than two years old.

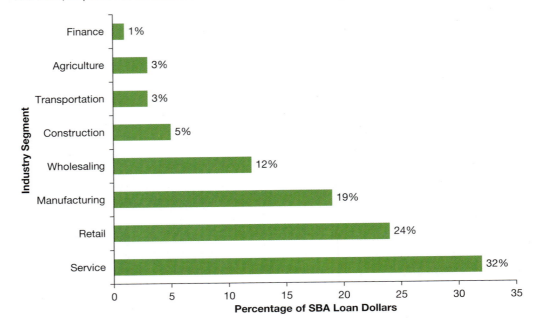

Note: Data totals 99% due to rounding.

local governments. In a typical arrangement, a private lender will provide 50 percent of the total value of the loan, the borrower 10 percent, and the certified development company the remaining 40 percent of the necessary funds. Because the 504 portion of the funds—that contributed by the certified development company—is 100 percent guaranteed by the SBA, the private lender's risk exposure is significantly reduced. The maturity for 504 financing is 10 years for equipment purchases and 20 years for real estate.[15]

In addition to the preceding loan programs, the SBA offers loan programs to support small businesses engaged in international trade and rural development, those with women owners, and those with working-capital needs. There is no doubt that the SBA plays a very significant role in providing debt financing for small businesses. However, the agency, like all other federal agencies, is subject to policy changes and budget cuts each year. The viability of the SBA in the future is dependent on its ability to effectively service the small business community.

One of the main criticisms of the SBA loan programs has been the amount of paperwork required, especially for relatively small loans. In response to this concern, the SBA recently created the **SBA Express program**.[16] Under this program, qualified small businesses can borrow up to $350,000 with the bank's own forms and receive a response within 36 hours. Additionally, there is a Microloan Program, which provides very small loans to start-up, newly established, or growing small business concerns. Under this program, the SBA makes funds available to non-profit community-based lenders (intermediaries), which in turn make loans to eligible borrowers in amounts up to a maximum of $35,000. The average loan size is about $13,000. Applications are submitted to the local intermediary, and all credit decisions are made on the local level. Each of these programs has been very successful. With the economic stimulus package, the SBA has changing requirements on some of these programs, making it even easier for small businesses to obtain financing.[17] Check out the www.sba.gov website for the most current information.

SBA Express program
A relatively new loan program available through the SBA that simplifies the paperwork that has historically been required.

State and Local Government Lenders. Many state and local governments lend money to entrepreneurs through various programs. As noted earlier, they can sponsor a certified development company to assist small businesses with the acquisition of fixed assets. Other loan programs are usually tied to economic development goals—for instance, some loans are made contingent on the number of jobs that will be created by the small business. Most state and local government programs have lower interest rates than conventional loans, often with longer maturities. It is clearly to your advantage to find out if these programs would be available to you.

Credit Card Start-Up Funding. Credit cards for financing small business? Your loan officer will say, "Don't use them." Your SCORE (Service Corps of Retired Executives) counselor will say, "Don't even think about it." The Kauffman Foundation states that for every $1,000 increase in credit card debt, the odds that the small business will fail increases by 2.2 percent. Credit cards have increased risk because while the personal credit history of the small business owner is used for the approval process, the credit limit is set higher since it is for business use with no increased collateral required. Today many small business owners are using credit cards as a partial source of funding, but this approach isn't for the faint of heart.

Diana Frerick loved to belt out Whitney Houston songs on karaoke nights. When she tried to turn her passion into a business, however, no one wanted to listen. Frerick used two credit cards to spend $5,000 on a karaoke system and music and started hosting private parties and corporate functions. Three years later, she and a partner opened Karaoke Star Store & Stage, again using her cards to pay for inventory and supplies. Now they employ 14 people and generate revenues of $2 million.

Credit cards are enticing because most offer extremely low introductory rates—3.9 percent, 2.9 percent, even 0 percent—for a limited time. When those introductory rates end, the annual percentage rate charged can jump as high as 22 percent within a matter of months. Think of it this way: If you aren't earning 22 percent on your equity, how can you afford to pay 22 percent for credit? Answer: You can't. Are you anxious to see how bankruptcy court works?

Funding your small business with credit cards, should only be for short-term situations in which you will be able to pay the debt off quickly. For example, if you have a solid client order, but you need money for items to fill the order.

If you choose to finance via credit cards, how do you tell if you are overextended?

- *You are unaware of your bills.* You should know how much you owe and whom you owe it to. Evaluate your credit report and your monthly credit card statement.

- *You are paying the minimum.* Pay off the credit card balances on a regular basis. If you are paying only the minimum payment allowed, it is a sign that you are in over your head.

- *You max out.* If your credit cards are close to or at their limit, you are in debt overload.

If you choose to use credit cards for financing, choose carefully and use wisely.

Trade Credit. The last major source of debt financing covered here is the use of **trade credit**, or *accounts payable*. Recall from Chapter 8 that accounts payable are the amounts owed by a business to the creditors that have supplied goods or services to the business. Although start-ups may find it difficult to obtain everything on credit right away, many manufacturers and wholesalers will ship goods at least 30 days before payment is required. This 30-day grace period is essentially a loan to the small business. Because no interest is charged for the first 30 days, the loan is "free." For this reason, you should take advantage of as much trade credit as possible.

trade credit
The purchase of goods from suppliers that do not demand payment immediately.

What If a Lender Says "No"?

Not every deal gets approved. Not every loan package is accepted. When rejection happens to you, get past the blow to your ego and try to learn what you did wrong. When a lender says, "no," do the following:

- Thank the lender for the time spent reviewing your package. Do not show resentment. Lenders almost always consider applications in a highly professional, objective manner. If you remain professional yourself, you will improve the odds of favorably impressing the lender when you return for future loans. Maintain the relationship.

- Ask what specific information, or lack thereof, counted against you. Federal regulations require a lender to prepare a detailed explanation for its loan rejection. Talk about the points cited, but don't argue—you are trying to learn as much as you possibly can. If you can make the changes suggested, ask when you can reapply.

- Ask the lender for specific, personal recommendations. Straight out ask for any personal advice the lender may have.

- Give the bank a reason to make the loan. Make sure you know exactly what you are asking for and the reason behind the request. Be prepared to tell your story effectively.[18]

- Understand that business loans are generally turned down for one (or more) of four main reasons: a poor credit score, lack of collateral, uncertainty of cash flow, and/or a poorly written business plan.[19]

- Ask whether the bank can rework your application so that it meets the lending criteria. This effort may require substantial changes in your business structure or adding personal collateral.

Sources of Equity Financing

From our discussion of debt financing, you know that lenders will expect entrepreneurs to provide their own funds—equity funds—at least 25 percent, and probably much higher, before approving a loan. The higher the risk assumed by the lender, the more of your own money you must put into the business. The most common sources of equity financing are personal funds, family and friends, partners, venture capital firms, small business investment companies (SBICs), angels, and various forms of stock offerings.

Bootstrapping via Personal Funds. Most new businesses are originally financed with their creators' funds. The essence of bootstrapping is stretching resources, both financial and otherwise, as far as they will stretch. The U.S. Department of Commerce estimates that nearly two-thirds of all start-ups are begun without borrowed funds. The first place most entrepreneurs find equity capital is in their personal assets. Cash, savings accounts, and checking accounts are the most obvious sources of equity funds. Additional sources are the sale of stocks, bonds, mutual funds, real estate, or other personal investments.

Han-Gwon Lung and Dan Foley bootstrapped their business, Tailored Ink. They had about a thousand bucks between them, but within two years they topped the $1 million plateau—with zero debt. How'd they do it?[20]

1. **Spend within your means.** Even with a full-time job, Lung stuck with frozen TV dinners and a cheap inflatable bed even though his friends were going through money faster than it was coming in. He realized that "you will never accumulate wealth if you spend it as soon as you get it. Debt and loans do not equal wealth." This requires delayed gratification.

2. **Save way more than you spend.** Saving takes discipline, but saving with business funding is even harder than personal. For example, say your business brings in $20,000 a month. Sounds good, but 20 to 40 percent of that revenue goes to taxes immediately, 25 percent is needed for business expenses, another 25 percent goes to living expenses . . . and $20,000 doesn't go as far as you thought it would. Han and Dan committed from the beginning to put most of their money back into the business and pay vendors before paying themselves.

3. **Always pay off your debts (or don't borrow at all).** The culture of the United States makes borrowing money seem normal, and it seems everyone does it for college, cars, houses, and businesses. But think of this scenario—say you charge $5,000 on your credit card and make the minimum monthly payment. At 15 percent interest, in 14 years you would have paid over $5,600 . . . and still owe the original $5,000!

Family and Friends. New businesses are often at least partially funded by the family and friends of the entrepreneurs. Family and friends are more willing to risk capital in a venture owned by someone they know than in ventures about which they know little or nothing. This financing is viewed as equity as long as there is no set repayment schedule. A best practice is to make an "arm's length" transaction and insist on preparing the same kind of documentation you would prepare if receiving funds from a total stranger.

Financing a business with capital from family and friends, however, creates a type of risk not found with other funding sources. If the business is not successful and the funds cannot be repaid, relationships with family and friends can become strained. You should explain the potential risk of failure inherent in the venture before accepting any money from family and friends. The key is to be sure you have a written contract with an investment letter that clearly outlines who approached whom about the funds in question and explains the specific terms of the funding.[21]

Partners. Acquiring one or more partners is another way to secure equity capital (see Chapter 10). Approximately 10 percent of U.S. businesses are partnerships. Many partnerships are formed to take advantage of diverse skills or attributes that can be contributed to the new business. For example, one person may have the technical skills required to run the business, whereas another person may have the capital to finance it. Together they form a partnership to accomplish a common goal.

Partners may play an active role in the venture's operation or may choose to be "silent," providing funds only in exchange for an equity position. The addition of one or more partners expands not only the amount of equity capital available for the business, but also the ability of the business to borrow funds. This is due to the cumulative creditworthiness of the partners versus that of the entrepreneur alone.

> "Partners may play an active role in the venture's operation or may choose to be 'silent,' providing funds only in exchange for an equity position."

Venture Capital Firms. *Venture capital firms* are groups of individuals or companies that invest a significant amount of dollars in new or expanding firms. VCs, as they are called, will make loans (but at high interest rates—say 20 percent), usually expect a higher rate of return (30 to 50 percent), and expect to have a sizeable ownership position in your business as their return on investment.[22] VC firms typically invest in companies they expect to sell within a few years. To be considered worthy of investment a company needs to show rapid, steady sales growth; proprietary new technology; a sound management team; and potential for being acquired by a larger company or initial public offering. Of the more than 600 venture capital firms operating in the United States, approximately 500 are private independent firms, about 65 are major corporations, and the rest are affiliated with banks. Obtaining capital from them is not easy.

A recent study showed that the average sum invested by venture capital firms is between $1.5 million and $2 million per business, with an overall range between $23,000 to more than $50 million. An excellent business plan is essential when approaching a venture capital firm, and a referral from a credible source—such as a banker or attorney known to the venture capital firm—may also be necessary. It takes an average of six to eight months to receive a potential investment decision. It has been estimated that less than 10 percent of the plans submitted to venture capital firms are ultimately funded.[23]

Venture capital firms rarely invest in retail operations. Instead, they tend to focus on high-technology industries, growth industries, and essential services. Ventures within these fields with strong, experienced management teams have the best chance of being funded. *Pratt's Guide to Venture Capital Success* is a good source of information on this source of financing.

Three engineers, Richard Yemm, Chris Retzler, and Dave Pizer, have created the "Sea Snake," a 180-meter mechanical sea monster that produces electricity when ocean waves hit the giant machine. While developing this new alternative energy source, Yemm sold another invention and used credit cards to work on his entrepreneurial idea. After building a prototype, the team was able to garner financial support from venture capitalists interested in the project. Today, 16 investors are helping to fund the company, Pelamis Wave Power, Ltd., as it further develops and sells this alternative energy technology.[24]

Small Business Investment Companies. *Small business investment companies (SBICs)* are venture capital firms licensed by the SBA to invest in small businesses. SBICs were authorized by Congress in 1958 to provide equity financing to qualified enterprises. In 1969, the SBA, in cooperation with the U.S. Department of Commerce, created *minority enterprise small business investment companies (MESBICs)* to provide equity financing to minority entrepreneurs. Any business that is more than 51 percent owned by members of a minority group or persons, or socially and economically disadvantaged Americans is eligible for funding.

SBICs and MESBICs are formed by financial institutions, corporations, or individuals, although a few are publicly owned. These investment companies must be capitalized with at least $500,000 of private funds. Once capitalized, they can receive as much as $4 from the SBA for each $1 in private money invested.

SBICs and MESBICs are excellent sources of both start-up and expansion capital. Like venture capital firms, however, they tend to have investment policies regarding geographic area and industry. There are approximately 300 SBICs and MESBICs currently in operation in the United States. They are listed in the *Directory of Operating Small Business Investment Companies* available from any SBA office.

Angels. An **angel** is a wealthy, experienced individual who has a desire to assist start-up or emerging businesses, frequently in companies in their communities. Often they provide funding for start-ups that will allow the business to grow to the point where a VC will then pick up the funding. Most angels are self-made entrepreneurs who want to help sustain the system that allowed them to become successful. Usually they are knowledgeable about the market and technology areas in which they invest.

According to a study on business angels, there are more than 250,000 such investors in the United States. A typical angel investment ranges from $20,000 to $50,000, although nearly

angel
A lender, usually a successful entrepreneur, who loans money to help new businesses.

one-fourth are for more than $50,000. An angel can add much more than money to a business, however. His business know-how and contacts can prove far more valuable to the success of the business than the capital invested.

Several types of angel investors exist. *Corporate angels* are typically former senior managers of Fortune 1000 companies. In addition to getting their cash, you may persuade them to fill a management position in your company (corporate angels generally do the biggest deals, ranging from $200,000 to $1 million). *Entrepreneurial angels* own and operate their own businesses and are looking for ways to diversify their portfolios. They almost always want a seat on the board, but rarely want a management spot (deals run from $200,000 to $500,000). *Enthusiast angels* generally do smaller deals ($10,000 to $200,000), are older and wealthy, and invest for a hobby. *Professional angels* include doctors, lawyers, accountants, and other professionals. They like to invest in companies that offer products with which they are familiar. They can offer value through their expertise. *Micromanagement angels* are very serious investors. They are typically self-made, wealthy individuals who definitely want to be involved in your company strategy.[25]

When approaching angel investors, some experience and an in-depth knowledge of your business are essential. Since most angels are entrepreneurs themselves, they have "been there" and can spot someone who doesn't know their business inside and out. Be prepared to answer all questions, including the tough ones, angels will ask, such as why are you purchasing that piece of equipment? Angels will see through "fluff" answers immediately.

Finding an angel investor is not easy. The best ways for an entrepreneur to locate one are to maintain business contacts with tax attorneys, bankers, and accountants in the closest metropolitan area and to ask for an introduction. Networking can be key.

> "Finding an angel investor is not easy. The best ways for an entrepreneur to locate one are to maintain business contacts with tax attorneys, bankers, and accountants in the closest metropolitan area and to ask for an introduction. Networking can be key."

Mergers and Acquisitions (M&A). Merging with a company flush with cash can provide a viable source of capital. Such transactions may trigger many legal, structural, and tax issues, however, that you must then work out with your accountant and lawyer. Deals for small to mid-sized companies have become increasingly popular as consolidation in technology-based industries occurs.

Stock Offerings. Selling company stock is another route for obtaining equity financing. The entrepreneur must consider this decision very carefully, however. The sale of stock results in the entrepreneur's losing a portion of the ownership of the business. Furthermore, certain state and federal laws govern the way in which stock offerings are made. Private placements and public offerings are two types of stock sales.

Private Placements. A *private placement* involves the sale of stock to a selected group of individuals. This stock cannot be purchased by the general public. Sales may be in any amount, but placements less than $500,000 are subject to fewer government-imposed restrictions and trigger less onerous disclosure requirements than those in excess of $500,000. If the company selling the stock is located and doing business in only one state, and stock is sold only to individuals within that same state, the sale is considered an *intrastate stock sale* subject only to that state's regulations. If the sale involves more than one state, then it is an *interstate stock sale,* and the federal Securities and Exchange Commission's regulations will apply.

What if one partner wants out of a business and the remaining partner or partners don't have the cash for a buyout? *Recapitalization* means rearranging the financial structure of a business—generally by using a combination of debt and third-party investors like private equity firms.

Public Offerings. A *public offering* involves the sale of stock to the general public. These sales always are governed by Securities and Exchange Commission regulations. Complying with these regulations is both costly and time-consuming. For public offerings valued between $400,000 and $1 million, the legal fees, underwriting fees, audits, printing expenses, and other costs can easily exceed 15 percent.

The first time a company offers its stock to the general public is called an **initial public offering (IPO)**. To be a viable candidate for an IPO, a company must be in good financial health and be able to attract an underwriter (typically a stock brokerage firm or investment banker) to help sell the stock offering. In addition, the market conditions must be favorable for selling equity securities.

There are three main reasons companies choose public offerings:

1. When market conditions are favorable, more funds can be raised through public offerings than through other venture capital methods, without imposing the repayment burdens of debt.

2. Having an established public price for the company's stock enhances its image.

3. The owner's wealth can be magnified greatly when owner-held shares are subsequently sold in the market.

One critical caution about public stock offerings is that they require companies to make financial disclosures to the public. If a company fails to live up to its self-reported expectations, shareholders can sue the company, charging that the company withheld or misrepresented important information.

Choosing a Lender or Investor

A key decision facing entrepreneurs is determining which sources of financing to pursue. Your choice will often be limited by the degree to which you meet the requirements of each lending or investing source. If you decide to pursue *debt financing*, you must have the minimum down payment or other capital requirements necessary to secure the loan. Assuming these requirements can be met, you will have to determine which lending source to approach. Usually the foremost criterion will be finding the lowest cost or interest rate available. However, other important lender-selection considerations are

initial public offering (IPO)
The first sale of stock of a business made available to public investors.

- *Size.* The lender should be small enough to consider the business owner an important customer, but large enough to service the business owner's future needs.

- *Desire.* The lender should exhibit a desire to work with start-up and emerging businesses, rather than considering them too risky.

- *Approach to problems.* The lender should be supportive of small businesses facing problems, offering constructive advice and financing alternatives.

- *Industry experience.* The lender should have experience in the business owner's industry, especially with start-up or emerging ventures.

The best guideline may be to seek the lenders with which you feel the most comfortable. A loan relationship can last for a decade or more. Finding a lending source that is pleasant to work with is often as important as finding the lowest cost of debt.

If you decide to pursue *equity financing*, you should consider the fact that close personal relationships can become strained when money is involved. Although the use of funds obtained from family members, friends, or partners is perhaps conceivable, none of these sources may be acceptable or feasible for personal reasons.

> "Although the use of funds obtained from family members, friends, or partners is perhaps conceivable, none of these sources may be acceptable or feasible for personal reasons."

Autonomy is another important consideration. Equity financing always requires that you give up a portion of ownership in the venture. If independence is critical to you, then think carefully about the source of equity you pursue.

The most important criterion in choosing investors should be matching what the business needs with what the investors can offer. If the business requires only money, then you should attempt to find a "silent" partner—one who is willing to provide capital without playing an active role in the management of the business. Conversely, if your business needs a particular type of expertise, in addition to money, then you should seek an investor who can provide management advice or other assistance along with needed capital. For example, a new business in a high-tech industry might pursue angel financing from a successful individual who has prospered in that industry.

Clearly, choosing a lender or investor takes time and patience. The process is similar to finding a spouse. The relationship that is forged between the entrepreneur and the source of financing can be long lasting and should be mutually beneficial.

Concept Check Questions

1. What kinds of businesses would depend on floor planning?

2. What does "pledging accounts receivable" mean?

3. What are the advantages of borrowing through the SBA?

4. Why do suppliers extend trade credit to other businesses? What are the advantages and disadvantages of using trade credit?

5. How do private placements and public offerings differ?

6. Discuss the types of interest rates that may apply to a loan.

7. What is the difference between a secured loan and an unsecured loan?

8. Of the approximately 500,000 companies that started in the year 2017, only 5,052 received $72 billion in funding from venture capitalists. If just this small percentage actually received venture capital, why do small business magazines print such a disproportionately large number of articles about venture capital?

9. How and why does a small business's capital structure change over time?

CHAPTER REVIEW

SUMMARY ▶▶

LO 9.1   Determine the financing needs of your business.

A straightforward process for determining financing need is to (1) list the assets required for your business to operate effectively and the needed expenses; (2) determine the market value or cost of each asset; (3) identify how much capital you are able to provide; and (4) subtract the total of the owner-provided funds from the total of the assets and expenses required. This figure represents the minimum amount of financing required.

LO 9.2   Define basic financing terminology.

To procure financing, you must understand the basic financial vocabulary. Each major form of capital (debt and equity) has unique terminology that defines the details underlying financing agreements.

Each form of capital has pros and cons that make it more or less desirable to the entrepreneur under given circumstances.

LO 9.3   Explain where to look for sources of funding.

The search for capital and the application process can be unsettling as you sort through the various sources of funds. Major sources of debt financing include commercial banks, finance companies, government lenders, and insurance companies. Sources of equity include personal funding sources, partners, venture capital firms, angels, and stock offerings. Finding capital is one of the most important tasks you face in starting and managing a business. A thorough understanding of the issues involved will enhance your chances of finding the best source for your business.

KEY TERMS ▶▶

angel **246**	floor planning **239**	policy loans **241**
balloon notes **239**	initial public offering (IPO) **248**	principal **234**
certified development company **241**	installment loans **239**	SBA Express program **242**
debt financing **234**	interest rate **234**	SBA loan **241**
demand note **239**	leverage **233**	secured loan **239**
dividends **236**	line of credit **238**	short-term assets **230**
equity financing **236**	loan security **237**	trade credit **243**
factoring **240**	long-term assets **230**	unsecured loans **238**
fixed-rate loan **235**	maturity **235**	unsecured term loans **239**
		variable-rate loan **235**

STUDENT STUDY SITE ▶▶

edge.sagepub.com/hatten7e

Ⓢ SAGE edge™ Sharpen your skills with SAGE edge!

SAGE edge for Students provides a personalized approach to help you accomplish your coursework goals in an easy-to-use learning environment. You'll find mobile-friendly eFlashcards and quizzes as well as multimedia resources to support and expand on the concepts presented in this chapter.

EXPERIENTIAL LEARNING ACTIVITIES ▶▶

9.1: Finance Terminology

LO 9.2: Define basic financing terminology.

Match the following definitions to the appropriate finance term.

1. _____ Covenants

2. _____ Fixed-Rate Loan

3. _____ Interest

4. _____ Comakers

5. _____ Leverage

6. _____ Equity Financing

7. _____ Loan Security

8. _____ Maturity

9. _____ Dividends

10. _____ Principal

11. _____ Compounding

12. _____ Debt Financing

    a. Monies borrowed from a creditor that must be repaid

    b. Monies supplied by investors in exchange for an ownership position in the business

c. Payments based upon the net profits of the business and paid to the owners of the equity capital

d. Original amount of money to be borrowed

e. Loan retains the same interest for entire length of time for which the money is borrowed

f. The interval at which you pay interest

g. Assurance to a lender the loan will be repaid

h. Money borrowed against money you already have

i. Creates a joint liability with the borrower

j. Restrictions on what the borrower can or cannot do

k. Price to borrow money

l. A loan whose interest rate changes over the life of the loan

m. The time period in which the loan must be repaid

9.2: Finding Capital for the Start-Up

LO 9.3: Explain where to look for sources of funding.

Austin has been snowboarding since he was two and is fanatical about the sport. He lives, breathes, and sleeps snowboarding. After trying multiple materials, Austin has created a new material for making snowboards that is lighter and more durable than anything currently on the market. Snowboards made from his material are basically indestructible, very light and with the right wax, extraordinarily fast. Austin is sure his product will be successful but to begin manufacturing his snowboards, he needs capital, a lot of capital. He will also need capital to create his marketing campaign. He is hopeful that a 2018 Olympic medal holder like Shaun White will begin using his snowboard and then endorse the product. This too will require a lot of money. Austin projects that to take his business from the successful idea stage to successful profitable stage will require $500,000. He has $50,000 cash he can immediately invest into his business. Austin is passionate about his product. He knows it will have a huge positive impact on the snowboarding industry worldwide.

Which of the following sources of capital and type of capital would you advise Austin to pursue and why? Be thoughtful and specific to ensure your capital recommendation fits Austin's needs.

Choose one of the following as your recommendation and explain why this would be the best source of capital for Austin's new business: commercial banks (secured or unsecured term loans), crowdsourcing, SBA loan, credit cards, venture capital firms, angel investors, or family and friends.

CHAPTER CLOSING CASE ▶▶

When the Bank Cuts the Cord

Kevin Semcken was wandering the aisles and browsing the booths at a technology conference in Denver. At the time, he was the head of HealthTek Ventures, a venture capital firm in Evergreen, Colorado. Semcken came across a two-person start-up company named Able Planet with a promising idea— headphones embedded with a magnetic coil to enhance sound quality—but a lousy business. Since Semcken only has partial hearing in his left ear, he was intrigued. He was hardly ever able to hear high-frequency sounds like those produced by cymbals. The guys at the Able Planet booth gave him two headsets—one with the coil and one without—while he listened to Dean Martin's "You're Nobody 'Til Somebody Loves You." "When I switched to the Able Planet headphones, I could hear the cymbals," says Semcken. "I was instantly a fan."

Being a venture capitalist, Semcken believed in the product so much he not only invested in Able Planet but he also eventually took over as CEO and chairman. Able Planet's LINX headphones won an award for innovation at the Consumer Electronics Show. Soon, the calls began pouring in and revenue jumped more than 1,000 percent, to $2 million.

Early the next year, Semcken got a call that every small business owner dreads. The loan officer for the bank Able Planet used was changing the terms of the $2.5 million line of credit it provided to Semcken's Wheat Ridge, Colorado-based audio-equipment business.

Under the new terms, the bank would no longer provide funding for the cost of raw materials and manufacturing. Able Planet had been a customer of that bank for almost three years and had never missed a payment. And though Able Planet was not yet generating a positive cash flow, Kevin was understandably stunned. Without those funds, he would have no way to pay for inventory demanded by retailers such as Walmart and Costco. "They waited until the last minute and dropped it on us," Semcken says.

Up until the moment of that phone call, Able Planet's business plan had been fairly simple. The company used the bank line of credit to fund the manufacturing of LINX Audio headphones with a price range of $24 to $299 a pair. For more than a year, Semcken had been using some of the funds generated by the headphones to produce more of them and some of it to develop a promising new technology.

The promising new technology was called Sound Fit, which would expand his product line beyond headphones—including hearing aids and Bluetooth devices. Sound Fit is a listening device designed to fit snugly in the opening of the ear canal, eliminating nearly all ambient noise. Semcken got the idea for Sound Fit from a previous investment in a company developing a balloon-like stent that expanded and contracted to prevent debris from blocking small arteries during heart surgery. Semcken thought something similar could work for the ear. He urged Able Planet's audiologists to create an inflatable disk that could conform to the size of an individual's ear canal. Such a device wouldn't fall out like earbuds would during jogging or other activities. They wouldn't rest awkwardly against the ear like Bluetooth devices. And Sound Fit would not require a costly fitting procedure like hearing aids.

Semcken had secured nondisclosure agreements from 30 potential customers for Sound Fit who were interested in seeing more. But before Semcken could move forward with any of these negotiations, he needed funds to create production-quality prototypes, as well as operating cash for the headphone business.

After Semcken finished the phone conversation with his banker, he did what all good business owners facing a problem do: identify all his alternatives. A common funding source for manufacturers is known as a factor. A factor loans against or purchases accounts receivables, but charges very high interest rates. He could shop for a less risk-averse bank. The company also had more than 20 angel investors who had recently kicked in $1.4 million. But that money was gone. What were the chances those investors would be willing to pitch in more so soon? Previously, Sound Fit's potential

customers might have been willing to fund the development of prototypes in exchange for a sweeter deal in the event that the technology panned out. Five companies seemed particularly hot on the product, but in a recession, none wanted any extra risk.

The timing of the bad bank news was especially unfortunate. High school and college graduation season was coming soon—one of the busiest times of the year. Following this, there would be back-to-school sales and then Christmas, which account for some 60 percent of annual sales. No money to fund production in January meant no significant revenue for almost the entire year.

Semcken sat down with two of Able Planet's board members, Rob Cascella and Steve Parker, both investors in the business. They advised Semcken to put Sound Fit on hold and redouble his efforts on LINX Audio. "When you're at the point where you're not generating operating cash flow," says Cascella, "you have to worry about today or you're not even going to be there in three years."

But Semcken wanted to continue negotiating with all 30 of Sound Fit's prospects. "The way you get a partner committed is out of fear they're going to lose it," he says. He was open to pushing LINX harder, but if he couldn't finance production of the headphones for existing customers, then expanding the line and finding new accounts would be out of the question. When he told Cascella and Parker that he wanted to ask Able Planet's other angel investors for a loan, they gave him the go-ahead. His offer: For every $100,000 loan they guaranteed, investors would get warrants for 30,000 shares at $3 apiece. Within three days, Semcken had a dozen takers. A representative at U.S. Bank, where Semcken kept his personal account, offered to make the loans, but only up to a certain amount. Semcken was hoping to raise some $1.5 million this way.

Trying to cover all his financial bases, Semcken had been scrambling to find a replacement for the company's $2.5 million line of credit. He traveled around the country to meet with 15 banks—but none were yet stepping up.

Questions

1. Kevin Semcken identified some possible alternative solutions to his financing problem. Did he come up with all possible alternatives, or can you think of more?

2. Do you agree with board member Rob Cascella, who told Kevin to concentrate on producing headphones and put

off the Sound Fit for later . . . or do you agree with Kevin, who sees Sound Fit as the future of Able Planet? Defend your choice.

3. As a small business consultant, what would you advise Kevin Semcken do to guide Able Planet through its financial storm?

Sources: Nitasha Tiku, "When Your Bank Stops Lending," *Inc.*, July 2009, 58–61; Christopher Schweitzer and Kevin Semcken, "Everyday Listening," *Audiologists*, March 2, 2010, www.audiology.advanceweb.com; Jay Palmer, "Technology Trader: Gadget of the Week: Phoning It In," *Barron's*, August 4, 2008; Christopher Schweitzer, "Mind the Porta! The Effect of Severe Microphone Inlet Occlusion," *Hearing Review*, June 2008, www.hearingreview.com; Christopher Schweitzer and Desmond Smith, "From Horsepower to Hearpower," *Hearing Review*, July 2009, www.hearingreview.com.

## CHAPTER 10

THE LEGAL ENVIRONMENT

How much would you spend for a pair of sneakers? A thousand dollars? That's the price for authentic Adidas Yeezys. Kanye West tweeted, "You probably got bootleg Yeezys on right now." Responses were split between loyalists who mocked fakes and those tempted by $99 fakes.

What is the big deal, you think? Maybe you've been tempted by a $35 Louis Vuitton purse or $20 Dolce & Gabbana sunglasses. Fakes cut into legitimate companies' revenue and force layoffs. Even worse is how the global counterfeit goods market is funded by large-scale criminal operations using exploitative practices forcing women and children to work in inhumane conditions. Profits from knockoffs fund illegal gangs, dictators, and global terrorism.

The U.S. Department of Commerce reports that U.S. businesses lose an estimated $200 billion annually to the counterfeiting of trademarked and copyrighted products. The International Chamber of Commerce also estimates that counterfeit goods of all kinds account for 6 percent of all world trade—about $600 billion. The electronics industry puts the number of fakes between 5 and 20 percent, costing about $1 billion per year.

A recent study by consulting firm KPMG notes several ways to mitigate counterfeiting. Among them, use *radio frequency identification (RFID)* and other product-tracking technologies, coordinate with trade groups and business partners to respond to counterfeiting, and partner with and assist police agencies in detecting and busting counterfeiters. Changing packaging can make a product harder to duplicate, but it will likely only take a few months for the counterfeiters to copy that also.

Imitation may be the sincerest form of flattery, but it's a huge problem for small businesses. Since most small

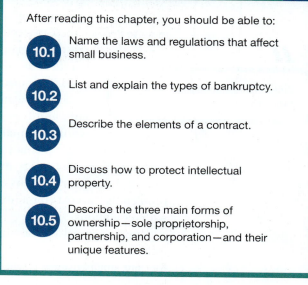

LEARNING OUTCOMES

After reading this chapter, you should be able to:

10.1 Name the laws and regulations that affect small business.

10.2 List and explain the types of bankruptcy.

10.3 Describe the elements of a contract.

10.4 Discuss how to protect intellectual property.

10.5 Describe the three main forms of ownership—sole proprietorship, partnership, and corporation—and their unique features.

business owners don't have the time, patience, or money to protect themselves, they are more than twice as likely to be victims of counterfeit fraud as big business.

Many small businesses sell their products via Amazon and are frustrated by cheap knockoff competition. Amazon tries to protect its legitimate business partners by fighting "fake reviews." Reviews put customers' minds at ease, drive sales, and push products up search rankings. Amazon also launched a mechanism for reporting counterfeit products.

Sources: Jenny Wolfram, "Why Kicking Out Counterfeit Crooks on Instagram Is So Important," *Entrepreneur*, October 22, 2017, www.entrepreneur.com/article/296783; Joe Keohane, "How Amazon Sellers Can Keep Things Real," *Entrepreneur*, April 4, 2017, www.entrepreneur.com/article/290455; Susan Houser, "Clone Wars," *JCK*, March 2014, 102–106; Kal Raustiala, "Fake It Till You Make It," *Foreign Affairs*, July/August 2013, 25–30.

Concept Module 10.1: Small Business and the Law

• **LO 10.1: Name the laws and regulations that affect small business.**

Would you like to live in a place with no laws? You could drive as fast as you wanted. You could drink alcohol at any age. You could do whatever you wanted, and, just think, there would be no taxes to pay because there would be no government making up rules and regulations! Although such absolute freedom might sound exciting at first thought, you don't have to picture this scenario for long to realize that it also includes no protection for any person or any group—it would be chaos. Orderly, civilized societies are built on laws.

We need laws to ensure fair competition between businesses, to protect the rights of consumers and employees, to protect property, to enforce contracts and agreements, and to permit

Master the content at
**edge.sagepub.com/
Hatten7e**

$SAGE edge™

bankruptcy when things go bad. We also need tax laws to collect the money needed for government to provide these protections. The balance of how much or how little protection we need or want changes over time. Through elections and open debate, our laws evolve to reflect the needs of and changes in society. But, as an old saying goes, "It's a good thing that we don't get half the government we pay for."

> "Orderly, civilized societies are built on laws."

Small business owners face a never-ending job of keeping up with the laws and regulations by which they must abide. One problem is that the wording of many laws and regulations is baffling and easy to misunderstand. A second problem for small businesses is the enormous amount of paperwork required to generate the many reports and records mandated by regulations. This paperwork imposes time and resource burdens on business owners who are often strapped for both. A third problem is the cost (for administrative and actual expenses) and difficulty in complying with regulations.

Running a small business does not require a law degree, but you do need two things to avoid trouble: a working knowledge of legal basics and a good lawyer. The best time to find a lawyer for your small business is when you are writing your business plan—not when you are already in trouble.

A study by the National Federation of Independent Business (NFIB) titled *Small-Business Problems and Priorities* showed the top 10 small business problems are split between costs, such as health care, and dealing with government regulations. NFIB senior research fellow Bruce Phillips noted, "Small business owners' most serious problems are politically generated, rather than spawned from free-market competition." Small business owners consider managing the daily burdens of health care costs, taxation, and regulation mandates to be far more difficult than what they do best—running a business. Figure 10.1 shows the top 10 responses from more than 3,500 small business owners to a 2016 survey dealing with cost- and regulation-related issues.

Regulations and the legal environment of small business cover a lot of ground. This chapter will discuss several major areas of business affected by the law: regulations, licenses, bankruptcy, contracts, and protection of intellectual property.

Small Business and Federal Regulations

All businesses have to follow all federal, state, and local laws and regulations (a legal rule created by a government agency), but small businesses face legal and regulatory standards that are different from the standards set for larger businesses. Go online to the Code of Federal Regulations (www.archives.gov/federal-register/cfr). You will see it is broken down into fifty titles, which in turn are broken into chapters, parts, sections, and paragraphs. Browse through this codification of general and permanent rules and regulations that fill 178,277 pages and with which American businesses, workers, and consumers must comply.[1] You will soon see why small business owners are so overwhelmed by regulations.[2]

Licenses and Permits. Only a few types of business require a federal permit, among them those selling alcohol or firearms; operating oversize vehicles or airplanes; importing or exporting plants, animals, or animal products; and broadcasting via the airwaves. Most businesses, however, do need some type of license and permit. The best place to start looking for the requirements is on the Small Business Administration (SBA) website (www.sba.gov), where you should search for both federal and state licenses and permits (the website changes format regularly, but the information is there).

Paying Overtime. If your business has annual revenue of greater than $500,000, you are likely covered under the Fair Labor Standards Act (FSLA) and required to pay overtime to

That's Bugging Me

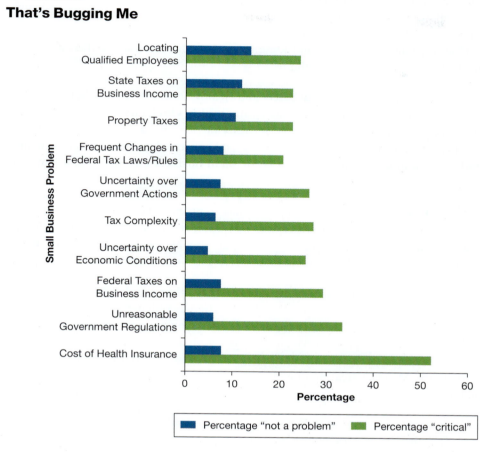

Small Business Problem (y-axis)

- Locating Qualified Employees
- State Taxes on Business Income
- Property Taxes
- Frequent Changes in Federal Tax Laws/Rules
- Uncertainty over Government Actions
- Tax Complexity
- Uncertainty over Economic Conditions
- Federal Taxes on Business Income
- Unreasonable Government Regulations
- Cost of Health Insurance

Percentage (x-axis): 0, 10, 20, 30, 40, 50, 60

■ Percentage "not a problem"   ■ Percentage "critical"

nonexempt employees who work more than 40 hours per week. If your business is below the $500,000 threshold, you must still pay overtime if you engage in "interstate commerce," which Congress defines as making phone calls, or exchanging mail or products to or from another state—so, pretty much every business.[3] Overtime pay means "time and a half," that is, the employee's normal hourly wage plus half that wage again for every overtime hour worked.

Job-Protected Leave. The Family and Medical Leave Act allows employees to take up to 12 weeks of unpaid leave for maternity or paternity, medical issues, or care for a family member without risking his or her job. Small businesses with fewer than 50 employees are exempt from this regulation.

Minimum Wage. The Fair Labor Standards Act currently has the federal minimum wage set at $7.25 per hour. Some states have set higher state-level minimums. If your small business has employees who are tipped (like food service), they can be paid a lower base rate.

Health Insurance. At this writing, the Affordable Care Act is undergoing further revisions, so stay tuned. Businesses with fewer than 50 full-time employees can purchase health insurance for them through the Small Business Health Options Program (SHOP) at healthcare.gov. Tax credits may apply if you cover at least half of your full-time employees' premium costs and you have fewer than 25 full-time employees.[4]

Workers' Compensation. Workers' Compensation is legally mandatory insurance your business purchases to cover work-related accidents. Injured employees receive medical care, death benefits, lost income, and vocational rehabilitation; you receive protection from lawsuits. Worker's Comp systems are regulated and administered by individual states so there is no single set of rules on benefits, coverage, or premiums.

Workplace Safety. The Occupational Safety and Health Administration (OSHA) was created by law in 1970 to assure workplace safety and health. OSHA has a labyrinth of rules regarding everything from asbestos to workplace violence.[5] Because even OSHA recognizes that its rules can overpower small businesses, it has created an online database of articles, handbooks, and guidelines specifically for small business (see www.osha.gov/dcsp/smallbusiness).

Paying Taxes. Competing with OSHA for the most complex and confusing regulations for small business is the Internal Revenue Service (IRS). You are responsible for paying federal taxes on the income your business brings in, self-employment tax, employment tax (if you have employees), excise taxes (depending on your industry) . . . plus state and local taxes.

Employee Classification. The IRS is the arbitror of whether people working for you are classified as employees or contractors. People classified as independent contractors are considered self-employed (for themselves) and therefore you are not required to withhold and pay income, Social Security, or Medicare taxes on that person. Classification is complicated but comes down to who controls the work, ability to fire, training, and who establishes work hours. Misclassification of employees as independent contractors comes with stiff penalties.

Nondiscrimination Employment Reporting. The Equal Employment Opportunity Commission requires businesses with more than 100 employees to annually report pay (and other information) by race/ethnicity, job category, and gender to assure compliance with federal nondiscrimination laws.

Environmental Protection. The Environmental Protection Agency regulates a patchwork of laws and regulations to assure that small businesses do not harm the environment. Examples include the Clean Air Act and the Clean Water Act, both of which deal with the disposal of materials your business would otherwise release into the environment. Your first stop should be the SBA's environmental regulation resource page.

Sales Tax. There is no federal sales tax, but if your small business sells online, you do need to collect state sales tax on sales in states in which your business has some physical presence (retail store, office, warehouse). Since sales tax is a major source of state and local government revenue, enforcement will come from state agencies.

Antitrust Laws. You might mistakenly think that the hundred-year-old federal Sherman Act would not still have application for small business—but it does. Say you run one of two food trucks operating in your community, and went to culinary school with the foodie who owns the other truck. You cannot mutually decide what prices you will each charge for tacos or mac and cheese or agree on territory without violating antitrust laws.

Truth in Advertising. The Federal Trade Commission (FTC) assures the public that companies are telling the truth in their advertising claims. Customers who suspect dishonesty report it to the FTC, in which case the business has to prove its claim. Medical and health claims

SMALL BUSINESS LEGAL WORRIES

Running a small business is complicated and problems can arise from many directions. The actual running of the business is seldom the biggest of those problems—legal issues rise to the top of that list. Here is the list:

- **Hiring and Firing:** Many small businesses operate under misinformation about terminating employment. The only federal law regulating employment deals with wages, hours, and discrimination—not termination of employment. If there is a mismatch between skills and responsibilities, or if an employee isn't doing the job, he can be fired "at will." Small business owners can avoid problems by creating an offer letter identifying the terms of employment, including a probationary period of 60 to 90 days.

- **Correct Legal Structure:** The most appropriate structure for your small business depends on several factors identified later in this chapter. But factors change with revisions such as the new tax code of 2018.

- **Protecting Your Name:** Your brand is a valuable asset, so make sure it is protected. Intellectual property (IP) protection comes in the form of a trademark and securing your domain name. When starting a new business, you need to be thinking about your domain name before day one. Trademark specialist Sonia Lakhany says, "Entrepreneurs and start-ups, particularly millennials, skip this step due to cost and budget reasons."

- **Protecting Your Trade Secrets:** Most small businesses never think of protecting their trade secrets, which are intellectual property, until it's too late. You do not have to be a high-tech company to own trade secrets. If your business makes salsa from an old family recipe, then that recipe has value. And you should protect it like Coca-Cola protects its formula.

- **Misclassification:** The IRS and the U.S. Department of Labor are taking an ever-closer look at how people working for your small business are classified—as employees or independent contractors. The National Law Review recommends that "employers regularly using independent contractors examine those relationships periodically to ensure that the classification remains defensible."

- **Be Careful How You Collect Data:** If your small business has any dealings in Europe, you should be aware of the General Data Protection Regulation. It requires permission from European consumers for using their data—or you can face fines as high as 4 percent of revenues. Be careful how you are collecting data from your U.S. customers also. Follow FTC guidelines.

Sources: Monica Zent, "7 Legal Issues Every Business Owner Needs to Address in 2018," *Inc.*, February 7, 2018, www.inc.com; Clare Curley, "Top Small Business Legal Issues," National Federation of Independent Business, January 9, 2017, www.nfib.com/resources/legal.

especially have to be backed by scientific studies. But statements about being "organic" or "green" are subject to substantiation also.

Licenses, Restrictions, and Permits

Because requirements for licenses and permits differ at the federal, state, regional, county, and city government levels, presenting a comprehensive list of all of them is not possible here.

Nevertheless, we can offer some general guidelines for finding information on regulations at each level.

- Double-check license and permit rules. Check with the appropriate government agency directly—don't rely on real estate agents, sellers, or anyone else's opinion.

- At the federal level, get an employer identification number for federal tax and Social Security withholdings. File Form 2553 if you are forming a corporation. Check with the appropriate agency for your specific type of business. For example, if you are starting a common-carrier trucking company, you should contact the Interstate Commerce Commission.

- At the state level, professionals, such as lawyers, dentists, and architects, need professional licenses. You need to register for a state tax number with the Department of Revenue. You need an employer identification number for state tax withholding. Special licenses are usually needed for selling liquor, food, gasoline, or firearms.

- At the regional level, several counties may form regional agencies that oversee environmental regulations and water usage.

- At the local level, permits and licenses to comply with local and county requirements will vary from place to place. You need answers from the local level—the local chamber of commerce and lawyers are good sources of information. Offices to consult would include the following:

  - City or county clerk
  - City or county treasurer
  - Zoning department
  - Building department
  - Health department
  - Fire department
  - Police department
  - Public works department

- If your business involves the sale or preparation of food, you will need not only a permit from a local health department, but also regular inspections. Local health departments may also be involved with environmental concerns, such as asbestos inspections, radon testing, and water purity testing.

Zoning Laws. You need to be absolutely sure how a property is zoned before you sign a lease. If it is not zoned properly, you can sign the lease with a contingency clause that the property will be rezoned. You can also apply to the local zoning commission to obtain a *variance*, which allows you to operate without complying with the regulation or without having the regulation changed.

Zoning laws control what a business can sell and where it can operate. They are typically used to control parking, waste disposal, and sign size and placement. You may not even be able to paint the building a certain color due to zoning restrictions. For example, a White Castle hamburger franchise in Overland Park, Kansas, was not allowed to paint the building white because a zoning ordinance prohibited white buildings.

How do zoning laws affect home-based businesses (see Chapter 7)? Technology is making it possible for you to be productive at work from the comfort of your own living room. But are zoning boards comfortable with that idea? Yes, for the most part. Although some zoning ordinances prohibit home businesses, most don't. Restrictions on what you can and can't do on the property are more common. Most zoning laws seek primarily to maintain the residential nature of the surrounding neighborhood.

You should check zoning laws before you start your business, whether or not it is home based. At the zoning department at city hall, find out about not only the written laws but also the attitudes held by administrators, citizens, and the business community. Find out if other home-based businesses are allowed. If you disagree with a zoning ruling, you may be able to appeal to a variance board, the city council, or local commissioners.

zoning laws
Local laws that control where and how businesses may operate.

CHOOSING AN ATTORNEY

A good attorney is hard to find, but it's well worth the effort to get one on your advisory team. What should you look for when choosing a lawyer or a law firm?

- **Excellence in working with people:** Like everyone else, some lawyers are good with people and some of them—are not. There will be times that your attorney will need to talk with your prospective buyers, sellers, employees, vendors, customers, shareholders, board members, and so on. A stereotypical trait that many people associate with attorneys is being combative. While that may be handy in the courtroom, little time will be spent there (hopefully) with your small business. What you need is someone who can work and play well with others.

- **A true long-term partner:** Every professional, from accountants to insurance agents, will play the long-term-partner card with you. But how do you tell? It begins with trust. You need to believe your attorney will always have <u>your</u> best interest at heart. This is important from the beginning, because as your business scales up, so does the importance of your legal counsel.

- **Sound judgment:** Many problems and situations you face will have clear-cut answers: yes/no; left/right; expand/contract; buy/sell. Where you need sound legal advice is in situations in the gray areas—when there is no clear direction. The relationship with your attorney takes time to develop, and over time you experience what kind of decision-maker she is.

Some small business owners wait until they need a lawyer, but in today's litigious society that's not the best idea. Finding a good one can be a solid competitive advantage for your small business.

Sources: Brian Hamilton, "3 Attributes to Look for in Your Lawyer," *Inc.*, August 24, 2017, www.inc.com; "Read This Before Hiring a Business Attorney," *Entrepreneur*, April 7, 2015, www.entrepreneur.com/article/242075; Mark Seibert, "9 Factors to Consider When Choosing a Franchise Attorney," *Entrepreneur*, March 30, 2016, www.entrepreneur.com/author/mark-siebert.

Concept Check Questions

1. Are the antitrust laws established in the late 1800s and early 1900s still pertinent in the 21st century? Why or why not?

2. How does the Federal Trade Commission protect consumers?

3. List and briefly explain the laws that protect people in the workplace.

4. What licenses are required by the owner of a small business?

5. Compliance with government regulations is sometimes burdensome for small business owners; what can they (and you) do to change the laws and regulations that influence small business in order to lessen the burden?

Concept Module 10.2: Bankruptcy Laws

- **LO 10.2: List and explain the types of bankruptcy.**

Bankruptcy is a remedy for becoming insolvent. When an individual or a business gets into a financial condition in which there's no other way out, the courts administer the estate for the benefit of the creditors. The Bankruptcy Reform Act of 1978 established eight chapters for businesspeople seeking the protection of bankruptcy. Three of these chapters—Chapters 7, 11, and 13—apply to most small business situations. Bankruptcy can accomplish one of two objectives: *liquidation*, after which the business ceases to exist, or *reorganization*, which allows the business owner to file a plan with the court that offers protection from creditors until the debt is satisfied.

bankruptcy
A ruling granted by courts to release businesses or individuals from some or all of their debt.

Chapter 7 Bankruptcy

Chapter 7 bankruptcy means that the business is liquidated, and all of the assets of the business are sold by a trustee appointed by the court. After the sale, the trustee distributes the proceeds to the creditors, who usually receive a percentage of the original debt. If any money is left over, it is divided among shareholders. About three of every four bankruptcy filings take place under Chapter 7.

Declaring bankruptcy does not necessarily leave you penniless and homeless. Most states have provisions allowing individuals to keep the equity in their homes, autos, and some personal property.

Bankruptcy may signal the demise of one business, but it could turn out to be an opportunity for you. For instance, imagine you are in business and one of your key suppliers goes bankrupt. What are your options? You could try to continue doing business with that firm for as long as possible. You could try to find a new supplier. Or you could use your knowledge of the bankrupt company and industry to your advantage, and buy the supplier at a bargain price, assuming you could operate the failed business more efficiently than the previous management.[6] Other strategic purchases could include buying a financially strapped competitor in an effort to increase your market share, or buying a business that is a customer in an effort to provide an outlet for your products.

The Bankruptcy Abuse Prevention and Consumer Protection Act of 2005 has caused some shifts in bankruptcy responsibilities. Individuals seeking Chapter 7 liquidation face increased responsibilities. While creditors have always had to show documentation of indebtedness—*proof of claim*—the burden is on the debtor to demonstrate that there is no reasonable alternative to the bankruptcy process. The debtor seeking liquidation must now prove an inability to pay his debts as they are due and demonstrate a good-faith attempt to resolve such a crisis without the court's help.

A controversial section in the bankruptcy code lies in the creation of a *means test* for eligibility to file under Chapter 7. The Bankruptcy Abuse Prevention and Consumer Protection Act requires a comparison of the debtor's income to the median income in the individual's home state. If the debtor's income is above the median and she is able to pay at least a minimal amount per month to creditors, she is now barred from Chapter 7 filing.[7]

Chapter 11 Bankruptcy

Chapter 11 provides a second chance for a business that is in financial trouble but still has potential for success. This type of bankruptcy can be either voluntary or involuntary. When you seek Chapter 11 protection, you must file a *reorganization plan* with the bankruptcy court. This plan includes a repayment schedule for current creditors (which may be less than 100 percent of the amounts owed) and indicates how the business will operate more profitably in the future. Only about 3 percent of bankruptcy filings take place under Chapter 11.

This reorganization protection keeps creditors from foreclosing on debts during the reorganization period. The business continues to operate under court direction. Both the court and the creditors must approve the plan, which also spells out a specific time period for the reorganization. If the business cannot turn operations (and profits) around, the likelihood of its switching to a Chapter 7 liquidation is great.

Chapter 13 Bankruptcy

Chapter 13 bankruptcy allows individuals, including small business owners, who owe less than $250,000 in unsecured debts and less than $750,000 in secured debts to pay back creditors over a three- to five-year period. As under Chapter 11, a repayment plan is submitted to a bankruptcy judge, who must approve the conditions of the plan. The plan must show

how most types of debts will be repaid in full. Some types of debts can be reduced or even eliminated by the court. About one-fourth of bankruptcies are filed under the provisions of Chapter 13.

Although much of the negative stigma attached to declaring bankruptcy of any type has decreased, this course of action is still not an "easy way out." Bankruptcy stays on your credit report for at least seven years. It is expensive and time-consuming. Chapters 11 and 13 may be better than liquidation, but they are not a solution to all of your problems.

> "Although much of the negative stigma attached to declaring bankruptcy of any type has decreased, this course of action is still not an 'easy way out.'"

Concept Check Questions

1. How are liquidation and reorganization used as different approaches to bankruptcy?

2. What chapters of bankruptcy law accomplish these objectives?

Concept Module 10.3: Contract Law for Small Businesses

- **LO 10.3: Describe the elements of a contract.**

A **contract** is basically a promise that is enforceable by law. Contract law comprises the body of laws that are intended to make sure the parties entering into a contract comply with the deal and provides remedies to those parties harmed if a contract is broken.

A contract does not have to be in writing to be enforceable. Although it is a good idea to get any important agreement down on paper to help settle future disputes, the only contracts that must be in writing are those involving one of the following:

- Sale of real estate

- Paying someone else's debt

- More than one year to perform

- Sale of goods valued at $500 or more

Even written contracts do not have to be complicated formal documents created by a lawyer. Although you may not want to rely on contracts that are too sketchy, a letter or memo identifying the parties, the subject, and the terms and conditions of the agreement can be recognized as a valid contract.

Elements of a Contract

The four basic conditions or elements a contract must meet to be binding are legality, agreement, consideration, and capacity.

Legality. A contract must have a legal purpose. For instance, you can't make a contract that charges an interest rate higher than legal restrictions allow. At the same time, just because a deal is unfair, it is not necessarily illegal. You can't get out of a deal later if you offer to pay $1,500 for a used computer that is worth only $150.

Agreement. A valid contract has a legitimate offer and a legitimate acceptance—called a "meeting of the minds." If a customer tells you his traveling circus will pay your print shop $600

> **contract**
> An agreement between two or more parties that is enforceable by law.

to print 200 circus posters and you say, "It's a deal," you have a legally binding contract. In this case, it is an oral contract, but it is just as legally binding as a written one.

Consideration. Something of value must be exchanged between the parties involved in the contract. Without consideration, the agreement is about a gift, not a contract. In the preceding example, the $600 and the 200 posters are the consideration. If the circus owner picks up the posters, pays you the $600, and says, "Wow, for doing such a great job, come to the circus and I'll give you a free elephant ride," can you legally demand to ride the elephant later? No, you got what you agreed to—the $600—but there was no consideration for the bonus.

Capacity. Not everyone has the capacity to legally enter into a contract. Minors and persons who are intoxicated or who have diminished mental ability cannot be bound by contracts. This is an important point to remember when running a small business. For example, if you sell a used car to a person younger than the age of 18, you could end up with a problem. The minor could take the car, run it without oil, smash it into a tree, and then ask you for his money back. You would be legally obligated to return the money because a contract with a minor is not binding.

Contractual Obligations

What can you do if a party with whom you signed a contract doesn't hold up her end of the deal? This scenario is called **breach of contract**, and you have several remedies available. Usually either money or some specific performance is used to compensate the damaged party. With either remedy, the intent of litigation is to try to put you back to where you were before the agreement was made.

Moneys awarded by a judge or arbitrator as a remedy for breach of contract are called **compensatory damages**. Go back to the circus poster example. If you were not able to complete the job as agreed and the circus owner had to pay someone else $800 to get the posters printed, you could be sued for $200 for breach of contract (probably in small claims court). Why $200? That amount represents the compensatory damages the circus owner suffered because you couldn't do the job for $600.

In some contract-dispute cases, money alone is insufficient to put a person back to his original state. In these cases, a judge may order a **specific performance** by the damaging party to make sure justice is done—in other words, requiring that party to do exactly what she agreed to do. Specific performance is awarded only if the item involved is unique and not substitutable. In this case, a judge will require the losing party to surrender the item in question.

Consider the case of buying an existing business for which the sales contract includes a *noncompete covenant*, which states that the previous business owner will not start or own a similar business within a specific geographic area for a certain amount of time. If the previous owner breaks the noncompete covenant and starts the same type of business, a single monetary award won't be enough. The judge can issue an **injunction**, which prohibits the previous owner from operating the new business for the duration of the agreement.

breach of contract
A violation of one or more terms of a contract by a party involved in the contract.

compensatory damages
Money awarded by the courts to a party of the contract who has suffered a loss due to the actions of another party.

specific performance
A nonmonetary award granted by the courts to a party of the contract who has suffered a loss due to the actions of another party.

injunction
A court order that prohibits certain activities.

Concept Check Questions

1. Name and explain the four elements that a contract must have to be valid.

2. Think of transactions you have entered into in the past: With whom were you agreeing, what was the agreement about, and what were the terms? When have you had a written contract with someone? When have you had an oral contract? Use several examples to analyze the process of buying a car, accepting a job, and ordering a pizza. What elements of contract law apply in each case?

Concept Module 10.4: Laws to Protect Intellectual Property

- ## LO 10.4: Discuss how to protect intellectual property.

Intellectual property is a broad term that refers to the product of some type of unique human thought. It begins as an idea that could be as simple as a new name or as complex as the invention of a new product. Intellectual property also includes symbols and slogans describing your business or product and any original expression, whether it takes the form of a collection of words (like a published book), an artistic interpretation (like a recording of a concert performance), or a computer program. These products of human thought have some value in the marketplace. A body of laws determines how, and for how long, a person can capitalize on his idea.

The forms of legal protection for intellectual property discussed in this section are patents, copyrights, and trademarks. Although commonly used, the term *protection* may be misleading when we are discussing intellectual property, because it implies defense, whereas patents, copyrights, and trademarks give the owner more offensive rights than defensive protection. They cannot prevent others from trying to infringe on your registered idea, but they can discourage such attempts by the threat of your taking them to court. Although these court challenges often do not prevail, the possibility that they might prevail reduces attempts to steal your intellectual property. In the United States, this right has been considered so essential a part of the country's economic functioning that it was written into the Constitution.[8]

©Shutterstock.com/SunnyGraph

Patents

A **patent** gives you the right to exclude someone else (or some other company) from making, using, or selling the property you have created and patented for a period of 17 years. To receive this protection, you have to file for a patent through the U.S. Patent and Trademark Office (PTO). With a patent application, you must pay both filing fees and maintenance fees. Three maintenance fees must be paid 4, 8, and 12 years after the patent grant, or the patent will expire before 17 years.

Although it is commonly believed that you have to hire a patent attorney to file a patent application, this is not the case. Actually, regulations require the PTO to help individuals who do not use an attorney. Hundreds of patents are granted each year to inventors who navigate the process solo. But just because you can complete the patent process without legal counsel, does that mean you should attempt it? It depends—particularly on factors like your comfort level with processing "red tape." Patent attorneys charge $3,000 to $5,000 to prepare a patent application. How many earth-changing widgets must you sell to cover that kind of overhead? If you are unsure of what the market for your widgets will be, books like *Patent It Yourself* by David Pressman contain all the instructions and forms you need to do it yourself.[9] Doing as much as you can yourself, while checking periodically with an attorney throughout the process, may be a reasonable compromise to offer you both expertise and cost savings.

The 2012 America Invents Act (AIA) changed the landscape for small businesses thinking about patent protection. The new law changes what makes an idea patentable or not, and the way others can challenge a new patent during the "post-grant review" process. Most important, the act moves from a "first-to-invent" basis to a "first-to-file" basis, which rewards the first person

intellectual property
Property that is created through the mental skills of a person.

patent
A form of protection for intellectual property provided to an inventor for a period of 17 years.

IP APP PROTECTION?

Entrepreneurs are changing some of their thought regarding intellectual property in the 21st century. In the past, companies have treated IP as an asset that must be kept out of the hands of others at all costs, but relaxing that paranoia is becoming less the exception and more the rule.

An interesting, and potentially dangerous, example is seen in the development of free and open-source software (FOSS). FOSS represents an incredible variety of utilities and programs published at no cost for the benefit of all comers. FOSS may be free to use, but may still be licensed. The challenge of creating open-source software and protecting your legal rights comes in writing the FOSS license form. Typical language is: "Nothing other than this License grants you permission to propagate or modify any covered work. These actions infringe copyright if you do not accept this License."

But the bottom line (literally) is that the success of a business is rarely tied to success in protecting IP.

Ninety-five percent of patents end up being of absolutely no commercial value. Even in the high-tech industry (where IP is everything), the rule of thumb in protecting patents is . . . don't bother. According to economics professor Glen Whitman, "The faster the pace of innovation, the less important will be the patent." In other words, superb execution trumps IP protection every time.

On the other hand, your app may be copyrightable. If you take this route, you need to file copyright registration on every significant version of that software to lock in your IP remedies for your company. In your code and on the screen displays, mark "©Year Company Name."

Sources: Art Mertes, "Are You Doing Enough to Protect and Monetize Your Intellectual Property?" *Entrepreneur,* September 6, 2017, www.entrepreneur.com/article/298237; Jeremy Quittner, "Have a New App? There May Not Be a Patent for That," *Inc.,* March 31, 2014, www.inc.com.

to file for a patent instead of the first person to think of the idea behind the patent.[10] Time and cost of the patent process coupled with **patent trolls** (companies known as *nonpracticing entities*, which own patents but never use them to create anything and make money by suing potential patent infringers) impede innovation.[11]

Three types of patents exist. The most common type is the *utility patent*, which covers inventions that provide a unique or new use or function. If you could come up with a new way to keep shoes on people's feet without using laces, buckles, Velcro fasteners, zippers, or other ways currently used, you would need to file for a utility patent.

Whereas utility patents cover use, *design patents* protect unique or new forms or shapes. If the new shape also changes the function of the object, then you need to apply for a utility patent. If looks alone are different, you need a design patent. For example, if you were to design a ballpoint pen that looked like a fish, but which served no other function than that of a ballpoint pen, you would file for a design patent on your invention.

The third patent type is a *plant patent*. Such a patent covers living plants, such as flowers, trees, or vegetables that can be grown or otherwise reproduced.

What Can Be Patented?. The PTO reviews each application and decides whether to grant a patent on the basis of four tests, which come from the following questions:

- Does the invention fit a statutory class?

- Is the invention useful?

- Is it novel?

- Is it nonobvious?

Patent trolls
Individuals or companies that hold patents for unscrupulous purposes such as stifling competition or launching patent infringement lawsuits.

The invention must fit into one of the five *statutory classes*—which means you must be able to call it a machine, process, manufacture, chemical composition, or combination of those terms.

The invention must provide some *legal utility*. That is, it must be useful in some way. If the invention has some commercial value, this test shouldn't be difficult to pass. If it doesn't, you will have a hard time building your small business on it. The invention must be possible to build and be workable to be granted a patent. You have to be able to show the examiner that the invention will operate as you say it will.

The invention must be *novel*. It must be different from all other things that have previously been made or described anywhere else in the world (called *prior art*). Meeting this test can be difficult since the definition of *novelty* may be confusing to everyone involved. Three types of novelty that meet this requirement are those created by (1) physical difference, (2) a new combination of existing parts, or (3) the invention of a new use.

The invention must be *nonobvious*. Although this rule is also difficult to understand, it is an important one. It means that the difference between your invention and other developments (or prior art) must not be obvious to someone with common knowledge in that field. The novelty of your invention needs to produce new or unexpected results.

The flowchart in Figure 10.2 can help you visualize the tests your invention must pass to get a patent.

Patent Search. Before you file a patent application, you should conduct a *patent search* to save time and money later. You can conduct this search yourself, or you can hire a patent agent or patent attorney to do it for you. You are searching for existing patents for inventions that are or may be similar to yours.

Start by coming up with several key words that could be used in describing your invention. These key words will be run through the primary patent reference publication at the PTO in Arlington, Virginia, called the *Index to the U.S. Patent Classification*. If you can't go to the PTO, you can search a Patent Depository Library. In these libraries, you can use the *Official Gazette of the U.S. Patent and Trademark Office*.

You can also conduct a patent search by subject or by specific patent via the internet. Such a search is done through the Shadow Patent Office. For more information, visit the PTO's home page at www.uspto.gov.

Patent Application. When submitting your patent application, you should include the following items:

1. Self-addressed, stamped postcard to show receipt of packet

2. Payment of the filing fee

3. Letter of transmittal

4. Drawings of your invention

5. Specifications, including

   a. Title or name of your invention

   b. Cross-reference of similar inventions

   c. Description of the field of your invention

   d. Prior art

   e. Features and advantages of your invention

   f. Drawing descriptions

   g. Description of how your invention works

   h. Conclusion

How Do You Get a Patent?

Here are the steps needed to receive a patent on your product.

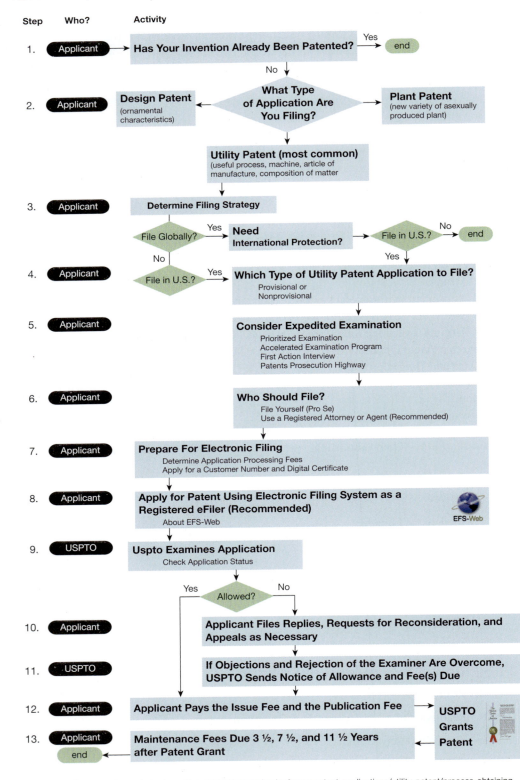

Source: https://www.uspto.gov/patents-getting-started/patent-basics/types-patent-applications/utility-patent/process-obtaining.

6. The claim, which specifies patent details that define the scope of your invention

7. An abstract, summarizing the whole project

8. A patent application declaration form that says you are the true inventor

9. A statement that you have not transferred patent ownership to anyone else

10. An information disclosure statement and a list of prior art[12]

A PTO examiner will review your application in the order in which it is received, meaning that it could be months or years before the review begins. The examination process can take from one to three or more years with revisions and amendments. If your patent is approved, you will be notified, and a copy of the application will be sent to the U.S. Government Printing Office.

Copyrights

A **copyright** is the protection of a literary, musical, or artistic work. Copyright laws protect the expression of ideas, not the ideas themselves, because lawmakers want to encourage the dissemination of ideas while protecting the rights of the original owner.

The length of copyright protection is the life of the author plus 50 years. If your corporation is the owner of a book's copyright, it will continue as owner for 75 years after the first publication, or 100 years after creation.

You don't have to register your work to receive copyright protection, but it does strengthen your rights to do so. If registered, you don't have to prove actual damages to collect up to $500,000 if someone violates your copyright. The act of creating the work begins the copyright protection, whether or not it is ultimately published. If you do choose to register your work, all you need to do is complete the proper forms and send the fees to the Copyright Office along with a copy of your work.

Many small businesses create computer software. Should they seek a patent or a copyright for their creation? Actually, software could qualify for either or both forms of protection, so which would be better? A patented computer program is difficult for competitors to simulate or design around, and the protection lasts for 17 years, but consider the disadvantages: Patents can be expensive, require a lot of work to apply for and search, and take several years to obtain. Windows of opportunity open and shut quickly in the software market. Your software may be obsolete before a patent can even be granted.

Copyrighting software is quick and inexpensive but doesn't provide the offensive punch of a patent. You can't copyright what a program does, only the specific way it is written. Thus, competing small business programmers only need to write the program for their software in a different manner to avoid copyright infringement.

What's the answer for "protecting" your software? Frankly, neither patents nor copyrights do a thorough job in this case. Protecting intellectual property for quickly changing industries and global markets is a serious problem that may become more so for small businesses and regulators in the near future.

Trademarks

A **brand** is a name, term, symbol, design, or combination of these elements that clearly identifies and differentiates your products from those of your competitors. A **trademark** is a registered and protected brand. Therefore, all trademarks are brands, but not all brands are trademarks. A trademark can include a graphic as well as a brand name. For example, not only is the Coca-Cola name protected, but the style of its script also makes it a trademark.

Your trademark rights remain in effect as long as you continue to use the trademark. This enduring nature offers an advantage over patents or copyrights. Trademarks are useful because they provide brand recognition for your product and are a good way to create an image in your customer's mind.

copyright
A form of protection for intellectual property provided to the creator of a literary, musical, or artistic work for a period of the creator's life plus 50 years.

brand
A name, term, symbol, design, or combination of these elements that clearly identifies and differentiates your products from those of your competitors.

trademark
A form of protection for intellectual property provided to the owner of a brand name or symbol.

A MATTER OF TASTE

The stories of companies like KFC, Coca-Cola, and McDonald's guarding their recipes for batter, syrup, and hamburger sauce are legendary. Triple-locked safes, binding contractual agreements, spies, and counterspies are all involved. A company's *trade secrets* are worth significant (sometimes staggering) amounts of money. Like any good secret, they are known to only a handful of people.

Many assets, such as chemical formulas or specific designs, are protected by patents. In exchange for the legal protection afforded by a patent, the patent holder must surrender the leverage of secrecy. That's because part of the patent application process involves a full explanation of the process or product. The PTO publishes all patent applications within 18 months of their filing. Protecting a trade secret is complicated by the fact that, unlike patents, copyrights, and trademarks, trade secrets do not fall under federal jurisdiction. They are regulated by individual state laws. Trade secrets must be *proved* to be secret to qualify for protection. At the very minimum, the owner must prove that procedures were in place to protect the information prior to any legal challenge.

Source: Geoffrey James, "Entrepreneurs Must Defend Intellectual Property Rights," *Inc.*, February 27, 2015, www.inc.com.

Question

1. Imagine that you have developed a unique formula for a soft drink that, upon entering a person's mouth, analyzes the drinker's DNA to determine his favorite flavor, and then the drink instantly realigns its chemical composition to become that flavor. Write a two-page paper describing how you can best protect this trade secret. Will you patent it? Why or why not?

Because there are more than 1 million trademarks in use in the United States, how do you find one that isn't already taken? As with the patent search, you can either do the *trademark search* yourself or hire someone to do it for you.

You can conduct a search yourself with the *Trademark Assistance Center* and file for a trademark with the Patent and Trademark Office, Washington, D.C., 20231 (www.uspto.gov) with an application and a $225, $275, or $400 fee (depending on options). You will find a series of informative videos on the PTO website—begin with *Basic Facts about Trademarks: What Every Small Business Should Know*. You can also register your trademark in your own state with the secretary of state at your state capitol.

Your trademark is worthless (and actually invalid) if you don't use it. Before your product is registered, use the symbol ™; after it is registered, use ®.

Concept Check Questions

1. What rights does owning a patent protect? How do you get this protection?

2. What tests must an invention pass to receive a patent?

3. What is the difference between a copyright and a trademark? Between a trademark and a brand?

4. What risk does an inventor assume when filing for a patent for an invention?

Concept Module 10.5: Forms of Business Organization

- **LO 10.5: Describe the three main forms of ownership—sole proprietorship, partnership, and corporation—and their unique features.**

One of the first decisions you will need to make in starting a business is choosing a form of ownership. This section will lead you through your options and present the advantages and disadvantages of each.

Several issues should be considered when making this decision. To what extent do you want to be personally liable for financial and legal risk? Who will have controlling interest of the business? How will the business be financed? The three basic legal structures you can choose for your firm are sole proprietorship, partnership, or corporation, with specialized options of partnerships and corporations available.

About 94 percent of nonemployer businesses that exist in the United States are sole proprietorships, making this the most common form of ownership (see Figures 10.3, 10.4, and 10.5).

▼ FIGURE 10.3

Ownership Forms of U.S. Businesses

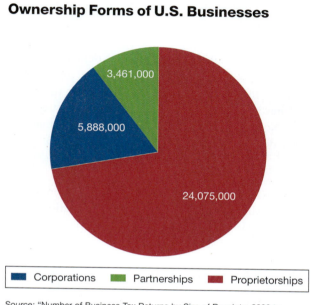

Legend: ■ Corporations ■ Partnerships ■ Proprietorships

Source: "Number of Business Tax Returns by Size of Receipts: 2000 to 2013," in *Statistical Abstract of the United States* (Washington, DC: ProQuest, 2018), table 767.

▼ FIGURE 10.4

Sales Revenue by Ownership Type

Legend: ■ Corporations ■ Partnerships ■ Proprietorships

Source: "Number of Tax Returns, Receipts, and Net Income by Type of Business: 1990 to 2013," in *Statistical Abstract of the United States* (Washington, DC: ProQuest, 2018) table 766.

▼ FIGURE 10.5

Net Income by Ownership Type

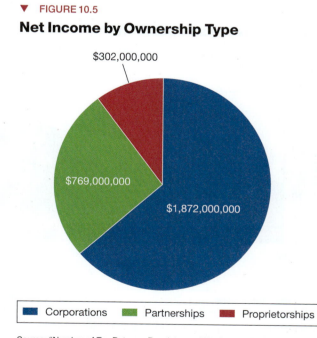

Legend: ■ Corporations ■ Partnerships ■ Proprietorships

Source: "Number of Tax Returns, Receipts, and Net Income by Type of Business: 1990 to 2013," in *Statistical Abstract of the United States* (Washington, DC: ProQuest, 2018), table 766.

Yet, while sole proprietorships represent 72 percent of all businesses, they account for only 4 percent of the total revenue generated by businesses and only 10 percent of the net profits earned. By comparison, corporations bring in 81 percent of business-generated revenue and 64 percent of the net income earned, even though they account for only 18 percent of the total number of businesses. Partnerships are also in the minority, with 10 percent of the total number of businesses, 15 percent of the revenue, and 26 percent of the net income earned.

Figure 10.6 shows that proprietorships increased in number and as a percentage of the total of the millions of small businesses that existed in the United States over the period of 1980 to 2013. This trend illustrates the rise of very small businesses. The number of corporations grew gradually, whereas the number of partnerships remained relatively constant. Changes in tax laws have varying effects on incentives for the different types of ownership, thereby affecting the number of businesses of each type that are formed.

> "You may have a smaller pie, but it's all your pie."

There is no single best form of organization. The choice depends on your short- and long-term needs, your tax situation, and your personal preferences, abilities, and resources. Don't confuse legal form of ownership with the size of the business. When you walk into a small neighborhood business, can you assume that it is a sole proprietorship? Not necessarily. A one-person flower shop may be a corporation, or a multimillion-dollar factory could be a sole proprietorship.

Sole Proprietorship

A sole proprietorship is a business that is owned and operated by one person. There are no legal requirements to establish a sole proprietorship. In most states, if you are operating under a name other than your full first and last legal names, you must register the business as a trade name with the state department of revenue.

Advantages. As the owner of a sole proprietorship, you have complete control of the business. The sole proprietorship is well suited to the aspiring entrepreneur's desire for independence. You don't have to consult with any partners, stockholders, or boards of directors. As a result of this independence, you are free to respond quickly to new market needs. Because you make all the

sole proprietorship
A business owned and operated by one person.

▼ **FIGURE 10.6**

Growth in the Business Population

While the number of all forms of ownership has risen, business tax returns show that the number of proprietorships has increased the most.

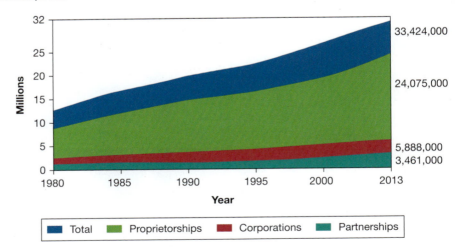

Source: "Number of Business Tax Returns by Size of Receipts: 1980 to 2013," in *Statistical Abstract of the United States* (Washington, DC: ProQuest, 2018), table 767.

decisions and bear all the responsibility, you do not have to share profits with anyone. You may have a smaller pie, but it's all *your* pie. No one else in the business tells you what to do, criticizes your mistakes, or second-guesses your decisions.

A sole proprietorship is easy to set up. There are fewer legal requirements and restrictions than with a partnership or a corporation. Legal and license costs are at a minimum. An inexpensive business license from the city or county clerk is all that is usually required—and sometimes not even that—unless your type of business requires special permits. For example, businesses selling food must be inspected by health departments. Otherwise, you need only hang your sign on the door and let the world know you are in business. The fast, simple way in which a proprietorship can be formed reduces start-up costs and stress.

The Internal Revenue Service (IRS) regards the business and the owner in a sole proprietorship as being a single entity. If your business shows a loss the first year or two (which is common), those losses can be deducted from any other income you have for the year. This tax advantage is short-lived, however. The tax code states that your business must make money three out of five years. According to the IRS, only money-making ventures are considered businesses. Anything else is a hobby. Even so, this deduction can give you a boost if you are starting your business on a part-time basis and have other income.

Just as proprietorships are easy to open, they are easy to close. If you choose, you can liquidate your assets, pay your bills, turn off the lights, and take your sign off the door, and you are then out of business. This is not the case with partnerships and corporations.

Disadvantages. The biggest disadvantage of a sole proprietorship is its **unlimited liability**. As a sole proprietor, you are personally liable for all debts incurred by the business. If the business should fail, you could lose more than you invested in it. Personal assets, such as your home and car, might have to be liquidated to cover the business debt. Thus, although there are few caps on the potential for return with a sole proprietorship, there are similarly few caps on the amount you could lose.

The sole proprietorship is the most difficult form of business for which to raise capital from outside sources. As one individual, you have access to fewer financial resources than a group of people could gather. Lenders believe their chances of seeing a return on their investment are reduced in a sole proprietorship and therefore are not as likely to loan money to this type of business.

The total responsibility of running a sole proprietorship may mean independence, but it can also be a disadvantage. Just as you are limited to the amount of capital you can raise, so you are limited to and by your own skills and capabilities. You may be an expert in some areas of running a business but be deficient in others.

Total responsibility can also mean a lack of continuity in the business. If you should become unable to work through illness, disability, or death, the business will cease to exist. Long vacations can become virtually impossible to take.

....
unlimited liability
The potential for an owner to lose more than has been invested in a business.

▼   TABLE 10.1

Balancing the Advantages and Disadvantages of Sole Proprietorships

Advantages	Disadvantages
Independence	Unlimited liability
Easy to set up	Limited resources
Easy to close	Limited skills
Tax benefits	Lack of continuity

Partnership

If two or more people are going into business together, they have two choices: form a partnership or form a corporation. A **partnership** is defined as an association of two or more persons to carry on as co-owners of a business for profit. Legally you can have a partnership without a written agreement (although it is not recommended), so the paperwork requirements for starting a partnership are about the same as those for a proprietorship.

When you form a partnership with friends, family, or associates, you may not think it is necessary to have a written agreement because you are so familiar with each other. You do. Problems are inevitable for every partnership, and the human memory is far too frail to depend upon in times of business difficulty. An agreement that is well thought out when the partnership is formed can save the business—and a friendship—later. Without a written agreement, a partnership operates according to the rules of the state under the Uniform Partnership Act (UPA). The intent of the UPA is to settle problems between partners. For example, without a written agreement that states otherwise, each partner shares equally in the profit and management of the business. The UPA is discussed in more detail later in this chapter.

> "An agreement that is well thought out when the partnership is formed can save the business—and a friendship—later."

Partners should bring complementary skills and resources to the alliance to give it a better chance of success. For instance, if one partner has creative abilities, the other partner should have a good business (financial) sense. Partners may also complement each other by providing different business contacts or amounts of capital. Think of the relationship this way: If both partners possess the same qualities, one of them probably isn't needed.

There are two types of partnerships: general and limited. Most of this discussion will focus on the **general partnership**, which is more common. In a general partnership, each partner faces the same personal liability as a sole proprietor. In a limited partnership, at least one of the partners has limited liability. This section will concentrate on general partnerships, with limited partnerships being discussed at the end of the section.

Advantages. The biggest advantage of partnerships should be the pooling of managerial talent and capital to create a product or service that is better than what any of the partners could have created individually (see Table 10.2).

Access to additional capital is an advantage of partnerships. Partners can pool their money. Moreover, credit is easier to obtain than for a proprietor. The reason is that the creditor can collect the debt from any one or all of the partners. Partnerships can also benefit from more management expertise in decision-making. With more partners involved, there is a higher chance of someone knowing what to do or having prior experience in any given situation.

Partnerships, like proprietorships, have a tax advantage in that the owners pay taxes as individuals. Therefore, profits are taxed only once on each partner's share of the income. The

partnership
An association of two or more persons to carry on as co-owners of a business for profit.

general partnership
A business structure in which the business owners share the management and risk of the business.

▼ TABLE 10.2

Balancing the Advantages and Disadvantages of Partnerships

Advantages	Disadvantages
Pooled talent	Unlimited liability
Pooled resources	Potential for management conflict
Easy to form	Less independence than proprietorships
Tax benefits	Continuity or transfer of ownership

partnership must file an informational return that reports how much money it earned or lost during the tax year and what share of the income or loss belongs to each partner.

Partnerships are easy to create. All you need are the appropriate business licenses and a tax number, and you're in business—for better or for worse.

Disadvantages. As with sole proprietorships, a disadvantage of partnerships is that the general partners carry the burden of unlimited liability. Each general partner's liability is not limited to the amount of his or her investment but rather extends to that partner's personal property as well. Even if the partnership agreement specifies a defined split in profits, each partner is 100 percent responsible for all liabilities.

In a partnership, you can be held liable for the negligence of your partners. A great deal of trust, a comprehensive agreement, and a good lawyer are, therefore, needed before opening such a business. Similarly, each partner can act as an agent of the partnership. In other words, any partner can enter into a contract for the partnership, incurring debt or other responsibilities, or selling assets, unless limited by the *articles of partnership*, discussed in detail later in this chapter. The choice of a business partner is much like choosing a partner for marriage. You need to know and be able to live with the other person's character, work habits, and values to make sure you are compatible.

The potential for managerial conflict within the partnership is one of the most serious problems that can threaten its viability. If partners disagree on matters that involve core issues, such as a future direction for the business, the partnership could literally split at the seams.

If a common reason to go into small business is independence, entering into a partnership limits that independence. For example, what happens if you want to reinvest profits in the business, but your partner wants to start holding your business meetings in Hawaii and have the company buy each of you new cars? Some resolution must be found, or the entire business could be in jeopardy. Being a partner requires compromise and cooperation.

Although the ability to raise capital is better with a partnership than with a proprietorship, a partnership still cannot usually gather as many resources as a corporation.

Another financial problem could occur when the partnership decides to retain some of its income and reinvest it in the business. All partners must pay income tax on their share of the partnership's income, even if they do not receive those funds. This requirement could prove financially difficult for some partners.

Continuity can also be a problem for partnerships. Difficulties may arise if a partner wants to withdraw from the partnership, dies, or becomes unable to continue in the business. Even if the partnership agreement identifies the value of each owner's share, the remaining partners may not have the financial resources to buy out the one who wants to leave. If a partner leaves, the partnership is dissolved. The remaining partners must find a new partner to bring in, contribute additional capital themselves, or terminate the business. This problem can be avoided in advance by including a *buy-sell agreement* in the *articles of partnership*, which will be discussed in detail later in this chapter.

The buy-sell agreement spells out what will happen if one of the partners wants to leave voluntarily, becomes disabled, or dies. A sensible solution is a "right of first refusal" clause, which requires the selling partner to give the remaining partners the first chance to buy the exiting partner's share. This proactive solution is highly recommended for all partnerships and corporations.

Limited Partnership. The **limited partnership** was created to avoid some of the problems of a general partnership while retaining its basic benefits. A limited partnership must have at least one general partner who retains unlimited liability and all of the other responsibilities discussed in the general partnership section. In addition, any number of limited partners with limited liability is allowed. Limited partners are usually passive investors. All they can lose

limited partnership
A business structure in which one or more of the owners may be granted limited liability as long as one partner is designated as a general partner with unlimited liability.

is the amount they invest in the business. With very few exceptions, limited partners cannot participate in the management of the business without losing their liability protection. Limited partnerships are a good way for the general partners to acquire capital—from the limited partners—without giving up control, taking on debt, or going through the process of forming a corporation.

The cost and complication of organizing a limited partnership can be as high as those for forming a corporation. A document called a *limited partnership agreement* is required in most states. This agreement identifies each partner's potential liability and the amount of capital each partner supplies. Most limited partnerships are formed for real estate investment because of the tax advantages to the limited partners, who can write off depreciation and other deductions from their personal taxes.[13]

Uniform Partnership Act. Signed in 1917 and revised in 1994, the Uniform Partnership Act (UPA) covers most legal issues concerning partnerships and has been adopted by every state in the union except Louisiana. The intent of the UPA is to settle problems that arise between partners. The best way for partners to protect their individual interests and the interests of the business is to draft their own articles of partnership (discussed below). Because two people can form a partnership with a simple verbal agreement, not all of them write such articles. Even without a written agreement, the UPA provides partners with some measure of protection and regulation, including the following provisions:

- All partners must agree to any assignment of partnership property.

- Each partner has one vote, no matter what percentage of the partnership she owns, unless a written agreement states otherwise.

- Accurate bookkeeping records are required, and all partners have the right to examine them.

- Each partner owes loyalty to the partnership by not doing anything that would intentionally harm the partnership or the other partners.

- Partners may draw on their share of the profits. This ability provides partners with access to their own capital.

- Salaries must be part of a written agreement. If a loss is incurred, partners must pay their share.

State-specific revisions to this act primarily involve the way in which a general partnership can become a *limited-liability partnership (LLP)*,[14] which is very similar to a *limited-liability company (LLC)*, which is discussed in detail later in this chapter.

Articles of Partnership. The formal contract between the principals, or people forming a partnership, is called the **articles of partnership**. The purpose of this contract is to outline the partners' obligations and responsibilities. As a legal document, it helps to prevent problems from arising between partners and provides a mechanism for solving any problems that do occur. A partnership agreement can save your business and your friendship. Articles of partnership usually specify the following items:

- *The name, location, and purpose of the partnership.* States the name of the partnership, where it is located, and why it exists.

- *The contribution of each partner in cash, services, or property.* Describes what each partner brings to the company.

articles of partnership
The contract between partners of a business that defines obligations and responsibilities of the business owners.

- *The authority of each partner and the need for consensual decision-making.* Specifies, for example, that large purchases (say, over $5,000) or contracts require the approval of a majority (or both) of the partners.

- *The management responsibilities of each partner.* Specifies, for example, that all partners must be actively involved and participate equally in the management and the operation of the business.

- *The duration of the partnership.* States whether the partnership is created to last indefinitely or for a specific period of time or for a specific project, such as building a new shopping center. The latter type of partnership is called a **joint venture**.

- *The division of profits and losses.* Specifies the distribution of profits or losses, which does not have to be exactly equal. The distribution could be allocated according to the same percentages that the partners contributed to the partnership. If not exactly equal, the division must be clearly stated.

- *The salaries and draws of partners.* States how the partners will be compensated, a decision that is made after the decision about how to divide profits and losses at the end of the accounting period. A *draw* is the removal of expected profits by a partner.

- *The procedure for dispute settlement or arbitration.* Describes a procedure for mediation or arbitration to solve serious disagreements, thus saving a costly trip to court.

- *The procedure for sale of partnership interest.* Provides veto power to partners in case one partner tries to sell his or her interest in the business.

- *The procedure for addition of a new partner.* States whether the vote for adding a new partner can be a simple majority or must be unanimous.

- *The procedure for absence or disability of a partner.* Describes the procedure for dealing with an accident, illness, or death of a partner.

- *The procedure and conditions for dissolving the partnership.* Describes what will happen if and when the partnership ends.

Corporation

The **corporation** is the most complicated business structure to form. In the eyes of the law, a corporation is an autonomous entity that has the legal rights of a person, including the ability to sue and be sued, to own property, and to engage in business transactions. A corporation must act in accordance with its charter and the laws of the state in which it exists. These laws vary by state.

This section is concerned with the type of corporation most common among small businesses—a **closely held corporation**. With this type of business, relatively few people (usually fewer than 10) own stock. Most owners participate in the firm's management, and those who don't are usually family or friends. By contrast, a corporation that sells shares of stock to the public and is listed on a stock exchange is called a **public corporation**. Public corporations must comply with more detailed and rigorous federal, state, and Securities and Exchange Commission (SEC) regulations, such as disclosing financial information in the company's annual report. These are different animals from the closely held corporations of small businesses.

This discussion will begin with the regular, or C, corporation. Later we will look at variations called the *S corporation* and the *limited-liability company (LLC)*. The **C corporation** is a separate legal entity that reports its income and expenses on a corporate income tax return and is taxed on its profits at corporate income tax rates.

joint venture
A partnership that is created to complete a specified purpose and is limited in duration.

corporation
A business structure that creates an entity separate from its owners and managers.

closely held corporation
A corporation owned by a limited group of people. Its stock is not traded publicly.

public corporation
A corporation that sells shares of stock to the public and is listed on a stock exchange.

C corporation
A separate legal entity that reports its income and expenses on a corporate income tax return and is taxed on its profits at corporate income tax rates.

Advantages. By far the biggest advantage of forming a corporation is the limited liability it offers its owners. In a corporation, the most you stand to lose is the amount you have invested in it. If the business fails or if it is sued, your personal property remains protected from creditors (see Table 10.3).

▼ TABLE 10.3

Balancing the Advantages and Disadvantages of Corporations

Advantages	Disadvantages
Limited liability	Expensive to start
Increased access to resources	Complex to maintain
Transfer of ownership	Double taxation[a]

[a]C corporation only.

As an example of how limited liability can be an advantage to a small business, consider the case of Kathy, owner of a local pub. Kathy is worried that one of her employees might inadvertently or intentionally serve alcohol to a minor or to an intoxicated person. If the intoxicated person were to get into an automobile accident, Kathy could be sued. In addition to buying liability insurance, Kathy has also incorporated her business so her personal assets will be protected in the event of a lawsuit.

Corporations generally have easier access to financing, because bankers, venture capitalists, and other lending institutions tend to regard them as being more stable than proprietorships or partnerships. Corporations have proved to be the best way to accumulate large pools of capital.

Corporations can also take advantage of the skills of several people and draw on their increased human and managerial resources. Boards of directors can bring valuable expertise and advice to small corporations. Also, because a corporation has a life of its own, it continues to operate even if its stockholders change. Transfer of ownership can be completed through the sale of the stock.

Disadvantages. Complying with requirements of the state corporate code poses challenges that are not faced by proprietorships or partnerships. Even the smallest corporation must file *articles of incorporation* (described later in this chapter) with the secretary of state, adopt bylaws, and keep records from annual stockholder and director meetings. Directors must meet to show they are setting policy and are actively involved in running the corporation. Fulfilling these requirements is necessary to prevent the IRS, creditors, or lawsuits from removing the limited-liability protection of a corporation. If a business does not meet these requirements, it is not considered to be operating as a corporation, and therefore forfeits the limited-liability protection of its directors and stockholders, leaving them personally responsible for liabilities. The process of denying limited-liability protection is referred to as "piercing the corporate veil."[15]

The legal and administrative costs incurred in starting a corporation can be a sizable disadvantage. *Self-incorporation kits* exist, but be careful about going through the incorporation process without the aid of an attorney. The cost of incorporating can easily reach $1,000 before the business is even open.

Corporate profits face double taxation in that the profits are taxed at the corporate level first and can be taxed again once the profits are distributed to stockholders. If a stockholder also works in the corporation, she is considered to be an employee and must be paid a "reasonable wage," which is subject to state and federal payroll taxes.

Even the limited liability that incorporation affords may not completely protect your personal property. If you use debt financing or borrow money, lenders will probably expect you to secure the loan with your personal property. Therefore, if the business must be liquidated, your personal property can be attached.

If you sell stock in your corporation, you inevitably give up some control of your business. The more capital you need to raise, the more control you must relinquish. If large blocks of stock are sold, you may end up as a minority stockholder of what used to be your own business. Raising capital in this way may be necessary for growth, but you lose some measure of control in the process.

Forming a Corporation. The process of incorporating your business includes the following steps: First, you must prepare **articles of incorporation** and file them with the secretary of state where you are incorporating. You must choose a board of directors, adopt bylaws, elect officers, and issue stock. At the time you incorporate, you must also decide whether to form a C corporation, an S corporation, or a limited-liability company (LLC), all of which will be described in this chapter.

You are not required to use an attorney to file articles of incorporation, but attempting the process and making a mistake could end up costing you more than an attorney would have charged for the job. Although states vary in their requirements, articles of incorporation usually include the following items:

- *The name of your company.* The name you choose must be registered with the state in which it will operate. This registration prevents companies from operating under the same name, which could create confusion for the consumer. Your corporation's name must not be deceptive about its type of business.

- *The purpose of your corporation.* You must state the intended nature of your business. Being specific about your purpose will give financial institutions a better idea of what you do. Incorporating in a state that permits very general information in this section allows you to change the nature of your business without reincorporating.

- *The names and addresses of the incorporators.* Some states require at least one incorporator to reside in that state.

- *The names and addresses of the corporation's initial officers and directors.*

- *The address of the corporation's home office.* You must establish headquarters in the state from which you receive your charter or register as an out-of-state corporation in your own state.

- *The amount of capital required at time of incorporation.* The proposed capital structure includes the amount and type of capital stock you issue at the time of incorporation.

- *Capital stock to be authorized.* In this section, you specify the types of stock and the number of shares that the corporation will issue.

- *Bylaws of the corporation.* A corporation's bylaws are the rules and regulations by which it agrees to operate. Bylaws must stipulate the rights and powers of shareholders, directors, and officers; the time and place for the annual shareholder meeting and the number needed for a quorum (the number needed to transact business); how the board of directors is to be elected and compensated; the dates of the corporation's fiscal year; and who within the corporation is authorized to sign contracts.

- *Length of time the corporation will operate.* Most corporations are established with the intention that they will operate in perpetuity. However, you may specify a duration for the corporation's existence.

Specialized Forms of Corporations

You have two other options to consider in addition to the C corporation. S corporations and limited-liability companies are corporations that are granted special tax status by the Internal

articles of incorporation
A document describing the business that is filed with the state in which a business is formed.

Revenue Service. A competent tax adviser can assist you to determine whether one of these options could provide a tax advantage for your business.

S Corporation. An **S corporation** provides you with the limited-liability protection of a corporation while allowing the tax advantages of a partnership. It avoids the double-taxation disadvantage of regular corporations and lets you offset losses of the business against your personal income tax. The S corporation files an informational tax return to report its income and expenses but it is not taxed separately. Income and expenses of the S corporation "flow through" to the shareholders in proportion to the number of shares they own. Profits are taxed to shareholders at their individual income tax rate.

To qualify as an S corporation, a business must meet the following requirements:

- Shareholders must be individuals, estates, or trusts—not other corporations.

- Nonresident aliens cannot be shareholders.

- Only one class of outstanding common stock can be issued.

- All shareholders must consent to the election of the S corporation.

- State regulations specify the portion of revenue that must be derived from business activity, not from passive investments.

- There can be no more than 75 shareholders.[16]

Limited-Liability Company. A relatively new form of ownership, the **limited-liability company (LLC)**, is quickly becoming a popular business form on its way to becoming the entity of choice for the future. First recognized by the IRS in 1988, LLCs offer the limited-liability protection of a corporation and the tax advantages of a partnership without the restrictions of an S corporation. The LLC is still evolving, so it is wise to keep a watchful eye on its development. For example, although the LLC is provided pass-through treatment of revenue for federal taxation purposes, individual states may tax it differently. Check with your tax accountant to see how LLCs are taxed in your state. Furthermore, some states allow the formation of an LLC by a single individual, in which case the IRS will treat it as a sole proprietorship.

Unlike the situation for C and S corporations, shares of stock do not represent ownership by the members. Rather, the rights and responsibilities of members are specified by the operating agreement of the LLC, which is like a combination of the bylaws and a shareholder agreement in other corporations. LLCs offer small business owners greater flexibility than either C or S corporations in that they can write the operating agreement to contain any provision desired regarding the LLC's internal structure and operations. In particular, LLCs are not constrained by the regulations imposed on C and S corporations dictating who can and cannot participate in them, what they can or cannot own, or how profits and losses will be allocated to members. For example, the owners of an LLC can allocate 50 percent of the business's profits to a person who owns 30 percent of the company. This distribution is not allowable in C or S corporations.

Although the requirements and rules that govern LLCs vary from state to state, there is some consistency. For example, almost every state requires an LLC designator (such as LLC, L.C, Limited Company, or Ltd.) in the business name. Still, it is a good idea to check your local regulations when starting an LLC.

You should seriously consider forming an LLC if you need flexibility in the legal structure of your business, desire limited liability, and prefer to be taxed as a partnership rather than as a corporation.

S corporation
A special type of corporation in which the owners are taxed as partners.

limited-liability company (LLC)
A relatively new type of corporation that taxes the owners as partners yet provides a more flexible structure than an S corporation.

Nonprofit Corporation. The **nonprofit corporation** is a tax-exempt organization formed for religious, charitable, literary, artistic, scientific, or educational purposes. Nonprofit corporations depend largely on grants from private foundations and public donations to meet their expenses. People or organizations that contribute to a nonprofit can deduct their contributions from their own taxes.

Assets dedicated to nonprofit purposes cannot be reclassified. If its directors decide to terminate the corporation, its assets must go to another nonprofit organization.[17] The details of forming and running a nonprofit corporation are beyond the interest of most readers of this book. To learn more about this business form, consult the sources listed in the endnotes.

Concept Check Questions

1. Sole proprietorships account for 76 percent of all U.S. businesses and generate 6 percent of all business revenue. Only 18 percent of all sole proprietorships are incorporated, but they generate 90 percent of all revenue. What do these statistics tell you about the two forms of ownership?

2. Under what conditions would you consider joining a partnership? Why would you avoid becoming a partner?

3. When would forming a limited-liability company be more advantageous than creating a C corporation or a partnership?

CHAPTER REVIEW

SUMMARY ▶▶

LO 10.1 Name the laws and regulations that affect small business.

The maze of federal, state, and local laws and regulations is a confusing place for small business. Specific laws that owners of small businesses should know include the Fair Labor Standards Act, Family and Medical Leave Act, Affordable Care Act, Equal Employment Opportunity Act, Clean Air and Water Acts, Sherman Act, and the Occupational Safety and Health Act.

LO 10.2 List and explain the types of bankruptcy.

The U.S. Bankruptcy Code is made up of nine chapters, only three of which apply to most small businesses (Chapters 7, 11, and 13). Chapter 7 uses liquidation, meaning that the business ceases to exist in an effort to provide the debtor with a fresh start. Liquidation involves selling all of the business assets and nonexempt personal assets and then distributing the proceeds among creditors. Chapters 11 and 13 allow the business owner to file a reorganization plan with the court that offers protection from creditors until the debt is satisfied.

LO 10.3 Describe the elements of a contract.

For a contract to be legally binding, it must have a legal purpose. Both parties must come to an agreement including a legitimate offer and a legitimate acceptance of that offer. Consideration, or something of value, must be exchanged. Finally, all parties must have the capacity to enter into a binding contract, meaning that they must not be underage, intoxicated, or of diminished mental ability.

LO 10.4 Discuss how to protect intellectual property.

Patents, copyrights, and trademarks are legal ways to protect intellectual property. A patent grants an inventor the exclusive right to make, use, and sell an invention for a period of 17 years. A copyright provides legal protection against infringement of an author's literary, musical, or artistic works. Copyrights usually last for the author's life plus 50 years. A trademark is a legally protected name, term, symbol, design, or combination of these elements used to identify products or companies. Trademarks last for as long as they are in use.

LO 10.5 Describe the three main forms of ownership—sole proprietorship, partnership, and corporation—and their unique features.

There are several choices for the form of ownership of your small business. The most common is the sole proprietorship. If you choose a partnership, you have the choice of a general partnership, in which all partners are fully liable for the business, or a limited partnership, in which at least one partner retains unlimited liability. A corporation offers its owners limited liability. In forming a corporation, you are creating a legal entity that has the same rights as a person. Variations of corporations include S corporations, limited-liability companies, and nonprofit corporations.

KEY TERMS ▶▶

articles of incorporation **279**
articles of partnership **276**
bankruptcy **261**
brand **269**
breach of contract **264**
C corporation **277**
closely held corporation **277**
compensatory damages **264**
contract **263**
copyright **269**

corporation **277**
general partnership **274**
injunction **264**
intellectual property **265**
joint venture **277**
limited-liability company (LLC) **280**
limited partnership **275**
nonprofit corporation **281**
partnership **274**

patent **265**
patent trolls **266**
public corporation **277**
S corporation **280**
sole proprietorship **272**
specific performance **264**
trademark **269**
unlimited liability **273**
zoning laws **260**

STUDENT STUDY SITE ▶▶

edge.sagepub.com/hatten7e

(S)SAGE edge™ Sharpen your skills with SAGE edge!

SAGE edge for Students provides a personalized approach to help you accomplish your coursework goals in an easy-to-use learning environment. You'll find mobile-friendly eFlashcards and quizzes as well as multimedia resources to support and expand on the concepts presented in this chapter.

EXPERIENTIAL LEARNING ACTIVITIES ▶▶

10.1: Contracts

LO 10.3: Describe the elements of a contract.

Answer the following question and explain your answer.

Kole has developed a successful business creating wonderful lawn ornaments out of concrete. In order to produce his ornaments, Kole needs a certain quality of sand to ensure the integrity and durability of his creations. He has been using a reliable aggregate supplier who has delivered the sand on a monthly basis for the last year. The supplier is now asking for an 18-month agreement on the delivery of 10 tons of sand at $50 a ton per month. Kole needs the sand on the 15th of each month in order to meet his production deadlines. The supplier has been in business over 15 years and Kole has had no issues with delivery or product quality since using the supplier. Kole would prefer not to enter into a contract, even though he does not intend to change suppliers. If the supplier insists on a contract, will a verbal agreement be sufficient in this instance? Address the following in your answer: legality, agreement, consideration, and capacity.

10.2: Form of Business Ownership

LO 10.5: Describe the three main forms of ownership—sole proprietorship, partnership, and corporation—and their unique features.

Choose a form of business ownership for Kaitlyn to use in opening her boutique.

Kaitlyn is excited about finally opening her own Total Beauty Makeover Boutique. She will be offering a total beauty package that will include hair styling, make-up consultations, manicures, pedicures and total skin care counseling. She will be using and selling her own line of make-up and beauty products that she has developed over the last five years. She has leased an amazing Victorian house in a prime location for her boutique. She envisions her services and products serving an age demographic from 14 to 75. She has obtained the needed financing to open her boutique and her products are developed and ready to be launched. Which form of business ownership should she use? List the advantages and disadvantages of the form of business ownership chosen.

CHAPTER CLOSING CASE ▶▶

To Sue or Not to Sue?

Jonathan Hoffman got an unpleasant surprise on a routine shopping outing. An employee had seen books and flashcards in a local Target that looked suspiciously like those made by his company, School Zone Publishing. Unfortunately, his employee was correct. The composition, fonts, language, and concepts screamed copycat. He turned a book over and it all made sense—the competing publisher was Dogs in Hats.

Peter Alfini started Dogs in Hats just two months before, after resigning as School Zone's vice president of national sales and marketing. As if to pour salt in Hoffman's wounds, Alfini had taken two former School Zone designers with him to Dogs in Hats. Now the competing workbooks and flashcards were beside Hoffman's on the shelves of School Zone's largest customer. Target accounted for about 10 percent of School Zone's sales.

Alfini claims that all of Dogs in Hats products came from his own ideas and resources. He had worked in educational publishing for more than a decade before joining School Zone. But Hoffman could not believe that Alfini had used what he learned at School Zone from product design and marketing to equipment and contacts to launch Dogs in Hats. Hoffman was infuriated.

Hoffman called an emergency meeting of his executive team—which includes his mother, Joan, the company's president and cofounder, and his sister, Jennifer Dexter, the vice president of design and development—and his attorney. They analyzed Alfini's products spread across the table. In one example, a School Zone alphabet flashcard featured a drawing of a blond girl in pigtails with green bows and a yellow shirt collar and with a blue capital G on the card's flip side. A Dogs in Hats alphabet flash card was nearly identical, except for the girl's hair color, which was brown. They all reached the same conclusion: School Zone's intellectual property had been stolen. The executive team had little choice but to take Dogs in Hats to court.

Summer sales data confirmed Hoffman's worst fears. School Zone revenue fell by 23 percent over one six-week period, when Dogs in Hats products were side by side with School Zone's products at Target. Hoffman became a man obsessed with preparing the legal case against Alfini. When he suspected one of his salespeople of passing company information to Alfini, he didn't know whom he could trust. In contrast to his normal management style, he limited access to the copy room and banned employees from the office on weekends and after hours. But he was doing what he had to do.

School Zone filed a complaint in federal district court in western Michigan listing 84 allegations against Dogs in Hats. Hoffman was seeking payment for damages and attorneys' fees. Furthermore, he was demanding that Alfini destroy all materials that infringed on School Zone's copyrighted and trademarked material. In Dogs in Hats' response to the complaint, Alfini denied most of the allegations, conceding only that he had hired former employees of School Zone and had reentered School Zone's property after resigning.

The extensive discovery process lasted for more than two years. School Zone had spent close to $200,000 on legal filings and attorneys' fees. Joan Hoffman and Dexter were begging Hoffman to drop the case. But Jonathan was haunted by the thought of what his father would have done. Hoffman's father Jim started School Zone in 1979 and had passed away a few months before the Alfini affair began. "Jim Hoffman would have fire in his eyes," his son believed. The company's attorneys had warned that if School Zone did not defend its marks now, it would be increasingly more difficult to do so in the future. So Hoffman wouldn't drop the case.

A judge magistrate sent the parties into mediation. Neither side should have been surprised; western Michigan courts regularly seek alternative means of resolving disputes over litigation. But Hoffman now faced a dilemma: whether to compromise via mediation and put an end to the case or to hold out for a shot at total victory in court.

Questions

1. Hoffman's gut told him to litigate aggressively. But do you think that was a smart move?

2. Should he settle? Or should he press his case before a judge?

3. Put yourself in Hoffman's place. What would you do?

Sources: Lora Kolodny, "Jonathan Hoffman Was Sure a Former Staffer Had Stolen His Company's Ideas," *Inc.*, September 2005, 55–56; Patrick Sauer, "Talk about Some Bad Hires," *Inc.*, March 2008, 74; Karyn Peterson, "A Smart Start," *Playthings*, November 2007, 12; and Troy Dreier, "Educational Software," *PC Magazine*, September 6, 2005, 149–184.

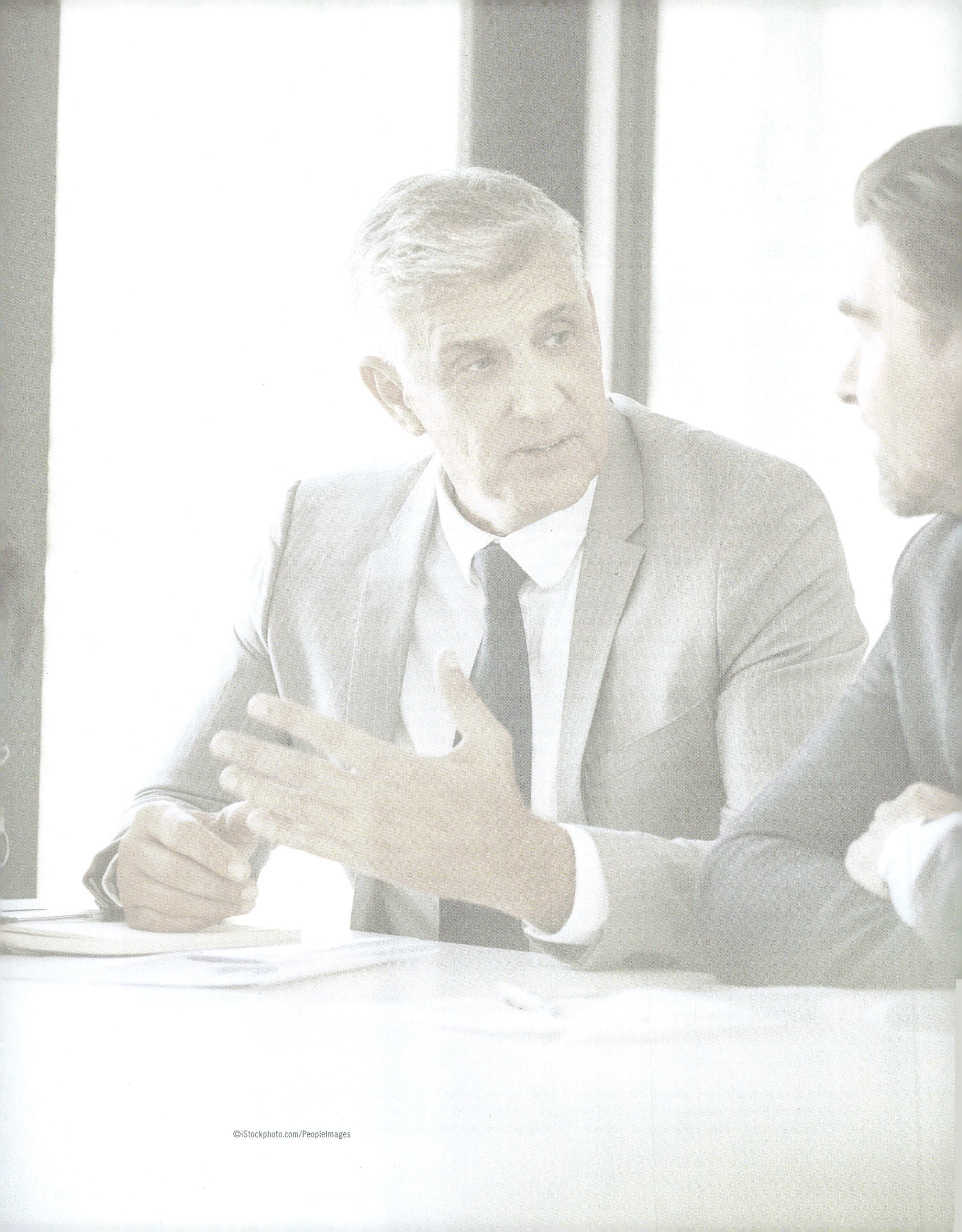

PART V

MARKETING THE PRODUCT OR SERVICE

CHAPTER 11

SMALL BUSINESS MARKETING

Strategy and Research

Surfing buddies Alex Schulze and Andrew Cooper took a trip to Bali to test the waves. After surfing all day, the pair sat on the beach and watched local fishermen heading out to fish at night. They were disturbed to see the amount of trash the small boats had to push through in order to get to open water. The budding entrepreneurs decided that ocean trash was a problem they had to help solve.

It's no small problem—have you heard of the Great Pacific Garbage Patch? Four ocean currents formed by wind currents and rotation of the planet are generally bounded by Japan, California, and Hawaii. The center of the 7.7 million square mile area tends to be very calm and stable with the circular motion drawing debris to the stable area where it becomes trapped. Such patches are made up almost entirely of tiny bits of plastic, called microplastics, which do not biodegrade but do break down into smaller and smaller pieces.

Alex and Andrew narrowed their options to organizing groups to remove trash from the ocean. Funding comes from making and selling recycled bracelets. 4Ocean was formed. Every bracelet purchased will remove one pound of trash from oceans and coastlines. The original blue 4Ocean Signature Bracelet is offered continually while a new color

Limited Edition is released every month—for $20 each. In its first year of operation in 2017, 4Ocean removed more than 250,000 pounds of trash, with a goal of making that a million pounds in 2018.

Because 4Ocean's cause resonates so strongly in people's minds and hearts, most of their marketing efforts have come from viral online campaigns—specifically via Facebook (with currently a half-million followers), Twitter (9,000 followers), Pinterest (37,000 monthly viewers), Instagram (330,000 followers), and YouTube (2,200 subscribers).

Sources: "Great Pacific Garbage Patch," National Geographic Society, September 19, 2014, www.nationalgeographic.org/encyclopedia/great-pacific-garbage-patch; https://4ocean.com/pages/our-story; www.facebook.com/4OceanBracelets.

Concept Module 11.1: Small Business Marketing

- **LO 11.1: Explain the importance of marketing in managing small businesses.**

What do you think of when you hear the term *marketing*? Do you think of selling and advertising? Probably, but marketing is actually much more than just selling or advertising. Marketing involves all the activities needed to get a product from the producer to the ultimate consumer. Management guru Peter Drucker has stated that businesses have two—and only two—basic functions: marketing and innovation. These are the only things a business does that produce results; everything else is really a "cost."[1] This is just as true for the one-person kiosk as it is for the largest corporate giant.

Of course, some selling will always be necessary, but the goal of marketing is to come as close as possible to making selling superfluous.[2] A truly customer-driven company understands what consumers want in a product and provides it so that its products, to a great extent, sell themselves. Of course, this is not easy. To paraphrase president Lyndon Johnson: Doing the right thing is easy; knowing the right thing to do is tough.

Marketing Concept

Many businesses operate today with a customer-driven philosophy. They want to find out what their customers want and then provide that good or service. This philosophy is called the marketing concept.

Businesses have not always concentrated their efforts on what the market wants. Before the Industrial Revolution and mass production, nearly all a business owner needed to be concerned about was making products. Demand exceeded supply for most goods, like boots, clothing, and saddles. People had to have these products, so about all a business had to do was to make them. This philosophy in which companies concentrate their efforts on the product being made is now called the **production concept** of business.

After the mid-1800s, when mass production and mass distribution became possible for manufactured products, supply began to exceed demand. Some selling was needed, but the emphasis remained on producing goods. World War II temporarily shifted resources from consumer markets to the military. After the war, when those resources were returned to the consumer market, businesses continued producing at capacity, and many new businesses were started. Managers found they could no longer wait for consumers to seek them out to sell all they could make. Although these companies still emphasized making products, they now had to convince people to buy *their* products, as opposed to the competition's, which inaugurated the *selling concept* of business.

The business philosophy that broadens the view of the marketing concept is called **relationship marketing**. Here a business owner recognizes the value and profit potential of customer retention; therefore, the guiding emphasis is on developing long-term, mutually satisfying relationships with customers and suppliers.

Of Purple Cows

In your travels you have most likely passed by many cows: black ones, white ones, brown ones, or some combination thereof. Unless you have a specific reason for noticing them, such as being in the cattle business, very few cows probably stand out in your mind. In fact, most people would classify cows as boring. Author Seth Godin makes an analogy between most products that consumers see daily with cows: Consumers see so many products that seem to be alike that they are all boring. But a purple cow? Drive by one of those, even if it is in a field with a whole herd of black, white, or brown cows, and it would get your attention. What products stand out in your mind as different? Krispy Kreme doughnuts? Netflix? Doing and creating things that are counterintuitive, phenomenal, and exciting are important ingredients to marketing small businesses.[3]

Small businesses can achieve the success that Godin discusses by avoiding the traps of convention and not being afraid to stand out from the crowd by offering unique products and marketing practices. "Purple cows" represent the creation of a competitive advantage or a *unique selling point (USP)*—topics that volumes have been written about. Take a look at Godin's *Purple Cow* for inspiration (you can read it in about an hour).[4]

Concept Check Questions

1. Marketing plays a key role in a small business's success. Can a small business succeed without adopting the philosophy underlying the marketing concept? Why or why not?

2. What would happen to a business without a marketing strategy? Why?

Concept Module 11.2: Marketing Strategies for Small Businesses

- **LO 11.2: Describe the process of developing a small business marketing strategy.**

Your **marketing strategy** should be decided in the early stages of operating your business. While marketing is critical to businesses of every size, it is often overshadowed in the minds of small business owners who are distracted by so many other factors. The marketing section of

TAKING ON THE BIG BOYS

The bigger and stronger the competition is, the better a small business's marketing strategy needs to be. That being the case, Amilya Antonetti may need *your* help with a marketing strategy. Antonetti is starting a business to break into the $4.7 billion U.S. laundry detergent market, competing directly with the likes of Procter & Gamble. The niche of the detergent market she seeks to fill is for hypoallergenic cleaning products. It was an idea she struck upon because her infant son had health problems aggravated by chemicals in the standard brands. She started her company, called SoapWorks, after conducting market research, primarily from other mothers of infants, and finding that many other families faced similar problems. Her annual advertising budget is limited to $60,000 (about what her huge competitors spend on one 30-second prime-time network TV ad), so she had to find different ways to let people know what SoapWorks would do for them.

Questions

1. If you were in Amilya Antonetti's place starting SoapWorks, what marketing strategy would you use to compete with Procter & Gamble and Clorox? How would you reach your target markets? How and where would you advertise? We talk about the power of word of mouth among our customers—how do you use it to your advantage as a small business marketer?

2. One of the biggest challenges SoapWorks faced was getting its products on the shelves of grocery stores. SoapWorks is in 2,500 stores from California to Florida, and the company had revenues of $5 million. How would you create such market penetration?

Sources: Isabel Isidro, "Amilya Antonetti: How a Family Need Spurred a Profitable Business," PowerHomeBiz, January 21, 2014, www.powerhomebiz.com; Charlotte Kelley, "Amilya Antonetti: Entrepreneur, CEO, Businesswoman and Mom Extraordinaire," NoLa Woman, accessed April 2018, http://nolawoman.com/articles/spotlight/women-in-the-news/226/.

the business plan is a good place for the small business owner to identify marketing strategies. Any potential investor will carefully inspect how you have laid out the marketing action that will drive your business.

A good marketing strategy will help you to be proactive, not reactive, in running your small business. Some marketing strategies unique to small businesses include:[5]

> "A good marketing strategy will help you to be proactive, not reactive, in running your business."

- **Build a strong online presence.** Without an online presence, your business does not exist in the mind of your market. You might think your local restaurant does not need to be online, but quite the contrary. A third of all mobile searches are related to location.

- **Collect reviews and testimonials.** Reviews are an important part of your online presence, ranking in local services, and acquiring new customers. Ninety-two percent of consumers say a 4-star rating will get them into a local business. Since positive reviews are so integral to your small business marketing strategy, get on multiple platforms to collect them (like Yelp, Google My Business, and TripAdvisor).

- **Make your customers say "Wow."** This is small business marketing? You bet it is. Many small business owners have heard that word-of-mouth is 10 times more effective than traditional promotion. But you cannot just hope it will happen. You have to generate it by continually exceeding customers' expectations.

- **Offer value-added marketing.** Especially when marketing to Millennials, good marketing does not mean peppering them with advertising. Dan Lobring of rEvolution states "Good marketing or advertising is about giving your audience a reason to care about your brand, showing them the 'why' they should care, and then making their experience as fans/consumers better for it."[6] See the 4Ocean example in the opening story of this chapter.

Small businesses in the service industries must pay special attention to marketing. When their service is one that customers could perform themselves, such as lawn mowing, a marketing strategy is critical. It is also often more difficult to differentiate or establish a brand image with services than with tangible products. Can the average car owner tell the difference between automatic transmissions that have been rebuilt by different shops? Probably not. A marketing strategy that communicates the benefits that consumers receive is crucial. However comprehensive or simple your marketing plan, it should include a description of your vision, marketing objectives, sales forecast, target markets, and marketing mix.[7]

Setting Marketing Objectives

Your marketing objectives define the goals of your plans. They can be broken into two groups: marketing-performance objectives and marketing-support objectives.[8] Objectives for *marketing performance* are specific, quantifiable outcomes, such as sales revenue, market share, and profit. For example, an objective of this type for a local insurance agency could be "to increase sales of homeowner's insurance by 10 percent in the next fiscal year." Objectives for *marketing support* are what you must accomplish before your performance objectives can be met, such as educating customers about your products, building awareness, and creating image.

Like any goal you want to accomplish in business, marketing objectives need to be (1) measurable, (2) action oriented by identifying what needs to be done, and (3) time-specific by targeting a date or time for achievement.

Developing a Sales Forecast

Your marketing plan should include a **sales forecast**, in which you predict your future sales in dollars and in units—in other words, what your "top line" will be. If you are writing a business plan for a start-up business, the sales forecast is one of the most important pieces of information you will gather. Why? Because that "top line" figure becomes the foundation for your pro forma income statements and cash flow statement. From your projected revenues, you will subtract your expenses and disbursements to see if and when you will make a profit.

Building Marketing Strategies

Forecasting is difficult, but it will help you establish more accurate goals and objectives. Your sales forecast will affect all sections of your marketing plan, including the choice of appropriate channels of distribution, sales force requirements, advertising and sales promotion budgets, and the effects of price changes.

A faulty sales forecast can do severe damage to a small business. Steve Waterhouse was an understandably excited sales manager when he reported in a budget meeting that one of his sales representatives had secured a $2 million order. Satisfying the order would require the company to invest $100,000 in new tools. The operations manager was not very excited, however, because the purchase order contained a clause allowing the customer to back out. The owner wisely decided to require a deposit for initial supplies before proceeding. After receiving $100,000 from the customer, the company purchased the required tooling. The customer then backed out of the deal. Crisis averted, but a close call nevertheless. What's the moral of the story? Be careful about projections based on "My sales rep says . . ."[9]

There are two basic ways to forecast sales: build-up methods and break-down methods. With a *build-up method*, you identify as many target markets as possible and predict the sales for each. Then you combine the predictions for the various segments to create a total sales forecast. For example, if you plan to open an ice cream shop, can you estimate how many ice cream cones you will sell in a year? Not very easily or accurately without some research. But you can estimate with some degree of accuracy how much you could sell in one day—especially if you spend several days outside an existing ice cream shop observing how many people go in and out, and roughly how much they are buying. From that daily sales figure, you can project sales for the week,

CREATING COMPETITIVE ADVANTAGE

ONLINE VIDEO MARKETING

One and a half billion users watch 1 billion hours of video on YouTube *every day*. If a video marketing strategy fits your small business, then you need to be on YouTube. But like all things online, you cannot just post a video—you have to get your video to rank at the top of searches.

Optimize your video title with key words—search for key words using Google Keyword Planner. Create an interesting thumbnail (an attractive shot from your video) to catch attention. If you create a YouTube channel, you don't just want viewers to watch one video and leave. Make a playlist where your next video plays automatically.

Since YouTube attracts so many eyeballs, you want some of them to be on your business. Consider the following topics for a winning video about you.

- Introduce details about a new product or service.
- Educate customers about your company/products.

- Convince potential customers via demonstrations and comparisons.
- Share testimonials from existing customers.
- Answer common customer questions.
- Offer a "behind-the-scenes" look into your company, telling your story.

With one of these goals in mind, you can create your core message and begin to think of how to communicate that message in video format. Your videos have to be short (three to six minutes is a good starting point). You have to stay on message (YouTuber's have notoriously short attention spans). Build in some type of "call to action."

Sources: Jason Rich, "Determining Your YouTube Strategy and Core Message," *Entrepreneur,* March 7, 2018, www.entrepreneur.com/article/309341; Syed Balkhi, "3 Quick Tips to Increase Your YouTube Ranking This Year," *Inc.,* April 19, 2018, www.inc.com; Salma Jafri, "How to Create YouTube Playlists (and Why They're Important)," *Entrepreneur,* June 22, 2017, www.entrepreneur.com/video/296168.

month, and year. Would you expect to sell the same amount per day in April? July? October? January? Probably not, so you would come up with a daily sales projection at different times of the year to allow for seasonal fluctuations.

With some types of products, of course, it is difficult to estimate daily sales. Then what? You may be able to use a *break-down method.* For this approach, you begin with an estimate of the total market potential for a specific product or an entire industry. This figure is broken down into forecasts of smaller units until you reach an estimate of how large a market you will reach and how many sales you will make. For example, if industry information from a trade association for a product you consider selling shows that 4 percent of a population will be in the market for your product at any given time, how many units and dollars of sales could you realistically generate? Do enough people live in your area, or can you reach enough of the target market for your business to be profitable?

Marketers use many other models in sales forecasting; unfortunately, most don't apply well to small businesses because they depend on historical data. You could assume that forecasting is built on sales—actually it is built on demand. There may not always be a big difference between the two, but what if you run out of an item for three months. Empty shelves mean zero sales, but don't assume that demand has gone away and drop the item.[10]

Identifying Target Markets

Market segmentation is the process of dividing the total market for a product into identifiable groups, or **target markets**, with a common want or need that your business can satisfy. These target markets are important to your business because they consist of the people who are more likely to be your customers. They are the people toward whom you should direct your marketing efforts. Identifying and concentrating on target markets can help you avoid falling into the trap of trying to be everything to everyone—you can't do it.[11]

target markets
Groups of people who have a common want or need that your business can satisfy, who are able to purchase your product, and who are more likely to buy from your business.

When asked about their target markets, many small business owners will respond, "We don't have specific target markets; we will sell to anyone who comes in the door." Of *course* you will sell to anyone who wants your product, but the point of segmenting target markets is to let the right people know about your product so that more people will want it. A market for your business must have three characteristics:

1. A need that your products can satisfy

2. Enough people to generate profit for your business

3. Possession of, and willingness to spend, enough money to generate profit for your business

To identify the most attractive target markets for your business, you should look for characteristics that affect the buying behavior of the people. Does where they live influence whether they buy your product? Does income, gender, age, or lifestyle matter? Do they seek a different benefit from the product than other groups do? These differences, called **segmentation variables**, can be based on geographic, demographic, or psychographic differences, or on differences in benefits received.

A small business owner should start (and occasionally revisit) the process of segmenting a market by committing to writing a description of "ideal" customers. For example, for a small accounting firm, that description could be "entrepreneurs in their early thirties to early fifties; owners of retail, service, or manufacturing firms with sales of $500,000 to $3 million." Ideal customer purchasing patterns could include this description: "When they are aware of a business need our accounting firm can solve, they want aggressive and innovative solutions. They don't have time to research solutions themselves." This preference pattern shows that our example accounting firm is segmenting on the basis of benefit received by customers. What makes such customers ideal ones for this firm? They actively want the skills of the professional services offered and are willing and able to pay for them.

> "Identifying and concentrating on target markets can help you avoid falling into the trap of trying to be everything to everyone—you can't do it."

Some methods of segmenting a market are more useful for certain businesses than others. For example, if males and females react to the marketing efforts of your business in the same way, then segmenting by gender is not the best way to identify a target market. When segmenting target markets, keep in mind that the reason for grouping people is to predict behavior—especially the behavior of buying from you.

A caveat for the future: Segmenting and targeting may not always be enough. The most common marketing strategy in the 1960s was **mass marketing**, or selling single products to large groups of people. Then, in the 1970s, **market segmentation** was used. Businesses took segmentation a step further in the 1980s with specialized **niche marketing**, which involves concentrating marketing efforts toward smaller target markets. The next step in the evolution of marketing came in the 1990s, with the emergence of **individualized marketing**, or customizing each product to suit the needs of individual customers. These trends in marketing techniques do not mean that businesses need to throw out every technique that has been used in the past. Rather, they indicate that businesses may need to add more tools to their marketing toolbox.

Technology allows us to conduct more individualized marketing by allowing us to track our customers with more precision. Individualized marketing, if taken to an extreme, could mean treating each person as a separate market (offering different products, different advertising, and different channels to each). Although this tactic is not always practical, technology has certainly made it possible.

When you're ready for more specific information on markets, check out the Census Bureau's website (www.census.gov). Here you'll find specific information by state and county regarding business patterns and census information. As you're researching the viability of a target market, you can check for the number and types of businesses already operating and the demographic

segmentation variables
Characteristics or ways to group people who are more likely to purchase a product.

mass marketing
Treating entire populations of people as potential customers for specific products.

market segmentation
Breaking down populations of people into groups, or target markets.

niche marketing
Segmenting populations of people into smaller target markets.

individualized marketing
Adjusting the marketing mix of a business to treat individual persons as separate target markets.

TARGET MARKETS OF ONE

With over 2 billion users on Facebook, do you wish your small business could advertise to just one? Well, you can. If you own a boutique bed and breakfast in Estes Park, Colorado, you can pitch to a couple who lives in Dallas, drives an SUV, registered as an Independent voter, is travelling to Rocky Mountain National Park, but has not booked a room for the night yet.

Targeting ads on Facebook is almost infinitely customizable. You have probably noticed ads that are tailored specifically to you based on your recent purchases, search history, or comments posted.

Facebook does use things like your Likes, demographics, and geographic area where you live. Things your Facebook friends do and like are factored in. For example, if one of your friends follows LL Bean, you will receive LL Bean ads on your feed. But these are just the beginning.

In Facebook's guide for advertisers, a business can refine who sees an ad based on exact Likes, postings to their timelines, what apps they use most, and/or what ads they have actually clicked on. You can also exclude or include people in groups such as renters of housing, political liberals, people who love woodworking, and on and on and on.

Custom audiences targets people who have already purchased from a site, or at least visited. For example, if you purchased the newest David Baldacci novel from Amazon (or listened to it via Audible) you can be shown Facebook ads for books similar to Baldacci's. You can use this type of customizing to determine who will receive ads for your small business's "lookalike audiences" who are similar to your target market but have not purchased from you yet.

One more category of Facebook advertising you can use are *dynamic ads*. This lets you target people who have already shown interest in your product, even if it was on another site. Dynamic ads can allow you to reach that Texas couple that had searched hotels on TripAdvisor within the last hour, but had not secured a room yet. Your Estes Park bed and breakfast ad can appear on their Facebook timeline.

Sources: Barbara Ortutay, "Why Facebook Ads Know So Much About You," *Inc.*, April, 16, 2018, www.inc.com; Lesya Liu, "5 Essentials for Connecting with Your Ideal Target Market on Social Media," *Entrepreneur*, January 3, 2017, www.entrepreneur.com/article/287192; www.facebook.com/business.

characteristics of that location's population. The Census Bureau is also fine-tuning its TIGER map service (https://www.census.gov/geo/maps-data/data/tiger.html), which provides census maps with street-level detail for the entire United States, all 50 states, and all counties in those states; cartographic design; and many other features. However, be aware that this site can be slow in creating the maps because of the large amount of data that must be transmitted.

Understanding Consumer Behavior

Whereas market segmentation and target marketing can tell you *who* might buy your products, it is also essential to your small business marketing efforts to understand consumer behavior—*why* those people buy. Information on consumer behavior comes from several fields, including psychology, sociology, biology, and other professions that try to explain why people do what they do. In determining why people purchase products, we will start with a stimulus–response model of consumer behavior called the *black box model* (see Figure 11.1). This model is based on the work of psychologist Kurt Lewin, who studied how a person's behavior is affected by the interactions of personal influences, such as inner needs, thoughts, and beliefs, and a variety of external environmental forces.

The *black box* is appropriate because it represents what goes on in the customer's mind that remains hidden from businesspeople. We can see the external factors that go in and the responses that come out, but we can't see the internal influences or the decision-making process.

A surprisingly short time ago, consumers bought almost everything they needed from a local retailer. E-commerce has changed that consumer behavior. An international research study by McKinsey in March 2018 studied how consumers research and purchase consumer packaged

Black Box Model of Consumer Behavior

Many internal and external factors influence consumer behavior.

Stimuli	Transformer	Responses
Marketing mix • Product • Price • Place • Promotion **Other** • Demographic • Economic • Situational • Social • Lifestyle *(External factors)*	**Black box (buyer's mind)** **Internal influences** • Beliefs/attitudes/ values • Learning • Motives/needs • Perception • Personality • Lifestyle **Decision-making process** • Problem solving • Information search • Alternate evaluation • Purchase • Postpurchase evaluation	**Purchase** • Product • Brand • Source • Amount • Method of payment No purchase

Source: The Black Box Model of Consumer Behaviour, from Warren Keegan et al., Marketing (Englewood Cliffs, NJ: Prentica Hall, 1992), 193.

goods (CPG), a category including cosmetics, food, beverages, and cleaning products. Seventy percent of respondents go online for CPG items. While U.S. consumers are seen as being tech-savvy, the highest multichannel shoppers were found in France (40 percent) and the United Kingdom (39 percent), followed by Germany (33 percent) and the United States (32 percent). Consumers quickly changed their behavior exchanging the instant gratification of examining products in person and purchasing them immediately in a retail store for the delayed gratification of waiting for products to be shipped and the convenience of not leaving their home. This behavior was statistically constant over all age groups.[12]

As a small business owner, closeness to your customers is an advantage in understanding the internal influences in customers' minds. Their beliefs, attitudes, values, and motives, as well as their perceptions of your products, are critical to your success. A small business owner needs to be aware of the steps of the mental decision-making process that consumers use in satisfying their needs. We all use them, even if we are not conscious of every step. People usually buy products as a solution to some problem or need in their lives, not just for the sake of buying something.

▲ Consumer behavior has shifted to online purchasing even for everyday items.

Thus, the first step in the decision-making process that leads to a purchase is *problem recognition*, which occurs when we are motivated to reduce a difference between our current and desired states of affairs. For example, consider a young couple expecting their first child, who realize they do not have a way to record events for future memories. They have recognized a problem. Now they begin the second step in the decision-making process: an *information search*. What products exist that can solve the problem identified in the first step? This search will usually lead consumers to read advertising, magazine articles, and ratings like those found in *Consumer Reports*. They also talk with salespeople, friends, and family members to learn more about products that will satisfy their needs.

These information searches usually turn up several possible solutions, which lead the consumer to the third step: an *evaluation of alternatives*. The parents-to-be need a camera to capture little junior for posterity, but the choices of a digital SLR, a four-thirds camera, a point-and-shoot camera, a small camcorder (like a GoPro), a full-scale camcorder, or a smartphone leave them with six alternatives to evaluate. As a small business owner, you enter the customers' decision-making process by being in their **evoked set** of brands or businesses that come to mind when considering a purchase. For example, if you need a pair of shoes, how many businesses that sell shoes come to mind quickly? Those stores are your evoked set for shoes. If your business does not come into customers' minds as a possible solution to their problem, you probably can't sell them too much. The purpose of most advertising (including small business advertising) is to get products into a customer's evoked set.

The most attractive alternative usually leads consumers to the fourth step, which is *purchase*, but many hidden factors can alter this decision. For example, the attitudes of other people can influence the purchase decision. If the prospective parents intended to buy a specific camera and learned that friends had trouble with that model, their decision to purchase would probably change.

Finally, the *post-purchase evaluation* occurs when the consumer uses the product and decides what his level of satisfaction is, which will affect your repeat sales. **Cognitive dissonance**, which, in this context, is the internal conflict we feel after making a decision, is a normal part of the process. If the parents in our example purchased an SLR camera without video capability, you might expect them to later think about the motion and sound that they could have received from a camcorder. As a small business owner, you try to reduce cognitive dissonance with return policies, warranties, and assurance that the customer made the right choice.

Concept Check Questions

1. What determines which type of sales forecast would be appropriate for a small business? Describe how a specific small business would implement the build-up approach.

2. Why is segmenting a niche market so crucial for a small business?

3. We all assume several different roles (parent, student, sibling, athlete, business owner, and so on) at any given time, and those roles affect our behavior as consumers. Describe how your various roles affect your purchases.

4. Segmentation is the process of breaking a population down into smaller groups and marketing to them. Is it possible for a small business to oversegment its market? How would that be dangerous?

Concept Module 11.3: Market Research

- **LO 11.3: Discuss the purpose of the market research process and the steps involved in putting it into practice.**

One of the major advantages that small businesses have over large businesses is close customer contact. Although this closeness can help you maintain your competitive advantage, you will

evoked set
The group of brands or businesses that come to a customer's mind when she thinks of a type of product.

cognitive dissonance
The conflict (i.e., remorse) that buyers feel after making a major purchase.

also need a certain amount of ongoing **market research** to stay closely attuned to your market. If you are starting a new business, you will need market research even more. In many fields customers don't know what they want so take care to not use marketing research as an inebriated person using a light post, for support rather than illumination.

The American Marketing Association (AMA) defines *market research* as the function that links the consumer, customer, and public to the marketer through information. That information can be used to identify and define marketing opportunities and problems; to generate, refine, and evaluate marketing actions; to monitor marketing performance; and to improve understanding of marketing as a process.

Big data and all of the implications that go with it impact every business from solo entrepreneurs to the largest companies. At the "big picture" level, big data is really about collecting, analyzing, and interpreting pieces of information that flow through your business. Even the smallest businesses produce data that can be analyzed, and decisions drawn from it—your website generating attention, your social media presence, your collection of credit cards. All can be analyzed to improve the customer experience. With some careful thought, big data approaches can be used to change how business is done.[13]

Not all market research conducted by small businesses is formal and intense. Most small business owners want to get information as quickly and as inexpensively as possible. One survey showed that most spend between one and six months and less than $1,000 conducting market research on the last product or service they launched.

Market research can be as simple as trash and peanuts—literally. Owners of small restaurants often inspect outgoing waste to see what customers leave on their plates uneaten. Why? Because customers may order a dish like crayfish and pineapple pizza for the novelty, but if most don't actually eat it, it should be taken off the menu. One creative discount merchant conducted an in-store market research project using peanuts. During a three-day promotion, customers were given all the roasted peanuts in a shell they could eat while in the store. At the end of each day, the empty hulls on the floor provided information about traffic patterns of people moving through the store. Piles of shells in front of displays showed the merchandise that was attracting particular interest.

There is one major factor signaling that small businesses should increase the amount of time and money they spend on market research: changing conditions. Because many markets and demographics change quickly, the businesses that emerge as winners are those that are *proactive* rather than *reactive*. Market research can give you information on what your customers are going to want as opposed to historical data that tell you what they used to want.

Some streetwise, down-and-dirty marketing research can be gathered from competitors. No, they will not voluntarily hand anything useful over to you, but you plant yourself in front of a competitor's store for a day or two, and notice how many people walk in. Now, how many walk out with a purchase? Can you get a feel for the average purchase size? This information could be very useful in making your sales projections if you have similar foot traffic.[14]

Small business owners who have been in business for longer than, say, two days have learned two things about market research: They need it, and it's expensive. Fortunately, customer feedback can be a click away. Several online survey tools make it possible for you to more effectively listen to customers and make informed business decisions. David Ambler, a partner in the Phelon Group, a Palo Alto, California, consultancy specializing in building customer relations reminds small business owners that "collecting data is one thing. Acting on it is another thing altogether. If you are unwilling or unable to act on survey data, then the survey is a waste of your customers' time and an unnecessary distraction for your organization."

> " "Small business owners who have been in business for longer than, say, two days have learned two things about market research: They need it, and it's expensive." "

market research
The process of gathering information about consumers that will improve marketing efforts.

big data
Huge amounts of information that are too large to process with traditional analytical methods but show conclusions via artificial intelligence and machine learning.

PPC OR SEO?

©Shutterstock.com/TarikVision

PPC stands for "pay-per-click," which is an internet marketing model where advertising companies pay a fee every time one of their ads is clicked. So, your small business would buy visits to your site. Search Engine Optimization (SEO) consists of techniques for search engine spiders to not only find your site, but also rank it at the top of search engine results.

So which is better for your small business's online marketing strategy? There is no single best answer.

Even though casual internet users don't realize it, Google, Bing, and other search engines update their algorithms dozens of times a year. Every update changes how SEO consultants and online marketers do their work. The old SEO game of stuffing key words into your site is pretty much dead. Google snuffed key word packing and other such crazy stuff with search algorithm changes made over the past couple of years. Compounding that, Google made search secure, which means you can't even see what key words brought a searcher to your site.

A recent study found that ads placed in a premium context (accessed for a fee) are viewed longer and have higher engagement than ads placed randomly in social media. Participants in the study freely browsed different websites and were shown ads in different contexts. Each respondent saw the same test ads in two different environments: a premium context and a social media site. Ads seen on a premium publisher site were viewed 17 percent longer and created 29 percent higher engagement.

Fortunately, by paying close attention to trends, search engine marketers define patterns that search engines prefer and what strategies they punish. Some of the strategies that do (and don't) work:

Do Be Unique: Every piece of content needs to be developed for your site and offer new information. Google actually devalues content when it only offers information that appears on other sites first.

Do Make Pages for Users: The bottom line is—websites that perform well satisfy users. If they like what you provide, they will share what you do. Some questions to determine usefulness:

- Does the page look trustworthy?
- Is the message clear?
- Does it provide helpful resources/information to users?
- Is the contact information visible?

Do Be Useful: There are really only a few motives that cause people to search online:

- Information: research, entertainment, news
- Communication: email, social networking, chatting
- Help: solving problems via forums and other communal sites
- Purchase: compare and/or buy products and services

All of your content needs to fulfill one (or more) of these roles.

Don't Use Tricks: As questionable marketing techniques catch on, Google identifies them and updates its algorithm to neutralize or punish them—leaving the questionable marketer back at square one.

Don't Use Link Schemes: These are tactics to gain bought or traded links to quickly inflate a reputation. Eventually these tactics are discovered and stopped by search engines.

Don't Force Key Words: The density of keywords has not been a strong factor since the late 1990s, but many marketers still cling to the practice. Including a key target word in your content is still recommended, but search engine ranking is determined by customer satisfaction.

Sources: Jason Parks, "PPC vs. SEO: What's Best for Your Business," *Entrepreneur,* April 12, 2018, www.entrepreneur.com/article/311355; Margo Aaron, "SEO Is Simpler Than You Think: 5 Things Every Beginner Needs to Know to Get It Right," *Inc.,* September 16, 2017; John Lincoln, "9 Thorough Guides That Will Teach You the Basics of SEO," *Inc.,* January 10, 2018, www.inc.com; Peter Roesler, "Study Suggests PPC Ads Have a Better, Longer-Lasting Effect on Consumers than Social Media," *Inc.,* February 12, 2018, www.inc.com.

Great sources for getting marketing research information that will actually help your small business are at "watering holes" where members of your target market tend to congregate:[15]

- LinkedIn or Facebook groups that are tied to your target customers

- Blogs or online discussion threads

- Industry groups and membership lists

- Spend a small amount of money to advertise on Google or Facebook to get a list of names of interested people. If no one responds—that's information too.

Market Research Process

The market research process follows five basic steps: identifying the problem, developing a plan, collecting the data, analyzing the data, and drawing conclusions (see Figure 11.2).

Identify the Problem. The most difficult and important part of the market research process is the first step—identifying the problem. You must have a clearly stated, concisely worded problem to generate usable information. Many people (novice and experienced researchers alike) have trouble with this step because they confuse problems with symptoms. For example, if you go to a physician complaining of a fever, the physician could prescribe medication that would bring your fever down. That step would not cure you, however, because an infection or other problem is actually causing your fever. Your physician will search until the problem is found and then fix it—not just mask the symptom. Similarly, declining sales in your small business is not just a problem—it is a symptom of another, underlying problem that is its cause. That underlying problem is what you would want to try to uncover with your research. Has the competition increased? Do your salespeople need retraining? Have your customers' tastes changed?

Your marketing "problem" does not always have to be something that is wrong. It could be something that is lacking or something that could be improved. You can use market research not only to solve problems but also to identify opportunities. Whatever your goal, your ability to complete this first step of the research process is important in guiding the rest of your research efforts.

Planning Market Research. Market research is often expensive, but a plan for how you will conduct your research project can help keep costs in check. Before you start, you must separate what is "critical to know" from what would be "nice to know." Your next step is to design a way to address the problem or answer the question that you have identified concerning your business. You can do it yourself, and you should keep it as simple as possible.

▼   FIGURE 11.2

Market Research Process

Conducting research on your markets involves a logical five-step process.

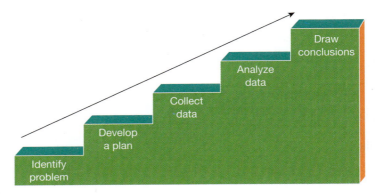

In planning your market research project, you need to do the following:

- Identify the types of information that you need.

- Identify primary and secondary sources of data.

- Select a sample that represents the population you are studying.

- Select a research method and measurement technique (phone survey, focus group, and so on) to answer your research question.

In conducting market research for your small business, you should choose a method that provides enough reliable data for you to make a decision with confidence. The method you choose must also use your limited time, money, and personnel efficiently.

Collecting Data. After you have identified the research problem and laid out a plan, you are ready to gather data. Although it sounds simple, don't get this order reversed. A common research error is to begin the process by gathering data and then trying to figure out what the information means and where to go with it—putting the cart before the horse. Determine what you need, and only then go get it. There are two basic types of data you may seek: secondary and primary.[16]

Secondary data are those that already exist, having been gathered for some other purpose. You should check secondary sources first, because they are less expensive than data gathered by conducting your own study. You may be able to solve your problem without an extended primary search.

The good news about secondary data is that the amount of available data is considerable. The bad news is this mountain of information can prove overwhelming.

A good place to begin your search of secondary data is your local library. Online databases like LexisNexis or Business Source Complete allow you to enter key terms into the program and immediately receive titles, abstracts, and entire articles from journals and periodicals. The U.S. Department of Commerce and the Small Business Administration (SBA) collect and publish data, which may help you. The Department of Commerce also publishes *Selected Publications to Aid Business and Industry*. Check the *Encyclopedia of Associations* for the thousands of trade, professional, technical, and industrial associations that exist. These associations compile information that can be very relevant to your business.

Among the best commercial sources of information are research and trade associations. Their information is industry specific and generally available only to association members, but it is thorough and accurate. If you are serious about getting into or being in business, the membership dues for these organizations are worthwhile investments.

Unfortunately, readily available secondary data are not always specific or detailed enough for your purpose, or they may be obsolete. In either case, you will need to gather your own primary data.

Primary data are qualitative or quantitative data that you collect yourself for your specific purpose. Both qualitative and quantitative data have their advocates and critics, but either can provide valuable information if collected and analyzed correctly.

Qualitative data refer to research findings that cannot be analyzed statistically. Such data are useful if you are looking for open-minded responses to probing questions, not yes-or-no answers.[17] Data can be obtained through *personal interviews* or *focus groups* (groups of six to ten people), which provide considerable depth of information from each person. Qualitative data do not lend themselves to statistical analysis, but they will help you look for trends in answers or obtain specific or detailed responses to your questions.

> "Unfortunately, readily available secondary data are not always specific or detailed enough for your purpose, or they may be obsolete. In either case, you will need to gather your own primary data."

secondary data
Marketing data that have been gathered, tabulated, and made available by an outside source.

primary data
Marketing data that a business collects for its own specific purposes.

Quantitative data are structured to analyze and report numbers, so as to help you see relationships between variables and frequency of occurrences. They are useful in providing information on large groups of people. Their less-probing questions yield results that can be analyzed statistically to show causation.

Because the questionnaire, via sites like www.SurveyMonkey, is such a popular small business research tool, the following advice is offered to increase its usefulness and enhance response rates.

- Try to make the questionnaire visually attractive and fun to answer. This will help keep it from ending up in the recipient's wastebasket.

- Try to structure possible responses. Instead of asking open-ended questions such as "What do you think of our product?" list answers that focus on specific issues such as reliability, quality, and price for respondents to check off.

- Don't ask for more than most people can remember. Annoying questions, like asking for the number of light bulbs a business uses in a year, can end the response.

- Don't use more than 20 words per question. People lose interest quickly if questions are too long.

- Be as specific and unambiguous as possible.

- Include a cover letter explaining the reason for the questionnaire. Say, "Thank you."

- Include a self-addressed, stamped return envelope to increase the response rate.

- Include a return date. A reasonable deadline will increase the number of responses and will let you know how long to wait before tallying the results.[18]

Other techniques of primary-data collection for small businesses are limited only by your imagination. The automobile license plates of many states show the county where the vehicle is registered. You can get an idea of where your customers live by taking note of the license plates in your parking lot. This information can help you determine where to aim your advertising. You can use the same technique by spending some time in your competitors' parking lots.

Advertisements that provide coded coupons or phrases in your broadcast advertising that customers can use to get a discount can help you determine the effectiveness and reach of your ads.

Data Analysis. Basically, *data analysis* is the process of determining what the responses to your research mean. Once data have been collected, they must be analyzed and translated into usable information. Your first step is to "clean" the data. This effort includes removing all questionnaires and other response forms that are unusable because they are incomplete or unreadable. Depending on the instrument or methodology used to gather data, you may need to code and examine the data to identify trends and develop insights. (An exhaustive description of data analysis is not appropriate for this text. For details of this process, refer to a source such as a market research text.)

For quantitative data, several software programs exist to aid in number crunching and transforming data into charts and graphs to make interpretation easier.

Presenting Data and Making Decisions. Market research that does not lead to some type of action is useless. Your research needs to aid you in making management decisions. Should you expand into a new geographic area? Should you change your product line? Should you change your business hours?

Conclusions based on your data analysis may be obvious. Data may fall out in such a way that you can see exactly what you need to do next to address the research problem identified in step 1.

Market research can provide you with information that will allow you to take proactive steps. This consideration is important because, as a small business owner, deciding what you need to do in the future is much more important than knowing what has happened in the past.

Limitations of Market Research

As important as market research can be for small businesses, it should be used with caution. Market research can provide you with a picture of what people currently know and expect from products or services, but it has limited ability to indicate what people will want in the future. Relying on market research exclusively for your marketing strategy and new product ideas is like driving a car while watching only the rearview mirror.

As noted in Chapter 1, small businesses provide many of the most innovative products that we use. Our economy and consumers depend on a stream of such innovations, but innovation does not come from market research. Peter Drucker notes that although the fax machine was designed and developed by U.S. companies, no U.S. companies began producing these devices for domestic consumption because market research indicated that there would be no demand for such a product.

Hal Sperlich designed the concept of the minivan while he was working for Ford, but when Ford didn't believe a market existed for such a vehicle (based on its historical market research), he switched to Chrysler. Sperlich says, "In ten years of developing the minivan, we never once got a letter from a housewife asking us to invent one." To the skeptics, that proved a market didn't exist.[19] Henry Ford is known for saying "If I would have asked my customers what they wanted, they would have answered 'faster horses.'"

Although market research works well for fine-tuning concepts for known products, customers don't have the foresight to ask for what they don't know about or don't know they need or want. There are two types of customer needs: those that customers can tell you about and those that customers have without realizing they have them. How many people were asking for drones or smart clothing 10 years ago?

There are two types of markets or customers for any given business: those served by the company's existing products and those not yet served—the company's potential customers. Market research can tell us the most about the spoken needs of a served market, but much room for growth can be found by exploring the three other sectors. So, think about it this way:

> "In ten years of developing the minivan, we never once got a letter from a housewife asking us to invent one."

- Marketing Research = useful for existing products/services when customer needs can be spoken in markets that are served.

- Marketing Research = NOT useful when customer needs are unspoken or markets are unserved.

When you are driving a car, you need to check the rearview mirror occasionally, just as you should check your current and past markets with market research. But the ideal is to concentrate on defining markets rather than reacting to them. An entrepreneur must go beyond what market research can tell.

Concept Check Questions

1. What is the significance of market research to the small business owner? How is market research defined, and what degree of complexity is necessary in the research plan for it to be valid?

2. Explain the market research process from a small business owner's perspective when he is trying to assess competitive advantage.

3. What types of data should be collected and analyzed to get a clear picture of the market for the good or service being produced?

4. Identify some valuable sources of information for the entrepreneur who is designing a market research plan to analyze competitive advantage.

5. What are some of the limitations of the process of market research? How can the entrepreneur offset these limitations?

6. What do you think is the biggest limitation for small businesses conducting market research? How could you use creativity to circumvent that limitation?

CHAPTER REVIEW

SUMMARY ▶▶

LO 11.1 Explain the importance of marketing to small businesses.

Marketing involves all the points of contact between your small business and your customers. Marketing is how you find out what they want and need; it is how you and everyone in your business treat customers; it is how you communicate with customers through selling and advertising. What could be more important?

LO 11.2 Describe the process of developing a small business marketing strategy.

Market segmentation is needed because no business can possibly be everything to everyone. Segmenting involves breaking down a population into target markets that have a common want or need that the business can satisfy. Target markets are the focus of a company's marketing efforts.

LO 11.3 Discuss the purpose of the market research process and the steps involved in putting it into practice.

Market research provides information about the people who are buying the products of a business. Conditions change, and the owner of a business must know about those changes to be proactive and maintain a competitive advantage. The steps of the market research process include problem identification, development of a plan, data collection, data analysis, and drawing conclusions. Market research can provide valuable information regarding people's current tastes, preferences, and expectations. It is useful in fine-tuning products that already exist for markets that are already known. Conversely, it is of limited use for markets that do not exist yet or for needs that customers do not realize they have.

KEY TERMS ▶▶

big data **296**

cognitive dissonance **295**

evoked set **295**

individualized marketing **292**

marketing strategy **288**

market research **296**

market segmentation **292**

mass marketing **292**

niche marketing **292**

primary data **299**

production concept **288**

relationship marketing **288**

sales forecast **290**

secondary data **299**

segmentation variables **292**

target markets **291**

STUDENT STUDY SITE ▶▶

edge.sagepub.com/hatten7e

$SAGE edge™ Sharpen your skills with SAGE edge!

SAGE edge for Students provides a personalized approach to help you accomplish your coursework goals in an easy-to-use learning environment. You'll find mobile-friendly eFlashcards and quizzes as well as multimedia resources to support and expand on the concepts presented in this chapter.

EXPERIENTIAL LEARNING ACTIVITIES ▶▶

11.1: Small Business Marketing: Strategy and Research Decision-Making

LO 11.2: Describe the process of developing a small business marketing strategy.

Zoe and Alec have just purchased their new home. It is in the suburbs, by great schools, awesome neighbors, wonderful running paths with an amazing yard and pool for entertaining. They have saved and planned for years to move into their dream home and finally have accomplished their goal. They are now moved in, settled, and ready to enjoy their new home. Alec went out on the patio this morning and noticed the pool had a green color to it, which he had not noticed previously, and he also realized the grass was getting tall. Somehow, in the excitement of buying their new home, neither of them had thought about how they were going to maintain their lawn and pool. The previous owners had left minimal pool supplies and no lawnmower or lawn care items. Alec went back in the house to talk to Zoe. What were they going to do?

Answer the following questions and help Zoe and Alec determine a course of action using the decision-making steps listed below. Using your smart phone or laptop, research actual answers for each step in the process. If lawn care and pool care are not relevant to your area, then choose a differing location and research that area. You must be able to defend your answers based upon the scenario and your research.

1. Problem recognition

2. Information search

3. Evaluation of alternatives—including evoked set

4. Purchase

5. Post-purchase evaluation

6. You own and operate a lawn care business. How and where do you successfully enter the above decision-making process in order to be the solution to the problem?

11.2: Small Business Marketing: Strategy and Research Target Market

LO 11.2: Describe the process of developing a small business marketing strategy.

Lacy has just returned from an incredible vacation in India where she was introduced to a new food that was amazingly wonderful—jackfruit. The jackfruit was readily available in most of the places she had visited and was a unique fruit, weighing up to 80 pounds. She had never eaten the fruit before and was amazed that its seeds could be eaten or ground into flour, the fleshy pods could be eaten and used as a meat substitute, and the ripe fruit could be used as a dessert with a sweet tropical fruit flavor. It was also highly nutritious, containing Vitamin C, potassium, and high levels of the B6 vitamin. Lacy had eaten jackfruit chips, jackfruit nuts, a milky jackfruit dessert, an iced jackfruit dessert, and a main dish in which jackfruit was used as a meat substitute. All the jackfruit variations had been very good. Lacy began wondering if there was a market for jackfruit in the United States. Which target market would buy this unique fruit?

Answer the following questions and help Lacy determine a target market for jackfruit. You must be able to defend your answers based upon the scenario and your Census Bureau research.

1. What need can the jackfruit satisfy?

2. Which demographic of people would potentially be most interested in jackfruit?

3. Are there enough people in this group to make selling jackfruit profitable?

4. Can the people in this group potentially afford jackfruit?

5. Go to census.gov and find two specific pieces of information on your chosen target market within a 100-mile radius of your location that addresses the above questions.

6. Which form of marketing will work best to reach your chosen target market: mass marketing, market segmentation, niche marketing, or individualized marketing? Why did you choose this form?

CHAPTER CLOSING CASE ▶▶

Active Analog Fun Business

Introduction to Children's Parties

The children's party market is no jelly and trifling matter. "It's a huge industry," Tim Jenkins writes after his interview with Amanda Frolich from Amanda's Action Kids. According to Frolich, "People spend an absolute fortune on their children's birthday parties and fortunately the recession hasn't affected our business."

Like Paul Lindley, founder of Ella's Kitchen, who used his parenting experience to launch a successful start-up, the party business with low barriers-to-entry sees numerous parent entrepreneur concepts. Michelle Hill incorporated her own party business called The Land of Make-Believe after spending hours creating props, themed food, and thinking up games suitable for her five-year-old son's shared birthday party. This birthday spectacular experience helped her identify a clear gap in the market.

According to Tim Jenkins, a modest £50 party spend per UK child equates to an annual £35 million for a single school-year group. With £250 not untypical for an outsourced party service, it is easy to value the industry in the hundreds of millions.

Business Model Essentials

Successful party concepts need a certain "wow" factor that is popular with the children, but also satisfies parents' social needs too. Thus, it is important to also consider appropriate services for parents. Maslow's hierarchy of needs framework perhaps offers some useful cues: shelter, comfort, psychological self-actualization—be that social linger space, self-service hot beverages, a glass of wine, or a latte bar. Party providers need to balance novelty with tried and tested formulas, perhaps offering evolving theme linkages that might anticipate new film releases, particularly sequels. They look to reduce parental hassle with branded off-the-shelf invitation cards and party bags that appeal particularly to cash-rich, often time-poor, parents.

Entrepreneur.com neatly summarizes the party service offering: "You'll plan the theme, provide costumes (unless guests arrive wearing their own), décor, food, favors and other assorted goodies, entertainment, and clean up afterward so parents can enjoy the festivities instead of running themselves ragged."

The business model usually has relatively low start-up costs—a website and a telephone number will generally suffice. Wardrobe,

The Land of Make-Believe party concepts include themes for cheerleaders, pirates, and fairies; cowboys and Indians; witches and wizards; Fairy Godmother, Teddy Bear picnic, glamor, and *Grease* the musical with Pink Ladies and T-Birds. Party concepts that tend to appeal more to boys, perhaps relying less on dressing up and dancing, include club energy sports, go-karting, football, army games, reptiles and pets, and fire engine–themed parties. Leisure venues also offer some stiff competition with swimming pool visits, laser quest, bowling, cinema, and restaurant visits also popular.

props, and base supplies are not insignificant items and should be carefully considered in financial planning. There is some wide variation in the complexity of offerings in the sector from a light touch and self-contained entertainer magician or comedian whose equipment might be limited to a costume, a music system, and some props that fit into a large suitcase or two to the full-service party-planning-solution provider offering a venue, full catering, the all-important candle-covered cake, decorations, and party bags. Three core components are required for a successful party operation, namely venue, catering, and entertainment. Fixed costs can be kept low, but are dependent on avoiding the purchase of a specialized vehicle and/or long-term premises by using a client-arranged venue. Children's party planning is clearly not a job for someone craving regular Monday through Friday, 9 a.m. to 5 p.m. hours. The ability to successfully interact with children and their parents, balancing controlled fun and calm authoritativeness, is particularly important but often rather taken for granted.

Marketing Communication Angles

A reputation for running successful parties is crucial to stimulate positive word-of-mouth referrals via parental social networks, accentuated by frequent contact at school pick-ups and drop-offs, but also on social media, and in particular parenting website communities such as mumsnet.com, which offers local listings, discussion boards, and advice-based content.

In addition to successfully hosting enjoyable parties, which should drive positive referrals, a number of low-cost marketing activities can be implemented to help generate future bookings such as

- Arranging to share a business card or small color flyer via the party bag that is often given to departing guests.

- Posting flyers at local clubs and church halls.
- Advertising in directories (telephone and web).
- Donating a free party to a school/community charity auction.
- Writing advertorial content accompanied by strong images in the local press (note parental permission and ethical issues around publishing photos of children).
- Creating a website and social media presence on key sites.
- Performing at community group/school events.
- Printing car stickers to build brand awareness and share web and telephone contacts.

Rugged Earth Adventures

One ex-army officer's start-up inspiration led to a birthday party business centered on a military outdoor adventure theme. Having experimented with a number of temporary locations, the business finally settled on a large piece of underutilized agricultural land that comprises a mix of scrub land, combined with lines of commercially unsuccessful shrubs and trees.

The customer segment that this business proposition appeals to is mostly parents of boys—approximately 75 percent of

participants are male, aged between 6 and 10 years. The children participate in a two-hour party that sees them run around outside in a natural environment. Issued with a foam bullet Nerf gun and protective glasses, participants are initially put into two teams, jungle versus desert, utilizing authentic British army terminology. A second game, the less frenetic snipers-and-seekers, is a form of hide-and-seek using realistic camouflage costumes. Then the young people are carefully instructed on how to thoroughly cook their own sausage, which is served as a hot dog, and the party concludes with toasted marshmallows. During one of the well-timed rest periods, a picnic basket is offered to the participants around the campfire with a variety of foods—an array that is low in chocolate and big on fruit and vegetables, which is appealing to parents, but it also includes less healthy but popular cupcakes and crisps.

With overprotective parents, toy guns that fire projectiles, and an open fire, the safety briefing is taken very seriously and uses a highly authoritative army style. Children are regularly reminded about safe behavior requirements around the fire pit, particularly when wearing flammable costumes. Compliant use of safety glasses is paramount, with regular and direct reinforcement of the safety rules taking place.

Hosting and supervising parents are made to feel at ease, provided with access to self-service hot and cold drinks and a place to perch. An informal satisfaction polling takes place just prior to the end around the campfire; positive responses are anticipated, thanks to a fairly simple formula that is well executed. The opportunity afforded to parents to relax while watching a group of children enjoy a totally stress-free afternoon is actually quite enjoyable.

The business income comes predominantly from weekend parties, with the current site offering a capacity of three or possibly four parties per day. Each party can entertain 10 to 24 young people and costs between £120 and £295 (£12 to £20/child, excluding cake and party bags, which are £5 per child extra). Activity days, attractive for dual working parents, are also offered during the Easter and summer school holidays, priced at £26 to £34 per day. The revenue generated covers operating costs after a very short operational period.

Discussion Questions

1. Currently the business strategy is to run one location. What might be the advantages and disadvantages of adopting this strategy to multiple sites?

2. Is the cost and effort of legally protecting the company's intellectual property a worthwhile investment?

3. Given the existing facilities and staff capabilities can you identify additional product offerings?

4. Using informed estimates to fill in the missing data, formulate a financial summary of the business in its current form. Forecast what these might look like in a year or two assuming the hoped for expansion has been realized. Would you invest in a business like this? Are there efficiencies of scale?

5. What additional revenue opportunities might the business investigate?

Sources: "Business Idea Center: Children's Party Planning," *Entrepreneur*, 2013, http://www.entrepreneur.com/businessideas/childrens-party-planning; Aisha Gani, "Five-Year-Old Misses Friend's Birthday Party and Gets Invoice for £15.95," *Guardian*, January 19, 2015, http://www.theguardian.com/uk-news/2015/jan/19/five-year-old-misses-friends-birthday-party-and-has-to-pay-1595; Bryony Gordon, The Children's Birthday Party Industry Is Completely Out of Hand," *Telegraph*, January 20, 2015, http://www.telegraph.co.uk/news/newstopics/howaboutthat/11355541/The-childrens-birthday-party-industry-is-completely-out-of-hand.html; M. Hill, "About us," The Land of Make Believe, http://www.landofmakebelieve.co.uk/intro.asp; Tim Jenkins, "Children's Parties Still Thriving," BBC, June 10, 2009, http://news.bbc.co.uk/1/hi/business/8091823.stm; W. King, (2013, October 11). Ella's Kitchen: It's in the Bag with Healthy Food for Baby," *Telegraph*, http://www.telegraph.co.uk/sponsored/technology/toshiba-technology/10363207/ellas-kitchen-healthy-baby-food.html; Geoffrey Levy and Richard Kay, "Kate's Family Has Eclipsed So Many of Their Poorer Relatives, So Just How Rich Are the Middletons?" *Daily Mail*, April 19, 2011, http://www.dailymail.co.uk/femail/article-1378288/Kate-Middletons-family-Just-rich-Middletons.html; C. Marshall, Steven Prokesch, and C. Weiser, "Competing on Customer Service: An Interview with British Airways' Sir Colin Marshall," *Harvard Business Review*, November-December 1995; Mr McDonut (website), http://www.mrmcdonut.co.uk/; Rugged Earth Adventures (website), http://www.ruggedearthadventures.com.

CHAPTER 12

SMALL BUSINESS MARKETING

Location

So you have a great product or service. Now where do you locate that product and how do you get that product to the right place so the consumer who is the end user can make the purchase? There are a variety of choices when it comes to the location for selling your product. We've all heard the statement: A critical key to the success of your business depends upon location, location, location. With today's technology, there are some new choices as well as more traditional choices when deciding where to locate.

Think—it's two minutes before class and you need caffeine. You run to the closest vending machine—fairly common occurrence, right? Vending machines can provide consumers access to a product 24/7 with no employee costs. Now think pizza, beer, and swimsuits? Not products we ordinarily think of finding in a vending machine. However, with today's technology and a global market, a consumer can get pizza for $5 with choice of toppings, and you can watch the machine knead dough and bake the pie in about three minutes in Italy, and dispense beer in the Czech Republic and swimsuits in New York, Los Angeles, and Miami right from a vending machine conveniently located with consumer goods.

Other surprising items that can be accessed via vending distribution (essentially making them available 24/7) like RollaSole comfortable shoes, mini works of art in reworked cigarette machines, or 63 shades of nail polish in Paris. Japanese clothing retailer, Uniqlo offers shirts and down jackets in tall machines in U.S. airports. Sprinkles Cupcake ATM has 15 locations stocked with cupcakes and cookies—you just select a flavor and a robotic arm will immediately dispense it for you. Even crazier example? The Dallas-based tattoo parlor Ems Street Tattoo's has vending machines that dispense a random design for just $100 (you still have to find an artist to do the actual tattoo work).

This chapter discusses how to get the product or service produced by your small business through distribution channels into locations where the end user, the consumer, can purchase and use the product.

Sources: Kaitlyn Wang, "Forget the Oreos: Here Are the 11 Craziest Things You Can Buy at a Vending Machine Right Now," *Inc.*, September 26, 2017, www.inc.com; Janine Popick, "Cashless Is Priceless: How Consumers Pay—Redefined," *Inc.*, October 22, 2013, www.inc.com; Dan Bova, "Car Vending Machines and New Emojis," *Entrepreneur*, March 26, 2018, www.entrepreneur.com/video/311033.

LEARNING OUTCOMES

After reading this chapter, you should be able to:

12.1 Describe small business distribution and explain how "efficiencies" affect channels of distribution.

12.2 Explain how the location of your business can provide a competitive advantage.

12.3 Discuss the central issues in choosing a particular site within a city.

12.4 Compare the three basic types of locations.

12.5 Explain the types of layout you can choose.

12.6 Present the circumstances under which leasing, buying, or building is an appropriate choice.

Concept Module 12.1: Small Business Distribution

- **LO 12.1: Describe small business distribution and explain how "efficiencies" affect channels of distribution.**

In this chapter, we will explore the role of product distribution, business location, and layout of your small business. In marketing terms, these functions are categorized as *place*. Of the *Four P's* of the marketing mix, place, or *distribution*, is especially significant for your small business because an effective distribution system can make or save a small business as much money as a hot advertising campaign can generate. In fact, distribution is about the last real bastion for cost savings—as techniques for tracking and individualizing promotion improve, as manufacturing becomes more and more efficient, and as employee productivity rises. Your choice of **distribution channel** is especially important when entering international markets, where you are not likely to have as many options for distribution as in the U.S. market.

distribution channel
The series of intermediaries a product passes through when going from producer to consumer.

Master the content at
**edge.sagepub.com/
Hatten7e**
$SAGE edge

direct channel
A distribution channel in which products and services go directly from the producer to the consumer.

indirect channel
A distribution channel in which the products pass through various intermediaries before reaching the consumer.

dual distribution
The use of two or more channels to distribute the same product to the same target market.

agents
Intermediaries who bring buyers and sellers together and facilitate exchanges.

brokers
Intermediaries who represent clients who buy or sell specialized goods or seasonal products.

In marketing, *distribution* has two meanings: the physical transportation of products from one place to the next, and the relationships between intermediaries who move the products—otherwise called the *channels of distribution*. There are two types of distribution channels: direct and indirect (see Figure 12.1). With a **direct channel**, products and services go directly from the producer to the consumer. Buying sweet potatoes and corn at a farmer's market, or a pair of sandals directly from the artisan who made them, are examples of sales through a direct channel. Other examples are buying seconds and overruns from factory outlets or through catalog sales managed by the manufacturer.

An **indirect channel** is so called because products pass through various intermediaries before reaching the consumer. Small businesses that use more than one channel (such as a swimsuit producer selling to an intermediary like a retail chain and directly to consumers via catalog sales) are said to use **dual distribution**.

Intermediaries include agents, brokers, wholesalers, and retailers.

Agents bring buyers and sellers together and facilitate the exchange. They may be called *manufacturer's agents*, *selling agents*, or *sales representatives*.

Brokers represent clients who buy or sell specialized goods or seasonal products. Neither brokers nor agents take title to the goods sold.

▼ FIGURE 12.1

Channels of Distribution

Channels of distribution are systems through which products flow from producers to consumers.

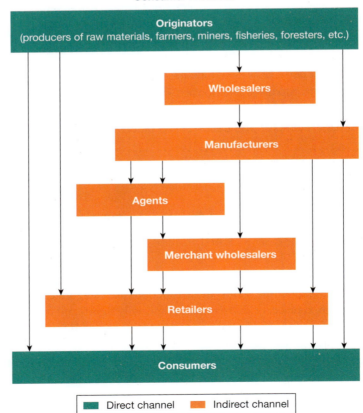

Wholesalers buy products in bulk from producers and then resell them to other wholesalers or to retailers. Wholesalers take title to goods and usually take possession.

Retailers sell products to the ultimate consumer. Retailers take title and possession of the goods they distribute.

The key word for evaluating a channel of distribution is *efficiency*—getting products to target markets in the fastest, least expensive way possible. Did you realize that about three-fourths of the money spent on food goes to distribution?

Does adding intermediaries to the channel of distribution increase the cost of getting the product to the consumer? Or does "doing away with the middleman" always mean savings to consumers? Although the latter has become a marketing cliché, it is not always true. Adding intermediaries can *decrease* the price to the consumer if each intermediary increases the efficiency of the channel. You can do away with the middleman, but you can't replace her function. Someone still has to do the job.

For example, if your business needs half a truckload of supplies every month from your main supplier 400 miles away, should you buy your own truck or have the supplies shipped via a *common carrier* (a trucking company that hauls products for hire)? If that were the only time you needed a truck, of course it would be cheaper to have the supplies shipped, even though it adds an intermediary to your channel of distribution. If you do away with the middleman—in this case, the trucking company—you must replace its function by buying your own truck, paying a driver, maintaining the vehicle, filing paperwork, and so on. The question here is not *whether* the functions of an intermediary are performed; the question is *who* performs them.

You need to be prepared to revise the way you get your products to consumers because the efficiency of channels can change. Currently, the fastest-growing distribution systems involve non-store marketing, including vending machines, telemarketing, and direct mail. Sometimes a break from the industry norm can create a competitive advantage for your business. When Michael Dell started the Dell computer company, he eliminated all of the usual intermediaries found in the personal computer market. Dell advertised and sold directly to consumers. This distribution strategy shot Dell into the Fortune 500.

Efficiencies in channels of distribution not only allow small businesses to offer goods more efficiently (and therefore more profitably), but also provide opportunities for starting new businesses. If you establish a firm that will increase the efficiency of an existing channel, you are providing a needed service, which is the basis for a good business.

Concept Check Question

1. How can a small business owner create competitive advantage with a channel of distribution?

Concept Module 12.2: Location for the Long Run

- LO 12.2: Explain how the location of your business can provide a competitive advantage.

Selecting a location for your business is one of the most important decisions you will make as a small business owner. Although not every business depends on foot traffic for its customers, just about any business can pick a poor location for one reason or another. For example, retail businesses need to be easily accessible to their consumers. A company that produces concrete blocks for construction must be located in an area that frequently uses that type of building material, if it is to keep down transportation costs. Manufacturing businesses need to consider locating near their workers, sources of raw materials, and transportation outlets.

wholesalers
Intermediaries who buy products in bulk from producers and resell them to other wholesalers or to retailers.

retailers
Intermediaries who sell products to the ultimate consumer.

People do not tend to go out of their way to find a business. Although Ralph Waldo Emerson had great literary success when he wrote, "If a man can make a better mousetrap than his neighbor, though he builds his house in the woods, the world will make a beaten path to his door," it's best not to take his advice literally when selecting a location for your business.

This chapter will follow the building location process from the broadest decisions (selecting a state or region) to the narrowest (designing a layout of your facilities). There are four essential questions you need to ask:

1. What region of the country would be best for your business?

2. What state within that region satisfies your needs?

3. What city within that region will best suit you?

4. What specific site within that city will accommodate your business?

Don't automatically jump to the fourth question. By beginning the site selection process broadly and then narrowing down your choices, you can choose a location that meets the needs of your target market and is near other businesses that are complementary to yours (see Figure 12.2).

To analyze a potential location for your business, you will want to consider the specific needs of your business in conjunction with your personal preferences. First, establish the criteria that

▼ **FIGURE 12.2**

Identification of Regional and Local Markets

Choosing the right location for your business may be a process of narrowing down the region, state, city, and neighborhood that are right for you.

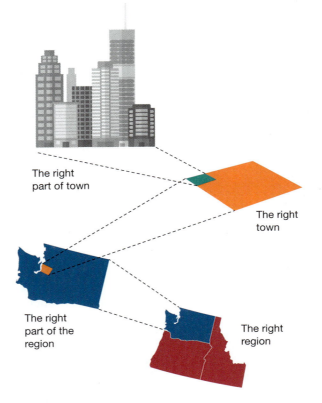

The right part of town

The right town

The right part of the region

The right region

are essential to your success. Then list those that are desirable but not mandatory. Examples of criteria include the following:

- Price and availability of land and water

- Quality and quantity of labor pool

- Access to your customers

- Proximity of suppliers

- Access to transportation (air, highway, and rail)

- Location of competition

- Public attitudes toward new businesses

- Laws, regulations, and taxes

- Your personal preference regarding where to live

- Financial incentives provided (tax breaks, bond issues, and guaranteed loans)

- Quality of schools

- Quality of life (crime rate, recreation opportunities, housing, cost of living, and cultural activities)

State Selection

Most small business owners start and operate their businesses in the area where they currently live. Other people, however, are anxious to relocate to another part of the country (or world) to run their small businesses.

The United States is a collection of local and regional markets rather than one big market. Business conditions vary from place to place. Economic booms and recessions vary from region to region. Markets and people's tastes vary from region to region as well, and these regional differences may influence the decision about where you should locate your business. For example, your recipe for deep-dish pizza may not set your business apart from the competition in Chicago, where that style of pizza is already very popular. By contrast, it may make your business unique in Flagstaff, Arizona, or Biloxi, Mississippi.

Every state, city, and town has an economic incentive to recruit businesses to relocate within their borders for the jobs and taxes contributed to their local economy. In exchange for commitments to relocate, businesses are offered reductions in sales taxes, enhanced tax credits for capital investment in business property (like machinery and equipment) and real property (like buildings and land), zoning and permit assistance, cash-grant incentives, low-interest loans, job training, and/or regulatory flexibility.

Where do you find information to compare and contrast the economic performance of regions, states, and cities? Several sources are available. Branding Facilities operates a website that highlights the economic development and site selection news broken down by every state (see https://businessfacilities.com/state-by-state-incentives-guide). Every year, *Inc.* magazine publishes its annual "Metro Report," which ranks job growth, population growth, business starts, growth in personal earnings, and employment pool data. *Fortune* magazine regularly includes information on regional and state economies in its "Looking Forward." *Business Week*, *Forbes*, the *Wall Street Journal*, *Entrepreneur*, and *USA Today* all regularly publish accounts of current regional and national information. The U.S. Census Bureau gathers data by geographic region every 10 years and maintains an extensive database.

CREATING COMPETITIVE ADVANTAGE

LOCATION, LOCATION, LOCATION

Relocating (or initially locating) a business is a huge decision—for the business owner, its customers, and especially the employees. There are many possible reasons for such a move. Some places are better than others for offering proximity to vendors or customers, tax burden or other financial incentives, cost of living, quality of life, or access to workforce talent. As with most business decisions, the benefits must outweigh the costs.

In its annual ranking of the "best-performing cities" in the United States, the Milken Institute shows the Sun Belt—running from the Southeast through the Southwest regions topping its list again for 2017. Orlando, Florida; Austin, Texas; and Nashville, Tennessee, among other cities have accelerating ecosystems for small businesses.

Such a big move (literally) takes thought and preparation. Consider the following questions:

- **Can you serve potential clients better in another region?** If you are selling to consumers, this question is best answered via marketing research. Location can be your competitive advantage if you can create a substantial list of clients in your new city.

- **Is the local business community welcoming of new entrants to the market?** As noted in this chapter, states and cities offer incentives to businesses considering relocation. But can you project how well your business will fit in after the incentives expire?

- **Is there a vibrant ecosystem of companies doing interesting things?** Small business success begets other small business success. A business climate is fertile ground for innovation. A great business city has a healthy mix of established traditional businesses to support and partner with new disruptors.

- **Is there a talent base motivated to stay?** Your growing business needs talent to run and grow. College towns are perfect for young companies in need of the skills young employees bring.

- **Can you get there from here?** A location with access to transportation into and out of the city is an important key for long-term viability. This applies both for people and for goods.

Location is one of the most significant competitive advantages you can build into your small business. Choose wisely.

Sources: Amy Osmond Cook, "Thinking of Moving Your Company? Think Fly-Over States." *Entrepreneur*, January 30, 2018, www.entrepreneur.com/article/307177; Anna Hensel, "The Hottest American Cities for New Businesses in 2017," *Inc.*, January 13, 2018, www.inc.com; Toby Nwazor, "5 Crucial Questions You Must Ask Before Moving Your Business," *Entrepreneur*, July 3, 2017, www.entrepreneur.com/article/295820; Remy Bernstein, "6 Questions You Should Ask Before Moving Your Company to a New Location," *Entrepreneur*, May 4, 2017, www.entrepreneur.com /article/293748.

Concept Check Questions

1. Why should the small business owner consider the demographics of an area when choosing a location for opening a new business? Name some sources of demographic information that are valuable tools to use in this evaluation.

2. When choosing a location for a new business, what are the most important criteria for the entrepreneur to consider? Explain the connection between type of business and location.

3. Why would a small business flourish in one area of the United States but fail in another region?

4. How can your business location affect customers' image and perception of your business?

Concept Module 12.3: Site Selection

- **LO 12.3: Discuss the central issues in choosing a particular site within a city.**

Whereas the total makeup of the U.S. marketplace is diverse and complex, neighborhoods tend to be just the opposite. People are generally more comfortable in areas where people like themselves live. Thus the cliché "opposites attract" doesn't usually hold true for neighborhoods. The reasons for this demographic fact can be a matter of practicality as much as preference. People of similar income can afford similarly priced houses, which are generally built in the same area. Neighborhoods also tend to contain clusters of similar age groups, religious groups, families, and cultural groups. These factors distinguish one neighborhood from another. They are therefore important to consider in locating your business.

To distinguish different neighborhood types, Nielsen Claritas has three systems to provide detailed demographic and segmentation information: PRIZM, P$YCLE, and Connexions. These systems provide information on consumer behavior including household affluence, likes, dislikes, lifestyles, purchase preferences, and media preferences based upon 66 segments. Some examples of the segments are Big Fish, Small Pond (older, upper-class college-educated professionals without kids); Back Country Folks (over 55, rural lifestyle, median income $33,000); and Park Bench Senior (retired singles with low-key sedentary lifestyles). Want to see what these systems have to say about your ZIP code? Go to www.mybestsegments.com and find out.[1]

Site Questions

Choosing the correct site involves answering many questions about each location being considered. You must find the right kind of site for your business. It must be accessible to your customers and vendors, and it must satisfy all legal requirements and economic needs of your business.

Type of Site

- Is the site located near target markets?
- Is the type of building appropriate for your business?
- What is the site's age and condition?
- How large is the trade area?
- Will adjacent businesses complement or compete with your firm?

Accessibility

- How are road patterns and conditions?
- Do any natural or artificial barriers obstruct access to the site?
- Does the site have good visibility?
- Is traffic flow too high or too low?
- Is the entrance or exit to parking convenient?
- Is parking adequate?
- Is the site accessible by mass transit?
- Can vendor deliveries be made easily?

Legal Considerations

- Is the zoning compatible with your firm?
- Does the building meet building codes?
- Will your external signs be compatible with zoning ordinances?
- Can you get any special licenses you will need (such as a liquor license)?

Economic Factors

- How much are occupancy costs?

- Are the amenities worth the cost?

- How much will leasehold improvements and other one-time costs be?

Traffic Flow

The number of cars and pedestrians passing a site strongly affects its potential for retail sales. If you are a retailer, you need to determine whether the type and amount of traffic are sufficient for your business. Fast-food franchises have precise specifications for number counts of vehicles travelling at specified speeds in each direction as part of their location analysis. State highway departments can usually provide statistics on traffic counts for most public roads.

Type of traffic is important, because you don't receive any particular benefit if the people passing your business are not likely to stop. For example, suppose you are comparing two locations for your upscale jewelry store—one in a central business district and the other in a small shopping center with other specialty stores in an exclusive neighborhood. Total volume of traffic by the central business district location will be higher, but you will enjoy more of the right type of traffic for your store at the small shopping center.

> "The synergy created from several similar businesses located together can be very beneficial, with customers coming to a specific area to 'shop around' before buying."

Other businesses in the area will affect the type of traffic. This explains why you often see automobile dealerships clustered together. The synergy created from several similar businesses located together can be very beneficial, with customers coming to a specific area to "shop around" before buying. Your chances of attracting customers in the market for an auto will be much greater in a location with complementary competition than if your location is isolated.

Some key questions to ask as you choose your location are

- Is your business going to be formal or laid back and casual? Your location should be consistent with your specific style and image.

- Are you on the correct side of the street for the flow of traffic? How many lanes of traffic must be crossed in order to reach your entrance?

- Do you have sufficient parking all times of the day? Is it easy to get to?

- Do you out-position your closest competitors in this area?

- What does the nearby competition look like? Sometimes having competitors nearby is good when customers like to comparison shop.

- For retail businesses, foot traffic is very important so you don't want to be tucked away.

- Is there an anchor store near you? Is your product differentiated from that product?

- Many older buildings don't have the necessary infrastructure to support the high-tech needs (like adequate electrical, air conditioning, and telecommunications services) of modern businesses.[2]

Concept Check Question

1. Explain the importance of knowing the legal requirements of an area before attempting to open a small business.

Concept Module 12.4: Location Types

● **LO 12.4: Compare the three basic types of locations.**

Commercial retail locations are available in many different forms. Think about businesses in your town. Service and retail businesses have several choices for types of locations: central business districts, shopping centers, and stand-alone locations.

Central Business Districts

The *central business district (CBD)* is usually the oldest section of a city. Although urban blight caused many businesses to desert CBDs in favor of the suburbs, many other CBDs have undergone a *gentrification* process, meaning that old buildings have been restored, or razed and replaced with new offices, retail shops, or housing. This planning and development, such as Denver's Larimer Square and Chicago's Water Tower Place, have created some of the best and most expensive locations for many types of retailers.

The advantages of locating in a CBD are that your customers generally will have access to public transportation; to a variety of images, prices, and services; and to many other businesses. The disadvantages can include parking availability, which is usually very tight and expensive; traffic congestion; possibly a high crime rate; older buildings; and sharp disparities between neighborhoods, in which one block can be upscale while the next is run-down.

Shopping Centers

Although concentrated shopping areas have existed for centuries, from the 1950s to 2005, the United States witnessed the "malling of America" with about 1,500 malls built. They have been on a long downward slide since 2005. Malls located in heavily populated, affluent areas still thrive, but many struggle or close. Those malls that maintain the right combination of attributes to succeed remain solid locations for small businesses taking advantage of the foot traffic that malls generate.[3]

Shopping centers and malls are centrally owned or managed, have balanced store offerings, and have their own parking facilities. **Anchor stores** are major department stores that draw people into the shopping center.

Over the last several decades, shoppers have come to demand the convenience of shopping centers. People living in the suburbs want to be able to drive to a location where they can park easily and find a wide variety of goods and services. Shopping centers have also gone through an evolutionary process, tending toward larger centers offering more variety, wider selections, and more entertainment. Have megamalls like the West Edmonton Mall or the Mall of America gone too far in this evolutionary process? Have they reached the point of being "too big"? Ultimately, the consumer market will decide.

Advantages shopping centers can offer to your business, compared with a CBD, include heavy traffic drawn by the wide variety of products available, closeness to population centers, cooperative planning and cost sharing, access to highways, ample parking, a lower crime rate, and a clean, neat environment.

A disadvantage of locating within a shopping center is the inflexibility of your store hours. If the center is open from 9 a.m. to 10 p.m., you can't open your store from noon until midnight. Your rent is often higher than in an outside location. The central management of the shopping center may restrict the merchandise you sell. Your operations are limited, membership is required in the center's merchant organization, and you face the possibility of having too much competition. Smaller stores may be dominated by anchor stores.

Shopping centers will continue to evolve rapidly. Aging centers are being renovated. As shoppers become more dependent on malls and shopping centers to supply their needs, more

anchor stores
Large retail stores that attract people to shop at malls.

service-oriented businesses, such as banks, health clinics, day care centers, and insurance offices, will be located in malls.

Stand-Alone Locations

Drawing in and keeping customers are difficult tasks, especially if you choose a freestanding, or stand-alone, location. With a freestanding location, your business must be the customers' destination point. Therefore, your competitive advantage must be made very clear to them. You must have unique merchandise, large selections, low prices, exceptional service, or special promotions to get them in.

Advantages of stand-alone locations include the freedom to set your own hours and operate the way you choose. You may have no direct competition nearby. More parking may be available, and rent may be lower than what you would pay at a shopping center.

Disadvantages of having your business in a stand-alone location include the loss of synergy that can be created when the right combination of businesses is located together. You have to increase your advertising and promotional spending to get customers in your door. You can't share operating costs with other businesses. You may have to build rather than rent.

If the goods or services that you offer are destination-oriented products (like health clubs, convenience stores, or wholesale clubs), a freestanding location may be the right choice for your business.

Service Locations

With some exceptions, the location decision for service businesses is just as important as it is for businesses selling tangible products. Services tend to be hard to differentiate, that is, to show how one is different from another. People will not go out of their way to visit a specific service business if they think there is very little difference between services, so car washes, video rental stores, dry cleaners, and similar services must be *very* careful about the convenience of their locations. With service businesses that visit the customer (like plumbers, landscapers, and carpet cleaners), location is not critical.

Incubators

In the early 1980s, government agencies, universities, and private business groups began creating business incubators to help new businesses get started in their area. Today, several hundred incubators operate in the United States, and their number is growing. Approximately 80 percent of business incubator graduates remain in business and they grow 22 times faster than start-ups not using an incubator, according to the International Business Innovation Association (InBIA).[4] Incubators offer entrepreneurs below-market rent prices, along with services and equipment that are difficult for start-up businesses to provide on their own. They encourage entrepreneurship, which contributes to economic development. Businesses are not allowed to take advantage of these benefits indefinitely, and they must "graduate" to outside locations as they grow. Choosing an incubator as your starting location can help you through the first months when your new business is at its most fragile. As noted earlier, a major advantage of incubators is that they charge lower-than-market rent.

▲ Mixed-use business incubators offer a wide variety of space, equipment, and programs like this one in Grand Junction, CO.

Incubators have huge economic impact on communities and small business owners. The incubator that your author has been associated with for two decades in Grand Junction, Colorado, formed in 1987 when the area suffered from an energy-related economic bust. With 35,000 square feet, the Business Incubator Center (BIC) hosts 50 to 65 tenants at any given time and works with over 1,000 clients each year. Since its inception, BIC has

THAT'S THE SPOT

Jodi has a problem. She has decided to go into business for herself selling used books, DVDs, CDs, and vinyl. She lives in a community of about 200,000 in the northeastern part of the United States. No other stores in the area specialize in the used products she will sell. Her community has a large regional shopping center with four anchor stores. Two sites the size she needs (approximately 2,000 square feet) are currently vacant in the mall.

The central business district is thriving, primarily with small boutique-type stores. The atmosphere is pleasant, with many trees, flower beds, and artistic sculptures lining the streets. The Downtown Business Association does a good job of arranging events like parades and music festivals to draw people to the CBD. One site with 2,500 square feet is available in the CBD.

The community has two primary traffic arteries lined with stand-alone commercial businesses. One stand-alone site is available that has ample parking and a traffic count of approximately 80,000 cars per day passing at 35 mph. This site is the right size, but it is not available to lease; she would have to buy the building. Foot traffic in the mall is the highest, but restrictions and lease payments are higher by far than in the other locations. Not as many people pass by the downtown location, but rent is much cheaper as well.

Questions

1. From the information you have been provided, and considering the advantages and disadvantages of the different types of locations mentioned in this chapter, where would you recommend that Jodi locate? Provide justifications for your recommendation.

2. What additional information would you want to have to make this location decision?

---

graduated over 250 new businesses with a greater than 80 percent existence rate after five years, helped launch over 600 companies that have generated more than $157 million in revenues, and created/retained over 9,500 jobs. That's a big impact for a community with an approximate population of 100,000.[5]

Martek Biosciences might not be a household name, but if you have children, you have probably benefited from its products. Martek graduated from the Technology Advancement Program Incubator in Columbia, Maryland. It develops and sells products derived from microalgae, including nutritional oils contained in infant formula that aid in the development of newborns' eyes and nervous systems.

Through the incubator, Martek had access to specialized facilities and equipment it would have been unable to use any other way. The scale-up lab helped company researchers determine whether a number of individual cells they had grown in the lab were scalable to a larger market. Martek now has license agreements with 13 infant formula manufacturers representing more than two-thirds of the world's wholesale infant formula market.[6]

New ideas inevitably beget new ideas. Incubators are operating at record numbers with some 45,000 start-ups operating in 2,200 incubators across 62 countries in 2018. Survival rate for participants is 87 percent, compared with 44 percent for companies that don't use incubators.

Support Services. Incubators typically provide office, production, and other equipment for tenants to share, items that young businesses often cannot afford by themselves. These items can improve your productivity as a young business, but they would cost a lot of money if you had to buy them outright. In an incubator, you can have access to such equipment and pay only when and if you use it. Receptionists, secretarial support, and shipping and receiving services are also available on a shared basis, so you don't have to add to your payroll.

> "Incubators typically provide office, production, and other equipment for tenants to share, items that young businesses often cannot afford by themselves."

▲ Incubators offer specialized space like commercial kitchens for culinary businesses.

Professional Assistance

Incubators often negotiate reduced rates with needed professionals like accountants and lawyers. They also offer training in cash flow management, marketing practices, obtaining financing, and other areas.

Networking. Incubators can put you in contact with other local businesses. A "family" atmosphere often develops between businesses located in incubators because all are at roughly the same stage of development. This atmosphere usually leads to an esprit de corps among tenants.

Financing. Incubators often have financial assistance available or access to other funding sources such as revolving loan funds, which can provide loans at lower than market rates.

Specialized Incubators. Arts incubators exist to provide assistance to artists, arts organizations, and creative enterprises in the early stages of development. They play the role of lowering barriers to artists turning their creations into businesses. In addition to assisting artists achieve a level of economic viability, such incubators engender improvement of a community's cultural programs, provide creative enhancement, attract other new businesses, boost tourism and visitor traffic, and increase community vitality.[7]

Concept Check Questions

1. What are the three location types and their subcategories?

2. Give an example of a type of small business that would have the greatest chance of succeeding in each location type. State your reason for selecting that particular business type by giving specific advantages.

3. The old adage "location, location, location" applies as well to cyberspace as it does to brick-and-mortar businesses. How does an internet-based business influence its "location"? Which of the principles of location discussed in this chapter apply to e-businesses? What other factors do they have to deal with?

Concept Module 12.5: Layout and Design

- **LO 12.5: Explain the types of layout you can choose.**

After you have selected a site, you need to lay out the interior of your business. If yours is a type of business that customers visit, most of your management decisions will be directed toward getting customers into your business to spend money. No matter what type of business you run, this is where the activity happens. How your location is laid out and designed is important because it affects the image and productivity of your business.

Legal Requirements

The Americans with Disabilities Act (ADA) requires businesses to be accessible to disabled customers and employees, with businesses having more than 14 employees required to accommodate disabled job candidates in hiring. This law affects the way every business operates. Buildings constructed after January 26, 1993, must meet stricter requirements than those built earlier.

NEW WAY WE WORK

▲ Co-working space offers shared facilities for a wide variety of freelance programmers, graphic designers, video producers, and many other small business owners.

Co-working space offers a new way for people to conduct business in shared space. A company called WeWork has been the proverbial 800-pound gorilla in that space since opening in 2010 and growing to 163 locations in 52 cities around the world.

WeWork's business model centers on renting real estate space via a variety of plans, cool designs, flexible leases, and services like high-speed internet, reception, mail, cleaning, coffee, and beer. It offers office culture to businesses too small to create that culture themselves.

For growing companies, WeWork offers a way to enter new cities without the hassle of scouting locations, negotiating contracts, designing the space, and hiring vendors. The 150,000 members of WeWork are largely packs of 20-somethings who pay anywhere from $220 a month for the use of a shared desk in an open common area to $22,000 a month for a 50-person office.

Weekly events that range from thought-leader panels to cheese tastings help nurture a strong team culture. Conference rooms, available for groups of 2 or 25, include audio-visual gear and an attractive ambiance.

The question that remains to be answered (in the long term, since co-working is relatively new) is whether co-working is a fad or signals a paradigm shift in the way we work. Research has shown that workers' primary problem with open or cubicle-filled offices is unwanted noise. But it's not just the noise that's the problem. In fact, some level of office banter in the background might actually benefit our ability to do creative tasks, as long as we don't get caught up in specific conversations. Rather than total silence, some people are more creative with a little background noise. This could explain why they can focus in a noisy coffee shop, but not in a noisy office.

The co-working space movement continues to grow in size, numbers, and variety. Spaces now feature specialization—for example, The Wing, in New York's Flatiron District features pale pink walls, cozy reading nooks, oversize bathrooms with stocked showers, and a library of books by female writers. A women-only and woman-centric workspace.

Sources: Steven Bertoni, "The Way We Work," *Forbes*, October 24, 2017, 64–72; David Burkus, "Why You Can Focus in a Coffee Shop but Not in Your Open Office," *Harvard Business Review*, October 18, 2017, 2–4; Maggie Wiley, "There's a Coworking Space for Everyone," *Entrepreneur*, December 2016, www.entrepreneur .com; Kate Rockwood, "Rethink the Workspace . . . and Build a Movement," *Entrepreneur*, June 2017, 58.

Some ADA requirements for customer accommodation include the following:

- Accessible parking must be provided with space for both the vehicle and an access aisle. An accessibility sign must also be located in front of the parking space to identify the parking spot.

- Access ramps must be provided in order to make the entrance accessible with the slope of the ramp not to exceed 1:12 (every inch of vertical rise must have at least one foot, or 12 inches, of ramp).

- Handrails must be provided whenever the ramp slope is more than 1:20 and the vertical rise is greater than six inches.

- Checkout aisles must be at least 36 inches wide.

- Door hardware must be easily grasped like a lever handle.

- Toilet facilities and water fountains must be accessible to people in wheelchairs.
- Self-service shelves, counters, and bars must be accessible to people in wheelchairs and to the visually impaired.[8]

Retail Layouts

The layout of your retail store helps create the image that people have of your business. It is important to display merchandise in an attractive, logical arrangement to maximize your sales and to make shopping as convenient as possible for your customers.

Three types of layouts are commonly used in retail stores in various combinations. The simplest type is the **free-flow layout**, which works well with smaller stores such as boutiques that sell only one type of merchandise (see Figure 12.3). As there is no established traffic pattern, customers are encouraged to browse.

A **grid layout** establishes a geometric grid by placing counters and fixtures at right angles in long rows (see Figure 12.4). It effectively displays a large amount of merchandise with tall shelves and many shelf facings. Supermarkets and drugstores tend to be set up with this layout, because it suits customers who wish to shop the entire store by moving up and down alternate aisles. But if customers can't see over fixtures or if they want only one or two specific items, they may find this layout frustrating.

The **loop layout** has gained popularity since the early 1980s as a tool for increasing retail sales productivity (see Figure 12.5). The loop sets up a major aisle that leads customers from the entrance, through the store, and back to the checkout counter. Customers are led efficiently through the store so as to expose them to the greatest amount of merchandise. At the same time, they retain the freedom to browse or cross-shop. This layout is especially good for businesses that sell a wide variety of merchandise, because customers can be routed quickly from one department of merchandise to another.

free-flow layout
A type of layout used by small retail stores that encourages customers to wander and browse through the store.

grid layout
A type of layout used by retail stores to move customers past merchandise arranged on rows of shelves or fixtures.

loop layout
A type of retail layout with a predominant aisle running through the store that quickly leads customers to their desired department.

▼ FIGURE 12.3

Free-Flow Layout

The free-flow layout encourages shoppers to browse.

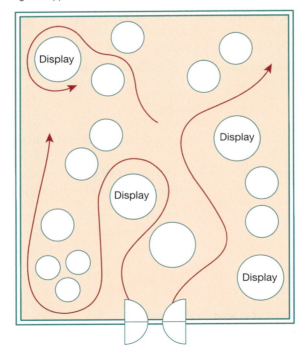

Grid Layout

The grid layout routes customers up and down aisles to expose them to a large quantity of merchandise.

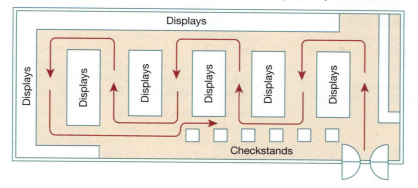

Loop Layout

The loop layout allows customers quick access to any department in the store.

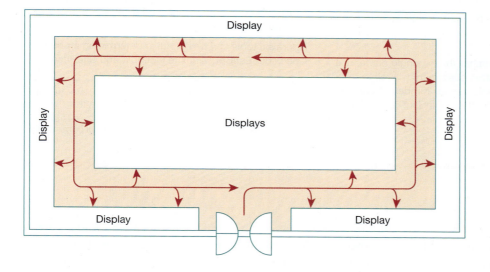

Service Layouts

Service businesses that customers visit, such as beauty shops and restaurants, need to be concerned about how their layout affects both their customers' convenience and the business's work flow. The image of these service businesses is just as strongly affected by layout as is the image of retail stores. Speed of service becomes more critical every year. Consider the decreasing amount of time needed for photo finishing—from one week, to two days, to one hour, to while you wait. Layout is critical to maintaining the speed and efficiency of service providers.

Manufacturing Layouts

The layout of a manufacturing business is arranged to ensure a smooth flow of work. The specific layout of your plant will depend on the type of product you make, the type of production process you use, the space you have available, and other factors, such as the volume of goods and amount of worker interaction needed. There are three basic types of manufacturing layouts, which may be combined as needed.

IF YOU'RE NOT ONLINE, YOU DON'T EXIST

Domain names have been the online real estate for businesses for two decades. As the title of this box says, in the minds of your customers you have to have an online presence in order to exist.

What has become more complicated now is that pretty much every word in the dictionary followed by dot-com is someone else's personal property. Almost 130 million domain names are already registered.

While dot-com is still the preferred URL, there are other options. Generic top-level domains, known as gTLDs, are new variations expected to become more relevant and change the way we search online. For example, if your small business deals in feline products, it would make sense for your domain name to be dot-cat. If your special skill is making rings, earrings, and bracelets out of exotic wood, wouldn't a domain name ending with dot-jewelry be better for building your online brand?

While staying in the realm of dot-com, some ways to come up with creative domain names include

- **Use a Catchy Phrase:** Rather than a single name, use a combination of words that customers will relate to your business. For example, realtor Kimberly Schmidt has the domain name GreatHomesInSanDiego.com. Pretty catchy.

- **Use a Call to Action:** Making your tagline your domain name builds your online brand presence and is memorable to your customers at the same time. For example TAG Heuer uses DontCrackUnderPressure .com. So, think about what action you want your market to take and turn it into a domain name.

- **Use a Valuation Company:** If you really want a domain name that is already registered, resist the urge to contact the owner. You have a better chance to obtain it (for less) via an intermediary.

Domain names are interesting digital assets. Assets have value, so what is a domain name worth if you want to buy one? Turns out there is huge variation in value. The vast majority are almost without value, while the record price is $35.6 million for insurance.com, sold in 2010. The closer a domain name is to a brand name—especially as a single word—and the more established a site is, the more value the domain name will generate.

Appraisal tools can be helpful in determining a price. Check out EstiBot, Website Outlook, and SitePrice.

Sources: Phil Lodico, "3 Keys to the Right Domain Name for Building a Brand," *Entrepreneur*, June 23, 2017, www.entrepreneur.com/article/295947; Alexandra Watkins, "5 Tips for Creating Memorable Domain Names," *Inc.*, April 5, 2018, www .inc.com; James Parsons, "How to Determine the Value of Your Domain Names," *Inc.*, June 20, 2016, www.inc.com.

Process Layout. With the **process layout**, all similar equipment and workers are grouped together so that the goods being produced move around the plant (see Figure 12.6). This layout is common with small manufacturers because of the flexibility it allows. The product being made can be changed quickly. An example of the process layout can be seen in a small machine shop, in which all the grinders would be in one area, all the drills would be in another area, and all the lathes would be in a third area. Restaurant kitchens commonly employ this type of layout as well, with the refrigerators in one place, the ovens in another, and a food preparation area elsewhere.

Another advantage of the process layout is that it minimizes the number of tools or equipment needed. For example, an assembly line (which uses a product layout) might require a company to purchase several grinding machines, one for each point where it is used on the assembly line. With a process layout, by contrast, fewer grinders need be purchased, and they can be used in one area. Because the machines operate independently, a breakdown in one does not shut down operations.

A disadvantage of the process layout is that when equipment is grouped together, increased handling is needed to move the product from one station to another when more than one task is performed. This effort can require additional employees. Because this layout is more general in nature, producing long runs of the same product would be less efficient than in the product layout.

process layout
A way to arrange a manufacturing business by placing all comparable equipment together in the same area.

Process Layout in a Restaurant Kitchen

In a process layout, similar equipment is grouped together in areas to complete specified tasks.

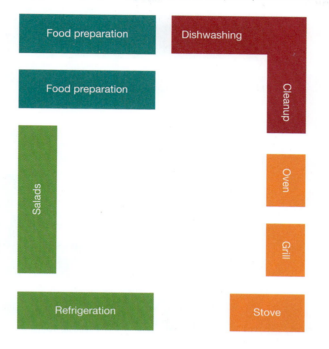

Product Layout. With a **product layout**, you arrange workers, equipment, and activities needed to produce a single product in a particular sequence of steps (see Figure 12.7). A product layout is best when you are producing many standardized products or using specialized equipment. Auto assembly lines, textile mills, and other continuous-flow assembly lines in which raw material enters one end of the line and finished products exit the other end are examples of a product layout. Material handling costs can be decreased and tasks can often be mechanically simplified so that skilled labor is not needed.

A restaurant that specializes in a product like bagels, pizzas, or cookies can make use of the product layout by moving through a sequence of steps to prepare the finished product. The kitchen can be arranged to store ingredients and mix the dough at one end of the counter before it is all moved to cold storage. Then batches can be removed and processed through a dough-rolling machine; prepared and mixed with other ingredients; and cooked, cut, and served in an assembly-line fashion. The layout works well for making that one product, but what if you want to diversify your menu to offer other food items like hamburgers, French fries, or tacos? You would have to set up separate product lines with new ovens, stoves, and counters for each new product—an expensive way to expand a menu.

A product layout is inflexible because it is costly and difficult to change the product that is being made. It is usually more expensive to set up than a process layout because more specialized machinery is needed. A breakdown anywhere along the line can shut down the entire operation. The specialization needed for a product layout eliminates this option for most small businesses because of cost reasons.

Fixed Layout. In a **fixed layout**, the product stays in one spot, and equipment, material, and labor are brought to it as needed for assembly. Types of businesses using this layout include

product layout
A way to arrange a manufacturing business by placing equipment in an assembly line.

fixed layout
A type of layout for a manufacturing business in which the product stays stationary while workers and equipment are brought to it.

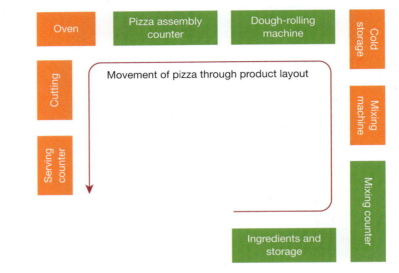

Product Layout in a Pizza Kitchen

In a product layout, workers, equipment, and activities are laid out according to the sequence of steps needed to make the product.

building construction, aircraft- and shipbuilding, and other large, immovable product production.

Home Office

Is a home-based business right for you? It is a popular option for business owners. Small Business Administration data show the share of businesses that are home-based has remained relatively constant over the past decade, at about 50 percent of all firms. Specifically, 60.1 percent of all firms without paid employees are home-based, as are 23.3 percent of small businesses with employees. The industries in which businesses are most likely to be home-based are information (70 percent); construction (68.2 percent); and professional, scientific, and technical services (65.3 percent).[9] Let's look at some advantages and disadvantages.

Advantages

- *Flexibility in scheduling personal, family, and business obligations.*

- *Low overhead expenses.* You are already paying for the space you live in and utilities.

- *No commute time.* Of course, that walk from the kitchen to the office can seem like a long one if you don't really feel like working.

- *Independence.* You can be your own boss and your own landlord. You have some degree of control over what work you accept and the schedule for doing it.

- *No office distractions.* A lot of time can be wasted in office settings chatting with people who "pop in."

Disadvantages

- *Interruptions.* It's hard for family and friends to understand that you really do have work to do.

- *Isolation.* Much of the social aspect of work can be lost without contact with others. A house can get very quiet and lonely.

- *Credibility.* Although home-based businesses are much more accepted today, being taken seriously as a business can be a challenge. This isn't a hobby, and you are not unemployed.

- *Work space.* Your working area may be cramped and not too private.

- *Zoning issues.* Be sure to check whether it is legal for you to operate a business out of your home.

The approaches to running a home business are as varied as the millions of entrepreneurs who own them. Equipment needs vary almost as much.

You must make sure that it is legal to operate a home-based business where you live. Some communities have adopted tough restrictions, such as not allowing a home office even for work you bring home from your "real" office. More typical concerns involve complying with zoning regulations that govern parking, signage, and types of businesses allowed in residential areas. Check with your local zoning board.

Concept Check Questions

1. What is the ADA, and how does it affect the small business owner's site layout and design plan?

2. What are the main types of layout plans, and what should the entrepreneur focus on when designing the layout plan for a new business?

Concept Module 12.6: Lease, Buy, or Build?

- **LO 12.6: Present the circumstances under which leasing, buying, or building is an appropriate choice.**

You have three choices of ownership for your location: leasing a facility, purchasing an existing building, or building your own. In this section, we will discuss the relative advantages of leasing or owning your building.

Leasing

A lease is basically a long-term agreement to rent a building, equipment, or other asset. The biggest advantage of leasing is the amount of cash you free up for other purposes. Not only do you avoid a large initial cash outlay through leasing, but you also reduce your risk during the start-up period. Once your business is established, your needs may change. Leasing your business premises can give you the flexibility to move to a bigger, better, or more suitable location in the future.

A disadvantage of a lease is that it may prevent you from altering a building to fit your needs. You also do not have long-term assurance that you can stay in the same location. The owner may decide not to renew your lease at the end of the term or may increase your rent payments. Leased space in shopping centers commonly requires a monthly fee based on square feet of space, plus a percentage of gross sales.

Review any lease with your lawyer before signing it. This advice holds true for any legal document, but with a lease there is a tendency to think, "These forms are pretty much standard," and thus ignore the advice to review them first. Remember who drew up the document—the lessor. Whom do you think the conditions of the lease will favor? Not you, the lessee. You may need to negotiate the provisions of the lease or *escape clauses*. These items can allow you to terminate the lease if your circumstances change drastically. You will also want to consider the lease's renewal options. Will the lease allow you to remain in the same location at the end of the lease period?

Leasehold improvements are important considerations to negotiate. They comprise the improvements you make to the property, such as upgrading lighting or plumbing, installing drop ceilings, building walls, and making other changes to the property. Of course, you cannot take these improvements with you when you leave, so try to negotiate rent payments in exchange for them. These are just a few of the factors you need to negotiate before signing a lease. Get all agreements in writing.

The best way to avoid disputes between landlords and tenants is for both parties to understand the lease agreement *before* it is signed. Because a lease will legally bind you for a long period of time, you should have the following questions answered to your satisfaction when you enter the deal:

1. *How long will the lease run?* The length of most leases is negotiable, with 3 to 10 years being typical and even one-year leases written with 10 one-year renewal options. In the past, landlords wanted the lease term to be as long as possible to hold down their vacancy rates. Now, in areas where vacant office space is at a premium, many businesses want long leases as a hedge against rising prices. For example, in New York City, an office tower may charge $60 per square foot a month for rent today, whereas the same offices rented for a monthly $16 per square foot only five years earlier.

2. *How much is the rent?* Be sure you know the dollar amount per square foot of space that the rent is based on for any location you consider. Find out how much you are paying for different kinds of space—you don't want to pay the same dollar amount for productive office space as you do for space like lobbies, hallways, mechanical areas, and bathrooms.

There are at least five types of leases, which calculate rent differently, though they are all based on square feet. In a **gross lease**, the tenant pays a flat monthly amount. The landlord pays all building operating expenses such as taxes, insurance, and repairs. Utility bills may or may not be included. In a **net lease**, the tenant pays some or all real estate taxes on top of the base rent. A **net-net lease** adds insurance to the tenant's responsibilities along with base rent and taxes. A net-net-net, or **triple-net lease**, requires tenants to pay not only the base rent, taxes, and insurance, but also other operating expenses related to the building, such as repairs and maintenance. A **percentage lease**, which is common in shopping centers or other buildings that include many different businesses, requires tenants to pay a base rent plus a percentage of gross income.

3. *How much will the rent go up?* To protect against inflation, most landlords include an **escalation clause** in leases, which allows them to adjust rent according to the consumer price index (CPI) or some other scale. You should not agree to pay the full CPI increase, especially if you are already paying part of the building operating expenses.

4. *Can you sublease?* There are many reasons why you might not be able to stay in a location for the stated duration of the lease, including, at the extremes, a failure of your business or becoming so successful that you need to move to a larger space. If you must move, can you rent your space to another tenant who meets the same standards the landlord applies to all other tenants?

5. *Can you renew?* Unless a clause is written into your lease that guarantees you the first right to your space at the end of the lease term, the landlord has no legal obligation to continue it. A formula for determining the new rent payment might be included in the renewal clause, or you might pay current market rate.

6. *What happens if your landlord goes broke?* A *recognition*, or *nondisturbance*, *clause* can protect you from being forced out or into a new lease should the property change ownership.

7. *Who is responsible for insurance?* Landlords should be expected to carry a comprehensive policy on the building that includes casualty insurance on the structure and liability coverage for

all public areas such as hallways and elevators. Building owners can require tenants to buy liability and content insurance.

8. *What building services do you get?* Your lease should state the specific services you can expect to receive, including any electricity use limits, cleaning schedules, and heating, ventilation, and air conditioning (HVAC). Note that, unlike residential rents, commercial space does not usually come with 24-hour HVAC service. (Monday through Friday from 8 a.m. to 5 p.m. and Saturday from 8 a.m. to 1 p.m. are normal.) This could produce some hot or cold working conditions if you work at other hours.

9. *Who else can move in?* Clauses can be written into leases that restrict direct competitors, or businesses that are exceptionally noisy or otherwise disruptive to others, from locating in adjoining spaces. Remember that such restrictions can become a problem to you if you need to sublease.

10. *Who pays for improvements?* Construction and remodeling become expensive quickly. Although you are usually allowed to make leasehold improvements, the building owner does not always have to pay for them. Improvements are an area wide open to negotiation in leases—make sure all agreements in this area are in writing.[10]

Purchasing

The decision to buy a building can be a difficult one. Ownership increases your upfront expenses and the amount of capital you need. The major expense of purchasing and remodeling can drain already stretched resources from other business needs.

With ownership, you gain the freedom of customizing the property any way you want. You know what your payments will be. At the same time, you are tied down to that location much more if you own rather than rent the property. Tax considerations enter the picture. Although lease payments are deductible business expenses, only depreciation on the building is deductible if you own it. Finally, the value of your investment is subject to the whims of the local real estate market. The value may appreciate or depreciate for reasons that have nothing to do with your own efforts. In the end, the choice comes down to economics and flexibility. Because most entrepreneurs are in business because of what they make or sell, and not in the "brick-and-mortar" business of real estate speculation, a majority will choose leasing.

Building

Building a new facility to meet your own specifications may be necessary if your business has unique needs or if existing facilities are not located where you need them, which may be the case in some high-growth areas.

As with buying an existing property, building a new facility greatly increases your fixed expenses. Will your revenues increase enough to cover these additional expenses? On the plus side, building a new facility may enable you to incorporate new technology or features that will lower your operating costs compared to using an older, existing building. Look at your *total* costs over the long term when making this decision.

Concept Check Questions

1. Compare and contrast the advantages and disadvantages of buying, building, or leasing space for a small business.

2. Most commercial leases are triple-net, rather than gross leases (like residential leases). What does that mean you are paying for each month in addition to the rent you pay per square foot?

CHAPTER REVIEW

SUMMARY ▶▶

LO 12.1 Describe small business distribution and explain how "efficiencies" affect channels of distribution.

The purpose of a channel of distribution is to get a product from a producer to consumers as quickly and cheaply as possible. Because distribution represents such a large portion of the price of many products, selecting the most efficient channel will help keep costs down.

LO 12.2 Explain how the location of your business can provide a competitive advantage.

Competitive advantages can be built on many factors. If the location choice of your business makes your product, good, or service more accessible to your customers, to the point where they buy from you rather than other sources, then location is your competitive advantage.

In deciding where to locate your business, you should consider the price and availability of land and water, the labor pool from which you can hire employees, accessibility to customers and suppliers, closeness of competition, adequacy of transportation, public attitudes toward new businesses, taxes and regulations, your personal preference about where you want to live, financial incentives offered, and the quality of life available.

LO 12.3 Discuss the central issues in choosing a particular site within a city.

The most appropriate site for your business is determined by answering specific questions related to matching the needs of your business with the type of site, accessibility, legal considerations, and economic factors.

LO 12.4 Compare the three basic types of locations.

The three types of locations you may choose are central business districts (CBDs), shopping centers, and stand-alone locations. The CBD for most cities and towns includes the original "downtown" area, so it is usually the oldest urban section. Shopping centers can range from small strip malls that serve the local neighborhood to very large regional malls that draw customers from hundreds of miles. A stand-alone location places your business apart from other businesses.

LO 12.5 Explain the types of layout you can choose.

For retail businesses, a free-flow layout encourages customers to wander and browse through the store. A grid layout moves customers up and down rows of shelves and fixtures. A loop layout features a wide central aisle that leads customers quickly from one department to another. For manufacturing businesses, a process layout groups all similar equipment and jobs together and provides the flexibility needed by many small manufacturers. A product layout arranges equipment and workers in a specific sequence to produce products in a continuous flow. With a fixed layout, the product being made stays in one place, while equipment, materials, and labor are brought to it.

LO 12.6 Present the circumstances under which leasing, buying, or building is an appropriate choice.

When deciding whether to lease, buy, or construct a building, you need to consider how long the building will be suitable for your business and whether you can afford to tie up your capital, which could be used for other purposes. Before leasing, you need to carefully examine the terms and conditions of the lease before signing it.

KEY TERMS ▶▶

agents **308**

anchor stores **315**

brokers **308**

direct channel **308**

distribution channel **307**

dual distribution **308**

escalation clause **326**

fixed layout **323**

free-flow layout **320**

grid layout **320**

gross lease **326**

indirect channel **308**

leasehold improvements **326**

loop layout **320**

net lease **326**

net-net lease **326**

percentage lease **326**

process layout **322**

product layout **323**

retailers **309**

triple-net lease **326**

wholesalers **309**

EXPERIENTIAL LEARNING ACTIVITIES ▶▶

12.1: Small Business Marketing: Location Channels of Distribution

LO 12.1: Describe small business distribution and explain how "efficiencies" affect channels of distribution.

Read the scenario and then decide which channel of distribution has been used, placing the letter that corresponds to your answer in the blank.

A. Retailers **D.** Brokers **G.** Indirect Channel

B. Agents **E.** Target Market **H.** Dual Distribution

C. Direct Channel **F.** Wholesalers **I.** Originator

1. _____ Jane is excited. She found a swimsuit she likes at a local retailer but they did not have her size. Tonight she is ordering the swimsuit in her size online.

2. _____ Brett grows wheat that he sells to a co-op, which then sells the wheat to a flour company, which then sells the wheat to a bakery, where Carrie buys her bread.

3. _____ Amy's business buys fresh produce in bulk from local farmers then sells the fresh produce to local restaurants and cafeterias.

4. _____ Kathy's store sells top-of-the-line cosmetics. Her customers range from high school girls to women over the age of 90.

5. _____ Jake is buying his first home. He is using an intermediary who is bringing him as the buyer of the house together with Stephen who is selling the house.

6. _____ Sally sells her fresh farm eggs to her neighbors every week.

7. _____ Nicole represents her buyer who purchases peaches for making jam. Nicole never takes title to the peaches.

Explain how a small business could add value in each channel of distribution listed above. Be specific.

12.2: Small Business Marketing: Location

LO 12.2: Explain how the location of your business can provide a competitive advantage.

Read the scenario and then answer the following questions.

Taylor and Rick are moving to a smaller community to raise their young son. While good for their business, the large metropolis where Baby Boutique is currently located is not where they want to be. Business has been great for the last five years and customers come from miles around to visit their store. They sell all things related to babies: bassinets, baby monitors, cribs, rocking chairs, clothing, scrapbooks, christening gowns, mobiles, toys, and much more. In fact, they will even come in and design your nursery, implement the design, and supply all the needed furnishings. Then as the baby grows, they will change out the furniture and décor to mature with the baby. Customer service is their top priority.

In order to be settled by the first day of school, time is of the essence. They contact a realtor in their new community, share the needs of their business, and ask her to find an adequate location, within the parameters of needed space, rent expense, and so on. The realtor finds a location for their store and sends them pictures. All looks good, and they sign a five-year lease. The next day, they, all their belongings, and their entire store are packed and ready to move.

They have rented a great house in a good neighborhood with an awesome school district and as soon as they arrive at their new home, they feel comfortable and welcomed. Not so as they drive up to the building on which they have signed a five-year lease. Driving to the location, they begin to get worried. They have gone from an upscale area to an area that is economically challenged. And as they drive up to their storefront, they note that on one side is a liquor store and on the other side is a pawnshop. Furthermore, the building is basically a steel warehouse with bars on the windows. All the traffic flow in the area appears to either divert to the liquor store or drive by the building. There are no other businesses within walking distance. Slowly they climb out of the moving truck. How will this new location work?

Answer the following questions about the site of this business. You must be able to defend your answers.

1.   Is the site located near their target markets? Who is their target market? Be specific.

2.   Is the type of building appropriate for the business?

3.   How large is the potential trade area for the business? Will people travel to their store?

4.   Will adjacent businesses complement or compete with their business?

5.   Will the natural traffic flow complement their business?

6.   What types of leasehold improvements and other one-time costs will be needed?

7.   In detail, describe the ideal location you would choose for this business, and be sure to include the socio-demographics of the target market.

CHAPTER CLOSING CASE ▶▶

Big-Box or Specialty Shop?

Lance Fried is an electrical engineer who loves to design new products. He and a buddy were watching surfers and scenery at the beach near his home in Del Mar, California, when the buddy dropped his 20 Gig iPod into a cooler full of water and ice. The trashed iPod gave Fried an idea—to make an MP3 player that would work underwater.

Fried spent months tinkering with his invention, a waterproof MP3 player designed specifically for athletes who need tunes while surfing, swimming, waterskiing, or snowboarding. Like most entrepreneurs, Fried had invested his personal savings but he had also somehow convinced half a dozen friends to work for him for free (pretty smooth).

By August 2004, Fried finished a working prototype and created his company called Freestyle Audio. The player was lightweight (40 grams), with a 40-hour battery, and lots of memory (for 2004). The headphones wrapped tightly around ears, and all of it was waterproofed using a proprietary technology. He projected to sell the units for $180.

It was then that Fried brought Greg Houlgate into the story. Houlgate was a friend who served on Freestyle's board and had worked as a sales strategist for a number of large sporting goods companies, including Callaway Golf. Houlgate showed the player to some of his contacts in the big-box retail world. "I've never had such a quick and positive response on any consumer electronics," he says.

Fried was amazed when Houlgate told him that major retailers—including Best Buy and Bass Pro Sporting Goods—wanted to put his gadget on their shelves side-by-side with players by giants like Apple and Sony. Fried knew that such a deal with just a single big chain could be worth an instant million dollars in revenue.

But the idea also scared Fried. Distribution via mass retailers had never been part of his San Diego start-up's plan. Instead, the idea always had been to start small, selling through specialty shops. A big-box strategy meant a whole new business plan—one that would involve mass production and a potentially huge up-front investment. Oh yeah, and retailers wanted the players in time for the holiday shopping season, which was just four months away.

How, or should, Freestyle capitalize on that interest? Fried quickly convened a meeting of his three-man board at Jimmy O's, a local ocean-view hangout. Houlgate presented the good news to the third partner, Mike Brower. "Mass distribution gets your name out fast and gives you an instant hit," Houlgate said. "Your vendors really start to take you seriously." That wasn't the only advantage. With mainstream retailers on board, it would be easier to attract investors. That part appealed to Fried, who was ready for money to come into rather than out of his own bank account.

But Brower, CFO of the popular sunglasses company Spy Optic, was not jumping on board. His experience working at sporting goods companies had always been to start small, get an influential niche group to love you, and go for bigger distribution deals only after that groundwork had been laid. How would Freestyle get its key customer groups—surfers and snowboarders—into big, unhip retail outlets like Best Buy and Bass Pro? And what would Freestyle have to give for the privilege of a good position on big-box shelves? "They'll make you a commodity if you don't know how to negotiate, asking for discounts that just kill your margins," Brower said.

Ramping up production would be no small feat in itself. It would require a significant capital investment. How could Freestyle find that kind of money? Would the company's manufacturing partners be able to maintain quality if orders suddenly spiked? How would the company get more attention than competing MP3 player brands manufactured by corporate giants and backed by multimillion-dollar marketing campaigns?

Fried had to make a huge decision—fast. The action sports retail trade show—where independent retailers go to test and order new gear to sell at their surf, dive, skate, and snowboard shops for the holiday season—was just weeks away. Making a big splash at the show had always been part of Freestyle's plan. If Fried signed on for a big-box deal, that plan would have to change.

Questions

1. Can Fried really say "no" to the big-box retailers? Why or why not?

2. What do you think Fried should do?

Sources: Lora Kolodny, "Case Study," *Inc.*, April 2005, 44–45; Brandi Stewart, "As Easy as MP3," *Fortune Small Business*, September 2007, 96; Darren Dahl, "Outside the Big Box," *Inc.*, April 2007, 54; Reed Albergotti, "For the Half Pipe," *Wall Street Journal*, December 22, 2007, W7.

## CHAPTER 13

SMALL BUSINESS MARKETING

Price and Promotion

©iStockphoto.com/martin-dm

When you hear the term "marketing influencer" do you immediately think King of Snapchat, DJ Khaled? Celebrities have huge online influence, but they are probably not right for small businesses (think $$$). What your small business actually needs are micro-influencers (those with fewer than 30,000 followers) because they actually drive 60 percent more target market engagement.

Marketing influencers have power because there is so much information about products online that consumers are afraid of misinformation and have lost much trust in other forms of advertising to the point of using ad blockers. Successful influencers have developed trust with specific groups of people in specific product categories. Over 88 percent of consumers trust online peer reviews more than traditional advertising. Thirty percent of consumers reported in a recent survey that they were more likely to purchase a product promoted by a noncelebrity blogger and 40 percent of Twitter users have made a purchase because of a Tweet from an influencer.

If you can find micro-influencers who are tapped directly into your target market, they are seven times more effective than celebrity influencers. But how do you know how much you should be spending for this influence? There are currently no universal pricing standards. Part of what you pay for depends on

- **Quality of content and photos:** Do shots come from a phone or DSLR to create an amateur or professional look?

- **Exclusivity:** Is the influencer working strictly for you or can she post for direct competitors at the same time?

- **Social reach:** How many followers does the influencer have across all platforms?

- **Social engagement:** How many interactions do the influencer's posts generate in terms of "likes," comments, and so on?

- **Usage rights:** Can your small business repurpose the influencer's posts for your own campaigns and social media?

Pricing by each individual post from an influencer is called a la carte. Currently as close as there is to an industry standard is one used by Instagram, with a formula of $100 for every 10,000 followers. About 84 percent of micro-influencers charge less than $250 for one branded Instagram post. Price bundling is the other common approach to paying for a group of posts. For example, a package of one blog post and two social posts will cost you between $200 and $1,500 (depending on the details, described in the bullet points above) with standard usage and no exclusivity, or $400 to $4,000 with extended usage rights and exclusivity.

Micro-influencer marketing provides a great new tool for both small business promotion and pricing practices. Let's look at some others.

Sources: Aj Agrawal, "What Startup Entrepreneurs Need to Know About the Influencer Marketing Landscape," *Entrepreneur*, April 6, 2018, www.entrepreneur.com/article/311535; Molly St. Louis, "Influencer Marketing Takes an Important Twist in 2018," *Inc.*, March 22, 2018, www.inc.com; Morgan Kaye, "How to Set the Right Price for Your Next Influencer Marketing Campaign," *Entrepreneur*, October 31, 2017, www.entrepreneur.com/article/303905.

Concept Module 13.1: The Economics of Pricing

- **LO 13.1: Identify the three main considerations in setting a price for a product.**

In the previous chapters, we discussed two components of marketing: product development and location (place). In this chapter, we will investigate the third and fourth components of the

Master the content at
edge.sagepub.com/ Hatten7e
$SAGE edge

marketing mix: price and promotion (completing the Four P's). We will consider why price is one of the most flexible components of a business's marketing mix, factors that must be considered in setting prices, strategies related to pricing, the use of credit in buying and selling, and ways to use the various media in communicating with your customers.

We deal with prices every day. The dollars you exchanged for a cup of coffee on the way to class, the tuition you paid for the semester, and the money you earn from a job all represent a form of price for goods and services.

Price is the amount of money charged for a product. It represents what the consumer considers the *value* of the product to be worth to them. The value of a product depends on the benefits received compared with the monetary cost. People actually buy benefits—they buy what a product will do for them. If consumers bought on price alone, then no Audi convertibles, Chanel handbags, or Godiva chocolates would ever be sold, because less expensive substitutes exist. People buy premium products like these because they perceive them to have higher benefits and increased quality that delivers value despite the higher cost. Typical consumers do not want the *cheapest* product available—they want the *best* product for the most reasonable price.

Price differs from the other three components of the marketing mix in that the product, place, and promotion factors all add value to the customer and costs to your business. Pricing lets you recover those costs. Although the "right" price is actually more of a range between what the market will bear and what the product costs, many elements enter into the pricing decision. For example, the image of your business or product influences the price you can charge.

Even though the pricing decision is critical to the success of a business, many small business owners make pricing decisions poorly. Total reliance on "gut feeling" is inappropriate, but so is complete reliance on accounting costs that ignore what is happening in the marketplace—what the competition is doing and what customers demand.

Three important economic factors are involved in how much you can charge for your products: competition, customer demand, and costs. Let's take a closer look at how each of these forces can affect your small business.

Competition

Your competitors will play a big part in determining the success of your pricing strategy. The number of competitors and their proximity to your business influence what you can charge for your products, because the competition represents substitute choices to your customers. The more direct competition your business faces, the less control you have over your prices. To survive in an industry dominated by giants, don't compete directly—differentiate. Offer your customers value—the best quality, service, and selection for their money.

> "To survive in an industry dominated by giants, don't compete directly—differentiate. Offer your customers value—the best quality, service, and selection for their money."

So why will customers come to your store, brand, or product as opposed to the competition? What sets your product apart? The following five areas are good places to start when thinking about what differentiates your product from the competition:

1. *Price*. While you may not be able to compete with the big-box stores, you do need to be sensitive to the economic climate. During a recession, consumers are much more careful about how they spend their scarce dollars. What is your competition doing in this arena? What can you do? Maybe you can bundle products, provide quantity discounts, provide frequent shopper rewards, and so forth.

2. *Added value*. How does your product or service add value to the customer? Is your product unique? Do you provide after-sale consultations? Can you provide one-stop shopping for more than one need? Does your price reflect this added value? Are you directly tying the added value to your price?

3. *Convenience.* How convenient are your location and your shopping hours for your customers? If your usual customer is a working mom, then you may need to open earlier in the morning so they can stop by after they have dropped off their children at school and before they go to work, or maybe open two evenings a week and the weekends. Check out the lifestyles of your customers and add convenience for them in the shopping process. Convenience is something for which customers will pay.

4. *Trust.* Do you have a family business that has been around for 50 years? If so, then advertise that fact. This is one area where you may be able to beat Walmart and other big box stores, if you have been in the community longer. Local testimonials that attest to not only the quality of the product but also the service that accompanies that product can be useful. Your pricing strategy should then incorporate this strategy. The customer will pay more because your business will be around to take care of them long after the product sale.

5. *Community member.* Do you participate in your local community? Maybe you sit on the school assessment committee or plant flowers at the local botanical garden. Demonstrate that you are very much a part of the community and plan to be so for a long time, and that you are giving back to the community. Again customers may be willing to pay more for a product when they know you are being a good steward in your community.

These are all factors that can help you show your customers how your product or service is different from the competition and how your price reflects these distinctions. Going back to our definition—customers buy benefits. Make sure the benefits your business provides are greater than the benefits the competition provides. Include price in this process but be aware that lower prices are not the only factor.[1]

Another factor in evaluating the competition can be the proximity of your competition. The closer the competition is geographically, the more influence it will have on your pricing. For example, if two service stations located across the street from each other had a price difference of 10 cents per gallon of gasoline, to which one would customers go? Conversely, the same price difference between stations located several miles apart may not have as dramatic an impact. Price competition presents a more difficult challenge for all businesses today because customers have more access to information about you and your competitors than you had about your own business even five years ago.[2]

The type of products sold will also have an impact on price competition. If you run a movie theater, then other theaters are not your only competition. In reality, your rivals include Netflix, athletic events, and even the opera. Don't think of yourself as being in the movie business—think of being in the entertainment business, because you are competing for entertainment dollars.

Therefore, you should monitor not only what other theaters are charging, but also what indirect, or alternative, entertainment services charge.

Today more small businesses are facing stiff competition from large competitors like Walmart and Amazon. Both of these retail giants have massive resource advantages, so no wonder small businesses feel intimidated. Can your small business compete? Of course you can. Probably not on price for identical items—they have economy-of-scale advantages from mass purchasing and distribution that can knock a small business out of a head-to-head price war, but there are other areas where small businesses excel, including the ones we discussed earlier: added value, being seen as a good community citizen, flexibility, superior product selection, and exceptional service, to name a few.

Research shows that prices drop anywhere from 1 to 3 percent when Walmart enters an area and sales can drop anywhere from 5 to 13 percent, depending on the business. In one study, however, sales in eating establishments and home furnishing stores actually increased by 2 to 3 percent when Walmart came to town. The stores most negatively impacted by Walmart were mass-merchandising stores. So how do you compete?

Small businesses have to get laser focused on their target market to compete against major competitors, regardless of whether they are online or brick and mortar.[3] Don't carry the same product lines as Walmart. Walmart focuses on national mid-tier, large-market-share products, and due to Walmart's price discounts you may not be able to compete against these brands. However, you can compete when it comes to top-tier or lower-tier brands. Most small businesses have tightly defined their market niche, and by offering superior products and service, for example, may still compete quite successfully. Identify your competitive advantage and then repeatedly tell your story—if a competitor's product is not totally safe or yours is eco-friendly, tell your customers! Amazon (or Walmart online) customers do not get instant gratification from purchasing online; Walmart customers have to, well, go to Walmart. If your small business offers awesome customer service (from immediate response to email and social media posts to handwritten thank-you cards), then customers have a reason to buy from you.

Small business survival depends on differentiation, not competing directly on price, especially against giant competitors.

Customer Demand

The second economic factor that affects the price you can charge for your products is *demand*—how much of your product do people want and what price are they willing to pay. Ordinarily, as price goes up, people buy less of a product, and as price goes down, people are willing to buy more of a product, an inverse relationship. The **demand curve** graphically demonstrates this relationship between price and quantity demanded, and since the relationship is inverse, the demand curve has a downward slope. See Figure 13.1.

Price elasticity is an important factor to take into consideration when discussing pricing. It determines the impact a change of price will have on the quantity of the product you will sell. For some products, like soda pop, if the price goes down (for example, when the product goes on sale), the consumer will buy considerably more of the product. On the other hand, milk is a product that we consume about the same quantity of regardless of the price increasing or decreasing. Price elasticity looks at this relationship between a change in price and the impact on quantity demanded. So if a small business owner has a product that is price sensitive or is elastic in economic terms, if the price is lowered, the consumer will buy more of the product, all other variables held constant. With an inelastic product, though, the price should not be lowered, or put on sale, since the consumer will not buy much more of the product even if it is cheaper. You could lose money putting an inelastic product on sale, all other variables being held constant.

If sales rise or fall more than prices rise or fall in percentage terms, demand for your product is price elastic. For example, assume the demand for your computer software is elastic (see Figure 13.1 again). If you drop your price by 5 percent, you would expect sales to increase by

demand curve
The number of units of a product that people would be willing to purchase at different price levels.

THE DANGER WITH DISCOUNTS

Many small business owners make the mistake of assuming that in a down economy, the only answer to decreasing sales is to lower price. Not a good idea. Customers quickly become conditioned to discounts, postponing purchases because they expect you to run yet another sale. Your price should be based upon your pricing strategy, and as such, any change in pricing should be made in order to facilitate accomplishing that strategy, not in response to the macro-economy. Price shoppers have zero brand loyalty.

Remember, customers buy benefits. Your job becomes, more than ever, to demonstrate to the consumer why they should be willing to pay the price you are asking for those benefits. Build your presentations around the benefits, not the price. A customer price objection just means that the customer does not yet understand how the benefits of the product will outweigh the cost. As the business owner, it is your job to show them, not just tell them, how the product meets and exceeds their needs.

Another mistake made is to cut store hours and lay off good employees. If your store is not open, you cannot sell. Make sure you carefully evaluate the cost of your labor against potential sales. How many sales do you need in order to pay for that employee being in the store one more hour? And unless you plan to close your doors, hang on to your best employees, remembering that there is more than money you can use to persuade good employees to stay.

A Pea in The Pod sells high-end clothing for women who are pregnant. Rather than joining the price-slashing herd of stores on Black Friday (the big shopping day after Thanksgiving), they do not even acknowledge it—no flashing signs, no piles of merchandise, no special promotions. A Pea in The Pod offers merchandise so specific and so valuable to its target market that it does not have to compete on price discounts.

A reason why you offer price discounts is your hope of selling enough additional units to offset the margin you lose because of the lower price. So you have to know how many units you need to sell to hit your breakeven point. See breakeven (B/E) analysis later in this chapter and augment with this formula on price discounting:

$$\text{B/E additional units} = \frac{\text{Units sold}\left(\text{old}\right) \times \left[\begin{array}{c}\text{Price}\left(\text{old}\right) - \\ \text{Price}\left(\text{discount}\right)\end{array}\right]}{\text{Price}\left(\text{discount}\right) - \text{Cost of goods sold}}$$

Any additional units sold above the breakeven volume will generate incremental profit.

If you do offer discounts, do so only for first-time buyers or for one week only. Or better yet, offer free delivery or after-sale consultations, or a discount on their next trip to see you. Rather than lower your price, which can also then damage your product perception, find other ways to lower the cost to the consumer, or add more value for the same price and make sure your customer recognizes the value you are adding. Always treat your customers well. Increasing attention paid to customers and increased attention to detail may not cost you anything but may return large rewards to you. Remember, without customers your business fails, regardless of the price you are charging.

Sources: Jessica Stillman, "Discounts Make You Dumb," *Inc.*, December 7, 2017, www.inc.com; Margo Aaron, "This Is What Happens When You Don't Discount Over the Holidays," *Inc.*, December 16, 2017, www.inc.com; Doug and Polly White, "Understanding the Math Behind Discounts," *Entrepreneur*, February 14, 2017, www.entrepreneur.com/article/289089.

---

more than 5 percent. Restaurant usage, personal boats, and fine china all tend to have elastic demand. Price elasticity also changes; products and market segments vary in the degree of elasticity depending on how consumers perceive their need for the product at that point in time.

If sales rise or fall less than prices rise or fall in percentage terms, demand for your product is price inelastic. You would expect the change in demand to be small after a change in your price (refer once more to Figure 13.1). Again using the milk example, if the price of milk increases by 10 percent, you would expect the demand for that product to change by less than 10 percent. After all, what else can you put on your morning cereal? Health care is price inelastic (at least without government intervention). Both staple necessities and luxury goods tend to have inelastic demand. If you absolutely have to have a product or service, you are less sensitive to price. If a product is truly a luxury, price becomes less of a concern. When demand for a product is inelastic, as with prescription drugs, a change in price will have little effect on the quantity you demand.

Demand Curves

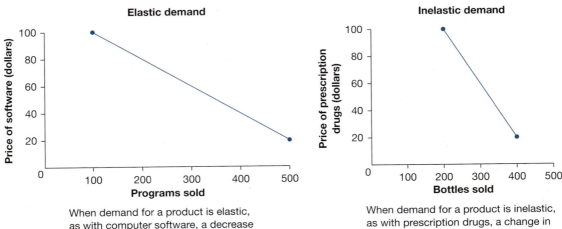

Elastic demand

Price of software (dollars) / Programs sold

When demand for a product is elastic, as with computer software, a decrease in price will cause an increase in demand.

Inelastic demand

Price of prescription drugs (dollars) / Bottles sold

When demand for a product is inelastic, as with prescription drugs, a change in price will have little effect on the quantity demanded.

Three factors influence the **price elasticity of demand** for a product:

1. *Availability of product substitutes.* The more alternatives that exist, the more price elastic a product tends to be. If the price of orange juice increases, you can always have apple juice, pomegranate juice, or even tea, making it elastic.

2. *Necessity of the product.* Necessary and luxury goods both tend to be price inelastic.

3. *The share of the purchase to the consumer's total budget.* Salt and toothpicks are inelastic since they represent such a small percentage compared to your overall budget.

The theory of the elasticity of demand is important for small business owners to understand in setting prices. How easily your customers can do without your product or how readily they can use something else in its place will affect what you can charge. Price elasticity can also let you know whether or not putting your product on sale will increase total revenue. Market research can provide price-sensitivity information about your product and should be evaluated for your product and services.

Costs

price elasticity of demand
The percentage change in quantity demanded for a product in response to a 1 percent change in price.

Earlier we stated that the "right" price is actually a range of possible prices. What your competition charges and what consumers are willing to pay set the ceiling for your price range. Your costs establish the floor for your price range. If you cannot cover your costs and make a profit, you will not stay in business.

Your total costs fall into two general categories: fixed costs and variable costs.

Total costs = Fixed costs + Variable costs

fixed costs
Costs that do not change with the number of sales made.

Fixed costs remain constant no matter how many goods you sell. In the short run, your fixed costs are the same whether you sell a million units or none at all. Costs such as rent, property taxes, and utilities are fixed. **Variable costs**, in contrast, rise and fall in direct proportion to sales. Sales commissions, materials, and labor tend to be variable costs.

variable costs
Costs that change in direct proportion to sales.

PRICING STRATEGY

Developing an effective pricing strategy can be tough. Without one, however, a small business will be fighting for survival. Read through the following two examples and answer the questions at the end.

Shake Smart

Kevin Gelfand and Martin Reiman cofounded their on-the-go healthy food start-up, Shake Smart, as a "functional nutrition" company targeting college students. They became friends as pledge brothers at San Diego State University. Their affordable, quick, and fresh options include customized protein shakes, acai bowls, and egg-white breakfast wraps. Of course, there are vegan, vegetarian, and gluten-free options. The pair wants to differentiate their small business by using healthy ingredients, innovative technology to keep overhead down, and fast service while still maintaining affordable prices for cash-strapped college students.

Drone MVP

Drones are hot—there were over 80 must-watch drone start-ups in 2018 alone. This level of competition overwhelms many people. Harrison Sheingberg and Louis Van Hove, who met at the University of Southern California, found the challenge to be fun. Rather than building drone hardware, Drone MVP is a platform that allows clients who need drone video footage to connect with drone pilots. Each has a problem Drone MVP solves: Clients have a hard time finding a pilot with specific skills at a reasonable price, while drone pilots have difficulty advertising their services to the right clients.

Questions

1. Working in teams of no more than three, choose one of the two examples to work on. Develop an outline for a comprehensive marketing strategy for the company and its product. Be specific in defining the product, place, price, and promotion aspects.

2. Once your team has developed its marketing strategy, find another team in the class that has worked on the same example. Take turns presenting your information to each other.

Sources: Emily Canal, "How Two Frat Brothers Turned Their College Smoothie Startup Into a $3.6 Million Company," *Inc.*, April 19, 2018, www.inc.com; Nathan Resnick, "6 of Today's Best Student-Run Startups," *Entrepreneur*, November 8, 2017, www.entrepreneur.com/slideshow/304118.

Take care of falling into the *capacity trap*—that is, accepting a lower price than usual because you have unused capacity. Unused capacity can take the form of an empty warehouse, a truck that is sitting idle, or a machine that is used only occasionally. When the opportunity arises to sell that capacity at a reduced rate, few people would refuse. They think about the money to be made on something that would otherwise go to waste but ignore the problems they create by charging significantly less than the service is worth. Along the way, they ignore the *cost of capital*; we invest in items like trucks and warehouses to make more money from them than if we had bought something else. There are also *opportunity costs*; low-margin sales tend to crowd out high-margin sales. For example, if business is slow in your small-job shop and you take on work at half your normal rate to avoid your machinery sitting idle, what happens when a full-pay job comes along? You don't have time to tackle it. Finally, do you think your existing customers won't find out that new customers are paying less than they are or have been for the same product or service? They will find out—and they will not be amused; they may feel betrayed. Certainly, they will demand the same discount. Bottom line: Don't erode your margins.[4]

> "Bottom line: Don't erode your margins."

Concept Check Questions

1. What can happen if the price of a product does not fit with the three other P's of the marketing mix?

2. Should a small business owner's judgment be used to determine prices if so many mathematical techniques have been developed for that purpose?

Concept Module 13.2: Breakeven Analysis

- **LO 13.2: Explain what breakeven analysis is and why it is important for pricing in a small business.**

By using the three cost figures discussed earlier (total fixed costs, unit price, and average variable cost) in a breakeven analysis, you can find the volume of sales you will need to cover your total costs. Your **breakeven point (BEP)** in sales volume is the point at which your total revenue equals total costs. In other words, how much of your product or service do you have to sell in order to cover all your costs? At breakeven, you are not making a profit. However, you are able to pay both your fixed and variable costs. So if your breakeven point is 35 CDs, that number means you must sell 35 CDs just to be able to pay your costs.

Figure 13.2 is an example of a BEP graph. Notice that the fixed-costs line runs horizontally because fixed costs don't change with sales volume. Fixed costs have to be paid regardless of the amount of product sold. Fixed costs are fixed—they do not change. The total-costs line begins where the fixed-costs line meets the *y-axis* of the graph, showing that even if you have sold nothing, you still have costs: your fixed costs. Total costs rise from that point at an angle, as variable costs and sales increase. The area between the total-costs line and the fixed-costs line represents your variable costs. The revenue line represents the number of units you will sell at any given price level—information you can derive from your demand curve. The point at which the revenue line meets the total-costs line is your breakeven point. The area above the BEP between the revenue and total-costs lines shows profit. The area below the BEP between the revenue and total-costs lines represents loss.

The slope and shape of the revenue line for your business will vary depending on your customer demand. The information needed to draw this line can come either from sales history or, if hard data are not available, from your personal best "guesstimate" of how much people will buy. You can also plot other revenue lines based on different selling prices. The revenue line in Figure 13.2 is based on product sales. Let's use the example of compact discs (CDs) selling for $13 each. You can also find your BEP for units with the following formula:

▼ **FIGURE 13.2**

Breakeven Analysis

When the price of a compact disk is $13, the breakeven point (BEP) would be reached when 50 CDs are sold and $650 of revenue are generated.

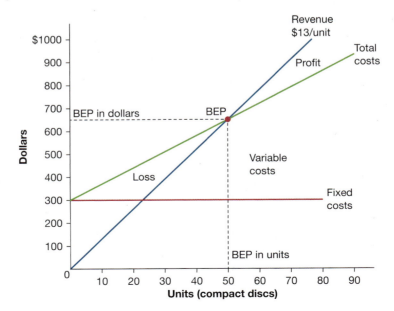

$$\text{BEP (units)} = \frac{\text{Total fixed costs}}{\text{Unit price} - \text{Average variable cost}}$$

where average variable cost equals total variable cost divided by quantity.

Using the data from Figure 13.2, we could calculate the BEP in units for a new CD of Christmas songs from Hatten and His Yodeling Goats. Total fixed costs to produce this musical masterpiece are $300. Variable costs run $7 per unit. Charging $13 per CD, we would have to sell 50 CDs to break even on the venture. (Would 50 people pay $13 to hear yodeling goats, or should Hatten keep his day job?)

$$\text{BEP (units)} = \frac{300}{13 - 7} = 50$$

If 50 people will not buy this CD, not only should Hatten keep his day job, he will also have to pay the $300 out of his own pocket since the fixed costs must be paid, even if he does go back to his day job. Fixed costs deserve careful consideration since even if you shut the doors to your business, you will likely still be paying the fixed costs incurred.

To calculate the BEP point in dollars, we need to find the average variable cost of our product. This is done by taking the total variable costs ($350) and dividing by the quantity (50). The following formula is used to calculate the BEP in dollars:

$$\text{BEP (units)} = \frac{\text{Total fixed costs}}{1 - \dfrac{\text{Average variable costs}}{\text{Unit price}}}$$

For our struggling musician's CD, we would find that at $13 per CD, the BEP would be $650.

$$\text{BEP (dollars)} = \frac{300}{1 - \dfrac{7}{3}} = 650$$

Again, unless Hatten feels certain he can sell $650 dollars worth of CDs to cover the fixed costs, he might want to explore another business venture.

What would happen to our BEP in dollars and our BEP in units if we changed the selling price to $20 each or $11 each? At $20 per CD, we would break even at only $400 in sales. At $11 per CD, we would break even at $880. Figure 13.3 illustrates what happens at different price levels.

Breakeven analysis is a useful tool in giving you a guideline for price setting. It can help you see how different volume levels will affect costs and profits. It can also help you to determine the amount of fixed costs you are willing to incur for your business. Let's say you want to open a small lawn-mowing service. You want to purchase a brand-new truck, trailer, and riding lawn mower. Regardless of whether you mow 1 lawn or 50 a day, these costs will have to be paid. Using breakeven analysis, you determine that in order to cover your costs, you must mow 50 lawns a day. Now you need to determine if there are 50 lawns to mow and whether you can logistically mow that many every day. If you cannot, then you have some options, like buying a used truck, trailer, and mower in order to reduce the fixed costs. Or you may realize, with the competition available both in providing the service and the price you can charge, a lawn-mowing business is not feasible. Breakeven analysis can be a quick initial check on the financial viability of your business idea.

How Price Changes Affect the Breakeven Point

When the price of a compact disk is changed to $11 or $20, the breakeven point also changes.

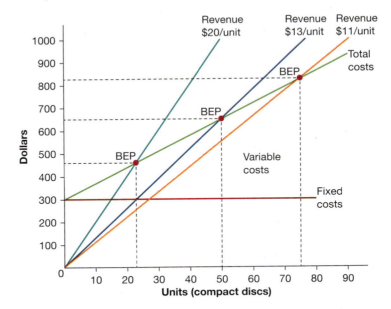

Another use for breakeven analysis is to tell you how many units you need to sell to earn your desired return. If Hatten and His Yodeling Goats wanted a return of $1,000, how many units would need to be sold?

$$\text{Target return} = \frac{\text{Total fixed} + \text{Desired profit}}{\text{Unit price} - \text{Average variable cost}}$$

$$\$1,000\,\text{return} = \frac{300 + 1,000}{13 - 7} = 217$$

When the sales price is $13 per CD, 217 CDs would have to be sold to generate a return of $1,000. Again, based upon your marketing research, what is the likelihood of that many CDs being sold? So now you have options. You can cut your fixed costs, raise your price, or be willing to accept less than the $1,000 return.[5]

Concept Check Questions

1. When would a small business owner be interested in using breakeven analysis?

2. A small business owner wants to use breakeven analysis but has trouble deciding which expenses are fixed and which are variable. What should she do next?

Concept Module 13.3: Price-Setting Techniques

- **LO 13.3: Present examples of customer-oriented and internal-oriented pricing.**

After taking competition, consumer demand, and your costs into consideration, you have made a start toward establishing your "right" price. You have a feel for what the price floor and price ceiling might be, but the price you finally choose will depend on the objectives and strategies you choose to pursue—what you are trying to accomplish in your business.

While one of the most difficult decisions you will make as a small business owner is the price you charge for your product, it is also one of the most critical decisions in the success of your business. Consider the following points when looking at product pricing.

The reason you are in business is to make money, which means you have to sell enough product at a high enough price to more than cover costs. Pricing your product too high can take you out of a market because consumers will not pay that much for your product or your competition will lower their prices. However, pricing your product too low can also cause problems since all costs, both fixed and variable, may not be covered. Consumers can also see low prices as an indication of low quality, to be discussed shortly.

How much will your customers pay? What is the income of your target market? Where does your product fit into their budget? What is your competition doing to lure your customers away?

Where is the market for your product going? Will sales increase? Are substitutes available? What is the likelihood other competitors will show up? Is it a fad item that won't be around long? What is your goal in pricing? Are you trying to gain market share? Are you conveying a quality product? How much product are you trying to sell? All of these questions tie back into what your pricing goal is.[6]

You have surely heard the old joke about the guy who buys 100 watermelons for $100 and sells them in bunches of 10 for $10. When asked how he expects to make money, he replies, "I'll make it up in volume." Okay, so it's not that funny, but you would be amazed how many people think they can grow their businesses merely by pricing their products cheaper than the competition. They assume that low prices will generate enough sales to make up for lower margins.

> "The reason you are in business is to make money, which means you have to sell enough product at a high enough price to more than cover costs."

Setting your prices too low is a dangerous trap. Take a hypothetical example: You think that some product is too expensive, so you decide to go into business selling that item for less than your competitors. If you sell for less, you have lower profit margins. Lower profit margins, in turn, mean less cash flow. Will you have an adequate cushion if an expense increases? After all, rents go up, utilities raise their rates, and so on. With lower profit margins, you'd need to cut costs—but where? Will you reduce wages and benefits? If so, will you be able to hire and retain good employees? Will you cut marketing costs? Will customers keep coming in the door, and, if they do, what kind of customers will they be? Low-price shoppers are the most fickle and most likely to switch to the next company that can offer your product for five cents less. Remember, we discussed that customers buy benefits. You can add value by more than just lowering price. Lowering your price may increase sales in the short run, but it's not a successful formula for growing in the long run. Customers want value, so when the value of your product exceeds the value of their money, they will buy.

As you see, price can't be everything—but you can't ignore it, either. Instead, you need a bona fide pricing strategy. Pricing strategies fall into two broad categories: customer oriented and internal oriented.

Customer-Oriented Pricing Strategies

Customer-oriented pricing strategies focus on target markets and factors that affect the demand for products. Such strategies include penetration, skimming, and psychological pricing. Both penetration and skimming strategies are based on knowing price elasticity, discussed earlier in this chapter. With an inelastic product, since there are not usually many substitutes, a skimming strategy can be used, setting prices higher. Higher prices can also be used purposefully to bring the customer's attention to specific product advantages. For elastic products that are much more price sensitive, penetration pricing may be a more effective strategy since even a small decrease in price can increase the demand for the product.[7]

Suppose you have the following pricing objectives:

- Increase sales.
- Increase traffic in your store.
- Discourage competitors from entering your market.

To accomplish these objectives and gain rapid market share, **penetration pricing** is the most appropriate strategy. Penetration pricing entails setting prices below what you might expect to encourage customers to initially try your product. This strategy is designed to keep competition from entering the market for your product. Although you make less profit on each unit, the trade-off is to remove the incentive for competition to enter, thereby, it is hoped, helping you build a long-term position in the market.

Suppose that you have a different set of pricing objectives:

- Maximize short- or long-run profit.
- Recover product development costs quickly.

If these are your objectives and you have a truly unique product, a strategy of **price skimming** may be appropriate. Price skimming involves setting your price high when you believe that customers are relatively price insensitive or when there is little competition for consumers to compare prices against. Skimming helps recover high development costs, so businesses with new-to-the-world inventions often use this strategy. It can also encourage consumers to look at your product and see what features make your product different and allow you to charge a higher price. When used purposefully as a strategy, skimming can arouse curiosity about your product and cause consumers to research it and discover its added benefits. Home electronics, for example, are often introduced using a skimming strategy. Think of the price declines in cell phones and headphones. These products usually have high development costs, but their unit costs fall as production increases. Of course, consumers have to be willing to pay a premium to be one of the first to own these new products. Skimming is not a long-term strategy. Eventually competition forces prices down.

Finally, suppose you have these pricing objectives:

- Stabilize market prices.
- Establish your company's position in the market.
- Build an image for your business or product.
- Develop a reputation for being fair with suppliers and customers.

To accomplish these objectives, you may employ one of the **psychological pricing** strategies, which aim to influence the consumer's reaction to prices of products. Such strategies include prestige pricing, odd pricing, and reference pricing.

People often equate quality with price, a belief that has led to a practice called **prestige pricing**. Prestige pricing is especially effective with goods whose quality is difficult to determine by inspection or for products that consumers have little solid information about. Products as diverse as jewelry, perfume, beer, and smoke detectors, or the services of law firms, can all be prestige priced.

In an experiment at Harvard Business School, graduate students were given two products, organic lettuce and free-trade coffee. When these two products were priced at an 80 percent premium, the graduate students were able to recall twice as much information about the products

penetration pricing
Setting the price of a new product lower than expected to gain fast market share.

price skimming
Setting the price of a new product higher than expected to recover development costs.

psychological pricing
Setting the price of a product in a way that will alter its perception by customers.

prestige pricing
Psychological pricing strategy used with goods whose quality is difficult to determine by inspection or for products about which consumers have little solid information.

and reasons/justifications why 80 percent more could be charged for those products. The students were also much more passionate about and willing to spend more dollars for these products. When products were then priced 10 percent higher or over 100 percent higher, the students did not spend time exploring the product benefits and simply chose their usual product. Pricing can be raised as long as it is neither too high nor too low.[8]

We are more likely to see goods priced at $4.98, $17.89, or $49.95 than at $5.00, $18.00, or $50.00—this is **odd pricing**. Research has yet to prove a positive effect of odd pricing, but proponents believe that consumers see $99.99 as a better deal than $100.00. Sales of some products seem to benefit from *even pricing* if you are trying to convey the image of quality. For example, pricing a diamond ring at $18,000 gives the appearance of being above squabbling over loose change.

Reference pricing is common in retail goods for which consumers have an idea of what the price "should be" and have a "usual" price for that item in mind. As discussed already, a product's price is supported by the value it generates for the customer; with reference pricing, however, the price can be changed without affecting the value. For example, a 12-pack of Coca-Cola is a commodity well recognized by most shoppers, who have a good idea of what a package of 12 cans of Coke is worth. If the price is dropped, customers are attracted to the product; conversely, if it is raised above that reference point, they are repelled.

If your customers are price sensitive to comparison prices of competing items, you may choose to use **price lining**. An example of price lining would be a men's clothing store that has ties at three different price points, such as $24.95, $33.95, and $44.95.

Markup. The amount added to the cost of a product in setting the final price. It can be based on selling price or on cost.

The **decoy effect** is based on price comparison to make a chosen product look more desirable. For example, if there are two choices of popcorn sizes at the concession stand at a movie theater, small for $3.00 and large for $7.00 most people will buy the small because they think they really don't need a large. But add a medium for $6.50 and the large looks like the best deal since it's just 50 cents more.[9]

For another example of the decoy effect, consider bottles of wine. Most people are not true experts in wine and base much of their purchase decision on price. Those people almost without fail, gravitate to the middle of the price range for their selected type of wine. The thought is to avoid the poor quality of the cheapest choice and the needless extravagance of the most expensive labels. Have you ever noticed a bottle of surprisingly expensive wine at a neighborhood store? If the cheapest bottles at that store are $3 and the highest priced bottle is $40, then people gravitate to the $10 to $12 bottles. But add a decoy $200 bottle and $20 to $25 bottles seem much more reasonable. The neighborhood store may never sell that $200 bottle of wine, but its existence increases the average sale price.

> "The neighborhood store may never sell that $200 bottle of wine, but its existence increases the average sale price."

Internal-Oriented Pricing Strategies

Pricing strategies that are internal oriented are based on your business's financial needs and costs rather than on the needs or wants of your target markets. If you use these strategies, make sure you don't price your products out of the marketplace. Remember that consumers don't care what your costs are; they care only about the value they receive. Internal-oriented strategies include cost-plus pricing and target-return pricing.

Cost-Plus Pricing

Probably the most common form of pricing is adding a specified percentage, a fixed fee, or **markup**, to the cost of the item. Although this type of pricing, called *cost-plus pricing*, has

---

odd pricing
Psychological pricing strategy in which goods are priced at, say, $9.99 rather than $10.00 in the belief that the price will seem lower than it really is.

reference pricing
Psychological pricing strategy common in retailing goods for which consumers have an idea of what the price "should be."

price lining
Grouping product prices into ranges, such as low-, medium-, and high-priced items.

decoy effect
A pricing technique that makes a specific product appear more desirable by adding a product and price that is slightly less attractive.

markup
The amount added to the cost of a product in setting the final price. It can be based on selling price or on cost.

ANCHORS, BUMPS, AND CHARMS

▼ FIGURE 13.4

Anchoring

Draw something similar to the above. Make the price tag hang off the sleeve. Change the tie color to blue and the suit color to gray.

Pricing our products—few areas of business involve so much science, yet so much art. Pricing involves rationality (ask an economics professor), costing, and predictability, with equal amounts of irrationality, emotion, and perception. Pricing involves anchors, bumps, and charms.

What is the best way to sell a $1,000 suit? Put it next to a $10,000 suit. Why? Because of a cognitive bias called *anchoring*, which is a tendency to heavily rely on the first piece of information we receive when facing a decision. If we see a suit priced at $100, then look at one priced at $1,000, the latter seems too expensive. The "anchor" for a price perception is found in the initial expectation.

Bumps give people an idea of quality grade. Think about equipment, styling, performance, economy, and features you would expect when looking at a new car that cost about $25,000. How would your expectations in those categories change if the price dropped to $12,500? Now, what if the price went to $45,000? Price range bumps tell us how to adjust our expectations.

Charm pricing means dropping just below a round number—that is, $49.99, rather than $50. Charm pricing may be irritating, but it has an effect on buying decisions.

While charm pricing does have an effect, it may not be ideal from the customer's perspective. Recent research shows that customers prefer round numbers. The developers of the physics-based puzzle video game *World of Goo* invited people to download the game for any price they wished using PayPal. More than 65,000 purchasers from 104 countries took them up on the deal paying anywhere from a penny to $150. What was really interesting was that 57 percent chose a round, whole number ending in zero.

Analysis of 1,301 gasoline purchases made from self-pump convenience stores showed similar results. Fifty-six percent were round, whole-dollar amounts, and another 4 percent ended in half-dollar amounts. Are you one of those people who try to stop the gas pump on zeros? If so (we can analyze *why* you do that another time), then you know the frustration of going over a little. The authors looked for this result and found that another 7 percent of the gas sales ended in .01—implying that the customer wanted to stop on an even dollar amount, but their reflexes were not fast enough. Ha!

Sources: Gregory Ciotti, "Pricing Psychology: 10 Timeless Strategies to Increase Sales," Help Scout, May 15, 2016, www.helpscout.net/blog/pricing-strategies; Justin Gray, "How to Raise Prices Without Losing Customers," *Inc.*, May 17, 2017, www.inc.com; William Morrow, "You Could Win a Price War With Amazon, Pricefixer, Netflix, Walmart, or Costco. Here's How," *Entrepreneur*, July 21, 2017, www.entrepreneur.com.

always been common in retailing and wholesaling, manufacturers also use this relatively simple approach. Markup can be based on either *selling price* or *cost*, and it is important to distinguish between the two.

For example, if an item costs $1.00 and the selling price is $1.50, the markup on selling price is 33.3 percent. Fifty cents is one-third of $1.50. However, using the same figures, the markup on cost is 50 percent. Fifty cents is one-half of $1.00. Markup based on cost makes your markup appear higher, even though the amounts are exactly the same. Most businesses base markup on selling price.

Effective use of markup depends on your ability to calculate the *profit margin* you need to cover costs. Formulas useful in calculating markup include the following:

$$\text{Selling price} = \text{Cost} + \text{Markup}$$

$$\text{Markup} = \text{Selling price} - \text{Cost}$$

$$\text{Cost} = \text{Selling price} - \text{Markup}$$

Target-Return Pricing. If you have accurate information on how many units you will sell and what your fixed and variable costs will be, *target-return pricing* will allow you to set your selling price to produce a given rate of return. To calculate a target-return price, add your fixed costs and the dollar amount you wish to make, divide by the number of units you intend to sell, and then add the variable cost of your product.

$$\text{Target return price} = [(\text{Fixed costs} + \text{Target return}) + \text{Unit sales}] + \text{Variable cost}$$

As an example, suppose demand for your product is 5,000 units. To meet this demand, you need a target return of $100,000. Your fixed costs are $200,000 and your variable costs run $50 per unit. Using this strategy, your price would be

$$\frac{200{,}000 + 100{,}000}{5{,}000} + 50 = 60 + 50 = 110 = \text{Your selling price}$$

Concept Check Questions

1. Of the pricing techniques described in this chapter, which one do you think is most commonly used by small businesses? Why?

2. What strategies should be considered if a small business is setting prices for a product that is to be exported? How do these strategies differ from those used in a domestic market?

3. As the owner of a small hometown drugstore, how would you prepare for a Walmart being built in your area?

Concept Module 13.4: Getting Paid

- **LO 13.4: Explain factors affecting small businesses getting paid.**

After establishing your pricing practices comes an even more important task: deciding how you will get customers to pay for their purchases. Payment methods include cash, check, credit, money order, cashier's check, or automatic withdrawal.

Obviously, accepting only cash really cuts down on those bad debts. But the trend is toward consumers carrying *less* cash, not more, so a cash-only policy will probably turn off many customers who would like to purchase with another form of payment. Most small businesses accept checks with adequate identification, such as a phone number and driver's license number, in case the bank returns the check for insufficient funds. For bookkeeping purposes, checks are treated the same as cash and actually make bank deposits easier.

The main reasons for your small business to extend credit are to make sales to customers you would not otherwise have reached and to increase the volume and frequency of sales to existing customers.

Extending Credit to Your Customers

Should you extend credit to your customers? Good question. Do your competitors? Will your sales increase enough to pay the finance charges? Will sales increase enough to cover the bad debts you will incur? Can you extend credit and still maintain a positive cash flow? Will credit sales smooth out fluctuations in sales volume?

Credit is broken down into two basic categories: trade credit and consumer credit.

Trade Credit. Trade credit refers to sales terms that one business extends to another for purchasing goods. As a small business owner, consider trade credit from both directions—extended to you from vendors and that you may extend to your customers. If you can purchase goods/services and are allowed to take 30, 60, or 90 days to pay for them, you have essentially obtained a loan for those items for that time period. Many new businesses can take advantage of trade credit even when no other form of financing is available. Be warned, however, that habitual late payment or nonpayment may cause your suppliers to cut off your trade credit and place your business on a COD—cash on delivery—basis.

If you extend credit to your business customers, you will need an accounts receivable system to keep cash flowing into your business. A very easy trap that growing new businesses fall into is the thought, "Get the sales now; work on improving profit margins later." This trap is especially serious for service businesses, whose largest expense is labor, which must be paid when the service is provided, not when the business owner is paid by the customer. Manufacturers also suffer from slow collection due to the long lag time between purchasing raw materials, labor, and inventory and the actual sale of the product. Not collecting your accounts receivable will negatively impact your cash flow and your ability to pay your expenses. If you don't collect on sales, they aren't sales.

> "If you don't collect on sales, they aren't sales."

Trade credit can be offered in several forms: extended payment periods and terms, goods offered on consignment, and payment not required until goods are sold. Credit lines are popular ways for one business to receive trade credit from another.

Consumer Credit. You have several choices regarding **consumer credit**, which is offered to your ultimate customers rather than to other businesses. You can carry the debt yourself, you can rely on a financial institution such as a bank to loan money to your customers, or you can accept credit cards.

If you wish to carry the debt yourself, you can set up an *open charge account* for customers. Customers take possession of the goods, and you bill them. Invoices are usually sent out monthly. You can encourage early payment by offering cash discounts or punishing late payment with finance charges. Open accounts must be managed carefully. As noted in Chapter 8, open accounts can absolutely kill cash flow and drain the life out of your business.

An *installment account* is frequently offered to customers who are purchasing big-ticket items (such as autos, boats, and appliances). Customers rarely have enough cash to pay up front for such items. With an installment account, they make a down payment and follow with monthly payments on the unpaid balance plus interest for an extended period of time. This type of financing is not quite as dangerous as the open account, because the product typically serves as collateral. Generally, small businesses exist to sell their products, whereas financial institutions are in business to sell money—so let them handle installment loans.

consumer credit
Credit extended by retailers to the ultimate customers for the purchase of products or services.

Alternatively, you may extend a *line of credit* to your customers. This system operates like a revolving credit account: You approve credit purchases for each customer up to a certain dollar limit. Lines of credit allow customers to buy goods without going through a new credit check for each purchase. Finance charges are paid on the unpaid balance monthly. Extending lines of credit can reduce the amount of paper in your credit application process, because a new application is not required for each purchase. This type of financing allows you to control the total amount of credit you extend.

To avoid the expense and inconvenience of maintaining your own accounts receivable, you can rely on *credit cards* as your source of consumer credit. Consumers' use of cash and checks is decreasing as a percentage of total consumer spending, whereas the use of credit and debit cards is skyrocketing.

For your small business to accept credit or debit cards, you need to use a third-party processing firm to manage the transaction between you and the bank issuing the card. Some processors have proprietary software that may not work with your online shopping cart, which can lock you into a situation you did not desire. In addition to swiping fees, processors often add annual or monthly fees, regulatory fees, compliance fees, and statement fees.

> "Consumers' use of cash and checks is decreasing as a percentage of total consumer spending, whereas the use of credit and debit cards is skyrocketing."

Convenience for customers comes at a price for businesses, however. Businesses must pay a percentage of each sale to the credit card company handling the sale. Although card companies offer discount rates for small businesses, transaction and statement fees will increase the amount you pay. The percentage that most small businesses pay to credit card companies varies according to the number of transactions made, but most small businesses are charged between 1.5 and 5 percent. Besides the percentage fee, each transaction may cost you anywhere between $.25 and $.50 as well as a minimum monthly transaction fee, plus a variety of set-up and other fees.[10] Make sure you understand the fee structure as well as the differing amounts you will be required to pay in order for your customers to use credit cards.

Online Credit Checks. For business credit requests, the Yahoo! web search site lists several merchant credit services that you can access through the web link capability. Just point your mouse to the one you want to investigate and click. In addition, Dun & Bradstreet provides a free search of millions of U.S. companies. Then, for a nominal fee, you can receive a Business Background Report that lists important credit information about the company you're investigating.

For about $225 per year, you can join the National Association of Credit Management, a membership organization that researches and reports on many small firms that are often overlooked by larger credit agencies. As a member, you can get a comprehensive report on a particular firm from the database, which includes about 6.5 million firms.

Collecting Overdue Accounts

Bill collecting is never fun, but it is critical for small businesses. The longer bills go unpaid, the worse your chances of collecting on the debt (see Figure 13.5).

Begin your collection process by telephone. On large accounts, call a couple of weeks after the receipt has been sent to verify with the customer that the invoice is correct. If you don't receive a check after 30 days, call again. Create a sense of urgency that the bill must be paid. Try to get a commitment for a certain amount by a specific day, like $100 by the 25th of the month. That puts the burden on the customer. If the customer is overdue, do not extend more credit. When you give credit to customers, you are now in the banking business, as well as your core business. If repeated calls lead you to believe that the customer is playing games, with little intention of paying what she owes, you have five choices: a letter service, an attorney, small claims court, a collection agency, or writing it off. Always remain

▼ FIGURE 13.5

Show Me the Money

The longer bills go unpaid, the less your chance of collecting.

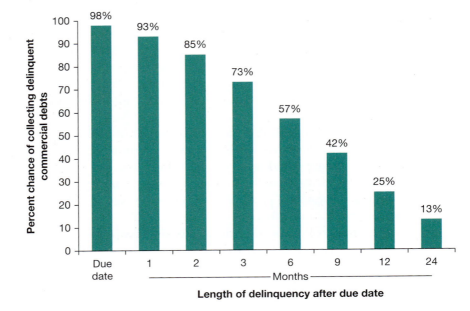

professional and try to stay on friendly terms. You can say something like "I really busted my tail to get the delivery to you on time. Will you please help us serve other customers by sending a check?"

You may want to consider taking online payments. With these systems, clients pay off their invoices within an average of 15 to 18 days of receiving them.[11]

To facilitate collections, pay attention to your invoices and credit applications. Always print your late-payment service charges on your invoices. Include a venue provision on your invoices if you are selling goods out of state so that any court case concerning the sale will be heard in a court of your choice. State the specific number of days a customer has to notify you of any problems with the shipment.

On your credit application form, ask customers to sign a release that authorizes creditors to disclose relevant information. This step will help you to spot credit problems in advance.

Concept Check Questions

1. Discuss the importance of remaining professional and friendly when trying to collect an unpaid bill.

2. What advantages and disadvantages are involved for a small business offering sales on trade credit?

Concept Module 13.5: Promotion

- **LO 13.5: Describe the advertising, personal selling, public relations, and sales-promotion tools that a small business owner uses to compile a promotional mix.**

The goal of a company's promotional efforts is to communicate with target markets. You have four major tools available when developing your *promotional mix*: advertising, personal selling, public relations, and sales promotions. The weight you choose to give to each of these tools will depend on (1) your *market*, (2) your *message*, and (3) the best *medium* that will communicate that message to your market.

Advertising and marketing are not synonymous. Understanding the difference will help you better tell your full story. Marketing is the systematic planning, analysis, and activity that communicate your competitive advantage to the people who would find value in it. Advertising is the paid outreach you make to prospective customers. Advertising supports marketing by creating exposure to what it is that you have to sell.

Advertising

Advertising is a way to bring attention to your product or business by publishing or broadcasting a message to the public through various media. Your choices of media include the following:

- *Print media:* newspapers, magazines, direct mail

- *Broadcast media:* radio, television, or online

- *Outdoor media:* billboards or posters placed to reach customers when they are away from home

The habits of your target market will affect your choice of advertising media. For example, if your target market is teenagers, online would be the most appropriate choice. The nature of your product will also help to determine the media selected. Does advertising for your product need to include color, sound, or motion to make it more attractive? The cost of your advertising is another important factor in choosing media vehicles. You should look at the total dollar amount that an ad costs and the cost per thousand people exposed to the message.

> "You should look at the total dollar amount that an ad costs and the cost per thousand people exposed to the message."

Advertising is critical, but it has some real downsides, including slow feedback, expense, difficulty cutting through clutter, and difficulty creating a personalized message. Choosing the appropriate advertising medium for your message is important. Advertising is about communicating with your target market. Which one should you use? It depends on where your target market looks for information. Don't immediately rule out any media (for example, just because YOU may not read newspapers doesn't mean you should not advertise in them IF your target market reads them). Let's take a look at your options.

Online

Advantages: Good selectivity of target markets; inexpensive. It is a highly visual medium and viewers love rich media, creative videos, GIFs, memes, and more. People interact better with visuals, and live video is the most effective because of its authenticity, and human connection.

Limitations: A case can be made that the internet is funded mostly through ads. Cookies can help target customers based on what those consumers view in browsers, but privacy concerns are making this harder to accomplish. Ad blockers are also a challenge; in January 2018, 11 percent of internet users had some type of ad blocker.[12] Advertising return on investment is expected to show results even as users grow more and more tired of ads. To enhance the effectiveness of advertising, it needs to grab attention, not blend in.

Newspaper

Advantages: Flexible; timely; covers local markets well; believable (because people read newspapers to get information); relatively inexpensive; can use color, coupons, or inserts.

Not every international market has the same levels of internet penetration—some countries still have high newspaper popularity.

Limitations: Why are newspapers (and all following mediums) even included in this section? Because they exist and while they do, some consumers still use them (45 years old and up with disposable income) and if they are in your target market you can reach them (recognizing that Facebook and Google account for more than 70 percent of all new advertising dollars). Other drawbacks include the short life of ads; number of ads per newspaper (causes clutter); poor photo reproduction; low pass-along value (meaning that newspapers are rarely read by more than one person).

All Television—Including Cable, Syndicated, and Spot

Advantages: Reaches large audience; combines sight, sound, and motion; perceived to be prestige medium.

Limitations: High absolute cost; having several ads run together increases clutter and decreases impact; short exposure time; ability of consumer to bypass the ads with DVR or mute with regular TV.

Direct Mail

Advantages: Can be targeted very specifically; message can be personalized; less space limitations than other media. Direct mail still works, while digital retargeting response rates average about .7 percent (less than 1 person in 100 responds—pretty inefficient). A direct mail postcard will generate a 4.25 to 5 percent response rate, and its use is also still growing. The 2017 Media Usage Survey revealed that 31 percent of marketers increased their use of direct mail, while another third held same as previous year.[13]

Limitations: Perceived as "junk mail"; high relative cost; mailing lists are expensive and often inaccurate.

Radio

Advantages: Can be targeted to specific audience; low relative cost; short lead time so ads can be developed quickly.

Limitations: People are often involved with other activities and do not pay full attention to ad; people cannot refer back to ad; competition for best time slots.

Magazine

Advantages: Target markets can be selected geographically and demographically; long life because magazines are often passed along; high-quality reproduction.

Limitations: Long lead time needed in purchasing ad; no guarantee of placement within magazine; higher relative cost than other print media.

Outdoor

Advantages: High, repeated exposure; low cost; little competition.

Limitations: Limited amount of message due to exposure time to ad; little selectivity of target market.

Miscellaneous. Known as *unmeasured media advertising,* miscellaneous advertising includes things like catalogs, ads on bus stop benches, and signage at sports fields. Many small businesses determine how much to spend on advertising by allocating a percentage of their total sales revenues. This percentage varies considerably by type of business (see Table 13.1).

Advertising Costs by Different Types of Businesses

Industry	Ad Dollars as % of Operating Income
New and Used Car Dealers	0.9%
Furniture and Home Furnishing Stores	3.6%
Electronics and Appliance Stores	1.9%
Hardware Stores	1.9%
Food and Beverage Stores	0.6%
Beer, Wine, and Liquor Stores	0.5%
Non-Store Retailers	2.6%
Software Publishers	4.5%
Commercial Banking	0.4%
Advertising and Related Services	4.3%
Food Services and Drinking Places	2.2%
Motor Vehicle Manufacturers	1.9%
Breweries	3.8%
Soft Drink Companies	3.6%

Source: Almanac of Business and Industrial Financial Ratios (2017) by Philip Wilson. Copyright 2017 by Walters Kluwer.

Advertising Objectives. Different types of advertisements help to accomplish different objectives. You may be trying to do any of the following:

- *Inform* your audience of the existence of your business, your competitive advantage, or product features and benefits.

- *Persuade* people to take an immediate action—such as buying your product.

- *Remind* people that your business or product still exists. Get them to remember what they received from your business in the past so that it remains in their evoked set.

- *Change the perception* of your business rather than trying to sell specific products. Generally called *institutional advertising*, advertising with this objective aims to build goodwill rather than to make an immediate sale.

It is a challenge to achieve these broad objectives with your advertising. Creating effective advertisements is both a science and an art. Originality, humor, and excitement can make your ad break through the clutter of other media, but, at the same time, these traits can obscure the real message of your ad. Communicating your message clearly while catching the viewer's attention is a tough balance to achieve. Consider these common strategies, all of which you might choose to achieve your advertising objectives:

> "Creating effective advertisements is both a science and an art."

- *Testimonials.* Use an authority or personal testimony from a celebrity to present your message. Athletes and movie stars attract attention, but their public images can change rapidly and must remain consistent with that of your business.

- *Humor.* Humor can grab the viewer's attention, but be careful who bears the brunt of the joke or you could offend some group and generate negative publicity for your business.

ONLINE BIG DOGS

Google and Facebook are the dominant online forces that you need to use to get attention and direct potential customers to your small business website (or wherever your sales platform is housed).

Google AdWords can be a very powerful tool to help your small business sell online. Done correctly, it can generate $2 in revenue for every dollar spent on advertising. Unfortunately, the "done correctly" part is not easy, but wasting money is. The service is complex and full of so many features that choosing what your small business will benefit from is confusing.

If you want to target key words using Google's pay-per-click (PPC) advertising, you pay Google every time someone searches for your word and clicks the PPC ad (which appears with the "Ad" label above and below the organic search results. As you might expect, some words are more expensive than others. "Business services" tops the list at $58.64. What does that mean? Each click is fifty-nine bucks. Get 100 clicks per day and you've spent $6,000 . . . and $2.2 million per year. The most expensive words are

1. Business Services: $58.64
2. Bail Bonds: $58.48
3. Casino: $55.48
4. Lawyer: $54.86
5. Asset Management: $49.86
6. Insurance: $48.41

Some see Facebook advertising as the magic bullet for selling. If only it were that easy. The reasons Facebook ads do NOT work are (1) misunderstanding ad metrics and results, and (2) no strategy in place. Your beginning points for metrics are

- Earnings per lead: EPL represents the revenue generated from one new lead. Take total revenue generated divided by the number of leads acquired to generate that revenue.

- Cost per lead: CPL is the cost to generate one new lead. Divide your total ad expenditure by the number of leads a campaign generated.

Numbers don't mean anything unless you can turn them into revenue. You need strategy to guide prospective customers from attention to a sale. Begin your strategy by connecting with people who do not know your business and capture their attention. At that point you can initiate a sales conversation. The bulk of Facebook advertising dollars are spent on lead generation. Finally, you are ultimately aiming to retarget prospects. Facebook retargeting is remarkably simple. It means to re-engage with people who came to your website, but did not make a purchase; they receive more of your ads so you can offer them a discount or free shipping.

Sources: Gene Marks, "5 Rookie Mistakes You Need to Avoid with Google AdWords," *Inc.*, January 15, 2018, www.inc.com; Amanda Bond, "Not Getting Results with Your Facebook Ads? Here Is Everything You Are Doing Wrong," *Entrepreneur*, August 3, 2017, www.entrepreneur.com/video/298156; Amanda Bond, "With Entrepreneurs Freaking Out After Facebook's Drastic Newsfeed Change, Here Are 4 Things You Can Do Right Now to Survive," *Entrepreneur*, January 15, 2018, www.entrepreneur.com/article/307505.

Advertising history is also full of very funny ads that did not generate a single dollar of additional revenue.

- *Sensual or sexual messages.* According to the cliché, "Sex sells." Sex is certainly used in a lot of ads, but research shows that it is not an effective way to get a message across. As with humor, using sex to attract attention is worthless if it doesn't translate into sales.

- *Comparative messages.* Naming competitors in your advertising is legal and quite common. It can be a very powerful way to position your product in customers' minds against another known entity—although it also gives your competitor free exposure.

- *Slice-of-life messages.* These messages may use a popular song or a brief scene from life to position your product. Music is a great way to transport people mentally back to another time in their life. Nostalgia can help create a brand identity for your product.

- *Fantasy messages.* These messages present an idealistic self-image of the buyer. What you are trying to do is link a product with a desirable person or situation. Certainly, this is what almost every beer or soft-drink commercial attempts—the message is "Drink this liquid and you will be beautiful, popular, and desirable." Right.

How do you tell if your advertising works? A common complaint among advertisers runs along this line: "I know that half of my advertising dollars are wasted, I just don't know which half." Measuring the effectiveness of your advertising is difficult. Is the cost of producing and running the ad justified by increased sales and profit? A few techniques might help you find out.

- *Response tracking.* Coded or dated coupons can let you compare different media, such as the redemption rate for coupons in newspapers compared with flyers handed out on the street.

- *Split ads.* Code two different ads, different media, or broadcast times to see which produces a greater response.

- *In-store opinions.* Ask in-store customers where they heard about your business, what they think, what you are doing right, and why they buy from you rather than from a competitor.

- *Telephone surveys.* Make random phone calls with numbers gleaned from customer files. Ask customers whether they have seen your advertising and what they think of it.

- *Statement questionnaires.* Drop a brief questionnaire in with the monthly bills you send out to ask customers if they are satisfied with the product or service and how they found out about it.

Advertising Development. Most small business owners plan their own advertising programs, which is usually more appropriate for them than hiring a professional producer. Even if you choose to use an advertising agency, you should still take active control of your advertising campaign. Remember, you cannot afford to buy a solution to every problem you will face. This is true with your advertising. Spending money will not automatically get you better advertising.

A common problem among self-produced advertisements is that business owners try to cram too much into them. Their reasoning is "This space costs a lot of money, so I am going to use every minuscule part of it." The result is usually an ad that is busy, unattractive, and uninteresting. Simplicity should be the rule here. White space draws the reader's attention. The same principle applies to package design: It doesn't have to tell the consumer everything.

> "I know that half of my advertising dollars are wasted, I just don't know which half."

Even though self-produced ads are appropriate for many small businesses, owners should at least investigate the options and promotions that outside professional advertising services make available.

Advertising Agencies. To mount an effective campaign, you may want to consider consulting an advertising agency. These businesses can help you by conducting preliminary studies, developing an advertising plan, creating advertisements, selecting the appropriate media, evaluating the effectiveness of the advertising, and conducting ad follow-up.

A small agency that specializes in and understands your type of business may be a better choice for a small business than a large agency. Ask your friends and colleagues for recommendations, and get samples of the agency's work before signing a contract. Remember that fees are often negotiable, so the agency's fees may be flexible.

Media Agencies. You can create your own advertising and hire a media buyer to coordinate the purchase of print space or broadcast time for your ads. Why would you choose to use a media buyer? If you have identified your specific target market, a media buyer can help coordinate your media mix to reach that market. Suppose you have designed a new line of blue jeans for urban girls from 13 to 17 years old. A media buyer can tell you in which magazine, on which radio station, or on which television show to advertise.

Art and Graphic Design Services. If you design your own ads and write your own copy but lack the artistic skills needed to produce the final piece of art or film, an art service can handle this task for you. Like the art director in an advertising agency, this service needs to work closely with the person writing your copy to coordinate the message.

Other Sources. Radio and television studios, newspapers, and magazines with which you contract to run your advertising can also produce ads for you. Their services generally cost less than those of an advertising agency.

Personal Selling

Personal selling involves a personal presentation by a salesperson for the purpose of making sales and building relationships with customers. There are many products not large enough, complex enough, or differentiated enough to warrant personal selling, but for those products that do, this technique is the best way to close the deal. Through personal selling, you are trying to accomplish three things: identify customer needs, match those needs with your products, and show the customers the match between their need and your product.

> "People seldom buy from someone they don't trust, so a successful salesperson must first earn a customer's trust."

Cost is the biggest drawback to personal selling. When you calculate what it costs for a salesperson to contact each prospect, you see that this strategy is much more expensive than the cost per person for advertising. Another drawback is that salespeople have gained a poor reputation because of the high-pressure tactics and questionable ethics a few of them employ. The biggest advantage of using personal selling is the flexibility of the presentation that becomes possible. A trained salesperson can tailor a presentation to the prospect around three aspects of the product:

- *Features:* What the product is

- *Advantages:* Why the product is better than alternatives

- *Benefits:* What the product will do for the customer

Customer expectations are rising. A good product at a fair price, offered by a well-trained sales staff, backed by a responsive customer service department, is just the starting point in a competitive marketplace. For your business to stand out, its products need to be tailored to the particular needs of your customers.

Once you start your own business and truly believe in your product, you have to sell. Even if the thought makes your palms sweat and your heart pump. You can push through your discomfort of selling to make your dream a success. You have many advantages going for you. You already know and believe in your product, so your enthusiasm is contagious. Push past rejection by remembering that it is professional, not personal, rejection. Be friendly, not pushy—your business/product exists because it solves a customer's problem. They just need to understand how.[14]

The personal-selling process involves seven steps:

1. *Pre-approach.* Before meeting with the prospective customer, a salesperson must acquire knowledge about the product and perhaps about the customer and his business.

2. *Approach.* Upon first meeting the customer, the salesperson tries to establish a rapport with her. People seldom buy from someone they don't trust, so a successful salesperson must first earn a customer's trust.

3. *Questioning.* To find out what is important to the customer, the salesperson will try to identify his needs as early in the process as possible.

4. *Demonstration.* The salesperson shows how the product will solve the customer's problem and meet her needs.

5. *Handling objections.* An effective salesperson will listen to what the customer is really saying. An objection shows that the customer is interested but needs more information. Would you raise objections to a salesperson if you were not really interested in a product? No, you would probably just walk away.

6. *Closing the deal.* When he senses that the customer is ready to buy, the salesperson should ask for the sale. Many sales are lost when a customer is ready to buy, but the salesperson continues to sell.

7. *Suggestion selling and follow-up.* An effective technique is *suggestion selling*, or recommending products that are complementary to those just sold. A follow-up phone call after a sale will build rapport and work toward creating a long-term relationship with the customer.

Public Relations

Public relations (PR) involves promotional activities designed to build and sustain goodwill between a business and its customers, employees, suppliers, investors, government agencies, and the general public. **Publicity** is an aspect of PR consisting of any message about your company communicated through the mass media that you do not have to pay for. Generally, PR works by generating publicity.

PR involves a variety of communication formats, including company publications such as newsletters, annual reports, and bulletins; public speaking; lobbying; and the mass media. Each format can have an appropriate use and benefit for your company's marketing effort.

The Business Card. Business cards may seem old-fashioned, but they are still an important marketing tool. An important image builder that is often overlooked and taken for granted is a 3.5-inch-by-2-inch paper rectangle—the business card. If done correctly and creatively, a business card not only provides information about your small business but also becomes hand-to-hand advertising.[15]

Your business card can build your personal brand. You're not stuck with boring paper. You can use stainless steel or gold metal cards. Taking a giant step beyond metal cards is Michelle Calloway, founder of Revealio. What Calloway has created is an augmented reality business card—point your phone at it and your screen will show logos, photos, videos, schematics, almost unlimited options. Pretty compelling business card.[16]

Business cards help people you meet at networking events match your face with your name. They give a reason to follow up with you after the event and provide a call to action, whether it is an email or a LinkedIn connection.

Sales Promotions

Any activity that stimulates sales and is not strictly advertising or personal selling is called a *sales promotion*. Special in-store displays, free samples, contests, trade show booths, and the distribution of coupons, premiums, and rebates are examples of sales promotions. These activities enhance but do not replace your advertising or personal selling efforts. They are most effective when used in intervals, because customer response decreases over time as customers become familiar with the promotions.

Trade Shows. Small business owners in every industry view trade shows as huge, promising, but somewhat overwhelming opportunities. They are prime real estate for meeting new vendors, suppliers, customers, partners, and media contacts. But, they are expensive for small companies.[17]

publicity
An aspect of public relations consisting of any message about your company communicated through the mass media that you do not pay for.

The 1.3 million-square-foot McCormick Place convention center in Chicago can seem like a very large place if you are a small business owner setting up for a trade show. Giant competitors set up booths that dwarf the displays of small businesses. Nevertheless, trade shows can generate big deals for small businesses.

Gregory Perkins uses bright lights, bold and colorful graphics, and 10-foot-tall displays to catch the attention of the 20,000 people attending Book Expo America. Perkins's business, Magic Image, sells African American greeting cards, calendars, and pocket planners. He does about a dozen shows a year, and they generate most of his $500,000 annual sales. At the Book Expo, Perkins caught a big fish of a deal when Target Stores placed a $30,000 order on the spot.

Research shows that trade shows can be more effective at generating sales than direct mail, telemarketing, or other sales strategies—but you have to develop some trade show savvy. To improve your odds of success at trade shows, try the following:

- Learn who the key players are in a niche (and how they compare)
- Meet the leaders in a company
- Conduct a competitive analysis
- Sit down with business partners
- Make sales and cut deals
- Meet potential allies
- Create serendipitous business opportunities
- Get inspired
- Make friends
- Keep going back

Customer Acquisition Cost

Finally, a calculation that is important in e-commerce is customer acquisition cost (CAC)—how much you have to spend in order to acquire a new customer. It is related to cost per action (CPA), which is the amount you have to spend to convert a customer (make a sale), but refers to both existing and new customers.

In its simplest form, CAC calculation is dividing your total dollars spent on all marketing linked to customer acquisition divided by your total number of new customers acquired. The numbers that go into what your small business specifically spends on acquisition is going to take some careful sorting, but you get the concept. For example, a company that spent $50,000 on advertising in a year, and generated 5,000 new orders would have a CAC of $10.

A CAC of $10 means nothing without context. If you own a BMW automobile dealership and have a CAC of $10, you would be thrilled due to the relative high price of your product. Part of understanding customer acquisition cost is getting the concept of customer lifetime value (CLV), or how much you make from a customer who repeatedly purchases from you for years. A $10 CAC is no big deal even if you are only making $20 net profit per customer, if that customer continues to buy once a month for 20 years.

Promotional Mix

In deciding how to combine each of your four tools into a promotional mix, you need to consider when each type of promotion may be appropriate. Advertising reaches so many people that it is good for creating awareness, but its power to stimulate action decreases quickly. Personal selling, by contrast, is the most effective tool for building customer desire for the product and prompting customers to take action. Because it requires one-on-one contact, however, it is less useful in creating awareness. Sales promotions are most effective with customers who are already interested in the product, but who may need prompting to make the purchase. Public relations builds awareness, but results in few immediate sales.

Concept Check Questions

1. What factors should be considered when a small business owner decides to advertise?

2. How would promotional mix decisions change for a small business that is expanding into a foreign market?

3. Much of the self-produced small business advertising is weak. Think of an example of a local small business that uses especially effective advertising. Why is it successful at communicating with its target market when so many are not?

CHAPTER REVIEW

SUMMARY ▶▶

LO 13.1 Identify the three main considerations in setting a price for a product.

The economic factors that have the largest influence on pricing are the prices charged by competitors, the amount of customer demand for your product, and the costs incurred in producing, purchasing, and selling your products.

LO 13.2 Explain what breakeven analysis is and why it is important for pricing in a small business.

Breakeven analysis ensures that your prices are set above total costs, allowing you to make a profit. It is also useful in estimating the needed demand for a product at different price levels. Finally, breakeven analysis shows how many units need to be sold to generate a target dollar return.

LO 13.3 Present examples of customer-oriented and internal-oriented pricing.

Customer-oriented price strategies, such as penetration pricing, skimming, and psychological pricing, focus on the wants and needs of your target customers and the number of units

of your product they will buy. Internal-oriented pricing involves setting your prices according to the financial needs of your business, with less regard for customer reaction.

LO 13.4 Explain factors affecting small businesses getting paid.

Small businesses extend credit to their customers to realize sales that would not have been made without credit, and to increase the volume and frequency of sales to existing customers. Credit is extended through open charge accounts, installment accounts, lines of credit, and acceptance of credit cards.

LO 13.5 Describe the advertising, personal selling, public relations, and sales-promotion tools that a small business owner uses to compile a promotional mix.

A promotional mix is the combination of advertising, personal selling, sales promotions, and public relations that best communicates the message of a small business to its customers.

KEY TERMS ▶▶

breakeven point (BEP) **340**	odd pricing **345**	psychological pricing **344**
consumer credit **348**	penetration pricing **344**	publicity **357**
decoy effect **345**	prestige pricing **344**	reference pricing **345**
demand curve **336**	price elasticity of demand **338**	variable costs **338**
fixed costs **338**	price lining **345**	
markup **345**	price skimming **344**	

EXPERIENTIAL LEARNING ACTIVITIES ▶▶

13.1: Small Business Marketing: Pricing and Promotion Breakeven Analysis

LO 13.2: Explain what breakeven analysis is and why it is important for pricing in a small business.

Read the scenario and then answer the following questions.

Alejandro and Peter wanted to start their own business providing yard care for the homeowners within a 20-mile radius of their home. They planned to provide all services themselves, ensuring quality service for their customers. While their home was in a subdivision populated by families with children, they were surround by subdivisions full of retirees. Alejandro and Peter were hoping to capture the retirees as the primary target market for their business.

After doing some initial research, they found there were four competitors in the area providing yard care services, and three of the four also provided landscaping services. The price charged weekly to mow a lawn, check sprinklers, and so forth averaged $30. Based upon research, it looked like $5 per lawn would cover variable costs. Fixed costs were another matter. They have no equipment and have heard horror stories about buying used equipment; however, the price difference is significant. Buying a used pickup, trailer, and riding mower would cost $12,000. If they purchased new equipment, the cost would be close to $25,000. How many yards would they

have to mow in order to break even, let alone make a profit with their proposed new small business? Was this even a viable business idea?

Answer the following questions.

1. Buying new equipment, how many lawns must be mowed just to break even.

2. Buying used equipment, how many lawns must be mowed just to break even.

3. If the mowing season is 120 days, how many lawns must be mowed every day using new equipment to break even?

4. If the mowing season is 120 days, how many lawns must be mowed every day using used equipment to break even?

5. Can they raise their price above $30 and if so by how much would you recommend raising price and why?

6. Alejandro and Peter come to you asking advice on their business idea? Should they begin their small business?

13.2: Small Business Marketing: Promotion

LO 13.5: Describe the advertising, personal selling, public relations, and sales-promotion tools that a small business owner uses to compile a promotional mix.

For each of the following scenarios, explain which advertising objective and which advertising strategy was used in the advertisement.

Advertising Objectives: Inform, persuade, remind, perception change

Advertising Strategies: Testimonial, humor, sensual, comparative, slice-of-life, and fantasy

1. A dish soap advertisement shows how this dish soap washes dishes so much better than any other dish soap available.

   Objective:

   Strategy:

2. This perfume advertisement shows a beautiful woman, who, wearing the perfume, magically shatters a wall that opens up to an elegant dinner party where she is the focus of the party.

   Objective:

   Strategy:

3. This advertisement shows a dog that desperately wants the dog treat from his owner. The dog is in such a hurry to get to the treat, he slides around the hardwood floor barely missing many obstacles in his way.

   Objective:

   Strategy:

4. This advertisement is for newborn diapers. The scene shows a Mom cuddling her baby for the first time with soothing music playing in the background.

    Objective:

    Strategy:

5. The scene shows a person who just picked up his carryout pizza. He gets out of his car, begins walking into his house and dramatically slips and falls, dropping his pizza. The advertisement then discusses how this pizza place offers pizza insurance and will remake the pizza for the customer, free of charge.

    Objective:

    Strategy:

6. The scene shows a famous movie actress using the beauty product that is being advertised. The actress is talking about how amazing the product is and how it works so well on her skin. She has used the beauty product for years with obvious amazing results.

    Objective:

    Strategy:

7. This cologne advertisement shows a well-shaped, good-looking man in a swimsuit diving deep into the water. As he jumps in, the cologne bottle appears in a spray of water. Water is part of the name of the cologne.

    Objective:

    Strategy:

8. The chewing gum advertisement shows a unicorn breaking through a wall with the person chewing the gum riding the unicorn. The person is now ready and eager for his meeting. The chewing gum has made all the difference.

    Objective:

    Strategy:

CHAPTER CLOSING CASE ▸▸

Social Media Implementation by SMEs: The Case of Luxury Food Stop

Luxury Food Stop is an award-winning independent grocery business located in a prime town center situation, in a busy market town in Northern Ireland. This third-generation family-owned business, established back in the 1800s, has prospered and grown, and now provides employment for over 100 staff. According to the European Union definition of small and medium-sized enterprises (SMEs), Luxury Food Stop can be categorized as a medium-sized firm. However, it must be acknowledged that in the retail sector many medium-sized firms demonstrate smaller-firm behaviors due to the contribution of part-time employees to their workforce. The company's brand is all about offering high-quality fresh foods, actively supporting local farmers and producers, and maintaining a colloquial relationship with its customers.

As customers enter the store, great care is taken by a friendly and helpful staff to give them a warm welcome and to greet them with attractive and eye-catching displays of fresh produce. This enticing environment encourages Luxury Food Stop's shoppers to pause and fill their baskets with first-class groceries. This helps to turn what might be a tedious chore into an enjoyable and traditional "market feel" experience.

To date, the grocery store's main approach to sales has been based on traditional retail marketing principles, for example, retail atmospherics, customer service, and stock merchandising. External marketing communications have been traditionally based upon newspaper advertisements.

Social Media Marketing in Luxury Food Stop

Two years ago Luxury Food Stop implemented social media as part of its marketing strategy. The store used three social media platforms, namely Facebook, Twitter, and Instagram. Currently, Luxury's Facebook platform has 1,268 page "likes" and in the month of October 2014, the company posted 20 times. Its Twitter account has 27 followers with 2 tweets and its Instagram account has 13 followers and 5 posts.

Although, the marketing manager has been encouraged by some positive response to Luxury's activity on social media, the online interaction with customers has not grown or progressed as first anticipated. This has caused the marketing manager to concentrate on Facebook and neglect Twitter and Instagram, which were last updated a year ago. This attitude of disinterest has created a negative rather than a positive impact on customers. The company has lost followers on Twitter and visits to its Instagram page have fallen.

Challenges of Harnessing Social Media Effectively for SMEs

With approximately 7,000 shoppers entering their store every week, customer relationships mean a lot to those at Luxury Food Stop. Many of these customers visit on a regular basis, but the marketing manager does not have a system to record and measure their in-store consumption patterns. This therefore makes it problematic to tailor social media marketing activities, notably Facebook, to specific categories of shoppers. The marketing manager remarked, "I don't know whether the people who liked us on our Facebook page are customers or not. . . . I imagine most of them are our customers . . . [although] quite a few would be staff as well."

In truth, the company doesn't really know how to capitalize on its social media presence. The marketing manager, who has no previous experience of using social media within a business context, has experimented and tried to learn about Facebook with the assistance of colleagues in the IT department. But the majority of the company's social media posts relate to staff, incorporating pictures of appetizing products available within their store.

Employees do occasionally research how other competitive food-related businesses use social media and the frequency and popularity of their posts, in relation to their own. Even so, no particular time is allocated to social media each week to create, plan, and update effective posts. In fact, the marketing manager acknowledged, "Social media is not our priority and never will be in the near future! . . . We play around with Facebook [but] there is no major strategy with it."

As an SME, Luxury Food Stop is often constrained in terms of time and human resources, which can mean that its staff is overstretched. A typical day for the marketing manager is spent on advertising, merchandising, pricing, purchasing, and signage plus many other "hands on" activities. Under the pressure of the day-to-day running of the store, the marketing manager said, "I do not have the time, the effort or the inclination to try to work out what it is that I need to do on Facebook to get a bigger hearing. It is not that important and I don't have the time for it." The marketing manager's lack of time, plus the obvious lack of expertise and motivation to use this marketing medium, has caused frustration and undue stress around the implementation of social media marketing. Unfortunately, the funds are just not there to bring in an expert who could help Luxury develop an effective social media campaign.

The Future of Social Media at Luxury Food Stop

The company could use, for example, the popular measurement tool Facebook Insight to determine important and relevant information regarding customers who visit its Facebook site, including their loyalty and the length of each visit. The marketing manager stated, "We don't really measure the effectiveness. Each week we look at the measures given us by Facebook and that is about it!" These measures provided by Facebook are limited to duration on website, number of unique visitors, level of engagement, and reach of postings. Social media measurement tools on Facebook Insight enable marketing managers to compile detailed information in order to analyze and evaluate customer data, resulting in better-informed management decisions.

The implementation of effective social media measurement would enable Luxury Food Stop to look forward and assess its plans for the coming year. This lack of vision and setting of SMART (specific, measurable, attainable, realistic, and timely) objectives keeps Luxury Food Stop from taking full advantage of the immense opportunities that social media offer.

Summary

This case study has examined the issues faced by an SME grocery retailer in the implementation of social media marketing. It has outlined the challenges, difficulties, and typical time constraints facing SME marketing managers in their day-to-day activities. In order to successfully implement effective social media marketing for an SME, marketing managers need to carefully choose the social media marketing platforms they use, plan their digital activities, prioritize social media marketing, set realistic objectives, and use relevant measurement tools to report their findings. Nevertheless, due to a number of inherent SME characteristics, their marketers are not capitalizing on the potential of social media channels.

Discussion Questions

1. The marketing manager of the Luxury Food Stop has opened two unproductive social media accounts. What are the dangers of doing this without any intention of continuously updating and maintaining them?

2. Discuss the other social media errors that the marketing manager may be creating for the company?

3. Provide examples of how marketing managers of SMEs can overcome their social media challenges?

4. What is the importance of the results to SMEs of measuring social media marketing activities?

5. Provide at least two examples of other social media platforms that Luxury could consider adopting, giving reasons for your choices?

6. Identify the choices of methods available to successfully implement social media marketing.

Sources: Go-Eun Choi, Peter Bolan, Karise Hutchinson, and Richard Mitchell, "Social Media Implementation by SMEs: The Case of Luxury Food Stop," Sage Knowledge: Business Cases, March 6, 2016, http://dx.doi.org/10.4135/9781473937581; Ian Fillis and Beverly Wagner, "E-Business Development: An Exploratory Investigation of the Small Firm," *International Small Business Journal* 23, no. 6 (December 2005): 604–634; Audrey Gilmore, David Carson, and Steve Rocks, "Networking in SMEs: Evaluating Its Contribution to Marketing Activity," *International Business Review* 15, no. 3 (June 2006): 278–293; Andrea Kaplan and Michael Haenlein, "Users of the World, Unite! The Challenges and Opportunities of Social Media," *Business Horizons* 53, no. 1 (2010): 59–68; Giovanni La Via and Antonio M. D. Nucifora, "The Determinants of the Price Mark-up for Organic Fruit and Vegetable Products in the European Union," *British Food Journal* 104, nos. 3/4/5 (2002): 319–336; Ogenyi Omar and Peter Fraser, "SME Retailing in the UK," in *Entrepreneurship Marketing: Principles and Practice of SME Marketing*, ed. Sonny Nwankwo and Ayuntunji Gbadamosi (London: Routledge, 2011).

MANAGING SMALL BUSINESS

PART VI

PROFESSIONAL SMALL BUSINESS MANAGEMENT

So what do small business owners do with the hours in the day? After all, it is their own business so they are the masters of their own time and activities, correct? Let's look at some young small business owners and the tasks they regularly perform. You might be surprised at the variety of activities required every day. Small business owners, literally, must do it all.

Bee Downtown

While attending North Carolina State University, Leigh-Kathryn Bonner's landlord would not let her install beehives on the apartment building where she lived, so she put two on the roof of Durham's American Underground, a business incubator, and Bee Downtown was launched. Over 100 client companies, (like Burt's Bees, IBM, and Chick-fil-A) have purchased hives installed on their business property and pay her for annual maintenance; they keep the honey, and the urban bee population flourishes. She says "It might take me twice as long to move a 60-pound beehive, but I'll do it in high heels and a dress coming out of a meeting with the New York Stock Exchange." She teaches beekeeping classes to employees, conducts research geared toward saving the bee population, and shows people how bees are a gateway to get people engaged with agriculture and sustainability. An impressive "beesness" (good one, Leigh-Kathryn).

No Cow

Daniel Katz is not your average 20 year old. He has started eight businesses that range from selling electronics to energy drinks to snakes. His latest venture, No Cow makes plant-based, dairy free No Cow Bars with lots of protein and little sugar. He also has a line of cookies and nut butter. For two years Daniel has been a one-person business. He says "I was working 18-hour days seven days a week, and buying

LEARNING OUTCOMES

After reading this chapter, you should be able to:

14.1 Describe the functions and activities involved in managing a small business.

14.2 Explain the stages of small business growth and their consequences for managing your business.

14.3 Discuss the significance of leadership and motivation in regard to employees of small business.

14.4 Discuss time and stress management as they relate to small business.

10-for-$10 canned vegetables to live off of and sleeping in the office on an air mattress." That dedication paid off. In two years, No Cow has grown to earn a $10 million annual revenue and substantial investment from the venture capital arm of cereal maker General Mills.

As you can see from these examples, running your own business requires a myriad of managerial skills that are used every day in a variety of ways. Small business owners seldom have the luxury of focusing on any one task until completed. They must be the proverbial jack-of-all trades. As you read through this chapter, you will learn how small business managers manage their businesses successfully through the functions of management: planning, organizing, leading, and controlling.

Sources: Michelle Cheng, "Rising Stars—Human Beeing," *Inc.,* May 2018, 25; Hannah Hayes, "Southerners of the Year 2017," *Southern Living*, accessed May 3, 2018, www.southernliving.com/culture/southerners-doing-good-2017; Diana Ransom, "Rising Stars—The Prodigy," *Inc.,* May, 2018, 26; John Kell, "General Mills' Venture Fund Invests in 20-Year-Old's Startup," *Fortune*, February 28, 2017, www.fortune.com.

Concept Module 14.1: Managing Small Business

- **LO 14.1: Describe the functions and activities involved in managing a small business.**

Businesses of every size must be managed or they will cease to exist. Although there are many similarities between managing a large business and managing a small one, significant differences also exist. Managing a small business is a complex job. You have to perform many activities well without the resources available to your large competitors. The expectations of customers, associates, and employees are increasing to the point where small businesses can rarely survive without understanding the tools and practices of professional management. In this chapter, we will investigate the processes of managing a growing business, of leading people, and of facing the concerns of a small business owner.

Master the content at
**edge.sagepub.com/
Hatten7e**

$SAGE edge™

Four Functions of Management

The major functions of **management** are generally accepted to be *planning, organizing, leading,* and *controlling.* To some extent, a manager performs these functions whether he is in charge of a large or a small operation; a for-profit or a nonprofit organization; or a retail, service, or manufacturing business.

These four functions are *continuous* and *interrelated* (see Figure 14.1). In other words, managers do each of them all the time. You don't have the luxury of getting out of bed in the morning and saying, "I think I am going to just organize today." Rather, you will have to do some planning, some organizing, a lot of leading, and some controlling every day.

These four functions are interrelated in that their achievement occurs as part of a progressive cycle. Planning begins the process, as the manager determines what to do. Organizing involves assembling the resources (financial, human, and material) needed to accomplish the plan. Leading is the process of getting the most output possible from those resources. Controlling is comparing what was initially planned with what was actually accomplished. If a deviation exists between what was planned and what was done, which is almost always the case, a new plan is needed, and the cycle begins again.

▼ **FIGURE 14.1**

Demand Curves

The functions of managing a business are continuous and interrelated.

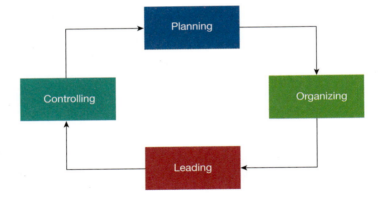

What Managers Do

Management is getting things done through people. When running a small business, you will have to spend a certain amount of time performing the actual duties and daily tasks of the business—probably more during the early stages in the life of the business and less later. You must decide where to strike a balance between doing and managing. This doesn't mean that managers don't "do" anything. Rather, it means that the time you spend on the daily tasks, like selling or writing new software or cleaning machinery, is time when you are not managing. Those tasks have to be done, and the small business owner is usually the one who has to do them, but managing a business is more than a collection of tasks.

First-time managers and business owners often think of management as doing the job they have previously done, only with more power and control. Rather, to use the analogy of a master chef, a novice business owner or manager must move from being the only person preparing and serving the food, to the master in the kitchen—planning the menu; insuring appropriate inventory is available for the dishes chosen; choosing the best combinations of meats,

PODCASTS: LISTEN, LEARN, AND TELL

To be a successful small business owner, you need to dedicate yourself to be in perpetual learning mode. What you face every single day as a small business owner is solving problems with creative solutions. The road to small business success is paved with speed bumps.

Fortunately, you have easy access to hundreds of podcasts that can help you through any specific situation or improve your business mindset. Some to consider as you search include

- **Entrepreneur on Fire:** One of the original podcasts on the topic, John Lee Dumas launched back in 2012. He states that he wants entrepreneurs to "emulate our successes and avoid our failures" via the telling of entrepreneurs' back stories and journeys.

- **The Gary Vee Audio Experience:** Gary Vaynerchuk has become quite a forceful voice via his podcast and YouTube channel (often punctuated by "colorful" language). He does provide insight into future trends and pioneering entrepreneurial solutions.

- **Freakonomics:** Critical thinking and problem solving involve a degree of thinking about things from a unique perspective. Stephen Dubner explores "the hidden side of everything" and unintended consequences.

- **How I Built This:** Guy Raz has fascinating conversations with the founders of about every well-known business you can think of, from Warby Parker to The Knot to Patagonia. Perfect listening for everyone starting, or growing, their own business.

On the topic of podcasts, 44 percent of American consumers listen to them, and 26 percent do so regularly. For you, and your small business, that means maybe you should consider launching your own podcast in addition to consuming them. The growth in popularity of podcasts is explained at least in part by the shift toward mobile, which is not going away soon.

Quality recording equipment is not expensive (relatively) and there are a lot of podcast platforms available, so you just need to find one that would be relevant to your industry and customers. Consider this approach to engaging with your customers and reinforce a message that is important to you and your business.

Sources: Jonathan Long, 5 Podcasts Every Entrepreneur Should Download Today," *Entrepreneur*, April 5, 2018, www.entrepreneur.com/article/311282; Jeremy Goldman, "Listen to These 13 Podcasts for a More Informed and Productive 2018," *Inc.*, January 3, 2018, www.inc.com; Jeff Haden, "5 Great Podcasts You Should Start Listening to Right Now," *Inc.*, April 2, 2018, www.inc.com; Aj Agrawal, "Why Podcasting Is the Next Marketing Frontier," *Entrepreneur*, April 27, 2018, www.entrepreneur.com/article/312537.

---

vegetables, fruits, and spices; and then bringing all the talents of the various kitchen crew together with perfect timing to ensure a great dining experience for the customer.

Although the four functions—planning, organizing, leading, and controlling—are as generally applicable today as they were in 1916 when they were first articulated by Henri Fayol, there is more to describing what managers *do*. Henry Mintzberg has gone into considerable depth searching for descriptions of how managers spend their time.[1]

First, rather than being reflective, systematic planners, managers tend to work at an unrelenting pace on a wide variety of activities that are brief and have little continuity. The front-line managers in Mintzberg's study averaged 583 activities per eight-hour day—one activity every 48 seconds. Even CEOs said that half of their activities lasted less than nine minutes, and only 10 percent took longer than an hour.

Second, rather than managers having no regular duties to perform, Mintzberg found that managers spend a lot of time on regular duties, such as performing rituals and ceremonies, negotiating, and dealing with the external environment. They receive visitors, take care of customers, and preside at holiday parties and other rituals and ceremonies that are part of their job, whether the business is large or small.

Third, even though management is often viewed as a technological science, information processing and decision making remain locked in the manager's brain. Managers are people who

> "First, rather than being reflective, systematic planners, managers tend to work at an unrelenting pace on a wide variety of activities that are brief and have little continuity."

depend on judgment and intuition more than on technology. Computers are important for the business's specialized work, but managers still greatly depend on word-of-mouth information to support almost all of their decisions. A manager's job is complex, difficult, and as much an art as a science.

Mintzberg suggests several important roles that a manager needs to fulfill so as to plan, organize, lead, and control successfully:

- Resource allocator role: Decides how resources are to be used

- Monitor role: Determines if quality control standards have been met

- Leader role: Determines the direction of the company

- Entrepreneur role: Keeps fresh new ideas and innovations flowing into the company

- Negotiator role: Continuously goes to bat for the resources needed for the success of the company[2]

As a manager, you must use your resources *efficiently* and *effectively*. The difference is more than an exercise in semantics. *Effectiveness* means achieving your stated goals. Having a helicopter fly you everywhere you go (across town to meetings, to the grocery store, to a ball game) is an effective way to travel. You get where you intend to go. But, of course, with the reality of limited resources, effectiveness cannot be your only goal. You need *efficiency*, too—that is, making the best use of your resources to accomplish your goals. In running a small business, you have to get the job done, but you have to contain costs as well. Wasting your limited resources—for instance, on helicopter rides—even though you achieve your goals, will lead to bankruptcy just as fast as if you were not making sales. A small business manager must balance effectiveness and efficiency to be competitive.

Jerry Murrell opened a hamburger and french fry business with his five sons in 1986 in Virginia. In 2002, they began selling franchises and by 2012 sales topped $1 billion, making it the fastest-growing restaurant chain in America. Today, Five Guys Burgers and Fries has 1,039 stores across the United States and Canada. In order to compete in this saturated market, Jerry chose to focus on quality control. The potatoes for the fries come from Idaho, the hamburger is never frozen, the buns are baked fresh daily and toasted on a grill, and the burgers are made to order. Due to the focus on quality, Jerry was reluctant to begin franchising, but his sons were insistent. In order to maintain the quality that is important to this business, it has two third-party audits in each store each week. One crew checks on customer service, and the other crew checks on kitchen safety. In this way, Five Guys Burgers and Fries has been able to grow successfully and still maintain the quality that gave the business its success in the beginning.[3]

Concept Check Questions

1. Give examples of efficiency and effectiveness in managing your everyday life.

2. Refer to the chapter-opening story. List two differing activities in which each manager engages.

Concept Module 14.2: Small Business Growth

- LO 14.2: Explain the stages of small business growth and their consequences for managing your business.

Growth is a natural, and usually desirable, consequence of being in business. Growth of your business can take several forms, albeit not necessarily all at once. You may see evidence of it in revenues, total sales, number of customers, number of employees, products offered, and facilities needed. It is something to be expected and planned for as your business evolves, but it should not be an end in itself. Bigger is not necessarily better. A sunflower is not better than a violet. And growth brings changes that may not always be positive ones.

As your business makes upward progress, you will experience "growing pains" just as people do when they move through childhood, adolescence, and adulthood. Signals of growing pains can be jobs that are not delivered on time, costs that continue to rise, the need to borrow additional money, a greater reliance on partners or employees, and increased risk taking. If growth is not managed appropriately, breakdowns in customer service and product quality can soon follow.

> "As your business makes upward progress, you will experience 'growing pains' just as people do when they move through childhood, adolescence, and adulthood."

Your Growing Firm

When a business grows in size by increasing its number of employees or its volume of sales, the way it is managed must also change. As it evolves from a bare-bones start-up to an expanded, mature firm, it may pass through roughly five stages—existence, survival, success, takeoff, and maturity.[4] Naturally, not all small businesses are the same size at start-up, nor do they all seek to achieve the same level of growth in maturity. Even so, these five stages provide a way to understand the changing needs of your business.

In the first, or *existence* stage, the owner runs the business alone (see Figure 14.2). Although not every business begins with one individual running (and being) the entire business, it is not uncommon. In fact, technology is making the solo type of business much more common than ever before. Online networks have allowed the creation of electronic cottage industries out of people's homes. Thus, although some people intentionally keep their businesses at the solo size, it also represents the first stage of growth. In fact there is even a new word to describe these business owners—*solopreneurs*.[5]

A business reaching the second stage, *survival*, has demonstrated that it has a viable idea; at this point, the key problem shifts from mere existence to generation of cash flow. Now the entrepreneur is no longer responsible for just her own efforts. She may need to hire employees if the business is to move forward. Hilda Kerne owns and operates a Lebanese food production company, Deleez Appetizers, in the Chicago area. The demand for this cuisine, which focuses on vegetarian dishes, has increased to the point where she is working 20 hours a day. Due to the popularity of the dishes, Hilda is looking at renting a larger facility and hiring her first employee. "It will kill me if I am going to work like this," she stated. However, hiring employees is expensive, particularly when looking at not only wages but also the hidden costs that must be addressed. While Hilda has discovered that hiring employees can be costly, so is working 20 hours a day every day.[6]

When the business grows to the point where employees operate in several departments, the entrepreneur must either become a professional manager or hire managerial expertise. In

▼ **FIGURE 14.2**

Five Stages of Business Growth

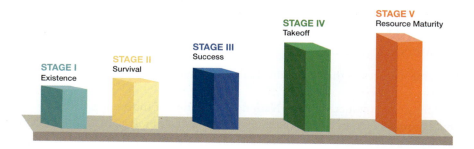

this third stage, *success*, the owner accepts a degree of disengagement as a level of supervision is added—employees to lead departments or divisions. Care must be taken that these supervisors understand the culture of the business they are joining and will work toward building it. At this point, the entrepreneur is performing less of the daily production personally and may not be in direct contact with parts of the company's efforts. He must turn loose more of the "doing" and assume more of the "managing." Giving up control in this way can be difficult, but delegation of authority and responsibility is something an entrepreneur must do to enable a business to grow.

In the fourth stage, *takeoff*, the business has grown to include multiple departments managed by numerous supervisors. As in the preceding stages, the owner remains the "head honcho," but now her responsibilities are more conceptual than technical in nature. In other words, rather than focusing on daily operations—making and selling the product or service—she will more intensely focus on managing the bigger picture, through long-range planning and overseeing supervisors, for instance. The business now needs someone to establish policies, handbooks, job descriptions, training, and budgets, and the owner will assume those executive duties. In this stage, the entrepreneur must go through the difficult metamorphosis of becoming a professional manager, hire someone else to run the business, and step out of the way, or sell the firm. The key problems in this stage are how to grow rapidly and how to finance that growth.

In the fifth stage, *resource maturity*, the company has arrived. The greatest concerns at this point are to consolidate and control the finances generated by rapid growth and to professionalize the organization. By this stage, the owner and the business are separate entities, both financially and operationally. The child the entrepreneur bore has grown up, moved out, and taken on a full life of its own. At this stage, it may be time for the organization to take a long, hard look at itself. Strategies and processes that have worked well in the past may need to be evaluated to see if they still remain effective. Many times the best person to do this organizational analysis is not the small business owner. The management team that is in place may have less of an emotional attachment and be able to more effectively look at needed changes.

None of these five stages is inherently better or worse than any of the others. Competitive advantage can be drawn from the speed and adaptability of a solo business or from the muscle achieved from growing a larger organization. Problems can also occur at every stage, although their magnitude is intensified when growth occurs too rapidly. Cash flow can turn negative, quality can suffer, and employees can lose sight of the vision of the business when growth is too rapid. Growth has to be managed, and it is not heresy to try to limit the size of your business.

Transition to Professional Management

The transition from entrepreneur to professional manager is difficult, because the skills or characteristics that were needed to establish and run the business in the start-up phase are not always the same skills needed to manage a larger business. The shift from thinking like an employee to thinking like a manager, from an entrepreneurial style of running a business to a managerial approach, can be more easily accomplished by considering the following:

- Clearly articulate your goals and vision to all.

- Adopt a managerial mindset.

- Use numbers to effectively and efficiently manage all resources, including your staff.

- Learn to delegate effectively.

- Implement processes that hold individuals accountable.[7]

In a recent study conducted by the National Federation of Independent Business (NFIB), 2,831 small business owners shared their insights about their most significant problem during

Measures of Small Business Problem Importance

Problem	2016 Rank	Mean	Standard Deviation	Percent "Critical"	Percent "Not a Problem"	2012 Rank
Cost of Health Insurance	1	2.27	1.84	52.3	7.7	1
Unreasonable Government Regulations	2	2.76	1.82	33.4	6.0	5
Federal Taxes on Business Income	3	2.91	1.86	29.3	7.6	6
Uncertainty over Economic Conditions	4	2.92	1.72	25.6	4.8	2
Tax Complexity	5	2.92	1.80	27.2	6.4	7
Uncertainty over Government Actions	6	3.04	1.86	26.3	7.4	4
Frequent Changes in Federal Tax Laws and Rules	7	3.28	1.84	20.7	8.0	8
Property Taxes (real, inventory, or personal property)	8	3.29	1.96	22.7	10.5	9
State Taxes on Business Income	9	3.33	2.00	22.7	11.9	10
Locating Qualified Employees	10	3.42	2.09	24.3	13.8	32

Source: Holly Wade, "Small Business Problems and Priorities," NFIB Research Foundation, August 2016, 12, https://www.nfib.com/assets/NFIB-Problems-and-Priorities-2016.pdf.

the previous year of operation (see Table 14.1). These owners evaluated 75 potential business problems and assessed their severity on a scale from 1 for a "Critical Problem" to 7 for "Not a Problem." A mean (average) was calculated from the responses for each problem.

Certain attributes distinguish professionally managed small businesses and can facilitate the process of transitioning from a solopreneur to a larger business. In order to make this transition, small business owners need to stop "running the show" to start "managing the show." To achieve that goal, consider the following:

- Develop an effective infrastructure—this is a must if the small business owner wants to retain control but not have to constantly micromanage every decision.

- Plan and manage growth—the biggest challenge here for the small business owner may be in the realization of how his role has now changed.

- Protecting the small business owner's time—the challenge again may be for the owner to stop doing things that he has always done. Delegation becomes key.[8]

The Next Step: An Exit Strategy

To every thing there is a season. There comes a time that every business must end. Unfortunately for many entrepreneurs, the arrival of this time means that the business could not sustain itself or them any longer and must cease to exist for that unhappy reason. But for many others, the business appears capable of continuing indefinitely. Then the question becomes, how long will *you* last? How will you and the business part ways? Just as you needed a plan to start this deal, so you need a plan to finish it. An exit strategy must be well planned. Not only can the process take a

> "Just as you needed a plan to start this deal, so you need a plan to finish it. An exit strategy must be well planned."

GROWING SMARTER

Ten years ago, Linda Turner was in an exercise class and saw a pregnant woman struggling through her routine. After class, Turner asked the woman if she knew of any products that would help her be more comfortable. Because none existed, she began developing a prototype of the BellyBra—a support device designed for women in their third trimester. The BellyBra has tank-top shoulder straps and fits snugly all the way down below the wearer's enlarged stomach area. Turner experimented with different fabrics, including white lace and CoolMax fabric that pulls heat away from the body.

The BellyBra prototypes tested well with consumers, but because Turner was a stay-at-home mom, she was not able to build a company at that time. She licensed the product to a company called Basic Comfort and became the firm's first employee. As the success of the BellyBra increased, Turner eventually left on friendly terms to go out on her own. She sold 1,000 units in her first year and 10,000 units in her second year. Some growth rate! She has now expanded her focus from obstetricians and gynecologists to selling on her internet site (www.bellybra.com).

Questions

1. Linda Turner will face different challenges as her company progresses through the five stages of growth described in this chapter. Describe how you believe her business would change in each stage.

2. Business growth that occurs too quickly can present some significant problems and challenges compared with a business that grows at a slow, steady pace (of course, zero growth or decline makes for a whole new set of problems). Describe the challenges of hypergrowth that Turner could face, and explain how she should respond as a small business owner.

Sources: Cynthia Griffin, "It's a Bra!" *Entrepreneur* 29, no. 4 (April 2001), 44; www.bellybra.com/about.

long time, but also there can be negative ramifications for your business if you do not plan the exit as carefully as you planned the start-up. Here are some tips to consider as you plan how you will end your business.

- Recognize when it is time to exit. Maybe the zest for the business is eluding you on a daily basis, maybe your mentor is suggesting it is time to quit, or maybe market conditions are changing. Pay attention to the small signs that may indicate it is time to exit.

- Watch out for your employees. You may be leaving, but your employees are probably planning on staying. Selling the business and changing management will cause uncertainty in their work lives that can cause additional employee stress.

- Make sure you have the right people in place as you leave. The management team you leave behind will be the people who take the business to the next level in the future. As much as possible, ensure that the people leading the charge will have the skills and resources needed to succeed.

- Follow your instincts. Look at the numbers, review the forecasts, analyze performance appraisals, but then pay attention to what you feel in your gut.[9]

You have three broad choices, with many themes and variations upon each: You can sell, merge, or close. None of the three is especially easy, but whether or not you have a strategy, you will exit sooner or later.

Consider these exit options:

- *Sell to a financial buyer.* This is someone like you who wants to buy and run a business.

- *Sell to a strategic buyer.* This could be company that wants to expand into your industry or a company in a similar business. Perhaps a competitor wants to buy more market share.

Such a buyer is more likely to pay market value, currently four to six times EBITDA (earnings before interest, taxes, depreciation, and amortization), as well as understand the intricacies of the business. Unless you want to continue to run the business after the sale, train your successor beforehand.[10]

- *Sell to a key employee or group of key employees.* This kind of deal is similar to selling to an individual buyer, but employee-buyers tend to be more intimately familiar with what they are purchasing. They will drive the price down, however, because they feel they deserve a lower price due to their years of service.

- *Sell to all employees via an employee stock ownership plan (ESOP).* This strategy is a great option for the seller if the business has a key group of motivated employees. You are much more likely to receive market price or even a premium because the ESOP will be based on a formal business valuation by a professional.

- *Take the company public.* This step takes a tremendous commitment, both physically and financially, to comply with all elements of the Securities and Exchange Commission (SEC) requirements. This option will often lead to loss of control over the company as management is faced with quarterly earnings reports that must meet estimates in order to maintain the stock price of the company.

- *Undertake a planned liquidation.* This approach involves running the business until the day you're done, then selling the assets. It takes a lot of planning and patience, and can be an emotional roller coaster.

Next comes *valuation*, in which the company's worth is in the eye of the beholder. There are as many ways to value a business as there are businesses, but the three most common are the *market approach* (what others have paid for comparable businesses), the *asset-based approach* (essentially the cost to re-create the operating assets of the business), and the *income approach* (how much a buyer could make from the business). See Chapter 6 for valuation approaches, remembering that any approach merely sets the beginning point for negotiation.

Concept Check Questions

1. Discuss some of the skills or characteristics that are needed by a manager in the start-up phase of a business, and explain how they differ from the skills or characteristics needed later to manage a larger, established firm.

2. Which exit strategy discussed in the chapter would you consider ideal? What would a downside of that strategy be?

3. Review the five stages of business growth. Which of these five would you aspire to for your own business? Be prepared to justify your answer.

Concept Module 14.3: Leadership in Action

- **LO 14.3: Discuss the significance of leadership and motivation in regard to employees of small business.**

Small businesses need managers who are also leaders, because building an organization requires every employee to contribute to productivity and efficiently use every resource. Owners of small businesses must be very visible leaders because they need to work closely with their people. The foundation of small business leadership is *credibility*. If people don't believe in the messenger, they won't believe in the message.

A lot of literature on management is devoted to an ongoing debate over management versus leadership. The debate began with a now famous statement from Warren Bennis:

"American businesses are overmanaged and underled."[11] Managers are more likely to be reactive, focusing on current information and making decisions based upon necessity. Leaders are much more active, shaping ideas and providing the vision for the organization. Managers establish processes, enable compromise, and limit choices within the context of organizational objectives. Leaders develop new approaches to problems, motivate followers to engage in the vision, and avoid routine, day-to-day tasks. Is one more important than the other? Not really, because running a small business takes a combination of *both* qualities. Vision without analysis produces chaos, and orderliness without passion produces rigid complacency. **Leadership** is the inspirational part of the many things a manager must do through directing and influencing team members—along with an amount of planning, directing, and controlling.

Where do small businesses find the next generation of leaders? Andy Medley and Scott Hill, owners of Indianapolis-based holding company CIK Enterprises, with 80 employees, grow their own. They run a manager's book group that meets weekly to discuss the theories of Jim Collins, Jack Stack, and other business thinkers. They call the program The Incubator. Managers nominate candidates based on enthusiasm, drive, and smarts. Only 10 percent of employees can participate at any given time. Those that come through to be future leaders will thrive, having been imbued with an understanding of the company culture. Hill states that "even if they don't want to do management, they'll come through saying, 'Hey, I learned a lot,' and they'll be better able to help in any way they can."[12]

Leadership Attributes

Numerous studies have been conducted in the area of leadership, using a variety of approaches. One of the major approaches to looking at leadership is to study the attributes that business leaders need in order to be successful, called the *trait approach* to leadership. Following are some of the traits found in most leaders.

Defining the Vision. Having a mental picture of where the company is going not only today but also tomorrow, a vision will always be an important part of leadership. Moreover, a good leader is able to describe that vision to others so that everyone is headed in the same direction and buys into the vision. A person with a vision that can't be put into action is a dreamer, not a leader.

Communication Ability. Constant communication is needed for a leader, not only to find out what is going on but also to let others know about the vision and the plans to implement the vision. The ability to communicate clearly with all groups of people ranks as one of the most important attributes a leader must possess.

Self-Confidence and Dependability. Leaders must believe in themselves and their ability to accomplish their vision. Leaders must demonstrate day in and day out their commitment and perseverance in pursuing the vision.

Adaptability. Leaders must be able to roll with the punches and take advantage of the opportunities presented. Resources, including people, must frequently be rearranged in order for the vision to be accomplished.

Commitment. Loyalty to one's company is more precarious in today's climate of economic uncertainty. With this being the case, it is more important than ever that leaders be seen as caring about the business and the employees. Passion for what is good for both the business and the workers can't be faked.

leadership
The process of directing and influencing the actions of members within a group.

LEADERSHIP IN A SMALL BUSINESS

So your small business needs you to not only be able to successfully manage, market, finance, and produce your product, but also lead? What are some key components necessary to lead your small business forward? On top of all your other tasks, how can you work in the now and also plan for the future? Here are some ideas on being a small business owner AND a leader.

- Take care of yourself first. A leader who is unhappy or ineffective will only bring in people who are the same.

- Leaders must develop a vision for the future, often with little data to fall back on. Maintaining the competitive advantage over time is essential to the success of the business and involves moving into new territory.

- Leaders help employees understand that vision in a way that allows employees to see how their positions fit in.

- Leaders must be prepared to fail. Not every idea, product, or new strategy will work. You must be able to pick yourself up, dust yourself off, and get back to work.

- Leaders must be fair. Employees want to know the process is equal for everyone and to be able to see and understand that process.

- Leaders need to demonstrate a certain amount of vulnerability. You cannot do it all well. Find key people who supplement and strengthen your areas of weakness.

- Leaders must develop a safe environment in which to make mistakes. If you want new ideas, new products, or new processes, employees must have the freedom to fail.

- Leaders get rid of the "bad" as soon as possible. Bad permeates the organization quickly. If it is bad, get rid of it whether it is a bad product, a bad supplier, or a bad employee.

- Leaders check frequently to see how others view their leadership capacity. It is easy to have a jaundiced view of your own leadership capabilities. Make sure you have at least one or two people who can accurately assess you and your leadership abilities and make appropriate suggestions when needed.

Sources: Abhi Golhar, "4 Most Critical Tactics for Great Leadership in 2018," *Inc.*, May 4, 2018, www.inc.com; Mike Kappel, "4 Leadership Methods for Empowering Employees and Building Strong Teams," *Entrepreneur*, May 6, 2018, www.entrepreneur.com/article/311610; Robert Sutton, "12 Things Good Bosses Believe," *Harvard Business Review*, May 28, 2010.

Creative Ability. Good leadership involves creating something that didn't exist before. A tolerance for ambiguity and risk taking is important as something different and new is created.

Ability to Follow Through. Leaders must make tough decisions, often based upon incomplete information with no guarantee of success. A leader needs a certain amount of toughness to make unpopular decisions or to stand against the majority when necessary in order to accomplish the vision.

Ability to Take Action. Small business leaders must realize that without action, all of the foregoing attributes are mere academic rhetoric. Leaders must also be able to make decisions, frequently with less-than-perfect information, and manage and set priorities on a daily basis as they persuade and motivate others to participate in accomplishing the vision.

Leadership attributes need to be practiced consistently to be effective. The subject of leadership is easy to talk about, but a challenge to demonstrate.[13]

Negotiation

The art of negotiation occurs continuously while running your small business, from the time the idea pops into your head until the day you harvest it. *Negotiation* can be defined as the communication process in which two or more people come together to seek mutual agreement about an issue. Negotiation can involve obtaining a certain action from someone, achieving approval from someone, or simply getting someone to agree with you. When you are raising money, hiring employees, shopping for suppliers, or signing contracts, you are negotiating. Whenever two or more people get together to exchange information for the purpose of changing their relationship in some way, they are negotiating. From merging onto the freeway in rush-hour traffic, to scheduling an appointment with a client, to deciding which television program to watch with your family, negotiation is involved.[14] Every negotiation ends with one of four possible outcomes:

- *Lose–lose.* Neither party achieves his needs or wants.

- *Win–lose.* One counterpart loses and the other wins.

- *Win–win.* The needs and goals of both parties are met, so they both walk away with a positive feeling and a willingness to negotiate with each other again.

- *No deal.* Neither party wins or loses since they agree at this time they cannot meet each other's needs and goals. This approach leaves the door open for negotiating at a later date since a win–lose or lose–lose did not occur.

Negotiation is so important to businesses of all sizes that we can see the free enterprise system at work by considering the sheer number of books written on the subject. The classic *Getting to Yes* has sold over 3.5 million copies since it was first published. *The Power of Nice, The Negotiation Tool Kit, The Art and Science of Negotiation, You Can Negotiate Anything, Negotiating Rationally,* and *The Art of the Deal* are other popular examples. Virtually every one of these books includes some simplistic examples, such as the Parable of the Orange, which goes like this: Two people each want an orange and agree finally to split the fruit in half. But it turns out that one side simply wanted the juice, and the other side wanted the rind. If only they had worked together to solve the problem, each side could have received what it wanted. Okay, so such simplistic solutions don't often turn up in the world of business. Nevertheless, there are some great pieces of advice in these tomes. Here's a sampling of some of the best:

- The goal should be win–win. If you wish to negotiate with this party again, both sides have to walk away feeling good about the outcome.

- Stay rationally focused on the issue being negotiated.

- Exhaustive preparation is more important than aggressive argument. The party with the most information often wins. You can never be overprepared in negotiating.

- Think through your alternatives. The more options you believe you have, the better your negotiating position.

- Know your BATNA—the best alternative to a negotiated agreement. Compare all outcomes to the BATNA you have developed before negotiations begin.

- Spend less time talking and more time listening and asking good questions. The more you understand the other party, the better the alternatives you can propose.

- Sometimes silence is your best response.

- Use one strong argument and repeat as needed. Do not dilute a strong argument with a weaker argument.

- Let the other side make the first offer. If you're underestimating yourself, you might make a needlessly weak opening move. You frequently have more power than you realize.

- Create a vision. How will this agreement benefit both parties?

- Don't walk into negotiations with a fallback position. If you are willing to compromise before you begin, you need to reevaluate your goals and alternatives.[15]

Delegation

By **delegation** of authority and responsibility, a manager gives employees the power to make many decisions that she would otherwise have to make, thereby giving her time to concentrate on more important matters. Delegation *empowers* employees, meaning that it increases their involvement in their work. Also, by holding employees more accountable for their actions, delegation allows managers to maximize the efforts and talents of everyone in the company.

Many small business owners are either unwilling or unable to delegate for several reasons. For entrepreneurs who have started a business, giving up control is difficult. Owners often know the business more thoroughly than anyone else and feel as if they *have* to make all the decisions so as to protect the business. They may feel that subordinates are unwilling or unable to accept responsibility. In reality, this attitude may become a self-fulfilling prophecy. If employees' attempts to take responsibility or to show initiative are squelched too often, they will either stop trying to show initiative or will leave the business.

Some small business owners simply misunderstand the meaning of management. They believe the only way to get the job done right is to do it themselves. That is a commendable attitude, but it can be counterproductive to being an effective manager, which, by definition, is someone who needs to get things done through other people.

Delegation is not the same as abdication. Nor is empowering people the same as instituting a pure democracy, where you simply count votes and the majority rules. In using delegation and empowerment, an effective leader is trying to encourage participation and take advantage of shared knowledge so that everyone can contribute. Of course, consensus can't always be reached, so sometimes the leader has to make a decision and go with it.

Some tips to help you delegate effectively:

- Understand the task and the results that are needed. Make sure needed authority as well as resources are provided.

- Choose the person carefully. Make sure the person has the needed skill set to successfully accomplish the task.

- Check on the progress of the delegated task before the completion date. See if additional information or resources are needed, and provide necessary feedback.

- Provide recognition and appropriate rewards when the task is successfully completed.[16]

Motivating Employees

The word *motivation* comes from the Latin *movere*, which means "to move." For our purposes, **motivation** is the reason an individual takes an action in satisfying some need. It answers the question of why people behave the way they do.

Motivation Theories. Some people say that one person cannot motivate another, that one can merely create an environment for self-motivation. Whether this is the case or not, as a small business manager, you will be interested in motivating your employees to accomplish the goals of the company. Many theories on motivation exist, and a thorough examination of each is not appropriate for this book, but you can obtain more information on the subject from texts on principles of management or organizational behavior. Here we will summarize two of the most well-known and accepted theories.

> "The goal should be win–win. If you wish to negotiate with this party again, both sides have to walk away feeling good about the outcome."

delegation
Granting authority and responsibility for a specific task to another member of an organization; empowerment to accomplish a task effectively.

motivation
The forces that act on or within a person that cause the person to behave in a specific manner.

One of the best known is Maslow's *hierarchy of needs*. Psychologist Abraham Maslow stated that people have in common a set of universal needs occurring in order of importance. The lowest-level needs are *physiological* (food, water, air, sleep, sex, and so on). *Safety and security* needs are the next level, followed by *social* needs, *esteem* needs, and then the highest-level need for *self-actualization*.

As a small business owner, you should be aware of the fact that your employees will not always manifest these needs in the same order. People will be at different levels of needs at different times—sometimes simultaneously—so a variety of ways to motivate their behavior is needed. For example, the use of money to motivate is often misunderstood, especially in terms of Maslow's hierarchy. Money is generally seen as providing for basic physiological needs and not being important to the higher-level needs. In fact, money is actually a motivator because it buys the time and resources needed for self-actualization. Social needs and esteem needs may be fulfilled through social events at the workplace or recognition from the manager and be more effective motivators than money, depending upon the person.

The biggest contribution of Maslow's theory to motivating employees is its recognition that people have needs that "pop up" and continue to require attention until they are satisfied. If a lower-level need pops up for an employee, he will not be able to concentrate on a higher-level need until the lower-level need is fulfilled. For example, if an employee receives a phone call from a school nurse informing him that his second-grade child had an accident and broke her arm on the playground, a safety need has popped up. This employee will probably not be very productive on the job until he can be sure the situation is under control, either by going to the school in person or by making other arrangements. Any effort to interfere with his handling of this need will create frustration and antagonism, which will undermine your employee's motivation and damage his attitude toward work.[17]

> "The biggest contribution of Maslow's theory to motivating employees is its recognition that people have needs that 'pop up' and continue to require attention until they are satisfied."

Another important motivational theory is Frederick Herzberg's *motivation-hygiene theory*. This theory is important to the small business owner because it recognizes that the factors producing job *satisfaction* are not the same as the factors that motivate employees to excel. Herzberg called things that cause people to feel good about their job *motivators* and things that people expect on the job *hygiene factors*. Since hygiene factors on the job are expected (such as safe working conditions or reasonable pay), the presence of these factors may create contentment among employees but not necessarily motivate them to excel (see Figure 14.3). To truly motivate your employees, motivational factors such as recognition, advancement, or job enrichment may be needed.

Look at the factors listed in Figure 14.3 that cause satisfaction on the job: achievement, recognition, the work itself, and responsibility. These provide intrinsic rewards to people. The practical application of Herzberg's theory gives a small business manager some direction in keeping employees satisfied on the job. Satisfaction may not translate directly into motivation, but it is a significant component in keeping employees on the job.

An underperforming employee can be assumed to be lacking in needed skills, but lack of talent is rarely the primary reason for a person to struggle at work. The *expectancy-value theory* gives a better explanation of motivation based on three factors:[18]

1. Our expectations about our own abilities (efficacy).

2. Our expectations about our environment (outcome).

3. How much importance we attach to the task at hand (value).

If, for instance, your employee just had a presentation that went very badly and she now questions her ability to present well, she may now be lacking confidence in her ability to do the job. This lack of confidence can be built back up by a good boss. Maybe she is

Relationship of Maslow's Hierarchy and Herzberg's Motivational Theory

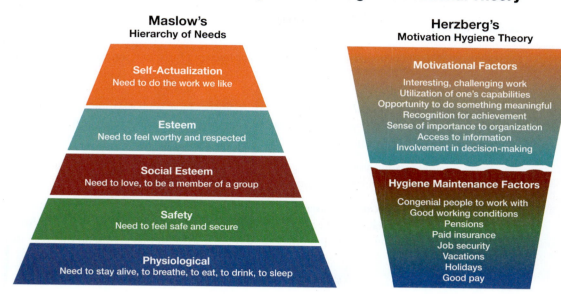

underperforming because she does not believe that her work will have an effect on the job to be done—like it doesn't matter what kind of job she does, the outcome will be the same. A conversation with this underperforming employee explaining and demonstrating the value of her contribution can be the fix. Finally, your employee may be confident and optimistic, but still not believe that the work she is doing is really "meaningful." Nobody likes to believe that they are assigned "busy work." You can show her how the work she does ties into the overall success of the small business.

Motivation Techniques. A key to motivating the employees of your small business is to know what is important to them. For instance, if you provide a motivational reward that they do not want, it is a kind of inadvertent punishment. Say you promise a "sweet year-end bonus" for the top performer for the month of December. You will probably set up healthy competition that increases morale and achievement. But if your sweet bonus turns out to be a fruitcake—and your employees don't care for fruitcake—don't expect your next incentive to be motivational.

Bill Mork is the owner of Modern of Marshfield, a furniture maker located in Marshfield, Wisconsin. Mork followed the popular advice of using recognition instead of cash to reward participants in his new employee-suggestion program. From the suggestions received, Mork and other managers picked a "colleague of the month," who was awarded with a special parking space and a big handshake in front of all the gathered employees.

The number of suggestions that came in as a result of the new program was underwhelming. One winner pleaded not to be chosen again, to avoid embarrassment and being called a "brown nose" by coworkers. As a result, Mork changed the whole program and added cash bonuses at each step. For any cost-saving suggestion made by an employee that was implemented by the company, the employee was given a bonus worth 10 percent of the estimated savings. An additional 10 percent of the savings was added to a fund to be split among all suggestion makers at the end of the year. Anyone who had contributed a suggestion was eligible for prize drawings, whether or not their suggestion was implemented. The "colleague of the month" is now chosen by previous winners rather than by managers.

Employees have taken a very different attitude toward the program since bonus checks were added.[19] Modern's sales have almost doubled. Each year Mork pays out $10,000 in rewards for about 1,200 suggestions submitted by 100 employees. Although that may sound like a lot of money, Mork estimates the savings generated by the suggestions to be five times that amount. This example suggests an answer to that long-asked management question, does money motivate? Apparently, at a very visceral level, *yes*.

Motivation Myths. So many motivation theories have been put forth that some misconceptions have resulted:

- *All employees need external motivation.* Some employees have such a strong internal drive that external techniques will not increase their motivation—though they still need your support, backing, and guidance.

- *Some employees don't need any motivation.* Motivation is the force that prompts every action—we all have to have motivation; it just comes from different sources.

- *Attempts to motivate always increase performance and productivity.* If our attempts to motivate involve incentives that employees do not desire, they can decrease performance. And some incentives can increase happiness and morale without producing an increase in productivity.

- *Money always motivates people.* Base salary is generally not a long-term motivator. A person who receives a raise may temporarily work harder but will soon rationalize, "I'm *still* getting paid less than I'm worth," and return to her previous level of productivity.

- *Intrinsic rewards provide more motivation than money.* As seen in the Bill Mork example, money—as a one-time bonus—does motivate at a visceral level.

- *Fear is the best motivator.* Workers who are afraid of a boss will work hard in the boss's presence, but may not have the business's best interests in mind. The best workers will also be looking for another job—so fear may drive out the very people the business needs the most.

- *Satisfied workers are always productive.* Happy people do not necessarily produce more. The goal of employee motivation is not to create a country club or amusement park atmosphere. Rather, the goal is to get everyone in the company to maximize his efforts so as to increase contributions (and earnings).

- *This generation of workers is less motivated than the last.* Most generations hold this attitude toward the following generation. While members of the so-called X generation have been mislabeled as "slackers," they have already produced notable entrepreneurs, including many who have been used as examples throughout this book.

Can You Motivate Without Using Money?. Money is not the only motivator. Employees value the recognition of their accomplishments and the contributions they make to the business. Here are some ideas on nonmonetary methods to use in recognizing and consequently motivating employees. And not one will negatively impact the company's profitability.

- Allow employees to be flexible in the hours that they work. A longer lunch or coming into work 30 minutes later, while usually not a problem for the company, can be very beneficial to the employee trying to balance family issues with work—and the cost is nothing.

- Give a handwritten thank you note. Take the time to write a short, yet specific, thank you to an employee who has gone above and beyond.

- Give a pass for a day off. Let employees earn extra days off to use as they like, spending time with their family or participating in a favorite activity.

CREATING COMPETITIVE ADVANTAGE

ADVANTAGEOUS CULTURE

Your small business will have a unique culture that starts on Day One. It is entirely up to you whether you shape it, or you can let the culture form itself. The conscious decisions you make to create your business's culture can be your competitive advantage.

Culture in a small business cannot be manufactured like a proverbial widget. Culture has to be nurtured with time and energy.

- **Create a culture that aligns with your core values.** Your small business is an extension of you—your personality, your interests, and your values. If your strength is being a collaborator, then build your culture on people who thrive on teamwork. Are you a work hard, play hard type? Then set your culture on high work expectations and fun celebrations. Create a culture that is a reflection of you.

- **Create a culture of complements.** Not the kind of compliments like "That's a lovely dress you're wearing, Mrs. Cleaver," but the kind that fill in gaps between company strengths and weaknesses. An orchestra of all one instrument does not sound as good as multiple sounds that create balance and harmony.

- **Create a culture of fun.** This advice can obviously be taken too far quickly, because you do have a business to run. Still, engaging employees in activities that are not just tedious work goes a long way in building a positive culture. Employees who are relaxed and comfortable with each other are happier and more productive.

- **Create a culture of believers.** A group of people who share a passion for a common goal is a powerful thing. Most successful companies of every size are filled with people who have "drank the Kool-Aid."

Zappos founder Tony Hsieh knows a lot about building corporate culture. His advice is to "Chase the vision, not the money." People who love coming to work and move in the same direction are the core of building and sustaining a strong culture.

Sources: Jacob Morgan, "Want a Competitive Advantage? Build Your Culture," *Inc.*, August 15, 2017, www.inc.com; Rajitha Boer, "Good Company Culture Removes Barriers Hindering Success," *Entrepreneur*, May 1, 2018, www.entrepreneur.com/article/312230; Monica Zent, "The 8 Essential Steps to Building a Winning Company Culture," *Entrepreneur*, November 7, 2014, www.entrepreneur.com/article/239475; Scott Schoeneberger, "You Built Great Culture, Now How Do You Leverage It for Great Work?" *Entrepreneur*, March 31, 2018, www.entrepreneur.com/article/310955.

- Celebrate employee birthdays. Make a birthday cake and have cake and coffee on the employee's birthday, or provide a birthday breakfast or lunch.

- Say, "Thank you." Too often we all forget the power of these two magical words. A simple, yet heartfelt, thank you for a job well done can be very motivating to employees.[20]

Employee Theft

Can you spot a thief in your business as easily as you can in the cartoons (you know, the guy with beady eyes, slick black hair, and a droopy moustache)? Of course you can't. But employee theft accounts for a staggering 7 percent of gross sales each year.[21] Small businesses are especially vulnerable because they have fewer defenses. Fraud and other employee abuse cost employers more than $50 billion per year. The U.S. Chamber of Commerce estimates that a third of business failures are related to employee theft. And 75 percent of employees admit to stealing products or money from their employers at least once. So what is a small business owner to do?

- Get a good small business insurance policy covering outside theft, employee theft, and/or computer fraud.

- Screen out potential problem employees at the hiring stage by administering a standardized test that indicates level of integrity, and conduct background checks before hiring.

- Create a culture of honesty with a written code of ethics and conduct. Instruct employees in how to spot problems and what to do about them (tell you).

- Set an example. Do not send mixed signals by taking money out of the register for personal use or using the business credit card for personal purchases. Employees pay attention to your behavior.

- Minimize the amount of cash on hand, and put excess cash in a safe.

- Never schedule an employee to work alone.

- Let everyone know that you look at every deposit and every check. Make sure that you get monthly bank statements delivered to your desk unopened.

- The most important point for small business: Divide up financial tasks. The person who keeps the books should not be the same person who keeps the money.

- Implement a zero tolerance policy. If an employee is stealing from the company, be prepared to implement the policy quickly and effectively.

Concept Check Questions

1. How can the owner of a small business apply Maslow's hierarchy of needs to working with employees?

2. What are positive and negative aspects of delegation?

3. As a business owner, in which of the leadership attributes discussed in the text are you the weakest? How could you help yourself improve in this area? How could others help you? What is your strongest leadership skill?

4. What is motivation? Can managers really motivate employees?

Concept Module 14.4: Special Management Concerns: Time and Stress Management

- **LO 14.4: Discuss time and stress management as they relate to small business.**

Beyond the standard functions of management lie many other duties and responsibilities. Besides running your business, you also have personal, family, and social activities. You must be a good manager of time and be able to keep stress at acceptable levels.

Time Management

As noted earlier, management is the *effective* and *efficient* use of resources. Most of us in business focus on our money: How much do I need? Where can I get it? We take the risking of our money seriously. But what is the most important component to making that money? What is a small business owner's most precious and most limited resource that can't be replaced? Time.[22]

> "What is a small business owner's most precious and most limited resource that can't be replaced?"

No one seems to have enough of it, yet everyone has the same amount—24 hours per day, 168 hours per week, or 8,760 hours per year. You can't store it, rent it, hoard it, sell it, or buy any more of it. So you had better use it wisely.

Few of us use time as effectively or as efficiently as possible. The key to effective time management for a small business owner is establishing priorities, investing time in what is important in life—and in the business. Thus time management is a goal-oriented activity. It requires that you prioritize what needs to be accomplished in any given day. Following are some indications that you are having problems with time management:

- You are frequently late for or forget meetings and appointments.

- You are consistently behind in responsibilities.

- You don't have enough time for basics—eating, sleeping, and family.

- You are constantly working and still miss deadlines.

- You are often fatigued, both mentally and physically.

How can you improve your effectiveness in using your time? A good starting point is to conduct a *time audit*. A time audit makes as much sense as conducting a financial audit, yet few small business managers can account for their minutes as precisely as they can their dollars. Why? They don't have time to conduct a time audit!

Begin your time audit by keeping a log to record your activities. Break days down into 15-minute intervals and keep track of what you do for about two weeks. When the log is complete, you can analyze how you have spent your time. Did you accomplish your most urgent tasks? Which activities were a waste of time and could be eliminated? In the end, the time audit should help you prioritize activities and set daily goals.

After you conduct your time audit, use these tips to your advantage:

- *Make a to-do list.* Write down and rank by importance what you want to accomplish each day. Make sure the most important activities receive top priority. The return you receive will be many times greater than the small amount of time you invest in this exercise.

- *Eliminate time wasters.* Combine similar tasks and eliminate unnecessary ones. Pay special attention to time spent in meetings.

- *Remember Parkinson's law.* "Work expands to fill the time available." If you schedule too much time to accomplish something, you'll probably set a pace to take that amount of time.

- *Schedule time for special projects and activities.* Other people can put appointments on your calendar; you can do the same, ensuring important tasks will get completed.

- *Know when you are most productive.* We all have a daily cycle. Some of us are "morning people." Some are "night owls." Schedule your work so that you handle your most demanding problems when you are at your best.

How late is late? Every culture has its own concept of time. In an experiment at California State University, Fresno, 200 students were surveyed in California and Brazil about their definition of "early" and "late." American students believed they were "late" for a lunch date when they made a friend wait for 19 minutes, compared with 34 minutes for the Brazilians. Does this finding mean anything to your small business? Yes, groups form "temporary cultures" that can be used to influence their attitude toward time.[23] Since perceptions of lateness vary, you need to clarify exactly what time employees are expected to be at work, to be back from lunch, and to show up for meetings.

Stress Management

One of the most ambiguous words in the English language is **stress**. There are almost as many interpretations of this term as there are people who use it, but technically, the stress response is actually the unconscious preparation to fight or flee that a person experiences when faced with a demand. Common usage leads us to think of stress as a negative thing, as if it were something to be avoided, yet there is a positive side to stress. Positive stress (called eustress) stimulates us to face challenges, motivates us to achieve, enhances our performance, increases efficiency, and adds excitement to life, as when you are anticipating a wedding or vacation. It produces favorable chemicals in our body—endorphins, serotonin, and dopamine—and is necessary for life and health. But the negative side of stress, called **distress**, entails unfavorable

stress
Emotional states that occur in response to demands, which may come from internal or external sources.

distress
The negative consequences and components of stress.

psychological, physical, or behavioral consequences, and this is the stress that we must learn to manage. It is also the stress that managers need to be aware of when dealing with employees, since this type of stress can decrease productivity, negatively impact customer relations, and increase absenteeism.[24]

For a situation to create distress for a person, two conditions are necessary: Its outcome must be uncertain, and it must be a matter of importance to the person. Another way to look at distress is as a mismatch that has occurred between the requirements to complete a task successfully and the resources that are available. Stress over time can lead to burnout, which, in turn, can decrease productivity dramatically.[25] Very few (if any) small businesses are "sure things" guaranteed to produce the outcome that the owner desires. Because small businesses are almost always the sole means of support for their owners, saying that they are extremely important to the owners is not an understatement. Therefore, both conditions causing distress exist in running a small business.

Other sources of stress that small business owners encounter include role conflict, task overload, and role ambiguity. *Role conflict* exists when we are faced with a situation that presents divergent role expectations. For example, a two-day business trip to meet with a potential client could help you land a large new account and prove very profitable for your business. But suppose taking the trip would cause you to miss your second grader's school play. The result is role conflict. The desire to attend both the meeting and the play—to be both a focused entrepreneur and a loving parent—creates a stressful internal conflict.

Task overload is another source of stress for a small business owner. More is expected of you than time permits—a common scenario in a small business. Unfinished work can be a sign of overload. In a business climate that calls for leaner organizations, work can pile up and more work can be taken on before existing jobs are finished. Unfinished work creates tension and uneasiness. If the pattern of taking on more and more continues, eventually an accumulation of unfinished work produces stress and decreases performance.

Role ambiguity occurs when you are not entirely sure what you should do in a situation. Owning a small business generally means that you don't have anyone to consult when problems arise and that you will have to make decisions on a wide variety of topics. Some people have a higher tolerance or preference for ambiguity than others, but it still produces stress.

Stress is cumulative—it builds up. Sales declining at the business, a key employee being unhappy, a child having discipline problems, and the transmission going kaput in the family car all can combine to form a lot of stress. Individual stressors that could be handled by themselves may combine and become overwhelming.

> "Stress cannot, and should not, be eliminated from everyday life, but it must be managed."

Stress cannot, and should not, be eliminated from everyday life, but it must be managed. There are three basic responses to stress: avoid the situation causing the stress, alter the situation so it no longer causes stress, or accept the situation. Realistically, for the small business owner, avoiding the business or altering the business may not be practical solutions. Acceptance of the situation and making positive changes over how we personally manage the stress may be the only true alternative. General recommendations for controlling your stress level include the following.

Preventive Stress Management

- Attempt to modify, reduce, or eliminate the source of distress. Any changes you can make in your schedule or role as business owner can help prevent distress from building to a dangerous level.

- Maintain a positive outlook. Optimism can pay big rewards when addressing stressful situations.

- Prioritize tasks and ensure there is a balance between the task that needs to be completed and the resources available. If not, you may need to rearrange resources.[26]

Relaxation Techniques. A few minutes of concentrated relaxation will prevent a build-up of distress. Practice a five-step relaxation exercise:

- First, sit in a comfortable position in a quiet location. Loosen any tight clothing.

- Second, close your eyes and assume a passive, peaceful attitude.

- Third, relax your muscles as much as possible—beginning with your feet and continuing to your head—and keep them relaxed.

- Fourth, slowly breathe through your nose and develop a quiet rhythm of breathing. After each exhale, quietly say "one" to yourself.

- Fifth, continue relaxing muscles and concentrate on breathing for 10 to 20 minutes. Open your eyes occasionally to check the time. It will take practice for you to learn to ignore distracting thoughts during relaxation, but soon this exercise can help you reduce stress.

Social Support Systems. Working in an environment that provides social and emotional support can help us deal with distress. Relationships within the workplace, family, church, and clubs provide emotional backing, information, modeling, and feedback.

Take Care of Your Health

- Exercise! A person's physical condition affects his response in stressful situations. Aerobically fit people have more efficient cardiovascular systems and better nervous system interaction, which allow them to deal with and recover from stressful events more quickly.

- Eat a balanced diet with plenty of water, fruits, and vegetables.

- Get enough rest. Sleeping in front of the television, catnapping, or sleeping for less than four to six hours a night does not provide the body the regenerative time it requires to be able to address the demands of the day.

If (once you own your own business) you find yourself struggling with any of the varied topics in this chapter, from motivating employees to battling stress, and cannot win the struggle alone, you may want to consider a fast-growing trend in small business—hiring a business coach. The practice is not unusual; managers have sought outside counsel ever since Machiavelli first advised a young prince. The number of business coaches has grown from 2,000 in 1996 to over 17,500 in 2016.[27]

Concept Check Questions

1. Are you a good manager of time in your personal life? How will this affect your ability to manage your time as a business owner?

2. Give examples of stress, eustress, and distress.

CHAPTER REVIEW

SUMMARY ▶▶

LO 14.1 **Describe the functions and activities involved in managing a small business.**

Managers plan, organize, lead, and control. To accomplish these functions, they perform many activities, such as developing relationships, negotiating, motivating, resolving conflicts, establishing information networks, making decisions, and continually learning.

LO 14.2 **Explain the stages of small business growth and their consequences for managing your business.**

In the earliest stage of many businesses' life, the entrepreneur acts alone. Many entrepreneurs even prefer to keep their businesses as one-person organizations. In the second growth stage, employees are added, so the entrepreneur often acts as a coach in getting work accomplished through other people. In stage three, a new layer of supervision is added, so the entrepreneur does not directly control all the people or activities of the business. In the fourth stage, takeoff, the business has grown to include multiple departments managed by numerous supervisors. By the fifth stage, the owner and the business are separate entities, both financially and operationally.

LO 14.3 **Discuss the significance of leadership and motivation in regard to employees of small business.**

Leadership means inspiring other people to accomplish what needs to be done. Leadership is part of a manager's job of providing the vision, passion, and creativity needed for the business to succeed.

Because management is getting things done through people, a small business manager must be able to motivate employees. The manager must therefore understand employees' behavior and recognize what is important to them. Maslow's and Herzberg's theories provide small business managers with frameworks for understanding motivation.

LO 14.4 **Discuss time and stress management as they relate to small business.**

Besides running your business, you must be a good manager of time and be able to keep stress at acceptable levels.

KEY TERMS ▶▶

delegation **377**

distress **383**

leadership **374**

management **366**

motivation **377**

stress **383**

STUDENT STUDY SITE ▶▶

edge.sagepub.com/hatten7e

⑤SAGE edge™ Sharpen your skills with SAGE edge!

SAGE edge for Students provides a personalized approach to help you accomplish your coursework goals in an easy-to-use learning environment. You'll find mobile-friendly eFlashcards and quizzes as well as multimedia resources to support and expand on the concepts presented in this chapter.

EXPERIENTIAL LEARNING ACTIVITIES ▶▶

14.1: Management: Four Functions

LO 14.1: Describe the functions and activities involved in managing a small business.

Jamie was just promoted to manager of the smoothie shop, where she had worked nights and weekends for the last two years. While Jamie had never held a management position, she felt confident in her new role. Yesterday and this morning she had been watching management training videos. Things were going great until two minutes ago. The owner of the store entered the store with a list of things for Jamie to do and the statement that the owner was on the way to Mexico to check out a potential new fruit supplier. Contact, other than email, would be difficult. Jamie momentarily panicked. She had been counting on the store owner as a mentor through the first couple of weeks as a new manager. Jamie glanced at the list in her hands, wondering what to do first. The list contained the following items: Create schedule for next two weeks, authorize payroll, make the cash deposit, create new marketing ad for upcoming flyer, hire Jamie's replacement, contact cleaning crew for monthly deep clean, order smoothie inventory, daily ensure enough cash/change in register, ensure food safety standards are met continuously, ensure quality customer service, order new uniforms for last two hires, ensure store cleanliness daily, order needed paper products, and contact pop company to evaluate contact for next year. As Jamie reached almost the end of the list, an employee walked into her office saying that the two employees scheduled to close tonight have both just called in sick.

1. For each item listed above, determine which of the four function of management that item falls under. Some items may fall under more than one category.

2. After categorizing the items into the four functions of management, prioritize the list of items with the most important item listed as number 1, that is, what should Jamie do first?

14.2: Management Leadership

LO 14.3: Discuss the significance of leadership and motivation in regard to employees of small business.

Form groups of 4–6 students. From each group, one person should be chosen as the leader. Have the group leaders go outside the classroom with the instructor so the instructor can provide instructions. The group members should not be able to overhear the conversation.

The instructor shares with the group leaders the following information. You are looking at three differing types of leaders.

Laissez-faire leaders: Leaders who are hands off and allow group members to make all decisions. The leader does no more than provide beginning information on the task to be completed.

Autocratic leaders: Leaders who dictate every decision and will not take any input from group members. They are truly "do it my way or no way."

Democratic leaders: Leaders who actively seek group member participation and advice in completing the task. The leader, in many ways, becomes just another group member.

Group Task

The task each student group must complete is to build a paper tunnel tall and wide enough for a golf ball to roll through. The **longest tunnel** will win the competition. No tape, glue, paper clips, and so on are allowed. The paper must hold together with no outside help. The tunnel must also stay upright for the length of the competition. All groups must have the same number of pieces of paper. There is a strict time limit of 10 minutes and the group leader must maintain their given leadership style for the activity. Halfway through, the instructor will provide one more piece of information about the tunnel layout.

CHAPTER CLOSING CASE ▶▶

Family Matters

Accurate Perforating Co. punches holes in sheet metal—LOTS of holes. The company, founded in 1940, perforates 40 million pounds of sheet metal annually (and, we assume, accurately) for industrial and architectural purposes.

Accurate's president Larry Cohen had a meeting scheduled with his bankers at the Chicago headquarters of Cole Taylor Bank, but he was not looking forward to it. The Chicago-based metal company owned by Cohen's family had run out of operating capital. Cole Taylor had loaned Accurate $1.5 million two years earlier. When the dreaded meeting finally arrived, the bank gave Cohen two choices: liquidate the business or find a new lender. Cohen was shocked by the ultimatum. "They were basically going to put us out of business," he says.

For decades, Cohen and his father, Ralph (the company founder), had focused on one thing: putting as many holes in as many sheets of metal as possible. They bought the metal from steel mills in the Chicago region, punched holes in it, and sold it in bulk to distributors, which then sold it to metal workshops. There the metal was fabricated and finished—that is, cut, folded to specification, and painted—and sold to manufacturers of products like speaker grilles and ceiling tiles. "We were really just selling tonnage," Cohen says. "We stayed away from sophisticated products, and as a result we wound up in a very competitive situation where the only thing we were selling was price."

Accurate's business model became increasingly unsustainable due to a worldwide glut of steel, forcing prices down. The costs of manufacturing steel climbed while its prices stayed flat, shrinking once-healthy profit margins. Most competitors found more profitable niches in fabricating, finishing, and selling metal directly to manufacturers, but Accurate survived through militant budgeting. "If we couldn't pay cash, we didn't do it," recalls

Cohen, who was unwilling to invest in the equipment required to become a fabricator. While times were so difficult, employees built perforating machines from scratch—repairing them only when absolutely necessary—and used outmoded manufacturing processes developed by the Cohen family way back in the 1940s. Annual revenue stayed between $10 million and $15 million for more than two decades. Accurate was decades behind the competition in terms of both technology and business strategy.

Aaron Kamins was the only member of the family's younger generation working at the company. Kamins was the 36-year-old nephew of Cohen who took over day-to-day operations as general manager. Even though decades behind the competition in both technology and business strategy, Kamins says, "There was a culture here that resisted change. Everyone was comfortable with what they were doing. We were making a living and that was that." Kamins, who had worked on Accurate's factory floor since graduating from college, hoped to steer the company in a new direction. With Cohen's approval, he borrowed $1.5 million from Cole Taylor Bank to purchase Semrow Perforated & Expanded Metals, a business in Des Plaines, Illinois, that produced and sold fabricated products. He hired two of the company's top executives, Mike Beck and Mike Zarnott, to oversee the division, along with 10 of Semrow's 40 factory workers.

Selling fabricated metal directly to manufacturers generated $1.5 million, but Beck, Accurate's director of new product development and engineering, and Zarnott, the company's director of sales and marketing, had bigger aspirations. They begged Kamins to break from the 1960s-type marketing. Kamins refused, being worried about diverting too much time and money away from the core commodity business, and Cohen agreed. "Everything I said about marketing Aaron thought was rubbish," says Zarnott, who struggled with a marketing budget of $15,000 a year— split between Yellow Pages ads and a listing in the Thomas Registry. Beck and Zarnott were not amused.

The next year brought a downturn period for Accurate. The Iraqi invasion made customers skittish. Orders fell by 50 percent. The bank "strongly recommended" that the company hire Stonegate Group, a turnaround firm in Deerfield, Illinois. Stonegate's primary recommendation was to renegotiate payment schedules with vendors. Meanwhile, Cohen liquidated half a million dollars in personal real estate to pay overdue bills. To cut costs, the company laid off 13 of its 85 employees.

Even with Stonegate's stellar advice, Accurate lost more than $500,000. Then came the meeting with Cole Taylor that December; the bank agreed to give Cohen a few weeks to devise a plan. He immediately began looking for a new lender but was able to borrow an additional $400,000 in loans from friends—just enough to purchase three months' worth of steel. That meant the company had 90 days to make some serious decisions about Accurate's future.

Liquidation seemed too dramatic because Cohen believed that Accurate could thrive with the right business model. Another alternative was to continue cutting costs and hope for a rebound in steel prices—a strong possibility due to growing demand from China. Beck and Zarnott's idea of scaling back the commodity business to focus on selling finished metal seemed like the smartest long-term strategy. But that alternative would take huge amounts of time and money to perfect the new manufacturing process, retrain factory workers, cultivate new clients, and revamp Accurate's nuts-and-bolts image—time and money they didn't have.

Cohen wrestled with the most difficult question: Should he replace his nephew with a more seasoned executive? Kamins had little formal business training. Was he the person to lead a turnaround? "I worried that we would just continue repeating all the mistakes that we had made," Cohen says. An outsider would offer a fresh perspective, but hiring a CEO would be expensive and time-consuming. Cohen felt like the owner of a baseball team with a losing manager. "I didn't know if a new guy would do a better job," he says. "I just knew the old guy wasn't doing a good job."

What do you think? Does Aaron Kamins deserve one last chance to save the company?

Questions

1. Put yourself in Larry Cohen's position. What would you see as your most immediate problem? What are your long-term problems?

2. Would you keep Aaron Kamins as CEO? Why or why not? If you fire him, who would do the job?

3. What do you recommend Cohen do to save Accurate Perforating?

Sources: Max Chafkin, "Case Study," *Inc.*, June 2006, 58–60; Allison Enright, "Not Just Metal with Holes," *Marketing News*, June 15, 2007, 7; Patrick Sauer, "Family Ties," *Inc.*, August 2007, 18; www.accurateperforating.com.

## CHAPTER 15

HUMAN RESOURCE MANAGEMENT

Heather Wilde proved that employee location does not matter. She worked at Evernote for six years from a sailboat and RV. Like a lot of people, Wilde wondered what work would be like from somewhere other than the same office every . . . single . . . day. She and friends were building the company Evernote and decided to join the ranks of digital nomads. Wilde was a founding employee at Evernote, an app designed for note taking, organizing, creating task lists, and creating an archive of notes.

Digital nomads are people who use a variety of telecommunication tools to stay in contact with employers and customers while roaming the planet.

A Gallup poll of 15,000 workers found that 43 percent of adults spend at least some of their time working remotely. Flexible schedules and the ability to work from home are top considerations in whether many employees accept a job (or stay in their current one).

With increased internet access improving in more corners of the world, working from anywhere has never been more possible. If your small business can utilize the skills of a digital nomad, you can save resources in terms of benefits, office space, and training.

After reading this chapter, you should be able to:

15.1 Discuss the importance of hiring the right employees.

15.2 Evaluate the advantages and disadvantages of the six major sources of employee recruitment.

15.3 Describe the four tools commonly used in employee selection.

15.4 Discuss the need for employee training and name the seven methods of providing this training.

15.5 Explain the two components of a compensation plan and the variable elements of a benefits system.

15.6 Profile an effective sequence for disciplining and terminating employees.

Sources: Heather Wilde, "Proof That Location Doesn't Matter," *Inc.*, July 28, 2017, www.inc.com; Lydia Belanger, "Evernote's Head of 'People' Explains How the Company Employs Tech Tools to Reinforce Its Values," *Entrepreneur*, March 14, 2018, www.entrepreneur.com/article/310249; Brian Hughes, "How to Run a Thriving Business as a Digital Nomad," *Entrepreneur*, April 16, 2018, www.entrepreneur.com/article/311981.

Concept Module 15.1: Hiring the Right Employees

- **LO 15.1: Discuss the importance of hiring the right employees.**

Are human resource management (HRM) issues important to small businesses? Can small business owners afford the time and cost of developing formal recruitment, selection, training, and benefits programs? Perhaps the more appropriate question is whether small business owners can afford *not* to spend the time and money on such programs? In today's marketplace, employees are one of the most valuable resources as well as a competitive advantage for businesses.

One of the most important decisions a small business owner makes is the hiring of the first and then successive employees. Not only do employees cause an increase in costs, but also hiring a bad employee can negatively impact the business. Employee turnover creates disruption in a company's overall productivity. The Society of Human Resource Management reports that on average 36 percent of all new hires fail within the first 18 months; 40 percent of senior managers hired from outside the company also fail within 18 months; and the cost of replacing employees can reach a third of their annual salary.[1]

As alarming as these figures are, they do not include other potential costs, such as defending against charges of discrimination, the loss of customer satisfaction, low employee morale, and wrongful-discharge suits. Once you find people to hire, you must find ways to retain and motivate them, which costs money. These costs may also increase as you implement more employee incentive and benefit plans.

Master the content at
**edge.sagepub.com/
Hatten7e**

$SAGE edge™

KEEPING YOUR MOST VALUABLE ASSET

Considering that employees are your small business's most valuable assets, how can you make sure you keep them? Other assets like equipment, inventory, and money don't just quit and walk away, so let's consider why people would.

Gallup conducts an annual report titled *State of the American Workplace*, gathering data from almost 200,000 employees. When asked the attribute that was most important when considering whether to leave their current job for another one, respondents stated *the ability to do what they do best*, which seems obvious. Wouldn't every small business owner or every manager want people to perform tasks at which they excel? Apparently, the evidence says "no." Factors ranked in order from the Gallup report are

- The ability to do what they do best.
- Greater work–life balance and better personal well-being.
- Greater stability and job security.
- A significant increase in income.

- The opportunity to work for a company with a great brand or reputation.

You may notice that money made the list, but did not top it, and *significant increase* indicates that if compensation is just OK, employees will stay. The interpersonal conditions that employees work in are important to them. Employees typically do not leave companies; they leave bosses, managers, and coworkers.

Small businesses are rarely able to compete for top talent based solely on compensation packages offered by large competitors. But when analyzing reasons why employees leave, there are many factors that allow small businesses to make retaining their best people a competitive advantage.

Sources: Marcel Schwantes, "Why Would People Consider Quitting Their Jobs, Exactly?" *Inc.*, May 14, 2018, www.inc.com; Ceren Cubukcu, "5 Reasons Why Your Employees Are Quitting," *Entrepreneur*, March 31, 2018, www.entrepreneur.com/article/311292; Justas Markus, "Mistakes That Make Your Employees Leave You," *Entrepreneur*, April 18, 2017, www.entrepreneur.com/article/292989.

All told, the costs and risks associated with HRM issues are too great for any company to ignore. Small business owners need to realize that their most valuable assets walk out the door each day at closing time.

Job Analysis

The recruitment process involves attracting talented individuals to your company. To achieve this goal, you must be able to (1) define the positions to be filled and (2) state the qualifications needed to perform them successfully. This endeavor requires that you conduct a job analysis, prepare a job description, identify a list of job specifications, and identify alternative sources of employees. While this list may seem long, time spent defining the job, describing the job, and determining the needed employee abilities is time well spent. Since the goal is to hire employees who fit the organization and who will stay, the following steps become critical in order to effectively hire.[2]

> "Small business owners need to realize that their most valuable assets walk out the door each day at closing time."

The **job analysis** indicates what is done on the job, how it is done, who does it, and to what degree. It is the foundation on which all other HR activities are based and, if necessary, defended in court. Although no single job-analysis technique has been endorsed by the courts or the Equal Employment Opportunity Commission (EEOC), both entities urge—and in some cases require—that the information from a job analysis be used to ensure equal employment opportunity.

The first step in completing the job analysis is to gain the support and cooperation of employees, because they often know best what the job involves. The next step is to choose the jobs that should be analyzed. Generally, the amount of time and money you have available, and the importance of the particular job to the company's overall success, will determine the order and the number of jobs you will analyze.

job analysis
The process of gathering all the information about a particular job, including a job description and the job specifications.

Step three involves identifying the job-analysis technique or techniques you will use to obtain information about each job. Although numerous techniques exist, for reasons of cost, ease of use, and time savings, the most commonly used technique is the questionnaire. Questionnaires typically seek to gather the following information: identification facts about the job, skill requirements, job responsibilities, effort demanded, and working conditions. Once you have analyzed your jobs, you are ready to prepare the job description and job specifications.

Job Description

A **job description** identifies the duties, tasks, and responsibilities of the position. Although a standard format for the job description (often termed the position description) does not exist, it is generally agreed that each job description should include the following elements:

- *Job identification.* The job title, location, or department within the company, and date of origin should be included in this introductory section. This section might also include the job code, salary range, pay classification, and analyst's name.

- *Job summary.* This summary should outline the jobholder's responsibilities, the scope of her authority, and superiors to whom she is to report.

- *List of essential duties.* Although this list may contain both essential and nonessential duties, the Americans with Disabilities Act (ADA) requires that each be clearly identified, because employment decisions may be based only on the essential components of the job. The duties should be listed in order of importance with the most important duties first. Any duty that will represent at least 5 percent of an employee's time should be included.[3]

- *Task statement.* Task statements detail the logical steps or activities needed to complete the overall duties. These statements should focus on the outcomes or results rather than on the manner in which they are performed. For example, a loading-dock worker might "move 50-pound boxes from the unloading dock to the warehouse" rather than "lift and carry 50-pound boxes from the unloading dock to the warehouse." Task statements help to identify the knowledge, skills, abilities, and educational levels needed to perform the job and help to establish performance standards for the position. In addition, these statements are valuable in complying with various federal and state employment provisions.

General working conditions, travel requirements, equipment and tools used, and other job-related data may also be included in the job description. To preserve your status as an at-will employer, which gives you the right to discharge an employee for any reason (discussed further later in this chapter), you may add a general-duty clause, such as "and other duties as assigned" or "representative tasks and duties," to indicate that your list is not comprehensive. This also assists employers when employees do not perform a task because "It's not in my job description." Figure 15.1 shows an example of a typical job (position) description.

Job Specifications

The **job specifications** indicate the skills, abilities, knowledge, experience, and other personal requirements a worker needs to successfully perform the job. In writing the specifications, take care to ensure the stated requirements are truly necessary for successful performance of the job. For example, in some cases, stating that a college degree is a requirement for a given job may be difficult, if not impossible, to prove if questioned by an EEOC representative. For this reason, you may wish to add a qualifier, such as "or equivalent," and always limit the specifications to those that are truly job related and necessary. Job specifications are often integrated into the job description, as shown in Figure 15.1.

job description
A written description of a nonmanagement position that covers the title, duties, and responsibilities involved in the job.

job specifications
The identification of the knowledge, skills, abilities, and other characteristics an employee would need to perform the job.

Sample Job Description

Job Title: Marketing Researcher

Department: Marketing

Reports To: Marketing Manager

Status: Non-Exempt

Summary: Employee is responsible for monitoring market conditions in local, regional, and national areas to determine sales potential for company's products and services.

Essential Duties and Responsibilities: All of the following, plus other duties as assigned. Employee will:

- Conduct marketing research and analyze data on customer demographics, preferences, and buying habits for the purpose of making intelligent marketing decisions.

- Prepare reports of marketing research conclusions, illustrating data graphically and explaining findings in written copy.

- Monitor internal and external environments including financial, technological, competitive, regulatory, and demographic factors so that market opportunities may be capitalized upon.

- Measure customer and employee satisfaction.

- Coordinate research to implement the organization's Integrated Marketing Communications (IMC) including print, broadcast, and online messages.

- Forecast and track marketing and sales trends.

- Measure effectiveness of marketing strategies and individual campaigns.

- Gather data on competitors and analyze price, sales, and distribution comparisons.

- Establish effective controls and corrective action needed to achieve marketing goals within designated budgets.

- Prepare monthly marketing activity reports.

Supervisory Responsibilities: None. Marketing Researcher is an autonomous staff position with no direct subordinates.

Qualifications: Requirements listed below represent the knowledge, skills, and/or abilities required to perform the job satisfactorily. Reasonable accommodations may be made to enable individuals with disabilities to perform the essential functions.

- *Education and/or Experience*—Bachelor's degree (BA, BS, or BBA) or equivalent required, Master's degree (MBA) preferred; or six years related experience and/or training; or equivalent combination of education and experience.

- *Language Skills*—Fluency in the English language with ability to read and analyze financial reports, legal documents, and industry trade journals. Ability to effectively communicate with customers, regulatory agencies, or members of the business community. Ability to effectively present information to top management, public groups, and/or boards of directors.

- *Mathematical Skills*—Knowledge of arithmetic, algebra, geometry, calculus, statistics and their applications. Ability to perform statistical operations such as frequency distribution, test reliability and validity, analysis of variance (ANOVA), correlation techniques, and factor analysis—and analyze using SPSS statistical software.

- *Analysis Ability*—Ability to define problems, collect data, establish facts, and draw valid conclusions.

- *Physical Demands*—Employee is regularly required to sit for extended periods of time. The employee is occasionally required to stand, walk, and lift up to twenty-five pounds. Reasonable accommodations may be made to enable individuals with disabilities to perform required duties.

Under Title VII and other anti-discrimination laws, you may not discriminate based upon gender, religion, race, color, or national origin. In order to choose only people from one of the protected groups listed, the employer must demonstrate specific job requirements that only this group possesses, termed bona fide occupational qualifications or BFOQs—for example, male clothing designers could legally advertise for male models only, where female models wouldn't be able to model men's clothing as intended.[4]

Concept Check Questions

1. What is the difference between a job analysis and a job description?

2. Discuss three key pieces of legislation that are used to prevent job discrimination.

Concept Module 15.2: Employee Recruitment

- **LO 15.2: Evaluate the advantages and disadvantages of the six major sources of employee recruitment.**

You may recruit employees from a variety of sources, each of which has advantages and disadvantages. The six major sources are help-wanted ads, employment agencies, internet job sites, executive recruiters (headhunters), employee referrals, and relatives or friends.

Internet Job Sites

Online job-posting sites like Indeed.com, Monster.com, Careeronestop.org (U.S. Department of Labor), and Careerbuilder.com provide access to millions of potential employees. Prices to list jobs vary by geographic location, industry, and the package you select. Trade associations you may belong to for your business also post job listings on their websites.

Be sure to write a compelling ad that stands out from all the rest. An advantage of online sites is that you are not limited to a certain number of words. Tell the story of your business and about the team you are assembling. Sell the advantages of your company and why the candidate should "buy."

Advertising for Employees

While online searching provides the primary tools now, don't overlook help-wanted ads in newspapers, trade publications, or local sources. They can generate a large number of responses. Ads can reach a wide, diverse audience of employees with unique or specialized skills.

Employment Agencies

Located in all states and most large cities, government-funded employment agencies focus primarily on assisting blue- or pink-collar employees, so they may not always offer the candidates you want. On the positive side, they allow you to obtain screened applicants at no cost. On the negative side, the quality of applicants may not be equal to that generated by some other sources. Private employment agencies can be useful in helping you find more-skilled employees. Fees for professional and management job candidates are usually paid by you, the employer.

Executive Recruiters (Headhunters)

Executive recruiting, or so-called headhunting firms, can be useful for small businesses looking for a key management person or two. Governmental employment agencies are much less expensive when looking for candidates for manual labor or other lower-level positions.

FINDING EMPLOYEES VIA LINKEDIN

Small business owners find hiring new employees to be stressful and time-consuming for the same reason many facets of small business are difficult—it's not a specialty you do often and you don't have a full-time HR department. LinkedIn is making that task easier for small businesses.

Small business owners should not see LinkedIn as a business-card collector, an email replacement, or a Facebook counterpart for business friends. As the premier business social media site it offers a lot of recruiting potential.

LinkedIn launched its hiring platform in 2018 as an end-to-end hiring solution for small businesses. The software is designed to combine LinkedIn's rich data set, existing sourcing tools, and new candidate management technology into a small business one-stop applicant-sourcing and candidate-hiring center. Twenty-two million people view jobs on LinkedIn every week. Ninety percent of LinkedIn members are open to considering a new job opportunity—if it's put right in front of them.

On the right side of the LinkedIn toolbar, you will see a pull-down tab—go to Talent Solutions. Here you can post jobs, with a choice for businesses that make either one to two hires per year, or those making three or more. Small businesses can choose the Recruiter Lite option for sourcing talent if only making a few hires per year. You can also post Career Pages to announce jobs you have available or showcase your company culture.

If *you* do not have a LinkedIn page yet (and intend a career in the world of business) you need to consider creating one. As either an employer or prospective employee, it truly can be the front page of the website for you. More influential decision makers, households with more than $100,000 income, and college graduates are on LinkedIn than receive print versions of the *Wall Street Journal* or the *New York Times*.

There are many advice sites for building a LinkedIn page (so look at several), but some highlights of what is desirable include

- **A Professional Photo:** As the point of first contact, a photo of you wearing business-formal or business-casual attire with a non-distracting background increases your appeal. People with profile photos receive 36 times more connections than those without.

- **A Professional Name:** Avoid gimmicky nicknames, key words, or numbers as part of your name.

- **A Headline:** Instead of standard "X position at Y company" be engaging, informative, and memorable.

- **A Compelling Professional Summary:** Writing one of these takes time and effort—but it's worth it. You are building the brand of "You."

- **Membership in Relevant Groups:** Groups enhance your contact-ability and allows others to reach you via the group messaging feature.

- **Add at Least Five Relevant Skills:** LinkedIn states that members with five or more skills are messaged 33 times more than those with none.

- **Publish Content:** It increases your visibility to employers and allows people to add you as a connection.

One more piece of LinkedIn advice—*BE NICE!!* As a professional connection site, this is not the place for you to post cranky, snarky, or profane comments.

Sources: Tamara Pupic, "The Future of Hiring, According to LinkedIn," *Entrepreneur*, December 6, 2017, www.entrepreneur.com/article/305630; Emily Conklin, "How to Become a LinkedIn Power User," *Entrepreneur*, November 11, 2017, www .entrepreneur.com/article/304419; www.linkedin.com.

Headhunting firms search confidentially for people who are currently employed and usually not actively seeking another job. Their services can be expensive. However, the process and results can be tailored specifically to your business.

Employee Referrals

Because your employees know the skills and talents needed to work in your company as well as the culture of your company, they can be a good source for finding people to fill slots. This inside-track approach to recruiting is not very costly and can generate qualified, highly motivated employees as long as your current employee morale is high and your workforce is somewhat large and diversified. On the downside, exclusive use of this source may perpetuate minority under-representation or create employee cliques. Moreover, in cases where the referral is not hired or does not work out, the referring employee may become resentful.

Relatives and Friends

The advantage of hiring relatives or friends is that you generally know beforehand of their abilities, expertise, and personalities. At the same time, no approach is more laden with long-term repercussions. The effects of a poor decision may be felt long after the desk has been cleared and the nameplate changed. According to Peter Drucker,

- Family members working in the business must be at least as able and hardworking as any unrelated employee.

- Family-managed businesses, except perhaps for the very smallest ones, increasingly need to staff key positions with nonfamily professionals.

- No matter how many family members are in a company's management, no matter how effective they are, one top job must be filled by a nonrelative.

- Before the situation becomes acute, the issue of management succession should be entrusted to someone who is neither part of the family nor part of the business.[5]

Other Sources

Job fairs, trade association meetings, and specialized internet sites run by professional organizations (accountants, environmental specialists, and so on) can be good sources of potential employees. Finally, don't forget the simple things, such as putting a "help wanted" sign in the window or a notice on the employee bulletin board.

Hiring decisions should not be made in haste. An incorrect decision can be costly to you and your business. Bad hires cut productivity causing reduced sales and revenue. The U.S. Department of Labor estimates that bad hires cost an average of a third of the employee's annual earnings. Hiring the wrong people is costly to small businesses not only by wasting recruiting and training dollars, but also losing the money that could have been used for a person who was a good fit in the first place. A recent survey of business owners showed that 95 percent indicated that a bad hire resulted in negative employee morale.[6] Hiring is an expensive process with many long-term consequences. Almost without exception, you are better off holding out for the best employee, rather than filling a position quickly. Keep the following factors in mind when trying to hire the best.

> "Almost without exception, you are better off holding out for the best employee, rather than filling a position quickly."

- Keep your focus on hiring the best. Don't settle for second best.

- Have a current written job description. Do not just use the last one written because it is convenient.

- Use a written rating system so that you don't forget about attributes of early candidates. This is also important if you have to defend your employee choice.

- "Overqualified" is better than "underqualified."

- A person with a long history of self-employment will, in all probability, return to self-employment as soon as possible. Hire this person as a consultant if you need her skills.

- Test specific skills and industry knowledge. You want to observe the candidate performing the work to be done (as closely as it can be duplicated) during testing.

- Check the candidate's background and all references thoroughly. While this may take time, it will pay off.

- Keep a written record of all terms of employment.

Concept Check Question

1. As a young business owner, you may soon be in the position of hiring one or more of your college friends in your own business. What are the advantages of hiring your friends? What are the potential pitfalls?

Concept Module 15.3: Selecting Employees

- **LO 15.3: Describe the four tools commonly used in employee selection.**

Once you have a pool of applicants from which to choose, you should match the applicants with the job requirements outlined in your job description and specifications. Four commonly used tools for selecting employees are the application form, the resume, the selection interview, and testing.

Application Forms and Resumes

Application forms and resumes contain essentially the same information. Both contain the candidate's name, address, telephone number, education, work experience, and activities. The difference between them is that applications are forms prepared by your company and the first formal contact the prospective employee has with your company. Resumes are personal profiles prepared by job candidates to highlight specific skills. Both have the following four purposes:

1. To provide a record of the applicant's desire to obtain the position

2. To provide a profile of the applicant to be used during the interview

3. To provide a basic personnel record for the applicant who becomes an employee

4. To serve as a means of measuring the effectiveness of the selection process

The application form need not be complex or long to achieve these objectives. It must, however, ask enough of the right questions to enable you to differentiate applicants on the basis of their knowledge, skills, and ability to perform the job. In addition, the application form should request the names of potential references and obtain the applicant's permission for you to contact each reference to discuss qualifications and prior job performance. Finally, it should include a notice that you are an at-will employer (discussed further later on in this chapter) and may therefore discharge an employee for cause or no cause and that any misinformation provided on the application form is grounds for immediate dismissal.

A caveat on resumes: They are sometimes the best fiction written, so view them with some degree of skepticism. You want to believe what people tell you, but check out all the facts, and contact previous employers.

Time and money constraints will prevent you from interviewing every candidate. Applications and resumes give you a screening tool to decide who to bring in for the next stage of the selection process—the interview.

Interviewing

Considered by many employers to be the most critical step in the selection process, the personal interview gives you a chance to learn more about the applicants; to resolve any conflicts or fill in any gaps in the information they provided; and to confirm or reject your initial impressions of them, drawn from the application or resume. The interview also gives you a chance to explain the job and company to the applicant. Always remember that you are selling your company to the potential employee as well as determining his suitability to join your company. If the applicant is a good fit, you want her to join your firm. But even if you don't hire this applicant, the image you create may well lead to another suitable person through a word-of-mouth referral.

To conduct an effective interview, you should do the following.

Be Prepared. Start by thoroughly reviewing the job description and job specifications. You must know what your needs are before you can find a person to fulfill them. Next, review the candidate's application form. Look for strengths and weaknesses, areas of conflict, and questions left unanswered or vaguely worded. Time spent during the interview should be used to dig deeper, not just review information already contained on the resume or in the cover letter.

Set the Stage for the Interview. Arrange to hold the interview at a time and location demonstrating its importance. Begin the interview on time. The location should provide privacy and comfort, and present the right image of your company. It should allow you to talk without interruptions. Taking telephone calls, answering employee questions, or working on another task while conducting the interview does little to ease the fears of the applicant and simply does not facilitate good communication or present a good image.

Use a Structured Interview Format. Develop a set of questions to ask each candidate so that you can compare their responses. The job description and specifications should be the source of the majority of your questions and the questions must be job related. Such a format will allow you to collect a great deal of information quickly, systematically cover all areas of concern, and more easily compare candidates on the basis of similar information. If interviewing several candidates, take notes on the answers provided by the candidates, so that you can remember and make comparisons later.

Use a Variety of Questioning Techniques. Although closed-ended questions are appropriate when looking for a commitment or for verifying information, they are very limiting. Consequently, you should use open-ended or probing questions that are related to the job. For example, rather than asking, "Have you ever dealt with an upset customer?" which can be answered with a yes or a no, instead ask, "How would you handle a customer who is upset with the quality of the product that was purchased from our store?" Open-ended, probing questions encourage the applicant to talk, providing you with a wealth of information and insight into the applicant's ability to communicate effectively.

No Matter the Type of Question, Make Sure That It Is Job Related. The EEOC requires that all job-interview questions be nondiscriminatory in nature. In other words, they must be devoid of references to race, color, religion, sex, national origin, or disability, and they must be job related. You should be able to relate each interview question to one or more of the items in your job description or job specifications and to show how the information obtained from the questions will be used to differentiate candidates.

Keep Good Records, Including Notes from the Interview. The EEOC construes any selection device as a test, and if a test results in underrepresentation of a protected group, it must be validated. Therefore, if the interview results in underrepresentation, the interview process must be validated. In the case of most small business owners, the problem is not one of questionable behavior or wrongdoing within this area, but rather one of inadequate documentation. You must be able to show that your decision to hire or not to hire was based on a sound business reason or practice as proven by your interview notes.

Questions NOT to Ask. In order to meet EEOC and other government guidelines, questions allowed during interviews must be job related and only job related. This is not the time to chitchat and discuss hobbies, families, and weekend activities. You are limited to information concerning how the person would handle the job and provide value to the company. In the back of your mind, a great mantra to repeatedly chant during an interview is "it must be job related, it must be job related." To avoid discrimination allegations, do NOT ask questions like these:

- How long have you been disabled? (You *can* ask if they can perform essential job tasks.)

- Do you have children or plan to have children in the near future?

- What was your maiden name?

- To which church do you belong, and how often do you attend?

- Have you ever been arrested? (You *can* ask whether the applicant has ever been convicted of a felony.)

- Do you own your own home, and how long have you lived there? Who lives with you at this address?

- How frequently and in what quantity do you drink alcohol? (You *can* ask if they use illegal drugs.)

- Do you have any religious obligations that would prevent you from working any day of the week or on any holidays?

- Can you make child care arrangements in order to work at night or on the weekends?

- What language do you most frequently speak?

- Do you have any kind of disability that would require reasonable accommodation?

- To which social clubs and organizations do you belong?

- Are you in a financially stable position personally?

- What is your weight?

- Have you ever filed a workers' compensation claim?

- What are the names and addresses of two relatives?

Testing

Employee testing has long been used by U.S. businesspeople to screen applicants. For the most part, prior to the 1971 Supreme Court decision in *Griggs v. Duke Power Co.*, employers were fairly free to do as they pleased in this matter.[7] Today, however, employers must be able to prove that their tests and other selection criteria are valid predictors of job performance. This can be done, according to the Supreme Court and the EEOC, through statistical or job-content analyses.

For small business owners, the process of statistically validating a test is generally far too time-consuming and expensive. Therefore, short of eliminating all tests, two options remain: purchasing preprinted tests from commercial vendors that have conducted the necessary standardization studies to ensure test reliability (although ultimate liability still rests with the employer) or using content-based tests. Although it is not an absolute defense, you are more likely to be able to prove a test's validity if the test is a sample or measure of the actual work to be performed on the job. For example, if a clerk's job involves counting back change to customers, then asking an applicant to count back change as a test is probably content valid and its use is therefore permitted.

Regardless of the type of test used, rarely should you use the results of a single test or indicator as the sole reason for hiring or not hiring an applicant. In addition, all test results should be kept strictly confidential and in a file other than the employee's personnel file. If you are unsure about a using a test, consult a lawyer who specializes in hiring law. Commonly used tests include the following.

Achievement, Aptitude, and Personality Tests.
These types of tests are given to measure specific skills a person has attained as a result of his experiences or education. These tests are easy and inexpensive to administer and score. Proving validity and job-relatedness, however, is another matter. Therefore, you should have a very compelling, business-related reason to justify their use during the selection process.

Performance (Ability) Tests.
Performance tests are administered to assess the applicant's ability to perform the job. The tests provide direct, observable evidence of performance. They are also easily administered, relate directly to the job, and are relatively inexpensive to conduct. Validity is generally not an overriding issue with performance testing. For a person with a disability, reasonable accommodations must be made during the test.[8]

Physical Examinations.
Often considered the last step in the screening process, physical examinations are given to discover any physical or medical limitations that might prevent the applicant from performing the duties of the job.

The ADA states that physical examinations can be required only after a conditional offer of employment and only if they are administered to all applicants in the particular job category.[9] In addition, you cannot disqualify individuals as a result of such examinations unless the findings show that the person would pose a "direct threat" to the health and safety of others.[10] All medical findings must be kept separately from general personnel files and be made available only to selected company personnel on a need-to-know basis.

Drug Tests.
Organizations are increasingly using drug tests to screen applicants, and with good reason. Although tests for illegal use of drugs are not considered tests under the ADA and are therefore not subject to its regulations, many state legislatures have imposed conditions under which drug tests may be administered, samples tested, and results used. Generally, to justify the cost and privacy concerns caused by these tests, you must be able to demonstrate a strong need for safety within your workplace or services.

With more states passing the legalization of marijuana, many businesses are starting to rethink drug testing policies for the first time in many years. Small businesses struggle with these decisions, due to limited legal and hiring expertise, because marijuana is still illegal under federal law.

The bottom line for small business owners: (1) if your business is regulated by a federal agency, such as the federal Department of Transportation, or a defense contractor, you are legally required to test for drugs—including marijuana; and (2) if your jobs include safety concerns, such as operation of potentially dangerous equipment or commercial driving, you should test for drugs even if they are legal in your state.[11]

Which Tests to Use? There are thousands of employee evaluations for you to choose from, but which one(s) should you use? Following are some of the most extensively validated, most respected instruments for cognitive ability and personality:

1. Watson-Glaser Critical Thinking Appraisal. This widely used cognitive test measures problem-solving skills, creativity, and other factors with 40 difficult questions ($10 to $20 per test).

2. Wesman Personnel Classification Test. This cognitive exam uses a combination of verbal and numerical questions to evaluate employees for decision-making roles ($7 to $15 per test).

3. Multidimensional Aptitude Battery II. This 303-question test of general mental ability, developed in 1998, is administered in 100 minutes. It measures ability to reason, plan, and solve problems ($190 for 25 tests).

4. Wonderlic Personnel Test. This classic test, developed in 1937, is probably most familiar to those who follow the NFL draft, as the football league administers it to college recruits. It takes only 12 minutes and is most appropriate for entry-level to mid-level jobs ($10 per test).

5. NEO Personality Inventory-Revised. This personality test measures respondents on five scales: neuroticism, extroversion, openness to experience, agreeableness, and conscientiousness ($245 for 25 tests).

6. 16PF. This personality test targeted for leadership positions includes 185 items measuring 16 personality factors ($8 to $30 per test).

7. Hogan Personality Inventory. This personality test consists of true-false questions that measure seven personality scales, such as ambition and prudence. This test has been around for about three decades, so responses can be compared to those of people actually doing most jobs in the United States ($25 to $175 depending on the amount of detail in the report).[12]

Hiring Independent Contractors versus Employees

You may decide that hiring employees is expensive and complicated so you want to take advantage of the services of independent contractors. With independent contractors you do not have to withhold Social Security and Medicare taxes, offer benefits, or several other things that you must provide for employees.

But be very careful, the Internal Revenue Service scrutinizes the way businesses classify their independent contractors and employees very closely. The determining factors fall into three main categories: behavioral control, financial control, and relationship of the parties. The IRS checklist has 20 factors when determining a worker's status, but here are the highlights:

Who has control? A worker is an employee if the person for whom he works has the right to direct and control him concerning when and where to do the work. The employer need not actually exercise control; it is sufficient that he has the right to do so.

Right to fire. An employee can be fired by an employer. A contractor cannot be fired so long as he or she produces a result that meets the specifications of the contract.

Training. An employee may be trained to perform services in a particular manner. However, contractors ordinarily use their own methods and receive no training from the employer.

Set hours of work. Workers for whom you set specific hours of work are more likely to be employees. Contractors, on the other hand, usually establish their own work hours.

A smart move is to draw up a simple document that spells out the duties of any independent contractors (IC) you use. It should state that the IC, not you the employer, is responsible for withholding any taxes. Tax law requires that you file with the IRS and give any person you pay more than $600/year a FORM-1099-MISC (Miscellaneous Income).[13]

This topic of IC/employee classification is taken very seriously by the IRS. If they find that you have misclassified a worker, a progression of fines and penalties await.

Concept Check Questions

1. When would you, as a small business owner, prefer to receive a resume than an application form?

2. Hiring an employee is a big step for a small business. How can you make a wise hiring decision if so many limitations are put on the interview questions you can legally ask?

Concept Module 15.4: Placing and Training Employees

- **LO 15.4: Discuss the need for employee training and name the seven methods of providing this training.**

You have hired your new employee—now what? **Employee orientation** is the process of introducing the new person to your business, to the current employees, and to your company culture and your way of doing things. The first few days and sometimes weeks on the job are critical for both employee success and productivity, and can be the difference between someone staying and leaving the organization. After the time, effort, and dollars spent getting to this point, you do not want to lose a good hire.

Orientation can be formal or informal, but regardless of the method used, there should be a process by which new employees are welcomed into the business. This can also be a critical component later in the event of a wrongful discharge claim. Some general purposes that should be accomplished during orientation include the following:

- Introduce the company. Talk about the history, the founders, the organization as a whole, and, more important, the culture. Knowing about the roots of a company is fundamental to helping a new hire become grounded.

- Don't treat the orientation like a catchall for everything a new employee needs to know. Give new employees a chance to interact with each other, not just sit and listen to presentations.

- Provide mechanisms to help the new employee adjust to this new environment. Think back to your first day on a new job and all the information you did not know. Little things like how to use the phone system to the time for breaks to how to log in to the computer system can be overwhelming. Finding a senior employee to assist in mentoring a new hire can be helpful. Just make sure there is a "fit" between the two and that the new hire feels comfortable going to the established employee with questions.

- Define job expectations. Make sure the new employee knows what she is expected to do. It is hard to hit the target if the target is unknown. Spend some time discussing procedures and expected outcomes.

- Consider going virtual. With so much online learning and webcasting, you don't have to have a physical orientation program.[14]

employee orientation
The process of helping new employees become familiar with an organization, their job, and the people they will work with.

HANDLING HARASSMENT

Sexual harassment is a topic that appears on every news feed featuring celebrities and notable names. The #MeToo and #TimesUp social media campaigns went viral and gained a lot of attention. But sexual harassment quietly affects small business and situations that do not make the news also.

Despite the pervasiveness of harassment in the workplace, a surprising number of businesses have no policies and training to prevent it. Only two-thirds of small businesses with employees have policies to protect those employees and themselves from legal liability.

John Malloy owned a manufacturing firm filled with male employees. Unfortunately, a female employee reported that a male colleague made comments that were a "blend of obscenities and sexual innuendo. Things you wouldn't say to your wife or mother." Malloy had recently put harassment policies in place and followed them sequentially. The male refused to show remorse and continued such talk. "We followed the procedure. He was suspended for a few days. He came back and resumed the same behavior. So we terminated him."

So what's a small business owner to do? Best practices suggest you should

1. **Respond quickly:** When an employee files a complaint, set up a meeting as soon as possible—within a couple of days—in private.

2. **Show empathy, not sympathy:** The employee wants and needs to be heard and taken seriously.

It is natural for the conversation to be laced with emotions but make clear that the point of the meeting is to determine facts before any conclusions are reached.

3. **Ask for lots of details during interviews:** Such as "Did anyone else witness the behavior?" Anything may be relevant.

4. **Ask how you can help:** The employee will undoubtedly be uncomfortable so intervening actions may be needed.

5. **Explain your organization's nonretaliation policy:** While harassment is to be taken seriously, so too is retaliation.

6. **Maintain neutrality:** If you find yourself unable to remain neutral, then you need to bring in someone who can be.

7. **Be thorough, but stay in touch:** As the small business owner, your most valuable asset in the process is integrity. Time is needed to discover all facts by interviewing all involved parties.

8. **Follow up:** Since such investigations do take time, check in with all parties on a regular basis.

Sources: Darren Heitner, "Do These 8 Things Immediately When an Employee Reports Harassment," *Inc.*, May 10, 2018, www.inc.com; Minda Zetlin, "54 Percent of Women Report Workplace Harassment," *Inc.*, March 15, 2018, www.inc.com; Renzo Costarella, "These Companies Are Battling Sexual Harassment by Teaching Employees to Recognize Unconscious Bias," *Entrepreneur*, December 1, 2017, www.entrepreneur.com/article/305324.

When an employee reports to work for the first time, she has many needs, some of which are more immediate than others. For example, the fear of not being at the right place at the right time, or of saying the wrong thing to the wrong person, generally far outweighs concerns over fringe benefits or the company's plan for future growth. Consequently, the order of the orientation presentation should be directed toward fulfilling the most pressing needs first.

If you as the small business owner are not conducting the orientation, ensure that the person in your organization who is doing it understands the importance and the process you expect. Employee turnover is expensive and retaining good employees begins on day one with an effective orientation to your business. Spend some time developing processes by which to start your new employees off right.

employee training
A planned effort to teach employees more about their job so as to improve their performance and motivation.

employee development
A planned effort to provide employees with the knowledge, skills, and abilities needed to accept new and more challenging job assignments within the company.

Employee Training and Development

Often overlooked by managers is the use of **employee training** and **employee development** as motivating tools. Training involves increasing the employee's knowledge and skills to meet a specific job or company objectives. It is usually task and short-term oriented. Development, by comparison, is more forward looking, providing the employee with the knowledge, skills, and abilities needed to accept a new and more-challenging job assignment within the company.

A trained workforce can give your business a competitive advantage that, once gained, is not easily duplicated by competitors. That advantage can be maintained and enhanced through an ongoing training-and-development program. Such a program helps prevent boredom and, consequently, increases retention rates for qualified personnel. Not only are turnover costs reduced, but also, over a period of time, the overall level of employee morale is raised. Finally, training and development assure your firm a place in tomorrow's competitive environment. New employee skills and abilities will inevitably be required as the business expands into new product lines, acquires new technologies, and strives to maintain or reach a higher level of customer service.

Ways to Train

Depending on the objectives of your training program, several techniques are available. The seven most common methods are on-the-job training (OJT), lecture, conferences, programmed learning, role-playing, job rotation, and correspondence courses.

On-the-Job Training. Everyone from the mail clerk to the company president experiences on-the-job training from the time he joins a company. This type of training entails learning the job while you are doing it. OJT is effective, but the small business owner should try to ensure that it is not the only type of training provided. The most familiar types of OJT are coaching and mentoring, in which a new employee works with an experienced employee or supervisor. This practice not only instructs new employees on how to operate equipment, but also ideally builds a bond between the employee, her mentor, and the business.

In order to be effective, OJT should encompass the following steps:

- Prepare the new employee for the training. What information is important to know before the employee even begins?

- Outline the task to be completed. Go over the steps and the processes to be used in successfully completing the job. Make sure the new employee knows where to get any required resources.

- Demonstrate the task. Break down the process into manageable steps the new employee can easily follow.

- Watch the new employee perform the task. After you have told and shown the new employee how to complete a task, watch to see if she understood your previous directions.

- Provide feedback. Once the employee demonstrates the task, let him know he did a good job or provide more information in order to help improve his process. Observing and providing feedback are critical steps in OJT.[15]

Lecture. Lecturing involves one or more individuals communicating instructions or ideas to others. The technique is often used because of its low cost, the speed with which information can be covered, and the large number of individuals who can be accommodated in each session. Employee participation is limited, however, and no allowance is made for individual employee differences.

Conferences. Also termed group discussions, the conference technique is similar to the lecture method, except that employees are actively involved in the learning. Although this technique produces more ideas than lecturing does, it takes more time, and only a limited number of employees can participate.

Programmed Learning. Programmed learning or instruction is achieved through use of a computer or printed text. The employee receives immediate feedback and learns at her own speed. This method works well for almost any type of training. However, outside materials must generally be purchased, and the learner must be self-directed and motivated for this technique to be effective.

Role-Playing. In the role-playing method, employees take on new roles within the company, acting out the situation as realistically as possible. If the sessions are videotaped, playing back the tapes allows for employee feedback and group discussions. Some employees find the technique threatening, and not all business situations lend themselves to this type of training.

Job Rotation. Job rotation allows employees to move from one job to another within the company. In addition to ensuring that employees have a variety of job skills and knowledge, the technique provides management with trained replacements in the event that one employee becomes ill or leaves the company. On the downside, job rotation does not generally provide in-depth, specialized training.

Correspondence Courses, Internet Classes, and Webinars. These techniques are especially useful for updating current knowledge and acquiring new information. Generally sponsored by a professional association or university, these techniques allow for specialized training without the employee having to leave work to attend. Accommodations will need to be provided if the training is to occur during work hours, but travel costs are significantly reduced using these methods. Webinars on a variety of topics are becoming more readily available and can be a great way to update skills or provide information on recent industry changes. With these techniques, the employee must be motivated to learn, and course costs may be high.

Concept Check Questions

1. What can a small business owner do in order to prevent sexual harassment from occurring, which is preferable to having to deal with it after the fact?

2. Review the section on training new employees. Give examples of types of jobs that would best lend themselves to each training method.

Concept Module 15.5: Compensating Employees

- **LO 15.5: Explain the two components of a compensation plan and the variable elements of a benefits system.**

Employees expect to be paid a fair and equitable wage. Determining what is fair and equitable is a challenging and ongoing task that involves primarily two components: wages and benefits. The U.S. Bureau of Labor Statistics reported that for March 2018, private industry employees, on average, made $33.72 an hour. Of that amount, $23.47 (69.6 percent) was wages and $10.75 (30.4 percent) was benefits. Of the $10.75 in benefits, 7.3 percent went to Medicare, Unemployment, and Workers' Compensation; 8.7 percent went to life, health, and disability insurance; 7.1 percent went to paid leave; and 5.3 percent went to retirement and other savings.[16]

Determining Wage Rates

Based on the Fair Labor Standards Act (FLSA), employees are classified as either exempt or nonexempt. Exempt employees are not covered by the major provisions of the FLSA, which specifies minimum wage, overtime pay, child labor laws, and equal-pay-for-equal-work regulations.

Hourly Wages. Most exempt employees are paid on a straight salary basis. Nonexempt employees, however, must be paid a minimum wage set by Congress (or your state government, if higher). These payments may take the form of hourly wages, salary, piecework rates, or commissions.

All-Salaried Employees. Some organizations are moving to an all-salaried workforce. These companies pay both exempt and nonexempt employees a salary (a fixed sum of money). Although still subject to FLSA provisions, this type of compensation plan removes the perceived inequity between the two "classes" of employees and fosters a greater esprit de corps.

Piecework Rates. Unlike salaried or hourly wage rates, the piecework rate is a pay-for-performance plan. Under a piecework rate, the employer pays an employee a set amount for each unit he produces. Some employers pay, as an incentive, a premium for units produced above a predetermined level of production. For example, an employee might receive $2 per unit for the first 40 units produced and $2.25 for any units above 40. Other plans might bump the straight rate for *all* units—from $2 to, say, $2.15—once the standard output quota of 40 units has been surpassed.

Commissions. Commissions represent another type of pay-for-performance approach. Some jobs, especially those in sales, are not easily measured in terms of units produced. Under a straight commission plan, the employee's wages can be based solely on her sales volume. Because employees often cannot control all of the external variables that affect sales, employers are increasingly paying these workers on a base-salary-plus-commission basis. Employees tend to favor this combination approach in which they are provided with a degree of income security during slow sales periods.

Still other employers are allowing their employees to "draw" against future commissions. This means that an employee may receive an advance from the employer during a slow sales period and repay the advance (draw) out of commissions earned during the remainder of the pay period or, in some cases, future pay periods. Such draws are particularly effective if sales fluctuate from month to month or from quarter to quarter.

Jim Lippie, CEO of consulting firm Thrive Networks of Concord, Massachusetts, paid salespeople via commission, but wanted to foster more teamwork. He considered switching them to salaries, but was concerned about decreasing motivation. Lippie then created a quarterly commissions pool shared equally by the six salespeople. Approximately one-third of their total compensation is tied to the performance of the whole sales team, and the rest is salary. Lippie says, "We've become much better at sharing information while spreading around both incentives and the risks."[17]

> "An incentive-pay program is a reward system that ties performance to compensation."

Incentive-Pay Programs

An incentive-pay program is a reward system that ties performance to compensation. Two common types of incentive-pay programs involve the awarding of bonuses and profit-sharing programs. **Bonuses** are generally doled out on a one-time basis to reward employees for their high performance. They may be given to either an individual employee or a group of employees. Bonuses are frequently awarded when an employee meets objectives set for attendance, production, sales, cost savings, quality, or performance.

bonuses
One-time rewards provided to employees for exceeding performance standards.

To be an effective motivator, a bonus must be tied to a specific measure of performance. The reason for which the bonus is being awarded must be communicated to employees at the time they are informed that they will receive it. The bonus should be paid separately from the employee's regular paycheck to reinforce its effect. In this way, the bonus is less likely to be viewed by employees as an extension of their regular salary and something to which they are automatically entitled.

Under a **profit-sharing plan**, employers usually make the same percentage of salary contributions to each worker's account on a semiannual or annual basis. The percentage of contributions varies according to the amount of profits earned, making the system highly flexible. Most employers believe these plans serve to motivate workers by giving them a sense of partnership with the employer. Profit-sharing plans are a mainstay of many small business owners' compensation plans.

Benefits

An employee **benefit** consists of any supplement to wages and salaries. Health and life insurance, paid vacation time, pension and education plans, and discounts on company products are examples. The cost of offering and administering benefits has increased greatly in recent decades—up from 25.5 percent of total payroll in 1961 to about 38 percent today. Often employees do not realize the market value and high cost of the benefits they receive.

According to the most recent *Employee Job Satisfaction* survey report, job security was number one on the list of very important contributors to job satisfaction, and benefits was number two. The opportunity to use skills and abilities, the work itself, and the organization's financial stability preceded compensation in the list of the top six contributors to employee satisfaction. Health care remains the most important benefit, with paid time off second on the list. Sixty-two percent of the respondents felt health care benefits were very important, and 66 percent said they were satisfied with the health care benefits provided to them by their employers compared to 71 percent of respondents who were very satisfied with their paid time off.[18]

As an employer, you are required by law to do the following:

- Provide time off for employees to vote, serve on a jury, and perform military service.

- Meet all workers' compensation requirements.

- Withhold Social Security retirement and disability, as well as Medicare and Medicaid from employees' paychecks, and pay the employer's percentage.

- Pay state and federal unemployment taxes, thus providing benefits for unemployed workers.

- Contribute to state short-term disability programs in states where such programs exist.

- Comply with the Federal Family and Medical Leave Act (FMLA) if your business has 50 or more employees. Check the requirements for your state. Some businesses with less than 50 employees may need to comply if state regulations so dictate.[19]

While you may need to in a competitive job market, you are not required to provide the following:

- Retirement plans

- Health plans—if over 50 FTE (full-time equivalent) employees, you must comply with the Affordable Care Act

- Dental or vision plans

profit-sharing plan
A plan in which employees receive additional compensation based on the profitability of the entire business.

benefit
Part of an employee's compensation in addition to wages and salaries.

- Life insurance plans

- Educational assistance

- Child care

- Discounts on products or services

- Paid vacations, holidays, or sick leave

With an increasing discontent and call for a new mix of benefits, the challenge for small business owners is to provide a mix of benefits that is both affordable for the employer and motivational for employees.

Flexible Benefit Packages. With the diversity in today's workforce, one benefit package seldom fits all. Since all employees do not have the same needs, a flexible-benefit package, or cafeteria plan, allows each employee to select the benefits that best suit her financial and lifestyle needs. Employees generally favor such plans due to their flexibility and pretax benefits.

Increasingly, flexible-benefit packages not only provide employees with a menu of benefits from which to choose, but also include choices between taxable and nontaxable benefits. Under the latter, IRS-approved plans, employees are allowed to purchase benefits with pretax dollars. In this way, they can reduce their taxable income while at the same time increasing their benefit options.

The advantages of flexible plans are not realized without additional costs. As the number and mix of benefits increase, so do administrative costs associated with activities such as record keeping, communications with employees, and compliance with government regulations. A second, but no less important, concern is that employees may select the wrong mix or types of benefits. Often employees do not worry about their benefits until they are actually needed, generally in response to a major illness or accident. Yet the law does not allow benefit choices to be changed during the plan year, so employees often find that their benefit options do not match their immediate needs.

Health Insurance. Because of steady cost hikes and complexity in understanding health insurance as changes abound in the Patient Protection and Affordable Care Act, only about half of America's small business offer health coverage to employees.[20] Health insurance is one of the most desirable benefits, so some options include

- Traditional indemnity plan: A selected insurance either pays health care provider directly or reimburses employees for covered amounts

- Managed care: Two common forms are Health Maintenance Organization (HMO) and Preferred Provider Organization (PPO). Under an HMO system, a firm signs a contract with an approved HMO that agrees to provide health and medical services to its employees. In return for the exclusive right to care for the firm's employees, the HMO offers its services at an adjusted rate. Unfortunately, employees often object to these plans because they are restricted to using the health care specialists employed or approved by the HMO.

- To overcome this objection, some companies are switching to PPOs. With a PPO, a firm or group of firms negotiates with doctors and hospitals to provide certain health care services for a favorable price. In turn, member firms encourage their employees, through higher reimbursement payments, to use these "preferred" providers. Employees tend to favor PPOs because they can see the doctors of their choice.

Retirement Plans. To assist employees in saving for their retirement needs, employers provide them with retirement, or pension, plans. Such plans present employees with an accumulated amount of money when they reach a set retirement age or when they are unable to continue working due to a disability. Retirement plans rate high on the list of benefits employees desire. Four common retirement options described here are individual retirement accounts, simplified employee pension plans, 401(k) plans, and Keogh plans.

- *Individual Retirement Accounts.* Individual retirement accounts (IRAs) allow employees to make tax-exempt contributions to a retirement account.

- *Simplified Employee Pension Plans.* A simplified employee pension (SEP) plan is similar to an IRA but is available only to people who are self-employed or who work for small businesses that do not have a retirement plan.

- *401(k) Plans.* Named after Section 401(k) of the 1978 Revenue Act, 401(k) plans allow small businesses to establish payroll reduction plans that are more flexible and have greater tax advantages than IRAs. As was true of the foregoing plans, the amount deferred and any accumulated investment earnings are excluded from current income and are taxed only when finally distributed (usually when the worker retires).

- *Keogh plans.* A tax-deferred pension plan available to self-employed individuals or unincorporated businesses for retirement purposes. Deductions to Keogh plans can be either defined-benefit or defined-contribution.

Concept Check Questions

1. List the advantages of a flexible-benefit package to employees and to the employer.

2. What factors influence the type and amount of employee benefits that a small business can offer?

Concept Module 15.6: When Problems Arise: Employee Discipline and Termination

- **LO 15.6: Profile an effective sequence for disciplining and terminating employees.**

Despite your best efforts at maintaining harmony in the workplace, sometimes problems may arise. When they do, you need policies established for discipline or dismissal of employees.

Disciplinary Measures

Discipline involves taking timely and appropriate action to change the performance of an employee or group of employees. The purpose of discipline is to ensure that company rules and regulations are consistently followed for the well-being of both the company and its employees. A fair and just disciplinary procedure should be based on four components: the employee handbook, performance appraisal, progressive approach, and appeal process.

Employee Handbook. The **employee handbook**, or policy manual, provides a comprehensive set of rules and regulations to inform employees of their rights and responsibilities in the employment relationship. To be effective, the rules and regulations must be up-to-date, easily understood, and, most important, communicated to employees. An effective way to achieve this latter goal is to go over the employee handbook during employee orientation and have employees sign a statement acknowledging its receipt. Following are suggestions for what to include in your employee handbook:

employee handbook
Written rules and regulations informing employees of their rights and responsibilities in the employment relationship.

- *The disclaimer.* Every employee handbook should have a disclaimer (it's a good idea to include it at the beginning and the end) specifying that the handbook is not a contract of employment. Without such a notice, a fired employee might attempt to sue you for breach of contract. A standard disclaimer about employment-at-will might state, "Nothing in this handbook should be construed to imply there exists a contract of employment. Employment with ABC Company is strictly at-will and can end upon the discretion of the employer."[21]

- *Employment policies.* Describe work hours, regular and overtime pay, performance reviews, vacations and holidays, equal employment opportunities, and other items that affect employment.

- *Benefits.* Relate insurance plans, disability plans, workers' compensation, retirement programs, and tuition reimbursement.

- *Employee conduct.* Explain your expectations on everything you classify as important, from personal hygiene to dress codes to employee development.

- *Glossary.* Every company has its own terms and jargon. Explain terminology important to your business. For example, Ashton Photo distinguishes between late ("not completed on time in a given department"), delayed ("production of a job has been suspended, awaiting information from the customer"), and on hold ("production of a job has been suspended for accounting reasons").

- *Organization chart.* Include charts and job descriptions to give employees a sense of their place in the organization and how all the parts of the business fit together.

In your employee handbook, don't try to include specifics on what people should do in every possible situation. You just want to communicate the broad principles of what the company believes in and how it expects people to perform.

Performance Appraisal. A well-designed **performance appraisal** system is the second essential component of a fair and just disciplinary policy. Not only does a sound performance-appraisal process document the need for possible discipline, but it also affords management the opportunity to address problem areas before they become disciplinary concerns. Performance evaluations should occur every six months, and more frequently during the probationary period. Copies of the evaluation should be included in the employee's personnel file. As performance evaluations occur, make sure benchmarks are established. These should be tied to the job description. Develop a process for the review and then follow that process with all employees. And lastly, meet with the employee to discuss the performance appraisal. Use this as a time to set goals for next year.[22] In addition, a well-defined performance-appraisal process will help to fulfill the third tenet of a good disciplinary procedure: a system of progressive penalties, discussed next.

Progressive Approach to Employee Discipline. The majority of American workers are "at-will employees," which means that the relationship can end for any reason (or no reason) as long as the employee is not being fired for discriminatory reasons (such as race, gender, or sexual orientation) or is not covered by an employment contract.[23] So, a small business owner may choose to establish a system of discipline, instituting steps to take before termination. This is called a **progressive approach to employee discipline**, in which discipline is incremental and increasingly forceful. Under most progressive systems, managers first issue an oral (informal) reprimand, then a written warning (formal notice), followed by suspension without pay, and finally discharge. Arbitrators and the courts generally favor progressive discipline over that of the

performance appraisal
A process of evaluating an employee's job-related achievements.

progressive approach to employee discipline
Discipline that is applied to employees in appropriately incremental and increasingly forceful measures.

hot-stove approach, except in cases of gross misconduct, such as theft or assault, when immediate discharge is warranted. Note that a record of any disciplinary action should be placed in the employee's file even if the reprimand is verbal. A written record is essential if termination occurs and to ensure that the discipline is in accordance with a union contract, if one exists. Write out what happened, what was said by both parties, and when it happened as soon as practical—after all, memories fade. Steps for a progressive disciplinary approach include the following:

- Determine whether discipline is needed. Is the problem an isolated incident or part of an ongoing pattern?

- Have clear goals to discuss with the employee. You should discuss the problem in specific terms. Indirect comments will not make your point clear. You must also state what you expect the employee to do. If the employee has no idea about your expectations after discussing a performance problem with you, she is likely to repeat past performance.

- Talk about the problem in private. Public reprimand is embarrassing both for the employee and for everyone who witnesses it. If you chastise an employee in public, you will lose trust and respect not only from that individual but also from those who observe the act.

- Keep your cool. A calm approach will keep a performance discussion more objective and prevent distraction by irrelevant problems.

- Watch the timing of the meeting. If the problem is not obvious and you schedule the meeting far in advance, the employee will spend time worrying about what is wrong. Conversely, if the problem is obvious, the meeting should be scheduled to give the employee plenty of time to prepare.

- Prepare opening remarks. Performance meetings will be more effective if you are confident in your opening remarks. Think them out in advance and rehearse them.

- Get to the point. Beating around the bush with small talk does more to increase the employee's anxiety level than to reduce it.

- Allow two-way communication. Make sure the disciplinary meeting is a discussion, not a lecture. You can get to the heart of the problem only if the employee is allowed to speak. Your intent is to arrive at a solution to a problem, not to scold the employee.

- Establish a follow-up plan. You and your employee need to agree to a follow-up plan to establish a time frame within which the employee's performance is to improve.

- End on a positive note. Highlight the employee's positive points so that he will leave the meeting with a belief that you want him to succeed in the future.[24]

Appeal Process. The final component of an effective disciplinary program is an **appeal process**. The most common appeal process in nonunion companies relies on an open-door policy, a procedure whereby employees seek a review of the disciplinary decision at the next level of management. For such a process to be effective, it must involve a thorough and truly objective review of the facts of the case by an executive of higher rank than the supervisor who applied the discipline. Open-door policies are appropriate for companies with many employees and levels of management. In the majority of small businesses, however, the only level of management is you—the owner. In that case, if an employee feels unjustly treated and is not satisfied with your decision, her only recourse is through the courts.

Dismissing Employees

Because dismissing an employee is the most extreme step of discipline you can exercise, it must be taken with care. Your legitimate reasons for dismissing an employee may include

appeal process
A formal procedure allowing employees to seek review of a disciplinary measure at a higher level of management.

A HAND IN THE TILL

Todd owns and manages a T-shirt shop in a small resort town. He has two full-time employees who have been with the business for more than three years. He also employs as many as five part-time employees, depending on the tourist season. They help him keep the shop open from 10:00 a.m. to 9:00 p.m. seven days a week. Todd opens the shop every day but typically has his employees close. Whoever closes the store follows a checklist of closing procedures, including ringing out the cash register, filling out the bank deposit, and putting the daily receipts in the safe, with $300 kept in a separate cash bag for the next day's opening cash on hand. As with many businesses, the cash drawer is often off by a small amount, but usually no more than a couple of dollars.

One day Todd opened the store and found that the cash drawer was short $35 for the previous day. Todd called a meeting that afternoon and told all seven employees that they would each have to chip in $5 to cover the shortage and that any time there was a shortage, they would have to split the reimbursement. Todd walked out of the room. The seven employees sat in disbelief.

Questions

1. Is Todd within his legal rights to take this action? If his actions are legal, what are some possible consequences?

2. How would you have handled the situation if you were Todd?

unsatisfactory performance of the job or changing requirements of the job that make the employee unqualified.

When it comes to discharging an employee, what you can and cannot do will be influenced to a large degree by two considerations. First, the decision to discharge an employee must be based on a job-related reason or reasons, not on race, color, religion, sex, age, national origin, or disability. Second, your ability to legally discharge an employee and the manner in which you may do so will be highly dependent on your at-will status. Under the **at-will doctrine**, unless an employment contract is signed, an employer has great leeway in discharging an employee, in that she has the right to discharge the employee for a good reason, a bad reason, or no reason at all. Within the past decade, however, the courts and some state legislatures have imposed one or more of the following restrictions on at-will employers. Check the laws of your state to find which apply to your business. And remember that an employee cannot be fired for union-related activities, even if a union does not exist in the company.

Implied Contract. An employer may be restricted in discharging an employee if an implied contract exists as a result of written statements in the company's employment application, employment ads, employee handbook, or other company documents. Verbal statements by company representatives to employees may also erode an employer's at-will status, as may an employee's record of long-term employment with the firm.

Good Faith and Fair Dealing. The good faith and fair dealing exception holds that the employer must have acted fairly and in good faith in discharging the employee. For example, an employee cannot be fired simply because he is about to become vested in the company's pension plan.

Public Policy Exception. Under the public policy exception, employers cannot discharge workers for exercising a statutory right, such as filing a workers' compensation claim, or performing public service, such as serving on a jury. Nor can an employee be fired for refusing to break the law or engaging in conduct that is against his or her beliefs— for example, refusing to falsify an employer's records to cover up possible misconduct on the part of the company.

at-will doctrine
Essentially means an employee hired for an indefinite period may be discharged for any or no reason, cause or no cause, unless specifically prohibited by law.

Proving Just Cause. In the event that a terminated employee seeks legal redress by filing a lawsuit against your business, whether or not you have acted in a manner consistent with the at-will principle will be decided by a judge. In all cases, you should be able to provide evidence of just cause for the dismissal, which generally implies due process and reasonability on your part. You are likely to have just cause if you can do the following:

- Cite the specific work-rule violation and show that the employee had prior knowledge of the rule and the consequences of violating it.

- Show that the work rule was necessary for the efficient and safe operation of the company and was therefore a business necessity.

- Prove that you conducted a thorough and objective investigation of the violation and, in the process, afforded the employee the opportunity to present his side of the story.

- Document that the employee was given the opportunity to improve or modify her performance (except in cases of gross misconduct or insubordination, when it is unnecessary).

- Show that there was sufficient evidence or proof of guilt to justify the actions taken.

- Show that you treated the employee in a manner consistent with past practices.

- Demonstrate that the disciplinary actions taken were fair and reasonable in view of the employee's work history.

- Document that the disciplinary action was reviewed by an independent party either within or outside the company prior to being implemented.

Firing employees is never a pleasant duty, and few managers handle the process well. That's because, whatever the facts of the dismissal, most managers feel bad about letting someone go. Ironically, expressing feelings of remorse can make the situation worse, giving the employee false hope. Instead, the best way to deal with the termination is to make it a quick, unambiguous act. Spell out exactly why you are letting the employee go, state clearly that the decision is final, and explain the details of the company's notice policy or severance. Then ask the employee to leave by the end of the week if possible and to sign a letter of acknowledgment, which will make it more difficult for him to reopen the discussion—or to sue. Above all, resist any attempts to turn the discussion into an argument.

Concept Check Questions

1. Explain the four components of an effective disciplinary system.
2. Define "at-will" employment status.

CHAPTER REVIEW

SUMMARY ▶▶

LO 15.1 Discuss the importance of hiring the right employees.

Some of the most valuable resources and competitive advantages a small business has are its employees. There are too many costs and risks involved in HR issues not to pay attention to them.

Job analysis is the process of determining the duties and skills involved in a job and the kind of person who should be hired to do it. A job description is part of the job analysis; it lists the duties, responsibilities, and reporting relationships of a job. Job specifications are another part of the job analysis; they identify the education, skills, and personality that a person needs to have to be right for a job.

LO 15.2 Evaluate the advantages and disadvantages of the six major sources of employee recruitment.

Help-wanted advertising reaches numerous potential applicants, but many of them will not be right for the job you are trying to fill. Employment agencies prescreen applicants so that you do not have to deal with as many people. The agencies run by the government are usually appropriate only for positions requiring lower-level skills. Private employment agencies and executive recruiters (headhunters) offer more expensive services but can help you find people with higher-level skills. Internet job sites offer limited resources, for a fee. Employee referrals are effective because your current employees know the skills and talents needed, but hiring in this manner can create cliques and build resentment if the new hire does not work out. Moreover, it can lead to underrepresentation of protected groups. Hiring friends and relatives gives you the advantage of knowing their abilities and expertise, but personal relationships can become strained on the job.

LO 15.3 Describe the four tools commonly used in employee selection.

In the selection process, you narrow the applicant pool generated by recruitment by trying to match the needs of your business with the skills of each person. Application forms and resumes, interviews, and testing are the most common tools of selection.

LO 15.4 Discuss the need for employee training and name the seven methods of providing this training.

To become a better, more productive worker, every employee needs to have his knowledge and skills enhanced through orientation and training. On-the-job training; lectures; conferences; programmed learning; role-playing; job rotation; and correspondence courses, Internet classes, and webinars are seven common techniques.

LO 15.5 Explain the two components of a compensation plan and the variable elements of a benefits system.

Employees can be compensated for their efforts with hourly wages, with straight salary, or on the basis of piecework or commission plans. Incentive-pay programs offer a way to motivate and reward employees above their base pay by paying bonuses or profit-sharing amounts. Common benefits included as part of a compensation package are flexible-benefit plans, health insurance, pension plans, and child care accounts. The most common pension plans adopted by small businesses are individual retirement accounts (IRAs), simplified employee pension (SEP) plans, 401(k) plans, and defined contribution plans.

LO 15.6 Profile an effective sequence for disciplining and terminating employees.

The progressive disciplinary system, favored by many managers today, begins with an oral reprimand, followed by a written warning, then suspension without pay, and, finally, termination from the company.

KEY TERMS ▶▶

appeal process **412**

at-will doctrine **413**

benefit **408**

bonuses **407**

employee development **404**

employee handbook **410**

employee orientation **403**

employee training **404**

job analysis **392**

job description **393**

job specifications **393**

performance appraisal **411**

profit-sharing plan **408**

progressive approach to employee discipline **411**

STUDENT STUDY SITE ▶▶

edge.sagepub.com/hatten7e

$SAGE edge™ Sharpen your skills with SAGE edge!

SAGE edge for Students provides a personalized approach to help you accomplish your coursework goals in an easy-to-use learning environment. You'll find mobile-friendly eFlashcards and quizzes as well as multimedia resources to support and expand on the concepts presented in this chapter.

EXPERIENTIAL LEARNING ACTIVITIES ▶▶

15.1 Human Resource Management—Interviewing

LO 15.3 Describe the four tools commonly used in employee selection.

Evaluate the following questions that could potentially be used during an interview. Place a "Yes" beside the question numbers that are acceptable to ask during an interview. Place a "No" beside the question numbers that should NEVER be asked during an interview.

1. What year did you graduate from high school?

2. How many years have you worked as a manager or in a supervisory capacity?

3. Do you plan to have a family in the future?

4. Are you available to work nights and weekends?

5. What is your native language?

6. How do you define success?

7. Are you bilingual and if so, what other languages do you speak?

8. Are you married?

9. Where do you see yourself in five years?

10. Do you belong to a church and if so, which one? How frequently do you attend?

11. Share with me your two most significant weaknesses.

12. What is your maiden name?

13. Which leadership style do you prefer to use and why?

14. What is your nationality of origin?

15. Share with me an example of a responsibility you have been given in the past and how you handled that responsibility?

16. Are you eligible to work in the United Sates? Can you, if hired, provide appropriate documentation?

17. Which organizations, outside of work, do you participate in and enjoy?

18. How would your supervisor or a coworker from your last job describe you?

15.2 Human Resource Management—Dismissing Employees

LO 15.6 Profile an effective sequence for disciplining and terminating employees.

Read the following case and answer the questions below:

Paige sighed. Letting Alex go had not been fun, and in fact, the last three months had not been fun. Alex had looked so promising at first. He had a great personality and worked well with the customers. He was always on time and willing to pick up extra shifts if needed, particularly the last shift of the day, which few employees wanted. He would even come in for a couple of hours at night just to help close, balance the daily transactions, balance the cash drawers, and straighten the store for the next morning. Since Alex had caught on so quickly, and was willing, Paige had gladly turned over closing the store to Alex four or five nights a week, which had allowed Paige to leave on time for the first time in months. Alex also had great marketing ideas and quickly became a leader on the sales team. With six new people, all hired at the same time, Alex had been a lifesaver.

Then, small discrepancies started showing up in the books at the end of the night and occasionally a piece of merchandise could not be found even though it was in the computer inventory system, which showed the item as being on the sales floor. At first Paige did not think too much of it. With six new people, mistakes were apt to occur, particularly on the cash register and in placing inventory on the floor. However, rather than getting better, the discrepancies had become more frequent and more expensive inventory started consistently disappearing. As a proactive move, Paige had called a staff meeting and reviewed all inventory and closing protocols with

all employees, not just the new staff. She then had all employees sign a statement that affirmed the employee understood all closing protocols and that employee theft was grounds for immediate dismissal. That had not stopped the problem. Next Paige had shifted schedules and placed differing people on opening and closing shifts. And much to her disappointment, whenever Alex did not work, there were no discrepancies at the end of the shift and no missing inventory. Paige had then pulled up the video feed that was constantly running and had closely reviewed the last six weeks. Without fail, each night Alex worked, the camera caught Alex either taking cash from the cash register and putting it in his pocket or putting inventory in a store bag by the cash register without ringing up the sale. Paige was disappointed. How could Alex do this? How could she have not figured this out more quickly?

Paige called Alex in yesterday and told him he was no longer employed. Glancing at her watch, she realized she had five minutes before HR called to review the disciplinary action she had taken. Paige hoped she made the right decision and followed the dismissal processes correctly.

1. Did Paige make the correct decision?

2. You are the human resources supervisor calling Paige to ensure due process was followed. Which questions do you need to ask? What information do you need from Paige?

CHAPTER CLOSING CASE ▶▶

Building a Team at Tagit

Philippa Bott and Ed Crossland formed Tagit in 2003 as an entrepreneurial venture. Each invested £25,000 in the idea of selling personalized sports clothing and memorabilia to anyone

wanting to purchase it. After exploring a number of markets, they finally struck a deep vein of successful contracts with schools and fitness centers, at which point Tagit took off. The company had a turnover of £2.75 million in 2014; now employing 80 people, it has a diverse and successful product portfolio and a database of over 21,000 customers.

The production process is simple. A team of designers create computer programs capable of translating logos and emblems into transferable designs. The final programs are loaded onto machines that either embroider or print the designs onto sweatshirts, school bags, baseball caps, sports equipment, and so on. These items, many of which are bespoke (custom-made), are then sold.

The employee relations' philosophy behind the company was articulated by Ed as one that was predominantly "selfish." He wanted to establish a place where he could enjoy going to work in the morning and stay happy all day. Intrinsic to this was his vision of an enjoyable nonhierarchical workplace where everyone was valued. This meant creating a workplace community based on "shared interests, while fostering an ethic of innovation and individual achievement—where Tagit employees have the capacity to affect and influence their own livelihoods." Philippa echoes this view. She talks enthusiastically about how she is "deeply driven by a need to see people within the company succeed. . . . I get a kick out of nurturing it [the company], seeing it grow and develop its people."

One of the interesting developments within the company linked to this philosophy has been its unique formulation of partnership practices and policies. Evolving as the company grew, this philosophy is epitomized by the slogan "Tagit is ours." This came to unique fruition when, unfortunately, Ed died and his widow sold 38 percent of her 45 percent stake in the company. Not one to miss an opportunity, Philippa ensured that the shares were offered to all of the staff.

In 2009, curious to evaluate their employee relations' philosophy and perhaps put it on a stronger footing, Philippa arranged for the entire company to hold a weekend workshop, creating a Tagit mission statement. The intention was to further examine the culture and formalize what each employee personified. However, the numbers who could attend were so small that the

process was postponed. Later a series of one-day workshops, held during working hours and led by an external facilitator, looked at how everyone behaved, and produced a model of what the participants believed their workplace activities and values involved. Starting with the question "Why are we here?" the workshops tracked the history of the company and, almost as an aside, debated the philosophical nature of democracy. The discussion led on to how a democratic work organization might be established within Tagit. Overall themes evolved and mini statements, encapsulating the ways in which the company operated—like "friendly atmosphere," "listening to one another," "flexibility," "our duties to one another"—were all recorded.

Deriving from all of this talk, the twin aspirations for the success of both Tagit and its individual employees were embodied in an updated mission statement:

> It is the mission of Tagit to offer people with shared goals and values the opportunity for continued personal and professional development, by cultivating a caring and rewarding environment where people feel inspired, respected and appreciated.

These core beliefs were incorporated into a number of formal employee relations' statements and policies. These policies were honed by a further workshop a year later. Again, everyone was involved. The core beliefs were elaborated on, and a model comprising five pillars was produced. This model epitomized the Tagit philosophy and became the rationale behind all of the company policies.

Each pillar is, in Philippa's words, "assigned a classic mutual exchange of rights with corresponding responsibilities." Each pairing is intended to articulate the mutual obligations between the company and its employees in a balanced way to "ensure that the company and the individual employee do not intrude too much on each other." Table 1 shows the pillars.

These pillars are now enshrined in the constitution of the company and any changes have to be agreed to by 76 percent of the

▼ TABLE 1

The Tagit Philosophy

	Pillar	Rights	Responsibilities
1.	Information and involvement	Access to information and involvement in decision-making	Open and honest participation
2.	Fair reward	Fair reward with no indecent salary differentials	Honest endeavor and commitment
3.	Shared prosperity	Shared prosperity through profit-sharing and share ownership	Persistence and full contribution to the Tagit effort
4.	Application of organizational values	To be treated with fairness, consistency, respect, and support	Protection and enhancement of the workplace community by showing fairness, consistency, respect, and support
5.	Development opportunities	Training opportunities for development	Commitment to meeting training objectives and to developing in harmony with the needs of Tagit

shareholders. Additionally, at an individual level, the model is incorporated into the employment contract. As Philippa said, "In a way it is an 'emotional contract' that we are asking people to sign, and we need them to think very carefully before they sign it."

Over the last few years workshops have discussed the pillars, added to the background documents, and the pages of explanatory notes have grown to more than 70. Redrafting has become imperative, perhaps all the more so because the company is now facing fierce competition (globally, not just nationally), redundancies are a possibility, and employees are questioning why security of employment has not been given a pillar of its own.

As the company has grown, the employees have been carefully chosen to fit in with the ethos espoused by the two founders. In the last nine months, however, particularly since the impact of austerity measures, there has been talk of job losses, and not everything has appeared quite so mutual. The last workshop called to reformulate the pillars was marked not by agreement but by dissent. Several employees claimed that the company obligations were, even if not *obviously* favoring the employer, ambiguous, and that the reciprocity was wearing thin. A recent recruit to the company, who had been working in Germany, suggested that formalizing the workshops in the style of a works council with union representatives speaking up for all of the employees, might be useful. Philippa was horrified and bemused. She felt that everyone had a duty to pull in the same direction, particularly when there was a problem, and that a works council would be an unnecessarily bureaucratic way of communicating with staff—something that she felt was already taken care of.

Discussion Questions

1. Evaluate the philosophy behind the company's way of working and analyze how it impacted perceptions of organizational justice both when the company was formed and later when redundancies were threatening.

2. To what extent do you think there is a partnership between the Tagit management and the workforce?

3. Where does the power lie?

4. Evaluate whether the possibilities of redundancies will strengthen or weaken the employee involvement activities at Tagit.

5. How would you advise the company to move forward from their present predicament?

Source: Cecilie Bingham, "Tagit," Sage Knowledge: Business Cases, January 2, 2018, http://dx.doi.org/10.4135/9781526439499.

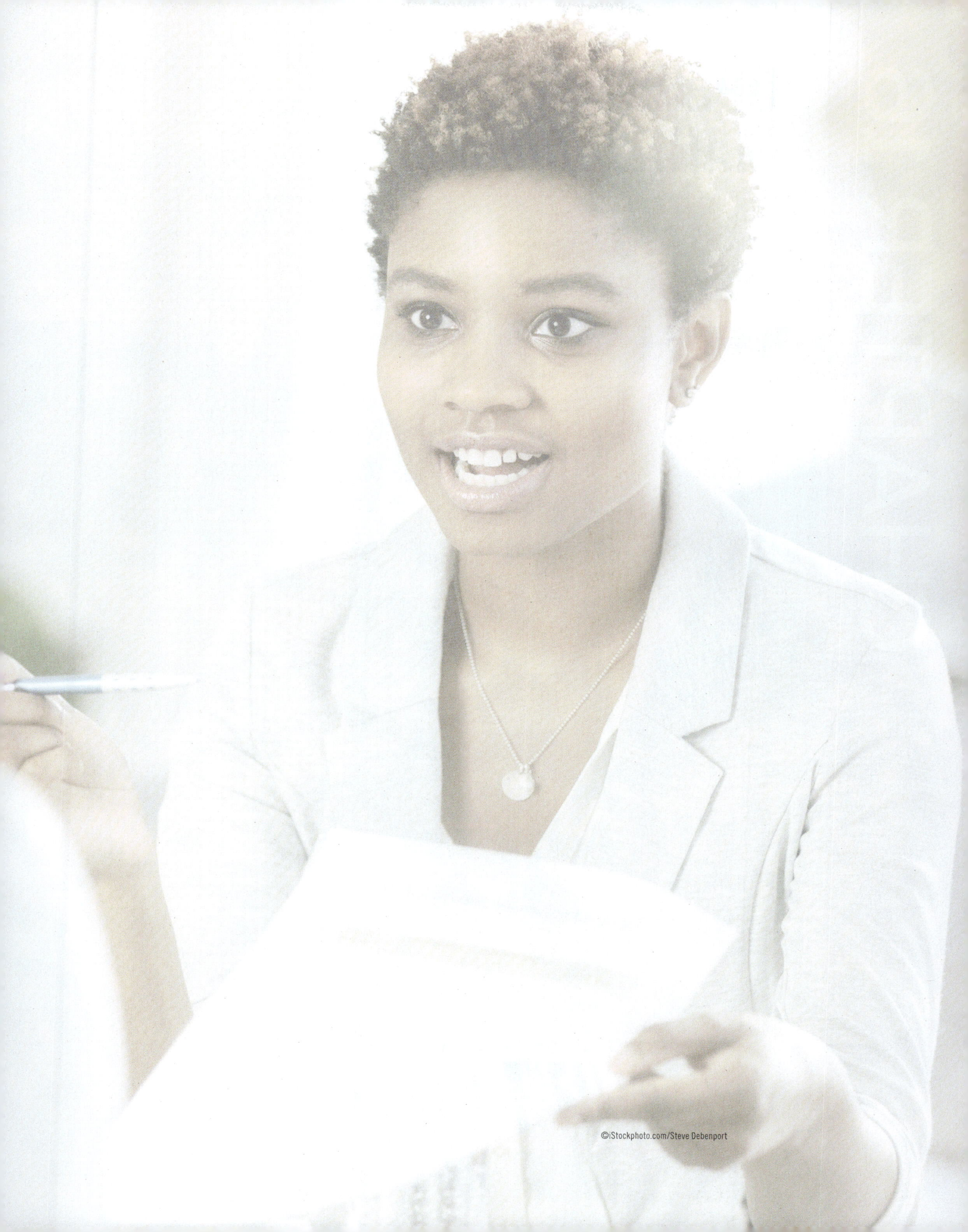

OPERATIONS MANAGEMENT

Think water, rocketing toward the sky. Think fire, blazing in the water. Think lights, illuminating the water. Think color, infusing the water. Think music, beckoning the water to dance. Think nothing short of—spectacular. This is why Mark Fuller, founder and CEO of WET, Water Entertainment Technologies, a *feature creator* as he likes to be called, has won awards such as Fast Company's 100 Most Creative People in Business and one of the Top 10 in the Design Industry. WET, a company based in Sun Valley, Idaho, has produced some of the most spectacular water fountain projects in the world. One of the latest fountains contains 1,500 water jets, 1,000 fog jets, and water streams that blast 500 feet in the air, all artfully and skillfully choreographed to music located in a 32-acre manmade lake at the foot of the world's tallest building, the Burj Khalifa in Dubai. And this is just one of his many creations. Las Vegas, Nevada, houses some of his best known, including the Fountains of Bellagio as well as the Las Vegas City Center.

The story of WET and Mark Fuller is an interesting one, beginning as a teenager when he built his own version of the Disney Jungle Cruise in his backyard, replete with underwater lights. He studied civil engineering in college and also built theatrical sets, combining his love of theater and engineering. After completing his master's degree from Stanford in mechanical engineering, he applied for a job with Disney. Disney definitely wanted to hire him after looking at the laminar fountain he had built, but did not know which position he fit. He became an "Imagineer," one of the group of people responsible for dreaming up new ideas for the parks. While still at Disney he started WET in 1983 in his garage, and like many small businesses, the company went through some difficult financial times, maxing out 13 credit cards attempting to stay afloat. Fuller's big break came in 1995, when Steve Wynn was creating the Bellagio. One of Wynn's employees had seen the fountains that Fuller had created at Disney and told Wynn about them. After Fuller made a trip to Vegas to meet with Wynn, the Fountains of Bellagio were conceived.

The engineering underlying the WET fountains is remarkable. Fuller invented water cannons that use compressed air to shoot water into the air. The shooters range from NanoShooters that have a range of 6 feet to XtreamShooters that can shoot water 500 feet into the air. The water can move so fast it literally breaks the sound barrier. He also invented new types of nozzles that he calls oarsmen, which are attached to underwater robotic arms that move forward and back and twirl. Today, all the component parts

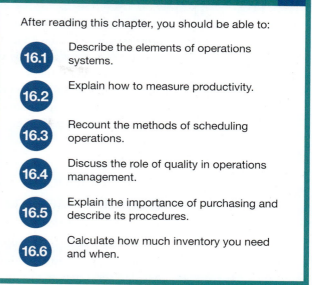

LEARNING OUTCOMES

After reading this chapter, you should be able to:

16.1 Describe the elements of operations systems.

16.2 Explain how to measure productivity.

16.3 Recount the methods of scheduling operations.

16.4 Discuss the role of quality in operations management.

16.5 Explain the importance of purchasing and describe its procedures.

16.6 Calculate how much inventory you need and when.

are made in-house. Nothing is outsourced, which Fuller believes gives WET a "competitive advantage" since the company can make changes quickly and efficiently as is needed on the dynamic projects it creates. The Fountains of Bellagio have 1,000 independently programmed nozzles, 5,000 lights, 200 speakers, and 33 technicians who keep the show running. Since the water is launched with compressed air, it requires only about 20 percent of the energy that big pumps would use. The water comes from wells that were originally drilled to irrigate a golf course on the site, using much less water than the golf course that was there.

WET is a great example of the operations system. It uses inputs that most of us take for granted—water, fire, color, and music—and transforms them into a remarkable phenomenon. John Seabrook says Fuller is the "fountain architect who gave water a voice." The output is a glorious show guaranteed to wow the viewer. Control systems are in place for the complicated process to ensure that each and every nozzle and shooter is functioning appropriately. The feedback comes not only from the computerized system running the shows but also from the applause of the crowds demonstrating their enjoyment. Mark Fuller and WET entice us to look at water with an entirely new perspective, transforming the usual into something spectacular.

Sources: Jonathan Gornall, "Dubai Fountain: The Stories Behind the Music," The National, January 28, 2018, www.thenational.ae; "WET Has Created Some of the World's Most Iconic Fountains," Fast Company, June, 21, 2017, www.fastcompany.com; The 100 Most Creative People in Business," Fast Company, June 2010, www.fastcompany.com; Jonathan Baran, "How Former Disney Engineers Turned Water into Big Business," *Fortune*, May 26, 2017, www.fortune.com.

This chapter focuses on operations management, sometimes referred to as OM, and the processes associated with it. The function of operations management has evolved over the last few decades from a narrow view of production, inventory, and industrial management into a broader concept that includes services. Indeed, the management of production and operations is critical to all small businesses, not just those involved in manufacturing. Every business performs an operations function—the processes and procedures of converting labor, materials, money, and other resources into finished products or services available for consumer consumption.

Concept Module 16.1: Elements of Operating Management

- **LO 16.1: Describe the elements of operations systems.**

Operations management systems contain five basic elements: inputs, transformation processes, outputs, control systems, and feedback. These elements must be brought together and coordinated into a system to produce the product or service—the reason for the business to exist.

Inputs

The **inputs** in an operations management system include all physical and intangible resources that come into a business. Raw materials are necessary as the things that will become transformed in a business. A company that makes in-line skates, for instance, must have polymers, plastics, and metals. Skills and knowledge of the people within the organization are other inputs. The in-line skate manufacturer needs trained workers that know how to fabricate the product. A management consulting firm, for example, needs people with special expertise who will provide recommendations for clients. For WET, the business featured at the beginning of this chapter, creativity and innovation become critical inputs to produce the product of the business. Money, information, and energy are resources all needed in varying degrees. Inputs are important to the quality of the finished product of the business. Remember the computer cliché "Garbage in—garbage out"? The idea holds true for operations management, too: You can't produce high-quality outputs from inferior inputs.

Transformation Processes

Once we have identified the inputs of a business, we can look at the processes that are used to transform them into finished products. **Transformation processes** are the active practices—including concepts, procedures, and technologies—that are implemented to produce outputs. Dry cleaners, for instance, take soiled clothing (inputs) and use chemicals, equipment, and know-how to transform them into clean clothing (the outputs of the business). WET takes water, fire, color, and music, along with vast amounts of creativity and technology, and transforms something we all use every day, water, into a totally new entertainment experience.

Outputs

Outputs, the result of the transformation processes, are what your business produces. Outputs can be tangible, such as a CD, or intangible, such as a doctor's diagnosis, or the entertainment experience of watching the Fountains of Bellagio.

Since a business's social responsibility, or obligation to the community, has become as serious a matter as product-liability and other lawsuits, we need to consider all the outputs a business produces—not just the beneficial or intended ones. When we look at the big picture of the transformation process, we see that employee accidents, consumer injuries, pollution, and waste are also outputs.

Control Systems

Control systems provide the means to monitor and correct problems or deviations when they occur in the operating system. Controls are integrated into all three stages of production—input, transformation, and output (see Figure 16.1). An example of a control system would be the use of electronic monitors in a manufacturing process to tell a machine operator that the product is not being made within the allowed size tolerance. In service companies, employee behavior is part of the transformation process to be controlled. A bank manager, for instance, might hire people to pose as new bank customers and then report back to the manager on the quality of service they received from tellers or loan officers. Control systems ensure that the quality of the product or service the customer expects occurs every time, like eating a Big Mac or a Krispy Kreme doughnut. The customer expects the same product and service with each purchase, regardless of location.

Feedback

Feedback is the information that a manager receives in monitoring the operation system. It can be verbal, written, electronic, or observational. Feedback is the necessary communication that links a control system to the inputs, transformation, and outputs. Once feedback is received, the cycle begins again since the transformation process is a continuous process, with any needed changes taking place throughout the process.

Concept Check Questions

1. Discuss the elements of an operations management system.

2. What would happen if the control systems were not included?

3. What would happen if the feedback were not included?

4. Describe your college's inputs, transformation processes, outputs, feedback, and control systems.

control systems
The means to monitor input, transformation, and output so as to identify problems.

feedback
Communication tools to connect control systems to the processes of a business.

▼ FIGURE 16.1
Control Systems

Every type of business takes inputs and transforms them into outputs.

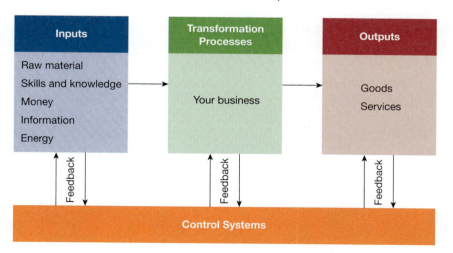

TRANSFORMING WET

Reread the chapter-opening vignette about WET. This vignette provides a lot of information about the company's products and processes. Find related articles about the company in the Buzz tab on its website (www.wetdesign.com).

Question

1. Using Figure 16.1 as a model, describe Water Entertainment Technology's inputs, transformation processes, outputs, feedback, and control systems.

Concept Module 16.2: Operations Management

- **LO 16.2: Explain how to measure productivity.**

Production broadly describes what businesses of all types do in creating goods and services. Computer hardware and software companies, health care providers, and farmers are all involved in production. Manufacturing is just one type of production, making goods as opposed to providing services or extracting natural resources. One of your highest priorities as a manager is to ensure that **productivity**—which is the measure of production, or output per worker—remains high. It is important to measure productivity so as to control the amount of resources used to produce outputs.

Operations Management for Manufacturing Businesses

Manufacturing is not often associated with small businesses. But the trade association American Small Manufacturers Coalition (www.smallmanufacturers.org) shows significant activity from its members (who have fewer than 500 employees) in a broad range of industry sectors—from food processors to machine shops to solid state circuitry assemblers. Within the 250,000 manufacturers in the United States, 99 percent of employees work for companies with fewer than 500 workers.[1] As you have seen through this entire book, small businesses exist because they solve specific problems, implement new technologies, and develop and improve a wide range of products.

Small manufacturers have the ability to offer specialized products that large manufacturers cannot make profitably. This ability to operate at a smaller scale provides a competitive advantage for niche manufacturers to operate in areas that have little or no competition from manufacturing giants.[2]

Manufacturing businesses can be classified by the way they make goods and by the time spent on making them. Goods can be made from flexible manufacturing, analytic or synthetic systems, using either continuous or intermittent processes.

Flexible manufacturing is very well suited for small businesses. It is almost exclusively done via computer numerical control (CNC) machines used to prototype and manufacture by cutting, carving, machining, and milling a wide variety of materials. CNC production is largely automated so it depends more on robot cells than people. Once the data are entered into the computers, the product can be made to precise specifications with very few people—perfect for niche small businesses. The downside is the initial cost of equipment.

Analytic systems reduce inputs into component parts so as to extract products. For example, automobile-salvage businesses buy vehicles from insurance companies or individuals to dismantle them for parts or scrap iron to sell. **Synthetic systems**, by contrast, combine inputs to create a finished product or change it into a different product. Thus, restaurants take vegetables, fruits, grains, meats, seafood, music, lighting, furniture, paintings, and a variety of human talents to create and serve meals.

productivity
The measure of outputs according to the inputs needed to produce them; a way to determine the efficiency of a business.

flexible manufacturing
Small-scale manufacturing utilizing CNC computer systems.

analytic systems
Manufacturing systems that reduce inputs into component parts so as to extract products.

synthetic systems
Manufacturing systems that combine inputs to create a finished product or change it into a different product.

Production by a **continuous process** is accomplished over long periods of time. Production of the same or very similar products goes on uninterrupted for days, months, or years. Microbreweries and wine makers are examples of small businesses that produce goods via a continuous process.

Production runs that use an **intermittent process** involve short cycles and frequent stops to change products. Small businesses using intermittent processes are also called job shops. Custom printing shops and custom jewelry makers are examples.

Can small businesses compete in a manufacturing sector long associated with gigantic factories? Yes, primarily because automation makes flexible production possible. Computers assist small manufacturers in determining raw material needs, scheduling production runs, and designing new products. Automation allows the retooling of production machines in seconds, rather than hours or days, so that shorter batches can be produced profitably. Machines can be programmed to perform many combinations of individual jobs and functions, rather than just one. With the help of computers, products and processes can be designed at the same time, rather than designing a product and then figuring out a way to make it.

Many small businesses are benefiting from the number of large businesses that are examining what they do best, determining that manufacturing is not their strongest suit, and farming out production to smaller specialty firms. This type of flexible contract production opens up many opportunities for entrepreneurs.

Changing the world of small business manufacturing is the Internet of Things (IoT), the network of physical devices, appliances, and equipment embedded with technology that enables objects to connect and exchange data. The IoT allows objects to be sensed or controlled to integrate the physical world with computer-based systems.

The IoT community of businesses has evolved through successful strategic partnerships to help each other build on their competitive advantages. Rabih Nassar, founder and CEO of IoT solutions firm Scriptr says "as demand for IoT technologies grows, entrepreneurs considering IoT solutions should look for ones that might help them achieve a competitive advantage. They should also assess their own competencies when rolling out IoT devices and find partners who help fill the gaps in experience to prevent any bottlenecks or project delays."[3]

Operations Management for Service Businesses

Service providers need and use operations management just as much as product manufacturers do. Both types of businesses take inputs and produce outputs through some type of transformation process. However, operations processes differ from one product and service to another, and some overlap. For example, manufacturers often offer repair services. Restaurants offer food products as well as services.

Traditionally, all service businesses were seen as intermittent-process businesses, because standardization didn't seem possible for businesses such as hair salons, accounting firms, and auto service centers. Today, in an effort to increase productivity, some service businesses are adopting continuous processes. For example, Merry Maids house cleaners, Jiffy Lube auto service, Fantastic Sam's family hair-cutting salons, and even chains of dentists located in malls are all using manufacturing techniques of continuous production. A notable difference between service and manufacturing operations is the amount of customer contact involved. Many services, such as hair salons, require the customer to be present for the operation to be performed, that is, service and delivery of the service occur at the same time. This makes the quality of the service of paramount importance. And many times this comes back to one of the most important inputs of a business—employees.

Consider the examples of product and service operations systems in Table 16.1.

continuous process
A production process that operates for long periods of time without interruption.

intermittent process
A production process that operates in short cycles so that it can change products.

SMALL BUSINESSES IMPACT THE IOT

The Internet of Things (IoT) evolves and expands quickly as companies, products, and applications connect. Small manufacturers from innovative consumer product makers to industrial and commercial hardware companies are leading the way. Let's look at a few:

- Nest—One of the pioneer companies in IoT, Nest is a significant player in Smart Home technology.

- Zebra—Zebra offers real-time visibility into everything from products to people in factories and supply chains. It gives physical things a digital voice.

- Click and Grow—A unique app for creating and managing gardens. App users just plug in and let technology take care of watering. Uses for this app can evolve to create self-sustaining environments anywhere.

- Flex—A small product design company that makes intelligent products for many industries and apps in the IoT environment. Its sketch-to-scale process helps other businesses integrate intelligent products and platforms creating connections and networks.

- Invoxia Trilby—Does your family communicate via Post-it Notes on the refrigerator? This smart portable speaker can go on your fridge (or anywhere else in the house) to leave digital messages or doodles for each other, set alarms, control home devices, or answer questions you pose from the internet.

- Samsara—This IoT platform offers companies tracking and monitoring of energy usage in buildings, and tracking of vehicles (like for fleet vehicle dash cams and GPS tracking).

- Stacey Higginbotham—OK, so not a small manufacturing company, but Stacey will open a world of information to you with her hosting of The Internet of Things podcast.

Sources: Angela Ruth, "25 Innovative IoT Companies and Products You Need to Know," *Entrepreneur*, August 18, 2017, www.entrepreneur.com/article/298943; Anna Johansson, "These 20 Influencers Will Lead the Internet of Things," *Inc.*, September 11, 2017, www.inc.com; Elizabeth Kiehner, "Is Your Business Ready for the M2M Era?" *Inc.*, August 31, 2017, www.inc.com.

What Is Productivity?

According to Chapter 14, as a manager, you are involved in planning, organizing, leading, and controlling. But how do you tell if and when you are reaching the goals that you have set? You can measure your success by assessing your *productivity*, the measure of output per hour worked, which is labor productivity, the most common productivity measure. Or, from another perspective, it is the amount of output produced compared to the amount of inputs used. Productivity can be described numerically as the ratio of inputs used to outputs produced. The higher the ratio, the more efficient is our operating system. You should

▼ TABLE 16.1

Product and Service Operations Systems

Inputs	Transformation	Outputs	Feedback
Restaurant			
Food	Cooking	Meals	Leftovers
Hungry people	Serving	Satisfied people	Complaints
Factory			
Machinery	Welding	Finished products	Defects
Skilled labor	Painting	Services	Returns
Raw material	Forming	Waste products	Market share
Engineering	Transporting	Plans	Complaints

constantly look for ways to increase outputs while keeping inputs constant or to keep outputs constant while decreasing inputs, both of which will increase your productivity. In a market that becomes more competitive daily, increasing productivity is key to profitability. The company that can do more with less is the company that succeeds.[4]

Ways to Measure Manufacturing Productivity

Productivity can be measured for your entire business or for a specific portion of it. Because many inputs go into your business, the input you choose determines the productivity you are measuring. The goal becomes to produce the optimal amount of output and to minimize costs in the process. Total productivity can be determined by dividing total outputs by total inputs:

Total productivity = Outputs/Labor + Capital + Raw materials + All other inputs

A variety of factors can go into lowering the productivity of your business, literally producing less output or using more resources to produce the same amount of output. These factors include

- Older technology, tools, or out-of-date processes can decrease the amount of output produced, increasing the costs of production. This in turn decreases your profitability.

- Lack of key materials or suppliers for the materials can stop production if the needed resources are not available.

- Lack of employees with the appropriate skills or employees who are not proficient in those skills can slow or even stop production in some instances.

- Not enough dollars to provide the needed resources. Money is also a necessary input, and too little can make all the other resources also unavailable or unavailable in the quantities needed.

If your software company sold $500,000 worth of software and used $100,000 in resources, your total productivity ratio would be 5. But you may not always want to consider all of your inputs every time. For example, because materials may account for as much as 90 percent of operating costs in businesses that use little labor, materials productivity would be an important ratio to track.

Materials productivity = Outputs/Materials

If 4,000 pounds of sugar are used to produce 1,000 pounds of candy, the materials productivity is 1,000 divided by 4,000, or 0.25, which becomes a base figure for comparing increases or decreases in productivity. Stated simply, you can increase the productivity of your business by increasing outputs, decreasing inputs, or a combination of both. Most productivity improvements come from changing processes used by your business, from your employees accomplishing more, or from technology that speeds production.

Productivity ratios can be used to measure the efficiency of a new process. Suppose that you run a furniture shop with a productivity ratio of 1:

Output/Input = Number of tables/Hours = 100/100 = 1

You have invented a new process that will save 20 percent on your labor costs. Now you can still produce the same number of tables (100) but take only 80 hours to produce them. Your new productivity ratio is 1.25:

New productivity ratio = 100/80 = 1.25

Unfortunately, your new process ends up increasing defects in the tables. To correct these defects, you have to increase labor hours to 120. Your productivity ratio is now 0.833:

$$\text{Corrected productivity ratio} = 100/120 = 0.833$$

Your corrected productivity ratio shows that it is back to the drawing board for your new process.

Ways to Measure Service Productivity

The importance of the service industries in the United States has grown over the last three decades. Approximately 80 percent of the U.S. workforce is employed in the service sector.

Productivity in service-related businesses has not grown as rapidly as productivity in manufacturing businesses because service businesses are more labor intensive and less standardization occurs. For example, you do not want your doctor giving you the same health care plan as he gives to your grandmother. Service-related businesses also usually require time spent one-on-one with or for the client-customer, often again without the benefit of standardization. So factories can substitute machines for people and increase output. Can service businesses do the same?

Providing quality service has its own unique set of challenges. The service and delivery of the service often occur at the same time. There is no opportunity to "remake" the product if it does not turn out "right." Say you are getting a haircut. The service and delivery are simultaneous, and if the hairdresser makes a mistake, there is no opportunity to pull the product and go back and remake it. The skill level of employees and the consistency of that skill level become critical in offering quality services.

You experience the problem facing service businesses in your daily life. Do you ever get overwhelmed with a to-do list that never seems to end? You wish you had more time, which is exactly how most service businesses attempt to increase productivity—by working longer hours.

Consider the Time Value Matrix by reviewing all the things you have to do and breaking them down into four categories: A Time, B Time, C Time, and D Time.

You are familiar with the Pareto Principle, where 80 percent of your efforts produce 20 percent of the results. In the Time Value Matrix, that 80 percent of your time that produces few results (email, meetings, interruptions) represents D Time. The other side, the 20 percent of your time that produces the vast majority of your results is called C Time. It is 16 times more valuable than D Time (4 times less input creating 4 times more output; see Figure 16.2).

▼ **FIGURE 16.2**

Application of the Pareto Principle to a Time Value Matrix

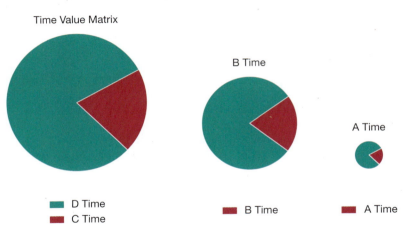

If we apply Pareto's Principle again—then 20 percent of the original 20 percent produces 80 percent of the original 80 percent of your results. That means that 4 percent of your effort (20 percent of 20 percent) creates 64 percent of your results. This 4 wonderful percent represents B Time. It could be a fabulous marketing campaign you launch generating a wealth of new customers.

Let's apply Pareto one more time. We get 1 percent (20 percent of 20 percent of 20 percent) of your time that generates 50 percent of all your results. This incredible 1 percent is A Time.

So it may be hard to distinguish tasks that are in the A or B activity levels. But think of how much more valuable they are than C or D activities! In running your small business, it's not enough to just put in long hours—identifying A and B activities not only upgrades your work, it makes your small business much more productive.[5]

Concept Check Questions

1. Define *productivity*.
2. How can identifying levels of activities be tied to productivity?

Concept Module 16.3: What about Scheduling Operations?

- **LO 16.3: Recount the methods of scheduling operations.**

Scheduling is a basic operations management activity for both manufacturing and service businesses that involves the timing of production. The purpose of scheduling is to put your plans into motion by describing what each worker has to do.

Scheduling is necessary to maximize levels of efficiency and customer service. For example, if a beauty shop schedules one haircut every 30 minutes, although each could actually be done in 20 minutes with no decrease in quality, the operator could be working one-third more efficiently. Three haircuts could be produced per hour rather than two. In contrast, a shop that schedules too much work cannot complete jobs on time, resulting in poor customer service and probably losing future business from customers who become aggravated by having to wait for their appointments. If you can schedule the exact amount of resources needed in order to meet your customer demand at a given time, you will optimize your resources and increase profitability.

Scheduling Methods

Most business operations use forward scheduling, backward scheduling, or a combination of the two methods. With **forward scheduling**, materials and resources are allocated for production when a job order comes in. Any type of custom production in which the product changes or in which demand is unknown in advance needs forward scheduling.

Backward scheduling involves arranging production activities around the due date for the product. You take the date on which the finished product must be delivered, then schedule in reverse order all material procurement and work to be done.

Henry L. Gantt devised a simple bar graph for scheduling work in any kind of operation. Developed in 1913, it still bears his name: the Gantt chart. This chart can be used to track the progress of work as a product makes its way through various departments (see Figure 16.3). It allows you to see the time required for each step and the current status of a job.

Routing

Scheduling involves routing, sequencing, and dispatching the product through successive stages of production. **Routing** shows the detailed breakdown of information explaining how your product or service will be produced. *Routing sheets* are the paper copies, and *routing files* are the electronic versions of this information. Needed information could include tooling

forward scheduling
Scheduling in which materials and resources are allocated for production when a job order comes in.

backward scheduling
Scheduling that involves arranging production activities around the due date for the product.

routing
Information showing the steps required to produce a product.

Gantt Chart

Stages of work in building a house can be scheduled in a Gantt chart.

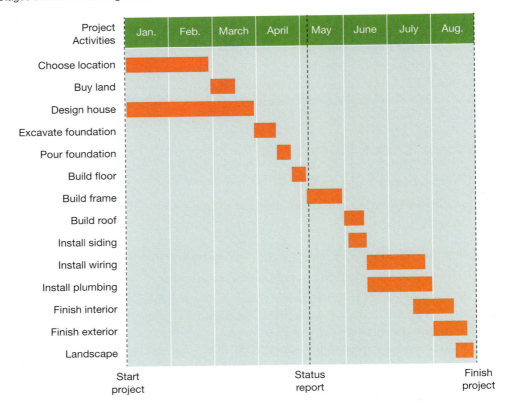

specifications and setups, the number of workers or operators needed, the sequence in which steps are to be taken, and the control tests to be performed.

Sequencing is the critical step of determining the order in which a job will go through your production system. Sequencing is most important when the job involves more than one department of your business, because a holdup in one department could cause idle time for another. Drafting a Gantt chart is a good way to track the flow of jobs between departments.

Dispatching

Dispatching is the act of releasing work to employees according to priorities you determined in planning the work sequence. Taxi companies often use *first-come, first-served* priority dispatching rules. A tailor may use an *earliest due date* rule, in which the order due first is dispatched first. A company that assumes that orders that will take the longest will be the largest (and most profitable) will use a *longest processing time* priority dispatching rule. Companies that make significant profit from handling charges and that reduce costs by completing more orders will use a *shortest processing time* priority dispatching rule.

sequencing
The order in which the steps need to occur to produce a product.

dispatching
Allocating resources and beginning the steps to produce a product.

Concept Check Questions

1. Explain the difference between forward and backward scheduling.

2. Give examples of products that would be suited to each of the dispatching rules.

Concept Module 16.4: Quality-Centered Management

- **LO 16.4: Discuss the role of quality in operations management.**

There is no quality more important to businesses today than just that—quality. In the recent past, many U.S. businesses lost tremendous market share to foreign companies for one reason: They had not paid enough attention to quality. Now, few industries and businesses, large or small, can afford *not* to pay attention to quality.

To manage a small business focused on quality, you must keep two things in mind about what the word **quality** means. First, from your customers' perspective, quality is how well your product or service satisfies their needs. Second, from your business's standpoint, quality means how closely your product conforms to the standards you have set.

All quality problems are related back to processes that did not work correctly. Or, conversely, all process hang-ups will result in quality issues. Consequently, analyzing the processes of your business is time well spent and will assist in increasing the quality of your business. Consider the following steps to ensure quality processes.

> "Perfection is not possible, but companies need to strive for it— that is, for zero defects."

- Develop clear guidelines on output requirements, and then communicate those requirements to all employees.

- Rather than correct problems, prevent problems, which is usually much less expensive.

- Implement control features for each step so a problem is identified and corrected early in the process.[6]

Six Sigma in Small Business

Six sigma is a methodology that emphasizes improving business processes in order to continuously meet and exceed customer expectations. Frequently, companies measure the quality of a product by tracking the **defect rate**. A defect rate is the number of goods produced that were out of the company's accepted **tolerance range**—the boundaries of acceptable quality. But how good is good enough? Is 99 out of 100 good enough? With a 1 percent defect rate, consider this: The U.S. Postal Service would lose more than 18,000 pieces of mail per hour!

Perfection is not possible, but companies need to strive for it—that is, for zero defects. **Six sigma** is the term that has come to signify the quality movement, not just in manufacturing but also throughout entire organizations where businesses are committed to looking at problems by extensively analyzing data and then ensuring end goals are met. Solving the underlying problem is central to six sigma. In statistical terminology, sigma denotes the standard deviation of a set of data. It indicates how all data points in a distribution vary from the mean (average) value. Table 16.2 shows different sigma levels and their corresponding defects per million.[7]

With a normal distribution, 99.73 percent of all the data points fall within three standard deviations (three sigma) of the mean—pretty good, but that is just for one stage of the production process. Products that have to go through hundreds or thousands of stages could still come out with defects.

If you choose six-sigma defects as your production goal, you will have 99.99966 percent of your products within your specification limits—only 3.4 defects per million! Even if your product has to go through 100 different stages, the defect rate will still be only 3,390 defects per million.

The concept of six sigma is not limited to producing goods in your small business. You can also apply it to customer satisfaction in your service business. Consider a company with 1,000 customers and 10 employees (or stages) that can affect customer satisfaction. The difference between three sigma

quality
How well a good or service meets or exceeds customers' expectations, or the degree to which a product conforms to established tolerance standards.

defect rate
The number of goods produced that are outside the company's boundaries of acceptable quality.

tolerance range
The boundaries a manager sets in determining the acceptable quality of a product.

six sigma
The tolerance range in which only 3.4 defects per million are allowed.

▼ TABLE 16.2

Sigma Levels and Defect Rates

Sigma Level	Defects per Million
3.0	66,810.0
3.5	22,750.0
4.0	6,750.0
4.5	1,350.0
5.0	233.0
5.5	32.0
6.0	3.4

WOMEN IN MANUFACTURING

An important issue in small business is recognizing the contributions that women leaders make in the field of manufacturing and operations. Collie Hutter and her husband founded Click Bond, which designs and manufactures high-performance fastening hardware and adhesive bonding processes for use in aerospace, marine, energy, and especially in airline sectors. She holds a BS in physics and an MBA from Wharton and was the inaugural recipient of the Manufacturing Institute's STEP Award for women for excellence in manufacturing. Her company creates products in factories in Nevada, Connecticut, and Europe that are used in virtually every plane flying. Interview questions for and responses from Collie Hutter provide the following insights:

- What is unique about her company? Click Bond manufactures proprietary products developed internally and therefore holds many U.S. and international patents.

- What does she do on a daily basis? As chairperson of a family-owned company that is in the process of passing operations to the next generation, Hutter guides family discussions to assure a smooth transition. She is involved in new directions in manufacturing and changes in management style.

- How did she get started in manufacturing? Her father's company manufactured transformer laminations. She started there in the quality assurance department and he encouraged her to make manufacturing a career.

- What are her biggest obstacles? Hutter tries not to see obstacles but sees many challenges. She sees the need to move much more swiftly in automating assembly processes in order to lower costs to customers . . . while maintaining quality and on-time delivery. Finding skilled workers is another challenge, so she is involved in workforce training and apprenticeship programs.

Hutter is obviously an impressive role model. Her story, and the stories of many other women in manufacturing, are important to showcase their accomplishments and lead the way for future women leaders in manufacturing.

Sources: Drew Greenblatt, "Extraordinary Women Manufacturing Business Leaders—Collie Hutter," *Inc.*, March 20, 2017, www.inc.com; Annie Conway, "Executive Gives Insight into Carson's Largest Manufacturer," *Northern Nevada Business Weekly*, January 25, 2018, www.nnbw.com; www.clickbond.com/about-us.

(499 dissatisfied) and four sigma (60 dissatisfied) is 439 dissatisfied customers. That represents 44 percent of your entire customer base![8]

Let's take a closer look at the basic components of a six-sigma quality program and the activities and tools needed.

Basic Components. The basic components of a six-sigma program include the actual improvement process and quality measurement. The actual improvement process involves the following steps:

1. Define products and services by describing the actual products or services that are provided to customers.

2. Identify customer requirements for products or services by stating them in measurable terms.

3. Compare products with requirements by identifying gaps between what the customer expects and what she is actually receiving.

4. Describe the process by providing explicit details.

5. Improve the process by simplification and mistake proofing.

6. Measure quality and productivity by establishing baseline values and then tracking improvement.

Two types of statistical analysis are used in six sigma—descriptive statistics and inferential statistics. Descriptive statistics is a useful tool for summarizing the data collected, usually including the use of measures of central tendency (the mean, median, and mode), variance, and standard deviation, along with distribution charts. Inferential statistics is the process of looking at a sample and then using statistical analysis to interpret results to your whole population of customers based upon that sample, and usually looking for relationships. Statistical tools used in this area include *probability*; *analysis of variance (ANOVA)*, which is used to identify where in the process this variation occurs (by location, person, or process step); and *regression analysis*, which is used to determine the magnitude of the effect these factors have on the process and to identify potential causes of variation.

One of the challenges of six sigma is implementation. There is no one way to implement six sigma in your business. There are no handy six steps you can check off. Many times the success or failure lies in the implementation of six sigma and the commitment and resources needed in order for successful implementation, particularly since it is not a one-time project. In order for six sigma to be effective, it is a process that can take years, not days, to successfully implement.[9]

> "In order for six sigma to be effective, it is a process that can take years, not days, to successfully implement."

Quality Activities and Tools.
The quality activities encompass ongoing management processes that businesses need to practice in a six-sigma program. They include participative management, short-cycle manufacturing, designing for manufacturing benchmarking, statistical process control (SPC), and supplier qualification. The improvement tools and analytical techniques include flowcharts (schematic representations of an algorithm or a process), Pareto charts (charts used to graphically summarize and display the relative importance of the differences between groups of data), histograms (the graphical versions of tables that show what proportion of cases fall into each of several or many specified categories), cause-and-effect diagrams (diagrams, also known as fishbone diagrams because of their shape, that show causes of certain events), and experimental designs (the designs of all information-gathering exercises where variation is present, whether under the full control of the experimenter or not).

The speed at which e-business is conducted fits like a glove with six-sigma principles, because these principles are aimed at enabling businesses to deliver just what customers need when they want it.

Small businesses that would like to achieve six-sigma status must work diligently to reduce the incidence of defects. Those that do will find six sigma to be not just a clinical phrase, but also the means toward achieving the ultimate goals of improved manufacturing and increased customer satisfaction.[10]

How Do You Control Operations?

The issue of quality affects the entire production process, so controls need to be built in at every stage. *Feed forward quality control* applies to your company's inputs. *Concurrent quality control* involves monitoring your transformation processes. *Feedback quality control* means inspecting your outputs. Each will be discussed here.

Feed Forward Quality Control.
Control of quality begins by screening out inputs that are not good enough. **Feed forward quality control** depends on every employee being a quality inspector and building better, long-term relationships with suppliers. When you have a long-term relationship with suppliers, they can help you achieve higher quality standards by continuously improving their products. Teamwork with your employees and cooperation with suppliers are keys to feed forward control.

Concurrent Quality Control.
Concurrent quality control involves monitoring the quality of your work in progress. To facilitate this type of monitoring, many small businesses are realizing the value of the international quality standards known as **ISO 9001** (pronounced ICE-oh 9001).

feed forward quality control
Quality control applied to a company's inputs.

concurrent quality control
Quality control applied to work in progress.

ISO 9001
The set of standards that certifies that a business is using processes and principles to ensure the production of quality products.

CREATING COMPETITIVE ADVANTAGE

LEAN MANUFACTURING

Lean manufacturing is an inventory-management and manufacturing strategy designed to reduce costs, increase productivity, and gain a competitive advantage. It revolves around the mantra of eliminating waste from the manufacturing process, with "waste" defined as any activity that does not add value from the customer's perspective.

Fortunately, just about every business has activities that do not add value. A good place to start is by exploring Lean Tools:

- **5S:** Organizing your work area with (1) sort (eliminate that which is not needed), (2) set in order (organize remaining items), (3) shine (clean and inspect work area), (4) standardize (write standards for above), and (5) sustain (regularly apply the standards).

- **Bottleneck Analysis:** Identifying parts of the manufacturing process that limit the overall throughput and improve the performance of the process.

- **Heijunka (Level Scheduling):** A form of production scheduling that intentionally produces small batches by sequencing products made in small groups.

- **Kaizen (Continuous Improvement):** A strategy where employees work together proactively for the purpose of regular, incremental improvements in the manufacturing process.

- **KPIs (Key Performance Indicators):** Metrics designed to track and encourage progress toward critical goals of the organization.

- **Root Cause Analysis:** A problem-solving methodology that focuses on resolving the underlying problem instead of applying quick fixes that only treat symptoms of the problem. A common approach is to ask "why" five times.

Lean manufacturing techniques move materials through the production process with the focus on reducing cost and time. Lean strategies can give a small business a sustainable competitive advantage, but it requires buy-in by all employees from the top down.

Sources: "Top 25 Lean Tools," Lean Production, accessed May 2018, www .leanproduction.com; Luanne Kelchner, "How Can Lean Manufacturing Help a Company Gain a Competitive Edge & Prepare for the Future?" Small Business Chronicle, accessed May 2018, www.smallbusiness.chron.com; JD Albert, "How to Figure Out Your Best Manufacturing Solution," *Entrepreneur*, March 28, 2016, www .entrepreneur.com/article/270144.

The purpose of the ISO 9001 standards is to document, implement, and demonstrate the quality assurance systems used by companies that supply goods and services internationally.

ISO standards do not address the quality of your specific products. Rather, compliance with them shows your customers (whether consumers or other businesses) how you test your products, how your employees are trained, how you keep records, and how you fix defects. ISO standards are more like generally accepted accounting principles (GAAP) to demonstrate appropriate processes have been used. Certification in the United States comes from the American National Standards Institute, www.iso.org.

An important tool for monitoring the quality of a product while it is being produced (concurrent control) is **statistical process control (SPC)**, the process of gathering, plotting, and analyzing data to isolate problems in a specified sample of products. Using SPC, you can determine the probability of a deviation being a simple, random, unimportant variation or a sign of a problem in your production process that must be corrected.

For example, if you are producing titanium bars that need to be 1 inch in diameter, not every single bar will measure exactly 1 inch. You need to calculate the probability that various deviations will occur by chance alone or because of some problem. If a sample bar measures 1.01 inches, you wouldn't be too concerned, because that amount of variation occurs by chance once in every 100 products. But if a sample bar measures 1.05 inches, a variation that occurs by chance only once in 10,000 products, you know a problem needs correction in your production process. See the control chart in Figure 16.4 for this example. A control chart consists of the following:

statistical process control (SPC)
The use of statistical analysis to determine the probability of a variation in product being random or a problem.

- Points representing averages of measurements of a quality characteristic in samples taken from the process and shown over a period of time

Control Chart

Are used to distinguish random from nonrandom variations in the production of goods.

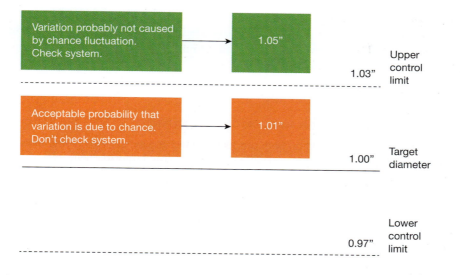

- A center line, drawn at the process mean

- Upper and lower control limits (called *natural process limits*) that indicate the threshold at which the process output is considered statistically unlikely

Another powerful tool for concurrent control is **benchmarking**, which allows the comparisons necessary for measurement. To identify or measure a competitive advantage for your small business, you must have a comparison base. Your products, services, and practices—almost anything related to your business that can be measured—can be benchmarked. Where can you find benchmark information? First, visit your local library reference section to find RMA's *Annual Statement Studies*. RMA (Risk Management Association) is second to none for providing small business industry averages. In addition, industry groups and trade associations often publish industry averages in journals, magazines, and newsletters.

Benchmarking can be used to improve every facet of your business. Some examples follow:

benchmarking
The process of comparing key points within your business with comparable points in another external entity.

Production Process	
• Methodology	• Facility needs
• Equipment needs	• Personnel needs
• Assembly time	• Quality control
• Inspection	• Cost considerations
• Parts availability	• Returns and repairs

Customer Service	
• Goods and services availability	• Returns, repair, and replacement
• Warranties and guarantees	• Feedback mechanisms (surveys, toll-free numbers, etc.)
• Cost considerations	

Feedback Quality Control. Inspecting and testing products after they are produced is called **feedback quality control**. Quality control inspectors may be used to check products. Rejected products will be discarded, reworked, or recycled.

A problem with many types of product inspection is that the product can no longer be used because it has to be cut up, taken apart, or disassembled to test and measure it. However, nondestructive testing of several metal and plastic parts is being perfected by using electromagnetic, magnetic-particle, liquid-penetrant, radiographic, ultrasonic, and acoustic-based methods.[11]

Concept Check Questions

1. What types of small businesses would benefit from having ISO 9001 certification?

2. This chapter concentrated on both productivity and quality. In running your small manufacturing business, can you increase both, or aren't they mutually exclusive?

Concept Module 16.5: Purchasing for Small Business

- **LO 16.5: Explain the importance of purchasing and describe its procedures.**

Your ability to offer quality goods at competitive prices depends on your purchasing skills. You need to seek the best value—the highest quality for the best price—for the goods, services, and equipment you purchase, because that is exactly what your customers will be expecting when they purchase your products. Price is therefore merely one of many factors to consider. You should also consider the consistency of your suppliers' quality, their reliability in meeting delivery schedules, the payment terms available, product guarantees, merchandising assistance, emergency delivery and return policies, and other factors.

Purchasing Guidelines

The following questions provide guidelines for evaluating your small business purchasing and inventory control:

- Are you using the proper sources of supply?

- Are you taking advantage of all purchase discounts?

- How do you determine minimum inventories and reorder points?

- Have you run out of raw materials or finished goods?

- What is the record of your current suppliers for quality, service, and price?

- Are you using minimum quantities or economic ordering quantities?

- What are your inventory holding costs?

- Do you know your optimal average inventory? Does it guide your purchasing policy?

- Could you improve your purchasing to increase profits?

- What is your inventory turnover ratio? How does it compare with the industry average?[12]

To illustrate the importance of purchasing to the profit of your small business, suppose your business spends $500,000 annually, has yearly sales of $1 million, and enjoys a profit margin of 10 percent or $100,000. If you were able to decrease the costs of your purchases by 3 percent, you would save $15,000—increasing your profits by 15 percent. To see the same profit increase through sales revenue, you would have to generate $150,000 in additional sales, or a 15 percent increase. This means that a 3 percent savings on the cost of purchased items has the same impact on your bottom line as a 15 percent increase in sales.

feedback quality control
Inspecting and testing products after they are produced.

Purchasing Basics

Whether you're purchasing inexpensive toilet paper for the employee bathroom or expensive components for your manufacturing process, you want to make good purchasing decisions—decisions that will get you the best possible product at the best possible price. To make your decisions wisely, it helps to know how the purchasing process *should* work. Let's look more closely at the steps in the purchasing process.

1. *Recognize, describe, and transmit the need.* If you're the only employee in your business, you'll have to rely on your own knowledge of your work processes to know *what* needs to be ordered and *when*. However, if your small business has other employees, you should train them to alert the person in charge of purchasing (yourself or another person whom you designate) of any needs. You'll probably want to standardize this process with a *purchase requisition* form that lists and describes the materials, supplies, and equipment that are needed. In addition, the purchase requisition should list the quantity needed, the date required, an estimated unit cost, a budget account to be charged, and an authorized signature. This form should also have at least two copies—one for the person who does the purchasing and the other for the person requesting the items.

> "The purchase requisition should list the quantity needed, the date required, an estimated unit cost, a budget account to be charged, and an authorized signature."

2. *Investigate and select suppliers and prepare a purchase order.* Once you know what's needed, you can begin to look for the best possible sources for obtaining the desired products. Because elsewhere this text describes the factors you need to examine in selecting a supplier, let's concentrate here on describing the *purchase order*, which is, in most instances, a legal contract document between you and the supplier—so you want to make sure you prepare it carefully.

Once you've selected a supplier, you should record on a serially numbered purchase order the quantity requirements, price, and delivery and shipping requirements accurately. If you have any quality specifications, they should also be described precisely. If you have any product drawings or other documents that relate to the order, these should be included as well. If you need to inspect sample products before an order is completed, be sure to specify what, when, and how much you want to sample. In other words, include all the data on your purchase order and word it so that it's clear to both you and the supplier what the specifications and expectations are.

You'll probably want to use a multipart purchase order form so that you and the supplier can keep track of the orders coming in and being fulfilled. In fact, purchasing experts say that seven is the minimum number of copies you'd want on a purchase order. Although you may consider this to be extreme, at least make sure that your purchase order form has enough copies so that both you and your supplier can keep track of the order in sufficient detail.

3. *Follow up on the order.* Although the purchase order represents a legal offer to buy, no purchase contract exists until the seller accepts the buyer's offer. The supplier accepts by either filling the order or at the very least notifying the purchaser that the order is being filled. By *following up* on the order by mail, email, fax, or phone call, you can keep on top of its status. If the goods you ordered are critically needed, the follow-up can be doubly important. (For important orders, you'll want to get written verification that your order was accepted.) Besides being a good way to keep on top of your purchasing activities, the follow-up helps you maintain good relations with your suppliers.

4. *Receiving and inspecting the order.* Once the order is received, you should inspect it immediately to confirm that it is correct. The supplier should have enclosed a *packing slip* with the order that you can compare against your copy of the purchase order. You should check for quantity as well as quality of the goods. If someone other than yourself checks orders, you'll probably want to use a *receiving report form* that indicates what's included in the order—quantity and quality. In fact, even if you're the person who checks the order, it would be smart to have some way of noting

the condition of the shipment, just in case you need this information in the future. If the order is correct, it's ready to go into inventory or into use. If there's a problem, you should contact the supplier immediately. Let the supplier know what the problem is and follow up with written *documentation* describing the problem. The supplier will let you know the procedure for handling the incorrect order.

5. *Completing the order.* The order isn't complete until you've paid the *invoice*—a bill that should be included with the order or might be sent later by the supplier—and prepared whatever accounting documents you need. Once you've completed this step, the purchasing process is complete.

Although the purchasing process as outlined here may seem burdensome and time consuming, keep in mind that being an effective and efficient purchaser makes an important difference in your small business.

Selecting Suppliers

Whom you buy from can be as important as *what* you buy. At the very least, supplier (or vendor) selection should be based on systematic analysis, not on guesswork or habit. Vendors are an important component of your operation.

Make-or-Buy Decision

A decision you must make in running your small manufacturing business is whether to produce your own parts and components or to buy them from an outside source. This choice is called the **make-or-buy decision**. Much of the decision rests on the availability and quality of suppliers.

The more specialized your needs or the more you need to hide design features, the more likely it is that you will have to make your own parts. But it is generally better to buy standardized parts (such as bolts) and standardized components (such as blower fans) rather than to make them.

The make-or-buy decision is not limited to manufacturing operations or functions. Service and retail businesses need to consider whether to outsource such functions as janitorial or payroll services. You could either use your own personnel for those services or hire another specialized business to produce them for you.

Concept Check Questions

1. Purchasing products or materials is obviously an important part of running a small business. What are the pros and cons of developing a relationship with a single vendor from which to purchase most of your products versus using multiple vendors and not depending on just one other company?

2. Consider the make-or-buy decision. Give three examples of situations in which a business should make, rather than buy. Give three examples of situations in which a business should buy, rather than make.

3. What factors should be considered when purchasing for a small business?

Concept Module 16.6: Managing Inventory

- **LO 16.6: Calculate how much inventory you need and when.**

Before considering how much inventory is needed, we should investigate the various meanings of the term **inventory**. Depending on the context, there are four common meanings of the term:

make-or-buy decision
The choice of whether to purchase parts and components or to produce them.

inventory
Goods a business owns for the completion of future sales. Also, the act of counting the goods held in stock.

1. The monetary value of goods owned by a business at a given time. "We carry a $500,000 inventory."

2. The number of units on hand at a given time. "We have 1,000 yo-yos in inventory."

3. The process of measuring or counting goods. "We inventory the office supplies every month."

4. The detailed list of goods. "I need to look at the inventory on the computer."

How Much Inventory Do You Need?

Managing inventory is like performing a balancing act. On one side of the scale, you have to keep an adequate supply of goods on hand. You don't want to shut down operations because you ran out of a needed part, and you don't want to lose a sale because customers find an empty shelf where they expected to find a product. On the other side of the scale, inventory represents money sitting idly on the shelf. And to complicate things further, the more you try to decrease the risk of running out of more obscure items, the more you increase the risk that some items will become obsolete.

Retail Business. An important factor in considering the inventory needs of many small retail businesses is the time needed to get fresh inventory in and the cost of reordering. If you can replace inventory quickly at a reasonable price, you can hold down your inventory costs by keeping fewer items yourself.

We introduced the Pareto Principle earlier in this chapter discussing service productivity. It applies to retailing also—about 80 percent of the firm's revenue will come from about 20 percent of the inventory. This principle reminds the small retailer to concentrate on the "vital few" rather than on the "trivial many."

> "Managing inventory is like performing a balancing act."

Service Industry. Even service businesses that aren't retail based must consider their inventory needs. For instance, a restaurant needs appropriate food and beverages, cleaning fluids, table service equipment, and miscellaneous supplies, such as menus, toothpicks, cash register tape, and check slips. Financial services firms need adequate supplies of paper, pencils, accounting forms, and other types of office supplies.

They might even need to have a supply of cash on hand to meet certain customer needs. Security firms need to keep items such as flashlights, mace or pepper spray, whistles or alarms, and, of course, office materials and supplies in their inventories. Auto repair shops must stock tires, batteries, wrenches, engine oil, grease, cleaning supplies, and other items. There are many other types of service businesses not mentioned here. The point is that small service-business managers should pay just as much attention to inventory control as their counterparts in manufacturing and retail.

Manufacturing Business. Inventory needs for a small manufacturer are different from those of retailers. Manufacturers' needs are based on production rate, lead time required to get in new stock, and the order amount that delivers the optimal economic quantity. Common techniques of manufacturers include just-in-time (JIT) inventory control and materials requirement planning (MRP), considered later in this chapter.

Costs of Carrying Inventory

There are several obvious and not-so-obvious costs of carrying inventory of any type. Financing is the most apparent cost of inventory. Because inventory is an asset, it must be offset by a liability—the cost of borrowing money or diverting your own cash from other uses. If you can sell merchandise and collect payment before you have to pay the supplier that provided you with the merchandise, you can avoid direct finance costs. Because that usually isn't the case, most inventory has a cash cost to the business.

Inventory **shrinkage** represents another cost to your business. Shrinkage can come from theft or spoilage. Employee theft and shoplifting by customers result in inventory that you had to pay for that is not available for sale. Spoilage is inventory you have purchased that is not fit for sale because of damage or deterioration.

Obsolescence, in which products become outdated or fall out of fashion, produces the same effect as spoilage: unrecoverable inventory costs caused by merchandise you can't sell. Such merchandise is known as dead stock. Obsolescence is a problem for a wide variety of businesses, but especially those in which styles, tastes, or technologies change quickly, such as clothing, automobile parts, and computer parts and accessories. You may be able to salvage some money from inventory that is obsolete (or on its way) through price reductions or recycling, but dead stock is still a major cost.

Holding costs are what you incur for keeping extra goods on hand—warehouse building expenses (either purchase and upkeep or rent), added utilities, insurance, and taxes on the building. In addition, there are expenses such as insurance on the value of the inventory and taxes on the inventory. Merchandise that spoils, becomes obsolete, depreciates, or is pilfered is considered part of the holding cost. Finally, you have interest expenses if you borrow money to pay for the goods.

Ordering costs are the expenses you incur in either ordering or producing inventory. Ordering costs tend to be fixed, meaning that they cost about the same no matter what quantity of goods you order. They include all the clerical expenses of preparing purchase orders, processing orders and invoices, analyzing vendors, and receiving and handling incoming products.

If holding costs were your only inventory expense, you would want to order as few items at a time as possible to minimize your cost of holding on to inventory. Ordering one part at a time would cut down on your storage expenses, but think of the cost in time, paper, and people needed to process that many order forms and receive goods one at a time—your total costs would go through the roof. Likewise, if ordering costs were your only inventory expense, you would want to send for as many goods as possible at one time to minimize your costs of ordering. Although your clerical needs would be cut by making out just one order, think of the size of the storage facility you would need and the cash-flow problems created by having all your money tied up in inventory.

In the real world, every business incurs both holding and ordering costs. Striving to maintain a balance between them is part of the difficult job of controlling inventory.

Controlling Inventory

Because inventory is such a significant expense, most businesses look carefully for ways to determine the appropriate levels of control for their inventory. *Inventory control* is the process of establishing and maintaining the supply of goods you need to keep on hand. It is important because inventory represents about 25 percent of a manufacturing firm's capital and as much as 80 percent of a retailer's capital. Many techniques are used to control inventory, with the best choice depending on the type of business and the kind of inventory. Several techniques are described in this section.

Reorder Point and Quantity

Controlling your inventory begins with determining when you need to restock inventory and how much you need to reorder. These considerations are called the *reorder point* and the *reorder quantity*, respectively. The time period that begins when an item is at its highest desired stocking level, continues as the item is used or sold, and ends when it is replenished is called an **inventory cycle**.

Suppose you are a retailer who sells a certain product—Elvis Presley statuettes—with an average weekly demand of 10 units (see Figure 16.5). The **lead time** (time from order placement until delivery) is two weeks. You would need to reorder when inventory drops to 30 Elvises so that you don't completely run out before the ordered items arrive. The reorder quantity would be 100 statuettes, so you would have a 10-week supply of goods on hand at your highest desired stocking level.

shrinkage
The loss of goods held in inventory due to theft or spoilage.

obsolescence
When products become outdated or fall out of fashion.

holding costs
Expenses related to keeping inventory on hand.

ordering costs
Expenses related to procuring inventory.

inventory cycle
The period of time from the point when inventory is at its highest level until it is replenished.

lead time
The period of time from order placement until the goods are received.

Inventory Cycles

An Inventory Cycle Lasts from the Time the Goods Are Used or Sold until They Are Replenished. The Reorder Point Indicates When You Need to Order Goods. The Reorder Quantity Is How Many Items You Wish to Put Back in Stock

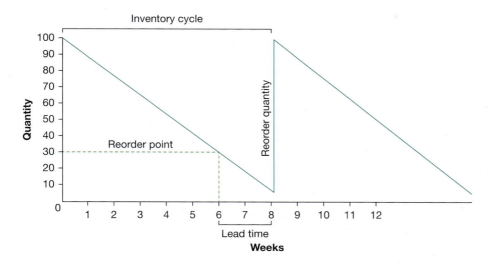

Visual Control

Many small businesses operate without a formal or complex inventory control system. If you run a one- or two-person business that sells a relatively narrow selection of items, *visual control* may be the only inventory system you need. Visual inventory control means that you look at the goods you have on hand and reorder when you appear to be running low on items. It depends on your being in the business during most business hours and on your knowing the usage rate and reorder time needed.

Economic Order Quantity

Economic order quantity (EOQ) is a traditional method of controlling inventory that minimizes total inventory costs by balancing annual ordering costs with annual holding costs for an item. EOQ balances these two types of costs to minimize your total costs (see Figure 16.6).

economic order quantity (EOQ)
A traditional method of controlling inventory that minimizes total inventory costs by balancing annual ordering costs with annual holding costs for an item.

▼ FIGURE 16.6

Economic Order Quantity

Economic Order Quantity (EOQ) Is a Way to Minimize Total Inventory Expenses by Balancing Holding Costs and Ordering Costs

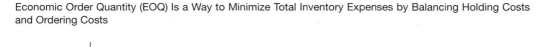

Several models exist for the EOQ approach that go beyond the scope of this book, so in practice you simply need to find a model that fits the cost structure of your business and use it. The basic model of EOQ makes three assumptions:

1. You can't take advantage of volume discounts.

2. You can accurately predict annual demand.

3. Your average inventory level is equal to your maximum level minus your minimum level divided by 2.

If your business meets these assumptions, you can use the following formula:

$$EOQ = \sqrt{\frac{2DO}{C}}$$

where

D = annual demand for the product (in units)

O = average ordering cost for one of the product (in dollars per year)

C = average holding cost for one of the product (in dollars per year)

To illustrate, imagine a sporting goods store that meets the three assumptions stated previously. This store usually sells 12,000 pairs of hiking boots per year. Its ordering costs are $10 per order. The holding costs run $0.96 per pair of boots per year. The EOQ for hiking boots for this store would be 500.

$$EOQ = \sqrt{\frac{2 \times 12,000 \times 10}{0.96}}$$

This result tells us that to minimize total inventory costs and balance ordering and holding costs, the sporting goods store would need to order 500 pairs of hiking boots at a time. In selling 12,000 pairs of boots and ordering 500 pairs each time, the store would need to order hiking boots 24 times per year.

$$Order per year = \frac{D}{EOQ}$$

$$24 = \frac{12,000}{500}$$

ABC Classification

In the process of handling many types of goods, some can get misallocated. A reason for misallocation can be that the person in charge of inventory is paying as much attention to an item that costs $5 and is sold twice a year as to items that cost $500 and are sold many times per month. An inventory system that helps to allocate more appropriate time and attention to items is **ABC classification**. This system classifies items based on the total dollar volume of sales each generates. To calculate the total dollar volume, multiply the cost of an item by the number of units sold annually. The greater the weighted dollar volume generated by an item, the more attention you will want to give it in your inventory control.

Items that generate high dollar volume will be classified in the A category and will receive the highest priority. Proportionately less attention will be given to the moderate-dollar-volume goods

ABC classification
An inventory control system that classifies items based on the total dollar volume of sales each generates.

in the B category, and low-dollar-volume items in the C category. A rule of thumb for percentage allocation for each group is shown in Table 16.3. The use of a computer database in your inventory control makes monitoring your ABC classification system relatively quick and easy to adjust if necessary.

▼ TABLE 16.3

ABC Inventory Classification

Classification	Percentage of Total Inventory Investment
A. High dollar volume	60–80
B. Moderate dollar volume	10–40
C. Low dollar volume	5–15

Concept Check Questions

1. Explain how the Pareto rule is important to a small business owner.

2. How can shrinkage affect an inventory system?

3. Assume that you are the owner of the sporting goods store used in the example of EOQ inventory control discussed above. You typically sell 14,500 sweatshirts per year. Your ordering costs are $10 per order. Holding costs are $0.60 per sweatshirt per year. What is your EOQ for sweatshirts? How many sweatshirt orders would you place per year?

4. When would an ABC classification inventory system be appropriate?

CHAPTER REVIEW

SUMMARY ▶▶

LO 16.1 Describe the elements of operations systems.

In developing a system for producing your product or service, your business takes inputs such as raw materials, skills, money, information, and energy, and transforms them in some way to add value to product outputs. You need to receive feedback at every stage to control the process.

Operating systems used by manufacturers are either analytic (systems that take inputs and reduce them into component parts to produce outputs) or synthetic (systems that combine inputs in producing outputs). The processes that manufacturers use are either continuous or intermittent. A continuous process produces the same good without interruption for a long period of time. An intermittent process is stopped with some frequency to change the products being made. Service businesses also take inputs and produce outputs through some transformation process. Most have used intermittent processes, but some have adopted continuous processes in an effort to increase productivity.

LO 16.2 Explain how to measure productivity.

The ratio of inputs used to produce outputs is called *productivity*. Productivity measures the efficiency of your entire business or any part of it. It can be improved by changing processes used by your business, by getting your employees to accomplish more, or by using some type of technology that speeds production. To calculate productivity, simply divide outputs by inputs.

LO 16.3 Recount the methods of scheduling operations.

Scheduling involves planning what work will need to be done and determining what resources you will need to produce your product or service. Forward scheduling is accomplished by having resources available and ready as customer orders come in. Backward scheduling is used when you plan a job around the date when the project must be done. Gantt charts are a useful backward-scheduling tool.

LO 16.4 Discuss the role of quality in operations management.

A company's tolerance range denotes the boundaries of acceptable quality. The defect rate indicates the number of products made that fall outside the tolerance range. Six sigma establishes a tolerance range of only 3.4 defects per million products produced. Statistical process control (SPC) is a procedure used to determine the probability of a deviation being a simple, random, unimportant variation or a sign of a problem in your production process that must be corrected.

Controlling operations enables you to measure what is being accomplished in your business. Feed forward quality control applies to your company's inputs. Concurrent quality control involves monitoring your transformation processes. Feedback quality control relies on inspecting your outputs.

LO 16.5 Explain the importance of purchasing and describe its procedures.

Purchasing is an important part of a small business because the goods or raw materials that you bring into your business become the products you will in turn have available to sell to your customers. A savings gained from the cost of purchased items has a larger effect on your profit level than an increase in sales revenue.

Small manufacturers must first decide whether to make the parts needed in their production or to purchase components from another business. Retailers must decide whether to hire personnel or to outsource needed services. Both of these are examples of the make-or-buy decision. Factors such as product quality, location of supplier, services that suppliers offer, and credit terms available need to be considered when selecting suppliers.

LO 16.6 Calculate how much inventory you need and when.

If your small business requires inventory, you must maintain a balance between having enough goods on hand to prevent lost sales due to items being out of stock and having inventory dollars lying idle on a shelf. Retailers and manufacturers need to heed the Pareto rule by paying attention to the "vital few" rather than the "trivial many" items in inventory. Shrinkage, obsolescence, holding costs, and ordering costs are factors to be considered in determining the inventory needs of your business.

To control your inventory, you must begin by determining your reorder point (when you need to reorder) and your reorder quantity (how much you need to reorder). Many small businesses depend on visual control to maintain inventory. Economic order quantity and ABC classification are common tools for controlling small business inventory.

KEY TERMS ▶▶

STUDENT STUDY SITE ▶▶

edge.sagepub.com/hatten7e

⑤SAGE edge™ Sharpen your skills with SAGE edge!

SAGE edge for Students provides a personalized approach to help you accomplish your coursework goals in an easy-to-use learning environment. You'll find mobile-friendly eFlashcards and quizzes as well as multimedia resources to support and expand on the concepts presented in this chapter.

EXPERIENTIAL LEARNING ACTIVITIES ▶▶

16.1: Operations Management

LO 16.1: Describe the elements of operations systems.

Identify which element (input, transformation process, output, control system, feedback) in the operations management system is represented in the following scenarios. Explain the element chosen. More than one element may be identified in each scenario.

1. A customer has just returned your product with the statement that the customer will never buy the product again.

2. The produce truck full of fresh vegetables has just made its daily delivery to your restaurant.

3. The timer is beeping on a batch of French fries needed for hungry customers.

4. The freshly baked bread for your amazing homemade sandwiches has just been taken from the oven and placed on the counter.

5. You are excitedly discussing the latest adventure movie you just watched as you leave the movie theater.

6. The camera store has taken your digital photo to produce a high quality canvas picture.

7. Each day you note which food and how much food remains on your customers' plates. If the same food shows up more than once, you go to the kitchen and ask the chef to check that product.

8. As you produce your product, small amounts of certain acids are released into the air, despite the air scrubbers you use.

9. Any unsold Krispy Kreme doughnuts are removed from the shelves at the end of each day.

10. Mike's Detail Service using labor, cleaning supplies, knowledge, and efficiency, details vehicles in under 15 minutes.

16.2: Operations Management: Productivity

LO 16.2: Explain how to measure productivity.

You are the newly hired manager at Ollie's Quick Change. The company prides itself and is known for providing oil changes for personal vehicles quickly and at a low cost, $25 for a standard oil change. Your first charge as a new manager is to increase the productivity of the store, which has dramatically decreased over the last year.

You have gathered the following data to use in analyzing productivity.

You have three full-time workers and several part-time employees. You decide to begin with the three full-time employees. Taylor produces 22 oil changes a day while Tim produces 20 oil changes a day. Allison is a recent hire with only two months' experience. Due to work schedules, Taylor works 7 hours a day while Tim and Allison work 8 hours a day.

When looking at materials used for the oil changes, Taylor uses $350 of supplies while Tim uses $275 of supplies, with Allison using $250 of supplies.

Each has a dedicated service bay and the needed tools/equipment for the job. Taylor receives a complaint at least once a week. Tim has received three complaints during the last 12 months and has a long list of repeat customers who ask for him specifically. Allison is quickly becoming the technician of choice by the female demographic who frequent the store.

After analyzing the data, what three pieces of information can you use to improve the productivity and profitability of Ollie's Quick Change?

CHAPTER CLOSING CASE ▶▶

Back in the Saddle

When Tom Pastorius opened Penn Brewery in 1986, he had modest goals—brew real German beer and serve it in a real German beer hall environment as the first craft brewery in Pennsylvania. Twenty-two years later, he was ready to step away. Pastorius had turned 65 when he retired from Penn Brewery, the company he had founded; then he sold his majority interest in the brewery and went to work as its president. Tom's wife, Mary Beth, was fine with the idea of retirement. The couple had had a great run building the local Pittsburgh microbrewery and restaurant. But the time had come to kick back a bit and enjoy life.

It didn't take long before Tom started to feel bored. He was also frustrated watching what the new owners were doing with his company—and he still owned 20 percent of it. He stayed on as president for five years. The proceeds allowed the couple to pay off their home mortgage, pay for their two sons to go to private colleges, and still have plenty left over for retirement.

The Pastorius family had built a successful microbrew production business, with Penn Pilsner being their flagship brand, making 15,000 barrels a year with $3.5 million in sales. Over the years, Penn Dark, Penn Weizen, Penn Oktoberfest, and other labels under their brand had racked up 14 medals at the Great American Beer Festival.

But Tom had been miserable working for the new owners. "I am not a good employee," he says. "I'm a solo act." Tom agreed with the new owners' strategy of turning Penn Brewery into a regional player. What he didn't like was the way they went about it. He fought over details such as installing a cooling system that he argued was too big for the operation. He unsuccessfully lobbied against a $120,000 billboard campaign. "We couldn't make enough beer to pay for it," he says. Sales went up, but expenses went up even more.

Tom couldn't take any more when the new owners announced that they would outsource manufacturing to The Lion Brewery in Wilkes-Barre, Pennsylvania, laying off 8 of the 10 brewery employees. The many Penn Pilsner fans were just as upset as Tom. "For beer people in Pittsburgh, Penn Pilsner was the Holy Grail," says Paul Cosentino, leader of the Boilermaker Jazz Band, which often played at the brewery's restaurant. "If it was no longer made here and it didn't taste the same, why should we buy it?" Sales were dwindling. Birchmere Capital, a Pittsburgh private equity fund that had purchased majority equity position, closed the restaurant and sold off much of the brewing equipment. "It was so hard to sit back and watch this place sink," says Tom.

Birchmere put the brewery up for sale. Tom started working on his business plan, beginning with a risk-benefit analysis. On the downside, the brewery was almost $1 million in debt. He would have to absorb the loss. The brand was tarnished. And he wasn't exactly young, but he still had plenty of experience and energy.

He would much rather be making beer in Pittsburgh than playing golf in Florida. If he didn't rebuild the business, then the value of his 20 percent stake would be zero. With his reputation, he knew he could bring the luster back to Penn Pilsner if he returned production to the Victorian-era redbrick building.

Mary Beth seemed determined to talk Tom out of buying back the brewery—and her opinion certainly mattered. For 17 years she had developed the traditional German menu, selling potato pancakes and bratwurst. The couple debated all through the summer, with their two grown sons eventually weighing in. "They ganged up on me," Mary Beth said. "They were proud of the brewery. It had been part of their childhood. They wanted to save it." But Tom Jr. says he also sympathized with his mother. "She knew it was a slippery slope," he says. Mary Beth had already launched a new business of her own, restoring historic buildings. She felt liberated away from the brewery. "It is the baby who never grows up," she says.

Questions

1. What alternatives does the Pastorius family have to resolve the conflict?

2. What operations management principles would apply to running a microbrewery?

3. What would your recommendation be to Tom and Mary Beth?

Sources: Cristina Rouvalis, "Case Study: When a Married Couple Disagree," *Inc.*, July 2010, 70–74; Sean Collier, "Penn Brewery Expanding to Two New Locations," *Pittsburgh Magazine*, March 5, 2018, www.pittsburghmagazine.com; www.pennbrew.com/our-story.

GLOSSARY

ABC classification: An inventory control system that classifies items based on the total dollar volume of sales each generates.

accounting: The system within a business for converting raw data from source documents (like invoices, sales receipts, bills, and checks) into information that will help a manager make business decisions.

accrual-basis method: A method of accounting in which income and expenses are recorded at the time they are incurred rather than when they are paid.

agents: Intermediaries who bring buyers and sellers together and facilitate exchanges.

aging schedules: A listing of a firm's accounts receivable according to the length of time they are outstanding.

analytic systems: Manufacturing systems that reduce inputs into component parts so as to extract products.

anchor stores: Large retail stores that attract people to shop at malls.

angel: A lender, usually a successful entrepreneur, who loans money to help new businesses.

appeal process: A formal procedure allowing employees to seek review of a disciplinary measure at a higher level of management.

articles of incorporation: A document describing the business that is filed with the state in which a business is formed.

articles of partnership: The contract between partners of a business that defines obligations and responsibilities of the business owners.

asset utilization ratios: Financial ratios that measure the speed with which various asset accounts are converted into sales or cash.

asset-based business valuation: A method of determining the value of a business based on the worth of its assets.

assets: Any resource that a business owns and expects to use to its benefit.

at-will doctrine: Essentially means an employee hired for an indefinite period may be discharged for any or no reason, cause or no cause, unless specifically prohibited by law.

average collection period: A measure of how long it takes a firm to convert a credit sale (internal store credit, not credit card sales) into a usable form (cash).

backward scheduling: Scheduling that involves arranging production activities around the due date for the product.

balance sheet: A financial document that shows the assets, liabilities, and owner's equity for a business.

balloon notes: A loan that requires the borrower to make small monthly payments (usually enough to cover the interest), with the balance of the loan due at maturity.

bankruptcy: A ruling granted by courts to release businesses or individuals from some or all of their debt.

benchmarking: The process of comparing key points within your business with comparable points in another external entity.

benefit: Part of an employee's compensation in addition to wages and salaries.

big data: Huge amounts of information that are too large to process with traditional analytical methods but show conclusions via artificial intelligence and machine learning.

bonuses: One-time rewards provided to employees for exceeding performance standards.

brand: A name, term, symbol, design, or combination of these elements that clearly identifies and differentiates your products from those of your competitors.

breach of contract: A violation of one or more terms of a contract by a party involved in the contract.

breakeven point (BEP): The point at which total costs equal total revenue and the business neither makes nor loses money.

brokers: Intermediaries who represent clients who buy or sell specialized goods or seasonal products.

business brokers: A business intermediary that brings sellers of their businesses together with potential buyers.

business failure: When a business closes with a financial loss to a creditor.

business-format franchising: A type of franchising in which the franchisee adopts the franchisor's entire method of operation.

business plan: A document describing a business that is used to test the feasibility of a business idea, to raise capital, and to serve as a road map for future operations.

business termination: When a business ceases operation for any reason.

C corporation: A separate legal entity that reports its income and expenses on a corporate income tax return and is taxed on its profits at corporate income tax rates.

capital intensive: A business that depends greatly upon equipment and capital for its operations.

cash budgets: A plan for short-term uses and sources of cash.

cash-basis method: A method of accounting in which income and expenses are recorded at the time they are paid, rather than when they are incurred.

cash flow: The sum of net income plus any noncash expenses, such as depreciation and amortization, or the difference between the actual amount of cash a company brings in and the actual amount of cash a company disburses in a given time period.

cash flow statement: A financial document that shows the amount of money a business has on hand at the beginning of a time period, receipts coming into the business, and money going out of the business during the same period.

cash-to-cash cycle: The period of time from when money is spent on raw materials until it is collected from the sale of a finished good.

certified development company: A nonprofit organization sponsored either by private interests or by state or local governments.

closely held corporation: A corporation owned by a limited group of people. Its stock is not traded publicly.

code of ethics: The tool with which the owner of a business communicates ethical expectations to everyone associated with the business.

cognitive dissonance: The conflict (i.e., remorse) that buyers feel after making a major purchase.

common-size financial statement: A financial statement that includes a percentage breakdown of each item.

comparables approach: A valuation technique to look at the value of comparable companies that have recently sold.

compensatory damages: Money awarded by the courts to a party of the contract who has suffered a loss due to the actions of another party.

competitive advantage: The facet of a business that is better than the competition's. A competitive advantage can be built from many different factors.

concurrent quality control: Quality control applied to work in progress.

consumer credit: Credit extended by retailers to the ultimate customers for the purchase of products or services.

continuous process: A production process that operates for long periods of time without interruption.

contract: An agreement between two or more parties that is enforceable by law.

control systems: The means to monitor input, transformation, and output so as to identify problems.

copyright: A form of protection for intellectual property provided to the creator of a literary, musical, or artistic work for a period of the creator's life plus 50 years.

corporation: A business structure that creates an entity separate from its owners and managers.

corridor principle: The idea that opportunities become available to an entrepreneur only after the entrepreneur has started a business.

creative destruction: The replacement of existing products, processes, ideas, and businesses with new and better ones.

current ratio: A financial ratio that measures the number of times a firm can cover its current liabilities with its current assets.

customer intimacy: Maintaining a long-term relationship with customers through superior service that results in a competitive advantage.

debt financing: The use of borrowed funds to finance a business.

debt ratio: A leverage ratio that measures the proportion of a firm's total assets that is acquired with borrowed funds.

decoy effect: A pricing technique that makes a specific product appear more desirable by adding a product and price that is slightly less attractive.

defect rate: The number of goods produced that are outside the company's boundaries of acceptable quality.

delegation: Granting authority and responsibility for a specific task to another member of an organization; empowerment to accomplish a task effectively.

demand curve: The number of units of a product that people would be willing to purchase at different price levels.

demand note: A short-term loan that must be repaid (both principal and interest) in a lump sum at maturity.

direct channel: A distribution channel in which products and services go directly from the producer to the consumer.

disclosure statements: Information that franchisors are required to provide to potential franchisees.

discounted cash flow: Valuation method based on future cash flows the business is projected to make.

dispatching: Allocating resources and beginning the steps to produce a product.

disrupt: In business context, disruption is making significant changes to the way business is done in a specific industry.

distress: The negative consequences and components of stress.

distribution channel: The series of intermediaries a product passes through when going from producer to consumer.

dividends: Payments based on the net profits of the business and made to the providers of equity capital.

double-entry accounting: An accounting system in which every business transaction is recorded in an asset account and a liability or owner's equity account so that the system will balance.

dual distribution: The use of two or more channels to distribute the same product to the same target market.

due diligence: The process of thoroughly investigating the accuracy of information before signing a franchise (or any other) agreement.

economic order quantity (EOQ): A traditional method of controlling inventory that minimizes total inventory costs by balancing annual ordering costs with annual holding costs for an item.

economy of scale: The lowering of costs through production of larger quantities.

employee development: A planned effort to provide employees with the knowledge, skills, and abilities needed to accept new and more challenging job assignments within the company.

employee handbook: Written rules and regulations informing employees of their rights and responsibilities in the employment relationship.

employee orientation: The process of helping new employees become familiar with an organization, their job, and the people they will work with.

employee training: A planned effort to teach employees more about their job so as to improve their performance and motivation.

entrepreneurship: The process of identifying opportunities for which marketable needs exist and assuming the risk of creating an organization to satisfy them.

entrepreneurship process: The stage of a business's life that involves innovation, a triggering event, and implementation of the business.

environmental factors: Forces that occur outside of the business that affect the business and its owner.

equity financing: The sale of common stock or the use of retained earnings to provide long-term financing.

escalation clause: A lease that varies according to the amount of inflation in the economy.

ethics: The rules of moral values that guide decision making, your understanding of the difference between right and wrong.

evoked set: The group of brands or businesses that come to a customer's mind when she thinks of a type of product.

executive summary: A condensed abstract of a business plan used to spark the reader's interest in the business and to highlight crucial information.

factoring: The practice of raising funds for a business through the sale of accounts receivable.

feasibility study: A tool for assessing parts of the business plan and determining if the idea will work.

feed forward quality control: Quality control applied to a company's inputs.

feedback: Communication tools to connect control systems to the processes of a business.

feedback quality control: Inspecting and testing products after they are produced.

financial ratios: Calculations that compare important financial aspects of a business.

fixed asset turnover: An asset utilization ratio that measures how efficiently a firm is using its assets to generate sales.

fixed costs: Costs that do not change with the number of sales made.

fixed layout: A type of layout for a manufacturing business in which the product stays stationary while workers and equipment are brought to it.

fixed-rate loan: A loan whose interest rate remains constant.

flexible manufacturing: Small-scale manufacturing utilizing CNC computer systems.

floor planning: A type of business loan generally made for "big-ticket" items. The business holds the item in inventory and pays interest, but it is actually owned by the lender until the item is sold.

forward scheduling: Scheduling in which materials and resources are allocated for production when a job order comes in.

franchise: A contractual license to operate an individually owned business as part of a larger chain.

franchise agreement: The legal contract that binds both parties involved in the franchise.

franchise fee: The one-time payment made to become a franchisee.

franchisee: The small businessperson who purchases the franchise so as to sell the product or service of the franchisor.

franchisor: The parent company that develops a product or business process and sells the rights to franchisees.

free-flow layout: A type of layout used by small retail stores that encourages customers to wander and browse through the store.

general ledger: A record of all financial transactions divided into accounts and usually compiled at the end of each month.

general partnership: A business structure in which the business owners share the management and risk of the business.

generally accepted accounting principles (GAAP): Standards established so that all businesses produce comparable financial statements.

goodwill: The intangible asset that allows businesses to earn a higher return than a comparable business with the same tangible assets might generate.

grid layout: A type of layout used by retail stores to move customers past merchandise arranged on rows of shelves or fixtures.

gross lease: A lease in which the monthly payment made by the tenant remains constant and the landlord pays the operating expenses of the building.

growth: Achievement of a critical mass in the business, a point at which an adequate living is provided for the owner and family, with enough growth remaining to keep the business going.

harvest: The stage when the owner removes him- or herself from the business. Harvesting a business can be thought of as picking the fruit after years of labor.

holding costs: Expenses related to keeping inventory on hand.

home-based business: A popular type of business that operates from the owner's home, rather than from a separate location.

hypergrowth: Businesses that are intentionally structured to grow at exceptional rates. Scalability is key to creating such growth.

implementation: The part of the entrepreneurial process that occurs when the organization is formed.

income statement: A financial statement that shows the revenue and expenses of a firm, allowing you to calculate the profit or loss produced in a specific period of time.

independent contractor: A person who is not employed by a business and, unlike employees, is not eligible for a benefit package.

indirect channel: A distribution channel in which the products pass through various intermediaries before reaching the consumer.

individualized marketing: Adjusting the marketing mix of a business to treat individual persons as separate target markets.

industry average analysis: A comparison of a firm's financial ratios to the industry averages.

initial public offering (IPO): The first sale of stock of a business made available to public investors.

injunction: A court order that prohibits certain activities.

inputs: All the resources that go into a business.

installment loans: A loan made to a business for the purchase of fixed assets such as equipment and real estate.

intangible assets: Assets that have value to a business but are not visible.

intellectual capital: The valuable skills and knowledge that employees of a business possess.

intellectual property: Property that is created through the mental skills of a person.

interest rate: The amount of money paid for the use of borrowed funds.

intermittent process: A production process that operates in short cycles so that it can change products.

inventory: Goods a business owns for the completion of future sales. Also, the act of counting the goods held in stock.

inventory cycle: The period of time from the point when inventory is at its highest level until it is replenished.

inventory turnover: An asset utilization ratio that measures the liquidity of the firm's inventory—how quickly goods are sold and replenished.

ISO 9001: The set of standards that certifies that a business is using processes and principles to ensure the production of quality products.

job analysis: The process of gathering all the information about a particular job, including a job description and the job specifications.

job description: A written description of a nonmanagement position that covers the title, duties, and responsibilities involved in the job.

job specifications: The identification of the knowledge, skills, abilities, and other characteristics an employee would need to perform the job.

joint venture: A partnership that is created to complete a specified purpose and is limited in duration.

journal: A chronological record of all financial transactions of a business.

labor intensive: A business that is more dependent on the services of people than on money and equipment.

lead time: The period of time from order placement until the goods are received.

leadership: The process of directing and influencing the actions of members within a group.

leasehold improvements: Changes that make a property more valuable, such as painting, adding shelves, or installing new lighting.

leverage: The ability to finance an investment through borrowed funds, increasing both the potential for return and the level of risk.

leverage ratios: Financial ratios that measure the extent to which a firm uses debt as a source of financing and its ability to service that debt.

liabilities: A debt owed by a business to another organization or individual.

licensing agreement: An agreement in which the owner of intellectual property grants another person (or another company) permission to produce that product.

limited-liability company (LLC): A relatively new type of corporation that taxes the owners as partners yet provides a more flexible structure than an S corporation.

limited partnership: A business structure in which one or more of the owners may be granted limited liability as long as one partner is designated as a general partner with unlimited liability.

line of credit: An agreement that makes a specific amount of short-term funding available to a business as it is needed.

liquidity ratios: Financial ratios used to measure a firm's ability to meet its short-term obligations to creditors as they come due.

loan security: Assurance to a lender that a loan will be repaid.

locus of control: A person's belief concerning the degree to which internal or external forces control his or her future.

long-term assets: Assets that will not be converted into cash within one year.

loop layout: A type of retail layout with a predominant aisle running through the store that quickly leads customers to their desired department.

macro-aging schedule: A list of accounts receivable by age category.

make-or-buy decision: The choice of whether to purchase parts and components or to produce them.

management: The process of planning, organizing, leading, and controlling resources to achieve the goals of an organization.

market research: The process of gathering information about consumers that will improve marketing efforts.

market segmentation: Breaking down populations of people into groups, or target markets.

marketing concept: The philosophy of a business in which the wants and needs of customers are determined before goods and services are produced.

marketing strategy: What the marketing efforts of a business are intended to accomplish and how the business will achieve its goals.

markup: The amount added to the cost of a product in setting the final price. It can be based on selling price or on cost.

mass marketing: Treating entire populations of people as potential customers for specific products.

maturity: The length of time in which a loan must be repaid.

maturity: The stage of the organization when the business is considered well established.

micro-aging schedule: A list of accounts receivable showing each customer, the amount that customer owes, and the amount that is past due.

mission statement: A description of the reason why an organization exists.

motivation: The forces that act on or within a person that cause the person to behave in a specific manner.

multiple method business valuation: A formula that applies a weighting factor based on the benefit the selling business owner has generated.

need to achieve: The personal quality, linked to entrepreneurship, of being motivated to excel and choose situations in which success is likely.

net lease: A lease in which the tenant pays a base monthly rent plus some or all real estate taxes of the building.

net-net lease: A lease in which the tenant pays a base monthly rent plus real estate taxes and insurance on the building.

net profit margin: A profitability ratio that measures the percentage of each sales dollar that remains as profit after all expenses, including taxes, have been paid.

niche marketing: Segmenting populations of people into smaller target markets.

noncompete clause: A provision often included in a contract to purchase a business that restricts the seller from entering the same type of business within a specified area for a certain amount of time.

nonprofit corporation: A tax-exempt corporation that exists for a purpose other than making a profit.

obsolescence: When products become outdated or fall out of fashion.

odd pricing: Psychological pricing strategy in which goods are priced at, say, $9.99 rather than $10.00 in the belief that the price will seem lower than it really is.

online business: A business that shares information, maintains customer relationships, and conducts transactions by means of telecommunications networks.

operational excellence: Creates a competitive advantage by holding down costs to provide customers with the lowest-priced products.

ordering costs: Expenses related to procuring inventory.

outputs: The tangible or intangible products that a business produces.

owner's equity: The amount of money the owner of a business would receive if all of the assets were sold and all of the liabilities were paid.

partnership: An association of two or more persons to carry on as co-owners of a business for profit.

patent: A form of protection for intellectual property provided to an inventor for a period of 17 years.

patent trolls: Individuals or companies that hold patents for unscrupulous purposes such as stifling competition or launching patent infringement lawsuits.

penetration pricing: Setting the price of a new product lower than expected to gain fast market share.

percentage lease: A lease in which the tenant pays a base monthly rent plus a percentage of gross revenue.

performance appraisal: A process of evaluating an employee's job-related achievements.

philanthropic goodwill: The level of social responsibility in which a business does good without the expectation of anything in return.

policy loans: A loan made to a business by an insurance company, using the business's insurance policy as collateral.

prestige pricing: Psychological pricing strategy used with goods whose quality is difficult to determine by inspection or for products about which consumers have little solid information.

price elasticity of demand: The percentage change in quantity demanded for a product in response to a 1 percent change in price.

price lining: Grouping product prices into ranges, such as low-, medium-, and high-priced items.

price multiples business valuation: A method of determining the value of a business based on applying specific appropriate multiples to revenue or free cash flow.

price skimming: Setting the price of a new product higher than expected to recover development costs.

primary data: Marketing data that a business collects for its own specific purposes.

principal: An amount of money borrowed from a lender.

private-label manufacturing: Producing products under another company's name.

pro forma financial statements: Financial statements that project what a firm's financial condition will be in the future.

process layout: A way to arrange a manufacturing business by placing all comparable equipment together in the same area.

product: A tangible good, an intangible service, or a combination of these.

product layout: A way to arrange a manufacturing business by placing equipment in an assembly line.

product leaders: A business that creates a competitive advantage based on providing the highest-quality products possible.

product life cycle: Stages that products in a marketplace pass through over time.

product-distribution franchising: A type of franchising in which the franchisee agrees to purchase the products of the franchisor or to use the franchisor's name.

production concept: The philosophy of a business that concentrates more on the product that the business makes than on customer needs.

productivity: The measure of outputs according to the inputs needed to produce them; a way to determine the efficiency of a business.

profitability ratios: Financial ratios that are used to measure the ability of a company to turn sales into profits and to earn profits on assets and owner's equity committed.

profit-and-loss statement: A financial document that shows sales revenues, expenses, and net profit or loss.

profit-sharing plan: A plan in which employees receive additional compensation based on the profitability of the entire business.

progressive approach to employee discipline: Discipline that is applied to employees in appropriately incremental and increasingly forceful measures.

psychological pricing: Setting the price of a product in a way that will alter its perception by customers.

public corporation: A corporation that sells shares of stock to the public and is listed on a stock exchange.

publicity: An aspect of public relations consisting of any message about your company communicated through the mass media that you do not pay for.

quality: How well a good or service meets or exceeds customers' expectations, or the degree to which a product conforms to established tolerance standards.

quick (acid-test) ratio: A financial ratio that measures a firm's ability to meet its current obligations with the most liquid of its current assets.

reference pricing: Psychological pricing strategy common in retailing goods for which consumers have an idea of what the price "should be."

relationship marketing: The philosophy of business that concentrates on establishing a long-term buyer–seller relationship for the benefit of both parties.

retailers: Intermediaries who sell products to the ultimate consumer.

return on assets: A profitability ratio that indicates the firm's effectiveness in generating profits from its available assets; also known as return on investment.

return on equity: A profitability ratio that measures the return the firm earned on its owner's investment in the firm.

routing: Information showing the steps required to produce a product.

royalty fees: The ongoing payments that franchisees pay to franchisors—usually a percentage of gross sales.

S corporation: A special type of corporation in which the owners are taxed as partners.

sales forecast: The quantity of products a business plans to sell during a future time period.

SBA Express program: A relatively new loan program available through the SBA that simplifies the paperwork that has historically been required.

SBA loan: A loan made to a small business through a commercial bank, of which a portion is guaranteed by the Small Business Administration.

secondary data: Marketing data that have been gathered, tabulated, and made available by an outside source.

secured loan: A loan that requires collateral as security for the lender.

segmentation variables: Characteristics or ways to group people who are more likely to purchase a product.

sequencing: The order in which the steps need to occur to produce a product.

serendipity: A fortunate discovery made by unplanned means.

service sector: Businesses in an economic sector that provide services, rather than tangible goods.

short-term assets: Assets that will be converted into cash within one year.

shrinkage: The loss of goods held in inventory due to theft or spoilage.

single-entry accounting: An accounting system in which the flow of income and expenses is recorded in a running log, basically like a checkbook.

six sigma: The tolerance range in which only 3.4 defects per million are allowed.

small business: A business is generally considered small if it is independently owned, operated, and financed; has fewer than 100 employees; and has relatively little impact on its industry.

small business management: The ongoing process of owning and operating an established business.

small business management process: The stage of a business's life that involves growth, maturity, and harvest.

social entrepreneurship: The process of creation and innovation of a new business with the passion of a social, cultural, or environmental mission.

social responsibility: The obligation of a business to have a positive effect on society on four levels: economic, legal, ethical, and philanthropic.

sole proprietorship: A business owned and operated by one person.

sources and uses of funds: A financial document used by start-up businesses that shows where capital comes from and what it will be used for.

specific performance: A nonmonetary award granted by the courts to a party of the contract who has suffered a loss due to the actions of another party.

statement of cash flow: A financial statement that shows the cash inflows and outflows of a business.

statistical process control (SPC): The use of statistical analysis to determine the probability of a variation in product being random or a problem.

strategic plan: A long-term planning tool used for viewing a business and the environments in which it operates in broadest terms.

stress: Emotional states that occur in response to demands, which may come from internal or external sources.

SWOT analysis: The step of strategic planning in which the managers identify the internal strengths and weaknesses of a business and the opportunities and threats that exist outside the business.

synthetic systems: Manufacturing systems that combine inputs to create a finished product or change it into a different product.

tangible assets: Assets owned by a business that can be seen and examined.

target markets: Groups of people who have a common want or need that your business can satisfy, who are able to purchase your product, and who are more likely to buy from your business.

times interest earned: A leverage ratio that calculates the firm's ability to meet its interest requirements.

tolerance range: The boundaries a manager sets in determining the acceptable quality of a product.

total asset turnover: An asset utilization ratio that measures how efficiently the firm uses all of its assets to generate sales; a high ratio generally reflects good overall management.

trade credit: The purchase of goods from suppliers that do not demand payment immediately.

trademark: A form of protection for intellectual property provided to the owner of a brand name or symbol.

transformation processes: What a business does to add value to inputs in converting them to outputs.

trend analysis: A comparison of a single firm's present performance with its own past performance, preferably for more than two years.

triggering event: A specific event or occurrence that sparks the entrepreneur to proceed from thinking to doing.

triple-net lease: A lease in which the tenant pays a base monthly rent plus real estate taxes, insurance, and any other operating expenses incurred for the building.

unlimited liability: The potential for an owner to lose more than has been invested in a business.

unsecured loans: A short-term loan for which collateral is not required.

unsecured term loans: A loan made to an established business that has demonstrated a strong overall credit profile.

variable costs: Costs that change in direct proportion to sales.

variable-rate loan: A loan whose interest rate changes over the life of the loan.

wholesalers: Intermediaries who buy products in bulk from producers and resell them to other wholesalers or to retailers.

window of opportunity: A period of time in which an opportunity is available.

zoning laws: Local laws that control where and how businesses may operate.

NOTES

CHAPTER 1

1. U.S. Small Business Administration, Office of Advocacy, "Frequently Asked Questions about Small Business," June 2016, https://www.sba.gov/sites/default/files/advocacy/SB-FAQ-2016_WEB.pdf.

2. Natalie Soroka, "Small and Medium-Sized Enterprises Reaching New Markets," U.S. Department of Commerce, May 2, 2017, www.commerce.gov/news/blog/2017/.

3. U.S. Small Business Administration, "Frequently Asked Questions," 2016.

4. U.S. Small Business Administration, "Frequently Asked Questions," 2016.

5. U.S. Small Business Administration, Office of Advocacy, "Frequently Asked Questions about Small Business," August 2018, https://www.sba.gov/advocacy/frequently-asked-questions-about-small-business.

6. U.S. Small Business Administration, Office of Advocacy, *Annual Report of the Office of Economic Research: FY2016* (Washington, DC: Author, 2017), https://www.sba.gov/sites/default/files/OER_Annual_Report_FY2016.pdf.

7. "Company Profile: New Belgium Brewing Co.," D&B Hoovers, December 12, 2017, www.hoovers.com.

8. Association for Enterprise Opportunity, *Bigger Than You Think: The Economic Impact of Microbusiness in the United States*, accessed December 12, 2017, https://www.aeoworks.org/publications/Bigger%20than%20You%20Think%20Report_FINAL_AEO_11.10.13.pdf.

9. John A. Byrne, "How Entrepreneurs Are Reshaping the Economy and What Big Companies Can Learn," *Business Week* (Enterprise ed.), October 1993, 12–18.

10. Major L. Clark and Radwan Saade, *The Role of Small Business in Economic Development of the United States: From the End of the Korean War (1953) to Present*, U.S. Small Business Administration (working paper), September 2010.

11. U.S. Department of Labor, Bureau of Labor Statistics, "Employment by Major Industry Sector" (table), October 24, 2017, www.bls.gov/emp/tables/employment-by-major-industry-sector/.

12. Small Business Act, Public Law 85–536 § 2, https://www.sba.gov/sites/default/files/Small%20Business%20Act_0.pdf, 3.

13. Kelly Edmiston, *The Role of Small and Large Businesses in Economic Development*, (Kansas City, MO: Federal Reserve Bank, 2007), www.KansasCityFed.org, 73.

14. Ely Portillo, David Perlmutt and Katherine Peralta, "Chiquita's Early Exit Raises Incentives Questions," *Charlotte Observer*, January 15, 2015, A1.

15. U.S. Small Business Administration, Office of Advocacy, "Frequently Asked Questions about Small Business," September 2012, www.sba.gov/advo.

16. U.S. Small Business Administration, Office of Advocacy, "Frequently Asked Questions about Small Business," August 2017, www.sba.gov/sites/default/files/advocacy/SB-FAQ-2017-WEB.pdf.

17. U.S. Small Business Administration, "Frequently Asked Questions," 2017.

18. Arnobio Morelix, *The Evolution of Entrepreneurship on College Campuses* (Kansas City, MO: Ewing Marion Kauffman Foundation, 2015), https://www.kauffman.org/currents/2015/10/the-evolution-of-entrepreneurship-on-college-campuses.

19. Reiva Lesonsky, "College Graduates Want to Start Businesses—But Are They Ready?" SmallBizDaily, June 24, 2014, www.smallbizdaily.com.

20. Louise Lee, "B-School Disrupt: Eight Startups Pitch Their Innovations," *Inc.*, November 2017, www.inc.com.

21. U.S. Census Bureau, American Fact Finder, *Statistics for All U.S. Firms by Industry, Gender, Ethnicity, and Race* (Washington, DC: Author, 2016), https://factfinder.census.gov.

22. National Association of Women Business Owners, *OPEN State of Women-Owned Businesses 2015* (Washington, DC: Author, 2015), www.nawbo.org/resources/women-in-business-owner-statistics.

23. U.S. Census Bureau, *Statistics for All U.S. Firms*.

24. Luke Cooper, "5 Organizations Helping Minority Startup Founders Succeed," *Entrepreneur*, October 24, 2016, www.entrepreneur.com/article/282529.

25. Faye Rice, "How to Make Diversity Pay," *Fortune*, August 8, 1994, 79–86.

26. J. A. Schumpeter, *Capitalism, Socialism, and Democracy* (New York: Harper & Row, 1943).

27. Joshua S. Gans, David H. Hsu, and Scott Stern, "When Does Start-up Innovation Spur the Gale of Creative Destruction?" *RAND Journal of Economics,* Winter 2002, 571–586.

28. Greg Satell, "2018: A Year to Begin New Shifts," *Inc.*, December 16, 2017, www.inc.com.

29. Anthony Breitzman and Patrick Thomas, *Analysis of Small Business Innovation in Green Technologies* (Washington, DC: U.S. Small Business Administration, Office of Advocacy, 2014), www.sba.gov/advo.

30. Bob House, "Embracing Innovation to Sustain a Competitive Edge," *Inc.*, October 30, 2017, www.inc.com.

31. "Business Failure and Dissolution," *Inc.*, accessed Dec. 16, 2017, www.inc.com/encyclopedia/business-failure-and-dissolution.html.

32. U.S. Small Business Administration, "Frequently Asked Questions," 2017.

33. R. L. Adams, "10 Reasons Why 7 Out of 10 Businesses Fail Within 10 Years, *Entrepreneur*, September 26, 2017, www.entrepreneur.com/article/299522.

34. Georgia McIntyre, "What Percentage of Small Businesses Fail? (And Other Similar Stats You Need to Know)," *Fundera Ledger*, August 29, 2017, www.fundera.com/blog/what-percentage-of-small-businesses-fail.

35. Geeta Nadkaeni, "What Failure Actually Says About Your Future," *Inc.*, November 28, 2017, www.inc.com/geeta-nadkarni/what-failure-actually-says-about-your-future.html.

36. Heather Wilde, "3 Tips from Failed Businesses That Will Keep You Afloat," *Inc.*, June 29, 2018, www.inc.com.

37. Jack Welch and Suzy Welch, "The Danger of Doing Nothing," *Business Week*, July 10, 2006.

38. McIntyre, "What Percentage of Small Businesses Fail?"

39. James Aley, "Debunking the Failure Fallacy," *Fortune*, September 6, 1993, 21.

40. Brian Headd, "Redefining Business Success: Distinguishing between Closure and Failure," *Small Business Economics*, vol. 21, 2003, 51.

41. "U.S. Divorce Rate Statistics," Statistic Brain Research Institute, accessed Dec. 16, 2017, www.statisticbrain.com/u-s-divorce-rate-statistics/.

42. "Graduation Rates," National Center for Education Statistics, December 2017, www.nces.ed.gov/fastfacts.

CHAPTER 2

1. Robert Hisrich, "Entrepreneurship/Intrapreneurship," *American Psychologist*, February 1990, 209.

2. P. VanderWerf and C. Brush, "Toward Agreement on the Focus of Entrepreneurship Research: Progress without Definition" (Proceedings of the National Academy of Management Conference, Washington, DC, 1989).

3. Denis Gregoire, Martin Noel, Richard Dery, and Jean-Pierre Bechard, "Is There Conceptual Convergence in Entrepreneurship Research? A Co-Citation Analysis of Frontiers of Entrepreneurship Research, 1981–2004," *Entrepreneurship Theory and Practice*, May 2006, 333–372.

4. Carol Moore, "Understanding Entrepreneurial Behavior: A Definition and Model," in *Academy of Management Best Paper Proceedings*, ed. J. A. Pearce II and R. B. Robinson, Jr. (46th Annual Meeting of the Academy of Management, Chicago, 1989), 66–70. See also William Bygrave, "The Entrepreneurial Paradigm (I): A Philosophical Look at Its Research Methodologies," *Entrepreneurship: Theory and Practice*, Fall 1989, 7–25; and William Bygrave and Charles Hofer, "Theorizing about Entrepreneurship," *Entrepreneurship: Theory and Practice*, Winter 1991, 13–22.

5. A. Shapiro and L. Sokol, "The Social Dimensions of Entrepreneurship," in *Encyclopedia of Entrepreneurship*, ed. J. A. Kent, D. L. Sexton, and K. H. Vesper (Englewood Cliffs, NJ: Prentice-Hall, 1992).

6. J. A. Schumpeter, *History of Economic Analysis* (New York: Oxford University Press, 1934).

7. William Gartner, "'Who Is an Entrepreneur?' Is the Wrong Question," *Entrepreneurship: Theory and Practice*, Summer 1989, 47. See also J. W. Carland, F. Hoy, W. R Boulton, and J. A. C. Carland, "Differentiating Entrepreneurs from Small Business Owners: A Conceptualization," *Academy of Management Review*, 1984, 354–359; William Gartner, "What Are We Talking about When We Talk about Entrepreneurship?" *Journal of Business Venturing*, 1990, 15–28.

8. Steven Covey, *The Seven Habits of Highly Effective People* (New York: Simon & Schuster, 1989), 95.

9. Peter Drucker, *Innovation and Entrepreneurship: Practice and Principles* (New York: Harper & Row, 1985).

10. Jess McCuan, "It's Good to Be King," *Inc.*, December 2003, 32.

11. Sanjay Goel and Ranjan Karri, "Entrepreneurs, Effectual Logic, and Over-Trust," *Entrepreneurship Theory and Practice*, July 2006, 480.

12. Jon Goodman, "What Makes an Entrepreneur?" *Inc.*, October 1994, 29.

13. David C McClelland, *The Achieving Society* (New York: Van Nostrand Reinhold, 1961). See also David C. McClelland, "Achievement Motivation Can Be Developed," *Harvard Business Review*, November/December 1965; David Miron and David McClelland, "The Impact of Achievement Motivation Training on Small Business," *California Management Review*, Summer 1979, 13–28.

14. Robert Brochhaus and Pamela S. Horwitz, "The Psychology of the Entrepreneur," in *The Art and Science of Entrepreneurship*, ed. Donald Sexton and Raymond W. Smilor (Cambridge, MA: Ballinger, 1986), 25–48.

15. T. S. Hatten, "Student Entrepreneurial Characteristics and Attitude Change toward Entrepreneurship as Affected by Participation in an SBI Program," *Journal of Education for Business*, March/April 1995, 224.

16. Michael O'Neal, "Just What Is an Entrepreneur?" *Business Week* (Enterprise ed.), 1993, 104–112.

17. U.S. Small Business Administration, Office of Advocacy, "Demographic Characteristics of Business Owners and Employees: 2013," April 28, 2015, www.sba.gov/sites/default/files/advocacy/Issue_Brief_6_Demographic_Characteristics_2013.

18. Leigh Buchanan, "What the Companies on the Inc. 5000 All Have in Common," *Inc.*, September 2015, www.inc.com/magazine/201509/leigh-buchanan/2015-inc5000-how-to-rocket-up-the-learning-curve.

19. Jerome Katz, "The Institution and Infrastructure of Entrepreneurship," *Entrepreneurship: Theory and Practice*, Spring 1991, 85–102.

20. "Best Schools for Entrepreneurs—Top 25 Undergrad Programs 2017," *Entrepreneur*, November 2016, www.entrepreneur.com.

21. Patrick Morris, "Small Businesses Lead the Way in Green Technology Innovation," U.S. Small Business Administration, Office of Advocacy, October 20, 2011, www.sba.gov/advocacy.

22. Mark Harrison, "Small Innovative Company Growth: Barriers, Best Practices and Big Ideas," U.S. Small Business Administration, Office of Advocacy, January 2015, https://www.sba.gov/sites/default/files/advocacy/FINAL_Innovation_Report.pdf.

23. Harrison, "Small Innovative Company Growth," 19.

24. Tucker Marion and Rifat Sipahi, "Early-Stage Firms and Delay-Based Inventory Control Using Decision-Making Tableaux," *International Journal of Production Research*, September 2010, 5497–5521.

25. Mark Malyszko, "Foul-Weather Gear: Strategies for Facing the Storm," *Accounting Today*, December 14, 2009, 31.

26. Monica Watarous, "Standout Product Launches in 2016," December 30, 2016, *Food Business News*, 1.

27. Mahesh Gupta, Chahal Hardeep, and Ramji Sharma, "Improving the Weakest Link: A TOC-Based Framework for Small Business," *Total Quality Management*, August 2010, 863–883.

28. Young Entrepreneur Council, "13 Best Practices for Building Solid Small Business Operations," Small Business Trends, November 1, 2017, www.smallbiztrends.com.

CHAPTER 3

1. Jason Haber, "5 Social Entrepreneurship Essentials," *Entrepreneur*, October 10, 2016, www.entrepreneur.com/article/271916.

2. Haber, "5 Social Entrepreneurship Essentials."

3. Fida Chaaban, "Social Entrepreneurship Is on the Rise: Soushiant Zanganehpour's Advice for 'Treps Acting as Agents of Change," *Entrepreneur*, October 22, 2015, www.entrepreneur.com/article/251981.

4. Chaaban, "Social Entrepreneurship Is on the Rise."

5. Gopal Kanji and Parvesh Chopra, "Corporate Social Responsibility in a Global Economy," *Total Quality Management*, February 2010, 119–143.

6. Milton Friedman and Rose Friedman, *Free to Choose* (New York: Harcourt Brace Jovanovich, 1980); Milton Friedman, *Capitalism and Freedom* (Chicago: University of Chicago Press, 1963), 133.

7. "Social Responsibility: 'Fundamentally Subversive'?" interview with Milton Friedman, *Businessweek*, August 15, 2006, www.businessweek.com.

8. Robb Mandelbaum, "The 83,000 Question: How Much Do Regulations Really Cost Small Business?" *Forbes*, January 24, 2017, www.forbes.com.

9. Stuart Dawson, John Breen, and Lata Satyen, "The Ethical Outlook of Micro Business Operators," *Journal of Small Business Management*, October 2002, 302–313.

10. Heather Huhman, "There Are No Excuses for Putting Off Social Responsibility," *Inc.*, September 18, 2017, www.inc.com.

11. Anne Murphy, "The Seven (Almost) Deadly Sins of High-Minded Entrepreneurs," *Inc.*, July 1994, 47–51.

12. "Measuring the Impact of Ethics & Compliance Programs," Ethics & Compliance Initiative, June 2018, www.ethics.org/knowledge-center.

13. Brenton Hayden, "Why the Golden Rule Must Be Practiced in Business," *Entrepreneur*, September 11, 2016, www.entrepreneur.com/article/281387.

14. O. C. Ferrell and John Fraedrich, *Business Ethics: Ethical Decision Making and Cases*, 11th ed. (Mason, OH: Cengage Learning, 2016), 10.

15. Josh Spiro, "How to Write a Code of Ethics for Business," *Inc.*, February 24, 2010, www.inc.com.

16. Heledd Jenkins, "A 'Business Opportunity' Model of Corporate Social Responsibility for Small- and Medium-Sized Enterprises," *Business Ethics: A European Review*, January 2009, 21–36.

17. Karen Klein, "A Push for 'Ethical Innovation,'" *Business Week Online*, February 3, 2010, 12.

18. George Manning and Kent Curtis, *Ethics at Work: Fire in a Dark World* (Cincinnati, OH: Southwestern Publishing, 1989), 77.

19. Scott Baca and Erin Nickerson, "Ethical Problems, Conflicts, and Beliefs of Small Business Professionals," *Journal of Business Ethics*, November 2000, 15–24.

20. Richard Kaleba, "Strategic Planning: Getting from Here to There," *Healthcare Financial Management*, November 2006, 74–78.

21. Charles Toftoy and Joydeep Chatterjee, "Mission Statements and Small Business," *Business Strategy Review*, November 2004, 41–44.

22. Darrell Zahorsky, "How to Write a Meaningful Mission Statement," The Balance, December 16, 2016, www.thebalance.com.

23. Tom Peters, *Thriving on Chaos* (New York: Knopf, 1988).

24. Catherine Clifford, "Kickstarter Wants to Be More Than a Crowdfunding Platform," *Entrepreneur*, March 11, 2016, www.entrepreneur.com/article/272350.

25. Melissa Dawn, "Internal Analysis Will Bring Out the Best in You—and Your Business," *Entrepreneur*, November 12, 2015, www.entrepreneur.com/article/252252.

26. Samuel Edwards, "3 Companies Using Speed as a Competitive Advantage," *Entrepreneur*, January 5, 2016, www.entrepreneur.com/article/253372.

27. Liri Andersson and Ludo Van der Heyden, "11 Leadership Guidelines for the Digital Age," *Entrepreneur*, July 12, 2017, www.entrepreneur.com/article/297071.

28. Michael Porter, "Know Your Place," *Inc.*, September 1991, 90–95.

29. Scott Mautz, "Science Says This is the Key to Sustainable Competitive Advantage (and It's Easy to Blow Off)," *Inc.*, April 18, 2017, www.inc.com.

30. Porter, "Know Your Place."

31. Robert Hartley, *Marketing Mistakes*, 9th ed. (New York: Wiley, 2004), 2.

32. O. C. Ferrell and Michail Hartline, *Marketing Strategy*, 5th ed. (Mason, OH: Cengage, 2011).

33. Fred Amofa Yamoah, "Sources of Competitive Advantage: Differential and Catalytic Dimensions," *Journal of American Academy of Business*, March 2004, 223–227.

34. Michael Porter, *Competitive Advantage: Creating and Sustaining Superior Performance* (New York: Free Press, 1985).

35. Aodheen O'Donnell, Audrey Gilmore, David Carson, and Darryl Cummins, "Competitive Advantage in Small to Medium-Sized Enterprises," *Journal of Strategic Marketing*, October 2002, 205–223.

36. Oren Harari, "The Secret Competitive Advantage," *Management Review*, January 1994, 45–47.

37. Marjorie A. Lyles, Inga S. Baird, J. Burdeane Orris, and Donald F. Kuratko, "Formalized Planning in Small Business Increasing Strategic Choices," *Journal of Small Business Management*, April 1993, 38–50.

CHAPTER 4

1. William A. Sahlman, *How to Write a Great Business Plan* (Cambridge, MA: Harvard Business School Press, 2008).

2. Norm Brodsky and Bo Burlingham, *The Knack: How Street-Smart Entrepreneurs Learn to Handle Whatever Comes Up* (Boston, MA: Portfolio Hardcover, 2008).

3. Mark Henrichs, "Do You Really Need a Business Plan?" *Entrepreneur*, March 2008, 104.

4. Nicole Gull, "Plan B (and C and D and . . .)," *Inc.*, March 2004, 40.

5. Rosalind Resnick, "Are Business Plans a Waste of Time?" *Wall Street Journal*, March 24, 2010, www.wsj.com.

6. Andrea Cooper, "Serial Starter," *Entrepreneur*, April 2008, 28.

7. Steve Blank, "Why the Lean Start-Up Changes Everything," May 2013, *Harvard Business Review*, 65–72.

8. Andrea Ovans, "What Is a Business Model?" *Harvard Business Review*, January 23, 2015, https://hbr.org/2015/01/what-is-a-business-model.

9. Martin Zwilling, "10 Most Common Business Models to Make a Profit," *Inc.*, November 17, 2017, www.inc.com.

10. Alexander Osterwalder and Yves Pigneur, *Business Model Generation* (Hoboken, NJ: John Wiley & Sons, 2010).

11. Don Hofstrand and Mary Holz-Clause, "Feasibility Study Outline," Iowa State University: Extension and Outreach, November 2009, www.extension.iastate.edu.

12. *Guidelines for Entrepreneurs* (pamphlet; Denver: Colorado Small Business Development Center).

13. Michael V. Copeland, "How to Make Your Business Plan the Perfect Pitch," *Business 2.0*, September 2005, 88.

14. Kayte Vanscoy, "Unconventional Wisdom," *Smart Business for the New Economy*, October 2000, 78–88.

15. William Sahlman, "How to Write a Great Business Plan," *Harvard Business Review*, July/August 1997, 101.

16. Nicole Gull, "Plan B (and C and D...)," *Inc.*, March 2004, 40.
17. Ralph Alterowitz and Jon Zonderman, "Financing Your New or Growing Business," in *Entrepreneur Mentor Series* (Irvine, CA: Entrepreneur Press, 2002), 113.
18. Guy Kawasaki, *The Art of the Start* (Boston, MA: Portfolio Hardcover, 2004), 188; Scott Clark, "Great Business Plan Is Key to Raising Venture Capital," *Portland Business Journal*, March 31, 2000, 36; and Dee Power and Brian Hill, "Six Critical Business Plan Mistakes," *Business Horizons*, July/August 2003, 83.
19. Tom Foster, "Kevin O'Leary: The 3 Keys to a Successful Pitch," *Inc.*, December 7, 2017, www.inc.com.
20. Foster, "Kevin O'Leary."
21. Jeff Haden, "How to Pitch: 18 Steps to Create and Deliver a Winning Pitch for Investors and Early Customers," *Inc.*, August 30, 2017, www.inc.com.

CHAPTER 5

1. Thomas Dicke, *Franchising in America: The Development of a Business Method, 1840–1990* (Chapel Hill: University of North Carolina Press, 1992), 13.
2. PricewaterhouseCoopers, *Economic Impact of Franchised Businesses: 2016*, vol. 4 (Washington, DC: International Franchise Association, Education and Research Foundation, 2016), www.franchise.org.
3. Mark Siebert, "The 9 Advantages of Franchising," *Entrepreneur*, December 4, 2015, www.entrepreneur.com/article/252591.
4. *The Franchise Handbook*, Franchise Times, https://www.franchisehandbook.com/.
5. "What Information Is Found in the FDD," International Franchise Association, www.franchise.org/what-information-is-found-in-the-fdd.
6. Andrew A. Caffey, "Hey, Get a Clue!" *Entrepreneur*, January 1, 2004, www.entrepreneur.com/article/66004.
7. Mark Siebert, "How to Franchise Your Business," *Entrepreneur*, May 10, 2010, www.entrepreneur.com/article/206498.
8. Siebert, "Franchise Your Business."
9. Gordon Tredgold, "7 Things You Need to Know Before Becoming a Franchise Owner," *Entrepreneur*, November 22, 2017, www.entrepreneur.com/author/gordon-tredgold.
10. Tredgold. "7 Things."
11. "Key Legal Questions to Ask," International Franchise Association, accessed May 10, 2010, https://www.franchise.org/key-legal-questions-to-ask.

CHAPTER 6

1. Bill Green, "When to Buy and When to Build: A Guide to Business Acquisitions," *Inc.*, October 10, 2017, www.inc.com.
2. Curtis Kroeker, "Buy the Small Business That's Right for You," *Inc.*, June 19, 2013, www.inc.com.
3. Darren Dahl, "How to Find a Business to Buy," *Inc.*, March 11, 2009, www.inc.com.
4. Curtis Kroeker, "5 Resources for Small Business Buyers," *Inc.*, May 22, 2013, www.inc.com.
5. "How to Buy a Business," *Entrepreneur* (Starting a Business series), www.entrepreneur.com/article/79638.
6. Peter McFarlane and Deborah Gold, "Do the Due," *CA Magazine*, August 1, 2003, 37–42.
7. "For Business Buyers and Sellers: A Guide," accessed May 28, 2010, https://us.businessesforsale.com.
8. Dalia Fahmy, "Deal Jitters?" *Inc.*, October 2005, 48.

9. Bill Broocke, "Buy—Don't Start—Your Own Business," *Entrepreneur*, March 22, 2004, www.entrepreneur.com/article/70058.
10. Ryan McCarthy, "Valuation Guide 2009—A Buyer's Market," *Inc.*, June 2009, 82–90.
11. Fred Steingold, *Legal Guide for Starting and Running a Small Business*, 11th ed. (Berkeley, CA: Nolo Press, 2009), 9–17.
12. John Warrillow, "How to Value Your Business," *Inc.*, March 4, 2015, www.inc.com.
13. John Burley, "How to Find Out What Your Company Is Worth (Without Wasting Your Money)," *Inc.*, April 6, 2017, www.inc.com.
14. U.S. Small Business Administration, "Buy an Existing Business or Franchise," accessed September 2018, www.sba.gov/business-guide/plan-your-business/buy-existing-business-or-franchise.
15. Ed Powers, "5 Key Numbers a Buyout Firm Uses to Value Your Company," *Inc.*, January 31, 2014, www.inc.com.
16. Bob House, "Common Approaches for Determining Business Value," *Inc.*, October 28, 2014, www.inc.com.
17. Ryan Caldbeck, "The Best Way to Set the Valuation of Your Company," *Inc.*, July 7, 2016, www.inc.com.
18. John Warrillow, "How to Value Your Business," *Inc.*, March 4, 2015, www.inc.com.
19. Paula Andruss, "5 Tips to Getting an Accurate Valuation," *Entrepreneur*, July 22, 2015, www.entrepreneur.com/article/246954.
20. Michael Sanibel, "The Art of Negotiating," *Entrepreneur*, August 24, 2009, www.entrepreneur.com/article/203168.
21. Darren Dahl, "Coming to Terms," *Inc.*, March 2010, www.inc.com.
22. Christine Lagorio, "7 Tips for Masterful Negotiating," *Inc.*, April 26, 2010, www.inc.com.
23. Danielle Fugazy, "Throwing Darts," *Mergers & Acquisitions: The Dealmakers Journal*, November 2009, 42–61.
24. Darren Dahl, "How to Close the Deal When Buying a Business," *Inc.*, March 11, 2009, www.inc.com/guides/buy_biz.
25. Aileron, "The Facts of Family Business," *Forbes*, July 31, 2013, www.forbes.com.
26. Ami Kassar, "Keeping It in the Family: Pros and Cons," *Inc.*, January 16, 2018, www.inc.com.
27. David Port, "The Family Business: Making Sure Both Stay Intact," *Entrepreneur*, March 24, 2010, www.entrepreneur.com/article/205684.
28. Marc Emmer, "How to Create a Successful Succession Plan for Your Family Business," *Inc.*, December 21, 2017, www.inc.com.
29. Emmer, "Succession Plan."
30. Claudio Fernandez-Araoz, Sonny Iqbal, and Jorg Ritter, "Leadership Lessons from Great Family Businesses," *Harvard Business Review*, April 2015, 83–88.
31. Manfred F. R. Kets de Vries, "Saving a Family Business from Emotional Dysfunction," *Harvard Business Review*, February 1, 2017, 2–5.
32. Fernandez-Araoz, Iqbal, and Ritter, "Leadership Lessons."
33. Christine Lagorio, "How to Run a Family Business," *Inc.*, March 5, 2010. www.inc.com.
34. Kets de Vries, "Saving a Family Business."
35. Josh Baron, "The Common Traps of Working in Your Family's Business," *Harvard Business Review*, November 6, 2017, 2–4.

CHAPTER 7

1. *Providing More Insight into the Small Business Owner* (Costa Mesa, CA: Experian Information Solutions, 2007), www.experian.com/whitepapers/BOLStudy_Experian.pdf.

2. U.S. Small Business Administration, Office of Advocacy, "Survey of Business Owners Facts," accessed May 2018, www.sba.gov.

3. U.S. Small Business Administration, Office of Advocacy, "Demographic Characteristics of Small Business Owners and Employees," accessed April 2015, www.sba.gov.

4. U.S. Small Business Administration, "Demographic Characteristics."

5. Rieva Lesonsky, "10 Things Small Business Owners Need to Know," SmallBizDaily, June 19, 2017, www.smallbizdaily.com.

6. "Most Small Businesses Have Less Than $400,000 in Annual Revenue," SmallBizLabs, October 20, 2016, www.smallbizlabs .com.

7. "Onmi-Channel Retail in 2017," Big Commerce and Square, accessed Feb 20, 2018, https://grow.bigcommerce.com/rs/695-JJT-333/images/the-omni-channel-selling-guide.pdf.

8. "Quarterly Retail E-Commerce Sales," news release, U.S. Census Bureau, February 16, 2018, www.census.gov/retail/ mrts/www/data/pdf/ec_current.pdf.

9. Kaleigh Moore, "4 Ways to Find Profitable Ideas for an Online Business," Inc., January 10, 2018, www.inc.com.

10. Maria Haggerty, "2 Ways to Grow Your Online Business in 2018," Inc., January 30, 2018, www.inc.com.

11. R. L. Adams, "To Make Money Online Do These 3 Things First," Entrepreneur, February 2, 2018, www.entrepreneur.com/ article/308180.

12. R. L. Adams, "17 Passive Income Ideas for Automating Your Cash Flow," Entrepreneur, April 3, 2017, www.entrepreneur .com/slideshow/299914.

13. Marco Carbajo, "5 Key Financial Tips When Starting a Home-Based Business," U.S. Small Business Administration Blogs, August 14, 2017, www.sba.gov/blogs/.

14. "Shocking US Home Based Business Statistics," IncFile Blog, March 21, 2017, www.incfile.com.

15. Maya Payne Smart, "There's No Place Like Home," Black Enterprise, February 2009, 79–81.

16. "Advantages and Disadvantages of a Home-Based Business," Strategy Plan One, January 16, 2012, www.strategyplanone .wordpress.com.

17. "63 Businesses to Start for Under $10,000, Entrepreneur, April 6, 2016, www.entrepreneur.com/slideshow/299290.

18. Larry Kim, "This Is Why You Need to Start a Side Hustle (and a Few Reasons Why You Shouldn't)," Inc., February 21, 2018, www.inc.com.

19. Adele Cehrs, "How to Make Money and Grow Your Business in the Gig Economy," Inc., October 30, 2017, www.inc.com.

20. David Shadpour, "The Gig Economy: Pioneering the Future," Forbes, January 19, 2018, www.forbes.com.

21. Shadpour, "The Gig Economy."

22. Kevin Daum, "The Gig Economy Is Exploding: Here Are the Rules Employers and Freelancers Must Follow to Survive," Inc., August 18, 2017, www.inc.com.

23. Nathan Resnick, "How This Entrepreneur Kept His Day Job While Starting a Business," Entrepreneur, February 10, 2017, www.entrepreneur.com/article/288510.

24. All data on Inc. 500 companies come from Inc., special issue, September 2013.

25. Jason Snell, "Test Driving the iPad," Macworld, June 2010; Diane Goldner, "Ahead of the Curve," Wall Street Journal, May 22, 1995, R16, small business edition.

26. John Case, "Why 20 Million of You Can't Be Wrong," Inc., April 2004, 102.

27. "The State of Small Business Report," Network Solutions, January 2010, www.grow smartbusiness.com.

28. David Kopcso, Robert Ronstady, and William Rybolt, "The Corridor Principle: Independent Entrepreneurs versus Corporate Entrepreneurs," in Frontiers of Entrepreneurship Research (Wellesley, MA: Babson College, 1987), 259–271.

29. Tim Blumerntritt, "Does Small and Mature Have to Mean Dull? Defying the Ho-Hum at SMEs," Journal of Business Strategy 25, no. 1 (2004): 27–33.

30. Phaedra Hise, "Where Great Business Ideas Come From," Inc., September 1993, 59–60.

31. Neil A. Martin, "Invincible Spirit," Success, October 1994, 24.

32. Michael Treacy and Fred Wiersema, "How Market Leaders Keep Their Edge," Fortune, February 6, 1995, 88–98.

33. David Freedman, "The Secret of Their Success," Inc., April 2010, 92–93.

CHAPTER 8

1. Doug and Polly White, "How and When to Grow Your Company's Accounting Function," Entrepreneur, October 11, 2016, www.entrepreneur.com/article/282896.

2. Justin Kulla, "Why Making Sure Your Accountant Is Good Should Be Your Top 2018 Priority," Inc., January 2, 2018, www .inc.com.

3. Jane Porter, "10 Questions to Ask Before Hiring a Tax Accountant," Entrepreneur, January 14, 2013, www.entrepreneur .com/article/225378.

4. Allen Beck, "The Cash Method for Small Business," Tax Advisor, October 2002, 623.

5. James J. Newhard, "Small Business Reporting: No More Force-Fitting into GAAP," Pennsylvania CPA Journal, Fall 2013, 1–3.

6. Rick Teberg, "Mom and Pop Shops," Journal of Accountancy, July 2003, 49.

7. Chris Joseph, "4 Categories of Financial Ratios," Small Business Chron, accessed March 5, 2018, http://smallbusiness .chron.com.

8. New York Society of CPAs, "10 Ways to Improve Small Business Cash Flow," Journal of Accountancy, March 2000, 14.

9. Daniel Akst, "The Survival of the Fittest," Fortune Small Business, February 2002, 77.

CHAPTER 9

1. U.S. Small Business Administration, Office of Advocacy, "FAQ about Small Business Finance," July 2016, www.sba.gov.

2. Abigail Thorpe, "Infographic: Alternative Lending for Small Business Owners," National Federation of Independent Business, February 21, 2018, www.nfib.com/resources/money.

3. Ed Van den Berg, "Outsourcing for SMEs," Credit Management, June 2009, 24–25.

4. Amanda Watt, "The Money-Go-Round," NZ Business, October 1, 2009, 58.

5. Boyd Farrow, "Can Your Company Raise Money? Ask These Questions First," Entrepreneur, January 17, 2018, www .entrepreneur.com/article/306523.

6. Jared Hecht, "How to Finance Taking Your Startup to the Big Time," Entrepreneur, February 15, 2018, www.entrepreneur .com/article/308343.

7. Debt vs. Equity Financing: Which Is Best for Your Business? National Federation for Independent Business, June 20, 2017, www.nfib.com/content/resources/money/ital-50036/.

8. Debt vs. Equity Financing, National Federation for Independent Business.

9. Jared Hecht, "How to Finance Taking Your Startup to the Big Time," *Entrepreneur*, February 15, 2018, www.entrepreneur.com/article/308343.

10. Chris Meyer, "Applying for a Business Loan? Make Sure Your Personal Information Is Protected," *Entrepreneur*, August 24, 2017, www.entrepreneur.com/article/298957.

11. Jared Hecht, "The Most Popular Types of Credit Lines Your Business Needs to Know," *Inc.*, April 27, 2016, www.inc.com.

12. James Sudakow, "This Practical Guide from Small Business Experts Covers Everything You'll Encounter Running a Business," *Inc.*, March 21, 2018, www.inc.com.

13. Eyal Lifshitz, "'Factoring' Family into Account," *Entrepreneur*, February 9, 2017, www.entrepreneur.com/article/288486.

14. www.sba.gov/funding-programs/loans.

15. www.sba.gov/financing /funding-programs/loans.

16. www.sba.gov/funding-programs/loans.

17. Emily Flitter, "SBA Widens 504 Loan Program," *American Banker*, June 25, 2009.

18. "College Student's Guide to Financing a Business," Commercial Capital Blog, March 29, 2018, www.comcapfactoring/com/blog.

19. "Guide to Financing a Business," Commercial Capital Blog.

20. Han-Gwon Lung, "4 Money-Management Tips to Help You Bootstrap Your Business," *Entrepreneur*, November 21, 2017, www.entrepreneur.com/article/304914.

21. *Angels: A Funding Source for Firms with Limited Revenue*, National Federation of Independent Business, April 22, 2003, www.nfib.com.

22. "Venture Capital," *Entrepreneur*, retrieved April 1, 2018, www.entrepreneur.com.

23. *State of the Field—Venture Capital*, Ewing Marion Kauffman Foundation, accessed April 1, 2018, www.kauffman.org.

24. Jeremy Lovell, "In the Land of the Loch Ness Monster, 'Sea Snake' Prepares to Ride the Waves," *Scientific American*, June 3, 2010, www.scientificamerican.com/article/sea-snake-prepares-to-ride-waves.

25. Dalia Fahmy, "Want Power and Money?" *Inc.*, April 2006, 44–46.

CHAPTER 10

1. Regulatory Studies Center, "Total Pages in the Code of Federal Regulations (1975–2016)," George Washington University, Columbian College of Arts & Sciences, https://regulatorystudies.columbian.gwu.edu/reg-stats.

2. Gretchen Schmid, "16 Need-to-Know Small Business Regulations," Fundera, March 24, 2017, www.fundera.com/blog/small-business-regulations.

3. "When Must Employers Pay Overtime?" Nolo, accessed April 14, 2018, www.nolo.com/legal-encyclopedia/employer-pay-overtime-laws-29928.html.

4. "Affordable Care Act Tax Provisions for Small Employers," Internal Revenue Service, accessed April 2018, www.irs.gov/affordable-care-act/employers/affordable-care-act-tax-provisions-for-small-employers.

5. "Occupational Safety and Health Administration," in *Entrepreneur Encyclopedia*, accessed April 2018, www.entrepreneur.com/encyclopedia/occupational-safety-and-health-administration.

6. Carol Roth, "6 Steps Resilient Entrepreneurs Take to Rebound from Bankruptcy," *Entrepreneur*, October 10, 2016, www.entrepreneur.com/article/283377.

7. "Lessons from the Brink of Bankruptcy," *Inc.*, August 5, 2014, www.inc.com.

8. "Constitution of the United States of America," Article I, Section 8, in Daniel J. Boorstin, *An American Primer* (Chicago: University of Chicago Press, 1966), 94.

9. David Pressman & Thomas Tuytschaevers, *Patent It Yourself*, 18th ed. (Berkeley, CA: Nolo Press, 2016).

10. Eyal Shinar, "U.S. Small Business Owed $825 Billion in Unpaid Invoices," *Entrepreneur*, November 20, 2016, www.entrepreneur.com/article/285233.

11. Jana Kasperkevic, "Small Businesses Are Ditching Patents in Droves," *Inc.*, May 2013, www.inc.com.

12. Kasperkevic, "Ditching Patents in Droves."

13. Fred Steingold, *Legal Guide for Starting and Running a Small Business*, 15th ed. (Berkeley, CA: Nolo Press, 2017).

14. "Limited Liability Partnership," in *Entrepreneur Encyclopedia*, accessed April 2018, www.entrepreneur.com.

15. Steingold, *Legal Guide*.

16. "Subchapter S Corporation," in *Entrepreneur Encyclopedia*, accessed April 2018, www.entrepreneur.com.

17. Society for Nonprofits, "Starting a Nonprofit Organization," June 2010, www.snpo.org/resources/startup.php.

CHAPTER 11

1. Peter Drucker, *People and Performance: The Best of Peter Drucker on Management* (New York: Harper's College Press, 1977), 90.

2. Drucker, *People and Performance*, 91.

3. Seth Godin, *Purple Cow: Transform Your Business by Being Remarkable* (New York: Portfolio, 2002).

4. N. Craig Smith, Minette Drumwright, and Mary Gentile, "The New Marketing Myopia," *Journal of Public Policy & Marketing* 29, no. 1 (Spring 2010), 4–11.

5. Kimberly de Silve, "7 Ways to Boost Your Small-Business Marketing," *Entrepreneur*, April 4, 2018, www.entrepreneur.com.

6. David Roe, "8 Tips for Marketing to Millennials," CMS Wire, April 16, 2018, www.cmswire.com/digital-marketing/8-tips-for-marketing-to-millennials.

7. Laurel Mintz, "Digital Marketing 101," *Inc.*, April 10, 2018, www.inc.com.

8. Kevin Clancy and Peter Krieg, "Getting a Grip," *Marketing Management*, Spring 2010, 19–23.

9. Michele Marchetti, "Advanced Planning," *Sales and Marketing Management*, May 2004, 16.

10. Anna Johansson, "Revamp Your Demand Forecasting With These 5 Tips," *Inc.*, Sept 21, 2016, www.inc.com.

11. Sally Dibb and Lyndon Simkin, "Implementation Rules to Bridge the Theory/Practice Divide in Market Segmentation," *Journal of Marketing Management* 25, no. 3–4 (2009), 375–396.

12. Peter Roesler, "New Research Reveals More Consumers Are Shopping Online for Everyday Items," *Inc.*, April 16, 2018, www.inc.com.

13. Kris Lahiri, "Big Data Is Changing Business in Some Surprising Ways," *Inc.*, March 30, 2018, www.inc.com.

14. Howard Tullman, "Does Your Customer Research Prove What You Already Know?" *Inc.*, December 13, 2017, www.inc.com.

15. Bill Aulet, "How Entrepreneurs Can Conduct Primary Market Research," *Entrepreneur*, April 19, 2017, www.entrepreneur.com.

16. Bill Aulet, "How Entrepreneurs Can Conduct Primary Marketing Research," Entrepreneur, April 19, 2017, www.entrepreneur.com/article/292962.

17. American Marketing Association, www.marketingpower.com.
18. U.S. Small Business Administration, www.sba.gov/starting_business/marketing/research.html.
19. Gary Hamel and C. K. Prahalad, "Seeing the Future First," *Fortune,* September 5, 1994, 70.

CHAPTER 12

1. "Market Segments Explained," Nielsen Claritas, retrieved April 2018, www.mybestsegments.com.
2. "10 Things to Consider When Choosing a Location for Your Business," *Entrepreneur,* May 20, 2015, www.entrepreneur.com/slideshow/299849.
3. Jonathan O'Connell, "The Fall—and Overhaul—of the American Mall," *Washington Post,* January 30, 2015, www.washingtonpost.com.
4. Jason Axelrod, "Incubating an Economy," *American City & County,* October 2017, 14–18.
5. "History," Business Incubator Center, www.gjincubator.org/about-us.
6. "Martek Biosciences," International Business Innovation Association (website), www.nbia.org/success_stories/success/.
7. Linda Essig, "Value Creation by and Evaluation of US Arts Incubators," *International Journal of Arts Management,* Winter 2018, 32–45.
8. "ADA Guide for Small Businesses," U.S. Small Business Administration, Office of Entrepreneurial Development and the U.S. Department of Justice, Civil Rights Division, retrieved August 21, 2018, www.slideshare.net/smallbusinessdotcom/ada-guide-for-small-business.
9. "Frequently Asked Questions," U.S. Small Business Administration, Office of Advocacy, June 2016, www.sba.gov/sites/default/files/advocacy/SB-FAQ-2016_WEB.pdf.
10. "Frequently Asked Questions," U.S. Small Business Administration.

CHAPTER 13

1. Bing Gordon, "Mastering the Art of Pricing: What the Textbooks Don't Teach You," June 29, 2015, www.entrepreneur.com/article/247805.
2. Gordon, "Mastering the Art of Pricing."
3. Pius Boachie, "4 Ways Small Businesses Can Compete Against Major Competitors," *Entrepreneur,* February 21, 2017, www.entrepreneur.com/article/287450.
4. Norm Brodsky, "The Capacity Trap II," *Inc.,* December 2003, 55–57.
5. Doug and Polly White, "How to Calculate 'Breakeven,'" *Entrepreneur,* May 24, 2016, www.entrepreneur.com/article/276296.
6. Gordon, "Mastering the Art of Pricing."
7. Marco Bertini and Luc Wathieu, "How to Stop Customers from Fixating on Price," *Harvard Business Review,* May 2010.
8. Bertini and Wathieu, "How to Stop Customers."
9. Darian Kovacs, "4 Psychological Techniques That Can Improve Your Product Pricing," *Entrepreneur,* November 15, 2017, www.entrepreneur.com/article/304687.
10. John Rampton, "Accepting Credit Cards 101: What Your Business Needs to Know," *Inc.,* January 29, 2017, www.inc.com.
11. Brian Hamilton, "Why Managing Accounts Receivable Could Save Your Business," *Entrepreneur,* September 17, 2014, www.entrepreneur.com/article/237523.

12. Eran Halevy, "How Marketing and Advertising Are Bound to Change in 2018," *Entrepreneur,* January 22, 2018, www.entrepreneur.com/article/306162.
13. Thorin McGee, "Media Usage Survey 2017," *Target Marketing,* February 13, 2017, www.targetmarketingmag.com/article/media-usage-survey-2017.
14. Justin Kulla, "Do You Have the Guts to Sell? These 5 Steps Will Get You Over Your Phobia," *Inc.,* November 13, 2017, www.inc.com.
15. Ceren Cubukcu, "Why You Still Need Business Cards," *Entrepreneur,* September 9, 2017, www.entrepreneur.com/article/300051.
16. Tracy Leigh Hazzard, "How Your Business Card Can Outshine Everyone Else's, Every Time," *Inc.,* February 2, 2018, www.inc.com.
17. John Pilmer, "Unlike Many Things That Are a Lot of Work, Trade Shows Are Worth It," *Entrepreneur,* September 20, 2017, www.entrepreneur.com/article/297907.

CHAPTER 14

1. Henry Mintzberg, "The Manager's Job: Folklore and Fact," *Harvard Business Review,* March/April 1990, 163–176.
2. Henry Mintzberg, *Mintzberg on Management: Inside Our Strange World of Organizations* (New York: Free Press, 1990).
3. Matthew McCreary, "The 5 Best Burger Franchises You Can Buy (and How Much They Cost)," *Entrepreneur,* August 16, 2017, www.entrepreneur.com/slideshow/298595.
4. Neil C. Churchill and Virginia Lewis, "The Five Stages of Small Business Growth," *Harvard Business Review,* May/June 1983, 30–50.
5. Damon Brown, "The Biggest Mistake Solopreneurs Make (and 3 Ways to Avoid it)," *Inc.,* March 30, 2018, www.inc.com.
6. Catherine Clifford, "Why a $14/ Hour Employee Costs $20," CNNMoney.com, March 26, 2010.
7. Per Bylund, "How Entrepreneurs Can Hone Their Management Skills to Fuel Production," *Entrepreneur,* April 25, 2017, www.entrepreneur.com/article/293280.
8. Aileron, "Small Business, Big Opportunity: Replacing Traditional Management with Holacracy, *Forbes,* October 9, 2017, www.forbes.com.
9. Martin Zwilling, "8 Reasons to Think About Your Business Exit Before You Even Start," *Inc.,* April 3, 2018, www.inc.com.
10. Candace Sjogren, "The Entrepreneurial Exit Strategy—Prepare Yourself," *Entrepreneur,* September 4, 2017, www.entrepreneur.com/article/299557.
11. Warren Bennis, "Why Leaders Can't Lead," *Training and Development Journal,* April 1989, 35–39.
12. Peter Barron Stark and Jane Flaherty, "How to Negotiate," *Training and Development,* June 2004, 52–55.
13. Sherrie Campbell, "7 Ways Modest Leadership Increases Team Success," *Entrepreneur,* January 4, 2018, www.entrepreneur.com/article/306883.
14. Melissa Lamson, "The Neverfail Model for Negotiation," *Inc.,* April 4, 2018, www.inc.com.
15. Sean Kelly, "10 Tips to Negotiate Like a Boss," *Entrepreneur,* January 6, 2019, www.entrepreneur.com/article/283625.
16. Jennifer Beukman, "Mastering the Art of Delegation," *Entrepreneur,* February 28, 2017, www.entrepreneur.com/article/289777.
17. Michael Cronin, "Motivation the Old-Fashioned Way," *Inc.,* November 1994, 134.

18. Jeff Miller, "3 Things You Need to Know About Employee Motivation," *Inc.*, January 13, 2017, www.inc.com.
19. Norm Brodsky, "The Most Important Resource," *Inc.*, February 2006, 61–62.
20. "25 Ways to Reward Employees without Spending a Dime," HRWorld.com, July 13, 2010.
21. "Employee Theft Statistics," Statistic Brain, March 1, 2018, www.statisticbrain.com/employee-theft-statistics.
22. Daniel Finley, "Master Time," *Advisor Today*, January 2010.
23. Alison Stein Wellner, "The Time Trap," *Inc.*, June 2004, 42.
24. Judith Ross, "Monitor and Manage Your Stress Level for Top Performance," *Harvard Management Update*, April 2009.
25. Jonathon Halbesleben, "Addressing Stress and Beating Burnout," *Healthcare Executive*, March/April 2010.
26. Bonnie Miller, "Hard Times," *Public Management*, April 2010.
27. Coeli Carr, "When It's Worth It to Pay $1,000 an Hour for a Business Coach," *Inc.*, October 2016, 85–86.

CHAPTER 15

1. Anna Verasai, "Cost of Employee Turnover vs. Retention Proposition," *The HR Digest*, March 16, 2018, www.thedrdigest.com.
2. *How to Develop a Job Description*, Society of Human Resource Management, February 14, 2018, www.shrm.org/resourcesandtools.
3. *Develop a Job Description*, Society of Human Resource Management.
4. "Bona Fide Occupational Qualification," FindLaw, May 2018, https://smallbusiness.findlaw.com/employment-law-and-human-resources/bona-fide-occupational-qualification.
5. Peter F. Drucker, "How to Save the Family Business," *Wall Street Journal*, August 19, 1994, A10.
6. Mariah DeLeon, "What Really Happens When You Hire the Wrong Candidate," *Entrepreneur*, April 9, 2015, www.entrepreneur.com/article/244730.
7. Griggs v. Duke Power Company, 401 U.S. 424 (1971).
8. Bridget Styers and Kenneth Shultz, "Perceived Reasonableness of Employment Testing Accommodations for Person with Disabilities," *Public Personnel Management*, Fall 2009.
9. Heather R. Huhman, "5 Ways to Make Your Company's Hiring Process More Fair," *Entrepreneur*, February 10, 2016, www.entrepreneur.com/article/270617.
10. Huhman, "Make Your Hiring Process More Fair."
11. Christopher S. Rugaber, "Some Business Owners Are Rethinking Their Drug Testing Policies," *Inc.*, May 4, 2018, www.inc.com.
12. Workpop, "Biggest Pros and Cons of Personality Tests as Hiring Tools," *Inc.*, August 7, 2017, www.inc.com.
13. "How the IRS Classifies Independent Contractors," *Entrepreneur*, February 18, 2013, www.entrepreneur.com/article/225773.
14. Alison Davis, "5 Oh-So-Simple Ways to Make Orientation So Much Better," *Inc.*, January 30, 2017, www.inc.com.
15. Bruno Neal, "Stop Following Joe Around," *T+D*, January 2010.
16. Bureau of Labor Statistics, "Employer Costs for Employee Compensation," news release, December, 2017, www.bls.gov/news.release.
17. "Ask Inc.," *Inc.*, June 2006, 61.
18. *Employee Job Satisfaction and Engagement*, Society of Human Resource Management, January 2016, 23. www.shrm.org.
19. *EBRI Databook on Employee Benefits*, Employee Benefit Research Institute, May 2018, www.ebri.org.
20. Tom Murphy, "Health Benefits Keep Vanishing at Small Businesses," *Inc.*, September 2017, www.inc.com.
21. Ruth Mayhew, "Why Are Disclaimers in Employee Handbooks Important?" Chron, accessed May 2018, www.chron.com
22. *Essentials of an Employee Handbook*, www.allbusiness.com/essentials-of-an-employee-handbook-745-1.
23. Alison Doyle, "Does an Employer Have to Provide Notice of Termination?" The Balance Careers, March 15, 2018, www.thebalancecareers.com.
24. John Boitnott, "How to Deal with Employees Who Insist on Always Getting Their Way," *Entrepreneur*, August 12, 2014, www.entrepreneur.com/article/236369.

CHAPTER 16

1. "Growing Our Economy by Helping Small Manufacturers Succeed," American Small Manufacturers Coalition, accessed May 2018, www.smallmanufacturers.org.
2. Martin Murray, "Small Business Guide to Manufacturing," The Balance Small Business, March 14, 2018, www.thebalancesmb.com.
3. Sheila Eugenio, "3 Ways Entrepreneurs Are Making IoT More User-Friendly," *Entrepreneur*, August 13, 2017, www.entrepreneur.com/article/292415.
4. Yasmin Gagne, "Productivity Gains Add Up over Time: How to Start Collecting," *Inc.*, April 11, 2018, www.inc.com.
5. David Finkel, "The True Secret to Increasing Your Productivity," *Inc.*, March 16, 2016, www.inc.com.
6. Bill Eureka, "The Process of Quality," *Material Handling Management*, May 2010.
7. Kirsten Terry, "Sigma Performance Levels—One to Six Sigma," iSix Sigma, accessed May 2018, www.isixsigma.com.
8. Terry, "Sigma Performance Levels."
9. Katerina Gotzamani, "Results of an Empirical Investigation on the Anticipated Improvement Areas of the ISO 9000:2000 Standard," *Total Quality Management*, June 2010.
10. Bill Carmody, "Top Six Sigma Consultant Saves Billions for Clients: Then Explains Why Most Process Improvements Fail Utterly" *Inc.*, May 15, 2017, www.inc.com.
11. *Introduction to Nondestructive Testing*, American Society for Nondestructive Testing, accessed May 2018, www.asnt.org.
12. "How to Create a Formal Purchasing Program," *Entrepreneur*, accessed May 2018, www.entrepreneur.com/article/79798.

INDEX